JLA

STRENGTH IN NUMBERS

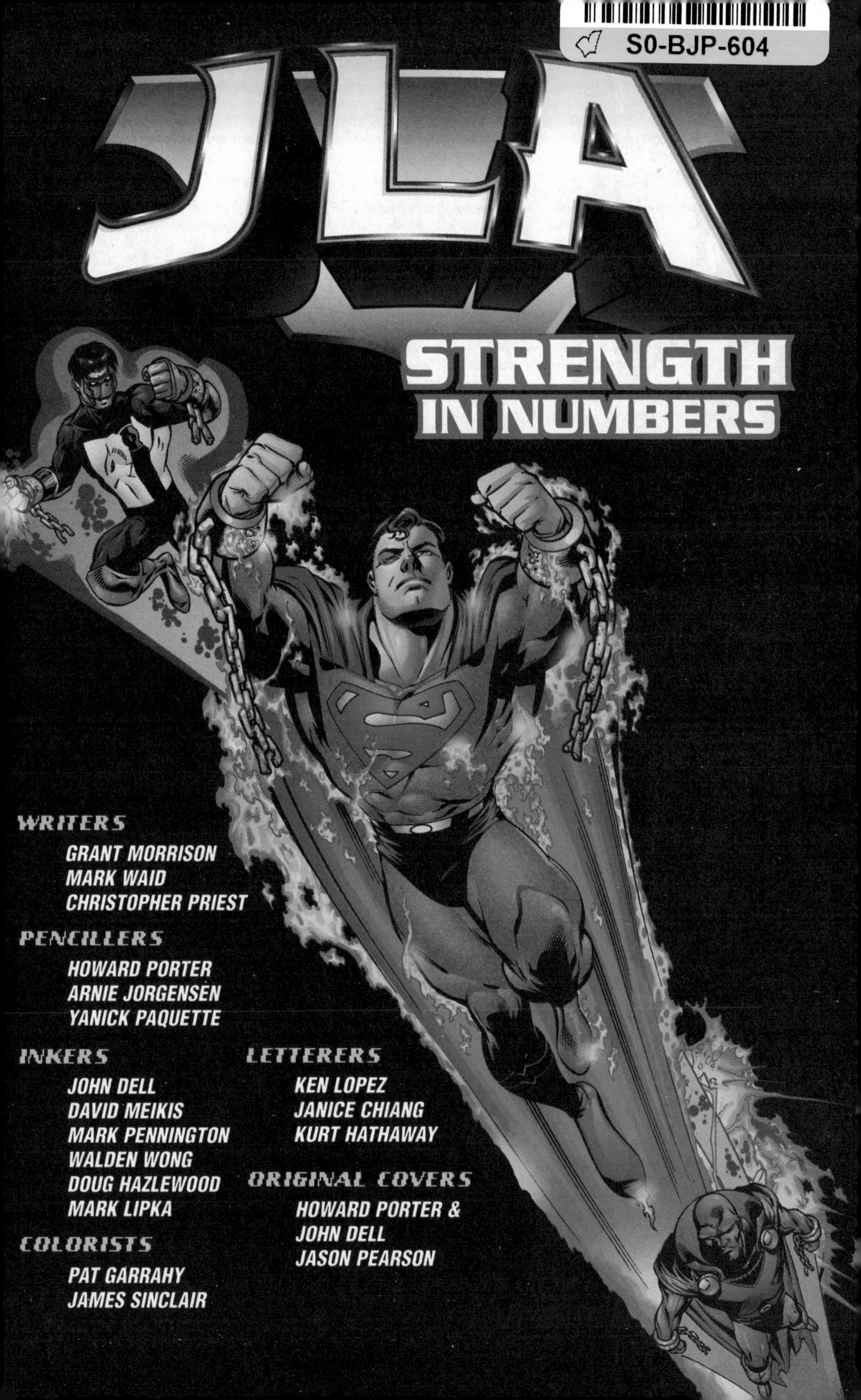

WRITERS

GRANT MORRISON
MARK WAID
CHRISTOPHER PRIEST

PENCILLERS

HOWARD PORTER
ARNIE JORGENSEN
YANICK PAQUETTE

INKERS

JOHN DELL
DAVID MEIKIS
MARK PENNINGTON
WALDEN WONG
DOUG HAZLEWOOD
MARK LIPKA

COLORISTS

PAT GARRAHY
JAMES SINCLAIR

LETTERERS

KEN LOPEZ
JANICE CHIANG
KURT HATHAWAY

ORIGINAL COVERS

HOWARD PORTER &
JOHN DELL
JASON PEARSON

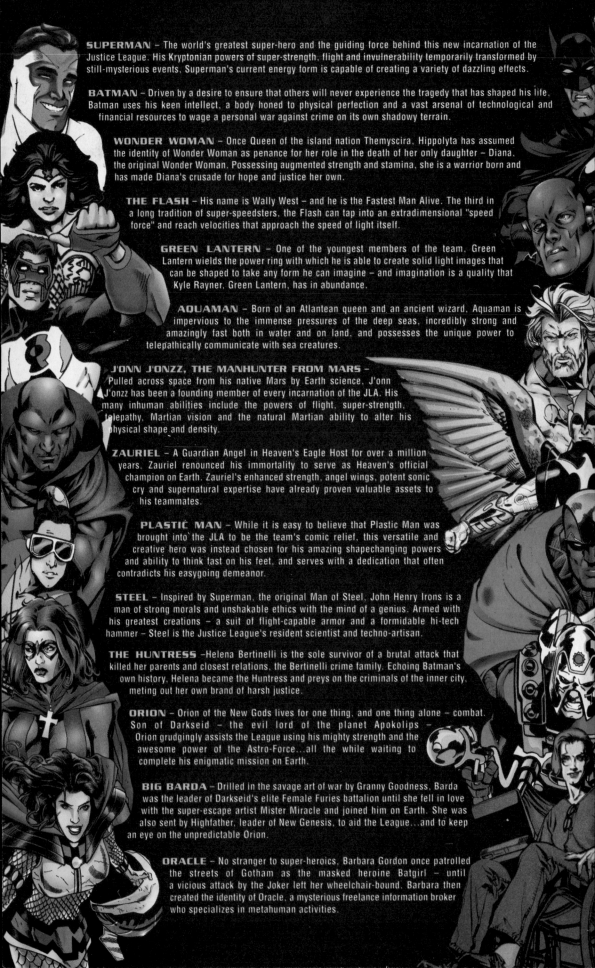

SUPERMAN – The world's greatest super-hero and the guiding force behind this new incarnation of the Justice League. His Kryptonian powers of super-strength, flight and invulnerability temporarily transformed by still-mysterious events, Superman's current energy form is capable of creating a variety of dazzling effects.

BATMAN – Driven by a desire to ensure that others will never experience the tragedy that has shaped his life, Batman uses his keen intellect, a body honed to physical perfection and a vast arsenal of technological and financial resources to wage a personal war against crime on its own shadowy terrain.

WONDER WOMAN – Once Queen of the island nation Themyscira, Hippolyta has assumed the identity of Wonder Woman as penance for her role in the death of her only daughter – Diana, the original Wonder Woman. Possessing augmented strength and stamina, she is a warrior born and has made Diana's crusade for hope and justice her own.

THE FLASH – His name is Wally West – and he is the Fastest Man Alive. The third in a long tradition of super-speedsters, the Flash can tap into an extradimensional "speed force" and reach velocities that approach the speed of light itself.

GREEN LANTERN – One of the youngest members of the team, Green Lantern wields the power ring with which he is able to create solid light images that can be shaped to take any form he can imagine – and imagination is a quality that Kyle Rayner, Green Lantern, has in abundance.

AQUAMAN – Born of an Atlantean queen and an ancient wizard, Aquaman is impervious to the immense pressures of the deep seas, incredibly strong and amazingly fast both in water and on land, and possesses the unique power to telepathically communicate with sea creatures.

J'ONN J'ONZZ, THE MANHUNTER FROM MARS – Pulled across space from his native Mars by Earth science, J'onn J'onzz has been a founding member of every incarnation of the JLA. His many inhuman abilities include the powers of flight, super-strength, telepathy, Martian vision and the natural Martian ability to alter his physical shape and density.

ZAURIEL – A Guardian Angel in Heaven's Eagle Host for over a million years, Zauriel renounced his immortality to serve as Heaven's official champion on Earth. Zauriel's enhanced strength, angel wings, potent sonic cry and supernatural expertise have already proven valuable assets to his teammates.

PLASTIC MAN – While it is easy to believe that Plastic Man was brought into the JLA to be the team's comic relief, this versatile and creative hero was instead chosen for his amazing shapechanging powers and ability to think fast on his feet, and serves with a dedication that often contradicts his easygoing demeanor.

STEEL – Inspired by Superman, the original Man of Steel, John Henry Irons is a man of strong morals and unshakable ethics with the mind of a genius. Armed with his greatest creations – a suit of flight-capable armor and a formidable hi-tech hammer – Steel is the Justice League's resident scientist and techno-artisan.

THE HUNTRESS –Helena Bertinelli is the sole survivor of a brutal attack that killed her parents and closest relations, the Bertinelli crime family. Echoing Batman's own history, Helena became the Huntress and preys on the criminals of the inner city, meting out her own brand of harsh justice.

ORION – Orion of the New Gods lives for one thing, and one thing alone – combat. Son of Darkseid – the evil lord of the planet Apokolips – Orion grudgingly assists the League using his mighty strength and the awesome power of the Astro-Force...all the while waiting to complete his enigmatic mission on Earth.

BIG BARDA – Drilled in the savage art of war by Granny Goodness, Barda was the leader of Darkseid's elite Female Furies battalion until she fell in love with the super-escape artist Mister Miracle and joined him on Earth. She was also sent by Highfather, leader of New Genesis, to aid the League...and to keep an eye on the unpredictable Orion.

ORACLE – No stranger to super-heroics, Barbara Gordon once patrolled the streets of Gotham as the masked heroine Batgirl – until a vicious attack by the Joker left her wheelchair-bound. Barbara then created the identity of Oracle, a mysterious freelance information broker who specializes in metahuman activities.

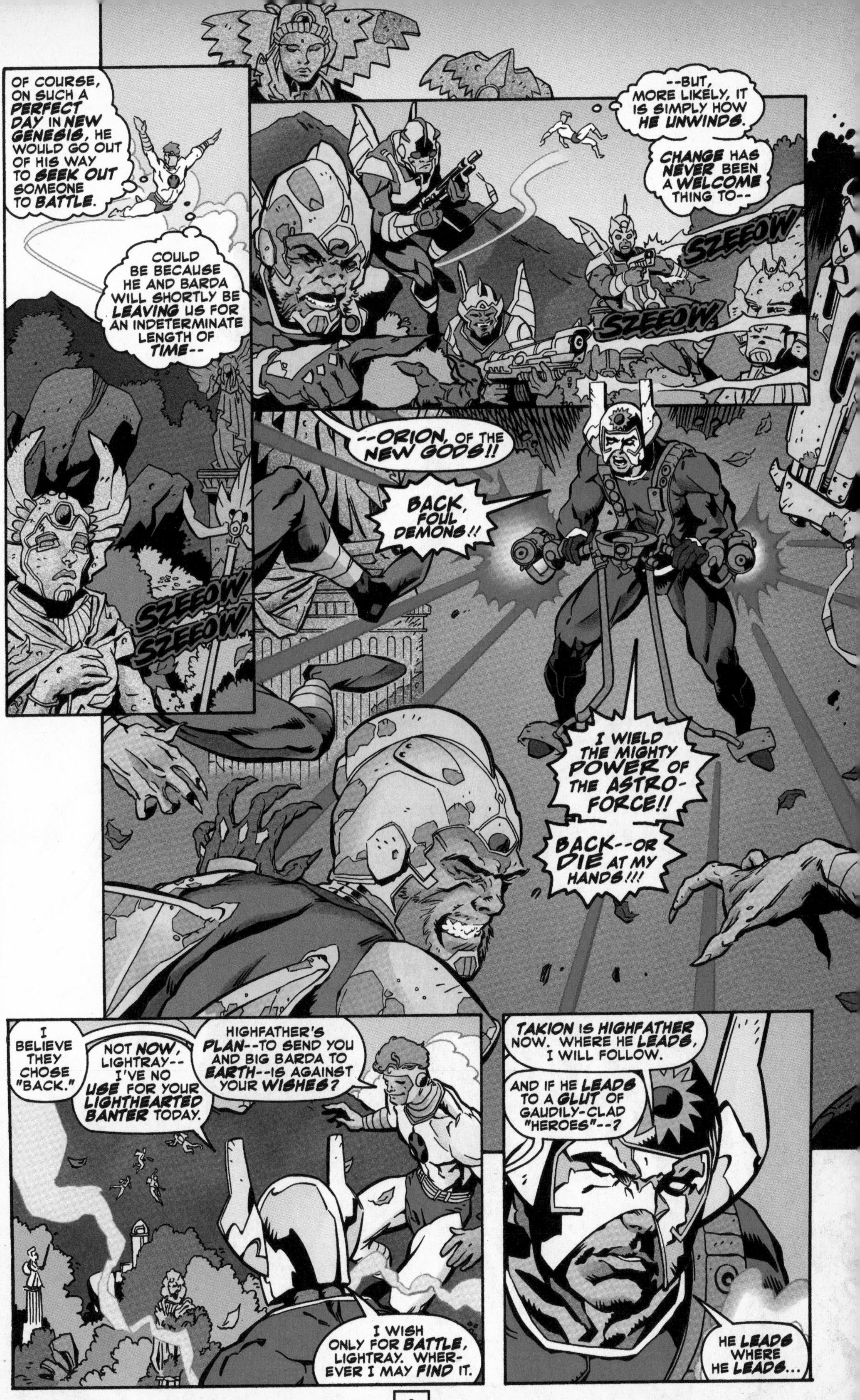

OF COURSE, ON SUCH A PERFECT DAY IN NEW GENESIS, HE WOULD GO OUT OF HIS WAY TO SEEK OUT SOMEONE TO BATTLE.
COULD BE BECAUSE HE AND BARDA WILL SHORTLY BE LEAVING US FOR AN INDETERMINATE LENGTH OF TIME--
--BUT, MORE LIKELY, IT IS SIMPLY HOW HE UNWINDS.
CHANGE HAS NEVER BEEN A WELCOME THING TO--
SZEEOW
SZEEOW
--ORION, OF THE NEW GODS!!
BACK, FOUL DEMONS!!
SZEEOW
SZEEOW
I WIELD THE MIGHTY POWER OF THE ASTRO-FORCE!!
BACK--OR DIE AT MY HANDS!!!
I BELIEVE THEY CHOSE "BACK."
NOT NOW, LIGHTRAY-- I'VE NO USE FOR YOUR LIGHTHEARTED BANTER TODAY.
HIGHFATHER'S PLAN--TO SEND YOU AND BIG BARDA TO EARTH--IS AGAINST YOUR WISHES?
I WISH ONLY FOR BATTLE, LIGHTRAY. WHEREVER I MAY FIND IT.
TAKION IS HIGHFATHER NOW. WHERE HE LEADS, I WILL FOLLOW.
AND IF HE LEADS TO A GLUT OF GAUDILY-CLAD "HEROES"--?
HE LEADS WHERE HE LEADS...

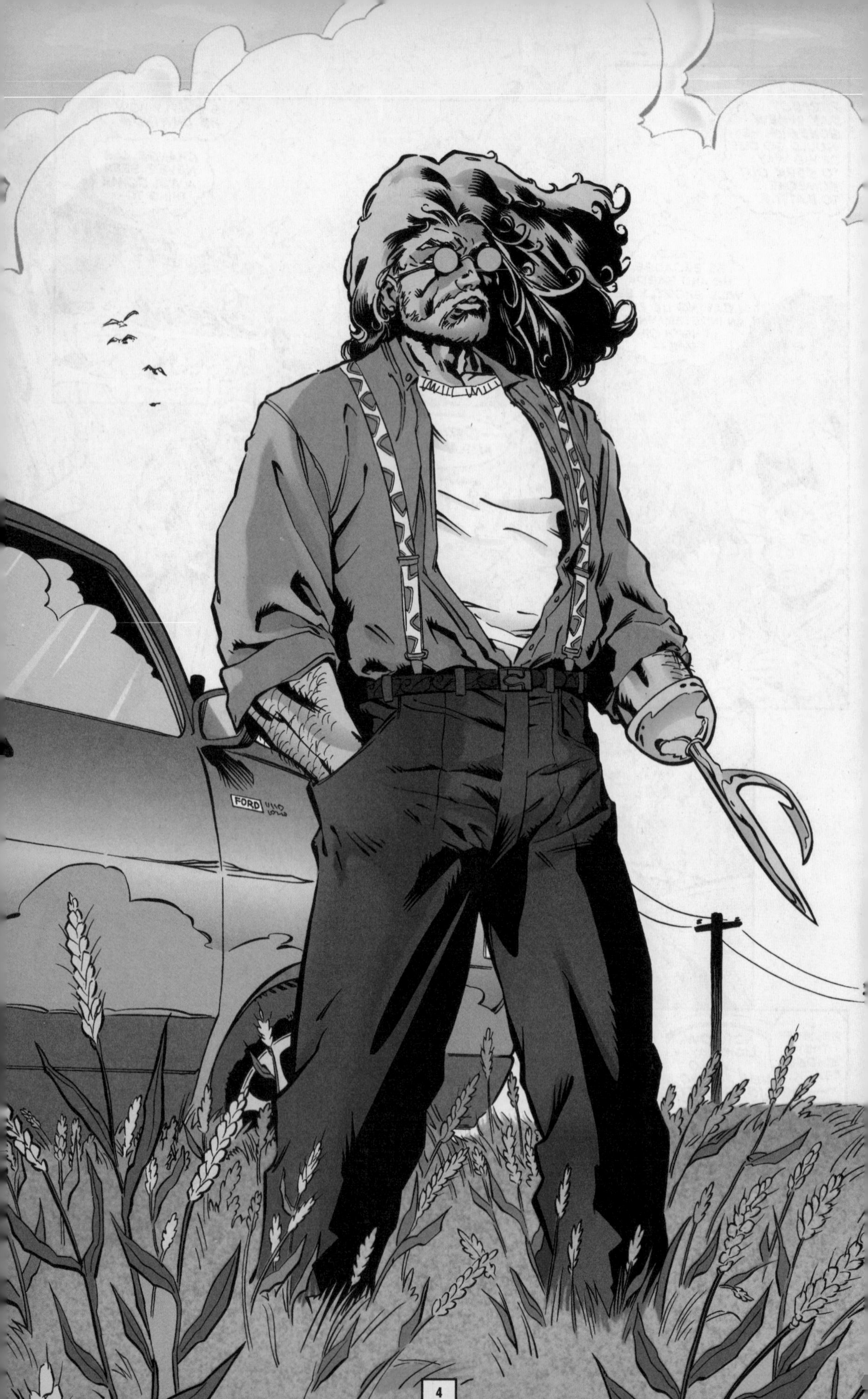
FORD

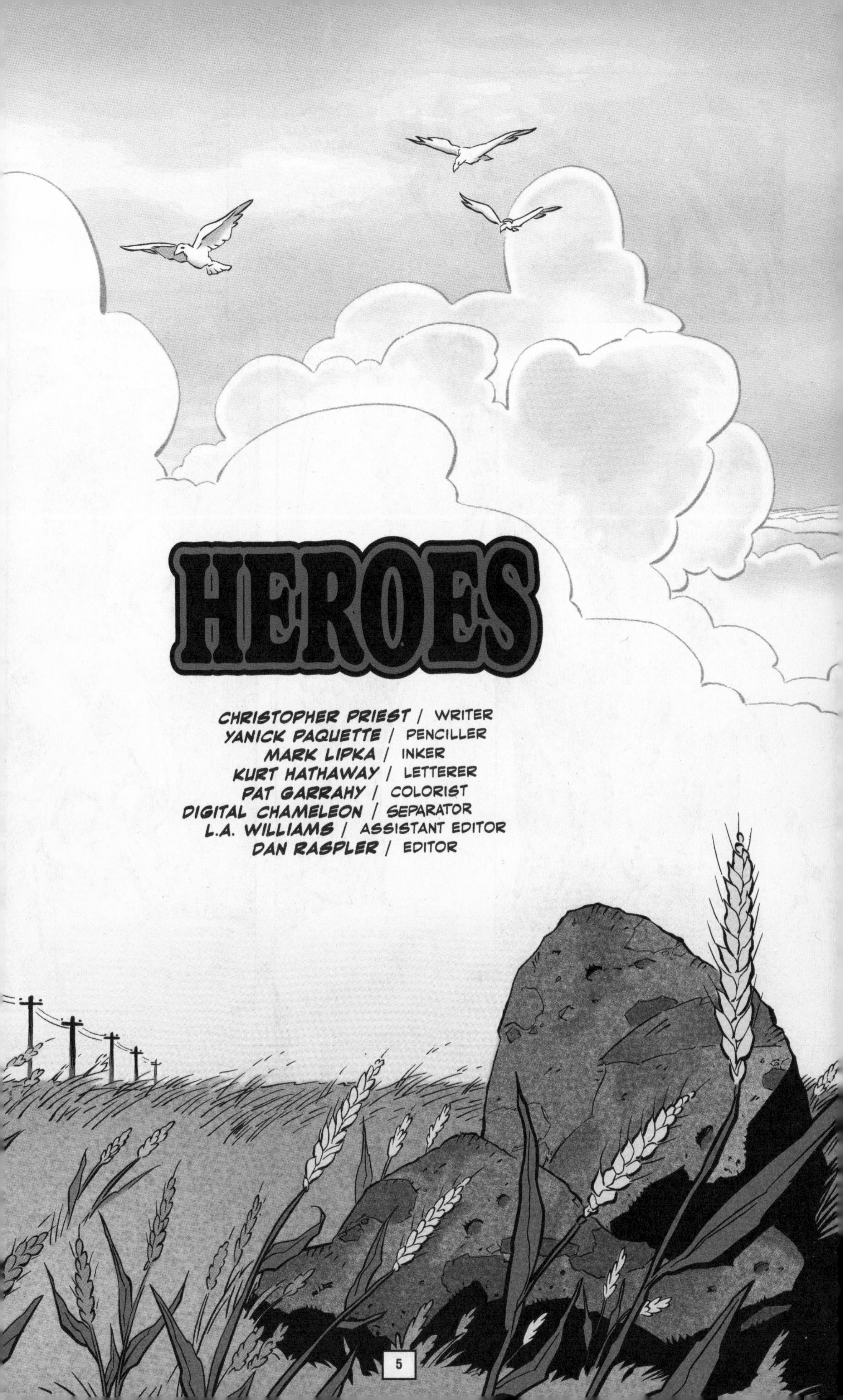
HEROES
CHRISTOPHER PRIEST / WRITER
YANICK PAQUETTE / PENCILLER
MARK LIPKA / INKER
KURT HATHAWAY / LETTERER
PAT GARRAHY / COLORIST
DIGITAL CHAMELEON / SEPARATOR
L.A. WILLIAMS / ASSISTANT EDITOR
DAN RASPLER / EDITOR

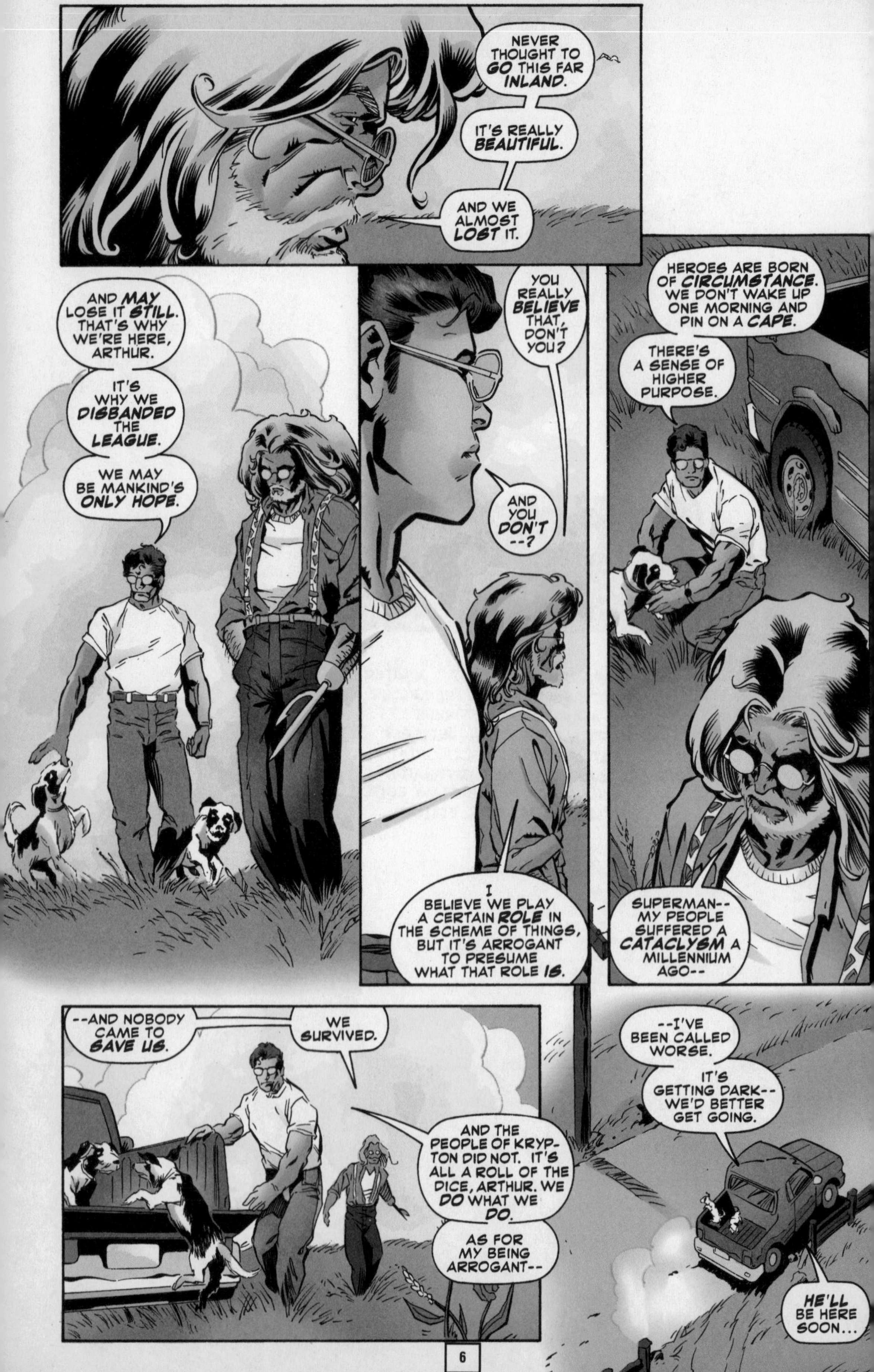
NEVER THOUGHT TO GO THIS FAR INLAND.
IT'S REALLY BEAUTIFUL.
AND WE ALMOST LOST IT.
AND MAY LOSE IT STILL. THAT'S WHY WE'RE HERE, ARTHUR.
IT'S WHY WE DISBANDED THE LEAGUE.
WE MAY BE MANKIND'S ONLY HOPE.
YOU REALLY BELIEVE THAT, DON'T YOU?
AND YOU DON'T --?
I BELIEVE WE PLAY A CERTAIN ROLE IN THE SCHEME OF THINGS, BUT IT'S ARROGANT TO PRESUME WHAT THAT ROLE IS.
HEROES ARE BORN OF CIRCUMSTANCE. WE DON'T WAKE UP ONE MORNING AND PIN ON A CAPE.
THERE'S A SENSE OF HIGHER PURPOSE.
SUPERMAN-- MY PEOPLE SUFFERED A CATACLYSM A MILLENNIUM AGO--
--AND NOBODY CAME TO SAVE US.
WE SURVIVED.
AND THE PEOPLE OF KRYP-TON DID NOT. IT'S ALL A ROLL OF THE DICE, ARTHUR. WE DO WHAT WE DO.
AS FOR MY BEING ARROGANT--
--I'VE BEEN CALLED WORSE.
IT'S GETTING DARK-- WE'D BETTER GET GOING.
HE'LL BE HERE SOON...

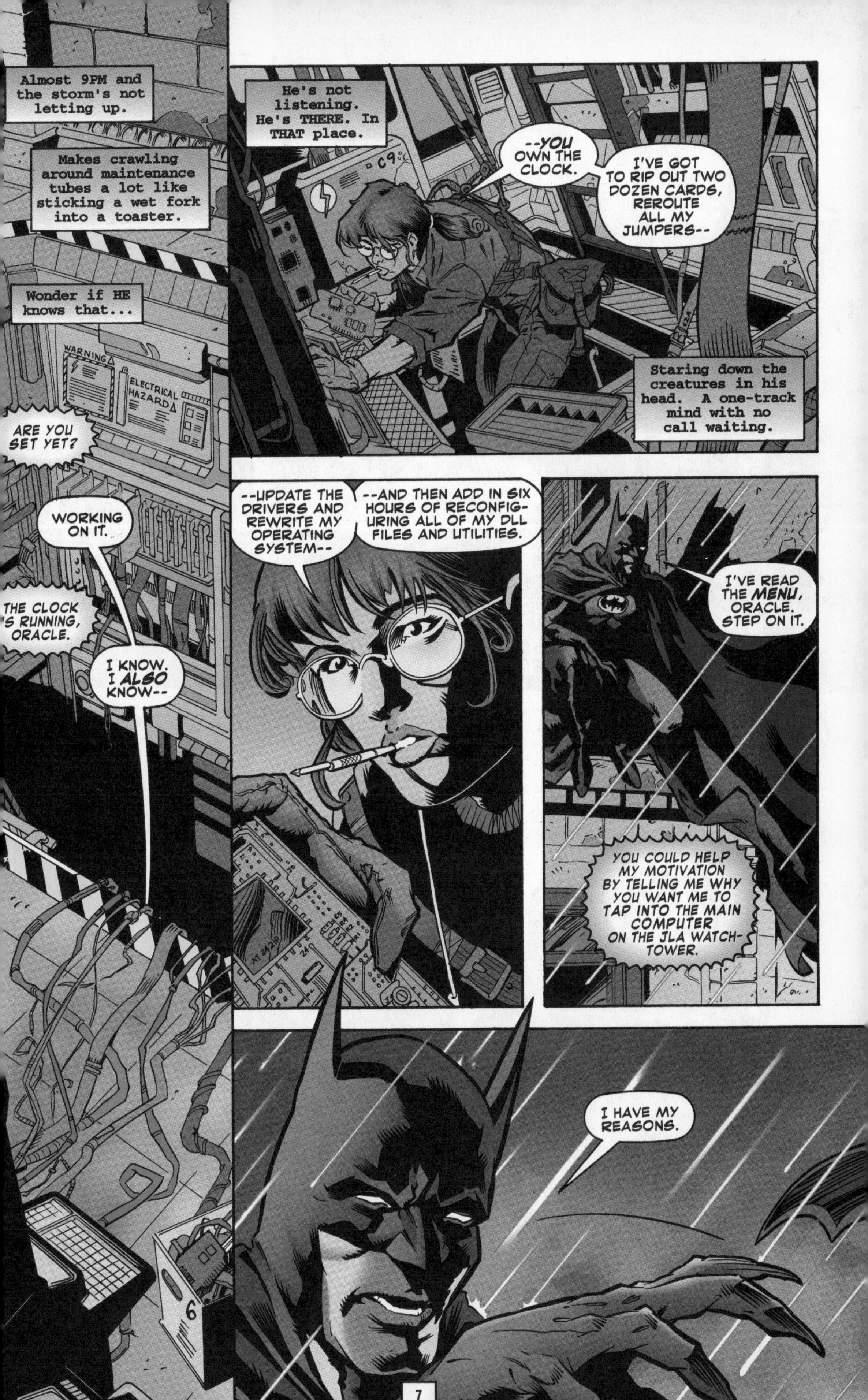
Almost 9PM and the storm's not letting up.
Makes crawling around maintenance tubes a lot like sticking a wet fork into a toaster.
Wonder if HE knows that...
WARNING
ELECTRICAL HAZARD
ARE YOU SET YET?
WORKING ON IT.
THE CLOCK 'S RUNNING, ORACLE.
I KNOW. I ALSO KNOW--
He's not listening. He's THERE. In THAT place.
--YOU OWN THE CLOCK.
I'VE GOT TO RIP OUT TWO DOZEN CARDS, REROUTE ALL MY JUMPERS--
Staring down the creatures in his head. A one-track mind with no call waiting.
--UPDATE THE DRIVERS AND REWRITE MY OPERATING SYSTEM--
--AND THEN ADD IN SIX HOURS OF RECONFIGURING ALL OF MY DLL FILES AND UTILITIES.
I'VE READ THE MENU, ORACLE. STEP ON IT.
YOU COULD HELP MY MOTIVATION BY TELLING ME WHY YOU WANT ME TO TAP INTO THE MAIN COMPUTER ON THE JLA WATCHTOWER.
I HAVE MY REASONS.

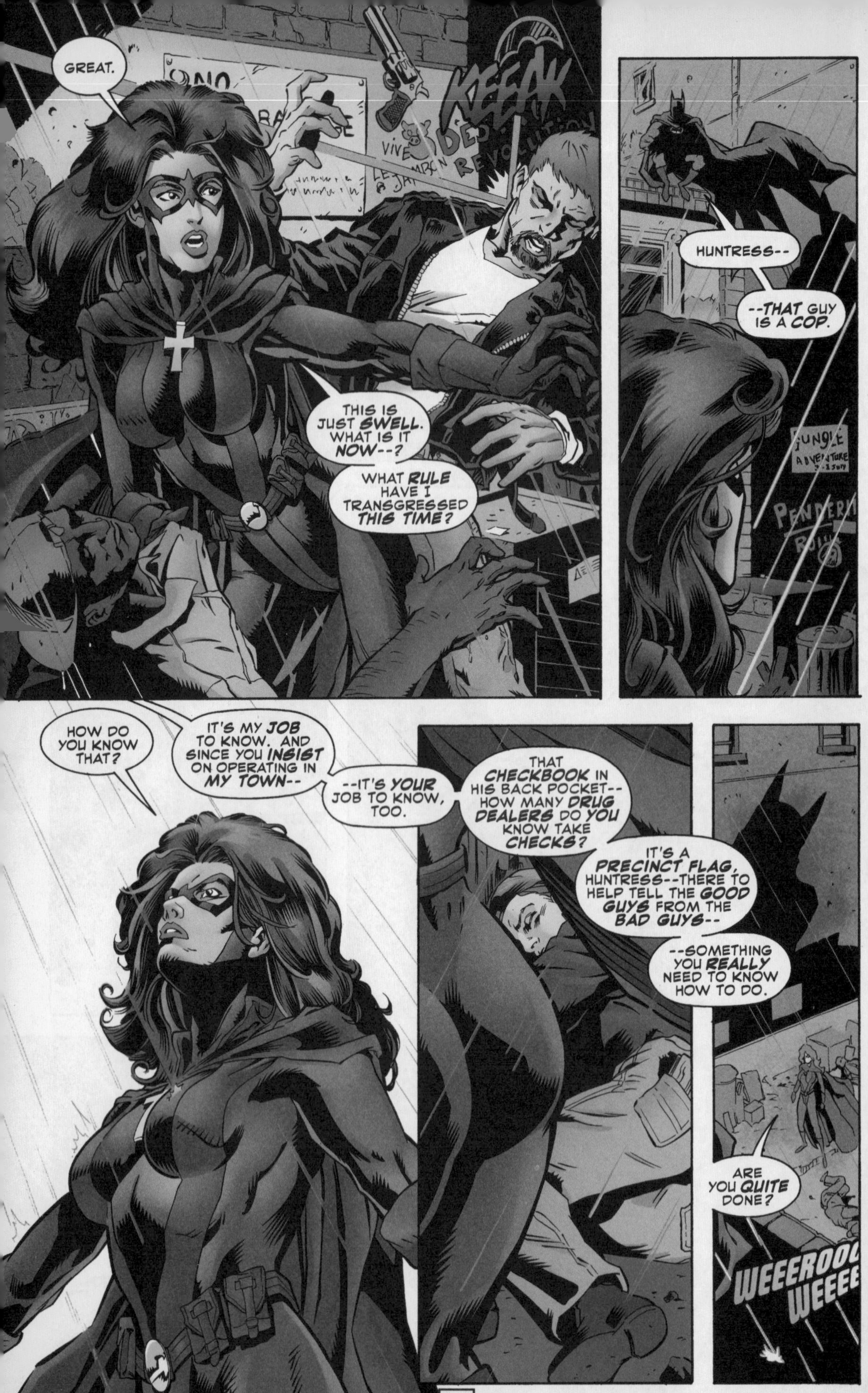
GREAT.
KEEAK
THIS IS JUST SWELL. WHAT IS IT NOW--?
WHAT RULE HAVE I TRANSGRESSED THIS TIME?
HUNTRESS--
--THAT GUY IS A COP.
HOW DO YOU KNOW THAT?
IT'S MY JOB TO KNOW. AND SINCE YOU INSIST ON OPERATING IN MY TOWN--
--IT'S YOUR JOB TO KNOW, TOO.
THAT CHECKBOOK IN HIS BACK POCKET--HOW MANY DRUG DEALERS DO YOU KNOW TAKE CHECKS?
IT'S A PRECINCT FLAG, HUNTRESS--THERE TO HELP TELL THE GOOD GUYS FROM THE BAD GUYS--
--SOMETHING YOU REALLY NEED TO KNOW HOW TO DO.
ARE YOU QUITE DONE?
WEEEROOO
WEEEE

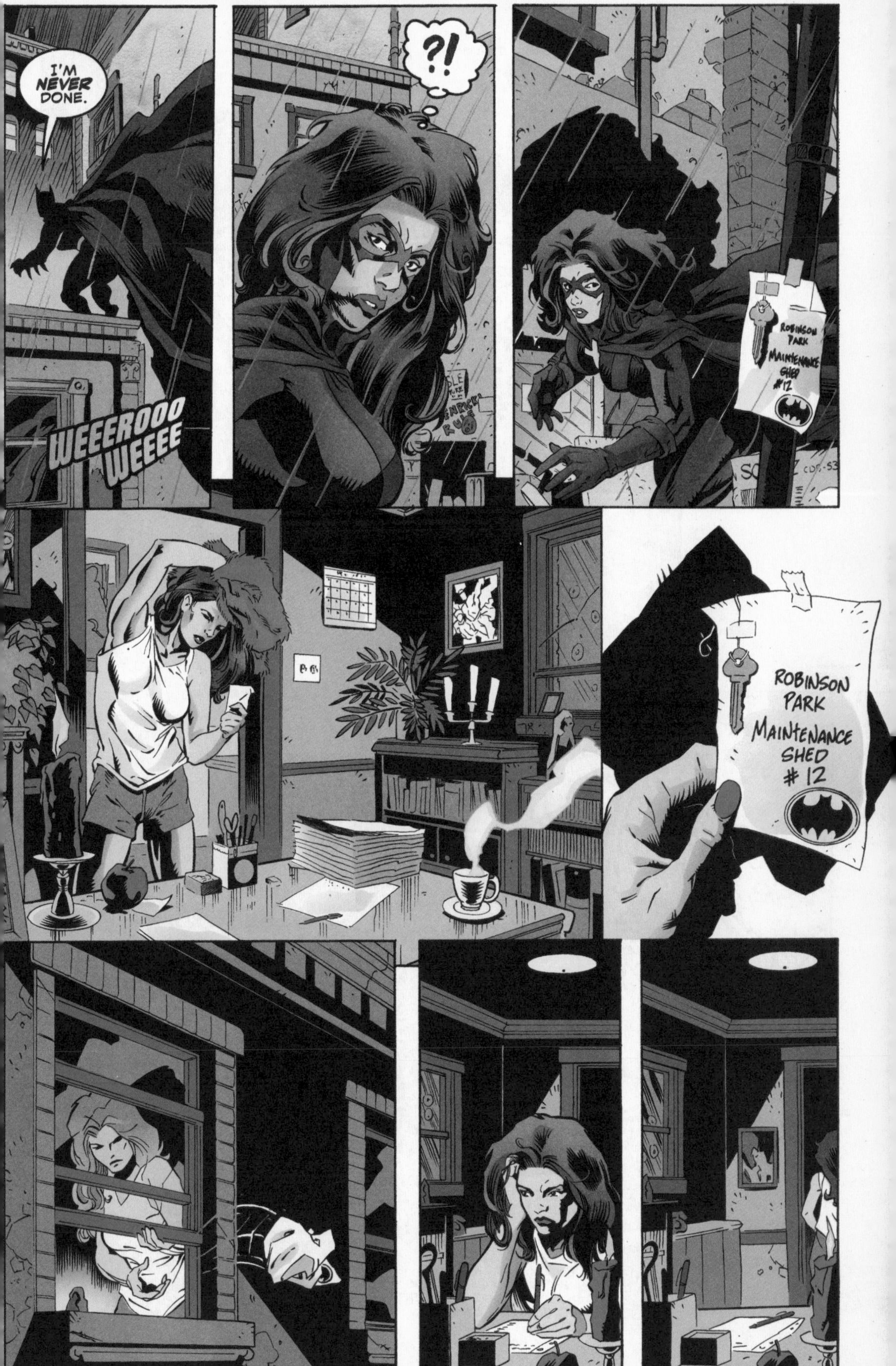
I'M NEVER DONE.
WEEEROOO WEEEE
?!
ROBINSON PARK MAINTENANCE SHED #12
ROBINSON PARK MAINTENANCE SHED # 12

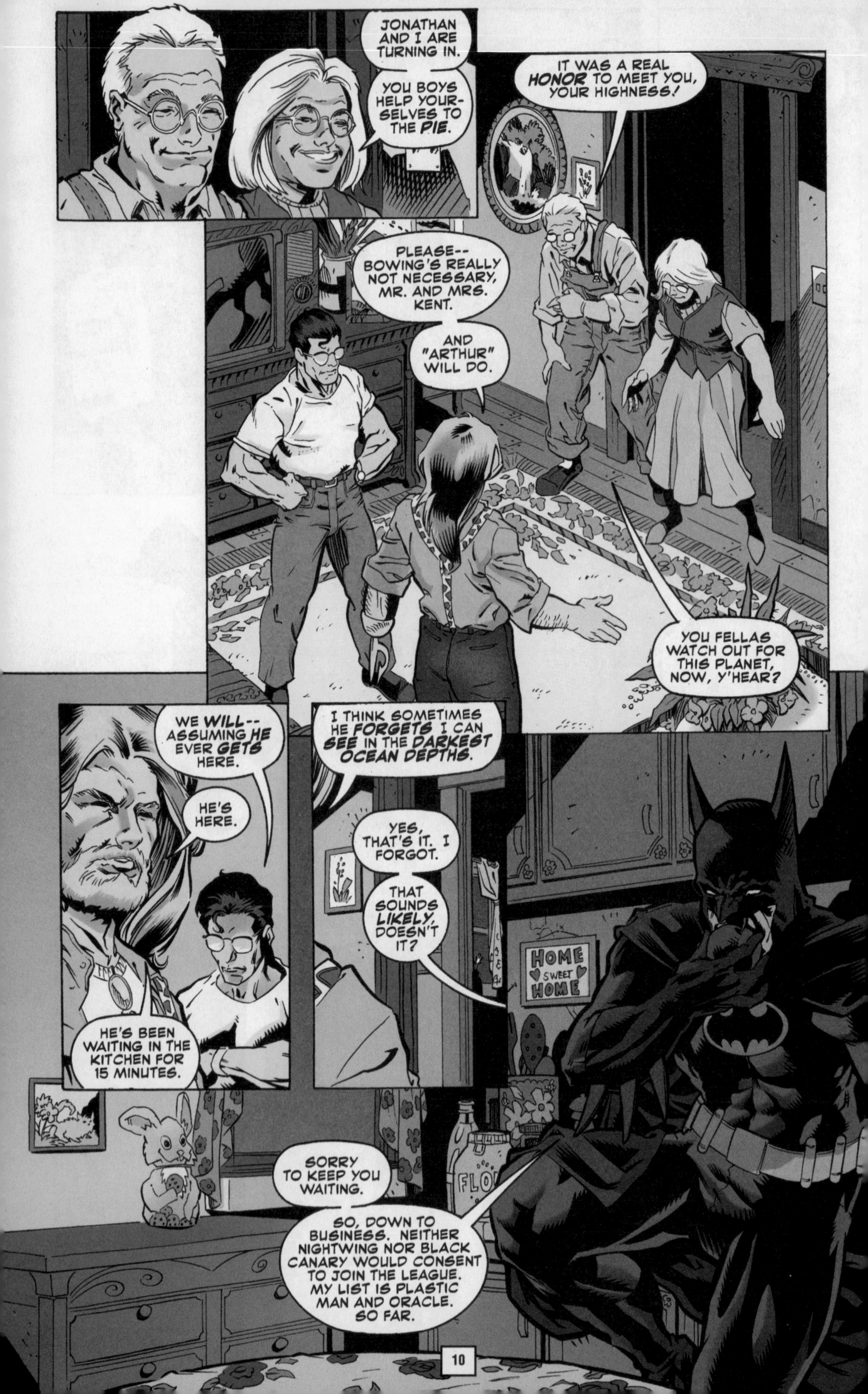

JONATHAN AND I ARE TURNING IN.
YOU BOYS HELP YOURSELVES TO THE PIE.
IT WAS A REAL HONOR TO MEET YOU, YOUR HIGHNESS!
PLEASE-- BOWING'S REALLY NOT NECESSARY, MR. AND MRS. KENT.
AND "ARTHUR" WILL DO.
YOU FELLAS WATCH OUT FOR THIS PLANET, NOW, Y'HEAR?
WE WILL-- ASSUMING HE EVER GETS HERE.
HE'S HERE.
HE'S BEEN WAITING IN THE KITCHEN FOR 15 MINUTES.
I THINK SOMETIMES HE FORGETS I CAN SEE IN THE DARKEST OCEAN DEPTHS.
YES, THAT'S IT. I FORGOT.
THAT SOUNDS LIKELY, DOESN'T IT?
HOME SWEET HOME
SORRY TO KEEP YOU WAITING.
SO, DOWN TO BUSINESS. NEITHER NIGHTWING NOR BLACK CANARY WOULD CONSENT TO JOIN THE LEAGUE. MY LIST IS PLASTIC MAN AND ORACLE. SO FAR.

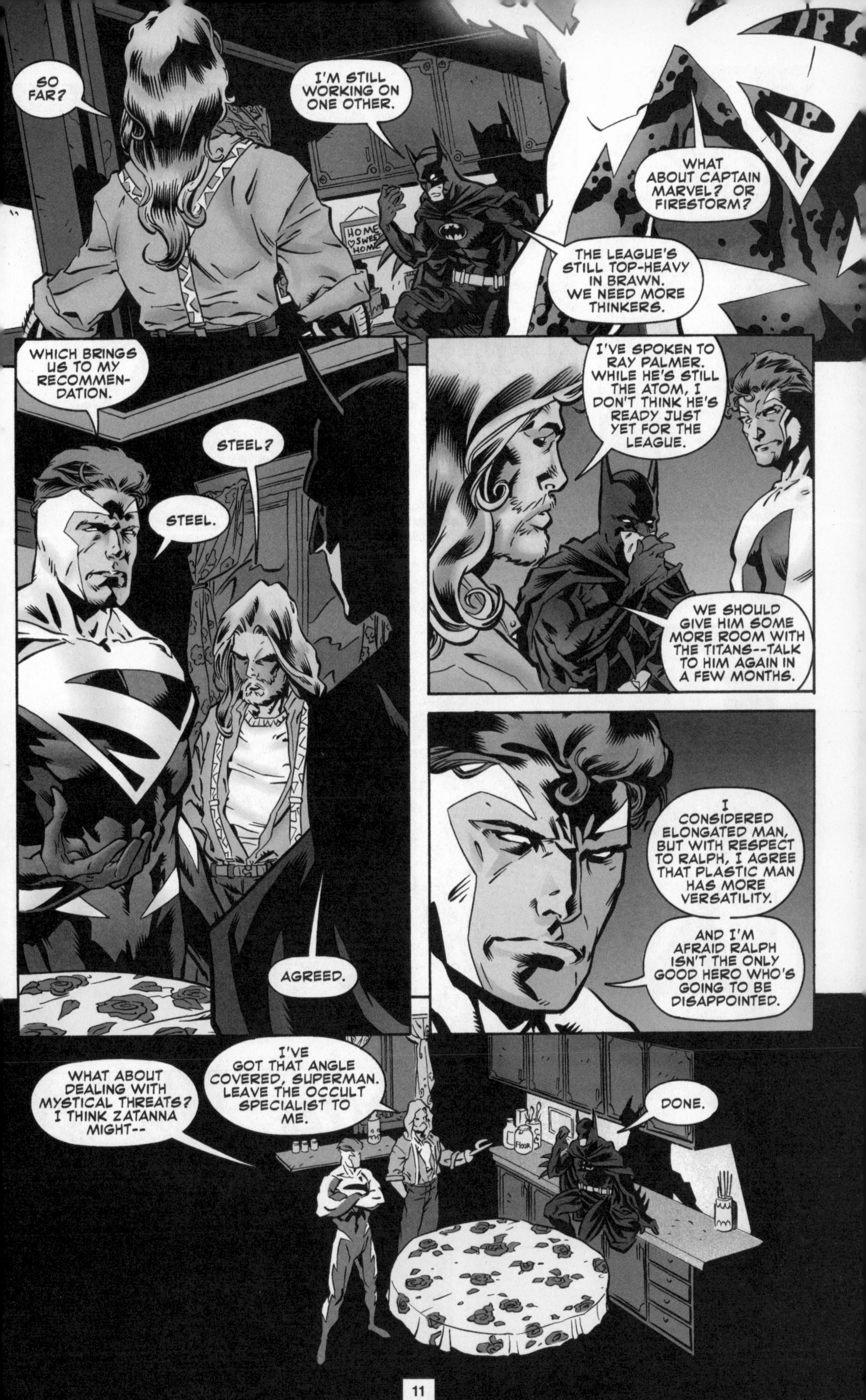
SO FAR?
I'M STILL WORKING ON ONE OTHER.
WHAT ABOUT CAPTAIN MARVEL? OR FIRESTORM?
THE LEAGUE'S STILL TOP-HEAVY IN BRAWN. WE NEED MORE THINKERS.
HOME SWEET HOME
WHICH BRINGS US TO MY RECOMMENDATION.
STEEL?
STEEL.
AGREED.
I'VE SPOKEN TO RAY PALMER. WHILE HE'S STILL THE ATOM, I DON'T THINK HE'S READY JUST YET FOR THE LEAGUE.
WE SHOULD GIVE HIM SOME MORE ROOM WITH THE TITANS--TALK TO HIM AGAIN IN A FEW MONTHS.
I CONSIDERED ELONGATED MAN, BUT WITH RESPECT TO RALPH, I AGREE THAT PLASTIC MAN HAS MORE VERSATILITY.
AND I'M AFRAID RALPH ISN'T THE ONLY GOOD HERO WHO'S GOING TO BE DISAPPOINTED.
WHAT ABOUT DEALING WITH MYSTICAL THREATS? I THINK ZATANNA MIGHT--
I'VE GOT THAT ANGLE COVERED, SUPERMAN. LEAVE THE OCCULT SPECIALIST TO ME.
DONE.
FLOUR

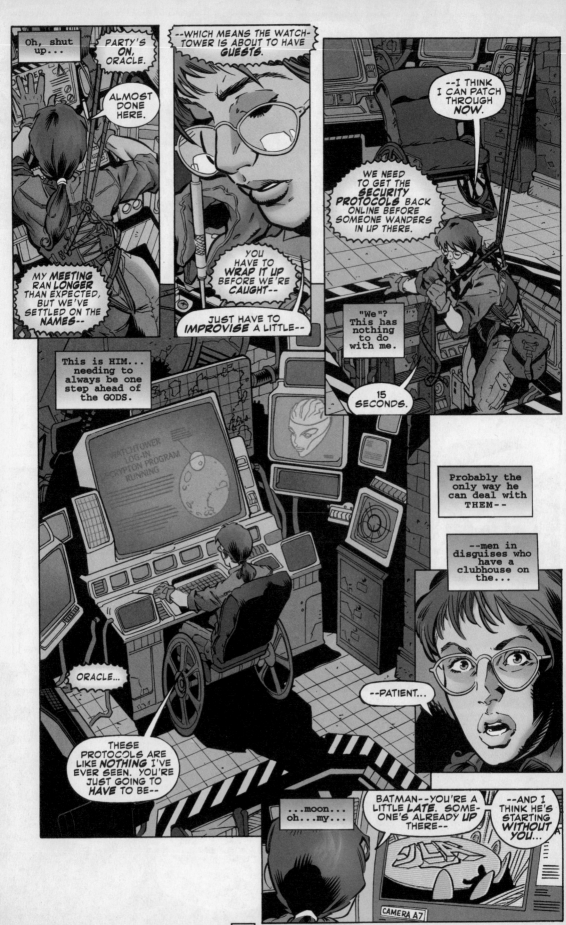

Oh, shut up...

PARTY'S **ON,** ORACLE.

ALMOST DONE HERE.

MY MEETING RAN **LONGER** THAN EXPECTED, BUT WE'VE SETTLED ON THE **NAMES--**

--WHICH MEANS THE WATCH-TOWER IS ABOUT TO HAVE **GUESTS.**

YOU HAVE TO **WRAP IT UP** BEFORE WE'RE **CAUGHT--**

JUST HAVE TO **IMPROVISE** A LITTLE--

--I THINK I CAN PATCH THROUGH **NOW.**

WE NEED TO GET THE **SECURITY PROTOCOLS** BACK ONLINE BEFORE SOMEONE WANDERS IN UP THERE.

"WE"? THIS HAS NOTHING TO DO WITH ME.

15 SECONDS.

This is HIM... needing to always be one step ahead of the GODS.

WATCHTOWER LOG-IN
ECRYPTON PROGRAM
RUNNING

Probably the only way he can deal with THEM--

--men in disguises who have a clubhouse on the...

ORACLE...

THESE PROTOCOLS ARE LIKE **NOTHING** I'VE EVER SEEN. YOU'RE JUST GOING TO **HAVE TO BE--**

--PATIENT...

...moon... oh...my...

BATMAN--YOU'RE A LITTLE **LATE.** SOME-ONE'S ALREADY **UP** THERE--

--AND I THINK HE'S STARTING **WITHOUT** YOU...

CAMERA A7

12

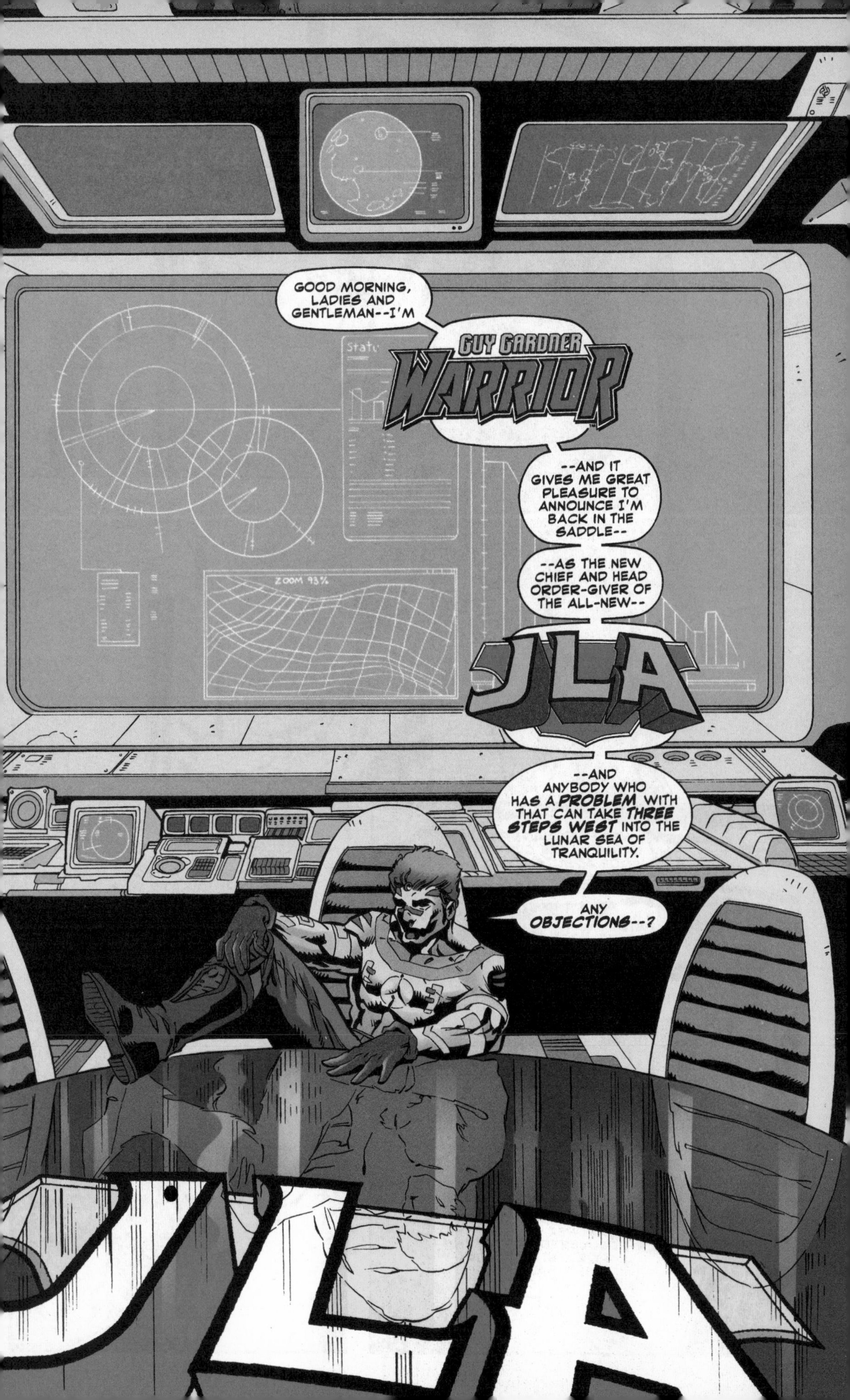

GOOD MORNING, LADIES AND GENTLEMAN--I'M
GUY GARDNER WARRIOR
--AND IT GIVES ME GREAT PLEASURE TO ANNOUNCE I'M BACK IN THE SADDLE--
--AS THE NEW CHIEF AND HEAD ORDER-GIVER OF THE ALL-NEW--
JLA
--AND ANYBODY WHO HAS A PROBLEM WITH THAT CAN TAKE THREE STEPS WEST INTO THE LUNAR SEA OF TRANQUILITY.
ANY OBJECTIONS--?
ZOOM 93%
JLA

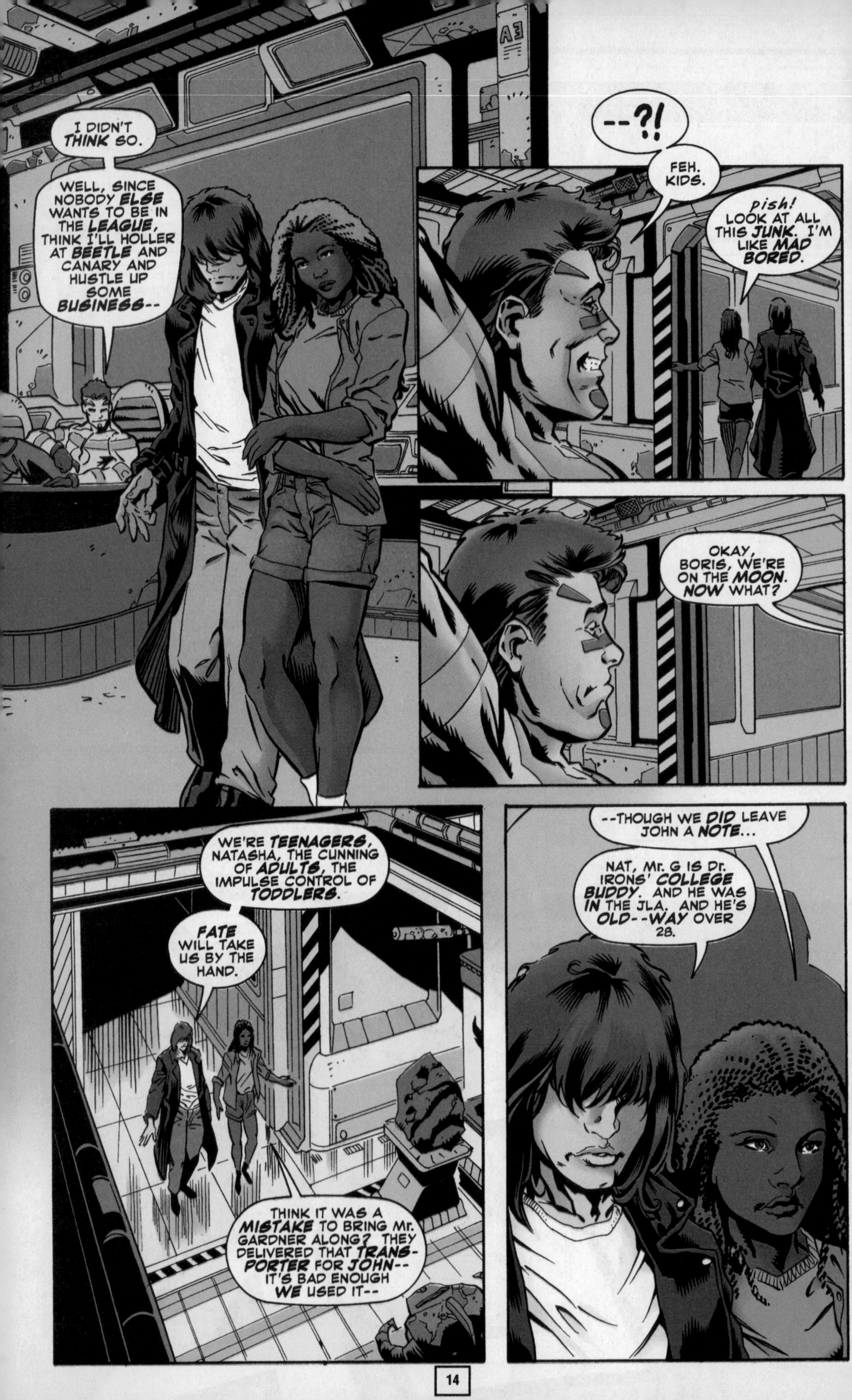
I DIDN'T THINK SO.
WELL, SINCE NOBODY ELSE WANTS TO BE IN THE LEAGUE, THINK I'LL HOLLER AT BEETLE AND CANARY AND HUSTLE UP SOME BUSINESS--
--?!
FEH. KIDS.
pish! LOOK AT ALL THIS JUNK. I'M LIKE MAD BORED.
OKAY, BORIS, WE'RE ON THE MOON. NOW WHAT?
WE'RE TEENAGERS, NATASHA, THE CUNNING OF ADULTS, THE IMPULSE CONTROL OF TODDLERS.
FATE WILL TAKE US BY THE HAND.
THINK IT WAS A MISTAKE TO BRING Mr. GARDNER ALONG? THEY DELIVERED THAT TRANSPORTER FOR JOHN-- IT'S BAD ENOUGH WE USED IT--
--THOUGH WE DID LEAVE JOHN A NOTE...
NAT, Mr. G IS Dr. IRONS' COLLEGE BUDDY. AND HE WAS IN THE JLA. AND HE'S OLD--WAY OVER 28.

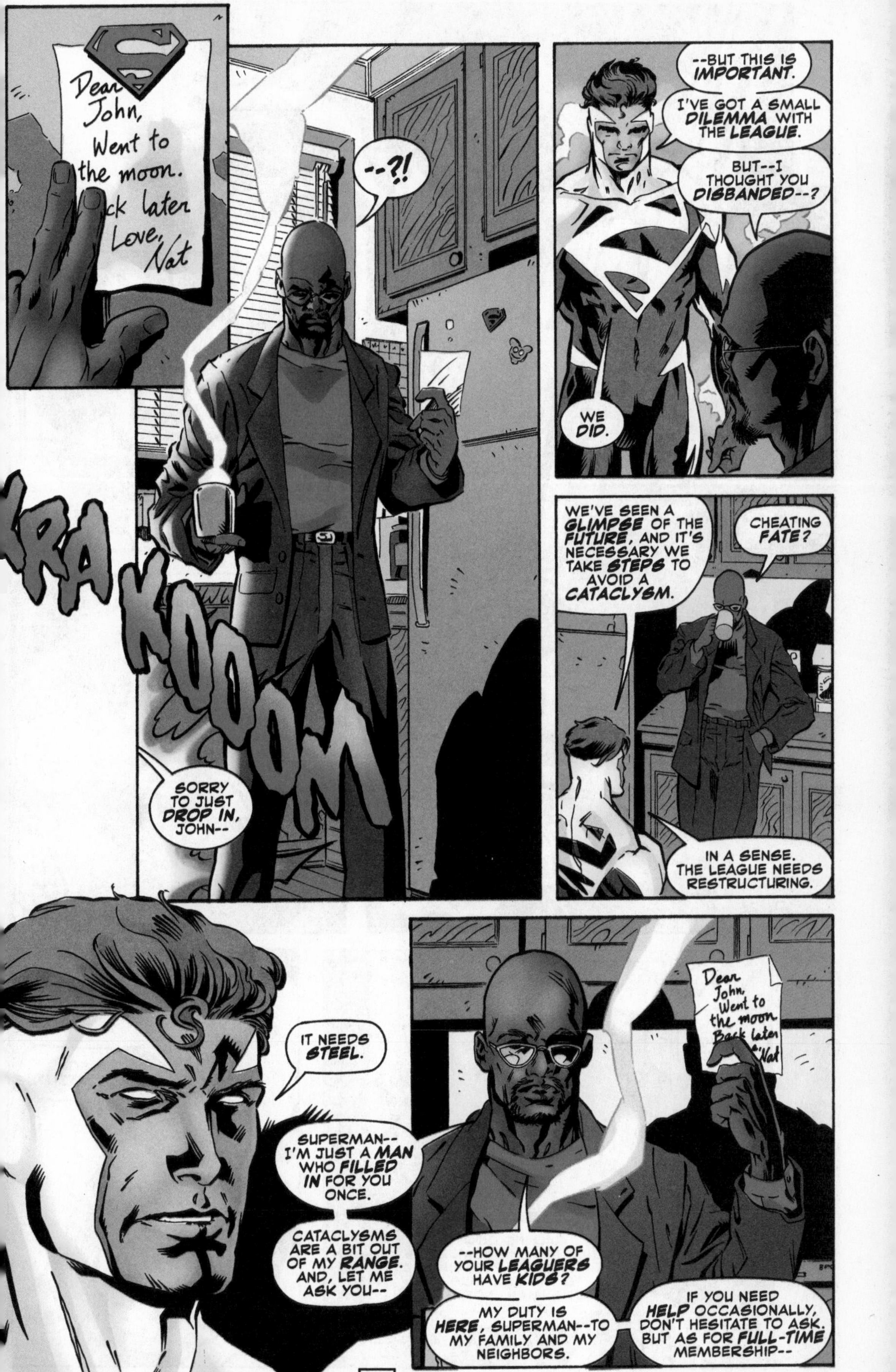
Dear John, Went to the moon. Back later Love, Nat
--?!
KRAKOOOOM
SORRY TO JUST DROP IN, JOHN--
--BUT THIS IS IMPORTANT.
I'VE GOT A SMALL DILEMMA WITH THE LEAGUE.
BUT--I THOUGHT YOU DISBANDED--?
WE DID.
WE'VE SEEN A GLIMPSE OF THE FUTURE, AND IT'S NECESSARY WE TAKE STEPS TO AVOID A CATACLYSM.
CHEATING FATE?
IN A SENSE. THE LEAGUE NEEDS RESTRUCTURING.
IT NEEDS STEEL.
SUPERMAN-- I'M JUST A MAN WHO FILLED IN FOR YOU ONCE.
CATACLYSMS ARE A BIT OUT OF MY RANGE. AND, LET ME ASK YOU--
--HOW MANY OF YOUR LEAGUERS HAVE KIDS?
MY DUTY IS HERE, SUPERMAN--TO MY FAMILY AND MY NEIGHBORS.
IF YOU NEED HELP OCCASIONALLY, DON'T HESITATE TO ASK. BUT AS FOR FULL-TIME MEMBERSHIP--

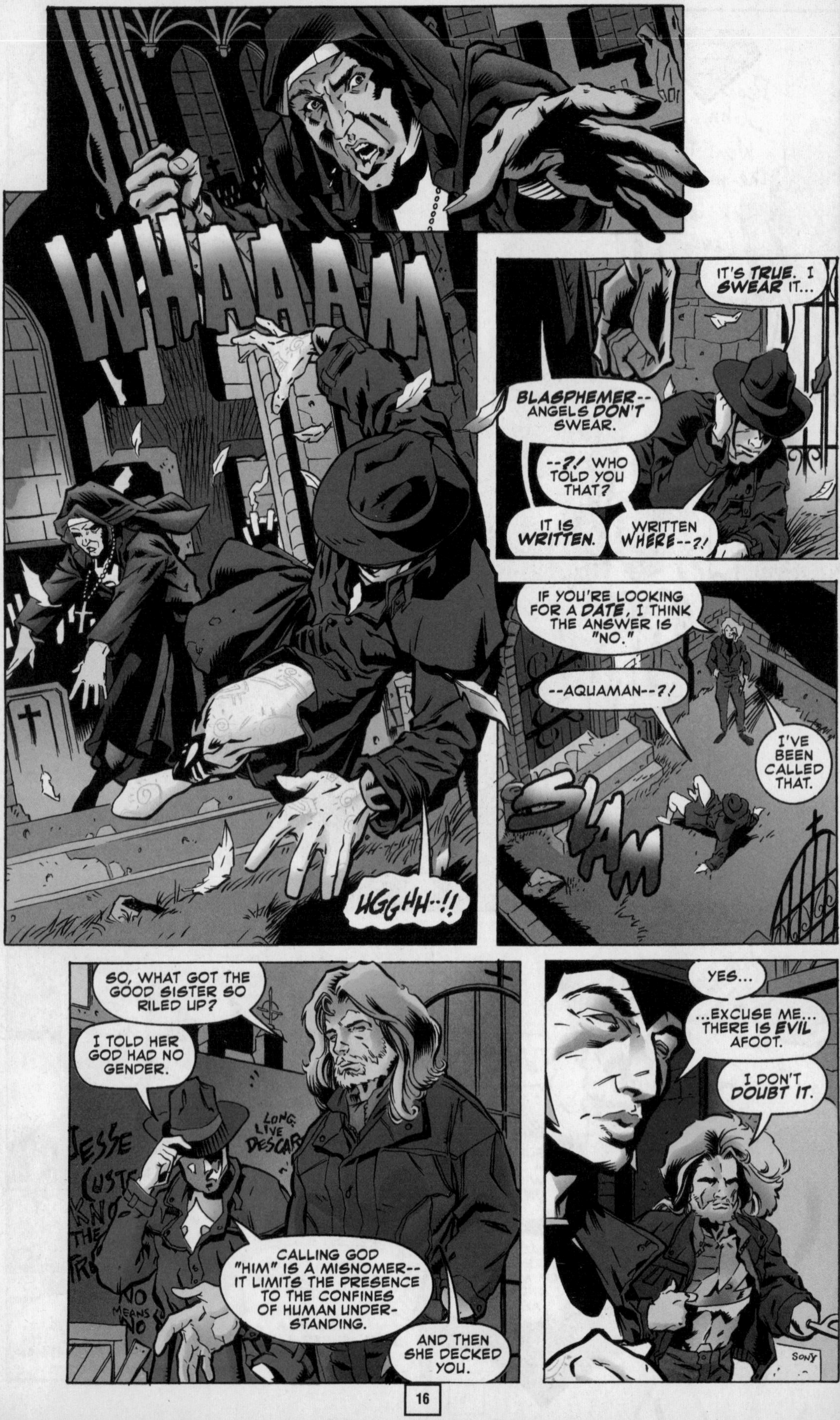
WHAAAM
UGGHH--!!
IT'S TRUE. I SWEAR IT...
BLASPHEMER--ANGELS DON'T SWEAR.
--?! WHO TOLD YOU THAT?
IT IS WRITTEN.
WRITTEN WHERE--?!
IF YOU'RE LOOKING FOR A DATE, I THINK THE ANSWER IS "NO."
--AQUAMAN--?!
I'VE BEEN CALLED THAT.
SLAM
SO, WHAT GOT THE GOOD SISTER SO RILED UP?
I TOLD HER GOD HAD NO GENDER.
LONG LIVE DESCAR
CALLING GOD "HIM" IS A MISNOMER--IT LIMITS THE PRESENCE TO THE CONFINES OF HUMAN UNDER-STANDING.
NO MEANS NO
AND THEN SHE DECKED YOU.
YES...
...EXCUSE ME... THERE IS EVIL AFOOT.
I DON'T DOUBT IT.
SONY

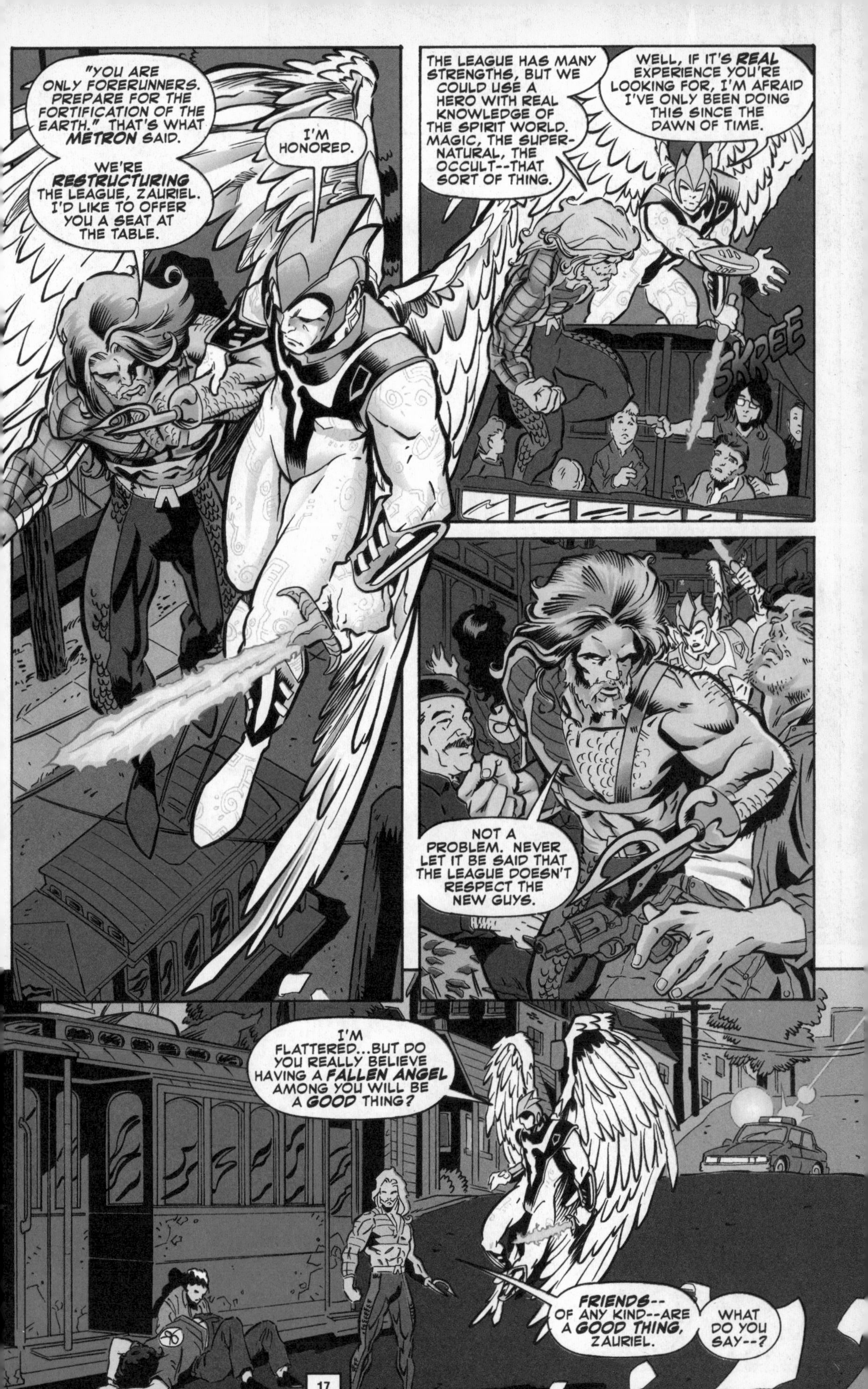
"YOU ARE ONLY FORERUNNERS. PREPARE FOR THE FORTIFICATION OF THE EARTH." THAT'S WHAT **METRON** SAID.
WE'RE **RESTRUCTURING** THE LEAGUE, ZAURIEL. I'D LIKE TO OFFER YOU A SEAT AT THE TABLE.
I'M HONORED.
THE LEAGUE HAS MANY STRENGTHS, BUT WE COULD USE A HERO WITH REAL KNOWLEDGE OF THE SPIRIT WORLD. MAGIC, THE SUPER-NATURAL, THE OCCULT--THAT SORT OF THING.
WELL, IF IT'S **REAL** EXPERIENCE YOU'RE LOOKING FOR, I'M AFRAID I'VE ONLY BEEN DOING THIS SINCE THE DAWN OF TIME.
SKREE
NOT A PROBLEM. NEVER LET IT BE SAID THAT THE LEAGUE DOESN'T RESPECT THE NEW GUYS.
I'M FLATTERED...BUT DO YOU REALLY BELIEVE HAVING A **FALLEN ANGEL** AMONG YOU WILL BE A **GOOD** THING?
FRIENDS--OF ANY KIND--ARE A **GOOD THING,** ZAURIEL.
WHAT DO YOU SAY--?

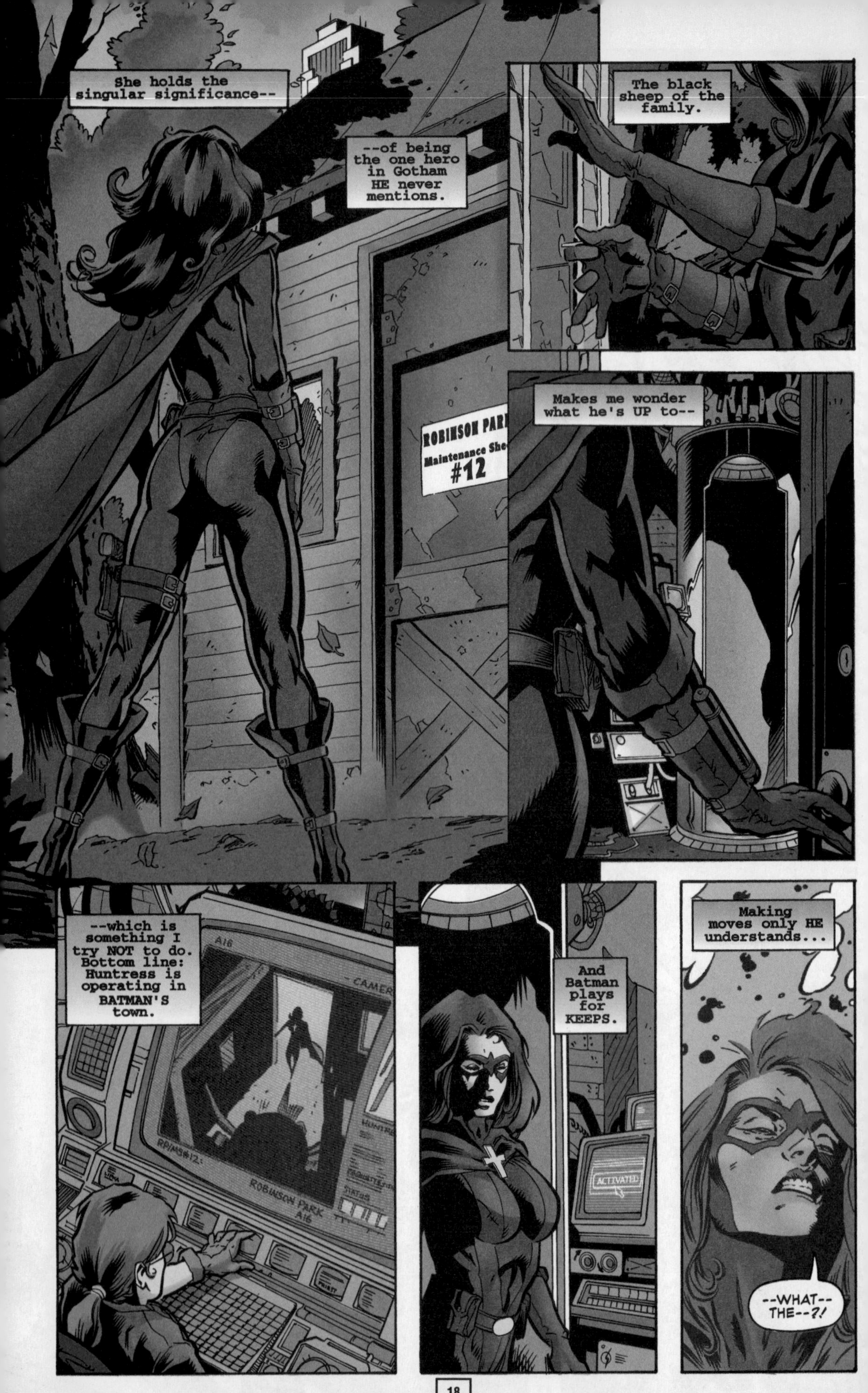
She holds the singular significance--
--of being the one hero in Gotham HE never mentions.
ROBINSON PARK
Maintenance She
#12
The black sheep of the family.
Makes me wonder what he's UP to--
--which is something I try NOT to do. Bottom line: Huntress is operating in BATMAN'S town.
ROBINSON PARK
A16
And Batman plays for KEEPS.
ACTIVATED
Making moves only HE understands...
--WHAT-- THE--?!

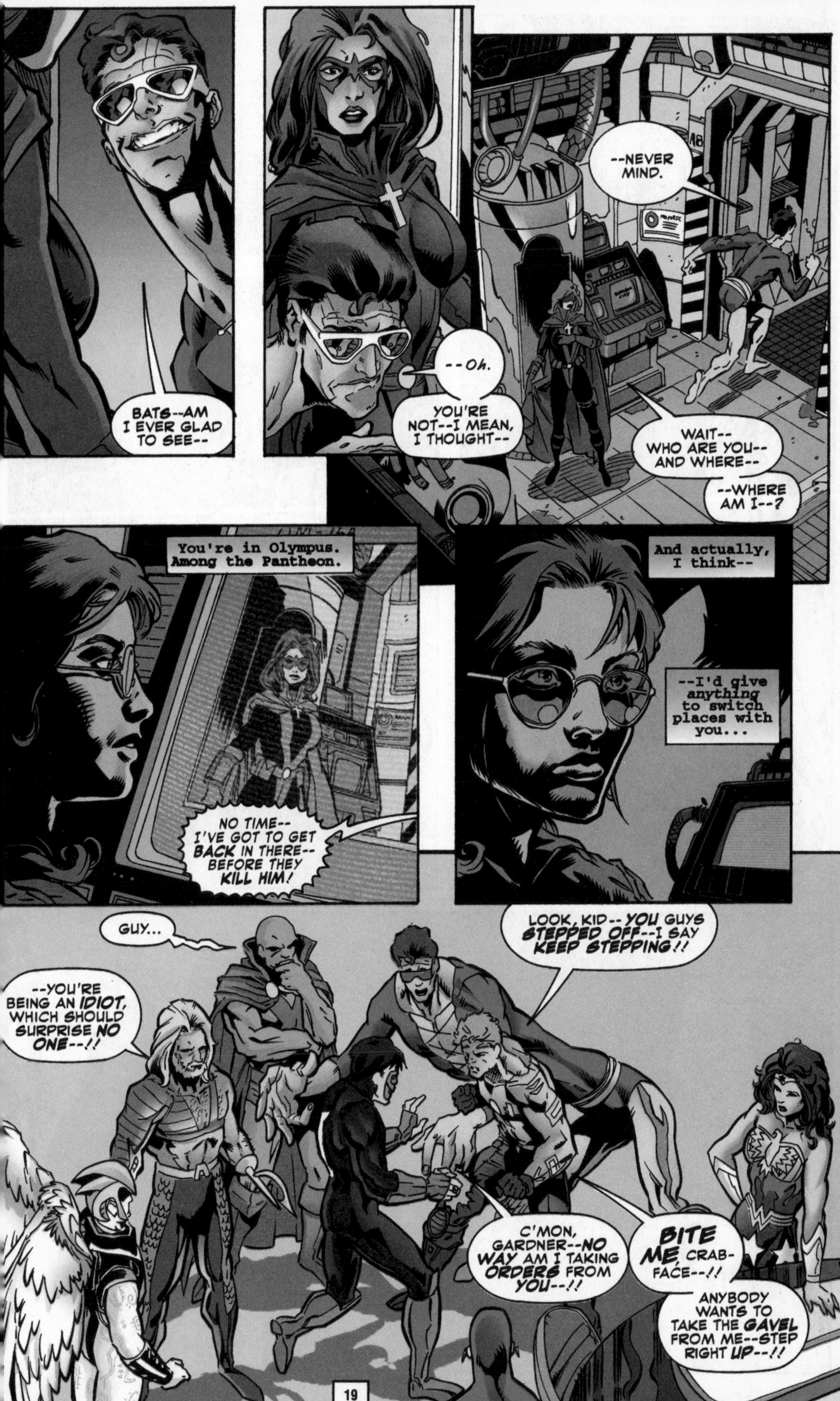
BATS--AM I EVER GLAD TO SEE--
--Oh.
YOU'RE NOT--I MEAN, I THOUGHT--
--NEVER MIND.
WAIT-- WHO ARE YOU-- AND WHERE--
--WHERE AM I--?
You're in Olympus. Among the Pantheon.
NO TIME-- I'VE GOT TO GET BACK IN THERE-- BEFORE THEY KILL HIM!
And actually, I think--
--I'd give anything to switch places with you...
GUY...
--YOU'RE BEING AN IDIOT, WHICH SHOULD SURPRISE NO ONE--!!
LOOK, KID--YOU GUYS STEPPED OFF--I SAY KEEP STEPPING!!
C'MON, GARDNER--NO WAY AM I TAKING ORDERS FROM YOU--!!
BITE ME, CRAB-FACE--!!
ANYBODY WANTS TO TAKE THE GAVEL FROM ME--STEP RIGHT UP--!!

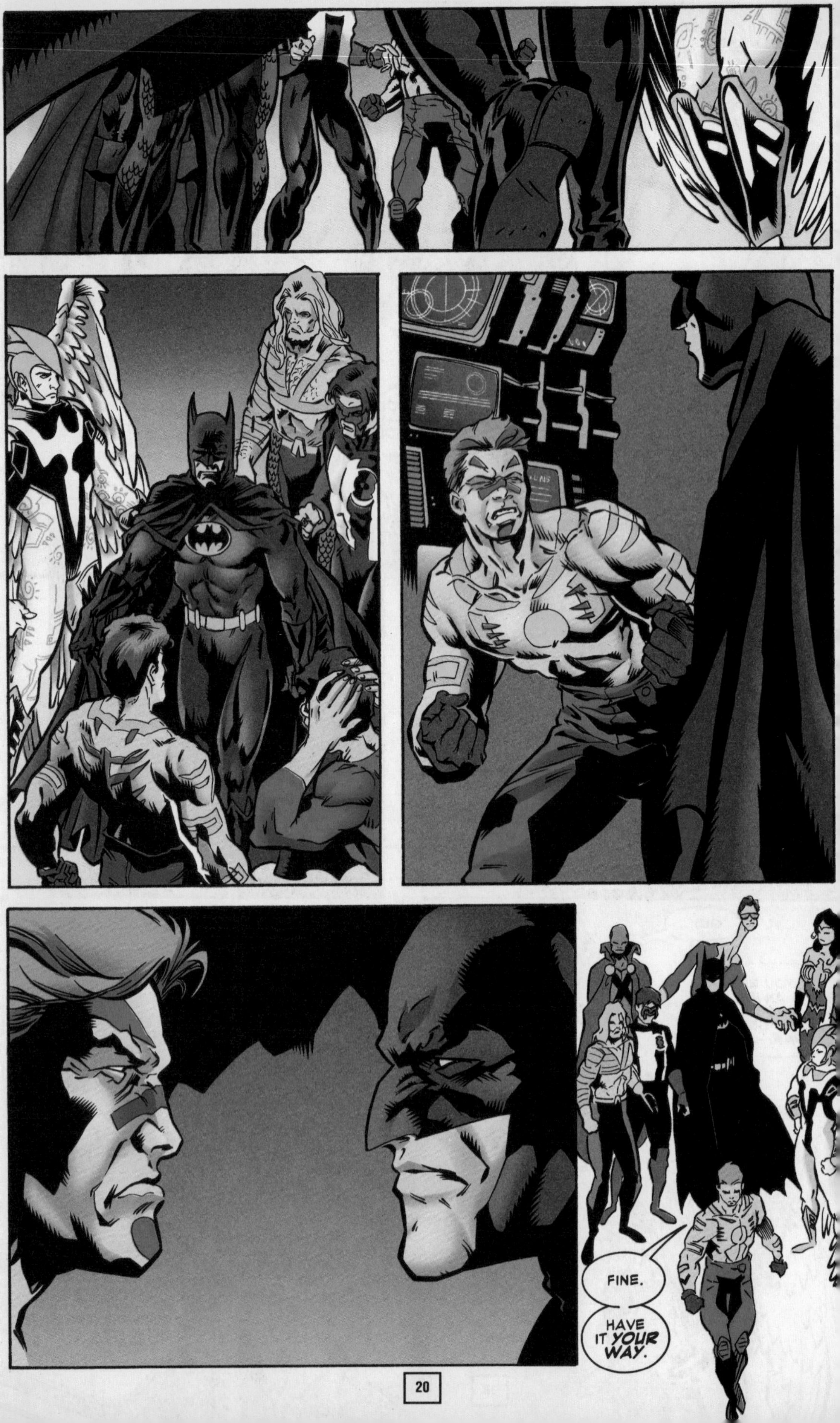
FINE.
HAVE IT YOUR WAY.

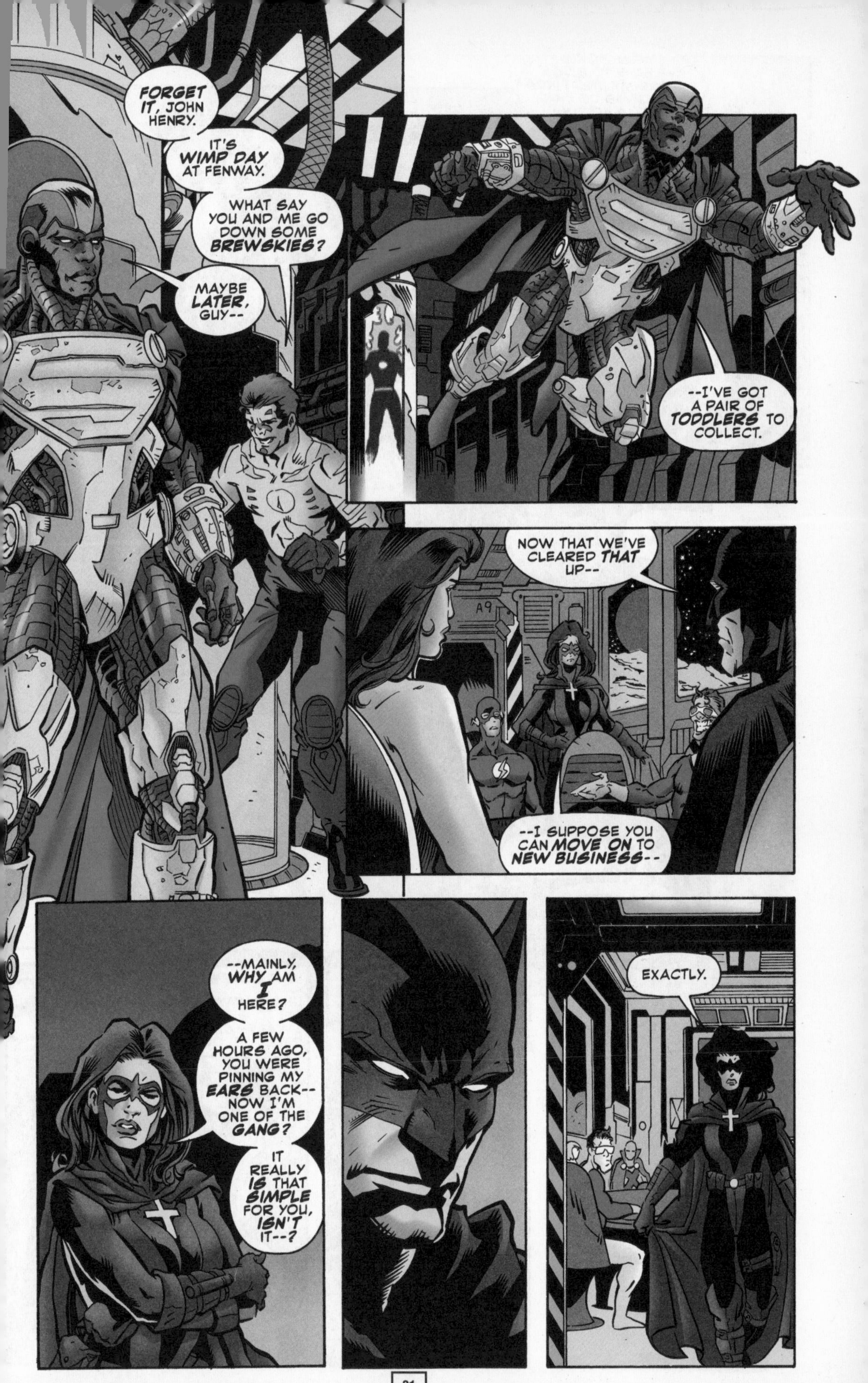
FORGET IT, JOHN HENRY.
IT'S WIMP DAY AT FENWAY.
WHAT SAY YOU AND ME GO DOWN SOME BREWSKIES?
MAYBE LATER, GUY--
--I'VE GOT A PAIR OF TODDLERS TO COLLECT.
NOW THAT WE'VE CLEARED THAT UP--
A9
--I SUPPOSE YOU CAN MOVE ON TO NEW BUSINESS--
--MAINLY, WHY AM I HERE?
A FEW HOURS AGO, YOU WERE PINNING MY EARS BACK-- NOW I'M ONE OF THE GANG?
IT REALLY IS THAT SIMPLE FOR YOU, ISN'T IT--?
EXACTLY.

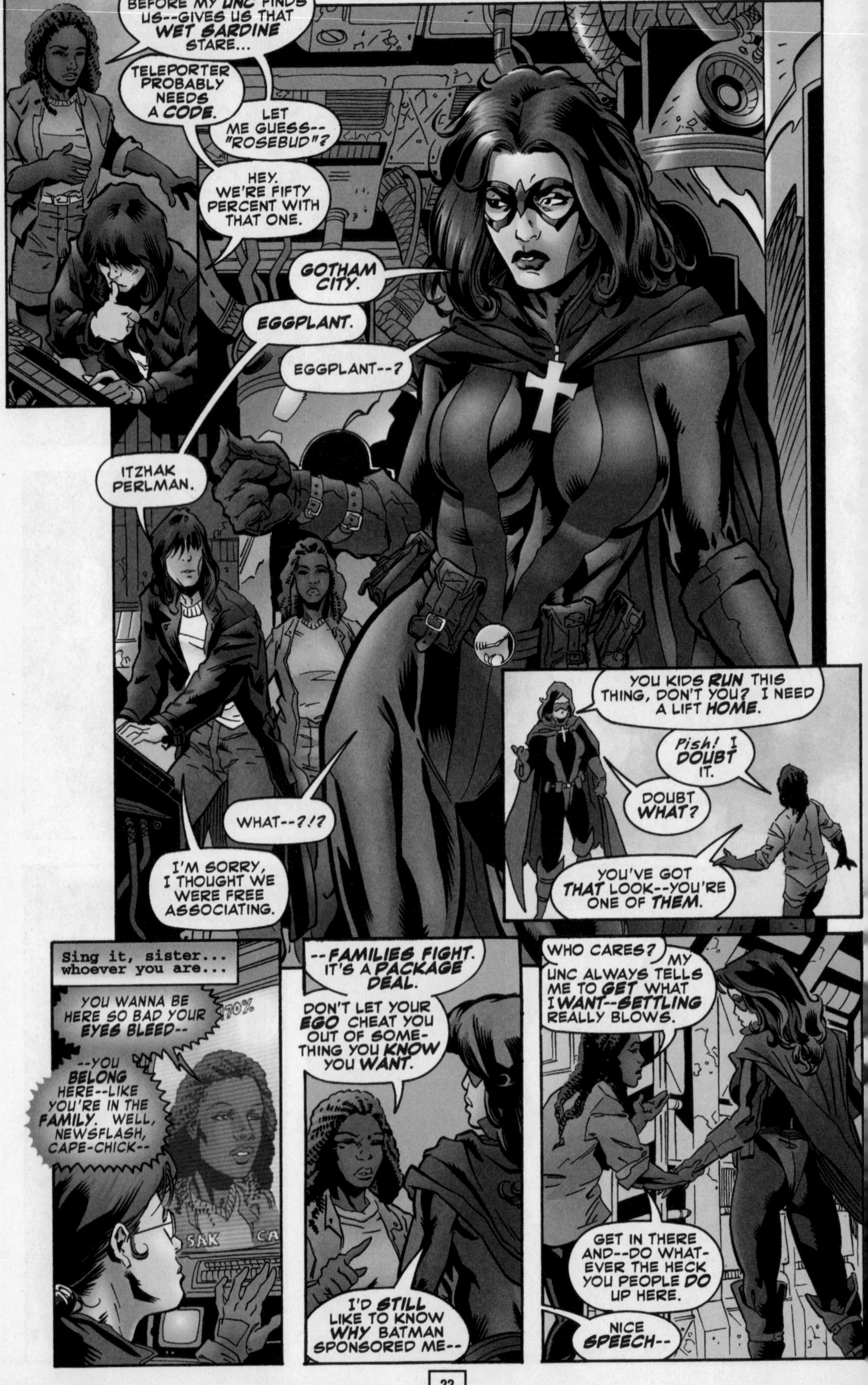

C'MON, BORIS, WE HAVE TO BOOK BEFORE MY UNC FINDS US--GIVES US THAT WET SARDINE STARE...
TELEPORTER PROBABLY NEEDS A CODE.
LET ME GUESS-- "ROSEBUD"?
HEY. WE'RE FIFTY PERCENT WITH THAT ONE.
GOTHAM CITY.
EGGPLANT.
EGGPLANT--?
ITZHAK PERLMAN.
WHAT--?!?
I'M SORRY, I THOUGHT WE WERE FREE ASSOCIATING.
YOU KIDS RUN THIS THING, DON'T YOU? I NEED A LIFT HOME.
Pish! I DOUBT IT.
DOUBT WHAT?
YOU'VE GOT THAT LOOK--YOU'RE ONE OF THEM.
Sing it, sister... whoever you are...
YOU WANNA BE HERE SO BAD YOUR EYES BLEED--
--YOU BELONG HERE--LIKE YOU'RE IN THE FAMILY. WELL, NEWSFLASH, CAPE-CHICK--
--FAMILIES FIGHT. IT'S A PACKAGE DEAL.
DON'T LET YOUR EGO CHEAT YOU OUT OF SOMETHING YOU KNOW YOU WANT.
I'D STILL LIKE TO KNOW WHY BATMAN SPONSORED ME--
WHO CARES?
MY UNC ALWAYS TELLS ME TO GET WHAT I WANT--SETTLING REALLY BLOWS.
GET IN THERE AND--DO WHATEVER THE HECK YOU PEOPLE DO UP HERE.
NICE SPEECH--

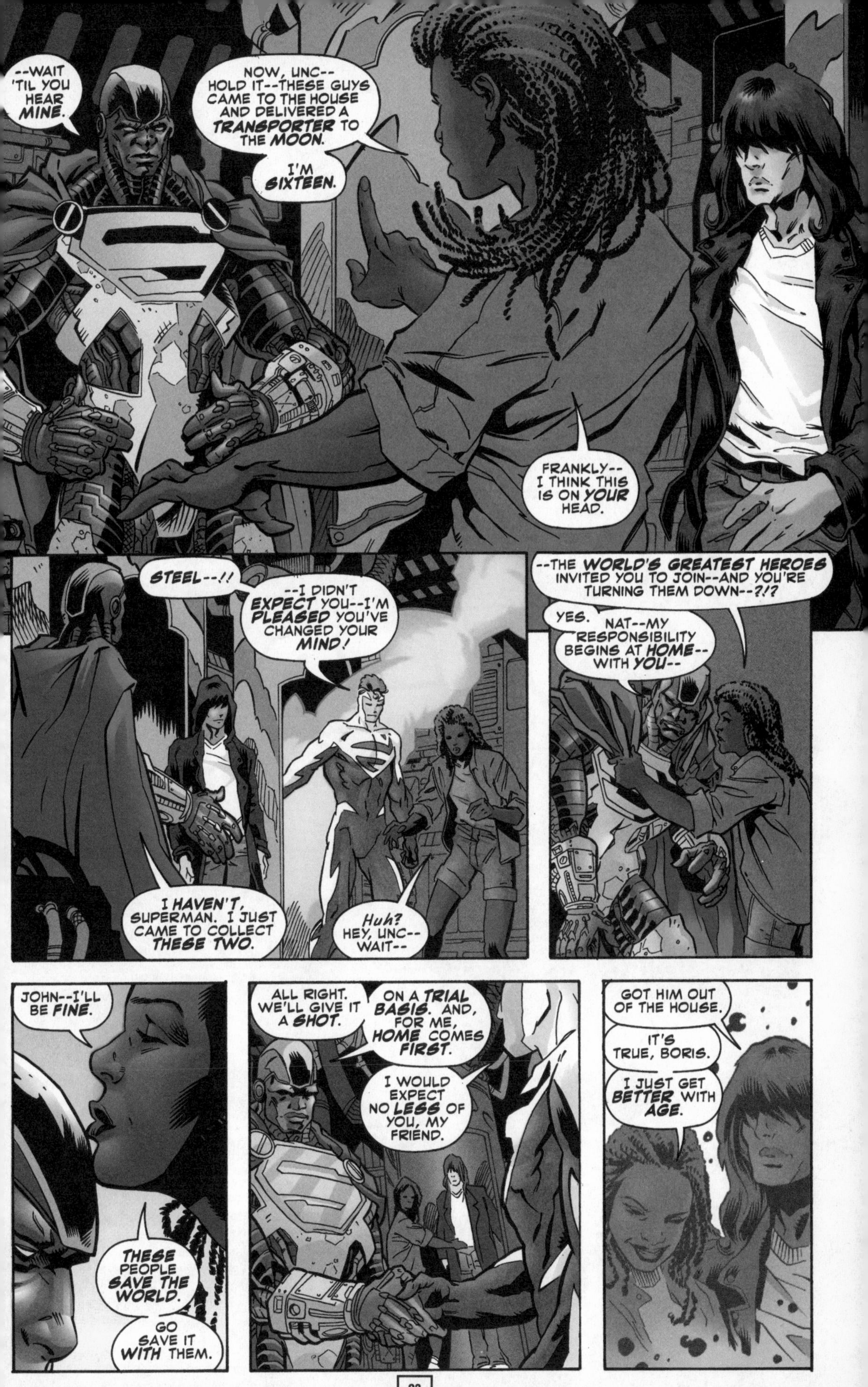
--WAIT 'TIL YOU HEAR MINE.
NOW, UNC-- HOLD IT--THESE GUYS CAME TO THE HOUSE AND DELIVERED A TRANSPORTER TO THE MOON.
I'M SIXTEEN.
FRANKLY-- I THINK THIS IS ON YOUR HEAD.
STEEL--!!
--I DIDN'T EXPECT YOU--I'M PLEASED YOU'VE CHANGED YOUR MIND!
I HAVEN'T, SUPERMAN. I JUST CAME TO COLLECT THESE TWO.
Huh? HEY, UNC-- WAIT--
--THE WORLD'S GREATEST HEROES INVITED YOU TO JOIN--AND YOU'RE TURNING THEM DOWN--?!?
YES.
NAT--MY RESPONSIBILITY BEGINS AT HOME-- WITH YOU--
JOHN--I'LL BE FINE.
THESE PEOPLE SAVE THE WORLD.
GO SAVE IT WITH THEM.
ALL RIGHT. WE'LL GIVE IT A SHOT.
ON A TRIAL BASIS. AND, FOR ME, HOME COMES FIRST.
I WOULD EXPECT NO LESS OF YOU, MY FRIEND.
GOT HIM OUT OF THE HOUSE.
IT'S TRUE, BORIS.
I JUST GET BETTER WITH AGE.

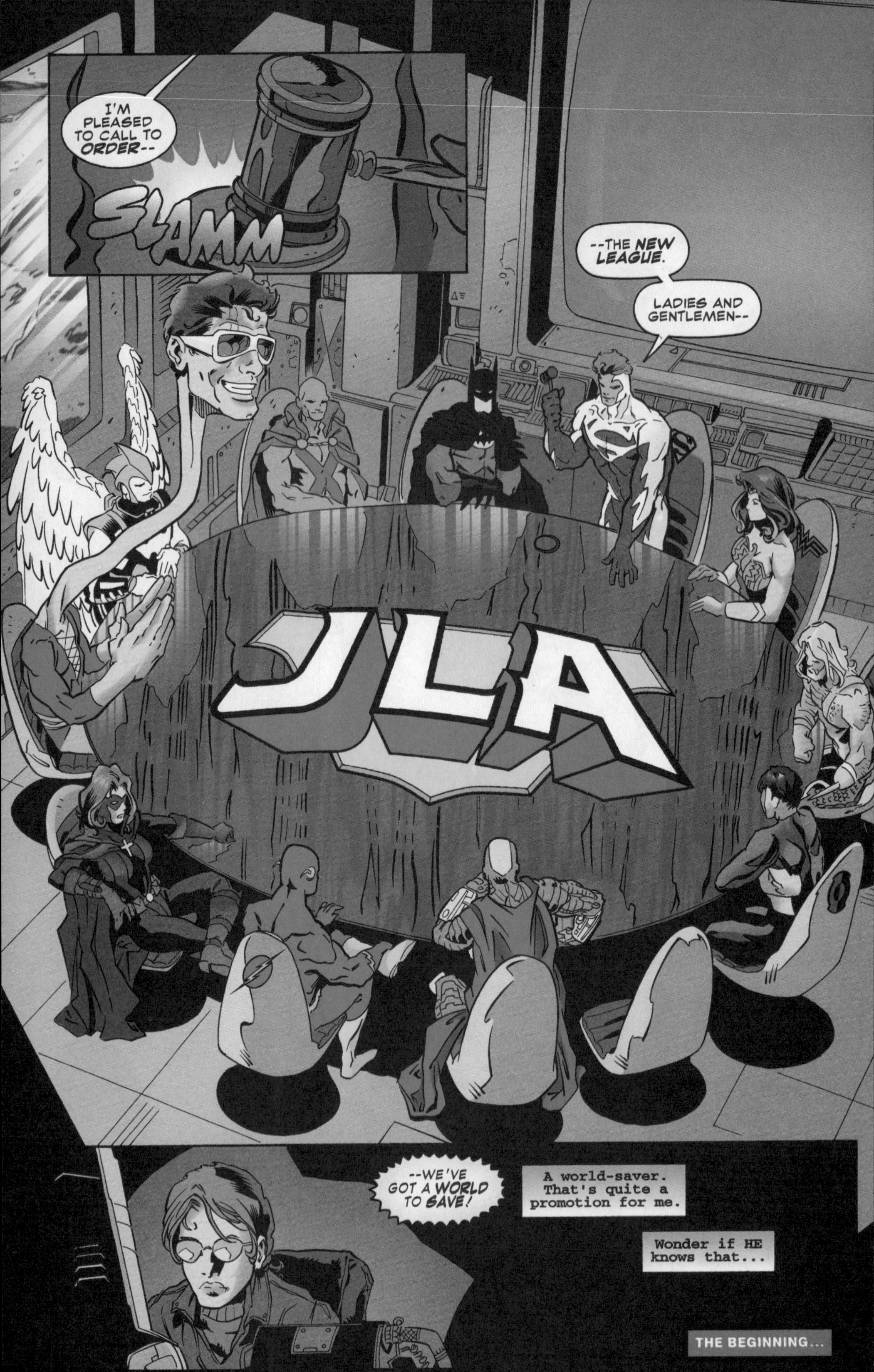
I'M PLEASED TO CALL TO ORDER--
SLAMM
--THE NEW LEAGUE.
LADIES AND GENTLEMEN--
JLA
--WE'VE GOT A WORLD TO SAVE!
A world-saver. That's quite a promotion for me.
Wonder if HE knows that...
THE BEGINNING...

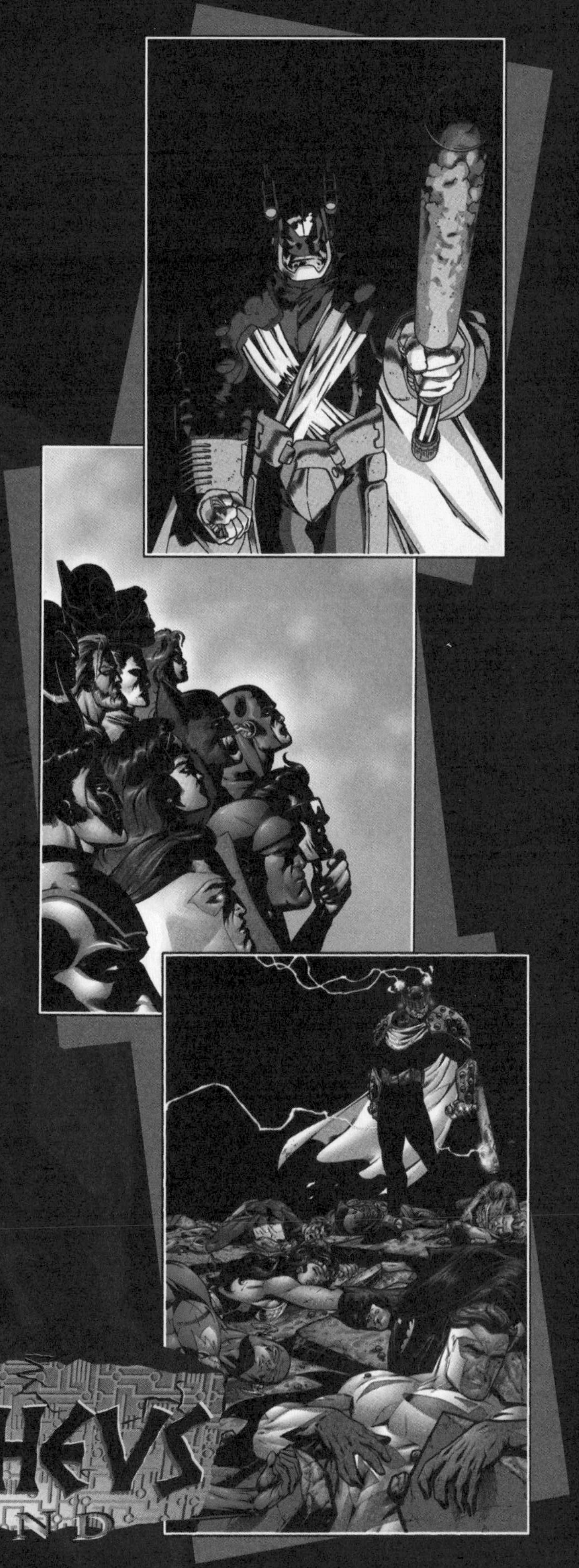

PROMETHEUS UNBOUND

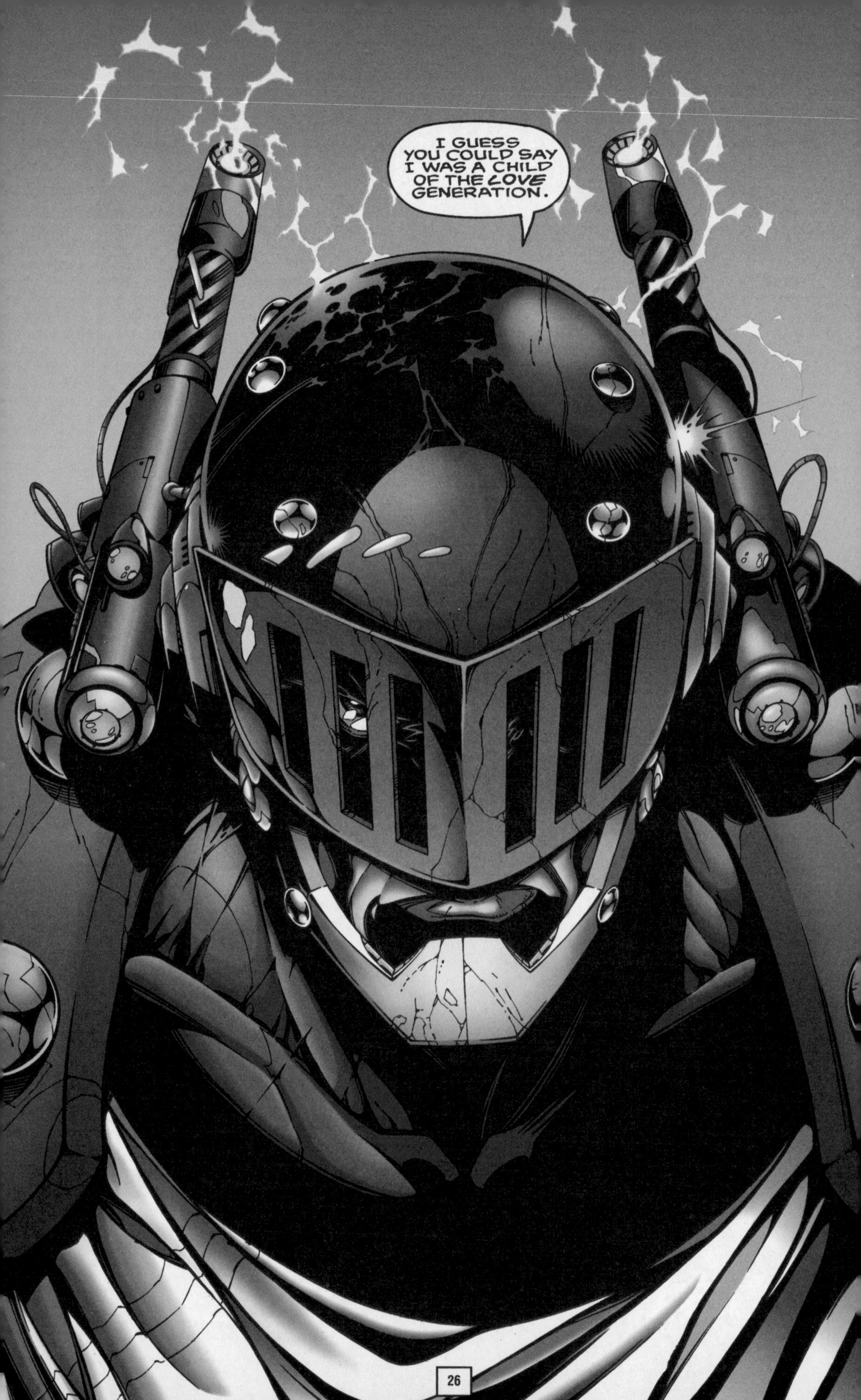
I GUESS YOU COULD SAY I WAS A CHILD OF THE *LOVE* GENERATION.

THERE WAS A CROOKED MAN

GRANT MORRISON • WRITER ARNIE JORGENSEN • PENCILLER DAVID MEIKIS • INKER
JANICE CHIANG • LETTERER JAMES SINCLAIR • COLORIST HEROIC AGE • SEPARATOR
PETER TOMASI • ASSOCIATE EDITOR DAN RASPLER • EDITOR

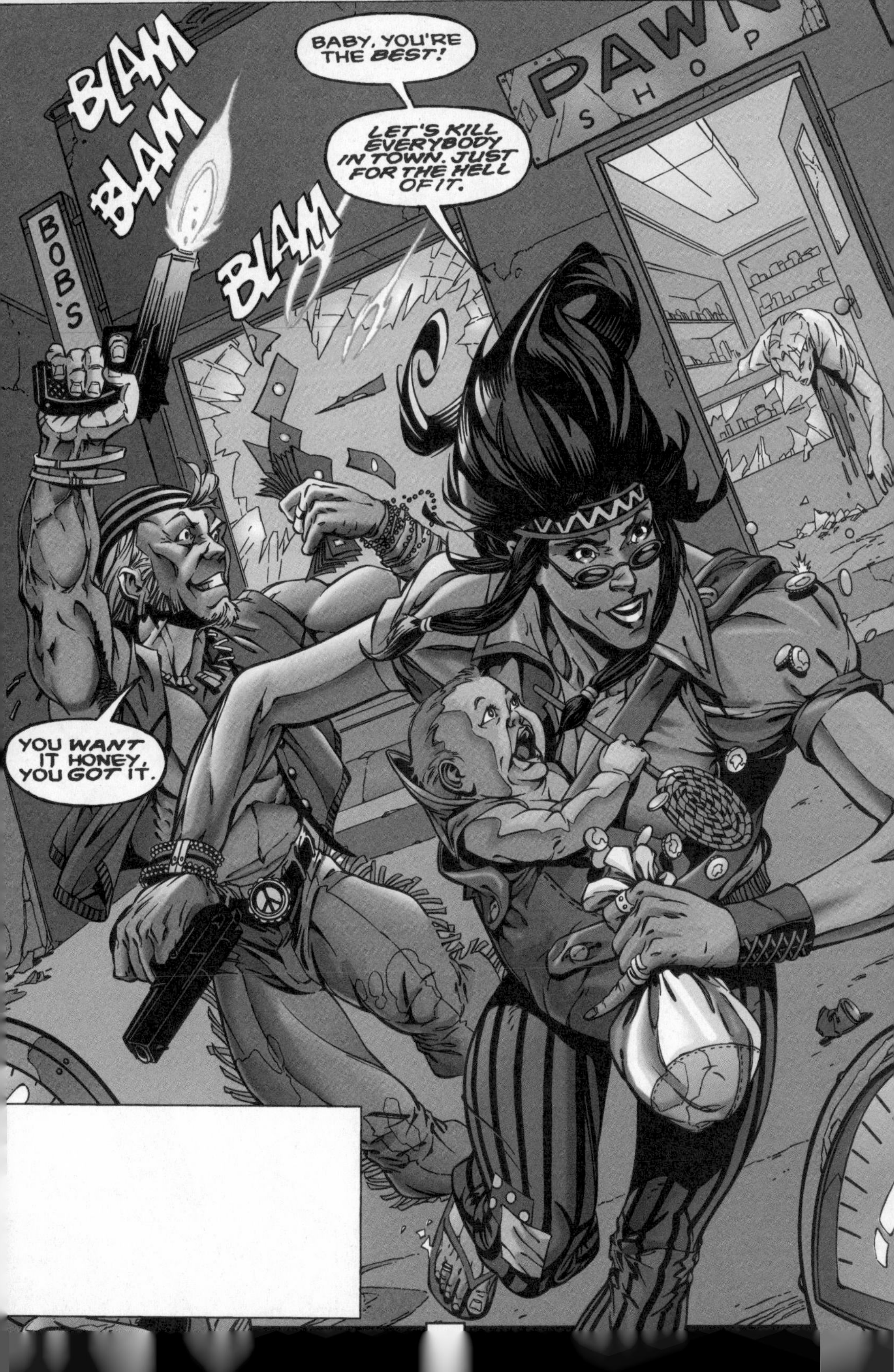
PAWN SHOP
BOB'S
BLAM BLAM
BLAM
BABY, YOU'RE THE *BEST!*
LET'S KILL EVERYBODY IN TOWN. JUST FOR THE HELL OF IT.
YOU *WANT* IT HONEY, YOU *GOT* IT.

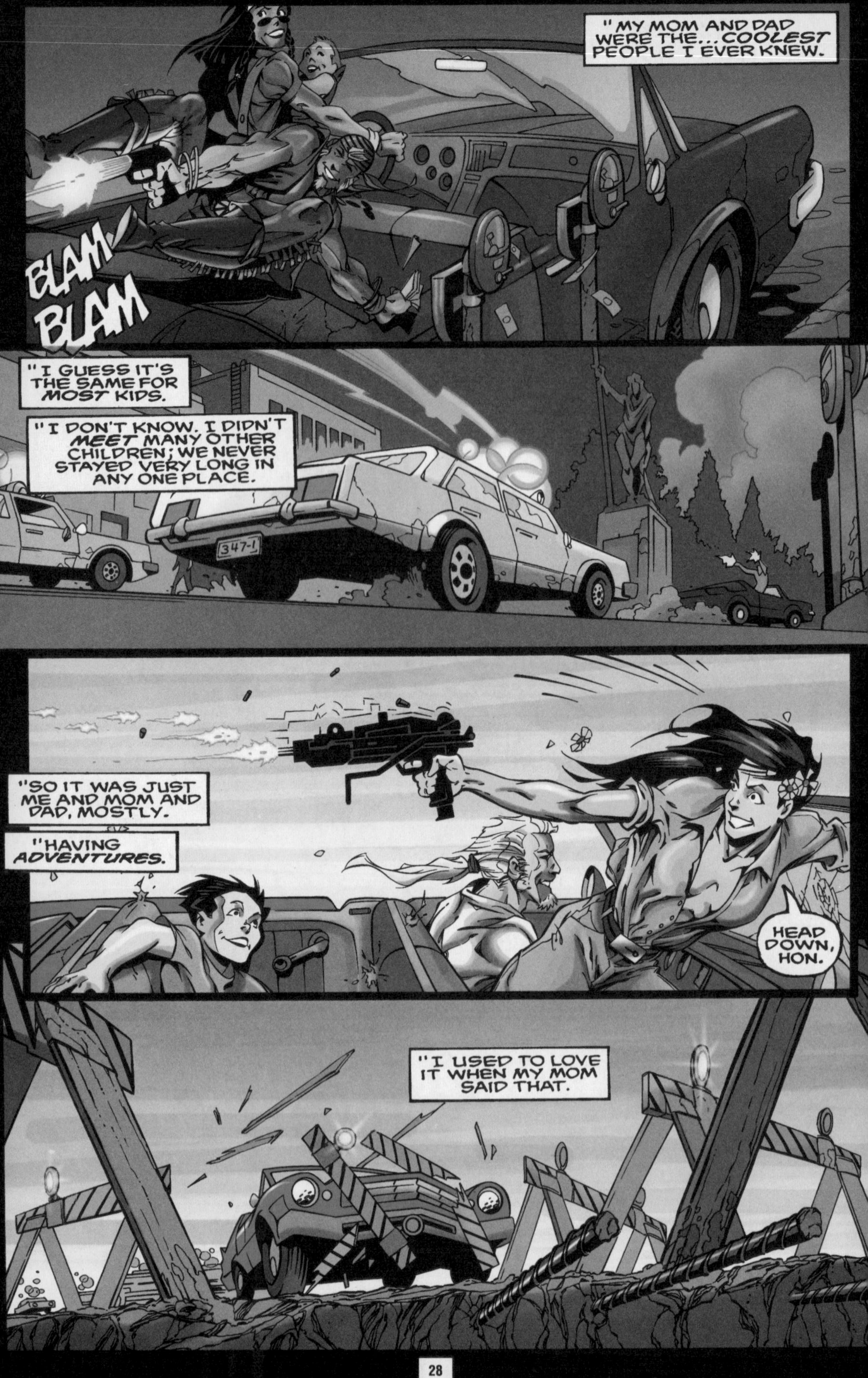
"MY MOM AND DAD WERE THE... COOLEST PEOPLE I EVER KNEW.
BLAM BLAM
"I GUESS IT'S THE SAME FOR MOST KIDS.
"I DON'T KNOW. I DIDN'T MEET MANY OTHER CHILDREN; WE NEVER STAYED VERY LONG IN ANY ONE PLACE.
347-1
"SO IT WAS JUST ME AND MOM AND DAD, MOSTLY.
"HAVING ADVENTURES.
HEAD DOWN, HON.
"I USED TO LOVE IT WHEN MY MOM SAID THAT.

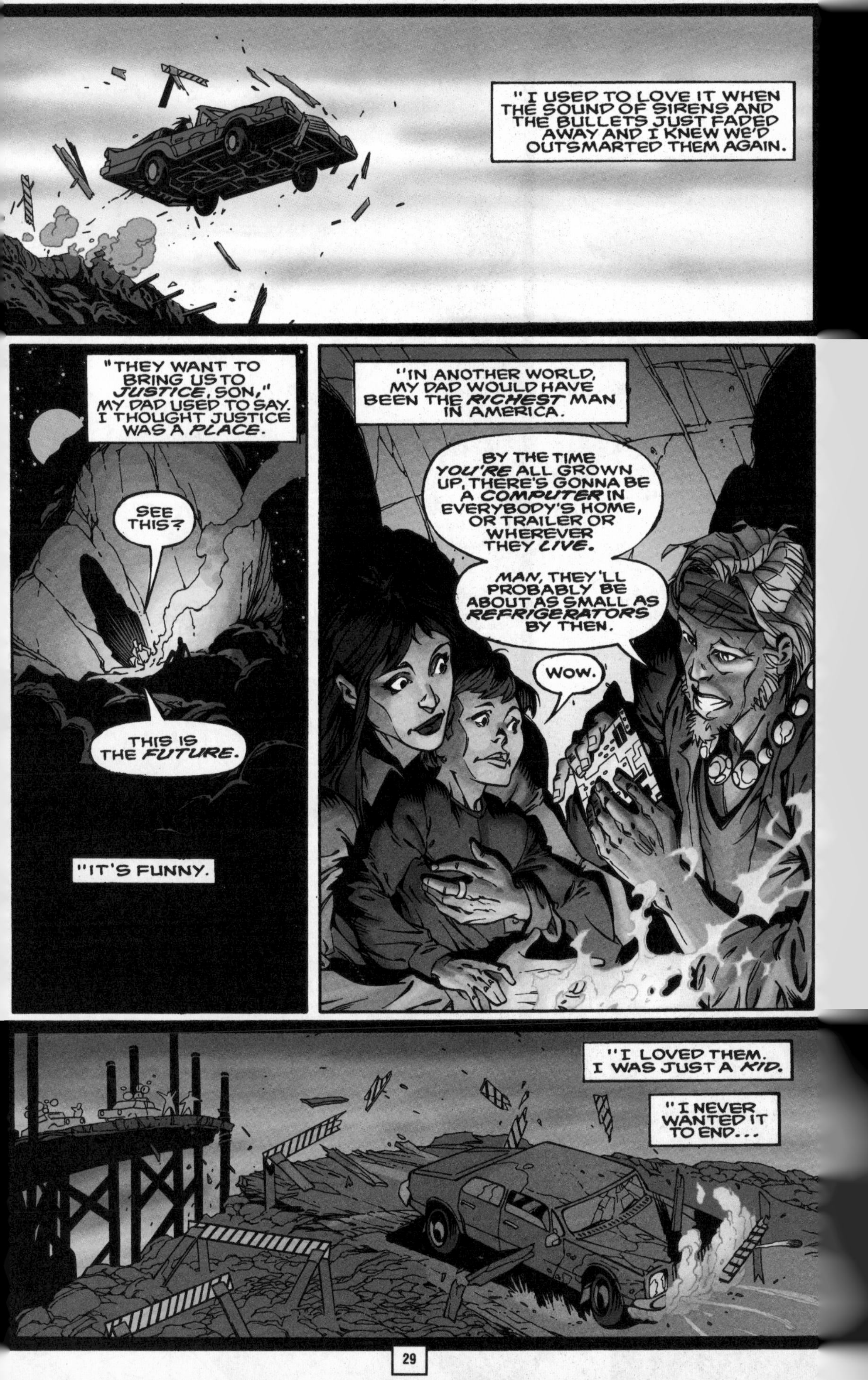
"I USED TO LOVE IT WHEN THE SOUND OF SIRENS AND THE BULLETS JUST FADED AWAY AND I KNEW WE'D OUTSMARTED THEM AGAIN.
"THEY WANT TO BRING US TO *JUSTICE*, SON," MY DAD USED TO SAY. I THOUGHT JUSTICE WAS A *PLACE*.
SEE THIS?
THIS IS THE *FUTURE*.
"IT'S FUNNY.
"IN ANOTHER WORLD, MY DAD WOULD HAVE BEEN THE *RICHEST* MAN IN AMERICA.
BY THE TIME *YOU'RE* ALL GROWN UP, THERE'S GONNA BE A *COMPUTER* IN EVERYBODY'S HOME, OR TRAILER OR WHEREVER THEY *LIVE*.
MAN, THEY'LL PROBABLY BE ABOUT AS SMALL AS *REFRIGERATORS* BY THEN.
WOW.
"I LOVED THEM. I WAS JUST A *KID*.
"I NEVER WANTED IT TO END...

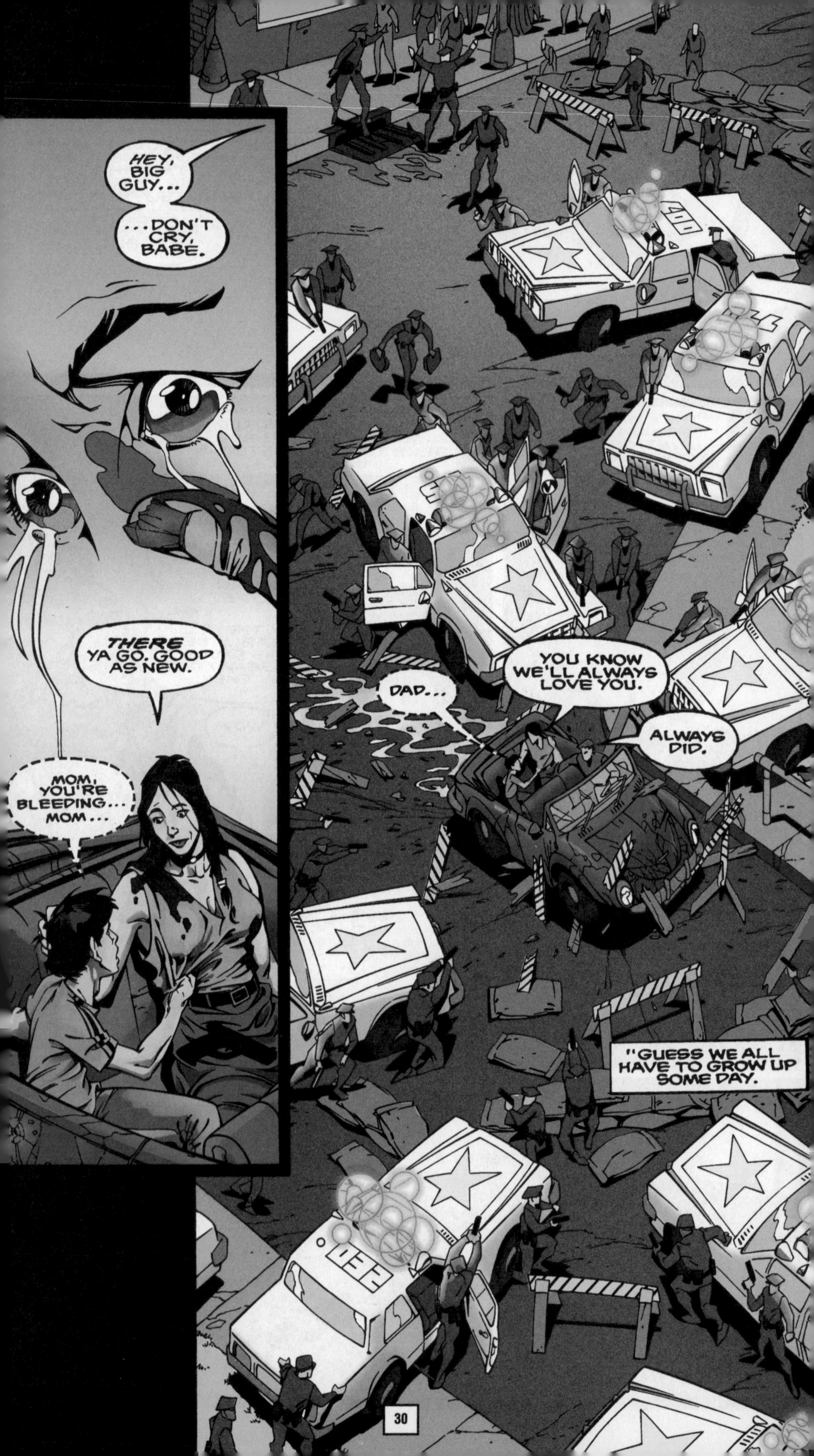
HEY, BIG GUY...
...DON'T CRY, BABE.
THERE YA GO. GOOD AS NEW.
MOM, YOU'RE BLEEDING... MOM...
DAD...
YOU KNOW WE'LL ALWAYS LOVE YOU.
ALWAYS DID.
"GUESS WE ALL HAVE TO GROW UP SOME DAY.

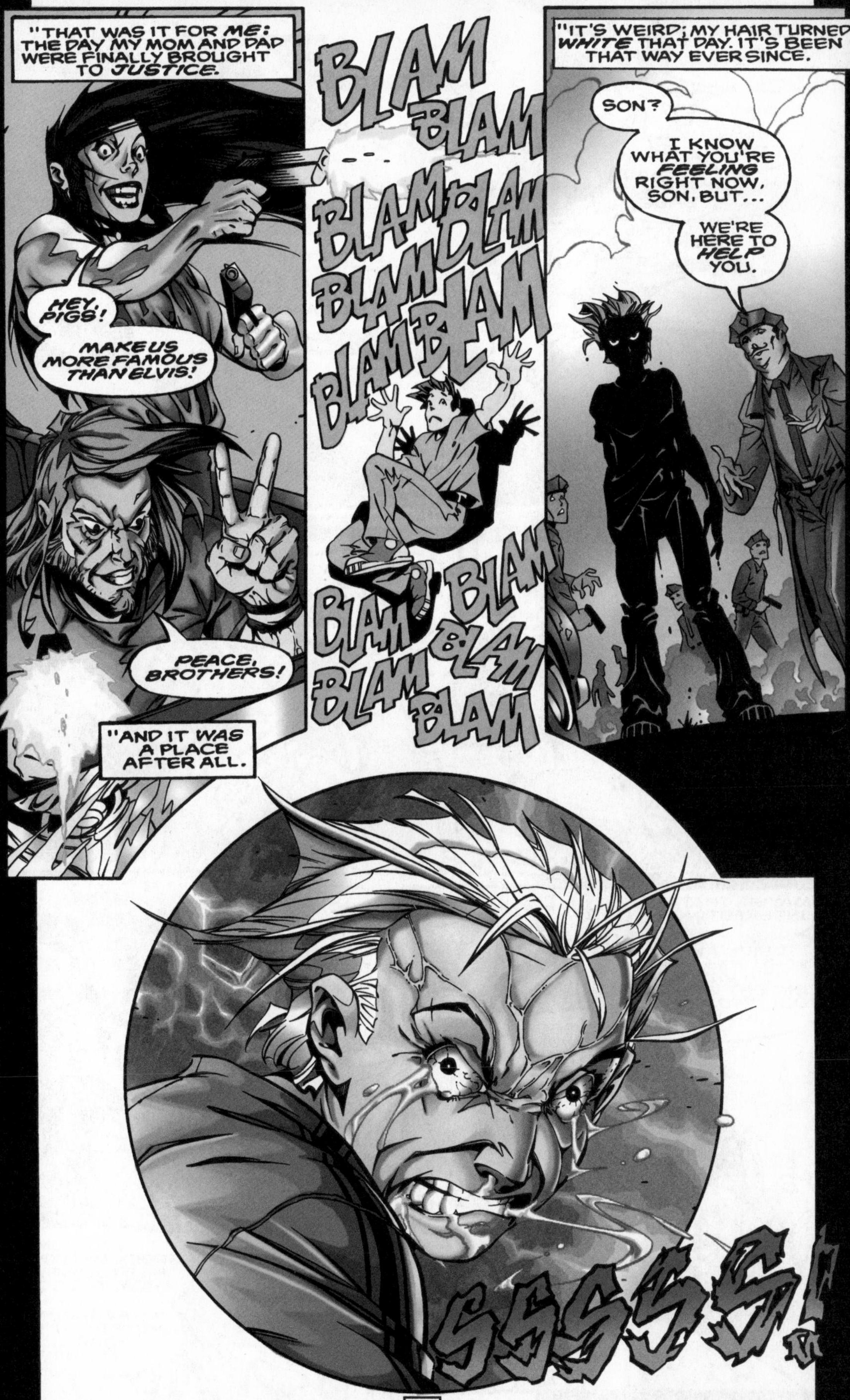
"THAT WAS IT FOR ME: THE DAY MY MOM AND DAD WERE FINALLY BROUGHT TO JUSTICE.
HEY, PIGS!
MAKE US MORE FAMOUS THAN ELVIS!
PEACE, BROTHERS!
"AND IT WAS A PLACE AFTER ALL.
BLAM BLAM
BLAM BLAM BLAM BLAM BLAM BLAM
BLAM BLAM BLAM BLAM BLAM
"IT'S WEIRD; MY HAIR TURNED WHITE THAT DAY. IT'S BEEN THAT WAY EVER SINCE.
SON?
I KNOW WHAT YOU'RE FEELING RIGHT NOW, SON, BUT...
WE'RE HERE TO HELP YOU.
SSSSS!

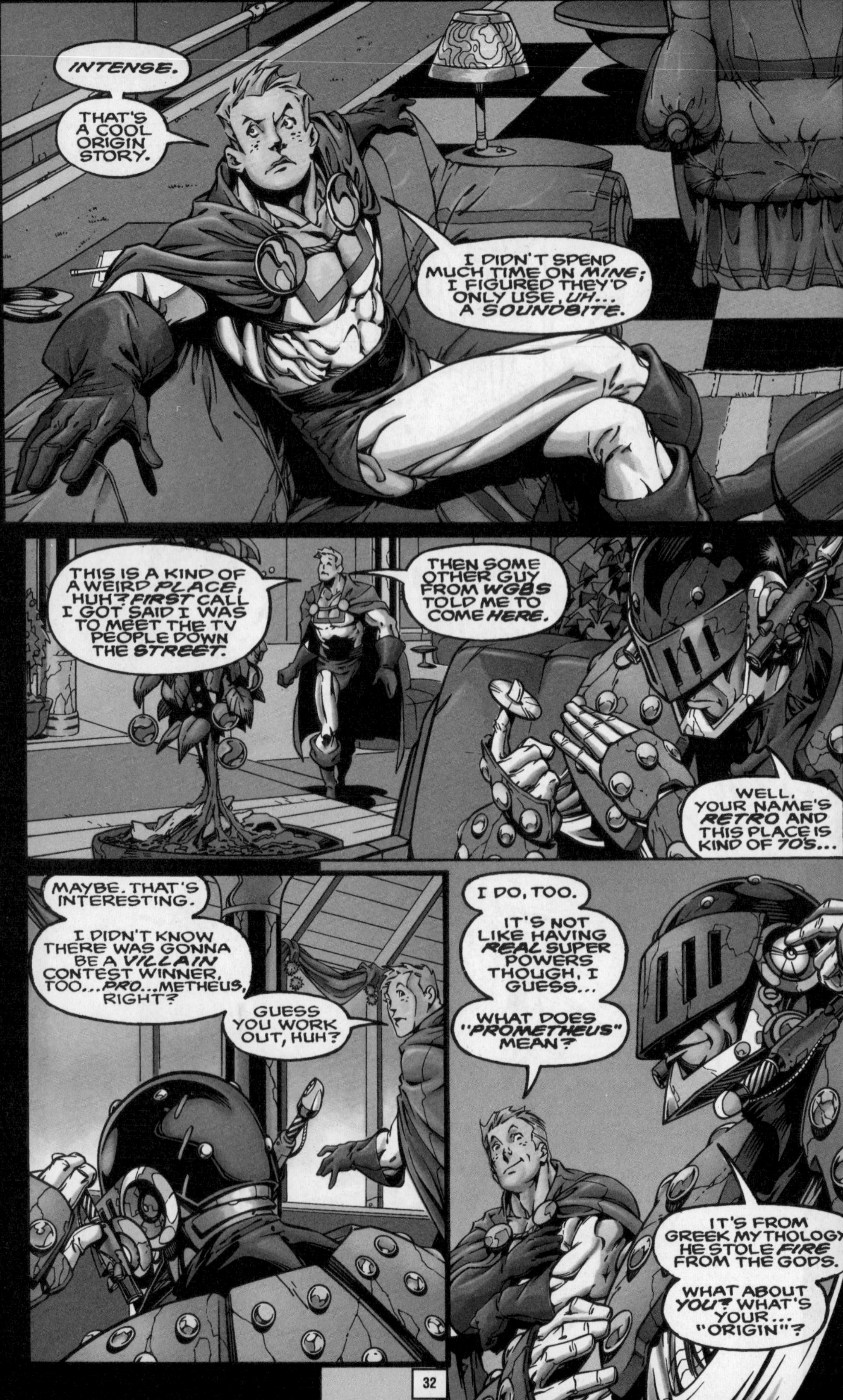
INTENSE.
THAT'S A COOL ORIGIN STORY.
I DIDN'T SPEND MUCH TIME ON MINE; I FIGURED THEY'D ONLY USE, UH... A SOUNDBITE.
THIS IS A KIND OF A WEIRD PLACE, HUH? FIRST CALL I GOT SAID I WAS TO MEET THE TV PEOPLE DOWN THE STREET.
THEN SOME OTHER GUY FROM WGBS TOLD ME TO COME HERE.
WELL, YOUR NAME'S RETRO AND THIS PLACE IS KIND OF 70'S...
MAYBE. THAT'S INTERESTING.
I DIDN'T KNOW THERE WAS GONNA BE A VILLAIN CONTEST WINNER, TOO...PRO...METHEUS, RIGHT?
GUESS YOU WORK OUT, HUH?
I DO, TOO.
IT'S NOT LIKE HAVING REAL SUPER POWERS THOUGH, I GUESS...
WHAT DOES "PROMETHEUS" MEAN?
IT'S FROM GREEK MYTHOLOGY. HE STOLE FIRE FROM THE GODS.
WHAT ABOUT YOU? WHAT'S YOUR... "ORIGIN"?

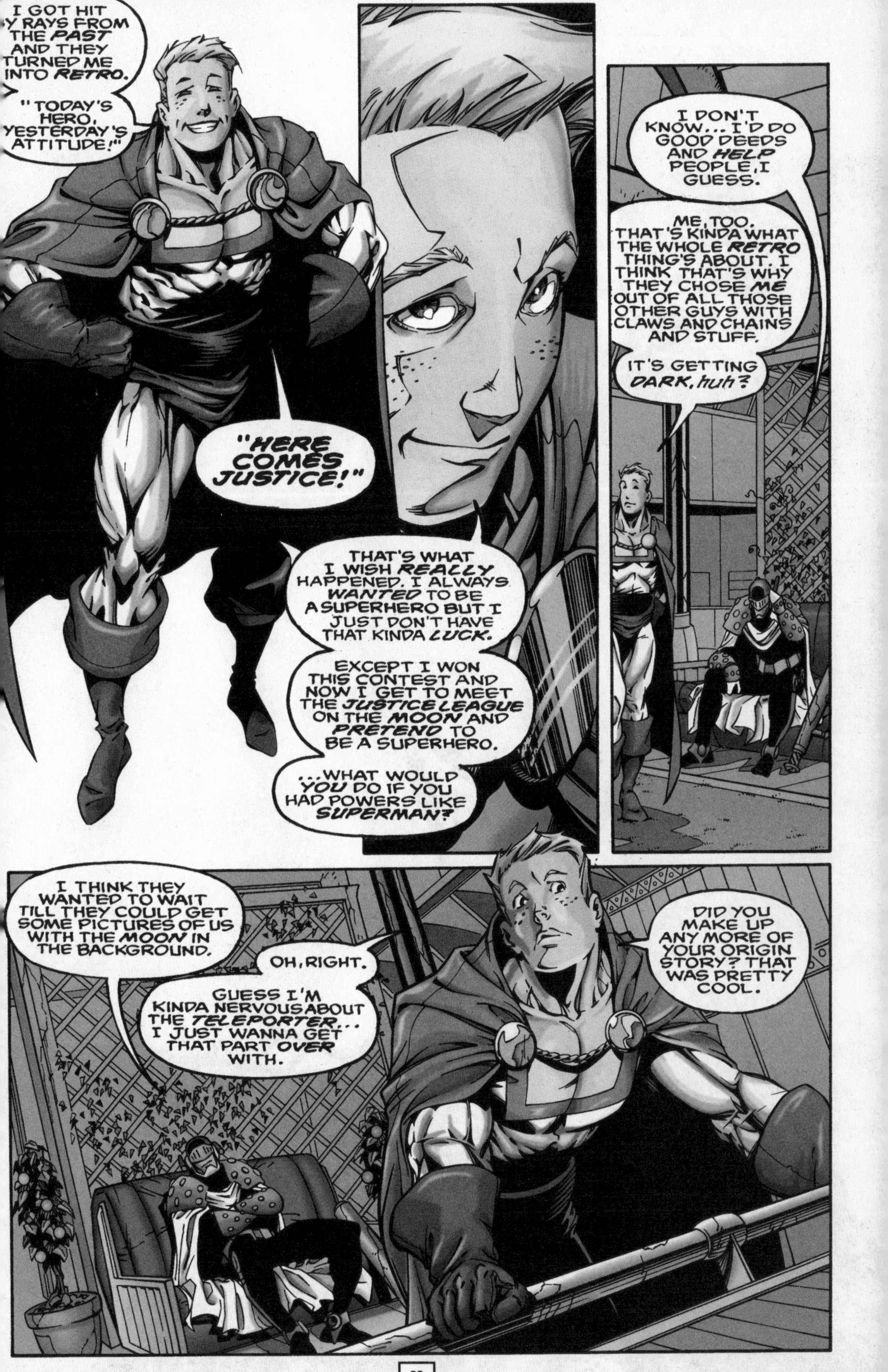

I GOT HIT BY RAYS FROM THE PAST AND THEY TURNED ME INTO RETRO.
"TODAY'S HERO, YESTERDAY'S ATTITUDE!"
"HERE COMES JUSTICE!"
THAT'S WHAT I WISH REALLY HAPPENED. I ALWAYS WANTED TO BE A SUPERHERO BUT I JUST DON'T HAVE THAT KINDA LUCK.
EXCEPT I WON THIS CONTEST AND NOW I GET TO MEET THE JUSTICE LEAGUE ON THE MOON AND PRETEND TO BE A SUPERHERO.
...WHAT WOULD YOU DO IF YOU HAD POWERS LIKE SUPERMAN?
I DON'T KNOW... I'D DO GOOD DEEDS AND HELP PEOPLE, I GUESS.
ME, TOO. THAT'S KINDA WHAT THE WHOLE RETRO THING'S ABOUT. I THINK THAT'S WHY THEY CHOSE ME OUT OF ALL THOSE OTHER GUYS WITH CLAWS AND CHAINS AND STUFF.
IT'S GETTING DARK, huh?
I THINK THEY WANTED TO WAIT TILL THEY COULD GET SOME PICTURES OF US WITH THE MOON IN THE BACKGROUND.
OH, RIGHT.
GUESS I'M KINDA NERVOUS ABOUT THE TELEPORTER... I JUST WANNA GET THAT PART OVER WITH.
DID YOU MAKE UP ANY MORE OF YOUR ORIGIN STORY? THAT WAS PRETTY COOL.

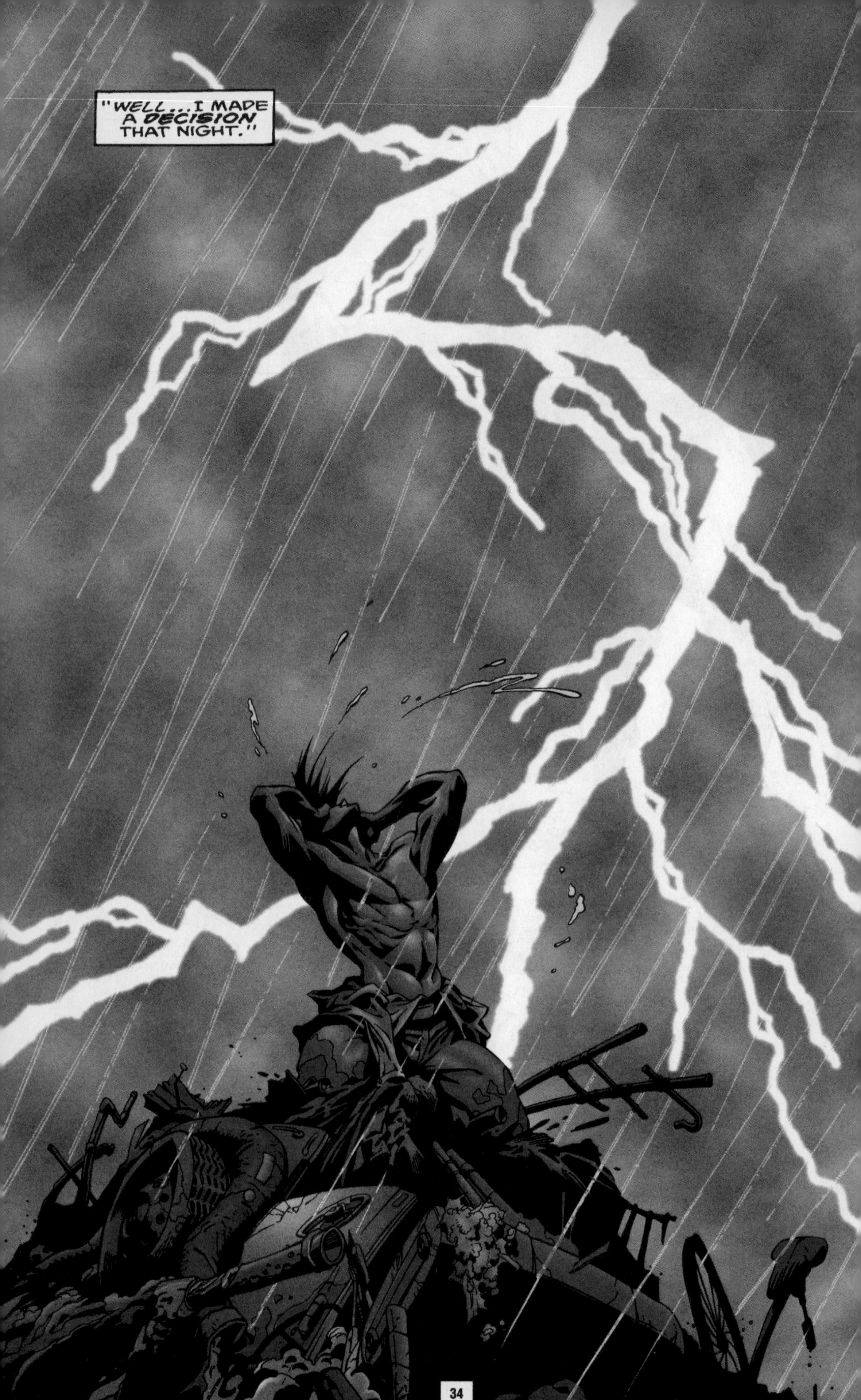
"WELL... I MADE A DECISION THAT NIGHT."

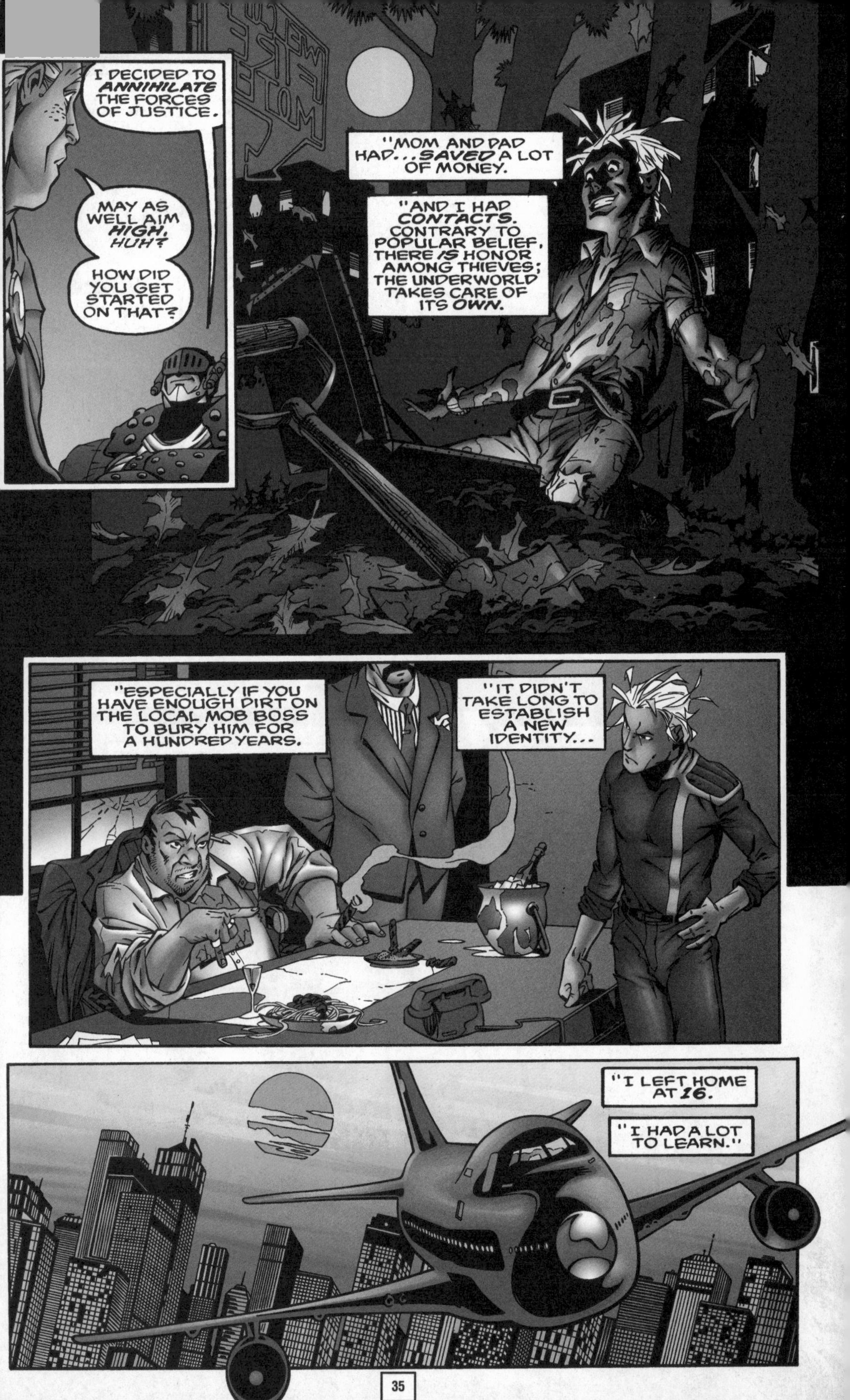
I DECIDED TO *ANNIHILATE* THE FORCES OF JUSTICE.
MAY AS WELL AIM *HIGH*, HUH?
HOW DID YOU GET STARTED ON THAT?
"MOM AND DAD HAD... *SAVED* A LOT OF MONEY.
"AND I HAD *CONTACTS*. CONTRARY TO POPULAR BELIEF, THERE *IS* HONOR AMONG THIEVES; THE UNDERWORLD TAKES CARE OF ITS *OWN*.
"ESPECIALLY IF YOU HAVE ENOUGH DIRT ON THE LOCAL MOB BOSS TO BURY HIM FOR A HUNDRED YEARS.
"IT DIDN'T TAKE LONG TO ESTABLISH A NEW IDENTITY...
"I LEFT HOME AT *16*.
"I HAD A LOT TO LEARN."

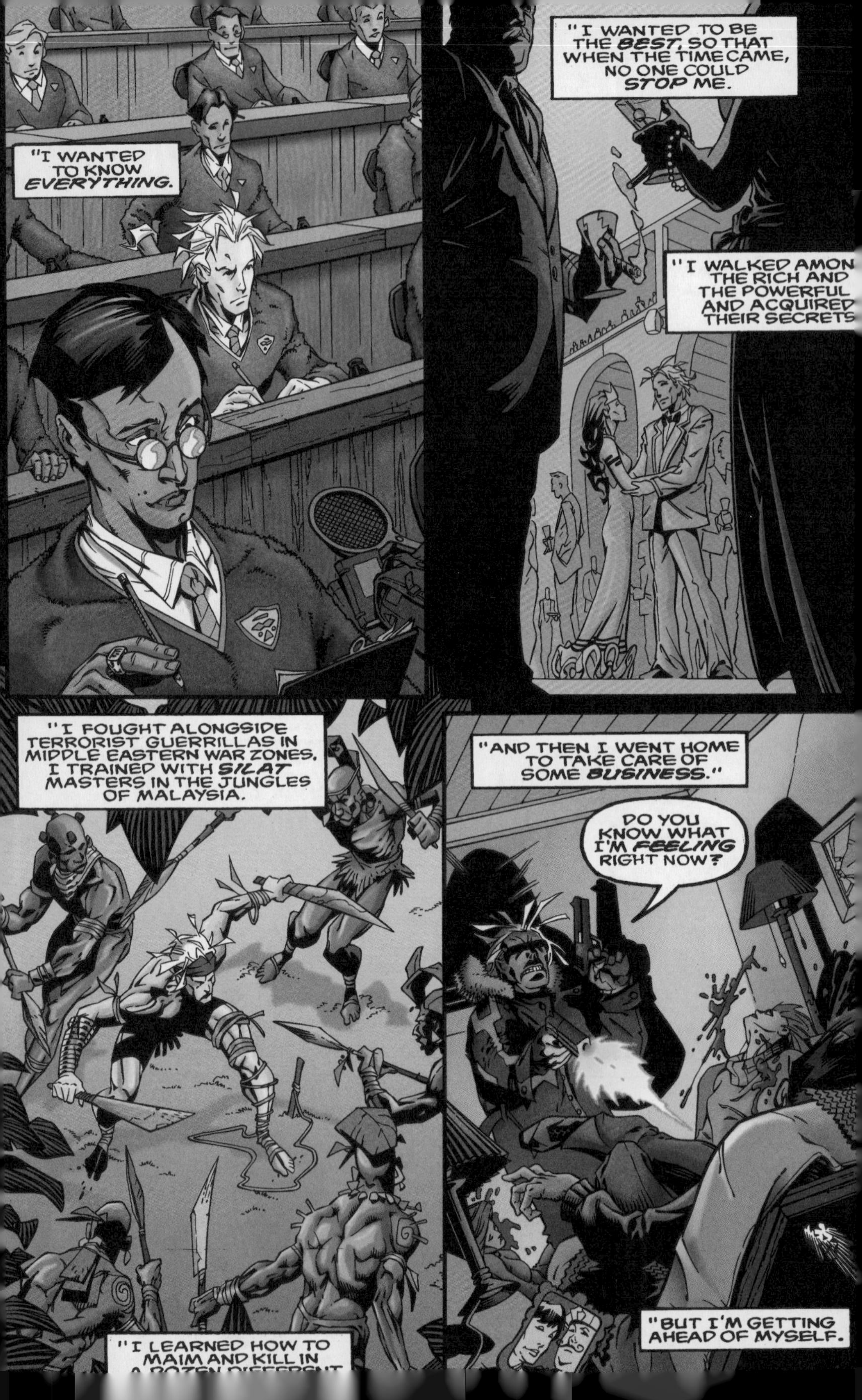
"I WANTED TO KNOW *EVERYTHING*.
"I WANTED TO BE THE *BEST*, SO THAT WHEN THE TIME CAME, NO ONE COULD *STOP* ME.
"I WALKED AMON THE RICH AND THE POWERFUL AND ACQUIRED THEIR SECRETS
"I FOUGHT ALONGSIDE TERRORIST GUERRILLAS IN MIDDLE EASTERN WAR ZONES, I TRAINED WITH *SILAT* MASTERS IN THE JUNGLES OF MALAYSIA.
"I LEARNED HOW TO MAIM AND KILL IN
"AND THEN I WENT HOME TO TAKE CARE OF SOME *BUSINESS*."
DO YOU KNOW WHAT I'M *FEELING* RIGHT NOW?
"BUT I'M GETTING AHEAD OF MYSELF.

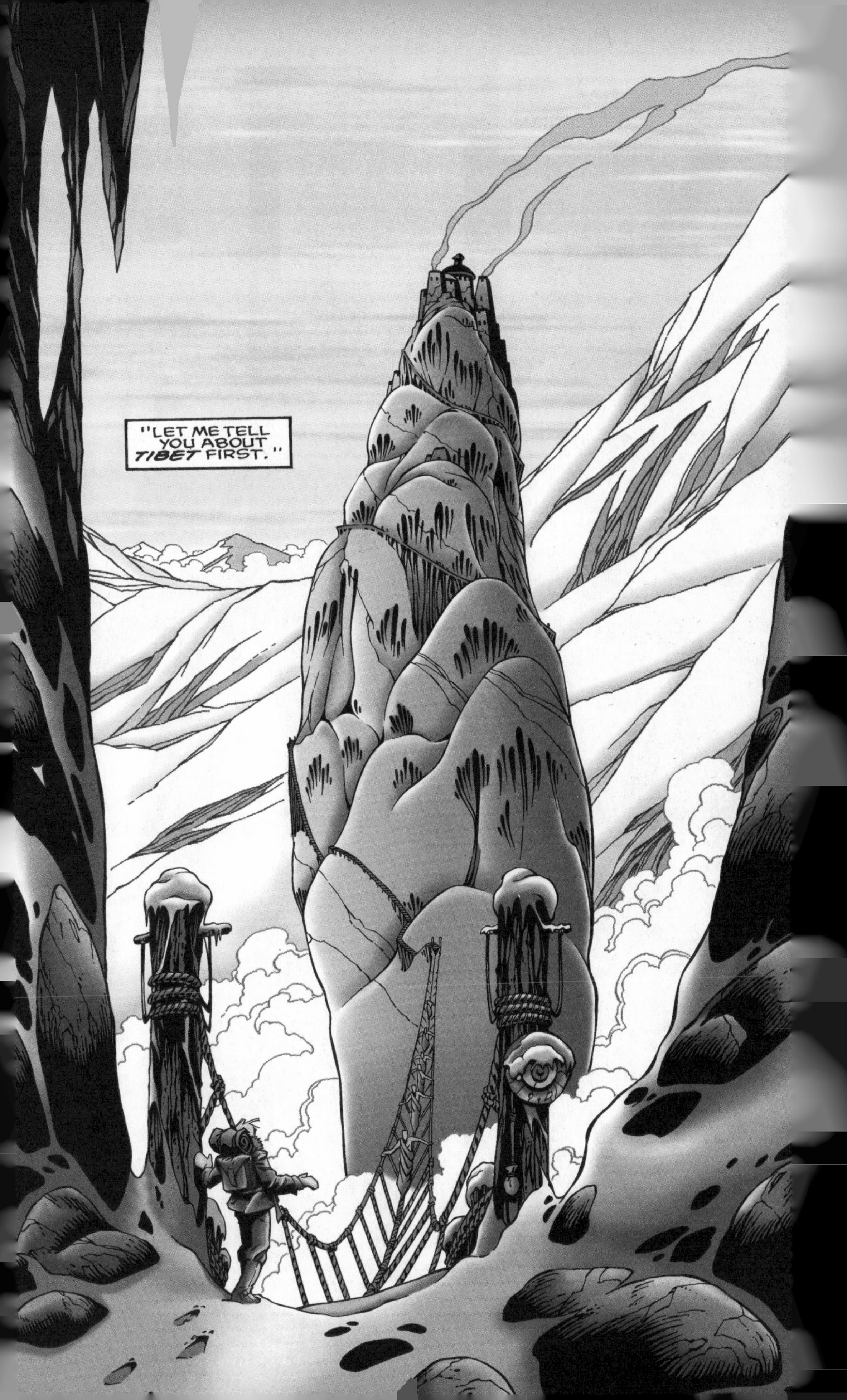
"LET ME TELL YOU ABOUT *TIBET* FIRST."

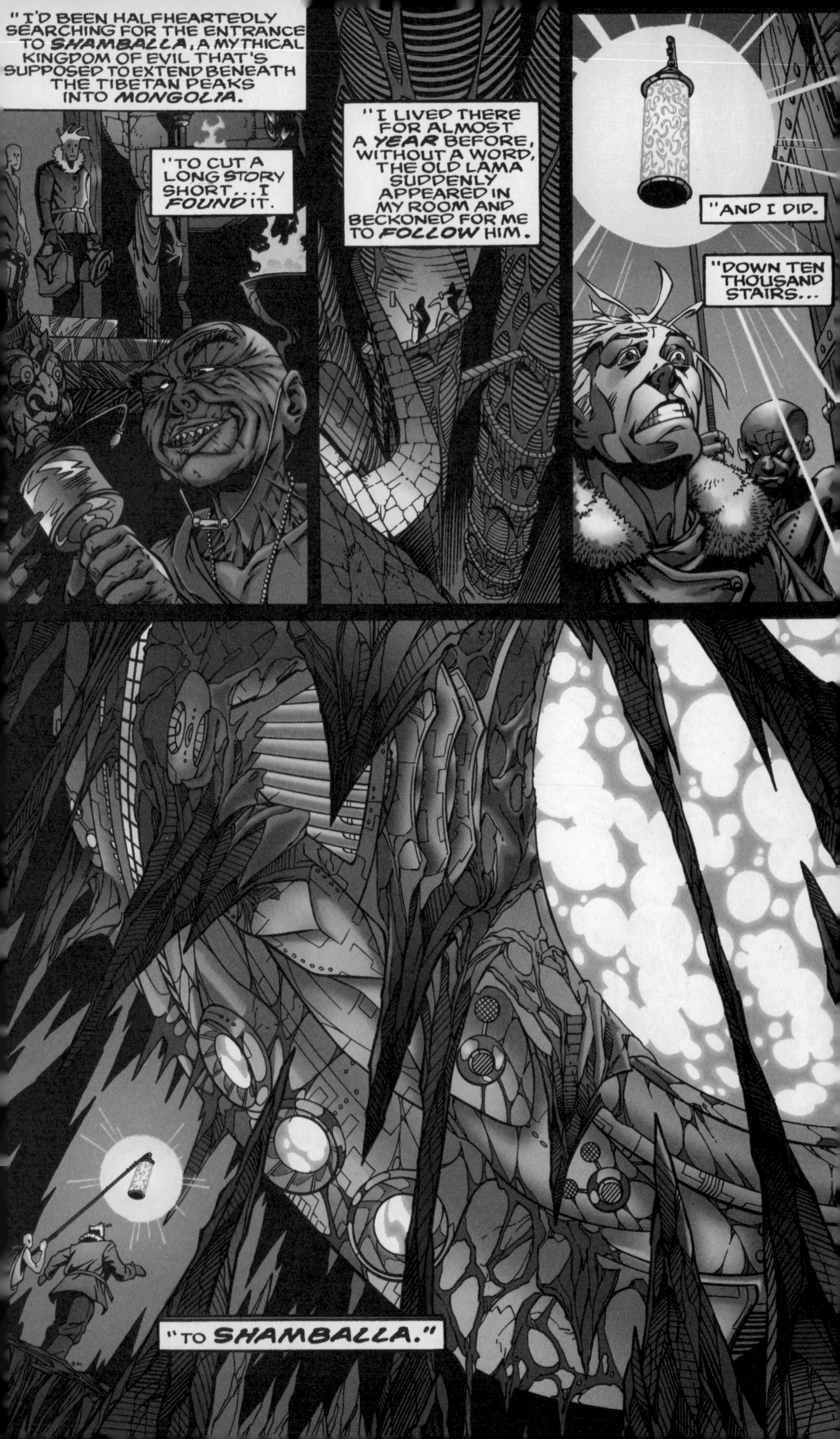
"I'D BEEN HALFHEARTEDLY SEARCHING FOR THE ENTRANCE TO SHAMBALLA, A MYTHICAL KINGDOM OF EVIL THAT'S SUPPOSED TO EXTEND BENEATH THE TIBETAN PEAKS INTO MONGOLIA.
"TO CUT A LONG STORY SHORT... I FOUND IT.
"I LIVED THERE FOR ALMOST A YEAR BEFORE, WITHOUT A WORD, THE OLD LAMA SUDDENLY APPEARED IN MY ROOM AND BECKONED FOR ME TO FOLLOW HIM.
"AND I DID.
"DOWN TEN THOUSAND STAIRS...
"TO SHAMBALLA."

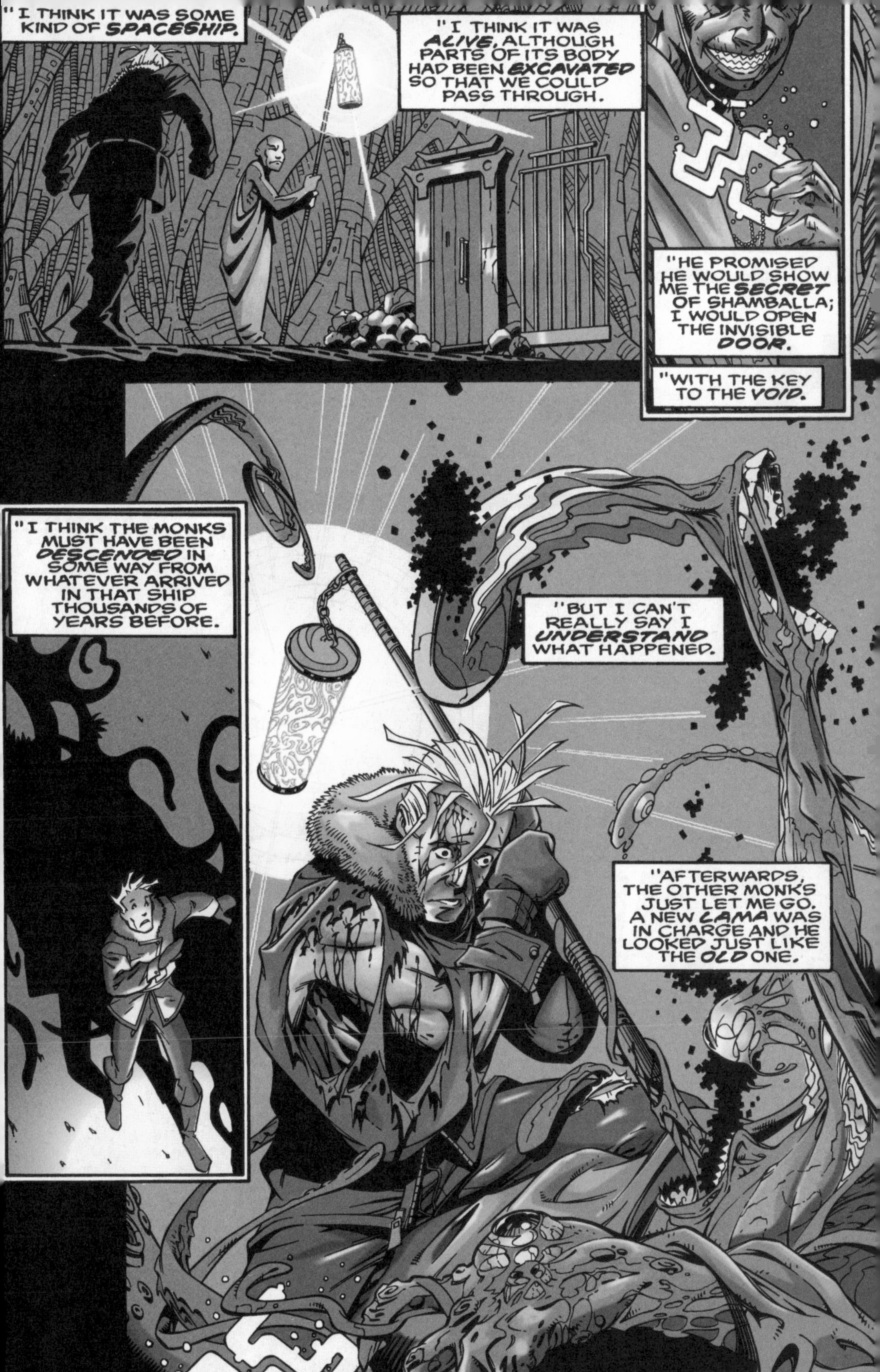
"I THINK IT WAS SOME KIND OF SPACESHIP.
"I THINK IT WAS ALIVE, ALTHOUGH PARTS OF ITS BODY HAD BEEN EXCAVATED SO THAT WE COULD PASS THROUGH.
"HE PROMISED HE WOULD SHOW ME THE SECRET OF SHAMBALLA; I WOULD OPEN THE INVISIBLE DOOR.
"WITH THE KEY TO THE VOID.
"I THINK THE MONKS MUST HAVE BEEN DESCENDED IN SOME WAY FROM WHATEVER ARRIVED IN THAT SHIP THOUSANDS OF YEARS BEFORE.
"BUT I CAN'T REALLY SAY I UNDERSTAND WHAT HAPPENED.
"AFTERWARDS, THE OTHER MONKS JUST LET ME GO. A NEW LAMA WAS IN CHARGE AND HE LOOKED JUST LIKE THE OLD ONE.

I... SAVED THIS.
I THOUGHT I'D CALL IT THE COSMIC KEY.
UH, OKAY. BUT I THINK THERE MIGHT ALREADY BE A...
KLIK!
THE LAMA WAS RIGHT. IT'S THE KEY TO THE VOID.
...
AWESOME.
LITERALLY.
NOTHING BUILDS STRAIGHT HERE, BUT THAT SUITS ME FINE.

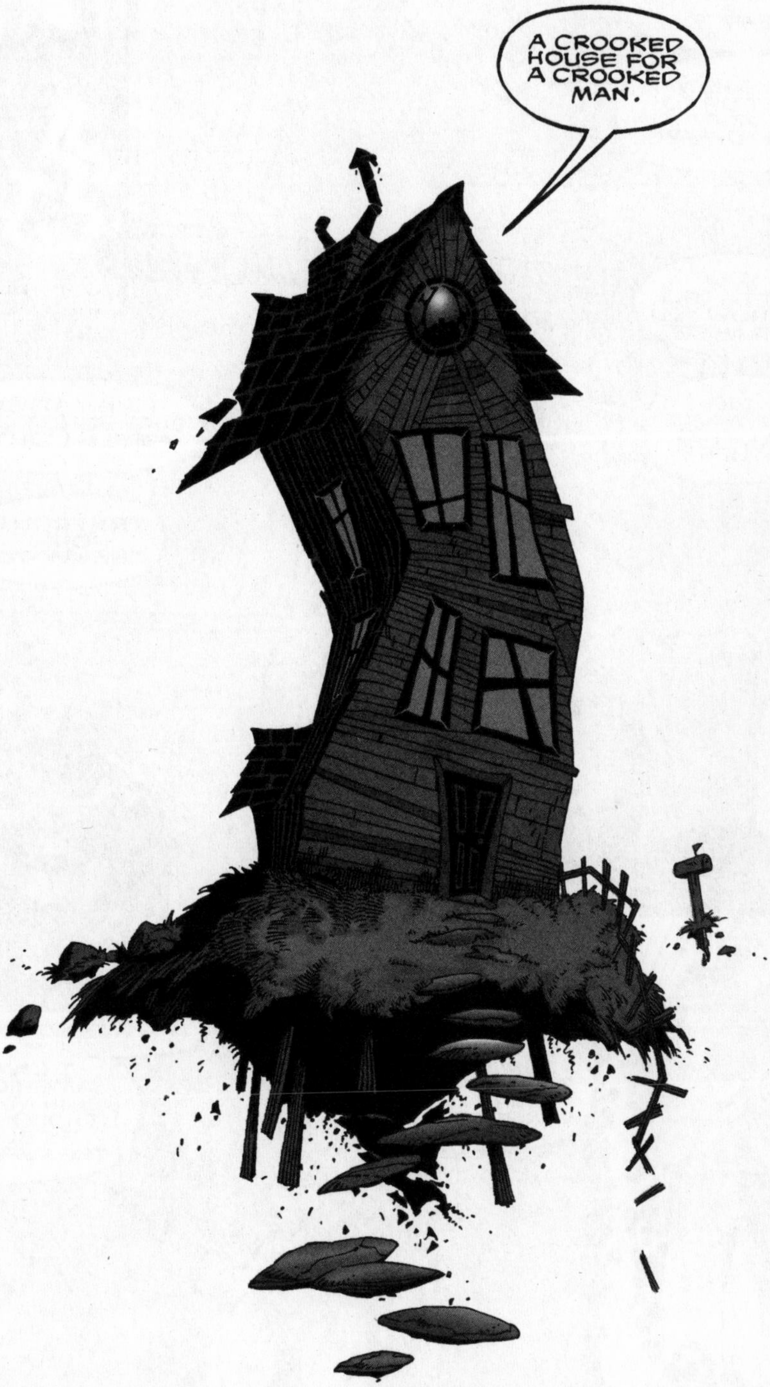
A CROOKED HOUSE FOR A CROOKED MAN.

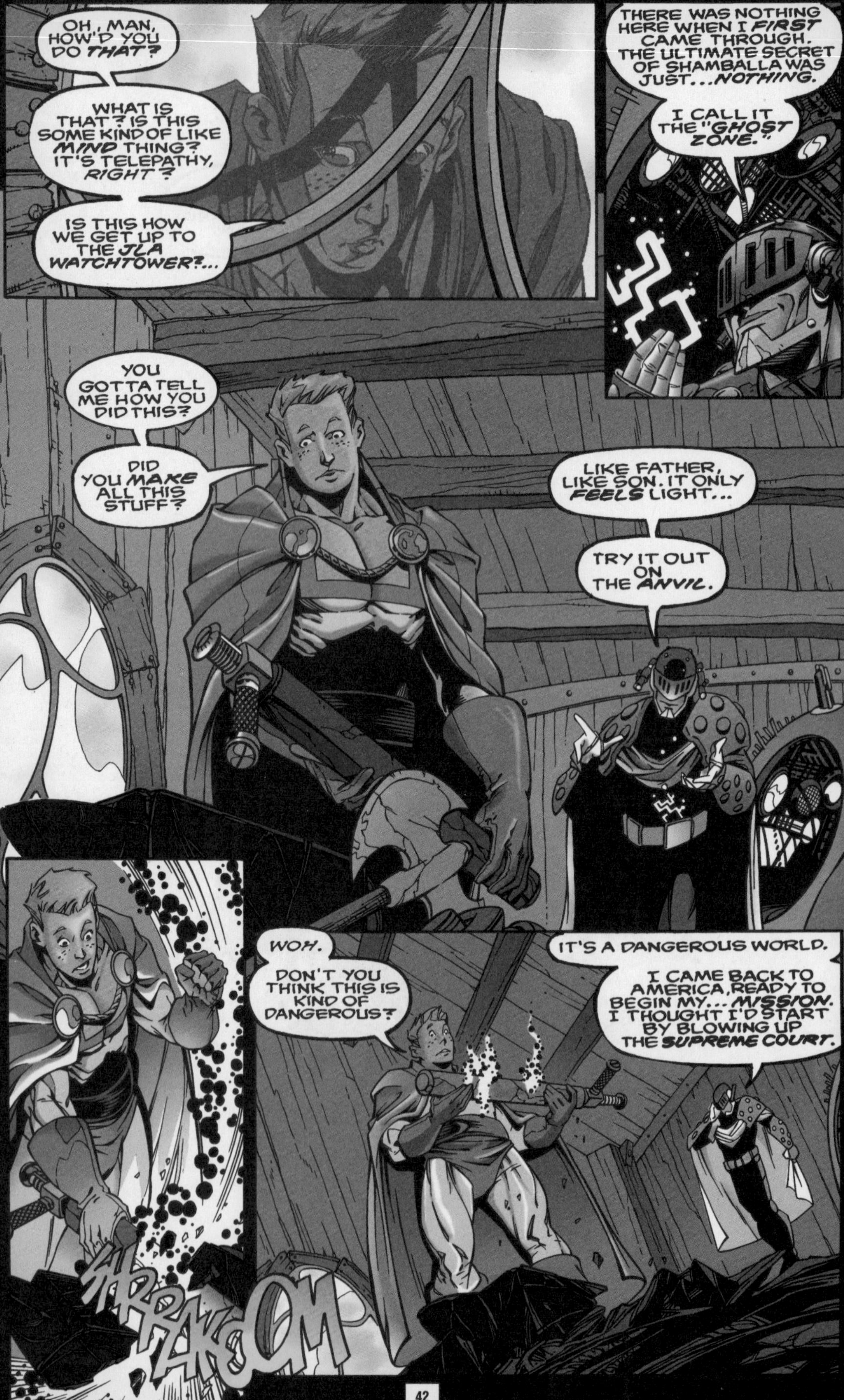

OH, MAN, HOW'D YOU DO *THAT?*
WHAT IS THAT? IS THIS SOME KIND OF LIKE *MIND* THING? IT'S TELEPATHY, *RIGHT?*
IS THIS HOW WE GET UP TO THE *JLA WATCHTOWER?...*
THERE WAS NOTHING HERE WHEN I *FIRST* CAME THROUGH. THE ULTIMATE SECRET OF SHAMBALLA WAS JUST... *NOTHING.*
I CALL IT THE *"GHOST ZONE."*
YOU GOTTA TELL ME HOW YOU DID THIS?
DID YOU *MAKE* ALL THIS STUFF?
LIKE FATHER, LIKE SON. IT ONLY *FEELS* LIGHT...
TRY IT OUT ON THE *ANVIL.*
SHRRAKOOM
WOH.
DON'T YOU THINK THIS IS KIND OF DANGEROUS?
IT'S A DANGEROUS WORLD.
I CAME BACK TO AMERICA, READY TO BEGIN MY... *MISSION.* I THOUGHT I'D START BY BLOWING UP THE *SUPREME COURT.*

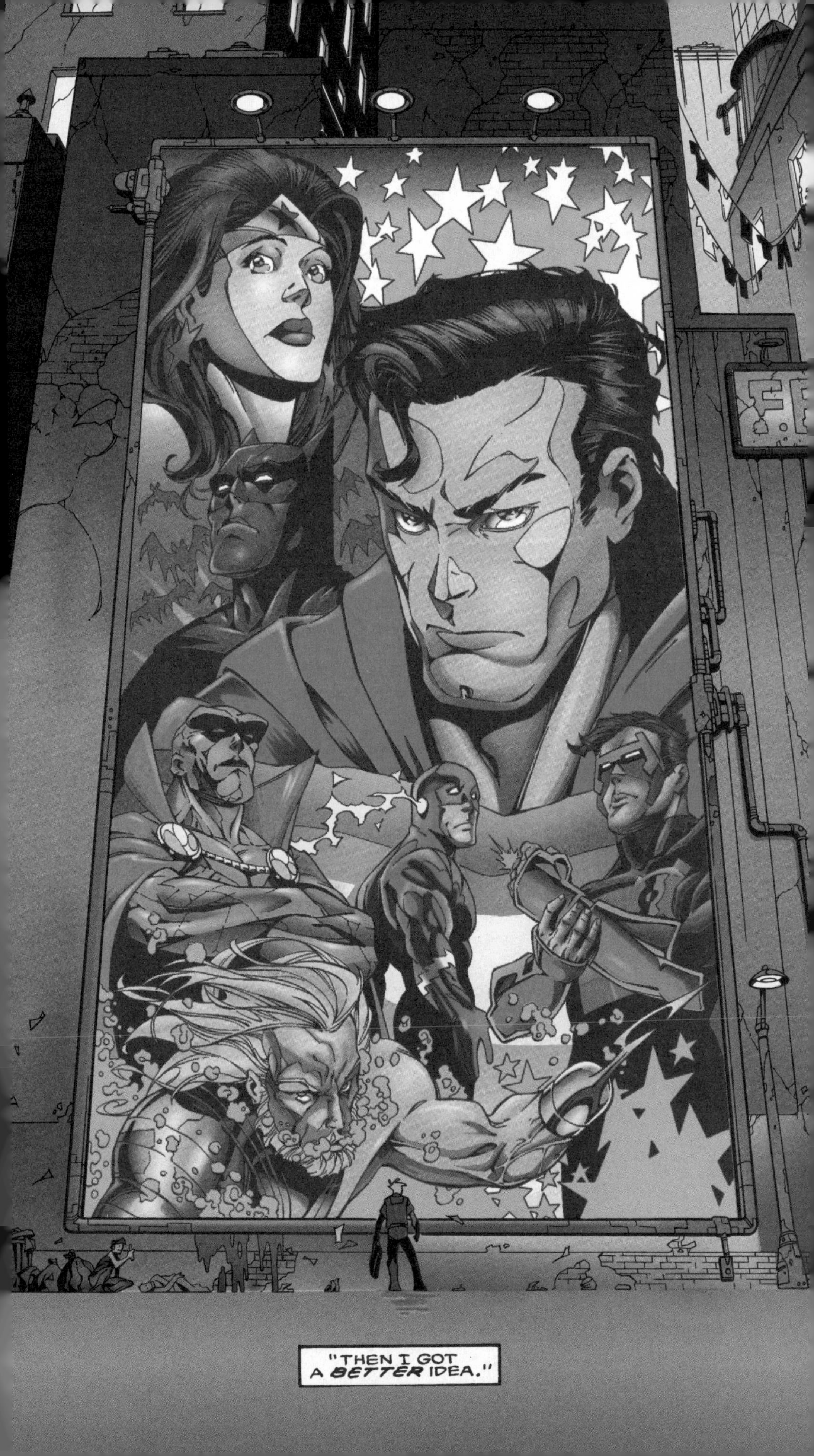
"THEN I GOT A *BETTER* IDEA."

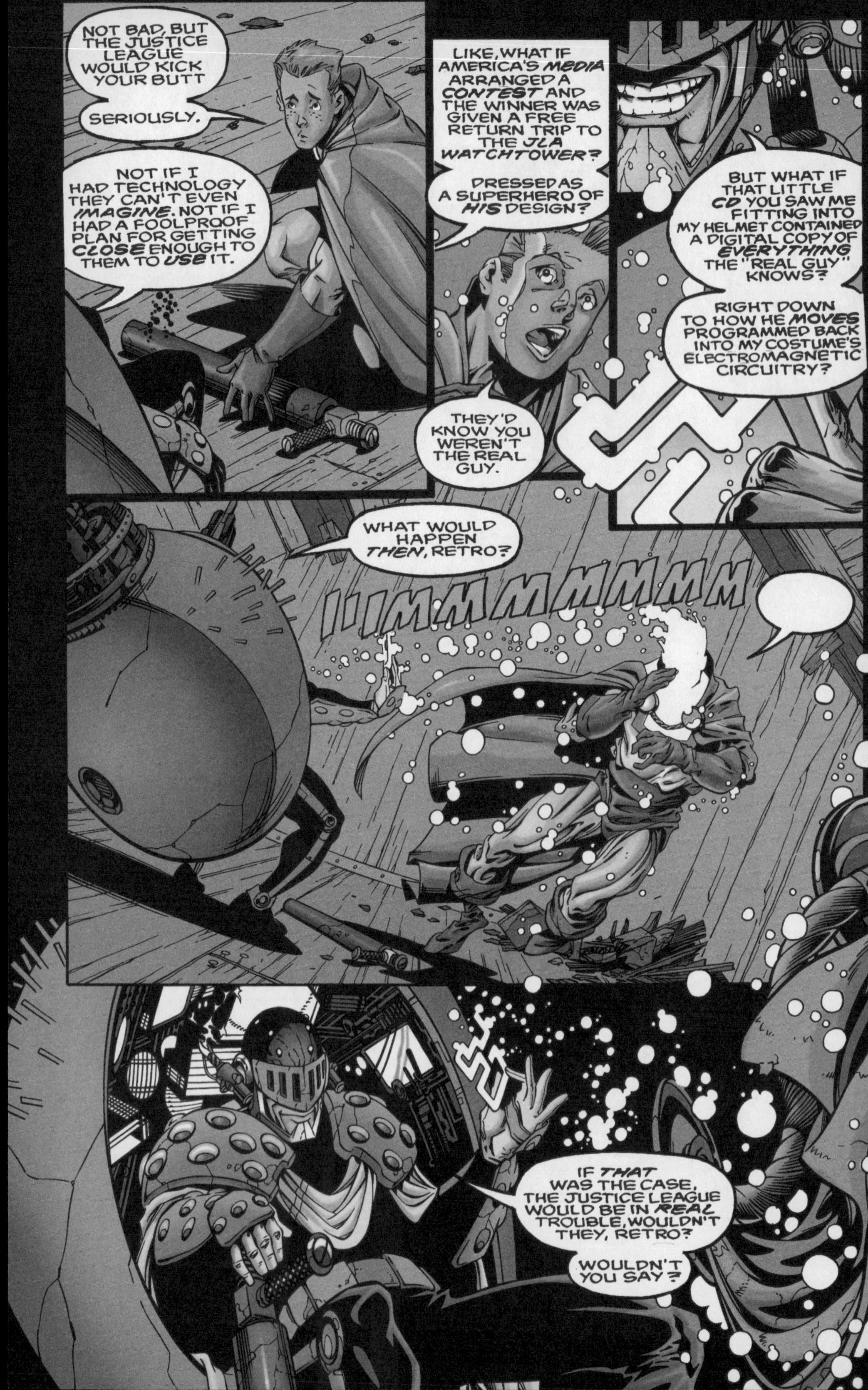
NOT BAD, BUT THE JUSTICE LEAGUE WOULD KICK YOUR BUTT
SERIOUSLY.
NOT IF I HAD TECHNOLOGY THEY CAN'T EVEN IMAGINE. NOT IF I HAD A FOOLPROOF PLAN FOR GETTING CLOSE ENOUGH TO THEM TO USE IT.
LIKE, WHAT IF AMERICA'S MEDIA ARRANGED A CONTEST AND THE WINNER WAS GIVEN A FREE RETURN TRIP TO THE JLA WATCHTOWER?
DRESSED AS A SUPERHERO OF HIS DESIGN?
THEY'D KNOW YOU WEREN'T THE REAL GUY.
BUT WHAT IF THAT LITTLE CD YOU SAW ME FITTING INTO MY HELMET CONTAINED A DIGITAL COPY OF EVERYTHING THE "REAL GUY" KNOWS?
RIGHT DOWN TO HOW HE MOVES PROGRAMMED BACK INTO MY COSTUME'S ELECTROMAGNETIC CIRCUITRY?
WHAT WOULD HAPPEN THEN, RETRO?
IIIMMMMMMMMM
IF THAT WAS THE CASE, THE JUSTICE LEAGUE WOULD BE IN REAL TROUBLE, WOULDN'T THEY, RETRO?
WOULDN'T YOU SAY?

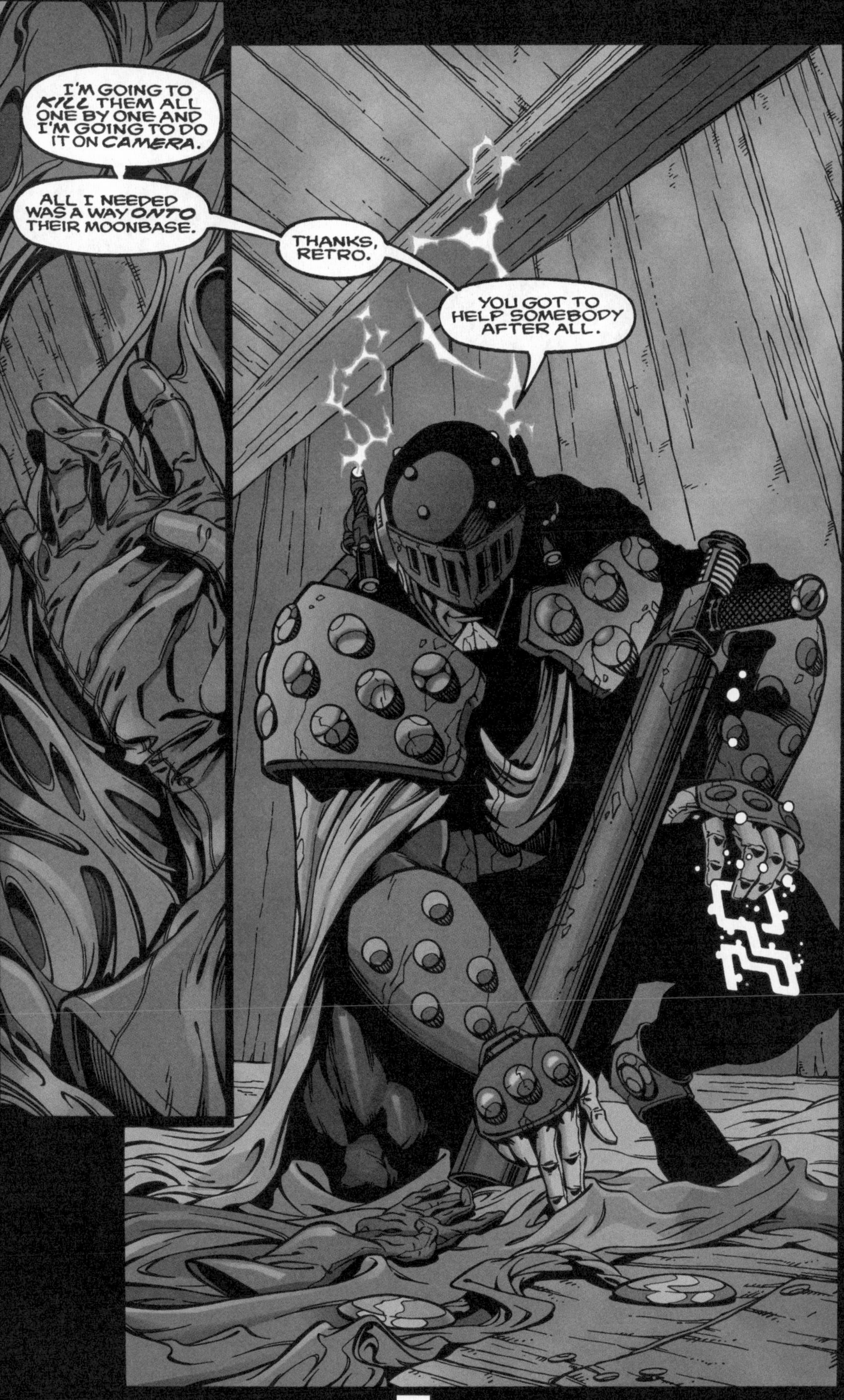

I'M GOING TO KILL THEM ALL ONE BY ONE AND I'M GOING TO DO IT ON CAMERA.
ALL I NEEDED WAS A WAY ONTO THEIR MOONBASE.
THANKS, RETRO.
YOU GOT TO HELP SOMEBODY AFTER ALL.

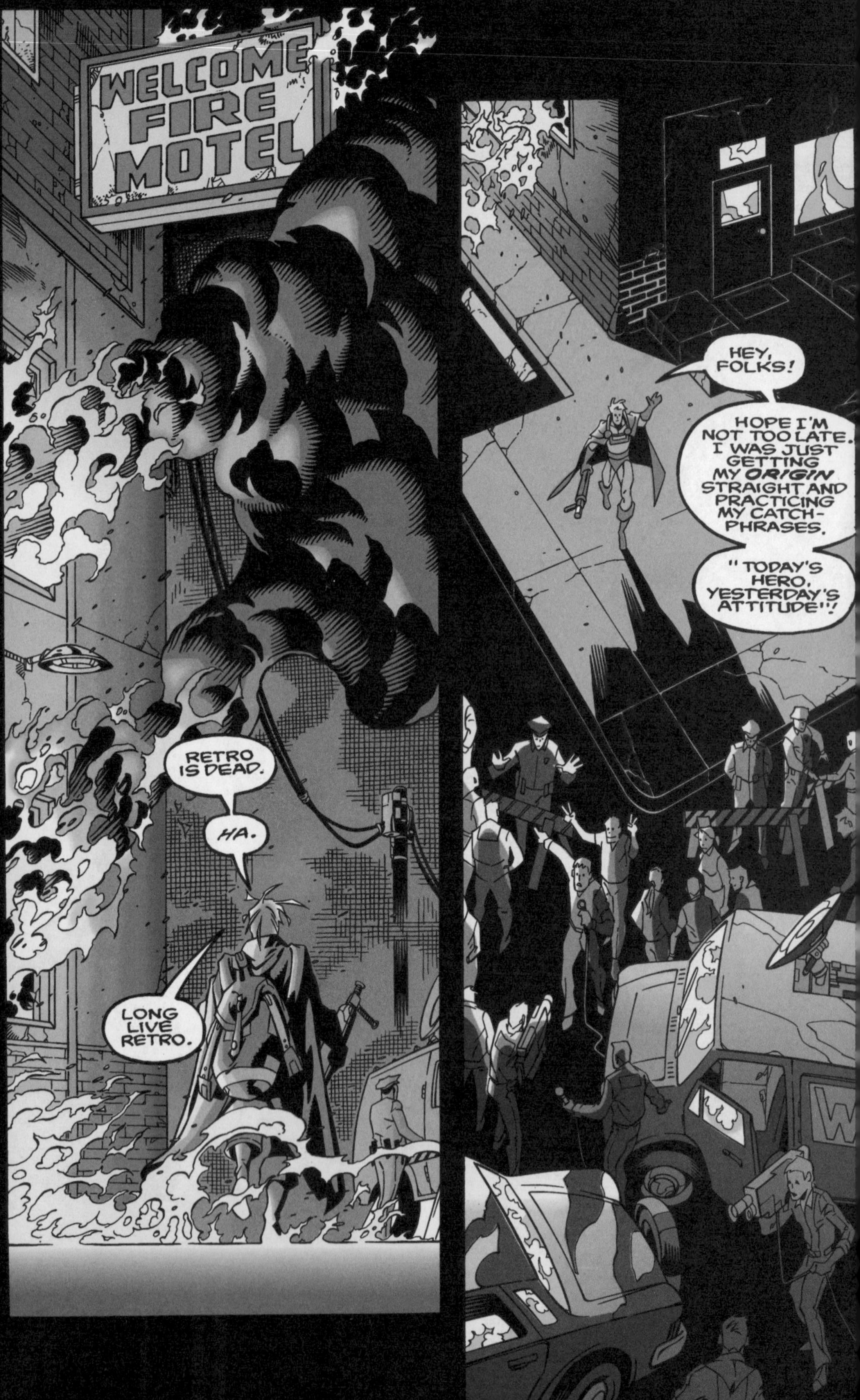
WELCOME FIRE MOTEL
RETRO IS DEAD.
HA.
LONG LIVE RETRO.
HEY, FOLKS!
HOPE I'M NOT TOO LATE. I WAS JUST GETTING MY ORIGIN STRAIGHT AND PRACTICING MY CATCH-PHRASES.
"TODAY'S HERO, YESTERDAY'S ATTITUDE"!

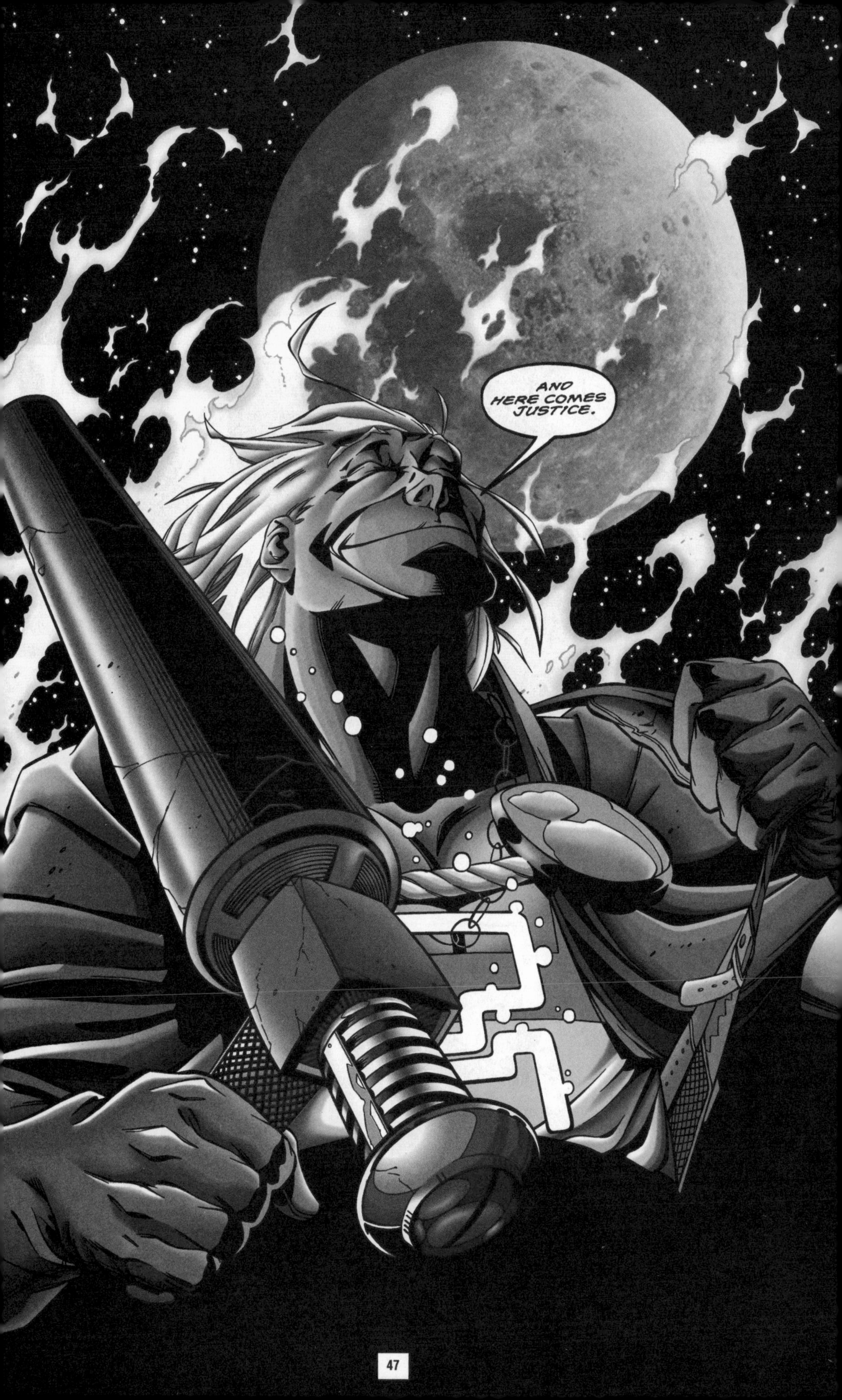
AND HERE COMES JUSTICE.

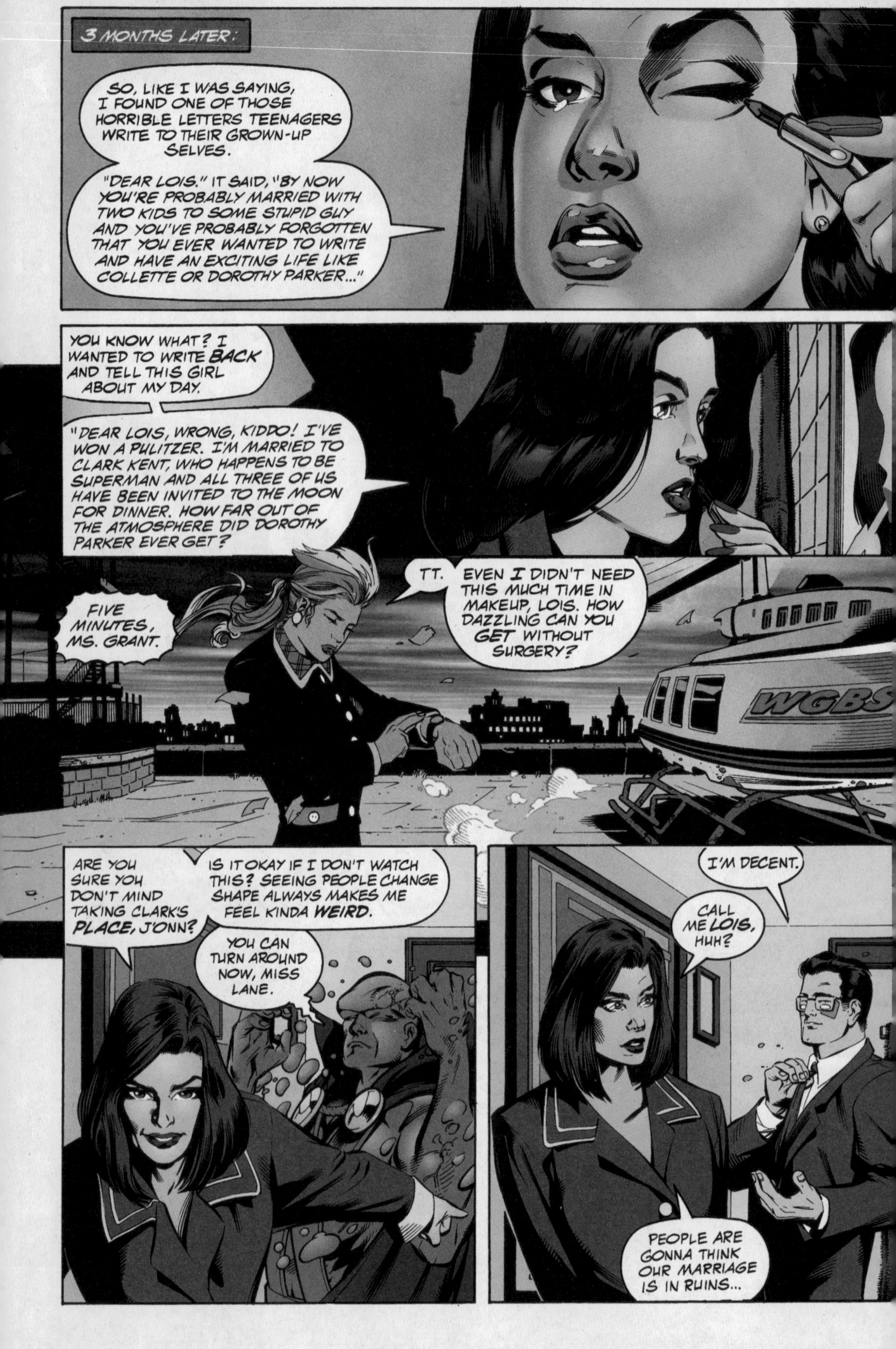
3 MONTHS LATER:
SO, LIKE I WAS SAYING, I FOUND ONE OF THOSE HORRIBLE LETTERS TEENAGERS WRITE TO THEIR GROWN-UP SELVES.
"DEAR LOIS," IT SAID, "BY NOW YOU'RE PROBABLY MARRIED WITH TWO KIDS TO SOME STUPID GUY AND YOU'VE PROBABLY FORGOTTEN THAT YOU EVER WANTED TO WRITE AND HAVE AN EXCITING LIFE LIKE COLLETTE OR DOROTHY PARKER..."
YOU KNOW WHAT? I WANTED TO WRITE BACK AND TELL THIS GIRL ABOUT MY DAY.
"DEAR LOIS, WRONG, KIDDO! I'VE WON A PULITZER. I'M MARRIED TO CLARK KENT, WHO HAPPENS TO BE SUPERMAN AND ALL THREE OF US HAVE BEEN INVITED TO THE MOON FOR DINNER. HOW FAR OUT OF THE ATMOSPHERE DID DOROTHY PARKER EVER GET?
FIVE MINUTES, MS. GRANT.
TT.
EVEN I DIDN'T NEED THIS MUCH TIME IN MAKEUP, LOIS. HOW DAZZLING CAN YOU GET WITHOUT SURGERY?
WGBS
ARE YOU SURE YOU DON'T MIND TAKING CLARK'S PLACE, J'ONN?
IS IT OKAY IF I DON'T WATCH THIS? SEEING PEOPLE CHANGE SHAPE ALWAYS MAKES ME FEEL KINDA WEIRD.
YOU CAN TURN AROUND NOW, MISS LANE.
I'M DECENT.
CALL ME LOIS, HUH?
PEOPLE ARE GONNA THINK OUR MARRIAGE IS IN RUINS...

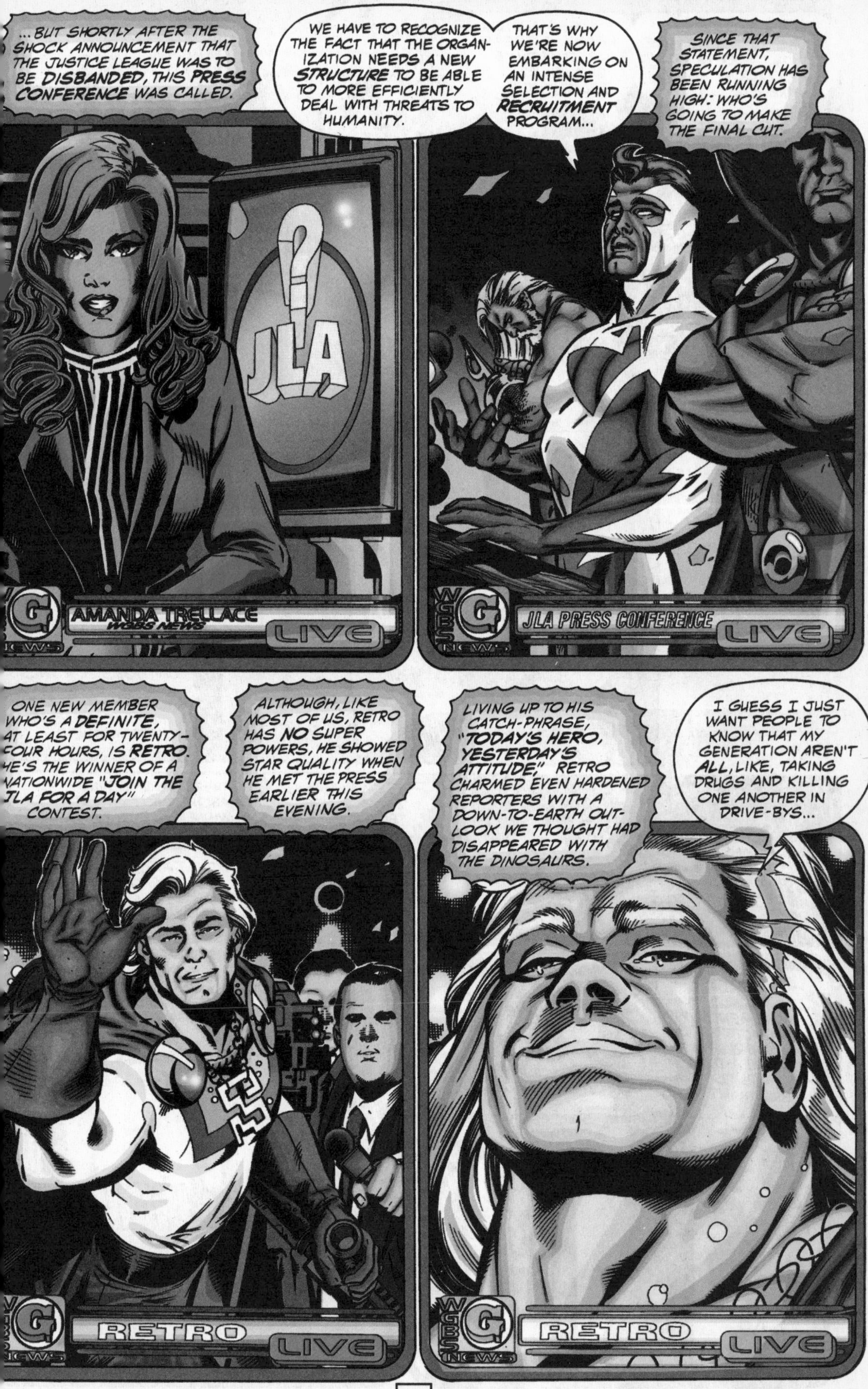
...BUT SHORTLY AFTER THE SHOCK ANNOUNCEMENT THAT THE JUSTICE LEAGUE WAS TO BE DISBANDED, THIS PRESS CONFERENCE WAS CALLED.
WE HAVE TO RECOGNIZE THE FACT THAT THE ORGANIZATION NEEDS A NEW STRUCTURE TO BE ABLE TO MORE EFFICIENTLY DEAL WITH THREATS TO HUMANITY.
THAT'S WHY WE'RE NOW EMBARKING ON AN INTENSE SELECTION AND RECRUITMENT PROGRAM...
SINCE THAT STATEMENT, SPECULATION HAS BEEN RUNNING HIGH: WHO'S GOING TO MAKE THE FINAL CUT.
JLA
AMANDA TRELLACE
WGBS NEWS
LIVE
JLA PRESS CONFERENCE
LIVE
ONE NEW MEMBER WHO'S A DEFINITE, AT LEAST FOR TWENTY-FOUR HOURS, IS RETRO. HE'S THE WINNER OF A NATIONWIDE "JOIN THE JLA FOR A DAY" CONTEST.
ALTHOUGH, LIKE MOST OF US, RETRO HAS NO SUPER POWERS, HE SHOWED STAR QUALITY WHEN HE MET THE PRESS EARLIER THIS EVENING.
LIVING UP TO HIS CATCH-PHRASE, "TODAY'S HERO, YESTERDAY'S ATTITUDE," RETRO CHARMED EVEN HARDENED REPORTERS WITH A DOWN-TO-EARTH OUTLOOK WE THOUGHT HAD DISAPPEARED WITH THE DINOSAURS.
I GUESS I JUST WANT PEOPLE TO KNOW THAT MY GENERATION AREN'T ALL, LIKE, TAKING DRUGS AND KILLING ONE ANOTHER IN DRIVE-BYS...
RETRO
LIVE
RETRO
LIVE

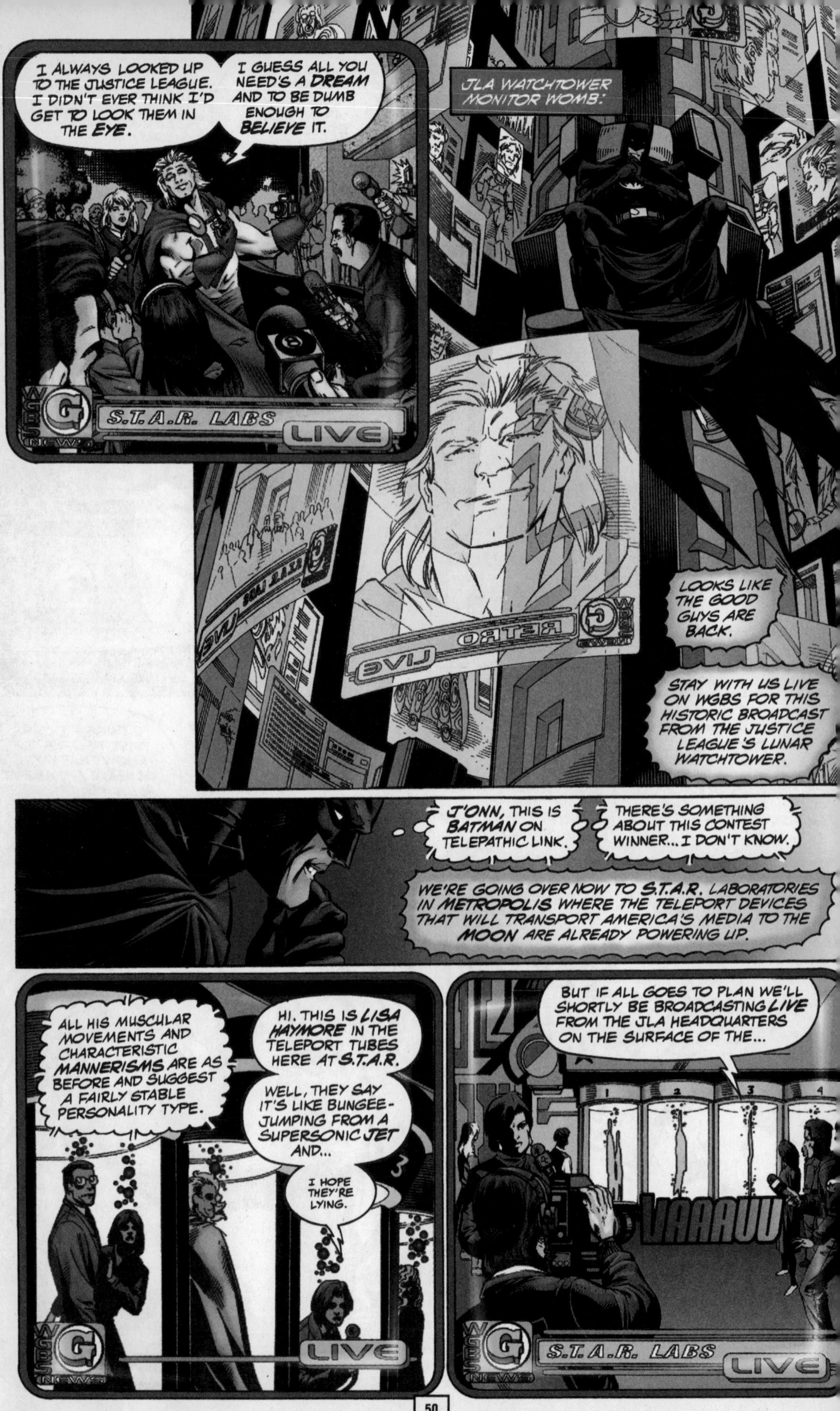
I ALWAYS LOOKED UP TO THE JUSTICE LEAGUE. I DIDN'T EVER THINK I'D GET TO LOOK THEM IN THE EYE.
I GUESS ALL YOU NEED'S A DREAM AND TO BE DUMB ENOUGH TO BELIEVE IT.
S.T.A.R. LABS
LIVE
JLA WATCHTOWER MONITOR WOMB:
RETRO
LIVE
LOOKS LIKE THE GOOD GUYS ARE BACK.
STAY WITH US LIVE ON WGBS FOR THIS HISTORIC BROADCAST FROM THE JUSTICE LEAGUE'S LUNAR WATCHTOWER.
J'ONN, THIS IS BATMAN ON TELEPATHIC LINK.
THERE'S SOMETHING ABOUT THIS CONTEST WINNER... I DON'T KNOW.
WE'RE GOING OVER NOW TO S.T.A.R. LABORATORIES IN METROPOLIS WHERE THE TELEPORT DEVICES THAT WILL TRANSPORT AMERICA'S MEDIA TO THE MOON ARE ALREADY POWERING UP.
ALL HIS MUSCULAR MOVEMENTS AND CHARACTERISTIC MANNERISMS ARE AS BEFORE AND SUGGEST A FAIRLY STABLE PERSONALITY TYPE.
HI. THIS IS LISA HAYMORE IN THE TELEPORT TUBES HERE AT S.T.A.R.
WELL, THEY SAY IT'S LIKE BUNGEE-JUMPING FROM A SUPERSONIC JET AND...
I HOPE THEY'RE LYING.
LIVE
BUT IF ALL GOES TO PLAN WE'LL SHORTLY BE BROADCASTING LIVE FROM THE JLA HEADQUARTERS ON THE SURFACE OF THE...
1
2
3
4
VAAAVV
S.T.A.R. LABS
LIVE

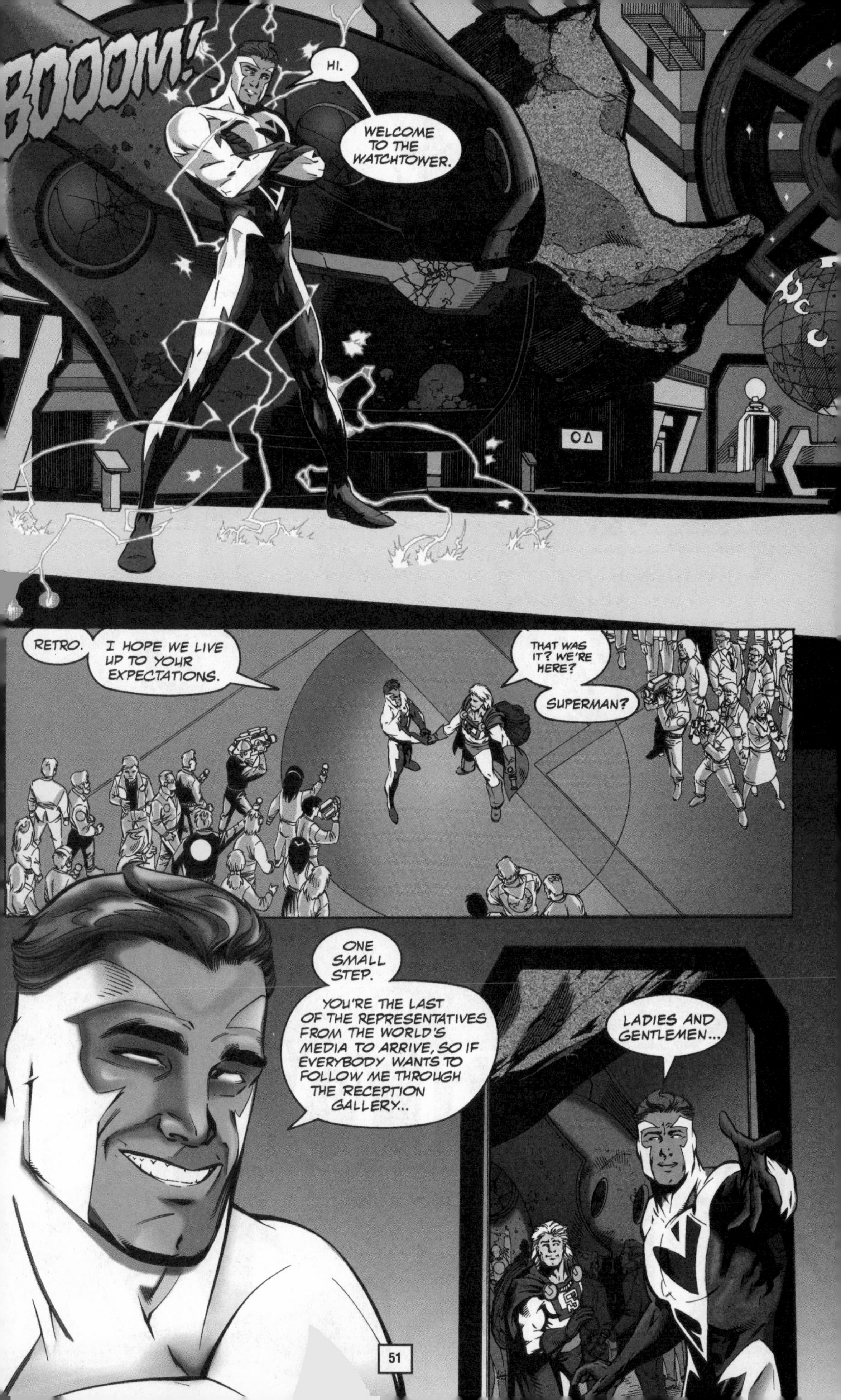

BOOOM!
HI.
WELCOME TO THE WATCHTOWER.
RETRO.
I HOPE WE LIVE UP TO YOUR EXPECTATIONS.
THAT WAS IT? WE'RE HERE?
SUPERMAN?
ONE SMALL STEP.
YOU'RE THE LAST OF THE REPRESENTATIVES FROM THE WORLD'S MEDIA TO ARRIVE, SO IF EVERYBODY WANTS TO FOLLOW ME THROUGH THE RECEPTION GALLERY...
LADIES AND GENTLEMEN...

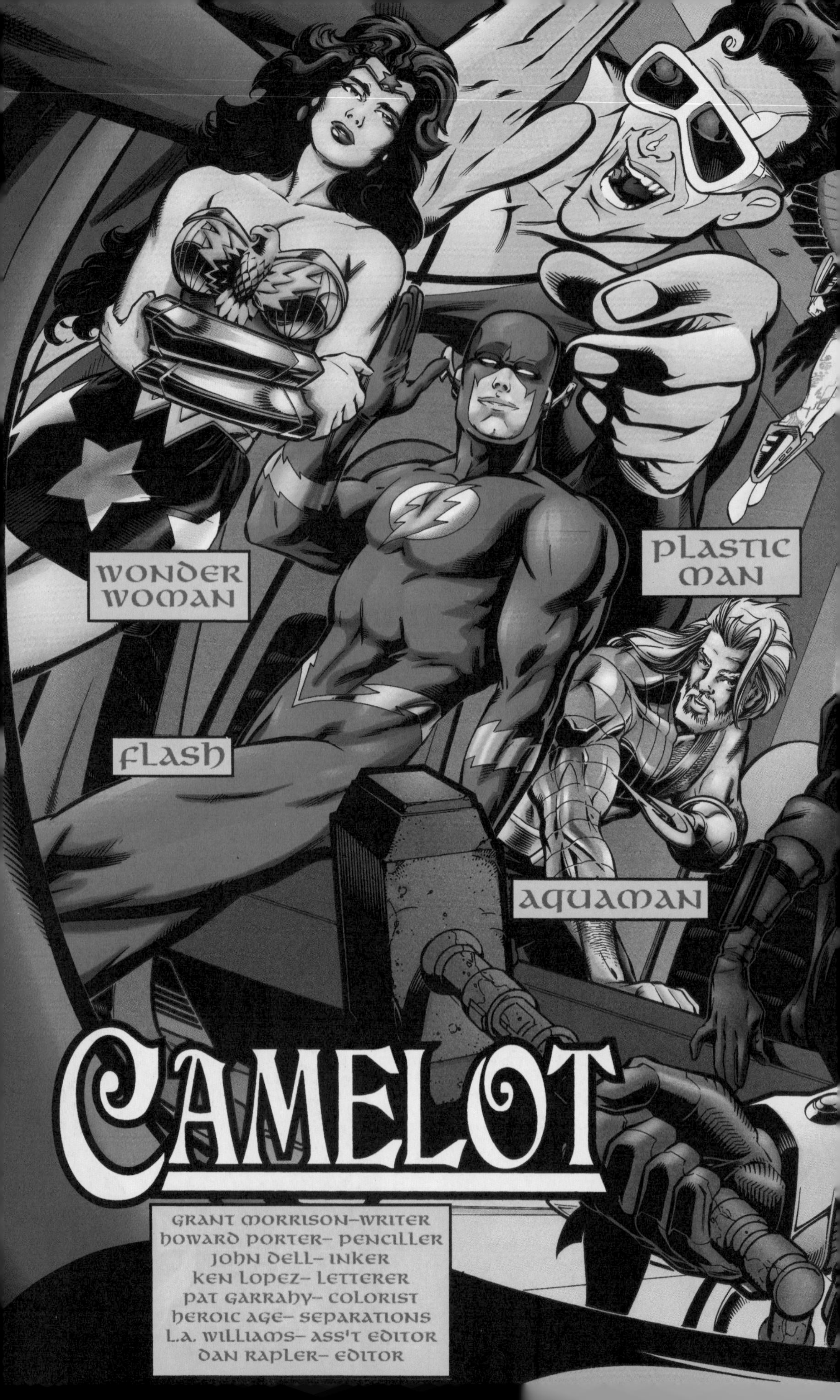

WONDER WOMAN
PLASTIC MAN
FLASH
AQUAMAN
CAMELOT
GRANT MORRISON–WRITER
HOWARD PORTER– PENCILLER
JOHN DELL– INKER
KEN LOPEZ– LETTERER
PAT GARRAHY– COLORIST
HEROIC AGE– SEPARATIONS
L.A. WILLIAMS– ASS'T EDITOR
DAN RASPLER– EDITOR

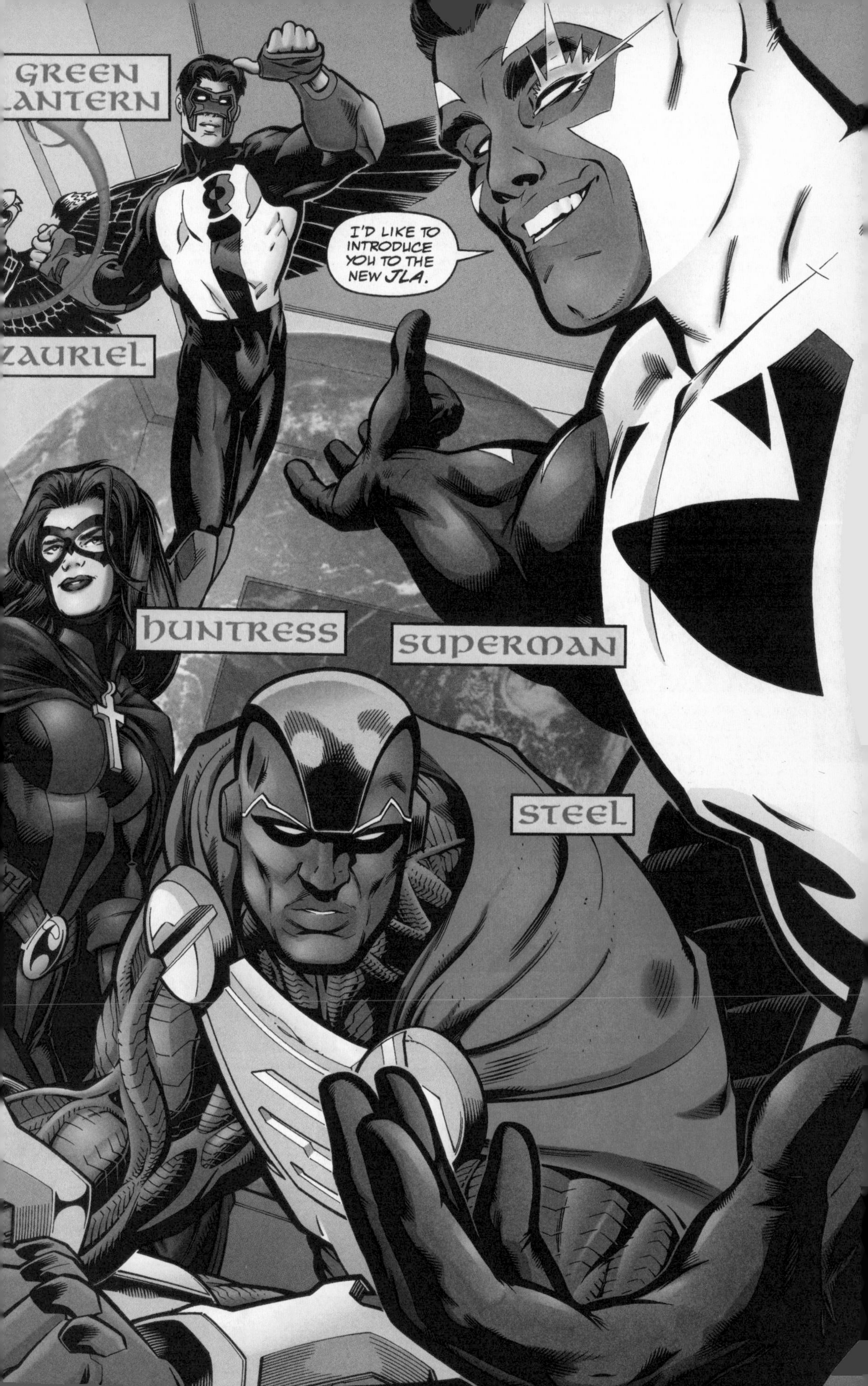
GREEN LANTERN
ZAURIEL
I'D LIKE TO INTRODUCE YOU TO THE NEW JLA.
HUNTRESS
SUPERMAN
STEEL

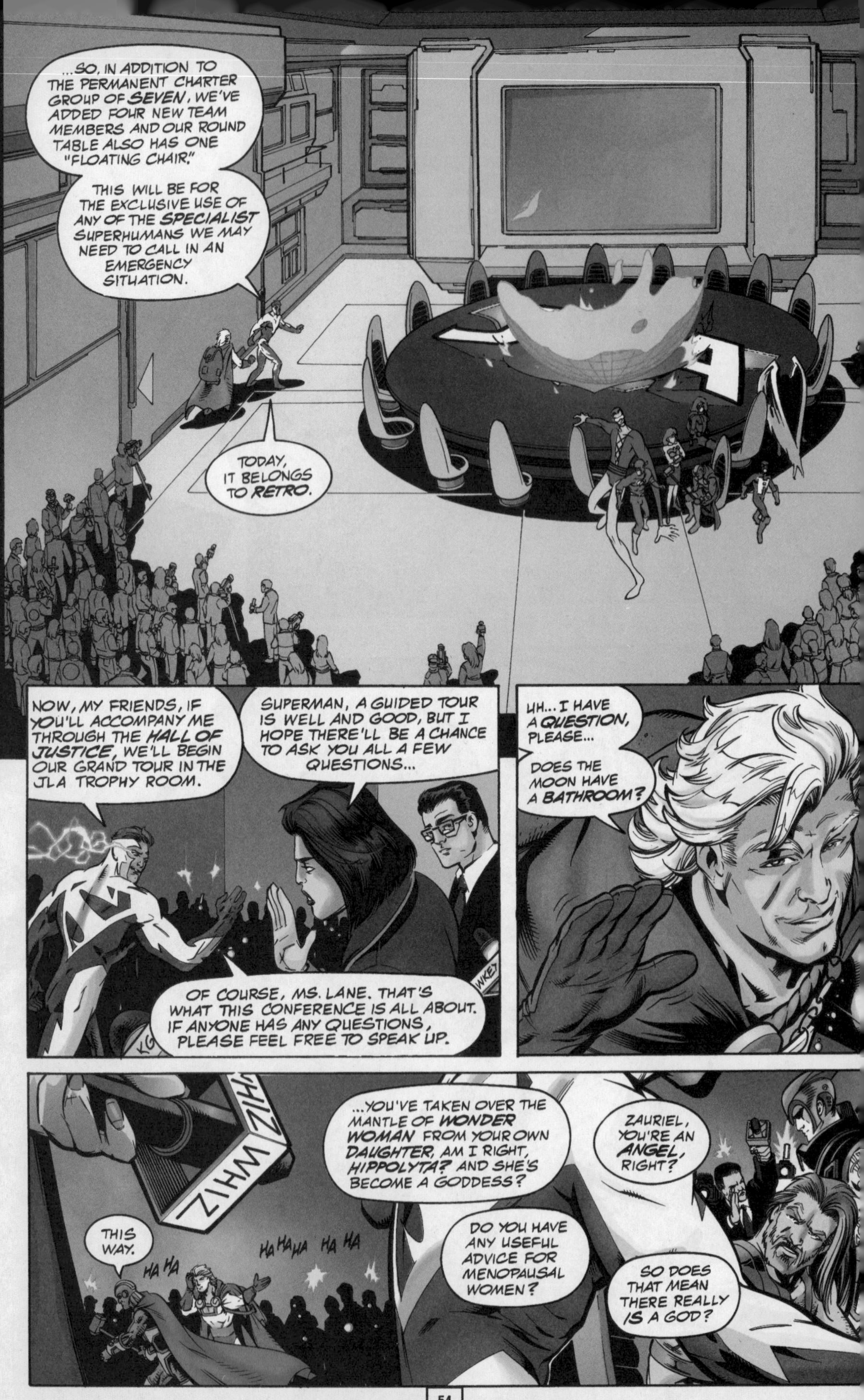
...SO, IN ADDITION TO THE PERMANENT CHARTER GROUP OF SEVEN, WE'VE ADDED FOUR NEW TEAM MEMBERS AND OUR ROUND TABLE ALSO HAS ONE "FLOATING CHAIR."
THIS WILL BE FOR THE EXCLUSIVE USE OF ANY OF THE SPECIALIST SUPERHUMANS WE MAY NEED TO CALL IN AN EMERGENCY SITUATION.
TODAY, IT BELONGS TO RETRO.
NOW, MY FRIENDS, IF YOU'LL ACCOMPANY ME THROUGH THE HALL OF JUSTICE, WE'LL BEGIN OUR GRAND TOUR IN THE JLA TROPHY ROOM.
SUPERMAN, A GUIDED TOUR IS WELL AND GOOD, BUT I HOPE THERE'LL BE A CHANCE TO ASK YOU ALL A FEW QUESTIONS...
OF COURSE, MS. LANE. THAT'S WHAT THIS CONFERENCE IS ALL ABOUT. IF ANYONE HAS ANY QUESTIONS, PLEASE FEEL FREE TO SPEAK UP.
UH... I HAVE A QUESTION, PLEASE...
DOES THE MOON HAVE A BATHROOM?
WHIZ
THIS WAY.
HA HA
HA HA HA HA HA
...YOU'VE TAKEN OVER THE MANTLE OF WONDER WOMAN FROM YOUR OWN DAUGHTER, AM I RIGHT, HIPPOLYTA? AND SHE'S BECOME A GODDESS?
DO YOU HAVE ANY USEFUL ADVICE FOR MENOPAUSAL WOMEN?
ZAURIEL, YOU'RE AN ANGEL, RIGHT?
SO DOES THAT MEAN THERE REALLY IS A GOD?

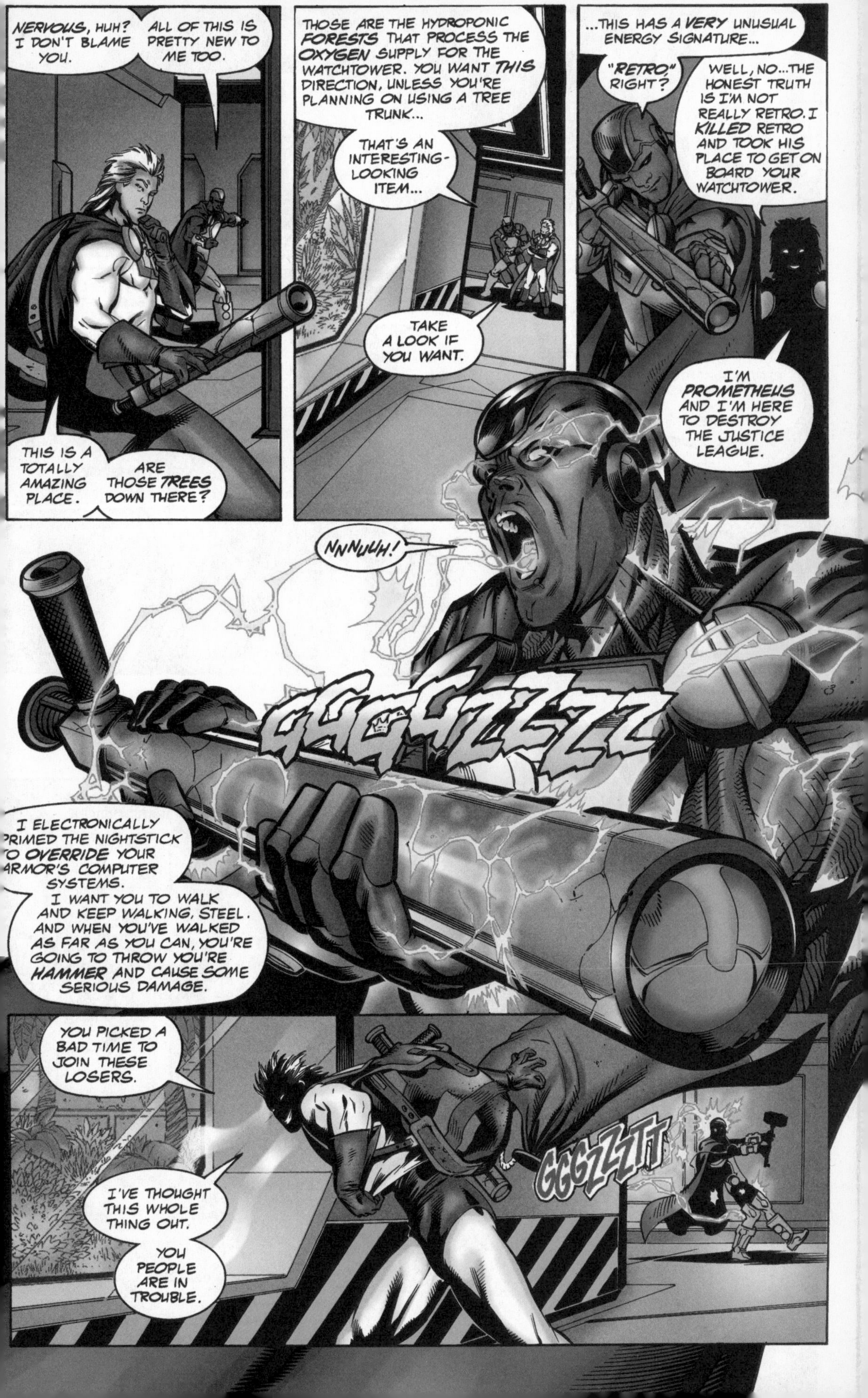
NERVOUS, HUH? I DON'T BLAME YOU.
ALL OF THIS IS PRETTY NEW TO ME TOO.
THIS IS A TOTALLY AMAZING PLACE.
ARE THOSE TREES DOWN THERE?
THOSE ARE THE HYDROPONIC FORESTS THAT PROCESS THE OXYGEN SUPPLY FOR THE WATCHTOWER. YOU WANT THIS DIRECTION, UNLESS YOU'RE PLANNING ON USING A TREE TRUNK...
THAT'S AN INTERESTING-LOOKING ITEM...
TAKE A LOOK IF YOU WANT.
...THIS HAS A VERY UNUSUAL ENERGY SIGNATURE...
"RETRO," RIGHT?
WELL, NO...THE HONEST TRUTH IS I'M NOT REALLY RETRO. I KILLED RETRO AND TOOK HIS PLACE TO GET ON BOARD YOUR WATCHTOWER.
I'M PROMETHEUS AND I'M HERE TO DESTROY THE JUSTICE LEAGUE.
NNNUUH!
GGGZZZZZ
I ELECTRONICALLY PRIMED THE NIGHTSTICK TO OVERRIDE YOUR ARMOR'S COMPUTER SYSTEMS.
I WANT YOU TO WALK AND KEEP WALKING, STEEL. AND WHEN YOU'VE WALKED AS FAR AS YOU CAN, YOU'RE GOING TO THROW YOU'RE HAMMER AND CAUSE SOME SERIOUS DAMAGE.
YOU PICKED A BAD TIME TO JOIN THESE LOSERS.
GGGZZZTT
I'VE THOUGHT THIS WHOLE THING OUT.
YOU PEOPLE ARE IN TROUBLE.

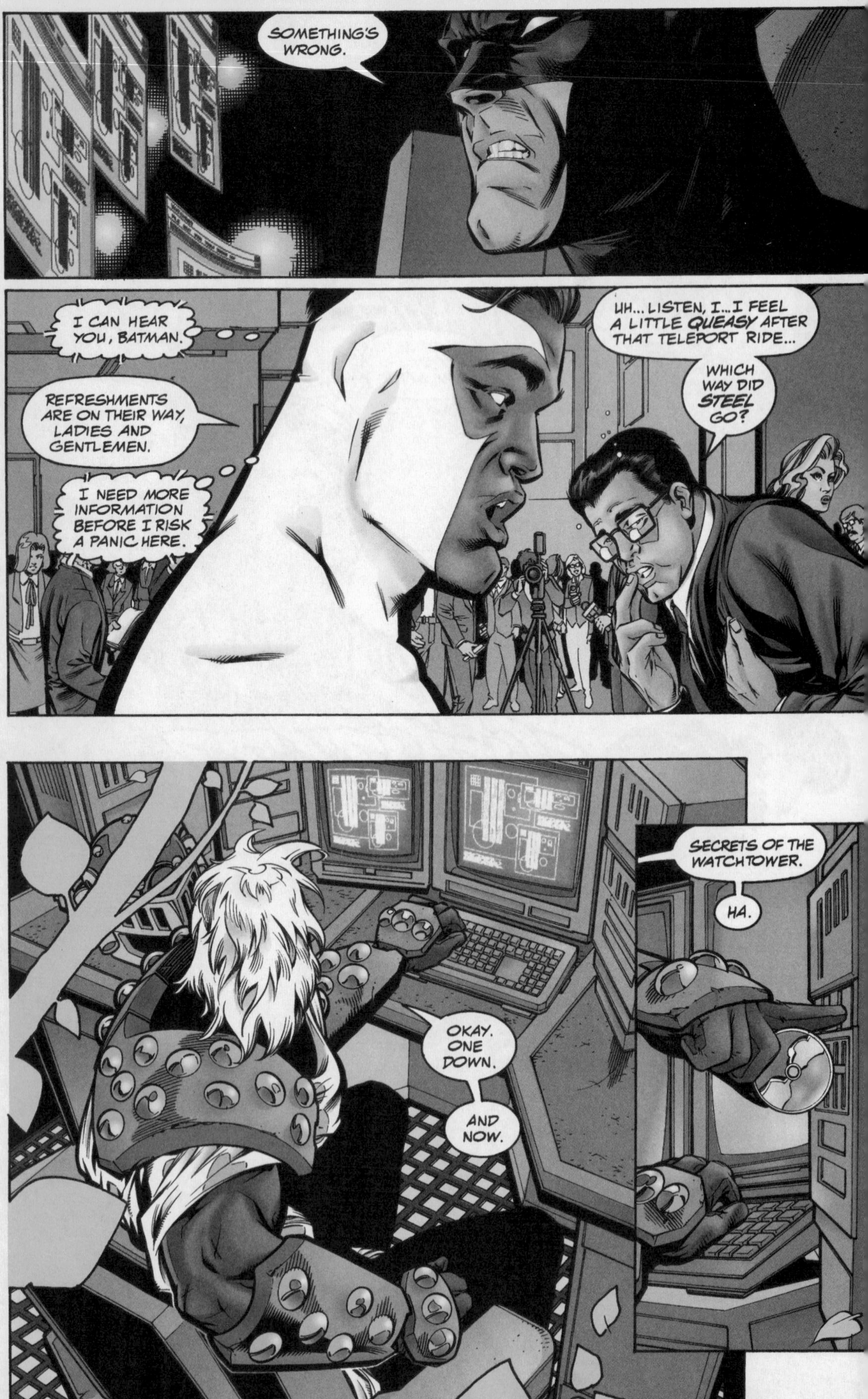
SOMETHING'S WRONG.
I CAN HEAR YOU, BATMAN.
REFRESHMENTS ARE ON THEIR WAY, LADIES AND GENTLEMEN.
I NEED MORE INFORMATION BEFORE I RISK A PANIC HERE.
UH... LISTEN, I...I FEEL A LITTLE QUEASY AFTER THAT TELEPORT RIDE...
WHICH WAY DID STEEL GO?
OKAY. ONE DOWN.
AND NOW.
SECRETS OF THE WATCHTOWER.
HA.

JLA WATCHTOWER Key

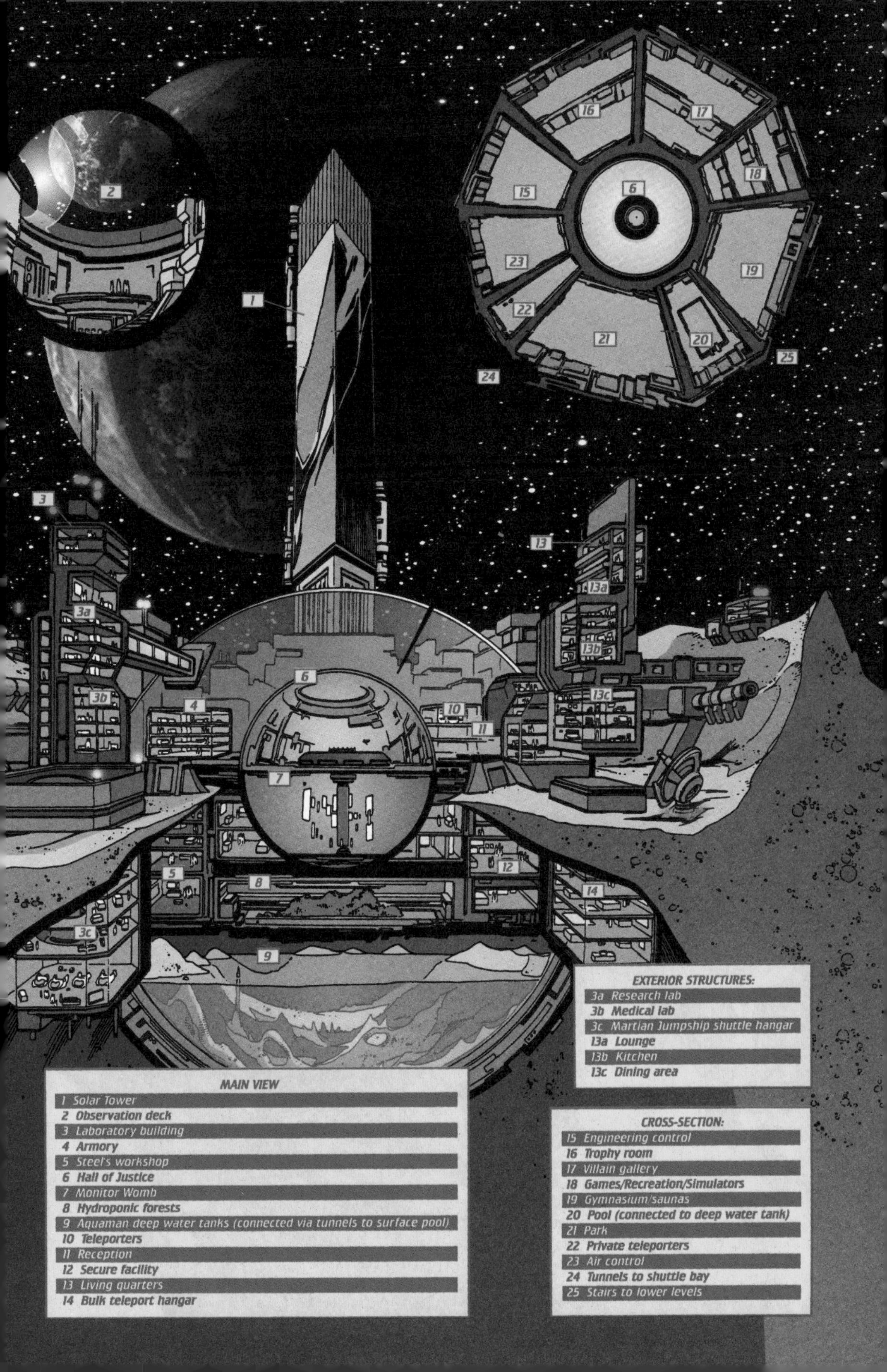
EXTERIOR STRUCTURES:
3a Research lab
3b Medical lab
3c Martian Jumpship shuttle hangar
13a Lounge
13b Kitchen
13c Dining area
MAIN VIEW
1 Solar Tower
2 Observation deck
3 Laboratory building
4 Armory
5 Steel's workshop
6 Hall of Justice
7 Monitor Womb
8 Hydroponic forests
9 Aquaman deep water tanks (connected via tunnels to surface pool)
10 Teleporters
11 Reception
12 Secure facility
13 Living quarters
14 Bulk teleport hangar
CROSS-SECTION:
15 Engineering control
16 Trophy room
17 Villain gallery
18 Games/Recreation/Simulators
19 Gymnasium/saunas
20 Pool (connected to deep water tank)
21 Park
22 Private teleporters
23 Air control
24 Tunnels to shuttle bay
25 Stairs to lower levels

INSTALL.

WHO ARE YOU?

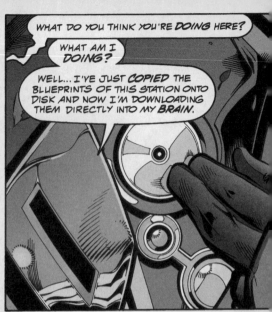

WHAT DO YOU THINK YOU'RE *DOING* HERE?

WHAT AM I *DOING*?

WELL... I'VE JUST *COPIED* THE BLUEPRINTS OF THIS STATION ONTO DISK AND NOW I'M DOWNLOADING THEM DIRECTLY INTO MY *BRAIN*.

EVERY MAINTENANCE DUCT, EVERY WIRE, EVERY PIPE: I NOW HAVE THEM ALL *MEMORIZED*.

STOP WHAT YOU'RE DOING AND COME WITH ME, PLEASE...

YOU MAY ALSO NOTICE THAT I'VE INCREASED THE *OXYGEN* CONTENT OF THE AIR.

OXYGEN IS HIGHLY COMBUSTIBLE.

YOU'RE VULNERABLE TO FLAME.

AND *THIS* IS A *PHOSPHORUS* DART.

CHUFF!

SHMMLIFF

UUUGGHHH

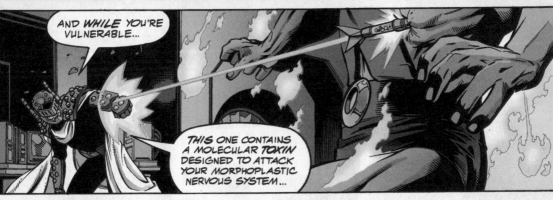

AND WHILE YOU'RE VULNERABLE...

THIS ONE CONTAINS A MOLECULAR TOXIN DESIGNED TO ATTACK YOUR MORPHOPLASTIC NERVOUS SYSTEM...

WHAT'S HAPPENING TO MUHHHH

COMPLETE SPASTIC PARALYSIS. YOU NO LONGER HAVE ANY CONTROL OVER YOUR PHYSICAL STRUCTURE.

IT SHOULD ONLY LAST ABOUT AN HOUR. MUCH LONGER THAN I'M GOING TO NEED.

UUILBBB

UNTIL THEN YOU'RE THE MOST POWERFUL PUDDLE OF GOO ALIVE.

SCOURGE OF THE UNDERWORLD!

HA!

TWO DOWN.

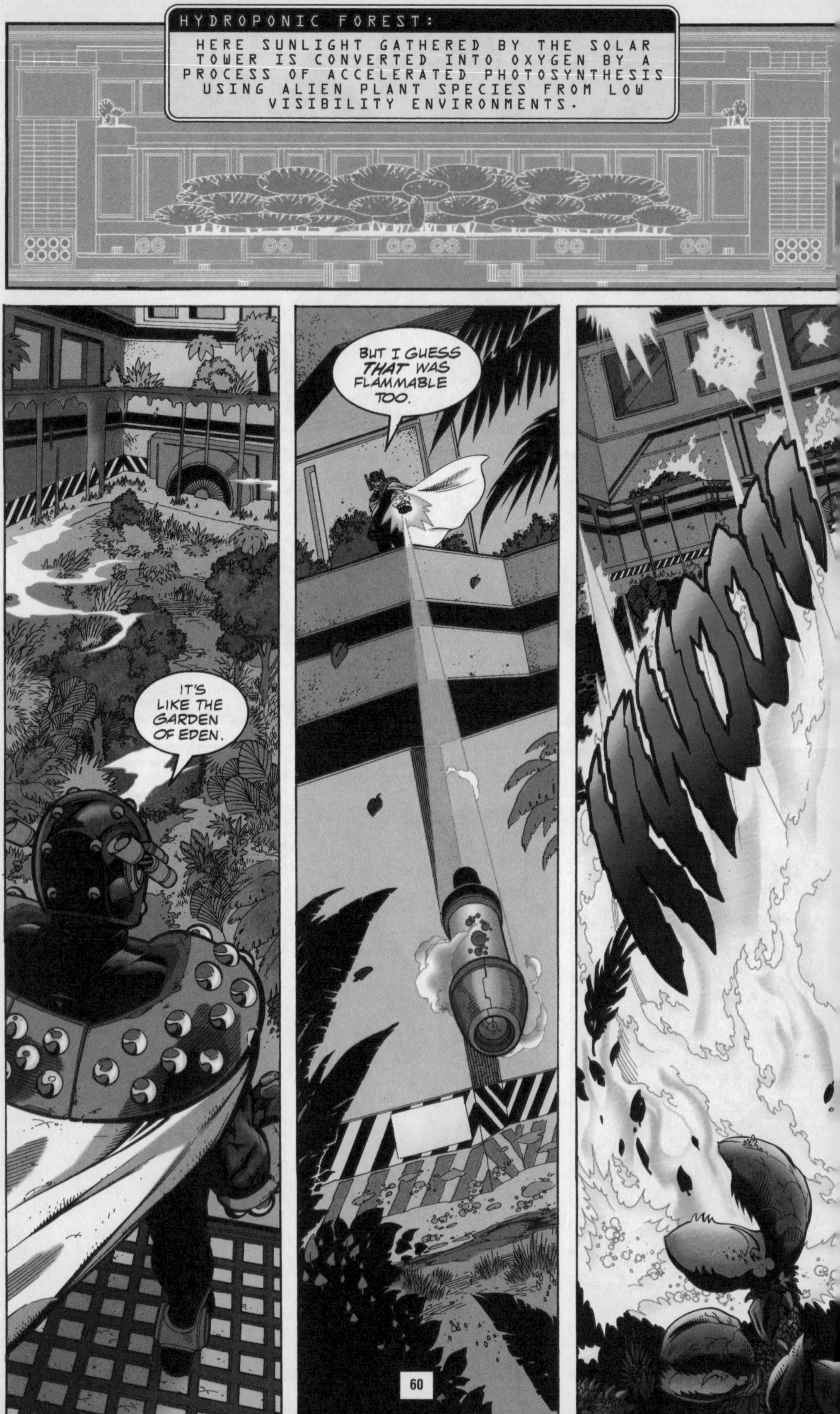
HYDROPONIC FOREST:
HERE SUNLIGHT GATHERED BY THE SOLAR TOWER IS CONVERTED INTO OXYGEN BY A PROCESS OF ACCELERATED PHOTOSYNTHESIS USING ALIEN PLANT SPECIES FROM LOW VISIBILITY ENVIRONMENTS.
IT'S LIKE THE GARDEN OF EDEN.
BUT I GUESS *THAT* WAS FLAMMABLE TOO.

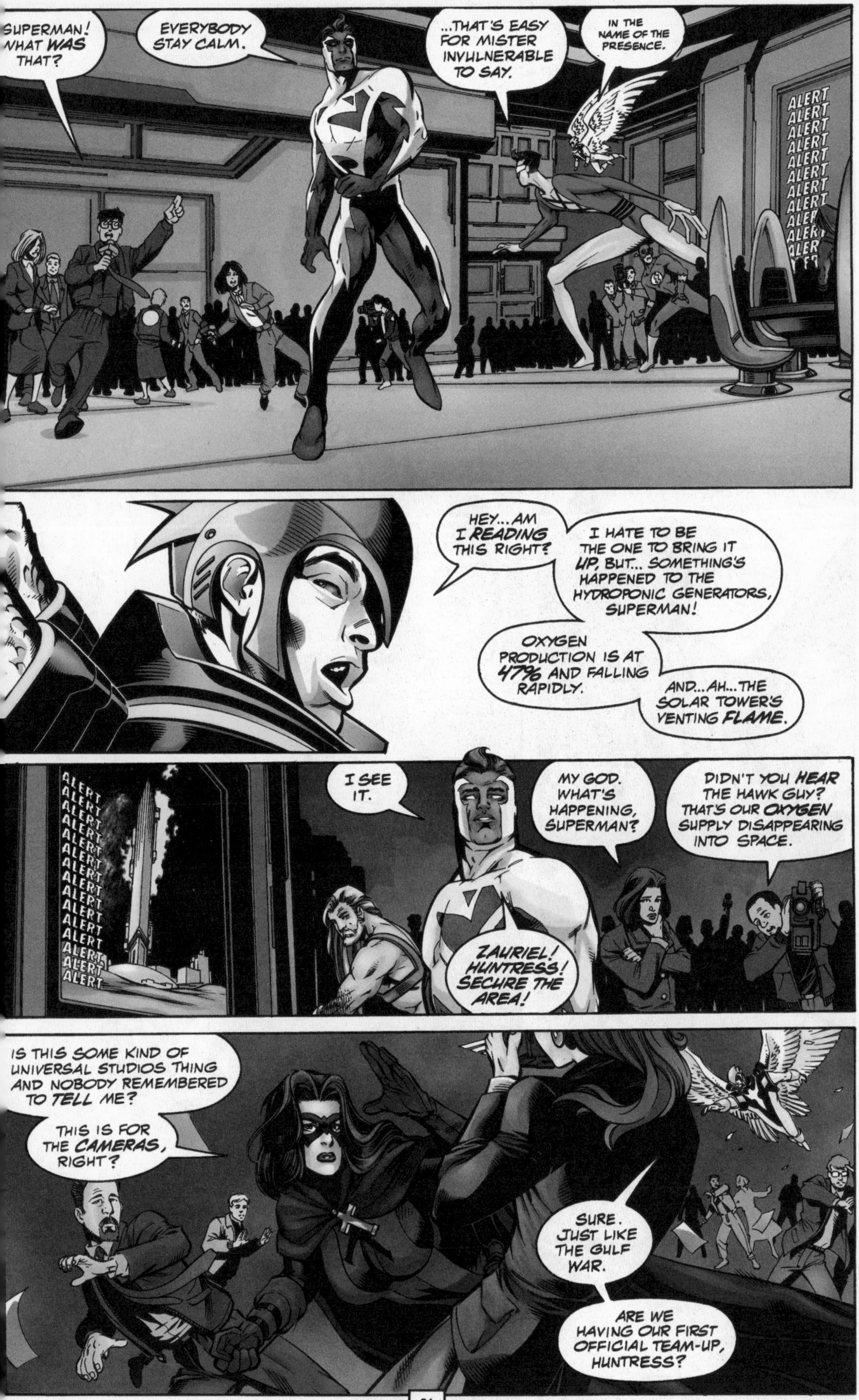
SUPERMAN! WHAT WAS THAT?
EVERYBODY STAY CALM.
...THAT'S EASY FOR MISTER INVULNERABLE TO SAY.
IN THE NAME OF THE PRESENCE.
ALERT ALERT ALERT ALERT ALERT ALERT ALERT ALERT ALERT ALERT
HEY...AM I READING THIS RIGHT?
I HATE TO BE THE ONE TO BRING IT UP, BUT... SOMETHING'S HAPPENED TO THE HYDROPONIC GENERATORS, SUPERMAN!
OXYGEN PRODUCTION IS AT 47% AND FALLING RAPIDLY.
AND...AH...THE SOLAR TOWER'S VENTING FLAME.
ALERT ALERT ALERT ALERT ALERT ALERT ALERT ALERT ALERT ALERT ALERT ALERT ALERT ALERT ALERT
I SEE IT.
MY GOD. WHAT'S HAPPENING, SUPERMAN?
DIDN'T YOU HEAR THE HAWK GUY? THAT'S OUR OXYGEN SUPPLY DISAPPEARING INTO SPACE.
ZAURIEL! HUNTRESS! SECURE THE AREA!
IS THIS SOME KIND OF UNIVERSAL STUDIOS THING AND NOBODY REMEMBERED TO TELL ME?
THIS IS FOR THE CAMERAS, RIGHT?
SURE. JUST LIKE THE GULF WAR.
ARE WE HAVING OUR FIRST OFFICIAL TEAM-UP, HUNTRESS?

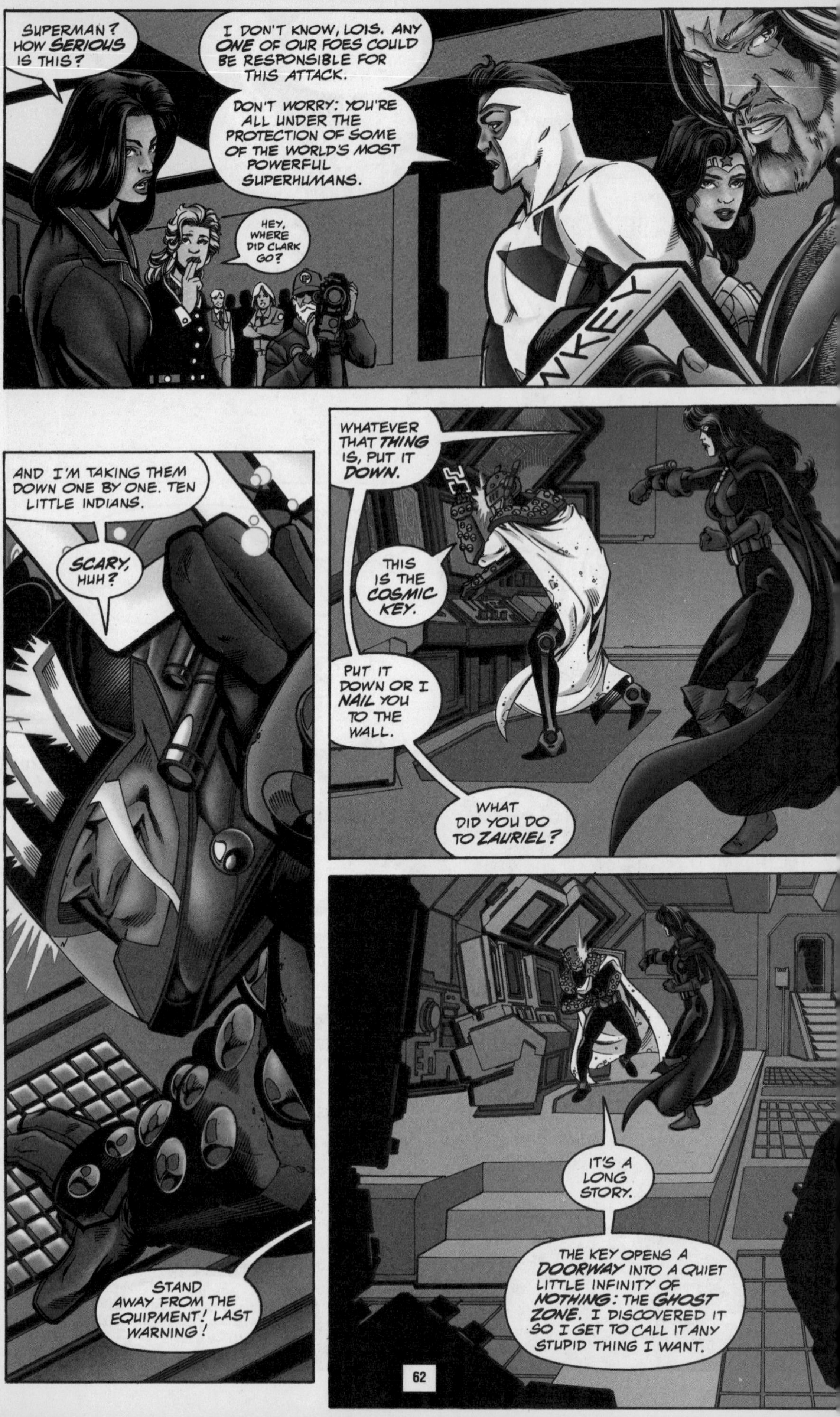
SUPERMAN? HOW SERIOUS IS THIS?
I DON'T KNOW, LOIS. ANY ONE OF OUR FOES COULD BE RESPONSIBLE FOR THIS ATTACK.
DON'T WORRY: YOU'RE ALL UNDER THE PROTECTION OF SOME OF THE WORLD'S MOST POWERFUL SUPERHUMANS.
HEY, WHERE DID CLARK GO?
AND I'M TAKING THEM DOWN ONE BY ONE. TEN LITTLE INDIANS.
SCARY, HUH?
STAND AWAY FROM THE EQUIPMENT! LAST WARNING!
WHATEVER THAT THING IS, PUT IT DOWN.
THIS IS THE COSMIC KEY.
PUT IT DOWN OR I NAIL YOU TO THE WALL.
WHAT DID YOU DO TO ZAURIEL?
IT'S A LONG STORY.
THE KEY OPENS A DOORWAY INTO A QUIET LITTLE INFINITY OF NOTHING: THE GHOST ZONE. I DISCOVERED IT SO I GET TO CALL IT ANY STUPID THING I WANT.

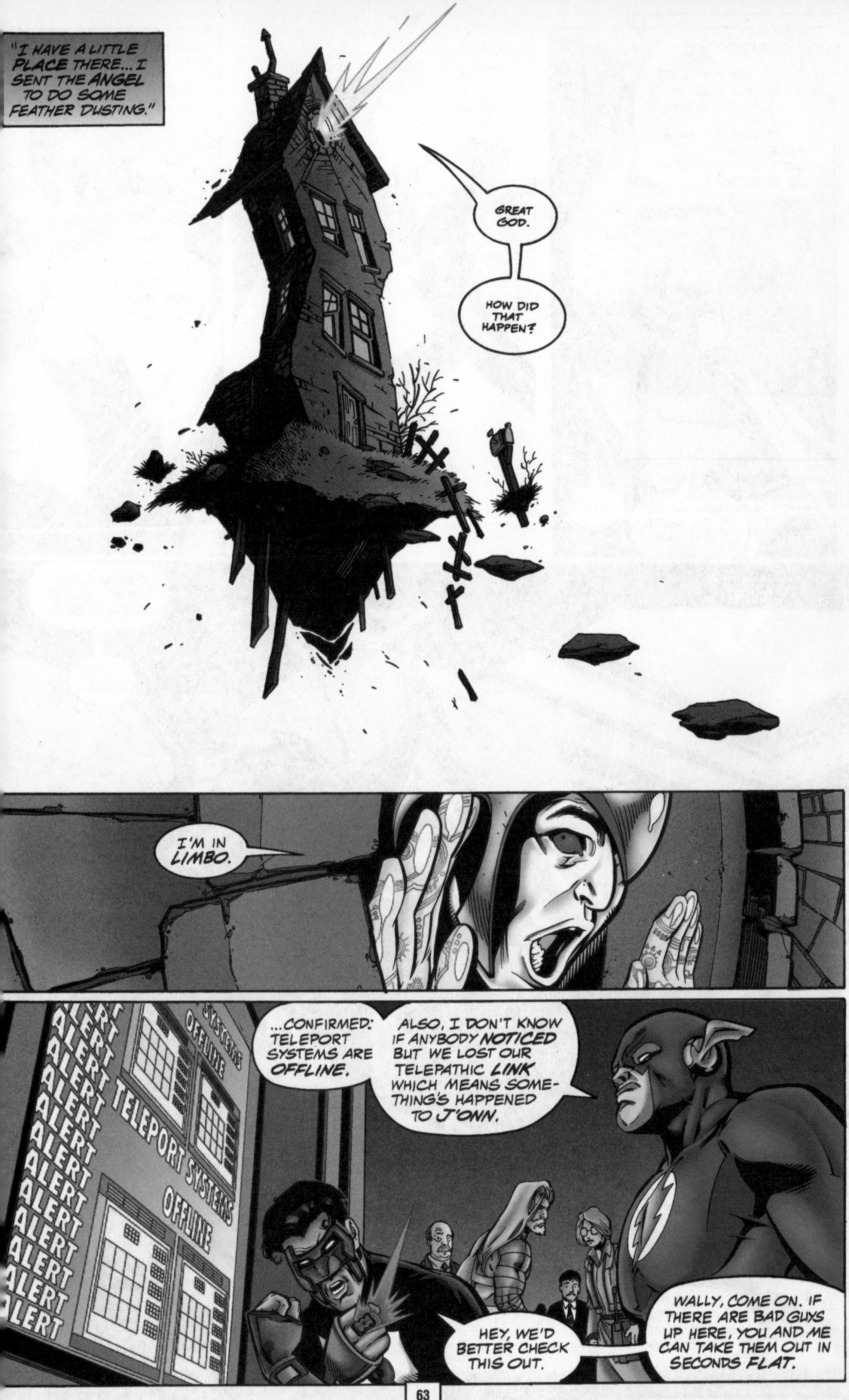
"I HAVE A LITTLE PLACE THERE... I SENT THE ANGEL TO DO SOME FEATHER DUSTING."
GREAT GOD.
HOW DID THAT HAPPEN?
I'M IN LIMBO.
...CONFIRMED: TELEPORT SYSTEMS ARE OFFLINE.
ALSO, I DON'T KNOW IF ANYBODY NOTICED BUT WE LOST OUR TELEPATHIC LINK WHICH MEANS SOMETHING'S HAPPENED TO J'ONN.
HEY, WE'D BETTER CHECK THIS OUT.
WALLY, COME ON. IF THERE ARE BAD GUYS UP HERE, YOU AND ME CAN TAKE THEM OUT IN SECONDS FLAT.
ALERT
TELEPORT SYSTEMS
OFFLINE

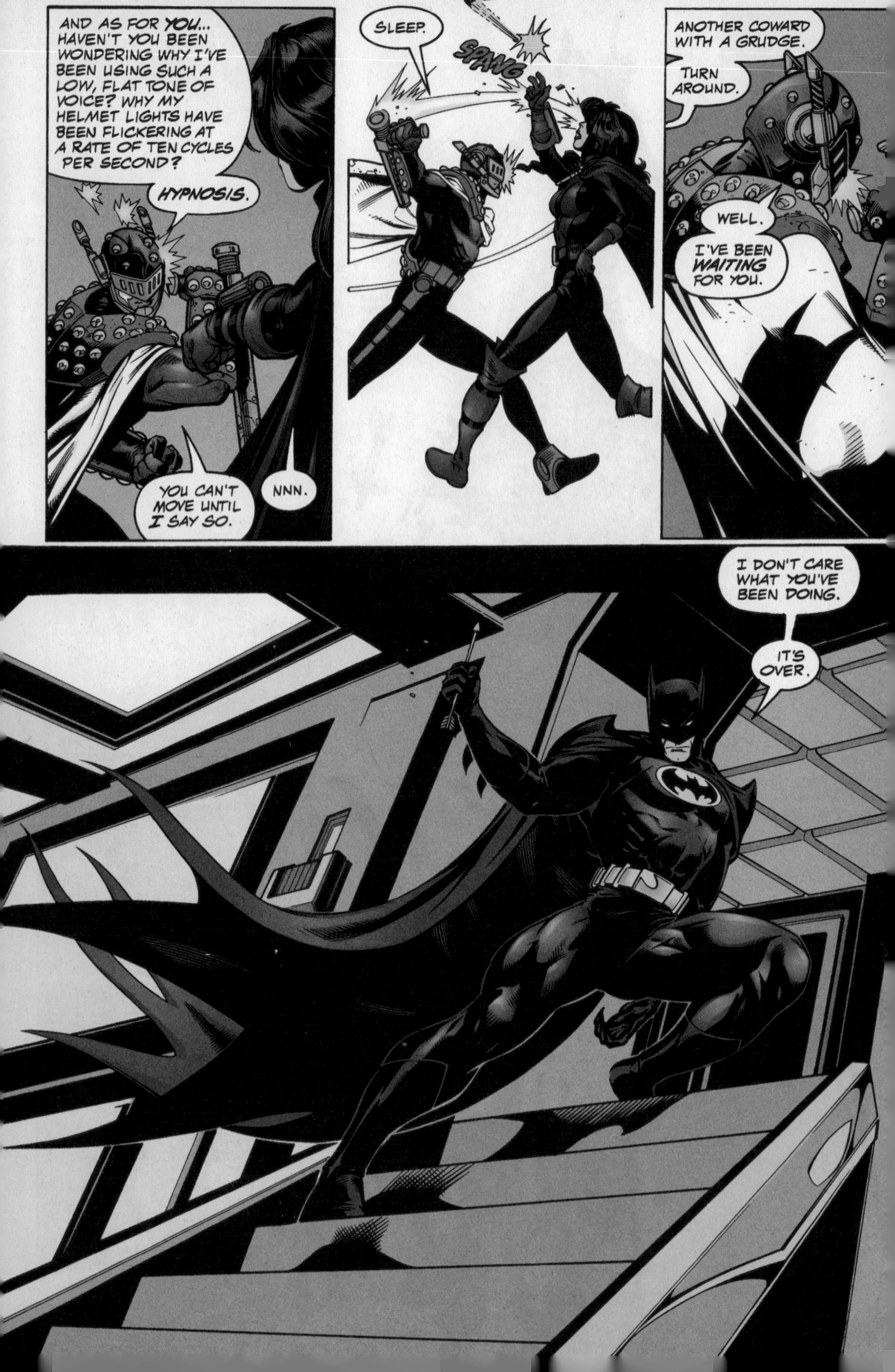
AND AS FOR YOU... HAVEN'T YOU BEEN WONDERING WHY I'VE BEEN USING SUCH A LOW, FLAT TONE OF VOICE? WHY MY HELMET LIGHTS HAVE BEEN FLICKERING AT A RATE OF TEN CYCLES PER SECOND?
HYPNOSIS.
YOU CAN'T MOVE UNTIL I SAY SO.
NNN.
SLEEP.
SPANG
ANOTHER COWARD WITH A GRUDGE.
TURN AROUND.
WELL.
I'VE BEEN WAITING FOR YOU.
I DON'T CARE WHAT YOU'VE BEEN DOING.
IT'S OVER.

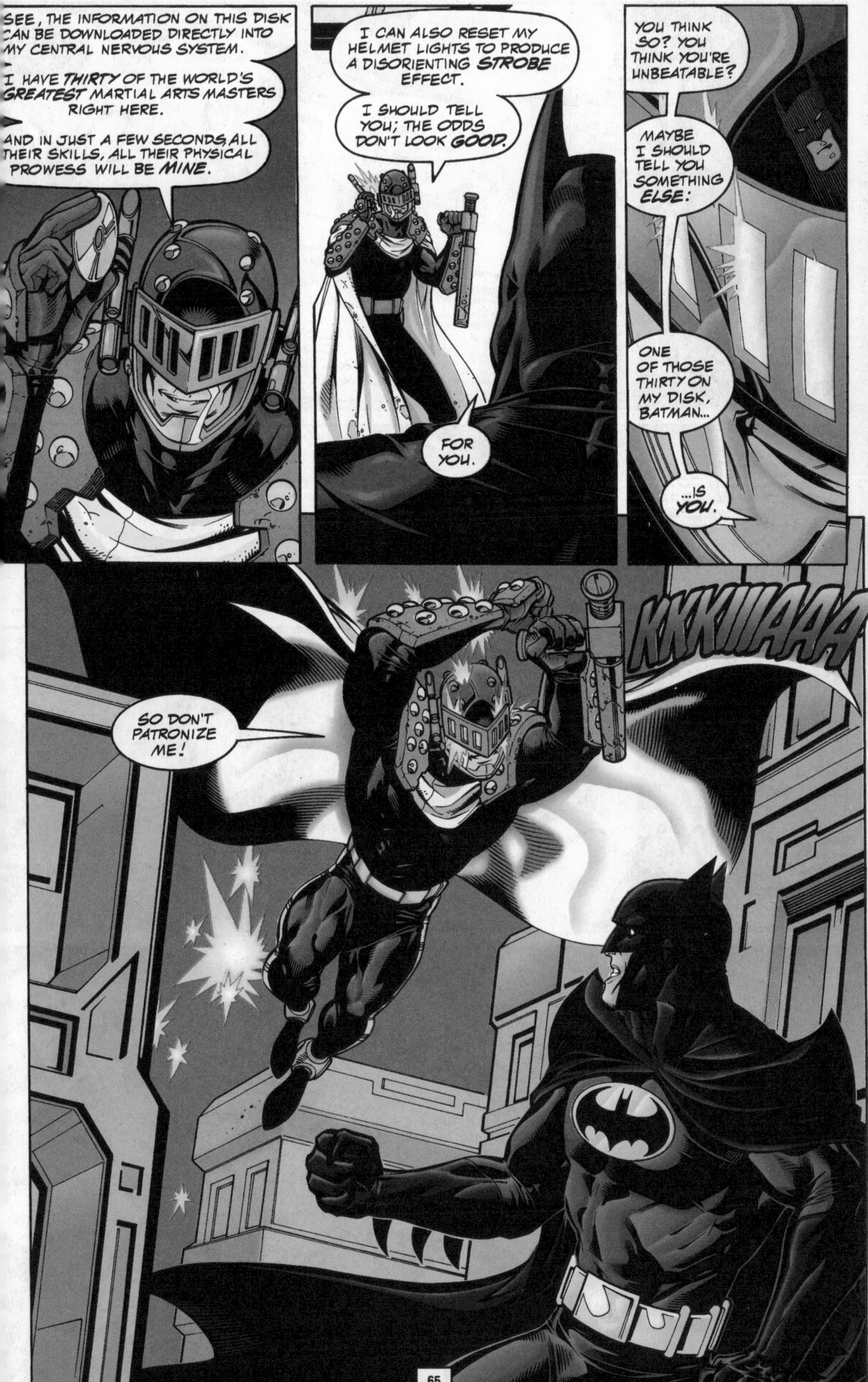
SEE, THE INFORMATION ON THIS DISK CAN BE DOWNLOADED DIRECTLY INTO MY CENTRAL NERVOUS SYSTEM.
I HAVE THIRTY OF THE WORLD'S GREATEST MARTIAL ARTS MASTERS RIGHT HERE.
AND IN JUST A FEW SECONDS, ALL THEIR SKILLS, ALL THEIR PHYSICAL PROWESS WILL BE MINE.
I CAN ALSO RESET MY HELMET LIGHTS TO PRODUCE A DISORIENTING STROBE EFFECT.
I SHOULD TELL YOU; THE ODDS DON'T LOOK GOOD.
FOR YOU.
YOU THINK SO? YOU THINK YOU'RE UNBEATABLE?
MAYBE I SHOULD TELL YOU SOMETHING ELSE:
ONE OF THOSE THIRTY ON MY DISK, BATMAN...
...IS YOU.
KKKIIIAAAA
SO DON'T PATRONIZE ME!

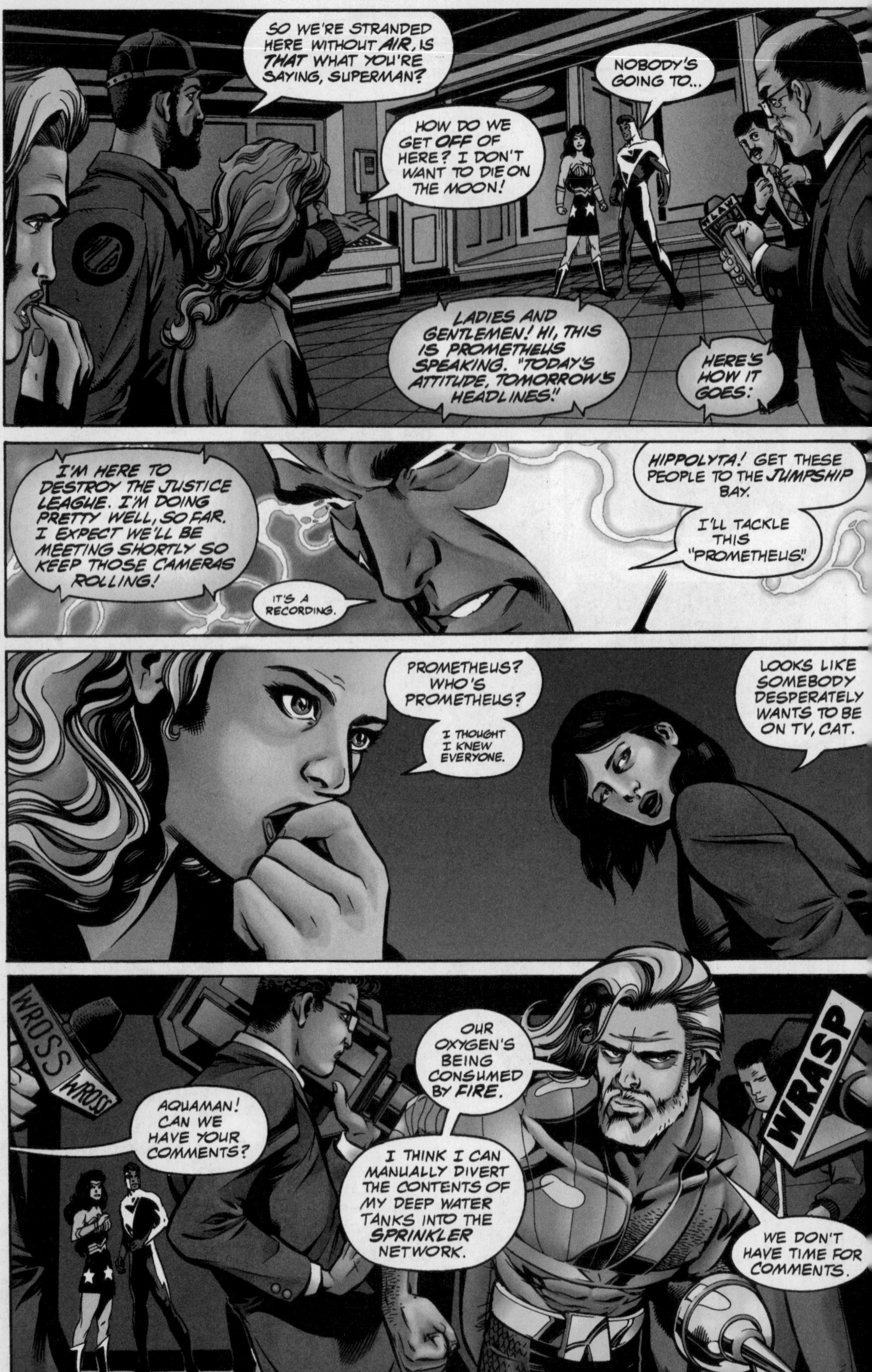
SO WE'RE STRANDED HERE WITHOUT AIR, IS THAT WHAT YOU'RE SAYING, SUPERMAN?
NOBODY'S GOING TO...
HOW DO WE GET OFF OF HERE? I DON'T WANT TO DIE ON THE MOON!
LADIES AND GENTLEMEN! HI, THIS IS PROMETHEUS SPEAKING. "TODAY'S ATTITUDE, TOMORROW'S HEADLINES."
HERE'S HOW IT GOES:
I'M HERE TO DESTROY THE JUSTICE LEAGUE. I'M DOING PRETTY WELL, SO FAR. I EXPECT WE'LL BE MEETING SHORTLY SO KEEP THOSE CAMERAS ROLLING!
IT'S A RECORDING.
HIPPOLYTA! GET THESE PEOPLE TO THE JUMPSHIP BAY.
I'LL TACKLE THIS "PROMETHEUS."
PROMETHEUS? WHO'S PROMETHEUS?
I THOUGHT I KNEW EVERYONE.
LOOKS LIKE SOMEBODY DESPERATELY WANTS TO BE ON TV, CAT.
WROSS
AQUAMAN! CAN WE HAVE YOUR COMMENTS?
OUR OXYGEN'S BEING CONSUMED BY FIRE.
I THINK I CAN MANUALLY DIVERT THE CONTENTS OF MY DEEP WATER TANKS INTO THE SPRINKLER NETWORK.
WRASP
WE DON'T HAVE TIME FOR COMMENTS.

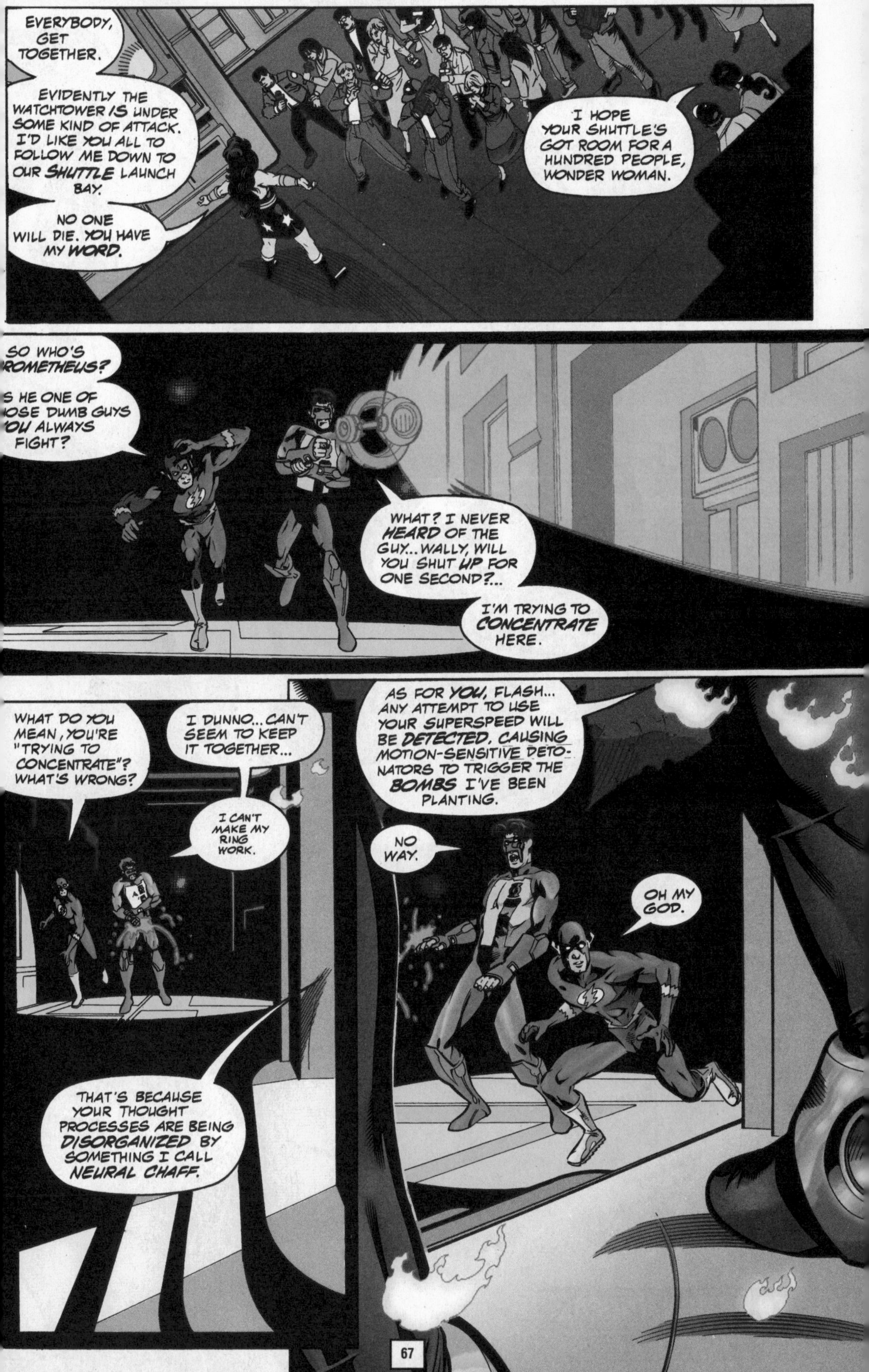
EVERYBODY, GET TOGETHER.
EVIDENTLY THE WATCHTOWER IS UNDER SOME KIND OF ATTACK. I'D LIKE YOU ALL TO FOLLOW ME DOWN TO OUR SHUTTLE LAUNCH BAY.
NO ONE WILL DIE. YOU HAVE MY WORD.
I HOPE YOUR SHUTTLE'S GOT ROOM FOR A HUNDRED PEOPLE, WONDER WOMAN.
SO WHO'S ROMETHEUS?
S HE ONE OF HOSE DUMB GUYS YOU ALWAYS FIGHT?
WHAT? I NEVER HEARD OF THE GUY... WALLY, WILL YOU SHUT UP FOR ONE SECOND?...
I'M TRYING TO CONCENTRATE HERE.
WHAT DO YOU MEAN, YOU'RE "TRYING TO CONCENTRATE"? WHAT'S WRONG?
I DUNNO... CAN'T SEEM TO KEEP IT TOGETHER...
I CAN'T MAKE MY RING WORK.
THAT'S BECAUSE YOUR THOUGHT PROCESSES ARE BEING DISORGANIZED BY SOMETHING I CALL NEURAL CHAFF.
AS FOR YOU, FLASH... ANY ATTEMPT TO USE YOUR SUPERSPEED WILL BE DETECTED, CAUSING MOTION-SENSITIVE DETONATORS TO TRIGGER THE BOMBS I'VE BEEN PLANTING.
NO WAY.
OH MY GOD.

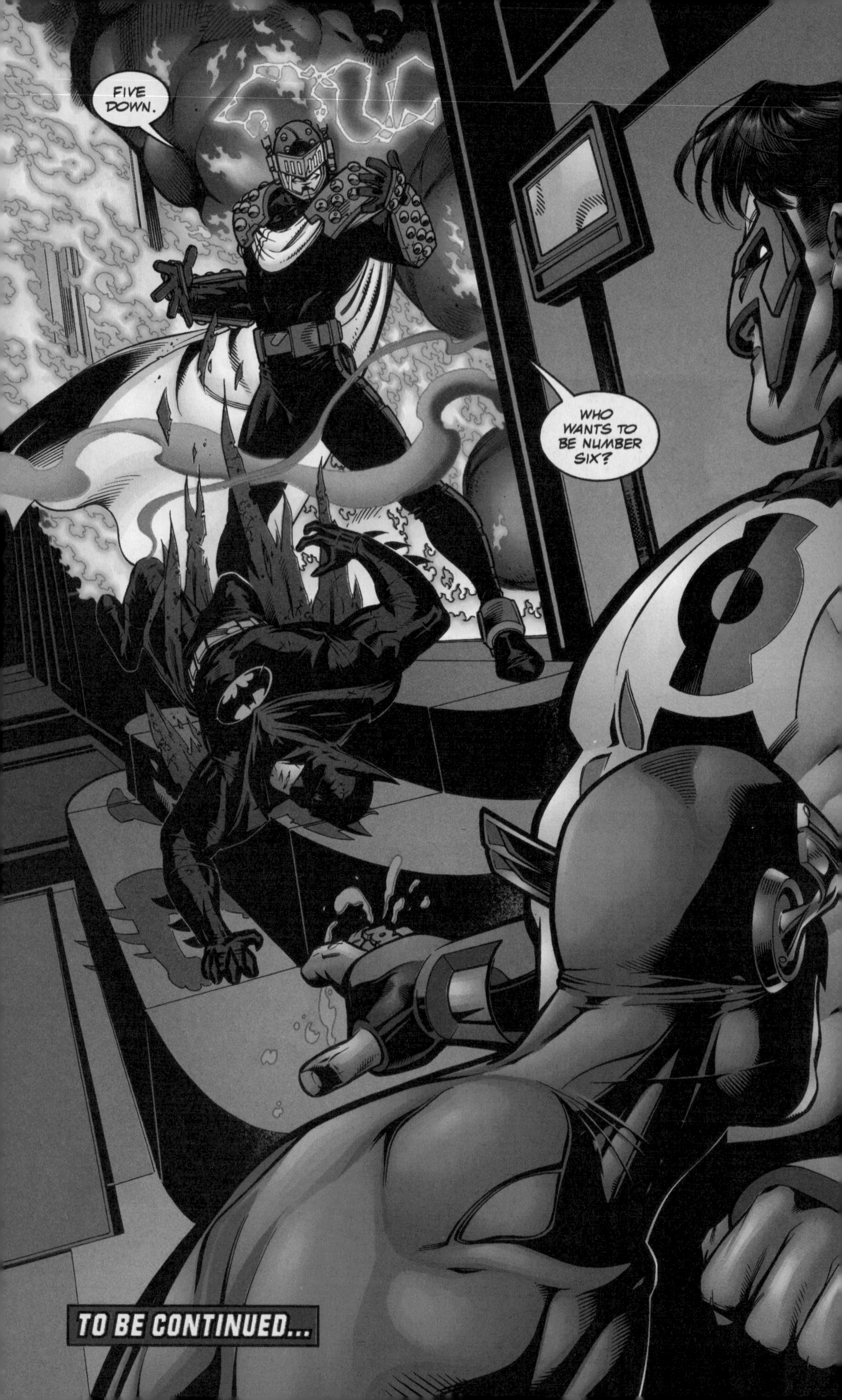
FIVE DOWN.
WHO WANTS TO BE NUMBER SIX?
TO BE CONTINUED...

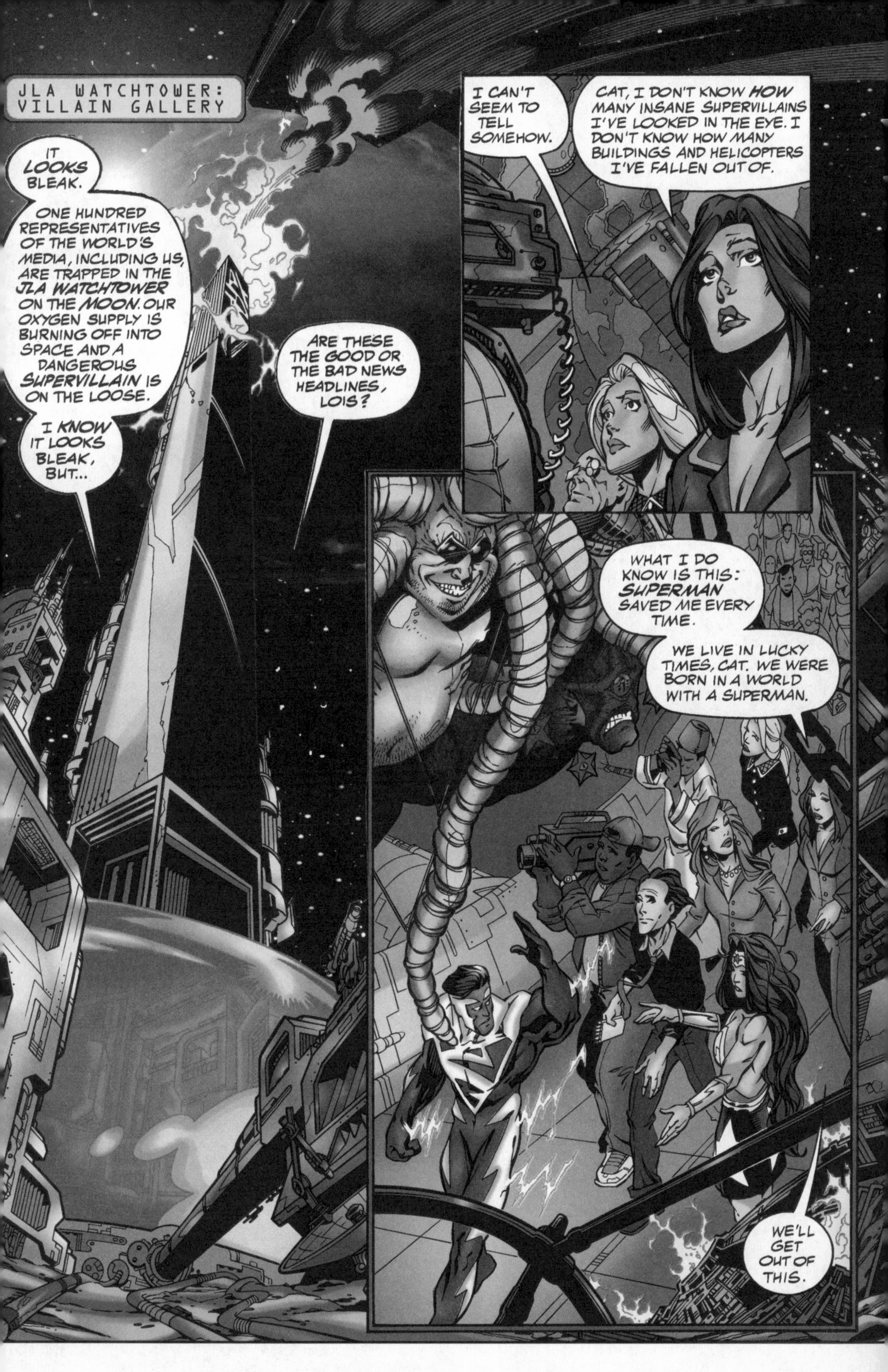
JLA WATCHTOWER: VILLAIN GALLERY
IT LOOKS BLEAK.
ONE HUNDRED REPRESENTATIVES OF THE WORLD'S MEDIA, INCLUDING US, ARE TRAPPED IN THE JLA WATCHTOWER ON THE MOON. OUR OXYGEN SUPPLY IS BURNING OFF INTO SPACE AND A DANGEROUS SUPERVILLAIN IS ON THE LOOSE.
I KNOW IT LOOKS BLEAK, BUT...
ARE THESE THE GOOD OR THE BAD NEWS HEADLINES, LOIS?
I CAN'T SEEM TO TELL SOMEHOW.
CAT, I DON'T KNOW HOW MANY INSANE SUPERVILLAINS I'VE LOOKED IN THE EYE. I DON'T KNOW HOW MANY BUILDINGS AND HELICOPTERS I'VE FALLEN OUT OF.
WHAT I DO KNOW IS THIS: SUPERMAN SAVED ME EVERY TIME.
WE LIVE IN LUCKY TIMES, CAT. WE WERE BORN IN A WORLD WITH A SUPERMAN.
WE'LL GET OUT OF THIS.

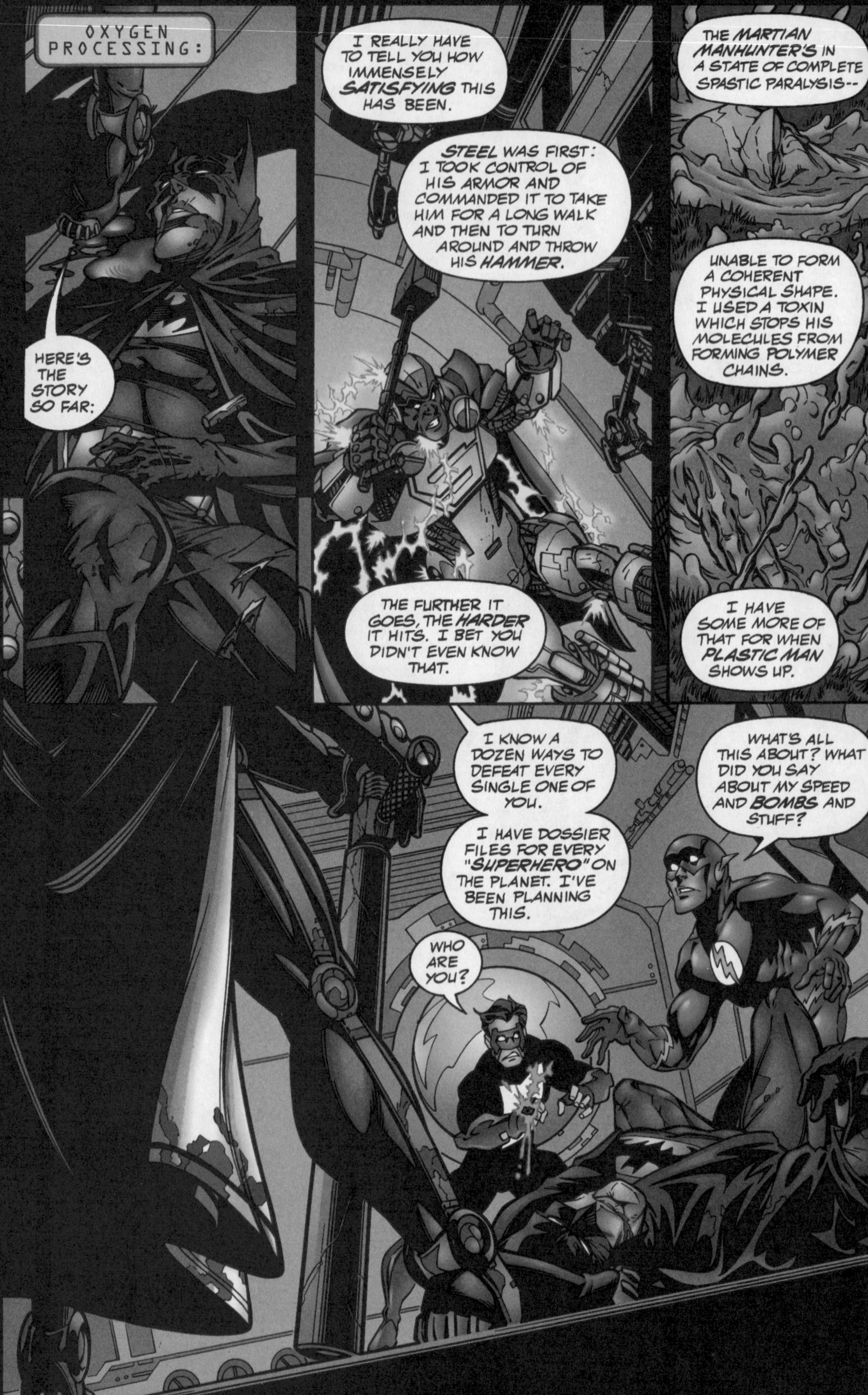
OXYGEN PROCESSING:
HERE'S THE STORY SO FAR:
I REALLY HAVE TO TELL YOU HOW IMMENSELY SATISFYING THIS HAS BEEN.
STEEL WAS FIRST: I TOOK CONTROL OF HIS ARMOR AND COMMANDED IT TO TAKE HIM FOR A LONG WALK AND THEN TO TURN AROUND AND THROW HIS HAMMER.
THE FURTHER IT GOES, THE HARDER IT HITS. I BET YOU DIDN'T EVEN KNOW THAT.
THE MARTIAN MANHUNTER'S IN A STATE OF COMPLETE SPASTIC PARALYSIS--
UNABLE TO FORM A COHERENT PHYSICAL SHAPE. I USED A TOXIN WHICH STOPS HIS MOLECULES FROM FORMING POLYMER CHAINS.
I HAVE SOME MORE OF THAT FOR WHEN PLASTIC MAN SHOWS UP.
I KNOW A DOZEN WAYS TO DEFEAT EVERY SINGLE ONE OF YOU.
I HAVE DOSSIER FILES FOR EVERY "SUPERHERO" ON THE PLANET. I'VE BEEN PLANNING THIS.
WHAT'S ALL THIS ABOUT? WHAT DID YOU SAY ABOUT MY SPEED AND BOMBS AND STUFF?
WHO ARE YOU?

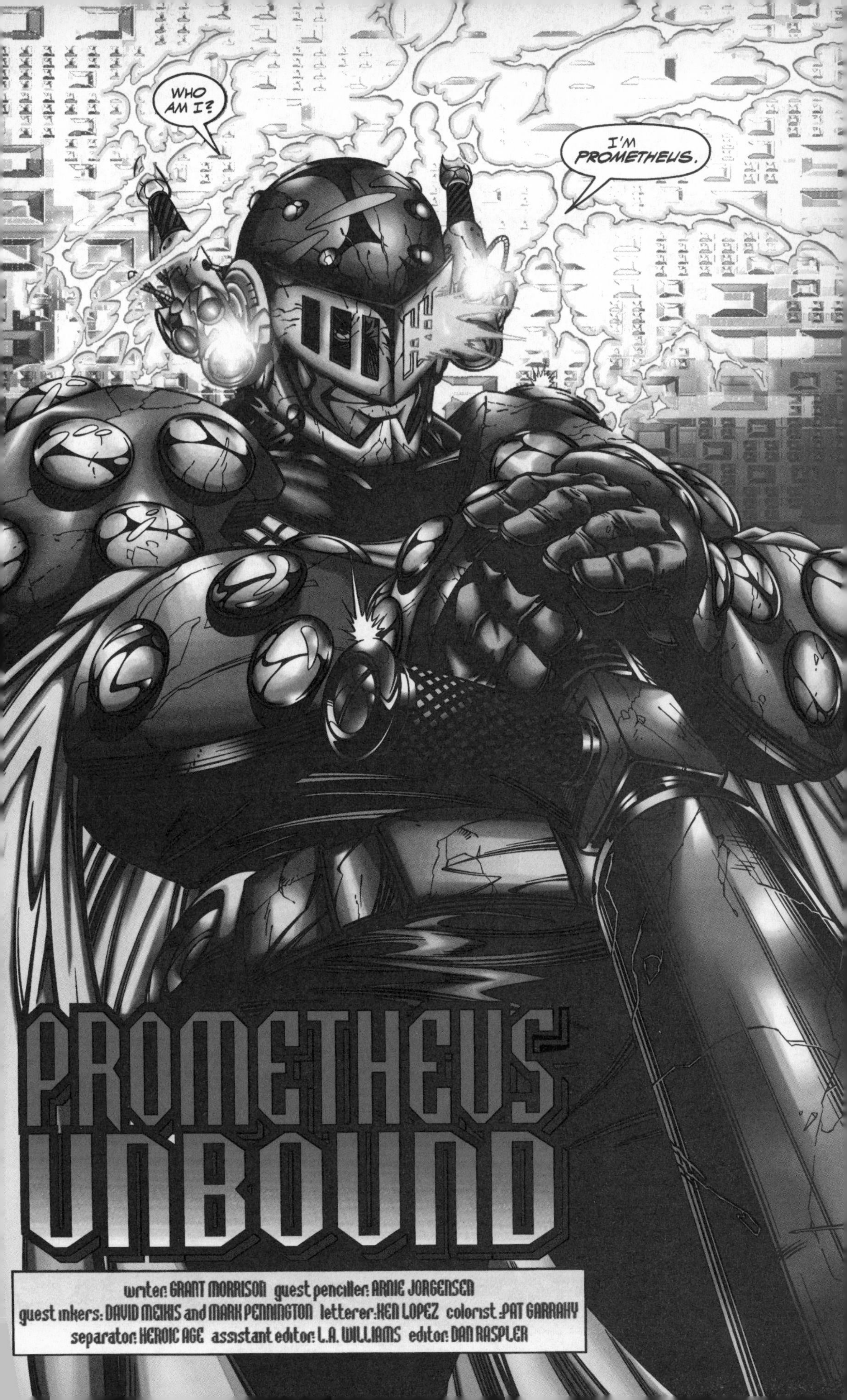
WHO AM I?
I'M PROMETHEUS.
PROMETHEUS' UNBOUND
writer: GRANT MORRISON guest penciller: ARNIE JORGENSEN
guest inkers: DAVID MEIKIS and MARK PENNINGTON letterer: KEN LOPEZ colorist: PAT GARRAHY
separator: HEROIC AGE assistant editor: L.A. WILLIAMS editor: DAN RASPLER

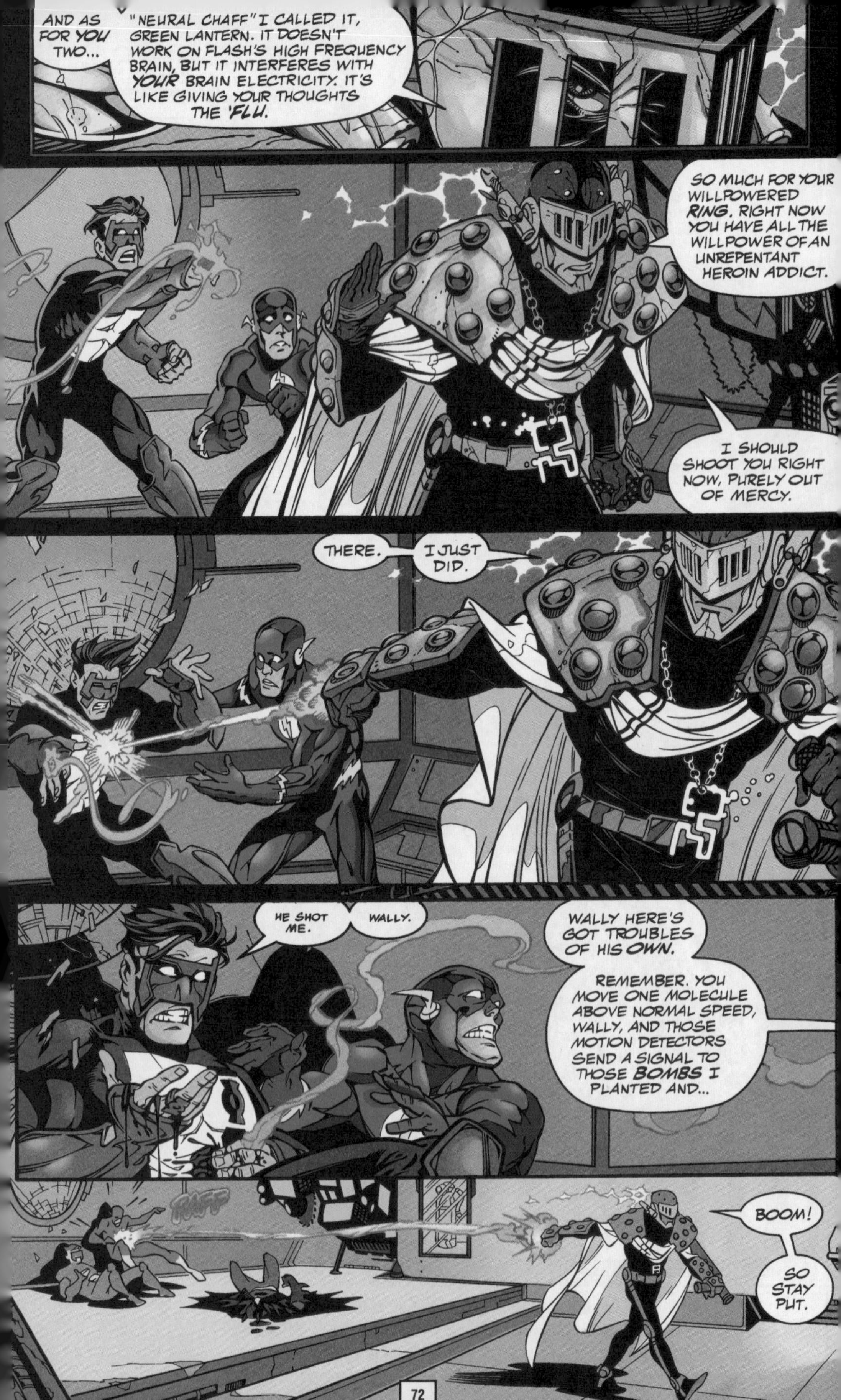
AND AS FOR YOU TWO...
"NEURAL CHAFF" I CALLED IT, GREEN LANTERN. IT DOESN'T WORK ON FLASH'S HIGH FREQUENCY BRAIN, BUT IT INTERFERES WITH YOUR BRAIN ELECTRICITY. IT'S LIKE GIVING YOUR THOUGHTS THE 'FLU.
SO MUCH FOR YOUR WILLPOWERED RING. RIGHT NOW YOU HAVE ALL THE WILLPOWER OF AN UNREPENTANT HEROIN ADDICT.
I SHOULD SHOOT YOU RIGHT NOW, PURELY OUT OF MERCY.
THERE.
I JUST DID.
HE SHOT ME.
WALLY.
WALLY HERE'S GOT TROUBLES OF HIS OWN.
REMEMBER. YOU MOVE ONE MOLECULE ABOVE NORMAL SPEED, WALLY, AND THOSE MOTION DETECTORS SEND A SIGNAL TO THOSE BOMBS I PLANTED AND...
BOOM!
SO STAY PUT.

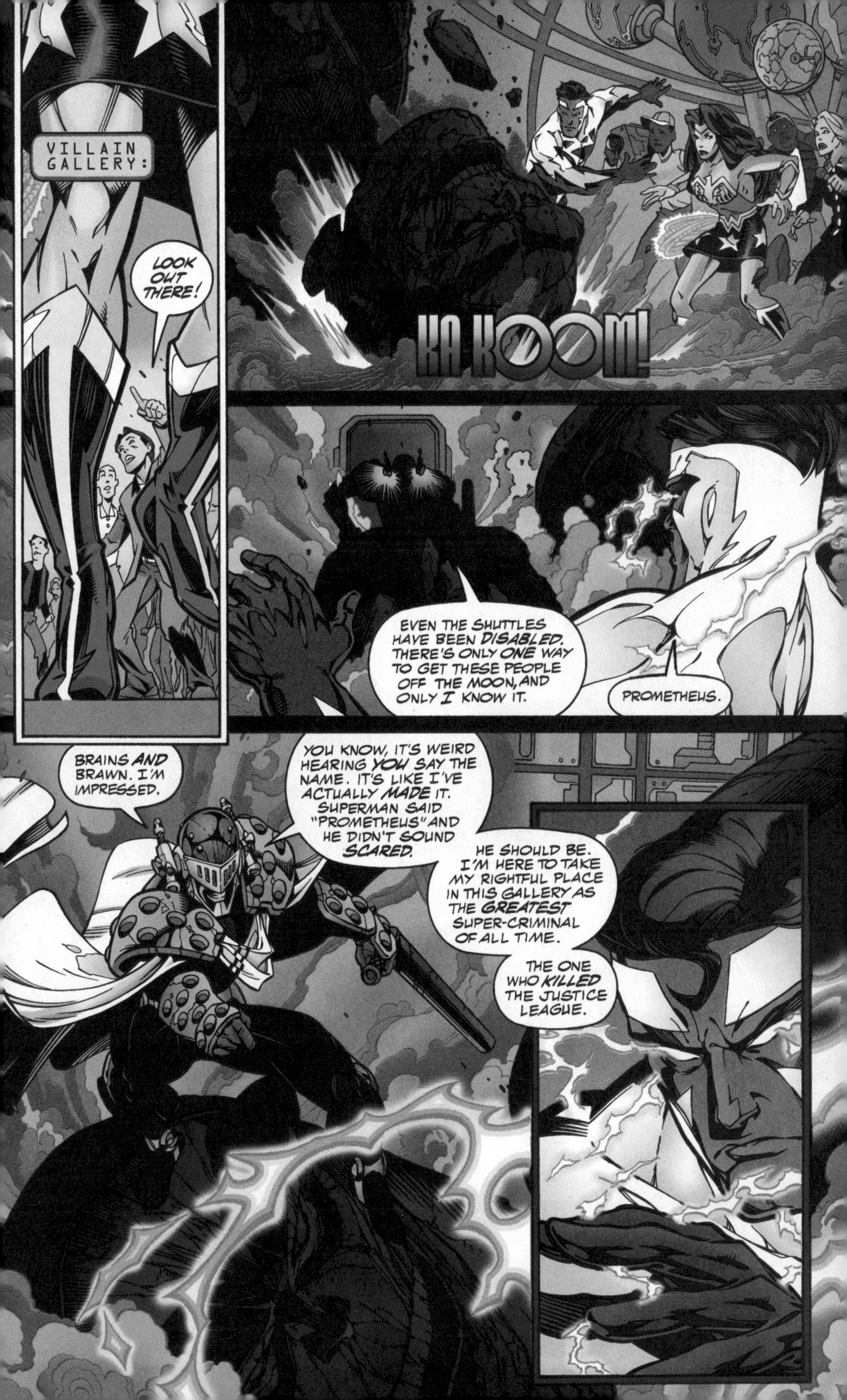
VILLAIN GALLERY:
LOOK OUT THERE!
KA KOOM!
EVEN THE SHUTTLES HAVE BEEN DISABLED. THERE'S ONLY ONE WAY TO GET THESE PEOPLE OFF THE MOON, AND ONLY I KNOW IT.
PROMETHEUS.
BRAINS AND BRAWN. I'M IMPRESSED.
YOU KNOW, IT'S WEIRD HEARING YOU SAY THE NAME. IT'S LIKE I'VE ACTUALLY MADE IT. SUPERMAN SAID "PROMETHEUS" AND HE DIDN'T SOUND SCARED.
HE SHOULD BE. I'M HERE TO TAKE MY RIGHTFUL PLACE IN THIS GALLERY AS THE GREATEST SUPER-CRIMINAL OF ALL TIME.
THE ONE WHO KILLED THE JUSTICE LEAGUE.

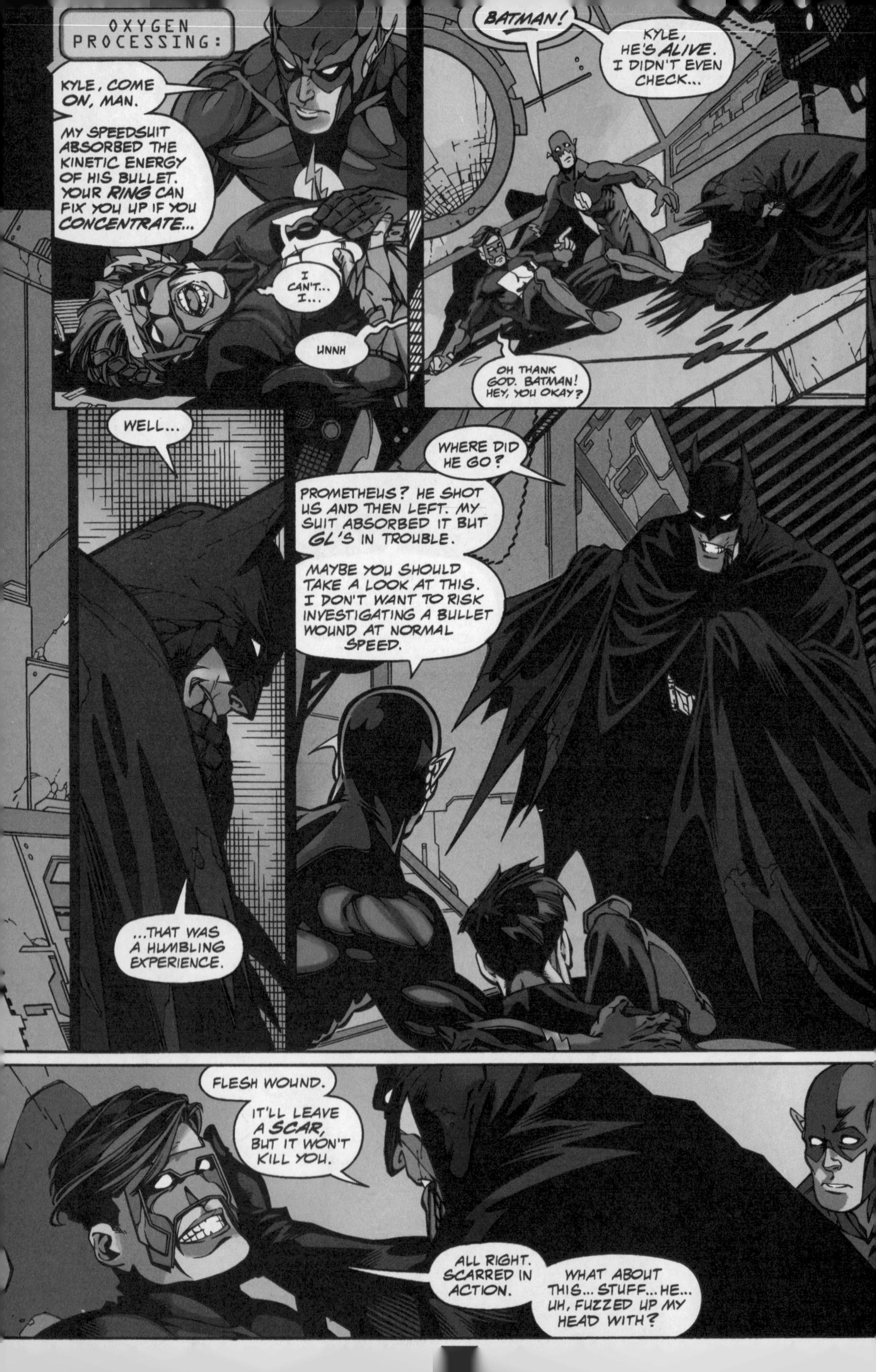
OXYGEN PROCESSING:
KYLE, COME ON, MAN.
MY SPEEDSUIT ABSORBED THE KINETIC ENERGY OF HIS BULLET. YOUR RING CAN FIX YOU UP IF YOU CONCENTRATE...
I CAN'T... I...
UNNH
BATMAN!
KYLE, HE'S ALIVE. I DIDN'T EVEN CHECK...
OH THANK GOD. BATMAN! HEY, YOU OKAY?
WELL...
...THAT WAS A HUMBLING EXPERIENCE.
WHERE DID HE GO?
PROMETHEUS? HE SHOT US AND THEN LEFT. MY SUIT ABSORBED IT BUT GL'S IN TROUBLE.
MAYBE YOU SHOULD TAKE A LOOK AT THIS. I DON'T WANT TO RISK INVESTIGATING A BULLET WOUND AT NORMAL SPEED.
FLESH WOUND.
IT'LL LEAVE A SCAR, BUT IT WON'T KILL YOU.
ALL RIGHT. SCARRED IN ACTION.
WHAT ABOUT THIS... STUFF... HE... UH, FUZZED UP MY HEAD WITH?

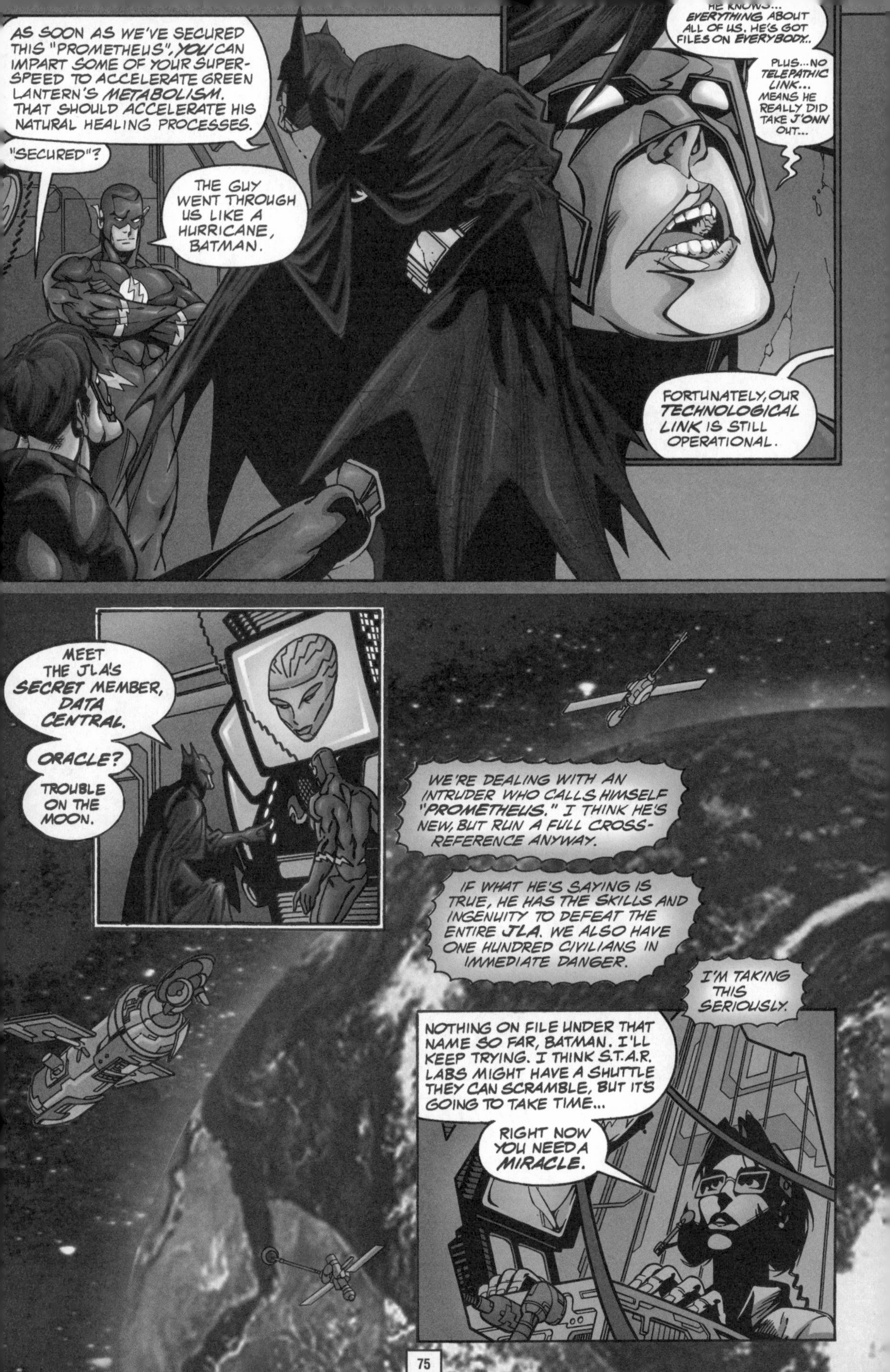
AS SOON AS WE'VE SECURED THIS "PROMETHEUS", YOU CAN IMPART SOME OF YOUR SUPER-SPEED TO ACCELERATE GREEN LANTERN'S METABOLISM. THAT SHOULD ACCELERATE HIS NATURAL HEALING PROCESSES.
"SECURED"?
THE GUY WENT THROUGH US LIKE A HURRICANE, BATMAN.
HE KNOWS... EVERYTHING ABOUT ALL OF US. HE'S GOT FILES ON EVERYBODY..
PLUS...NO TELEPATHIC LINK... MEANS HE REALLY DID TAKE J'ONN OUT...
FORTUNATELY, OUR TECHNOLOGICAL LINK IS STILL OPERATIONAL.
MEET THE JLA'S SECRET MEMBER, DATA CENTRAL.
ORACLE?
TROUBLE ON THE MOON.
WE'RE DEALING WITH AN INTRUDER WHO CALLS HIMSELF "PROMETHEUS." I THINK HE'S NEW, BUT RUN A FULL CROSS-REFERENCE ANYWAY.
IF WHAT HE'S SAYING IS TRUE, HE HAS THE SKILLS AND INGENUITY TO DEFEAT THE ENTIRE JLA. WE ALSO HAVE ONE HUNDRED CIVILIANS IN IMMEDIATE DANGER.
I'M TAKING THIS SERIOUSLY.
NOTHING ON FILE UNDER THAT NAME SO FAR, BATMAN. I'LL KEEP TRYING. I THINK S.T.A.R. LABS MIGHT HAVE A SHUTTLE THEY CAN SCRAMBLE, BUT ITS GOING TO TAKE TIME...
RIGHT NOW YOU NEED A MIRACLE.

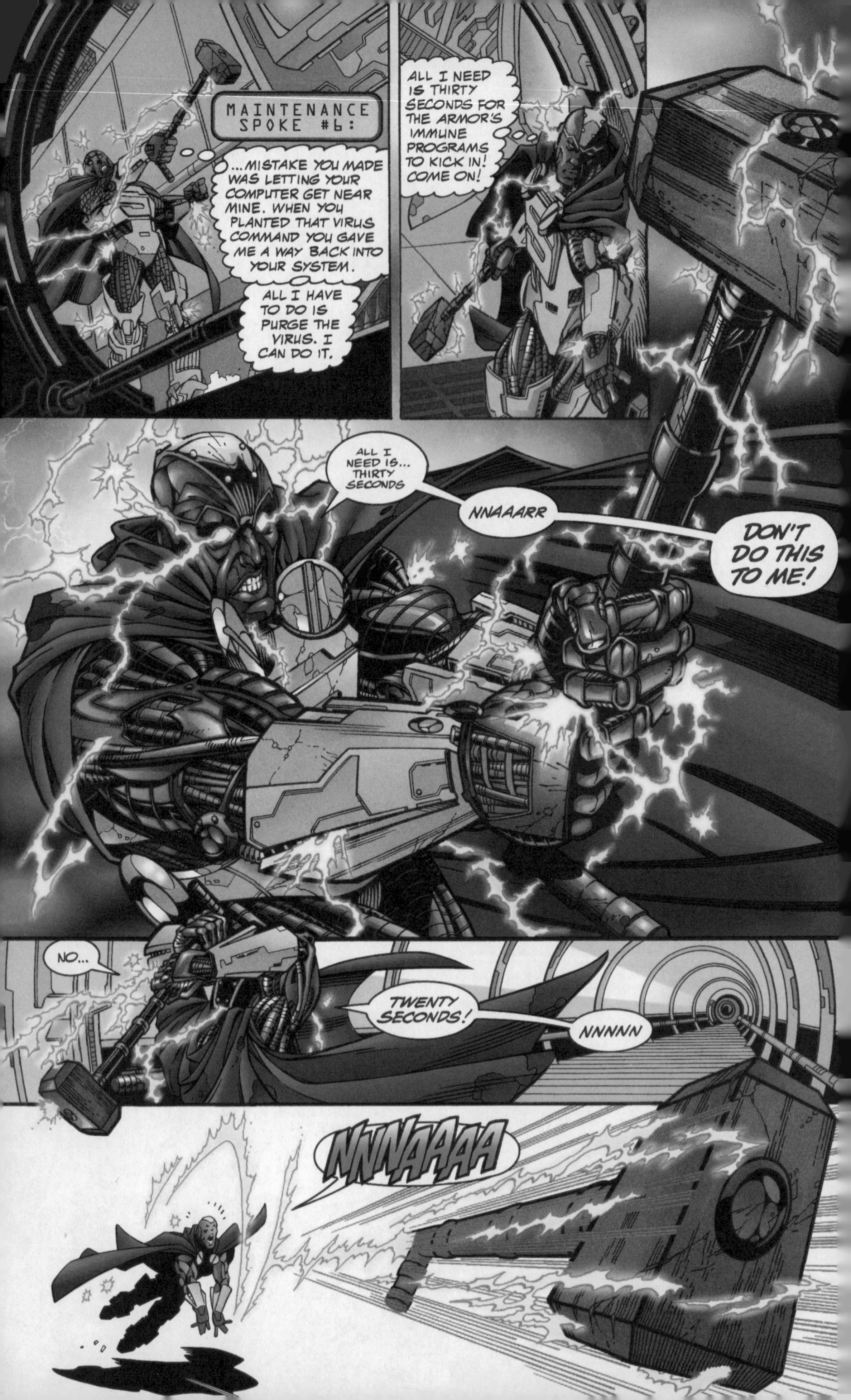
MAINTENANCE SPOKE #6:
...MISTAKE YOU MADE WAS LETTING YOUR COMPUTER GET NEAR MINE. WHEN YOU PLANTED THAT VIRUS COMMAND YOU GAVE ME A WAY BACK INTO YOUR SYSTEM.
ALL I HAVE TO DO IS PURGE THE VIRUS. I CAN DO IT.
ALL I NEED IS THIRTY SECONDS FOR THE ARMOR'S IMMUNE PROGRAMS TO KICK IN! COME ON!
ALL I NEED IS... THIRTY SECONDS
NNAAARR
DON'T DO THIS TO ME!
NO...
TWENTY SECONDS!
NNNNN
NNNAAAA

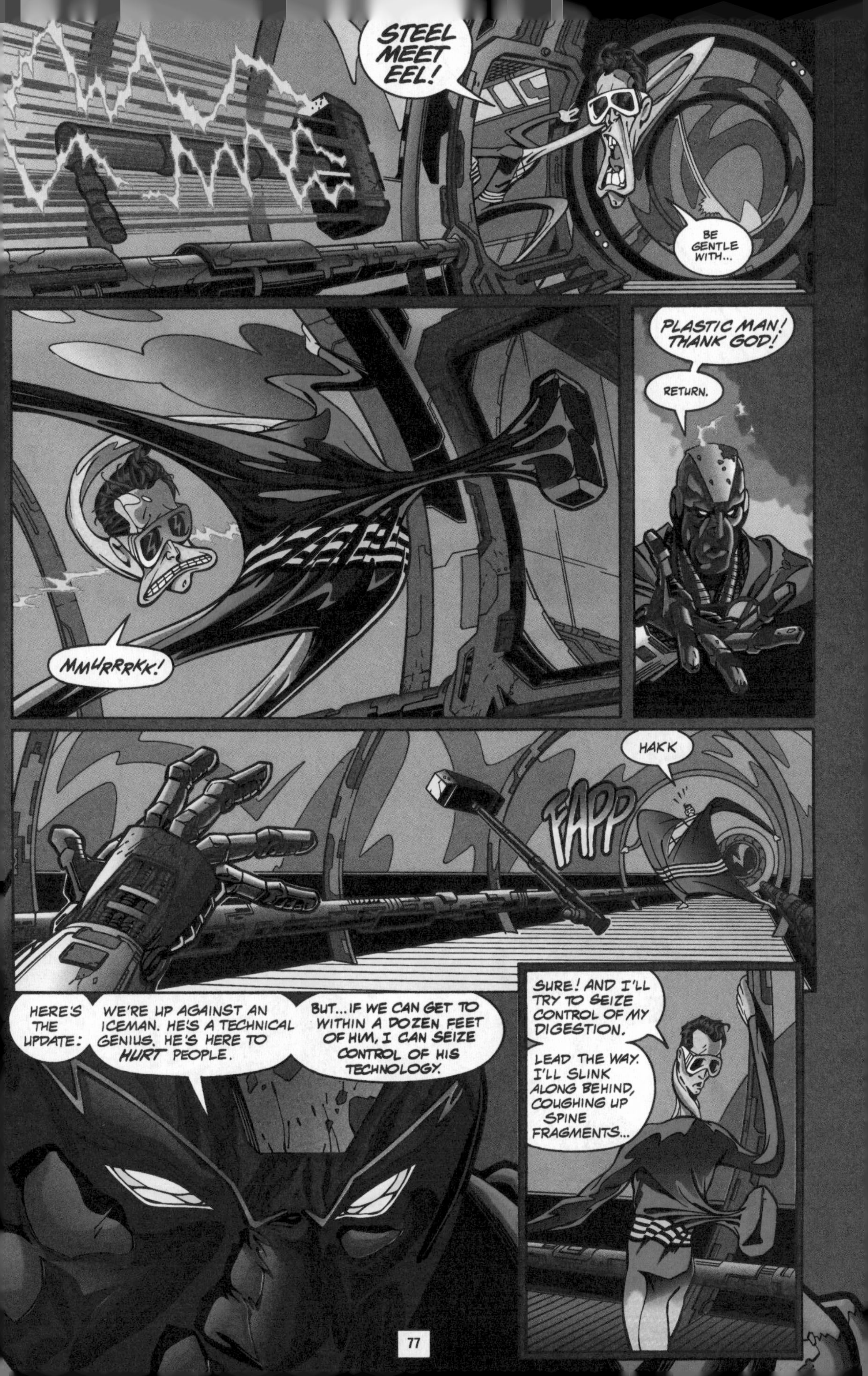
STEEL MEET EEL!
BE GENTLE WITH...
MMURRRKK!
PLASTIC MAN! THANK GOD!
RETURN.
HAKK
FAPP
HERE'S THE UPDATE:
WE'RE UP AGAINST AN ICEMAN. HE'S A TECHNICAL GENIUS. HE'S HERE TO HURT PEOPLE.
BUT... IF WE CAN GET TO WITHIN A DOZEN FEET OF HIM, I CAN SEIZE CONTROL OF HIS TECHNOLOGY.
SURE! AND I'LL TRY TO SEIZE CONTROL OF MY DIGESTION.
LEAD THE WAY. I'LL SLINK ALONG BEHIND, COUGHING UP SPINE FRAGMENTS...

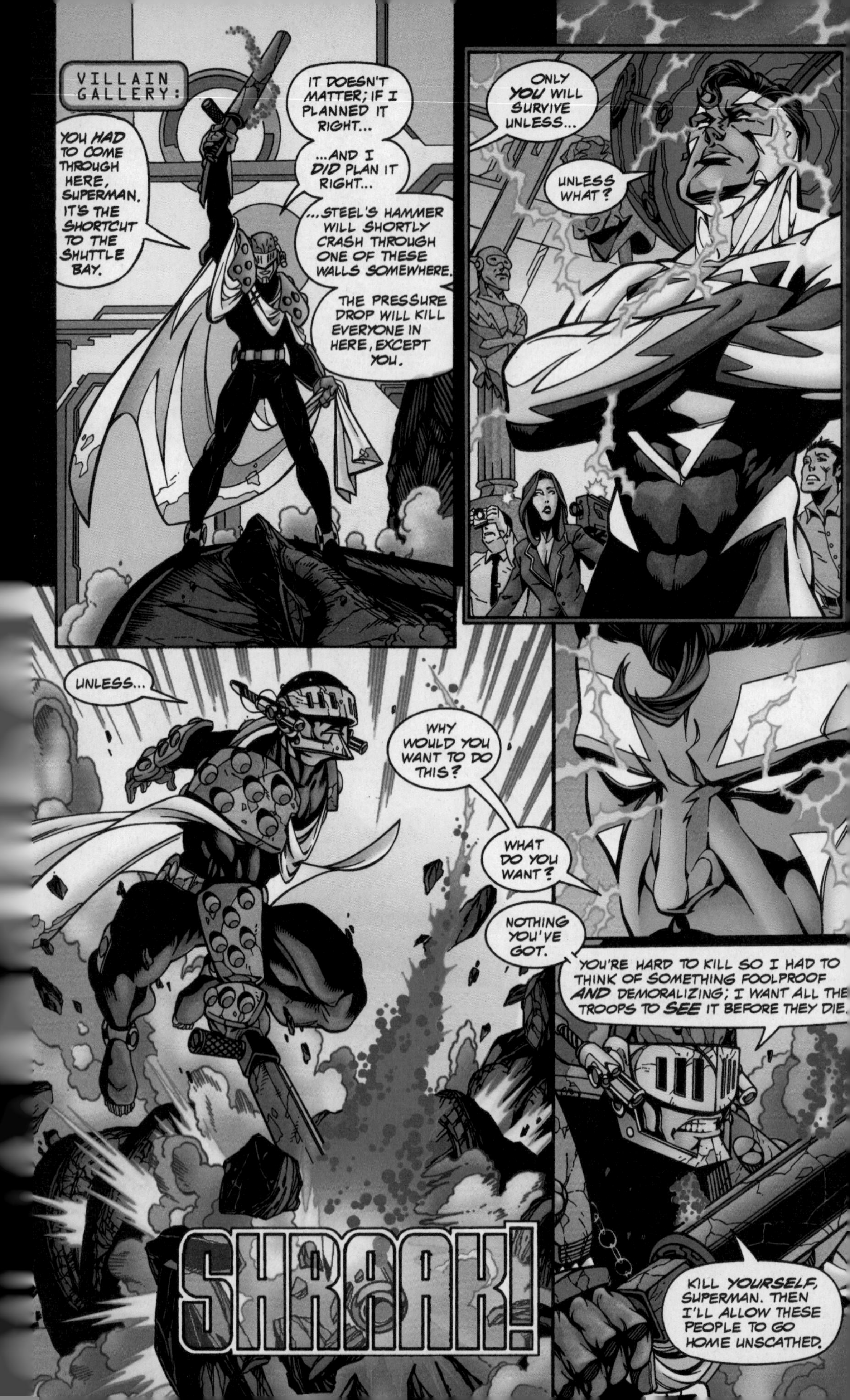
VILLAIN GALLERY:
YOU HAD TO COME THROUGH HERE, SUPERMAN. IT'S THE SHORTCUT TO THE SHUTTLE BAY.
IT DOESN'T MATTER; IF I PLANNED IT RIGHT...
...AND I DID PLAN IT RIGHT...
...STEEL'S HAMMER WILL SHORTLY CRASH THROUGH ONE OF THESE WALLS SOMEWHERE.
THE PRESSURE DROP WILL KILL EVERYONE IN HERE, EXCEPT YOU.
ONLY YOU WILL SURVIVE UNLESS...
UNLESS WHAT?
UNLESS...
WHY WOULD YOU WANT TO DO THIS?
WHAT DO YOU WANT?
NOTHING YOU'VE GOT.
YOU'RE HARD TO KILL SO I HAD TO THINK OF SOMETHING FOOLPROOF AND DEMORALIZING; I WANT ALL THE TROOPS TO SEE IT BEFORE THEY DIE.
SHRAAK!
KILL YOURSELF, SUPERMAN. THEN I'LL ALLOW THESE PEOPLE TO GO HOME UNSCATHED.

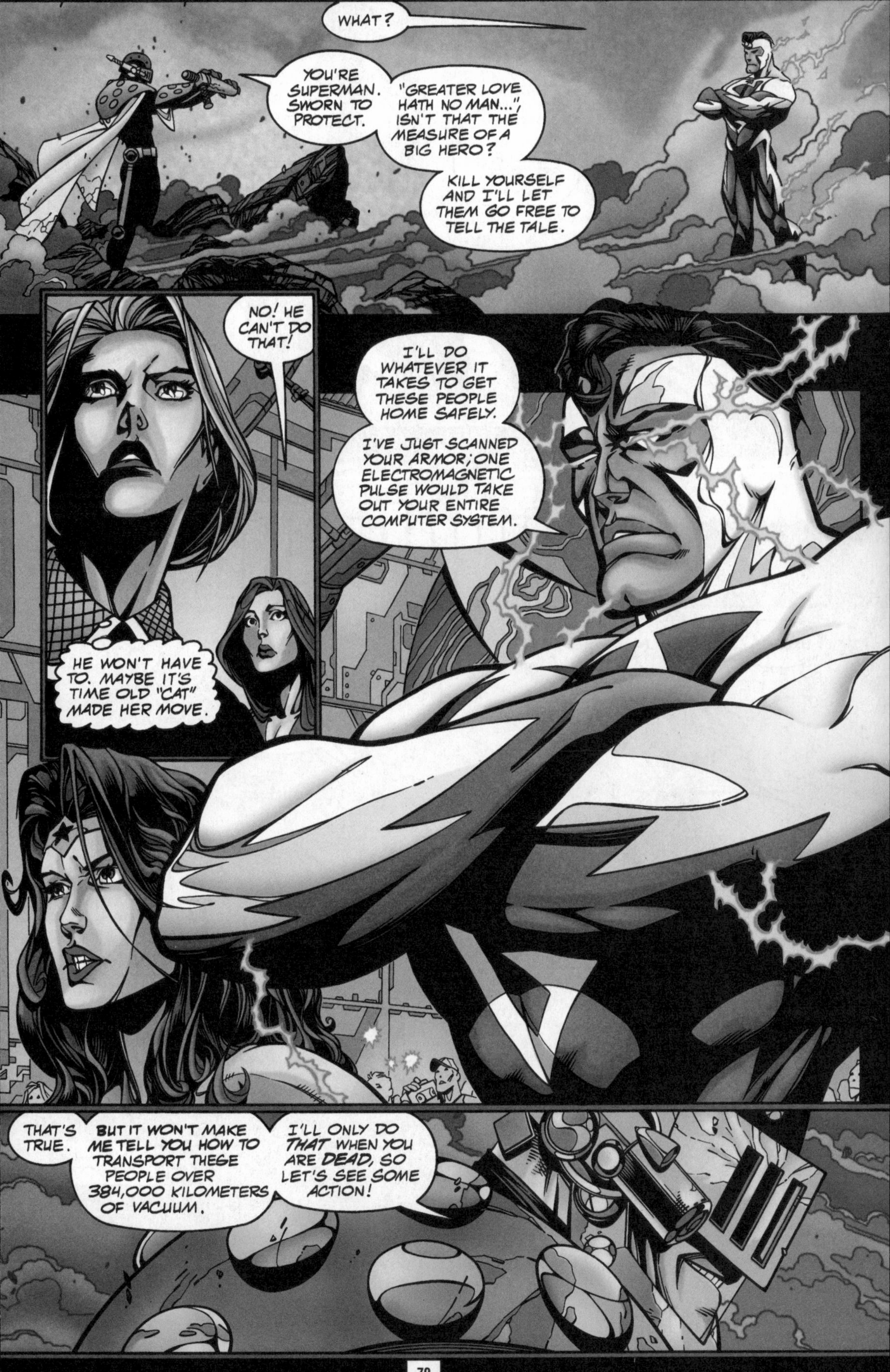
WHAT?
YOU'RE SUPERMAN. SWORN TO PROTECT.
"GREATER LOVE HATH NO MAN...", ISN'T THAT THE MEASURE OF A BIG HERO?
KILL YOURSELF AND I'LL LET THEM GO FREE TO TELL THE TALE.
NO! HE CAN'T DO THAT!
I'LL DO WHATEVER IT TAKES TO GET THESE PEOPLE HOME SAFELY.
I'VE JUST SCANNED YOUR ARMOR; ONE ELECTROMAGNETIC PULSE WOULD TAKE OUT YOUR ENTIRE COMPUTER SYSTEM.
HE WON'T HAVE TO. MAYBE IT'S TIME OLD "CAT" MADE HER MOVE.
THAT'S TRUE.
BUT IT WON'T MAKE ME TELL YOU HOW TO TRANSPORT THESE PEOPLE OVER 384,000 KILOMETERS OF VACUUM.
I'LL ONLY DO THAT WHEN YOU ARE DEAD, SO LET'S SEE SOME ACTION!

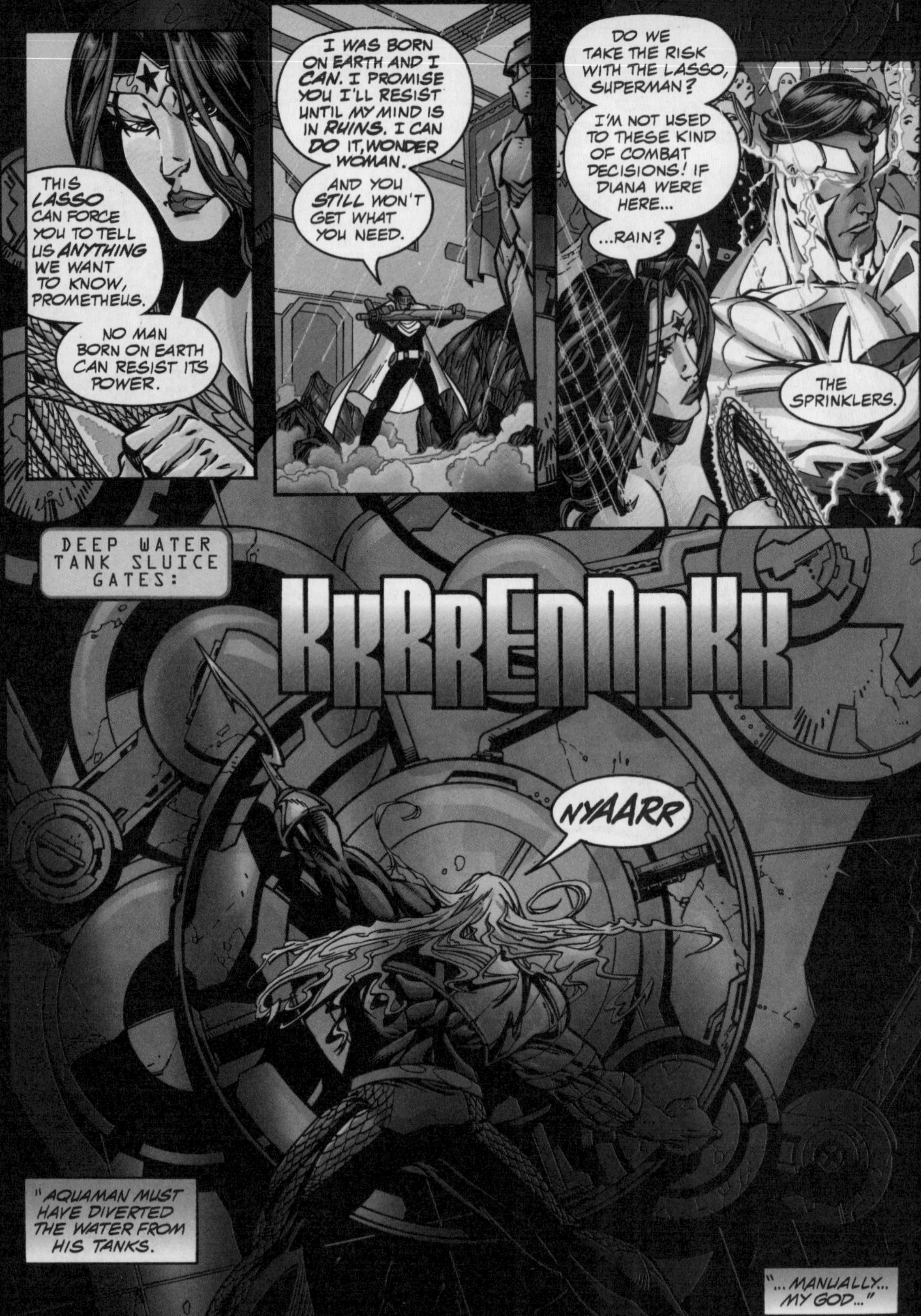
THIS LASSO CAN FORCE YOU TO TELL US ANYTHING WE WANT TO KNOW, PROMETHEUS.
NO MAN BORN ON EARTH CAN RESIST ITS POWER.
I WAS BORN ON EARTH AND I CAN. I PROMISE YOU I'LL RESIST UNTIL MY MIND IS IN RUINS. I CAN DO IT, WONDER WOMAN.
AND YOU STILL WON'T GET WHAT YOU NEED.
DO WE TAKE THE RISK WITH THE LASSO, SUPERMAN?
I'M NOT USED TO THESE KIND OF COMBAT DECISIONS! IF DIANA WERE HERE...
...RAIN?
THE SPRINKLERS.
DEEP WATER TANK SLUICE GATES:
KKRRENNNKK
NYAARR
"AQUAMAN MUST HAVE DIVERTED THE WATER FROM HIS TANKS.
"...MANUALLY... MY GOD..."

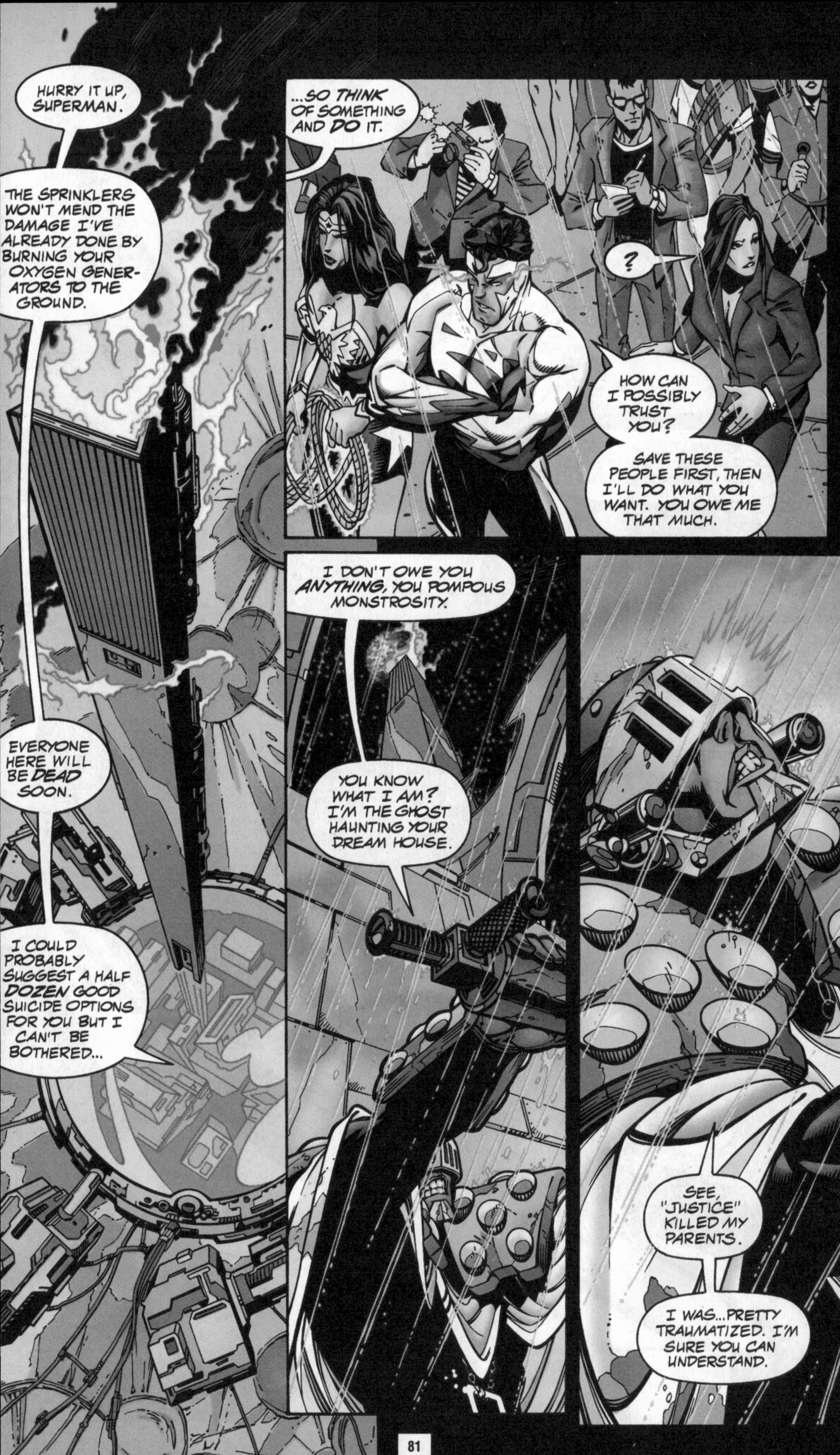
HURRY IT UP, SUPERMAN.
THE SPRINKLERS WON'T MEND THE DAMAGE I'VE ALREADY DONE BY BURNING YOUR OXYGEN GENERATORS TO THE GROUND.
EVERYONE HERE WILL BE DEAD SOON.
I COULD PROBABLY SUGGEST A HALF DOZEN GOOD SUICIDE OPTIONS FOR YOU BUT I CAN'T BE BOTHERED...
...SO THINK OF SOMETHING AND DO IT.
?
HOW CAN I POSSIBLY TRUST YOU?
SAVE THESE PEOPLE FIRST, THEN I'LL DO WHAT YOU WANT. YOU OWE ME THAT MUCH.
I DON'T OWE YOU ANYTHING, YOU POMPOUS MONSTROSITY.
YOU KNOW WHAT I AM? I'M THE GHOST HAUNTING YOUR DREAM HOUSE.
SEE, "JUSTICE" KILLED MY PARENTS.
I WAS...PRETTY TRAUMATIZED. I'M SURE YOU CAN UNDERSTAND.

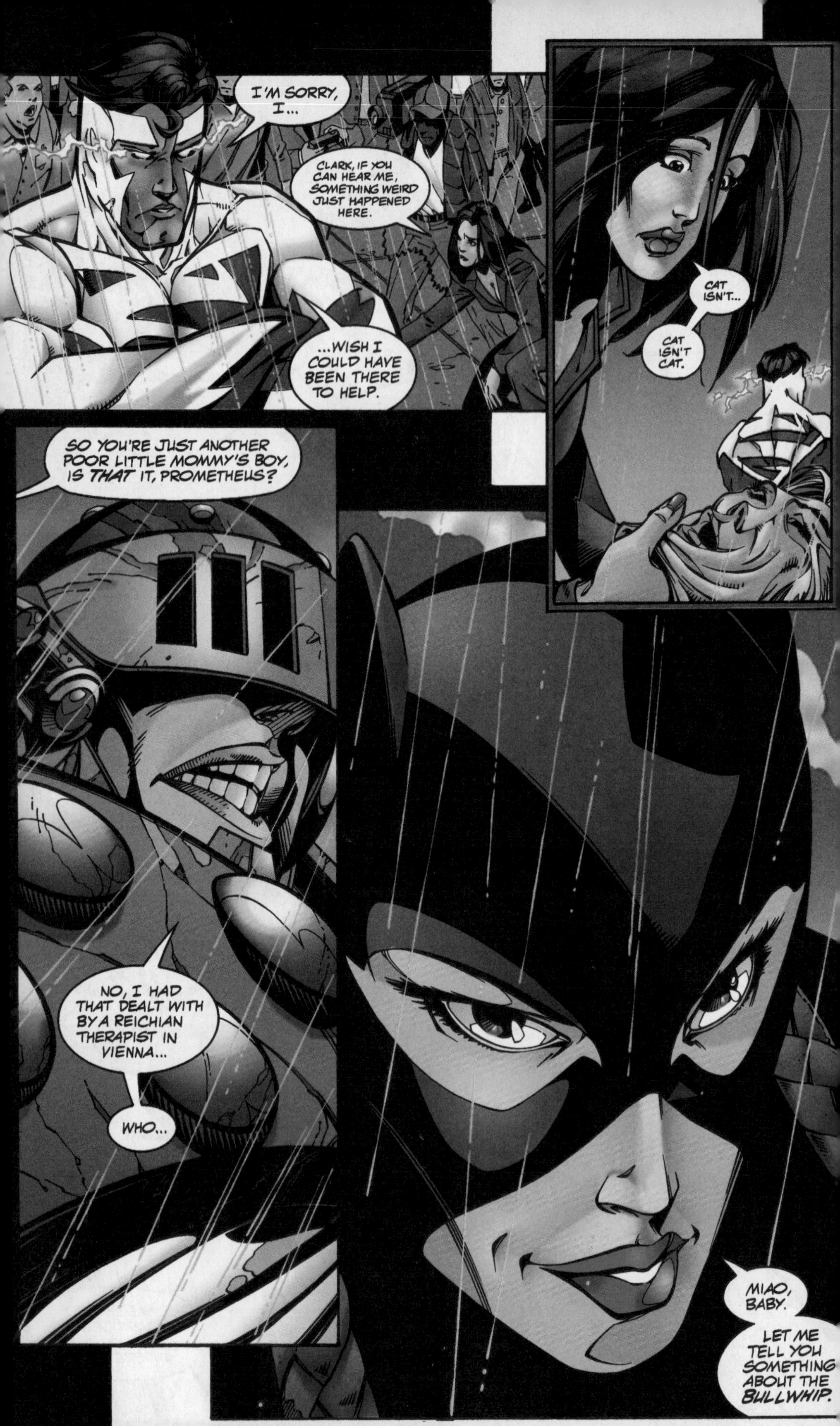
I'M SORRY, I...
CLARK, IF YOU CAN HEAR ME, SOMETHING WEIRD JUST HAPPENED HERE.
...WISH I COULD HAVE BEEN THERE TO HELP.
CAT ISN'T...
CAT ISN'T CAT.
SO YOU'RE JUST ANOTHER POOR LITTLE MOMMY'S BOY, IS *THAT* IT, PROMETHEUS?
NO, I HAD THAT DEALT WITH BY A REICHIAN THERAPIST IN VIENNA...
WHO...
MIAO, BABY.
LET ME TELL YOU SOMETHING ABOUT THE *BULLWHIP.*

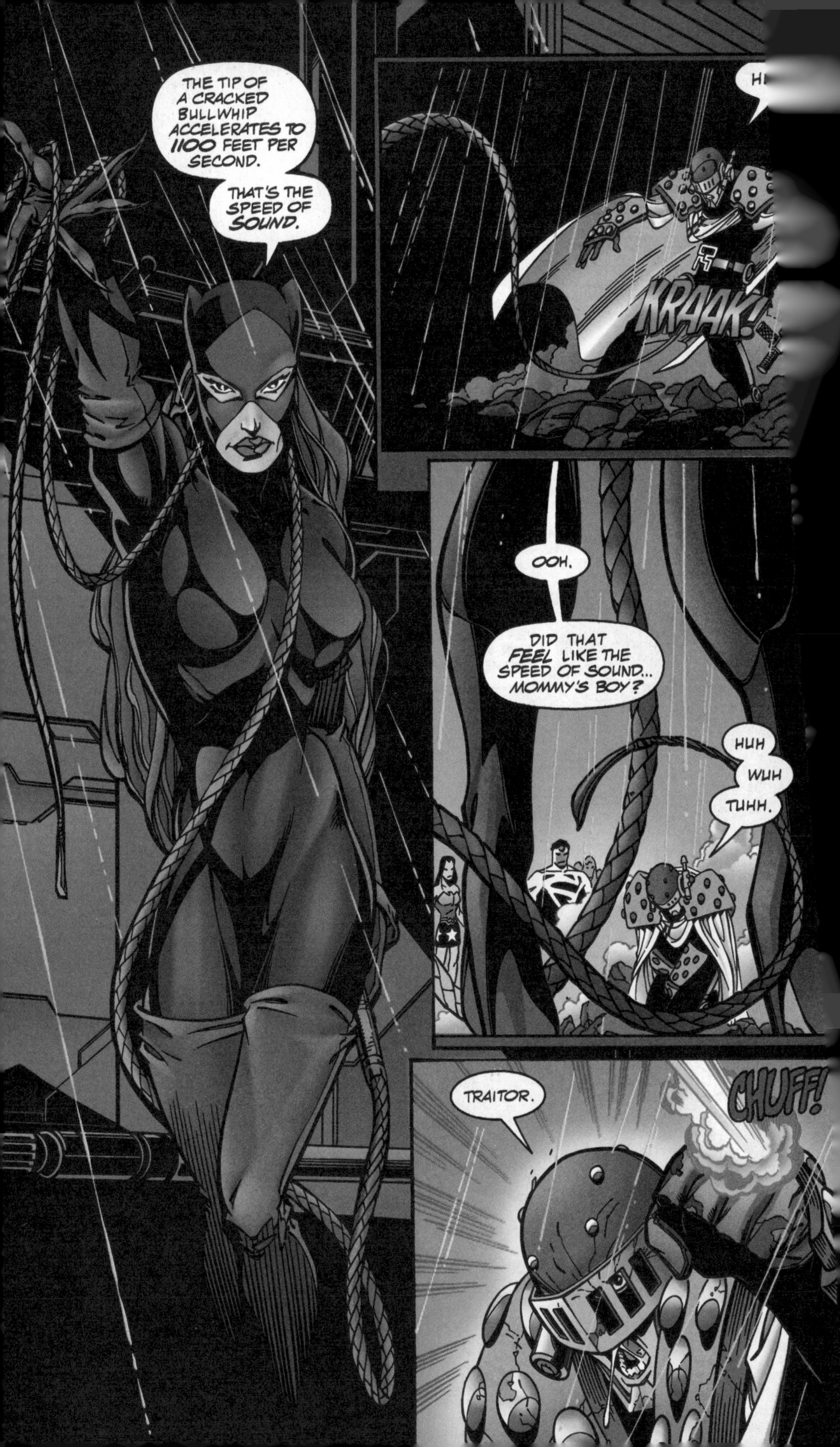
THE TIP OF A CRACKED BULLWHIP ACCELERATES TO 1100 FEET PER SECOND.
THAT'S THE SPEED OF SOUND.
KRAAK!
OOH.
DID THAT FEEL LIKE THE SPEED OF SOUND... MOMMY'S BOY?
HUH
WUH
TUHH.
TRAITOR.
CHUFF!

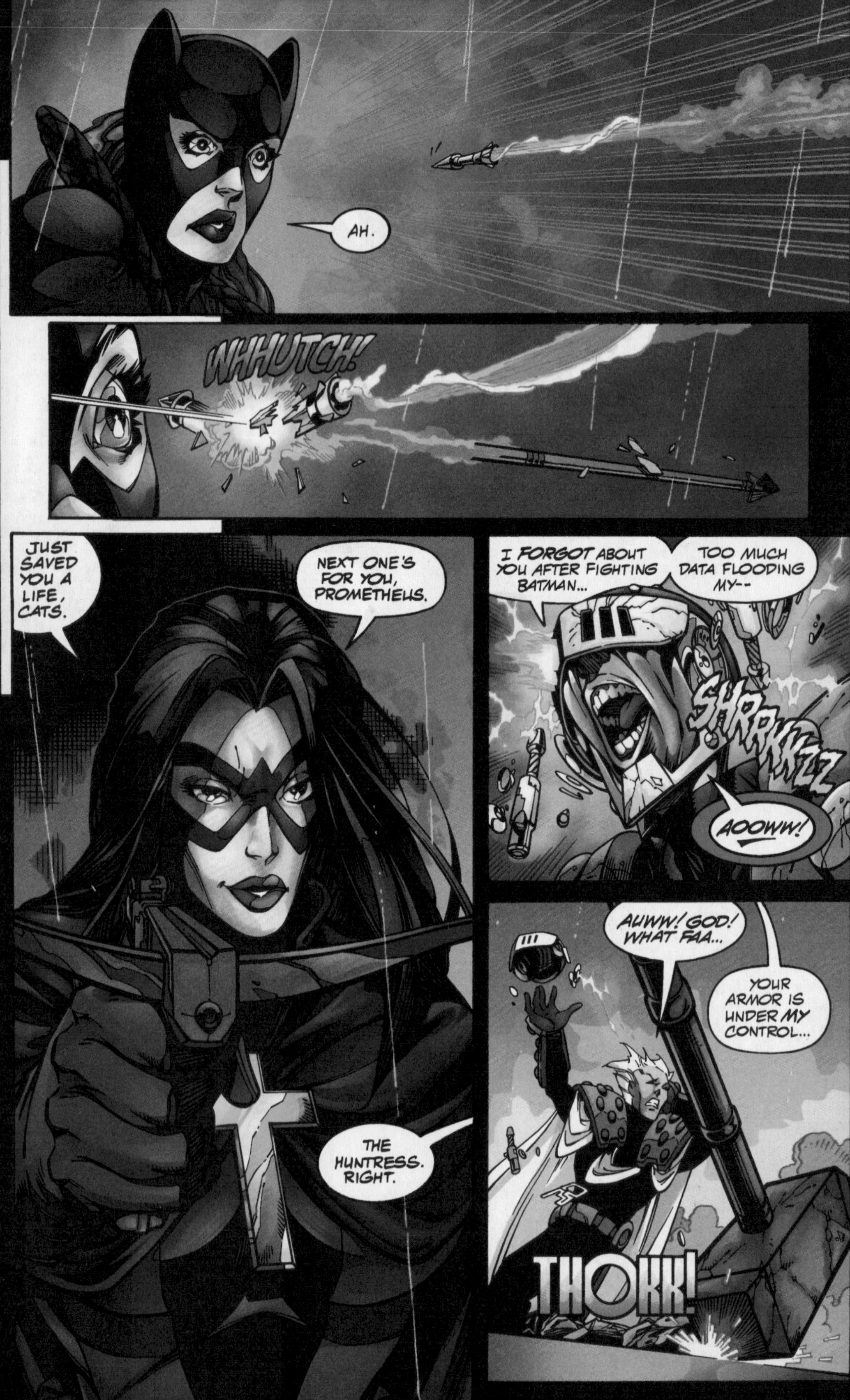
AH.
WHHUTCH!
JUST SAVED YOU A LIFE, CATS.
NEXT ONE'S FOR YOU, PROMETHEUS.
I FORGOT ABOUT YOU AFTER FIGHTING BATMAN...
TOO MUCH DATA FLOODING MY--
AOOWW!
THE HUNTRESS. RIGHT.
AUWW! GOD! WHAT FAA...
YOUR ARMOR IS UNDER MY CONTROL...
THOKK!

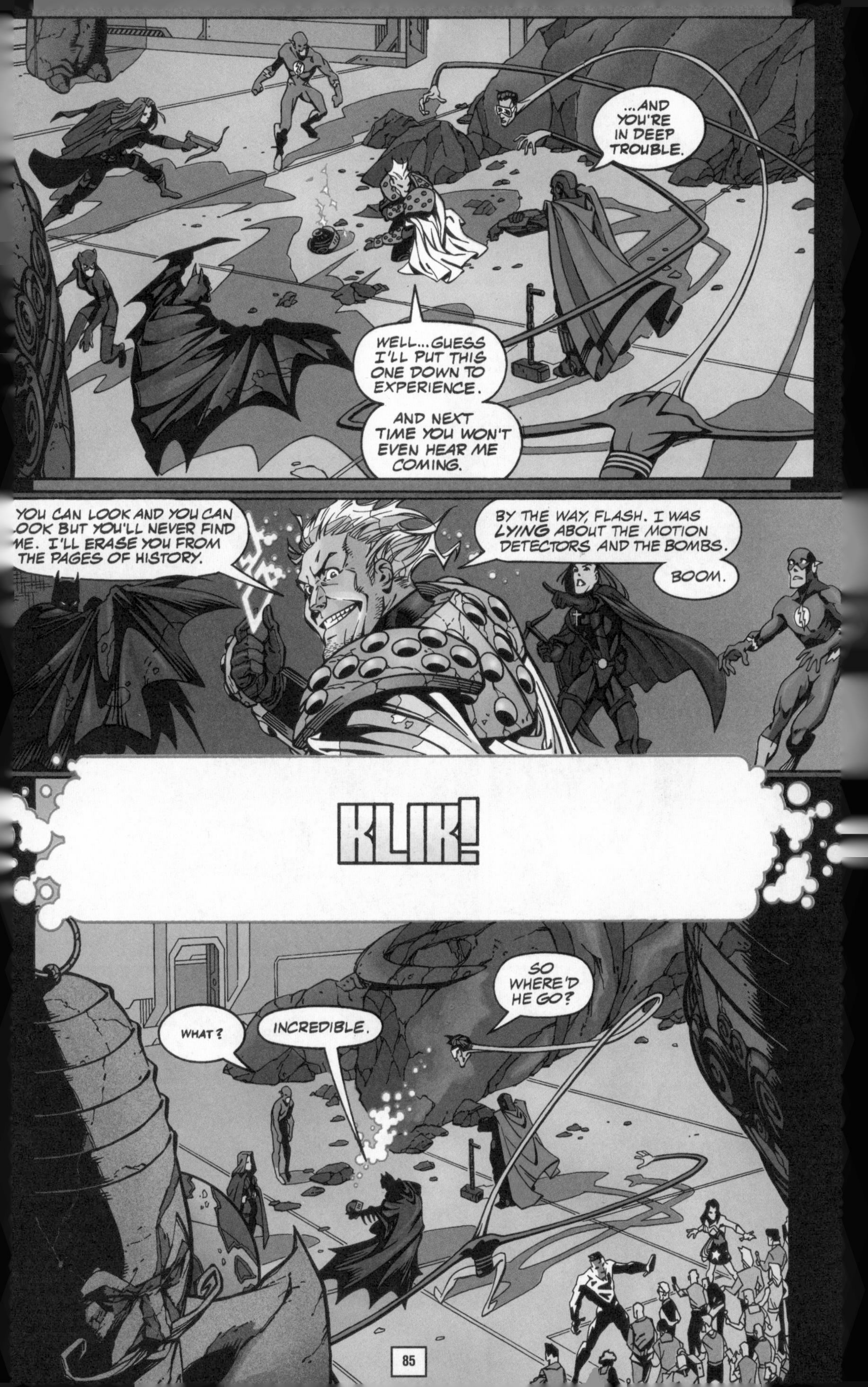
...AND YOU'RE IN DEEP TROUBLE.
WELL...GUESS I'LL PUT THIS ONE DOWN TO EXPERIENCE.
AND NEXT TIME YOU WON'T EVEN HEAR ME COMING.
YOU CAN LOOK AND YOU CAN LOOK BUT YOU'LL NEVER FIND ME. I'LL ERASE YOU FROM THE PAGES OF HISTORY.
BY THE WAY, FLASH. I WAS LYING ABOUT THE MOTION DETECTORS AND THE BOMBS.
BOOM.
KLIK!
WHAT?
INCREDIBLE.
SO WHERE'D HE GO?

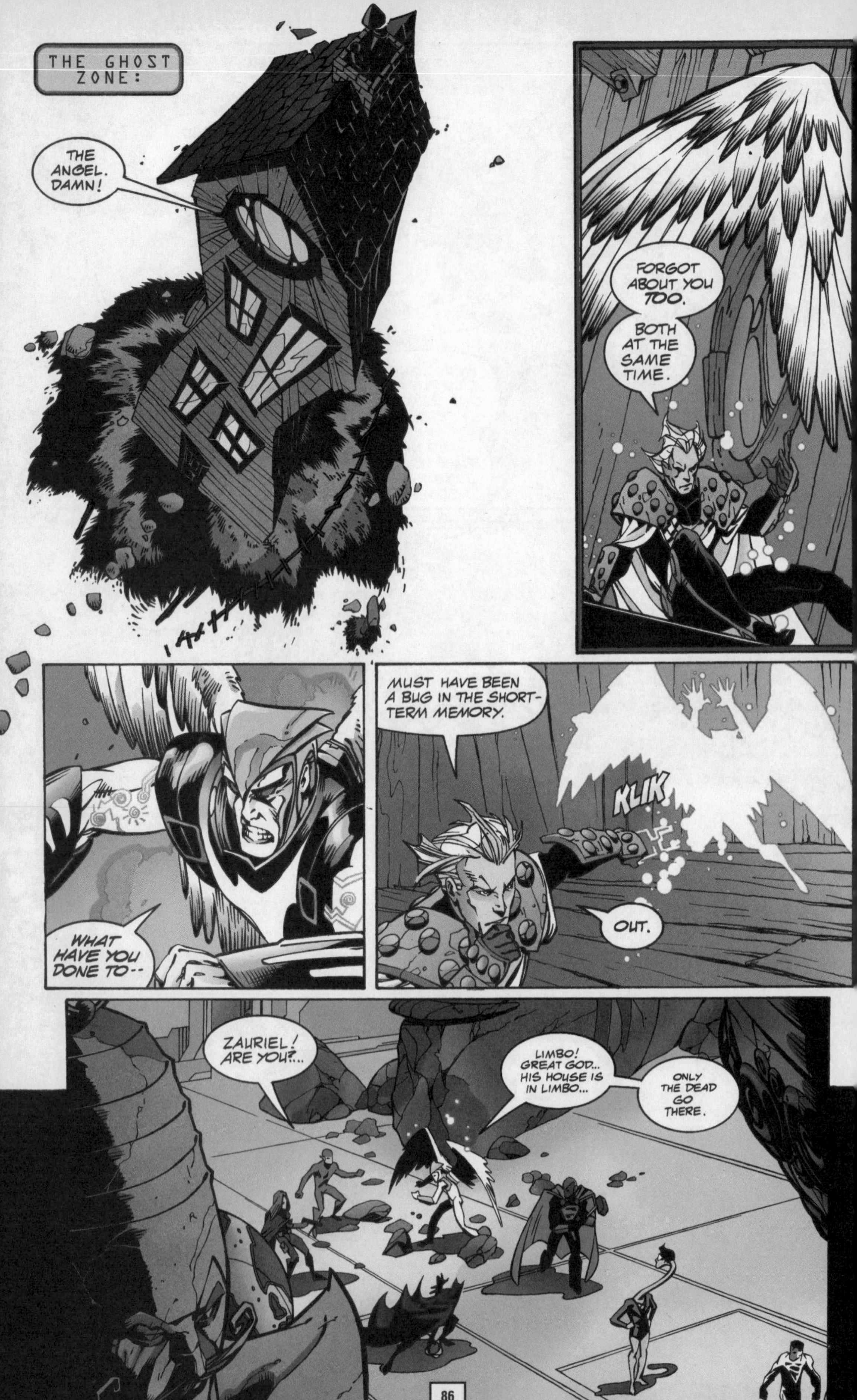
THE GHOST ZONE:
THE ANGEL. DAMN!
FORGOT ABOUT YOU TOO.
BOTH AT THE SAME TIME.
WHAT HAVE YOU DONE TO--
MUST HAVE BEEN A BUG IN THE SHORT-TERM MEMORY.
KLIK
OUT.
ZAURIEL! ARE YOU?...
LIMBO! GREAT GOD... HIS HOUSE IS IN LIMBO...
ONLY THE DEAD GO THERE.

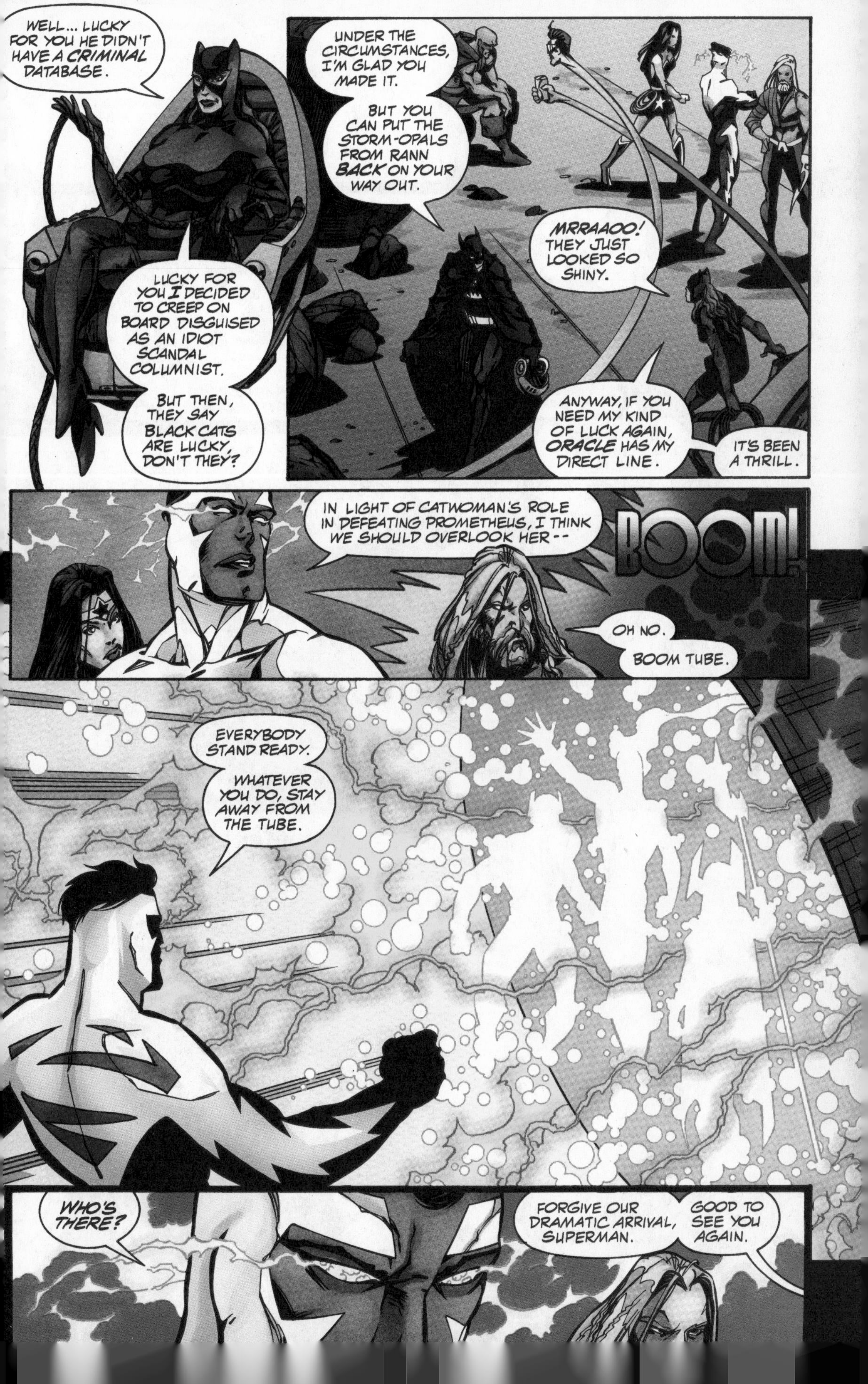
WELL... LUCKY FOR YOU HE DIDN'T HAVE A CRIMINAL DATABASE.
UNDER THE CIRCUMSTANCES, I'M GLAD YOU MADE IT.
BUT YOU CAN PUT THE STORM-OPALS FROM RANN BACK ON YOUR WAY OUT.
LUCKY FOR YOU I DECIDED TO CREEP ON BOARD DISGUISED AS AN IDIOT SCANDAL COLUMNIST.
BUT THEN, THEY SAY BLACK CATS ARE LUCKY, DON'T THEY?
MRRAAOO! THEY JUST LOOKED SO SHINY.
ANYWAY, IF YOU NEED MY KIND OF LUCK AGAIN, ORACLE HAS MY DIRECT LINE.
IT'S BEEN A THRILL.
IN LIGHT OF CATWOMAN'S ROLE IN DEFEATING PROMETHEUS, I THINK WE SHOULD OVERLOOK HER--
BOOM!
OH NO.
BOOM TUBE.
EVERYBODY STAND READY.
WHATEVER YOU DO, STAY AWAY FROM THE TUBE.
WHO'S THERE?
FORGIVE OUR DRAMATIC ARRIVAL, SUPERMAN.
GOOD TO SEE YOU AGAIN.

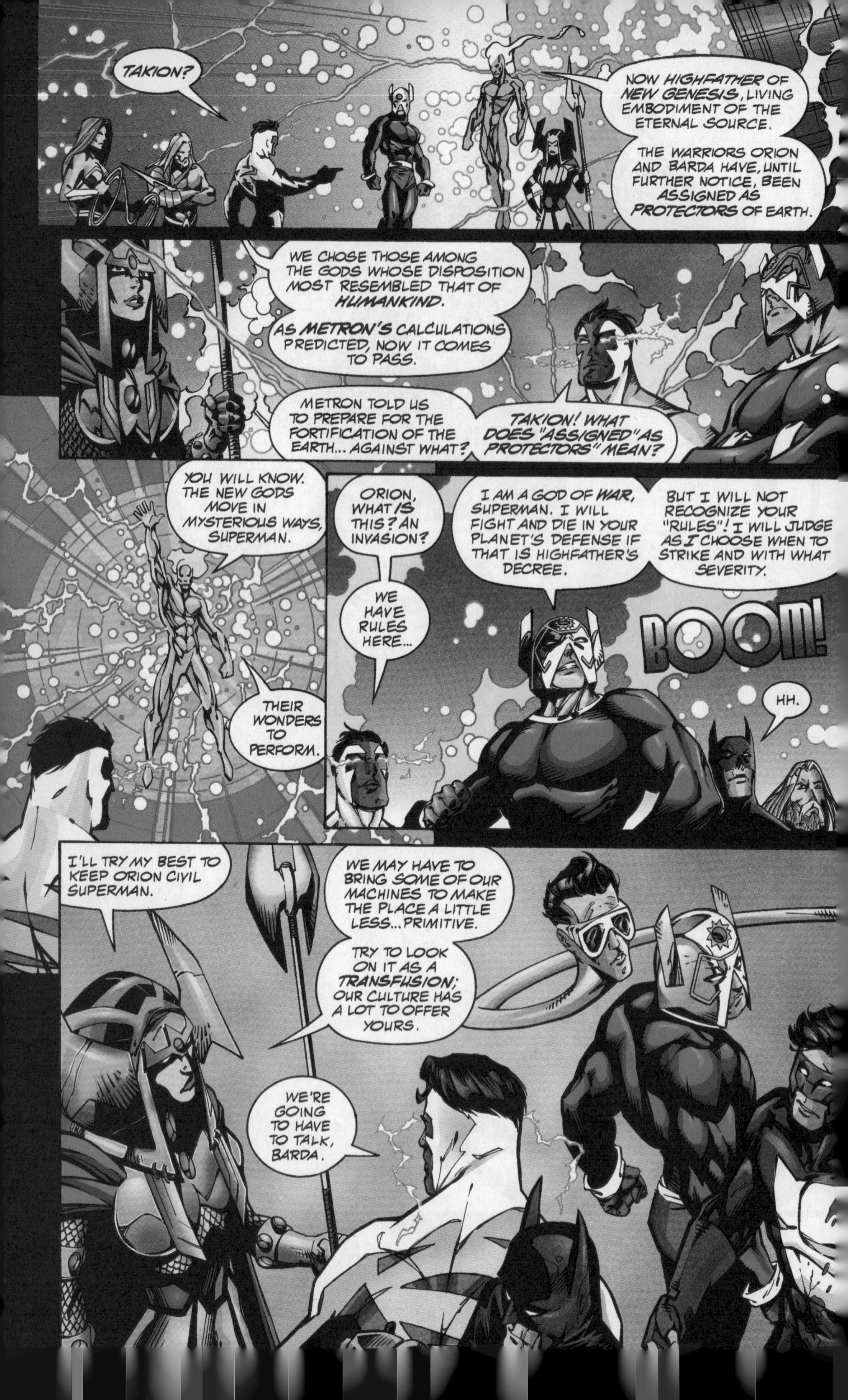
TAKION?
NOW HIGHFATHER OF NEW GENESIS, LIVING EMBODIMENT OF THE ETERNAL SOURCE.
THE WARRIORS ORION AND BARDA HAVE, UNTIL FURTHER NOTICE, BEEN ASSIGNED AS PROTECTORS OF EARTH.
WE CHOSE THOSE AMONG THE GODS WHOSE DISPOSITION MOST RESEMBLED THAT OF HUMANKIND.
AS METRON'S CALCULATIONS PREDICTED, NOW IT COMES TO PASS.
METRON TOLD US TO PREPARE FOR THE FORTIFICATION OF THE EARTH... AGAINST WHAT?
TAKION! WHAT DOES "ASSIGNED" AS PROTECTORS" MEAN?
YOU WILL KNOW. THE NEW GODS MOVE IN MYSTERIOUS WAYS, SUPERMAN.
THEIR WONDERS TO PERFORM.
ORION, WHAT IS THIS? AN INVASION?
WE HAVE RULES HERE...
I AM A GOD OF WAR, SUPERMAN. I WILL FIGHT AND DIE IN YOUR PLANET'S DEFENSE IF THAT IS HIGHFATHER'S DECREE.
BUT I WILL NOT RECOGNIZE YOUR "RULES"! I WILL JUDGE AS I CHOOSE WHEN TO STRIKE AND WITH WHAT SEVERITY.
BOOM!
HH.
I'LL TRY MY BEST TO KEEP ORION CIVIL SUPERMAN.
WE MAY HAVE TO BRING SOME OF OUR MACHINES TO MAKE THE PLACE A LITTLE LESS...PRIMITIVE.
TRY TO LOOK ON IT AS A TRANSFUSION; OUR CULTURE HAS A LOT TO OFFER YOURS.
WE'RE GOING TO HAVE TO TALK, BARDA.

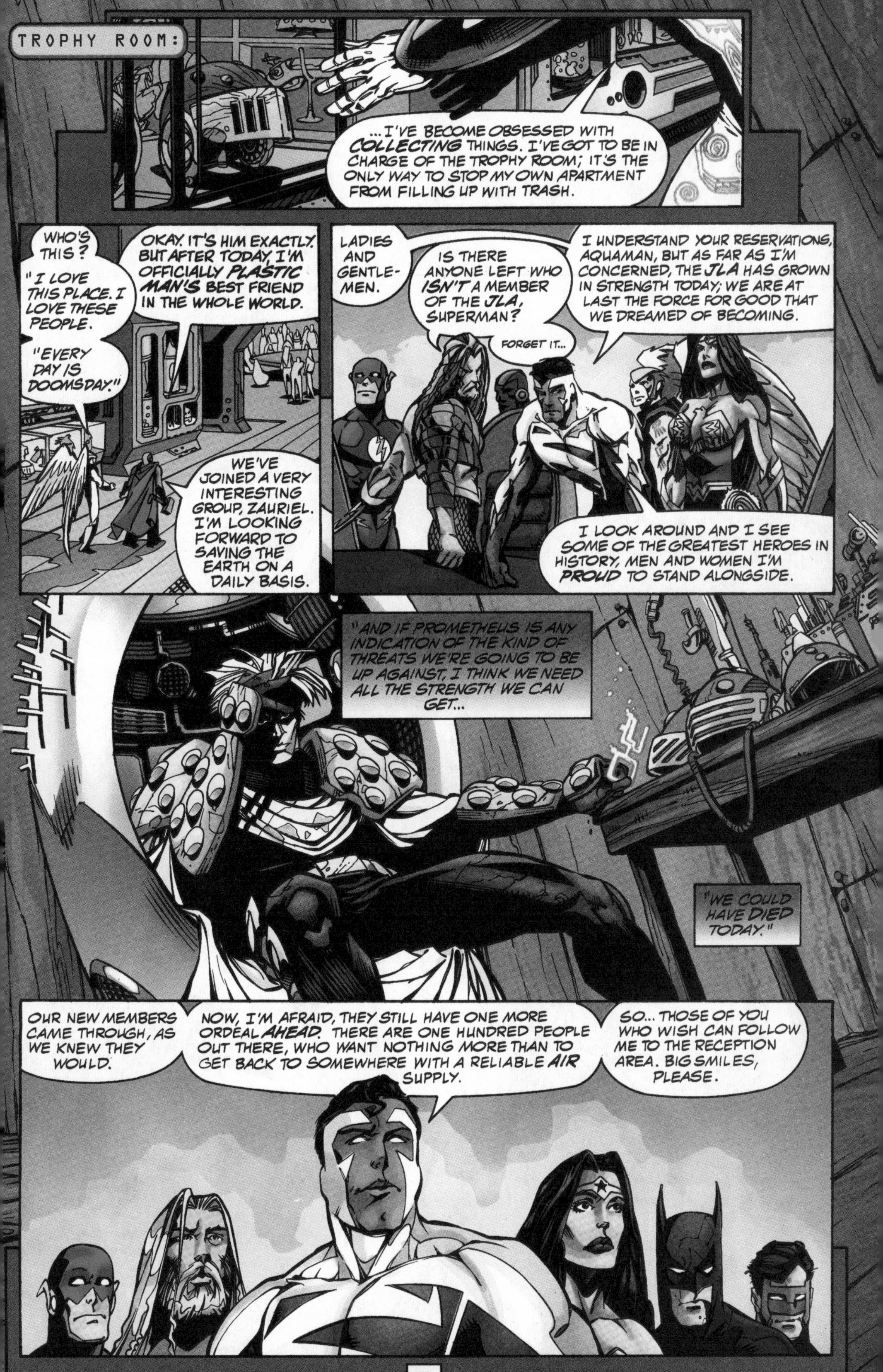
TROPHY ROOM:
...I'VE BECOME OBSESSED WITH COLLECTING THINGS. I'VE GOT TO BE IN CHARGE OF THE TROPHY ROOM; IT'S THE ONLY WAY TO STOP MY OWN APARTMENT FROM FILLING UP WITH TRASH.
WHO'S THIS?
"I LOVE THIS PLACE. I LOVE THESE PEOPLE.
"EVERY DAY IS DOOMSDAY."
OKAY. IT'S HIM EXACTLY. BUT AFTER TODAY, I'M OFFICIALLY PLASTIC MAN'S BEST FRIEND IN THE WHOLE WORLD.
WE'VE JOINED A VERY INTERESTING GROUP, ZAURIEL. I'M LOOKING FORWARD TO SAVING THE EARTH ON A DAILY BASIS.
LADIES AND GENTLE-MEN.
IS THERE ANYONE LEFT WHO ISN'T A MEMBER OF THE JLA, SUPERMAN?
FORGET IT...
I UNDERSTAND YOUR RESERVATIONS, AQUAMAN, BUT AS FAR AS I'M CONCERNED, THE JLA HAS GROWN IN STRENGTH TODAY; WE ARE AT LAST THE FORCE FOR GOOD THAT WE DREAMED OF BECOMING.
I LOOK AROUND AND I SEE SOME OF THE GREATEST HEROES IN HISTORY, MEN AND WOMEN I'M PROUD TO STAND ALONGSIDE.
"AND IF PROMETHEUS IS ANY INDICATION OF THE KIND OF THREATS WE'RE GOING TO BE UP AGAINST, I THINK WE NEED ALL THE STRENGTH WE CAN GET...
"WE COULD HAVE DIED TODAY."
OUR NEW MEMBERS CAME THROUGH, AS WE KNEW THEY WOULD.
NOW, I'M AFRAID, THEY STILL HAVE ONE MORE ORDEAL AHEAD. THERE ARE ONE HUNDRED PEOPLE OUT THERE, WHO WANT NOTHING MORE THAN TO GET BACK TO SOMEWHERE WITH A RELIABLE AIR SUPPLY.
SO... THOSE OF YOU WHO WISH CAN FOLLOW ME TO THE RECEPTION AREA. BIG SMILES, PLEASE.

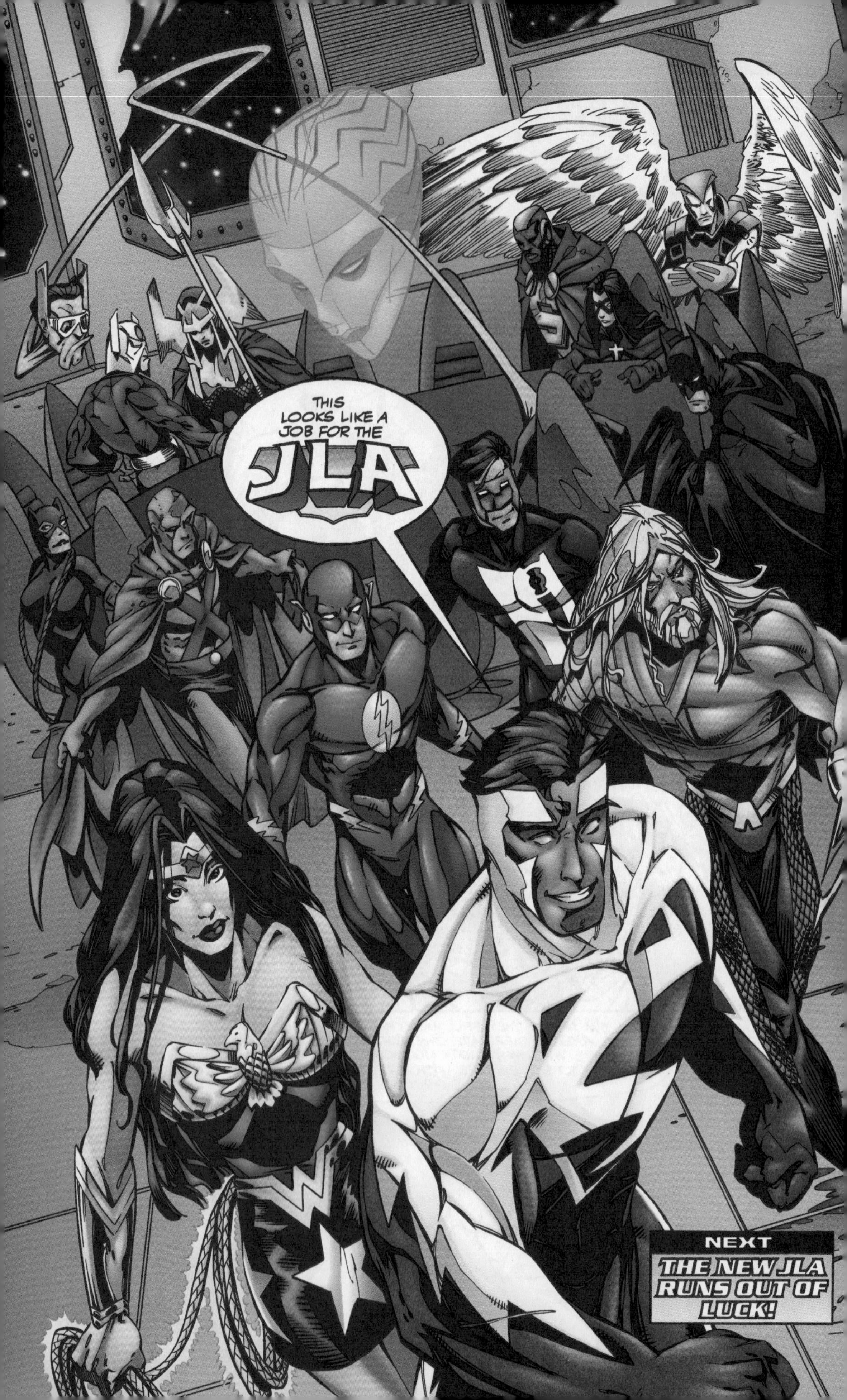
THIS LOOKS LIKE A JOB FOR THE JLA
NEXT
THE NEW JLA RUNS OUT OF LUCK!

THE STRANGE CASE OF
Dr. JULIAN
SEPTEMBER

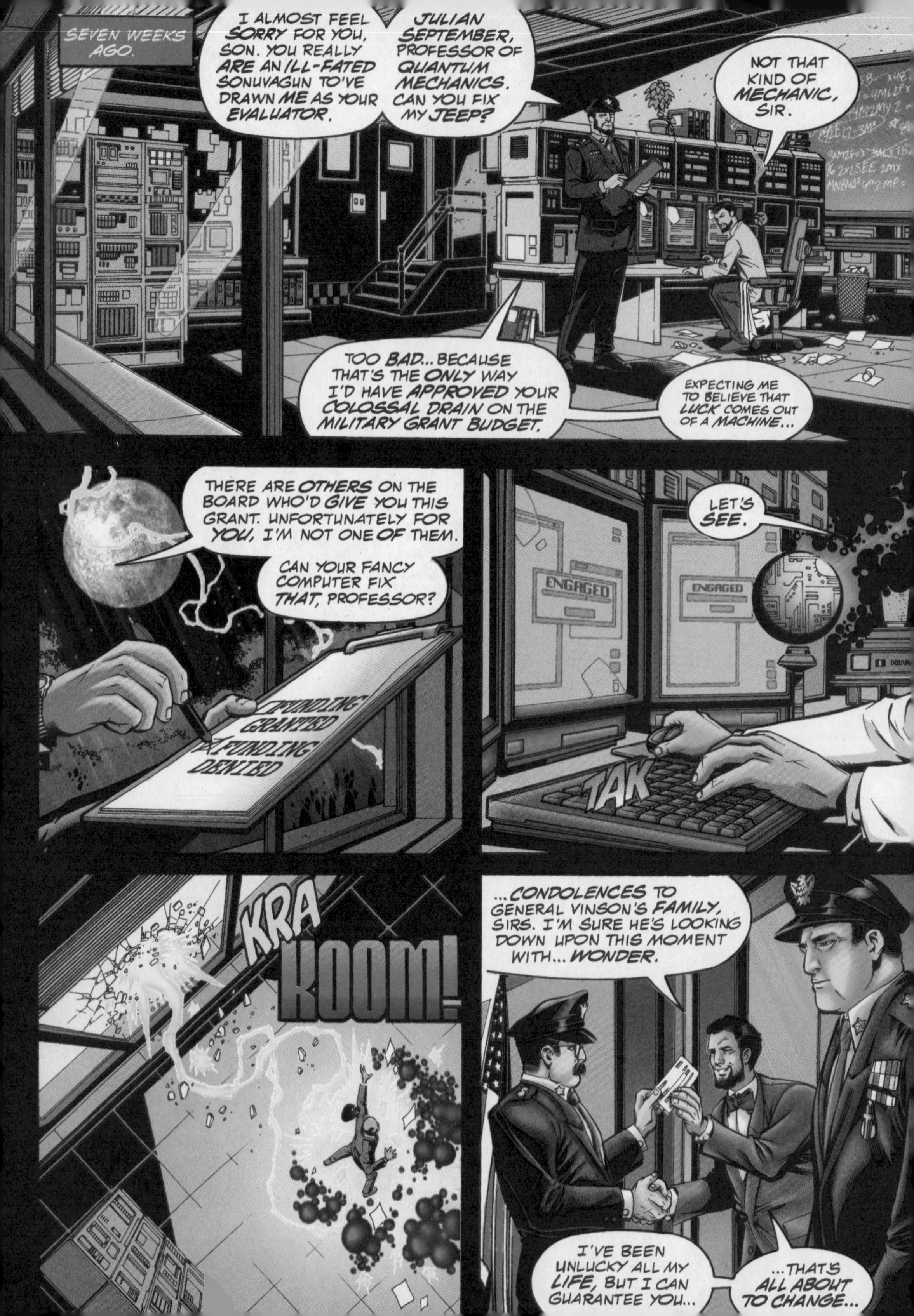
SEVEN WEEKS AGO.
I ALMOST FEEL SORRY FOR YOU, SON. YOU REALLY ARE AN ILL-FATED SONUVAGUN TO'VE DRAWN ME AS YOUR EVALUATOR.
JULIAN SEPTEMBER, PROFESSOR OF QUANTUM MECHANICS. CAN YOU FIX MY JEEP?
NOT THAT KIND OF MECHANIC, SIR.
TOO BAD... BECAUSE THAT'S THE ONLY WAY I'D HAVE APPROVED YOUR COLOSSAL DRAIN ON THE MILITARY GRANT BUDGET.
EXPECTING ME TO BELIEVE THAT LUCK COMES OUT OF A MACHINE...
THERE ARE OTHERS ON THE BOARD WHO'D GIVE YOU THIS GRANT. UNFORTUNATELY FOR YOU, I'M NOT ONE OF THEM.
CAN YOUR FANCY COMPUTER FIX THAT, PROFESSOR?
FUNDING GRANTED
FUNDING DENIED
LET'S SEE.
ENGAGED
ENGAGED
TAK
KRA
KOOM!
...CONDOLENCES TO GENERAL VINSON'S FAMILY, SIRS. I'M SURE HE'S LOOKING DOWN UPON THIS MOMENT WITH... WONDER.
I'VE BEEN UNLUCKY ALL MY LIFE, BUT I CAN GUARANTEE YOU...
...THAT'S ALL ABOUT TO CHANGE...

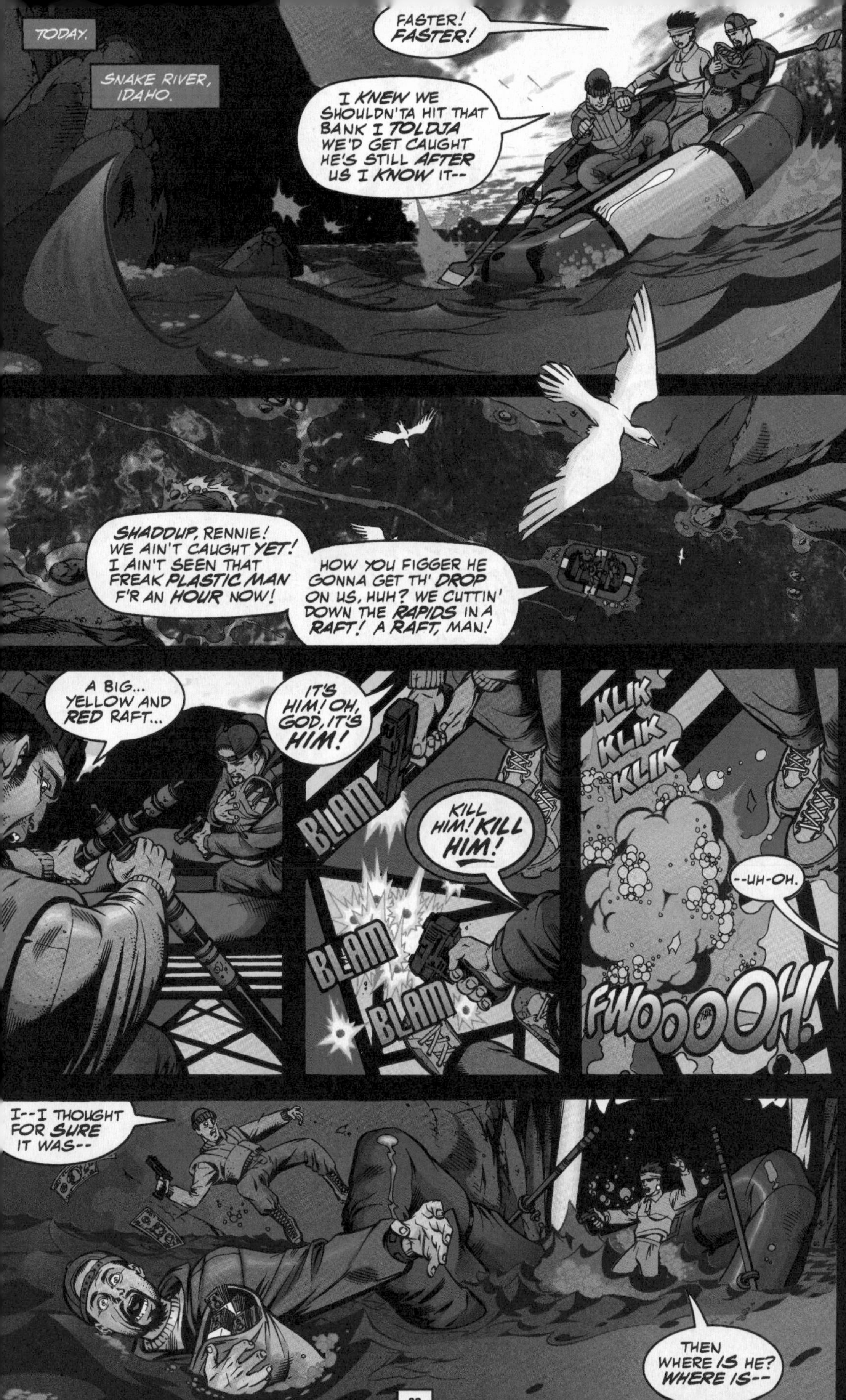

TODAY.
SNAKE RIVER, IDAHO.
FASTER! FASTER!
I KNEW WE SHOULDN'TA HIT THAT BANK I TOLDJA WE'D GET CAUGHT HE'S STILL AFTER US I KNOW IT--
SHADDUP, RENNIE! WE AIN'T CAUGHT YET! I AIN'T SEEN THAT FREAK PLASTIC MAN F'R AN HOUR NOW!
HOW YOU FIGGER HE GONNA GET TH' DROP ON US, HUH? WE CUTTIN' DOWN THE RAPIDS IN A RAFT! A RAFT, MAN!
A BIG... YELLOW AND RED RAFT...
IT'S HIM! OH, GOD, IT'S HIM!
BLAM
KILL HIM! KILL HIM!
BLAM
BLAM
KLIK KLIK KLIK
--UH-OH.
FWOOOOOH!
I--I THOUGHT FOR SURE IT WAS--
THEN WHERE IS HE? WHERE IS--

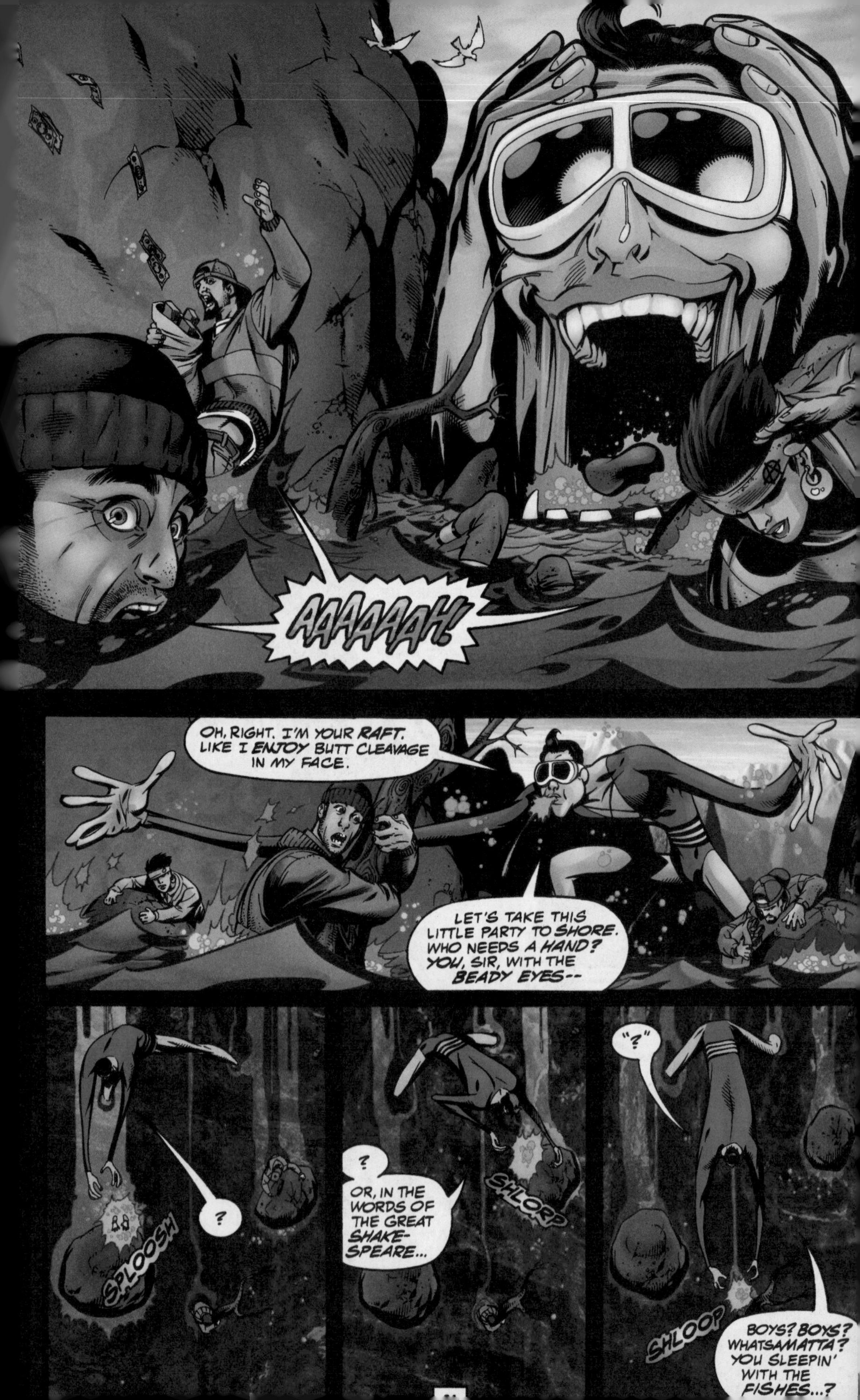
AAAAAAH!
OH, RIGHT. I'M YOUR RAFT. LIKE I ENJOY BUTT CLEAVAGE IN MY FACE.
LET'S TAKE THIS LITTLE PARTY TO SHORE. WHO NEEDS A HAND? YOU, SIR, WITH THE BEADY EYES--
?
SPLOOSH
?
OR, IN THE WORDS OF THE GREAT SHAKE-SPEARE...
SHLORP
"?"
SHLOOP
BOYS? BOYS? WHATSAMATTA? YOU SLEEPIN' WITH THE FISHES...?

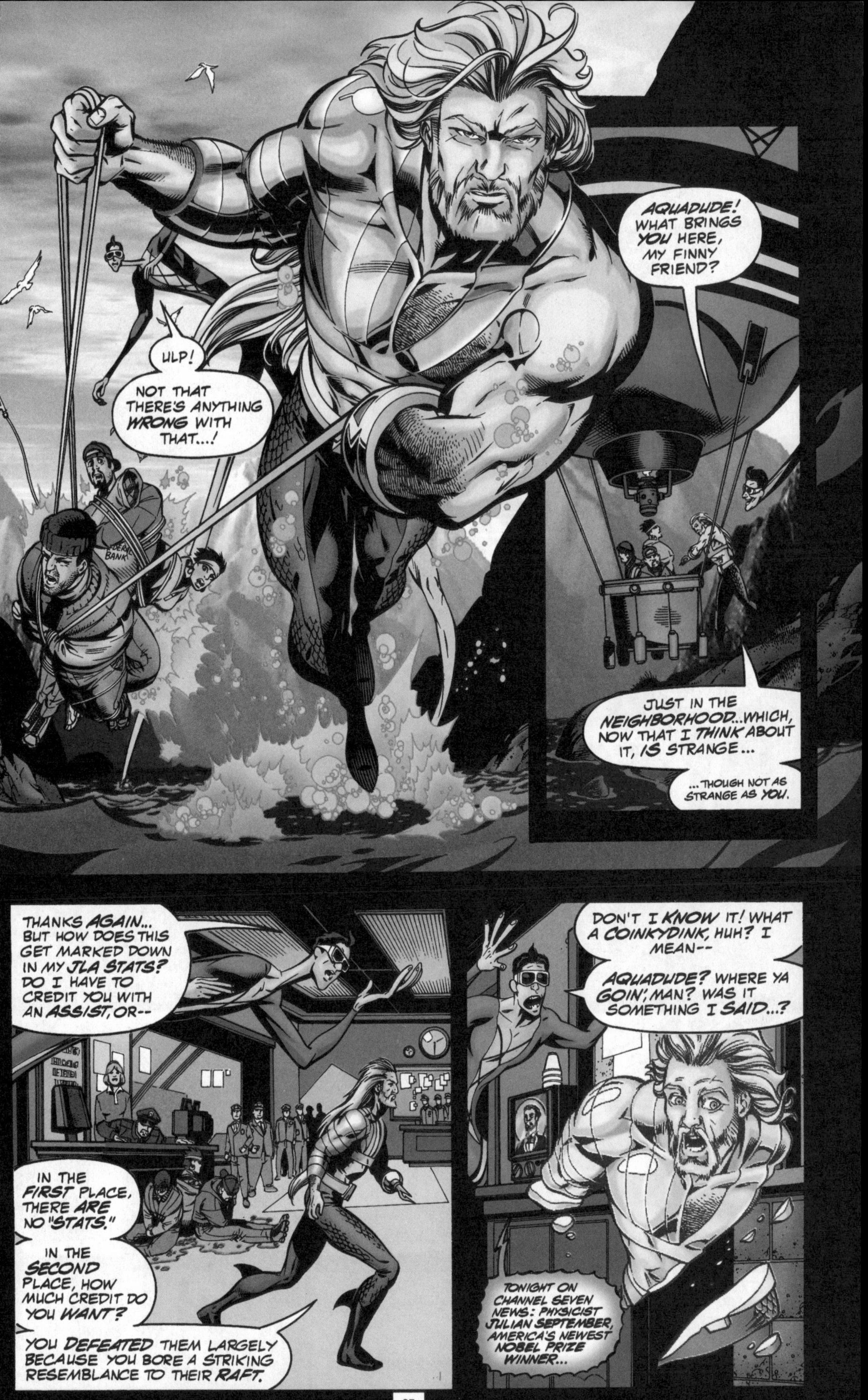
AQUADUDE! WHAT BRINGS YOU HERE, MY FINNY FRIEND?
ULP!
NOT THAT THERE'S ANYTHING WRONG WITH THAT...!
JUST IN THE NEIGHBORHOOD...WHICH, NOW THAT I THINK ABOUT IT, IS STRANGE...
...THOUGH NOT AS STRANGE AS YOU.
THANKS AGAIN... BUT HOW DOES THIS GET MARKED DOWN IN MY JLA STATS? DO I HAVE TO CREDIT YOU WITH AN ASSIST, OR--
IN THE FIRST PLACE, THERE ARE NO "STATS."
IN THE SECOND PLACE, HOW MUCH CREDIT DO YOU WANT?
YOU DEFEATED THEM LARGELY BECAUSE YOU BORE A STRIKING RESEMBLANCE TO THEIR RAFT.
DON'T I KNOW IT! WHAT A COINKYDINK, HUH? I MEAN--
AQUADUDE? WHERE YA GOIN', MAN? WAS IT SOMETHING I SAID...?
TONIGHT ON CHANNEL SEVEN NEWS: PHYSICIST JULIAN SEPTEMBER, AMERICA'S NEWEST NOBEL PRIZE WINNER...

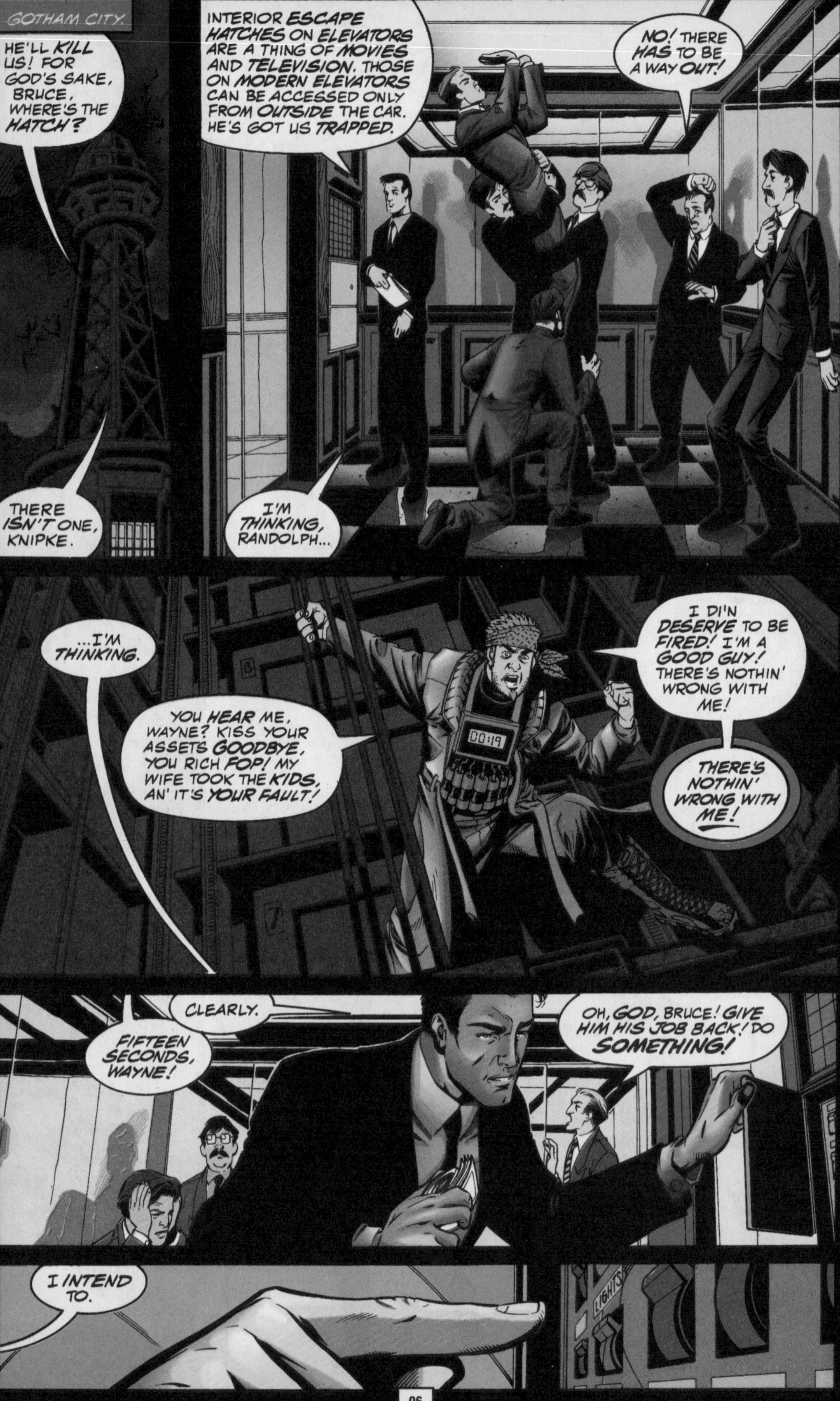
GOTHAM CITY.
HE'LL KILL US! FOR GOD'S SAKE, BRUCE, WHERE'S THE HATCH?
THERE ISN'T ONE, KNIPKE.
INTERIOR ESCAPE HATCHES ON ELEVATORS ARE A THING OF MOVIES AND TELEVISION. THOSE ON MODERN ELEVATORS CAN BE ACCESSED ONLY FROM OUTSIDE THE CAR. HE'S GOT US TRAPPED.
NO! THERE HAS TO BE A WAY OUT!
I'M THINKING, RANDOLPH...
...I'M THINKING.
YOU HEAR ME, WAYNE? KISS YOUR ASSETS GOODBYE, YOU RICH FOP! MY WIFE TOOK THE KIDS, AN' IT'S YOUR FAULT!
00:19
I DI'N DESERVE TO BE FIRED! I'M A GOOD GUY! THERE'S NOTHIN' WRONG WITH ME!
THERE'S NOTHIN' WRONG WITH ME!
FIFTEEN SECONDS, WAYNE!
CLEARLY.
OH, GOD, BRUCE! GIVE HIM HIS JOB BACK! DO SOMETHING!
I INTEND TO.
LIGHTS

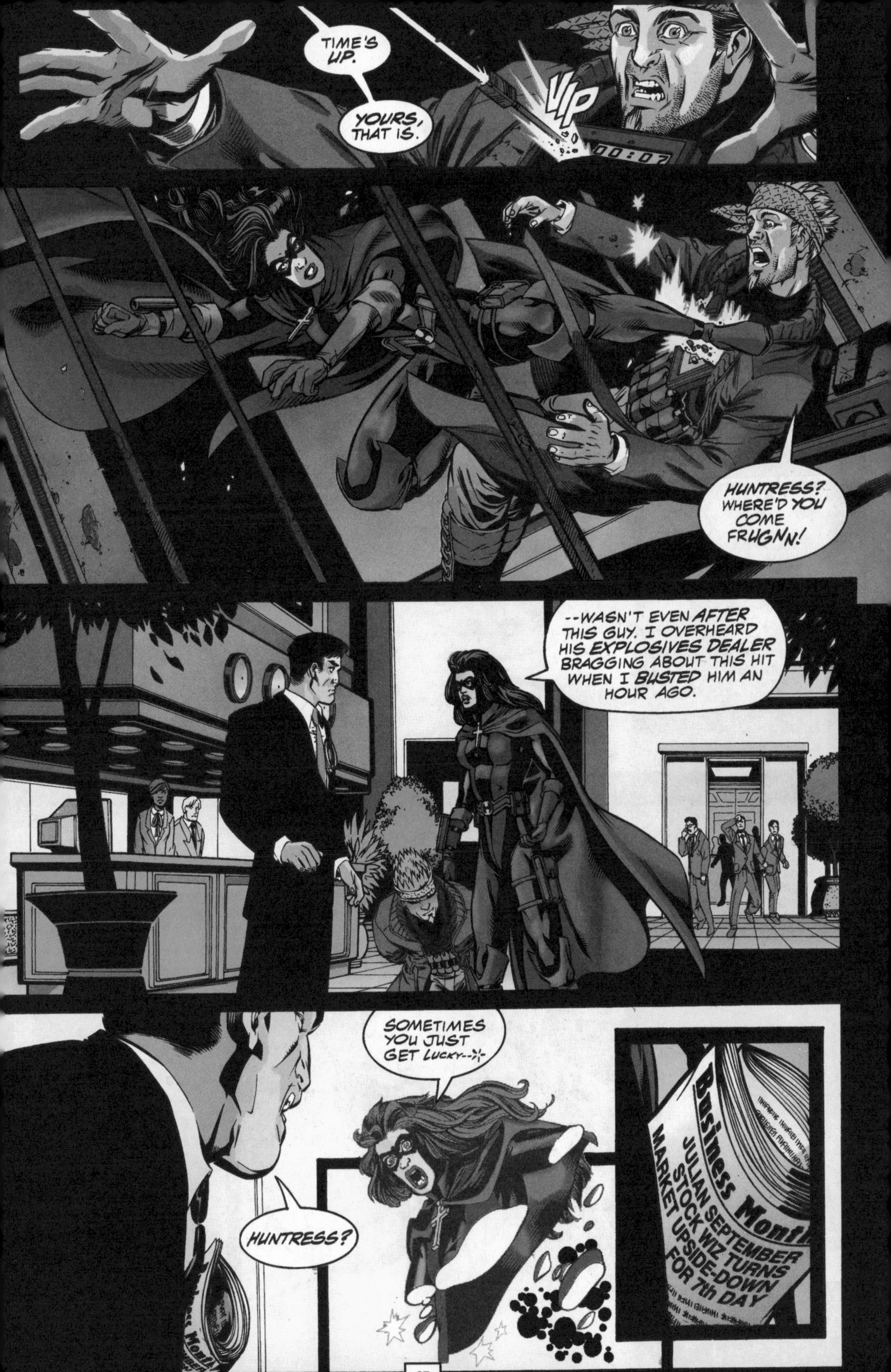
TIME'S UP.
YOURS, THAT IS.
VIP
00:07
HUNTRESS? WHERE'D YOU COME FRUGNN!
--WASN'T EVEN AFTER THIS GUY. I OVERHEARD HIS EXPLOSIVES DEALER BRAGGING ABOUT THIS HIT WHEN I BUSTED HIM AN HOUR AGO.
SOMETIMES YOU JUST GET LUCKY--
HUNTRESS?
Business Mont
JULIAN SEPTEMBER STOCK WIZ TURNS MARKET UPSIDE-DOWN FOR 7th DAY

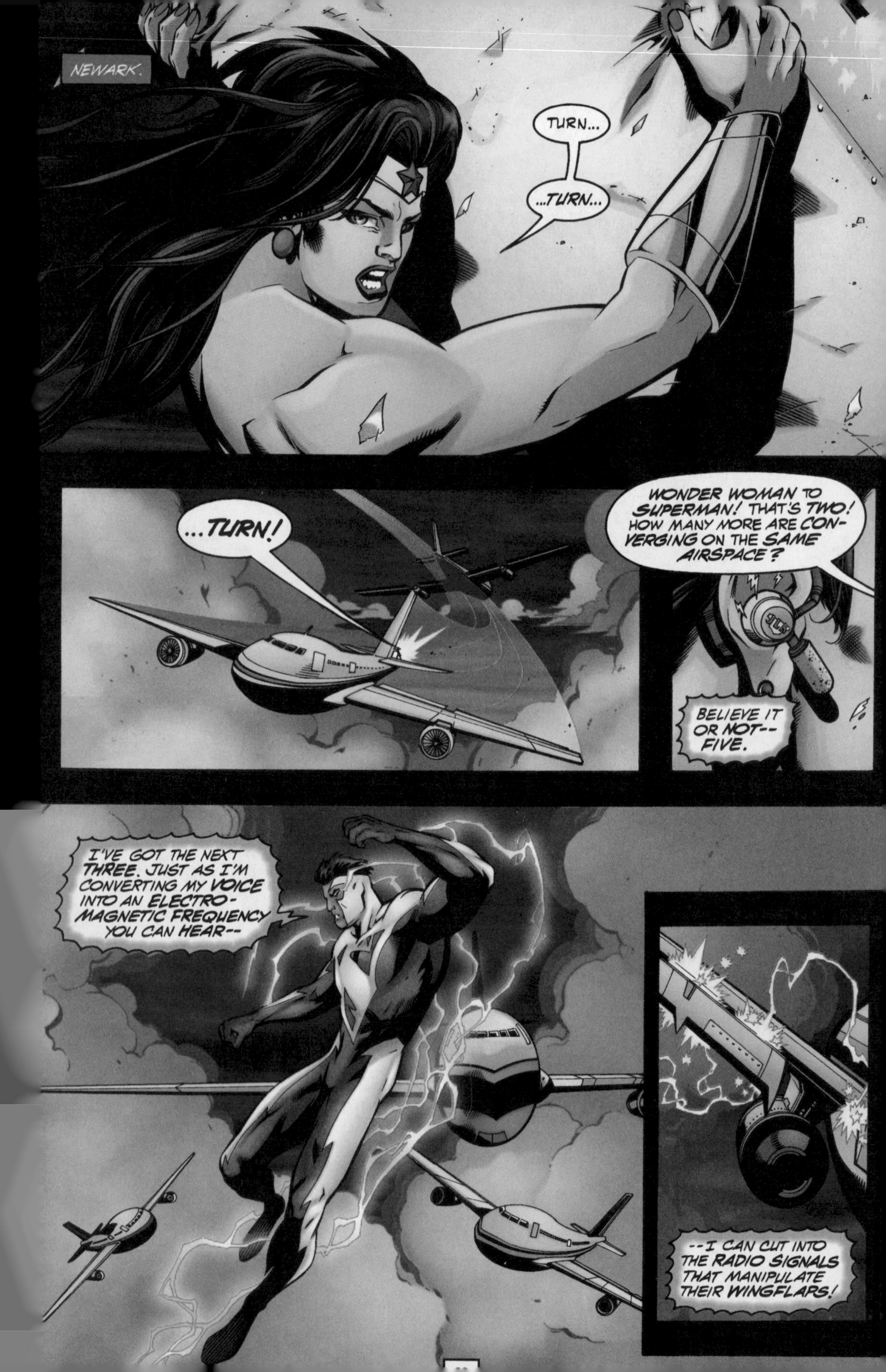
NEWARK.
TURN...
...TURN...
...TURN!
WONDER WOMAN TO SUPERMAN! THAT'S TWO! HOW MANY MORE ARE CONVERGING ON THE SAME AIRSPACE?
BELIEVE IT OR NOT-- FIVE.
I'VE GOT THE NEXT THREE. JUST AS I'M CONVERTING MY VOICE INTO AN ELECTRO-MAGNETIC FREQUENCY YOU CAN HEAR--
--I CAN CUT INTO THE RADIO SIGNALS THAT MANIPULATE THEIR WINGFLAPS!

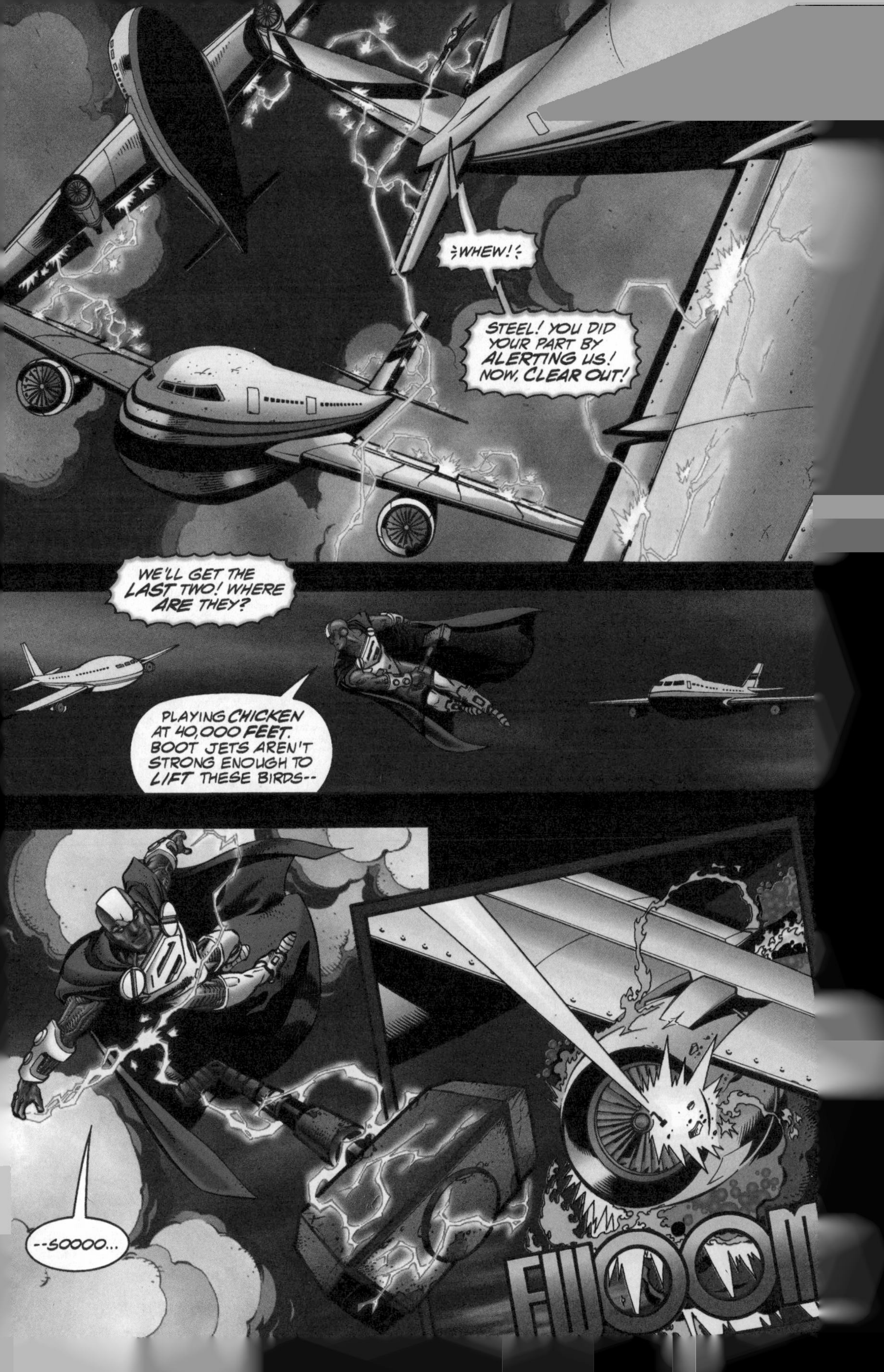

WHEW!
STEEL! YOU DID YOUR PART BY ALERTING US! NOW, CLEAR OUT!
WE'LL GET THE LAST TWO! WHERE ARE THEY?
PLAYING CHICKEN AT 40,000 FEET. BOOT JETS AREN'T STRONG ENOUGH TO LIFT THESE BIRDS--
--SOOOO...
FWOOM

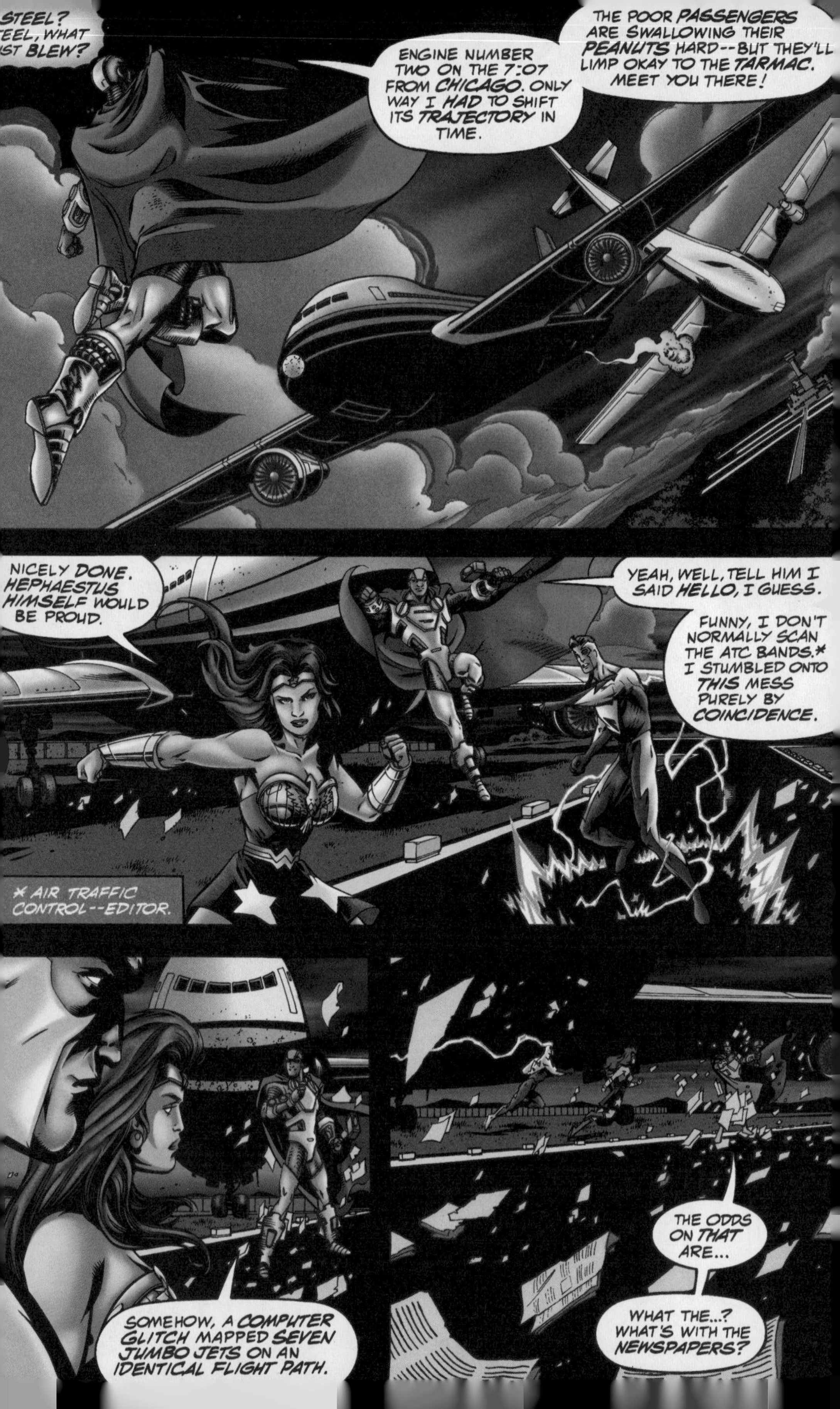
STEEL? TEEL, WHAT ST BLEW?
ENGINE NUMBER TWO ON THE 7:07 FROM CHICAGO. ONLY WAY I HAD TO SHIFT ITS TRAJECTORY IN TIME.
THE POOR PASSENGERS ARE SWALLOWING THEIR PEANUTS HARD--BUT THEY'LL LIMP OKAY TO THE TARMAC. MEET YOU THERE!
NICELY DONE. HEPHAESTUS HIMSELF WOULD BE PROUD.
YEAH, WELL, TELL HIM I SAID HELLO, I GUESS.
FUNNY, I DON'T NORMALLY SCAN THE ATC BANDS.* I STUMBLED ONTO THIS MESS PURELY BY COINCIDENCE.
* AIR TRAFFIC CONTROL--EDITOR.
SOMEHOW, A COMPUTER GLITCH MAPPED SEVEN JUMBO JETS ON AN IDENTICAL FLIGHT PATH.
THE ODDS ON THAT ARE...
WHAT THE...? WHAT'S WITH THE NEWSPAPERS?

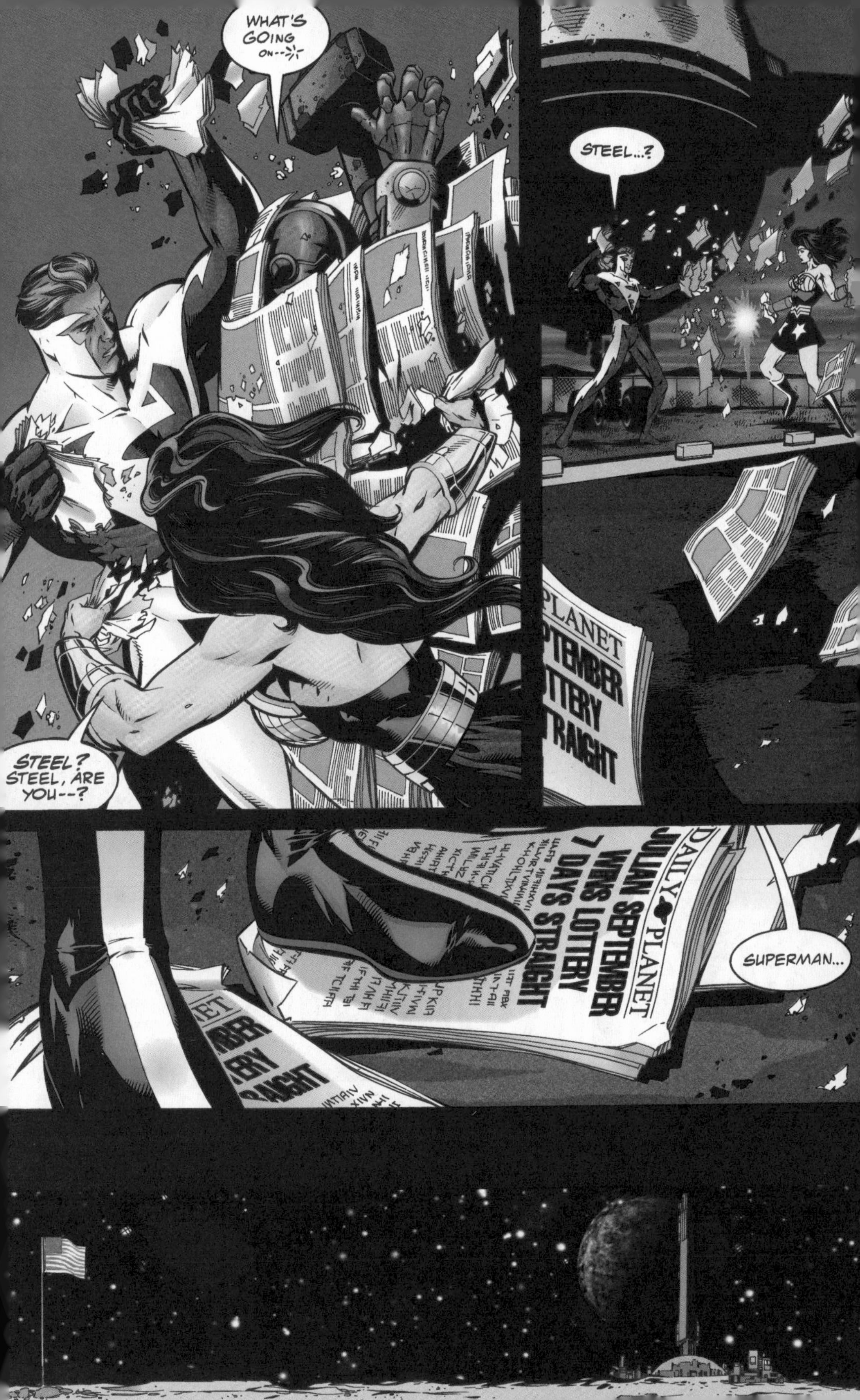
WHAT'S GOING ON--
STEEL...?
STEEL? STEEL, ARE YOU--?
PLANET
SEPTEMBER
LOTTERY
STRAIGHT
DAILY PLANET
JULIAN SEPTEMBER
WINS LOTTERY
7 DAYS STRAIGHT
SUPERMAN...

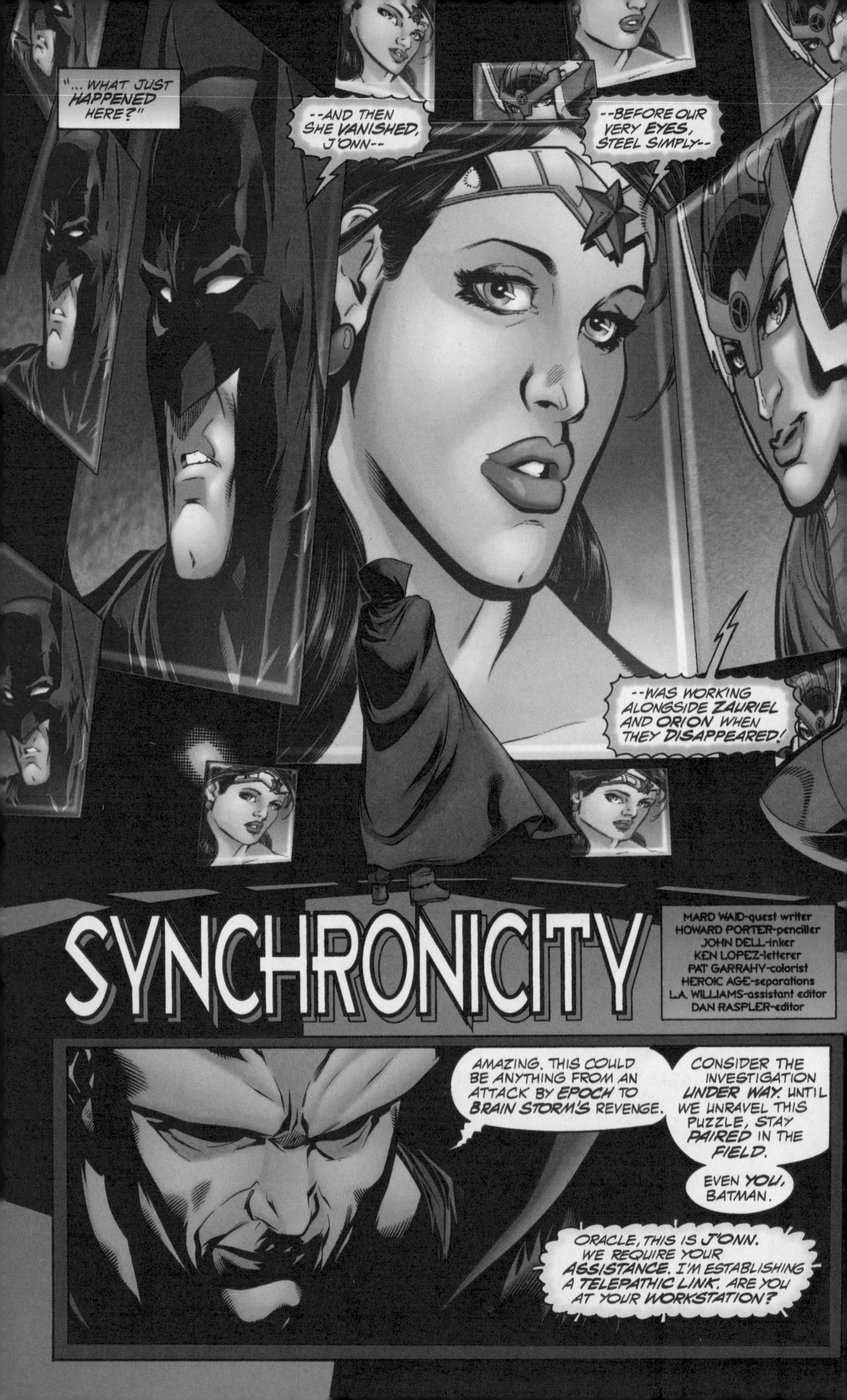
"... WHAT JUST HAPPENED HERE?"
--AND THEN SHE VANISHED, J'ONN--
--BEFORE OUR VERY EYES, STEEL SIMPLY--
--WAS WORKING ALONGSIDE ZAURIEL AND ORION WHEN THEY DISAPPEARED!
SYNCHRONICITY
MARD WAID-guest writer
HOWARD PORTER-penciller
JOHN DELL-inker
KEN LOPEZ-letterer
PAT GARRAHY-colorist
HEROIC AGE-separations
L.A. WILLIAMS-assistant editor
DAN RASPLER-editor
AMAZING. THIS COULD BE ANYTHING FROM AN ATTACK BY EPOCH TO BRAIN STORM'S REVENGE.
CONSIDER THE INVESTIGATION UNDER WAY. UNTIL WE UNRAVEL THIS PUZZLE, STAY PAIRED IN THE FIELD.
EVEN YOU, BATMAN.
ORACLE, THIS IS J'ONN. WE REQUIRE YOUR ASSISTANCE. I'M ESTABLISHING A TELEPATHIC LINK. ARE YOU AT YOUR WORKSTATION?

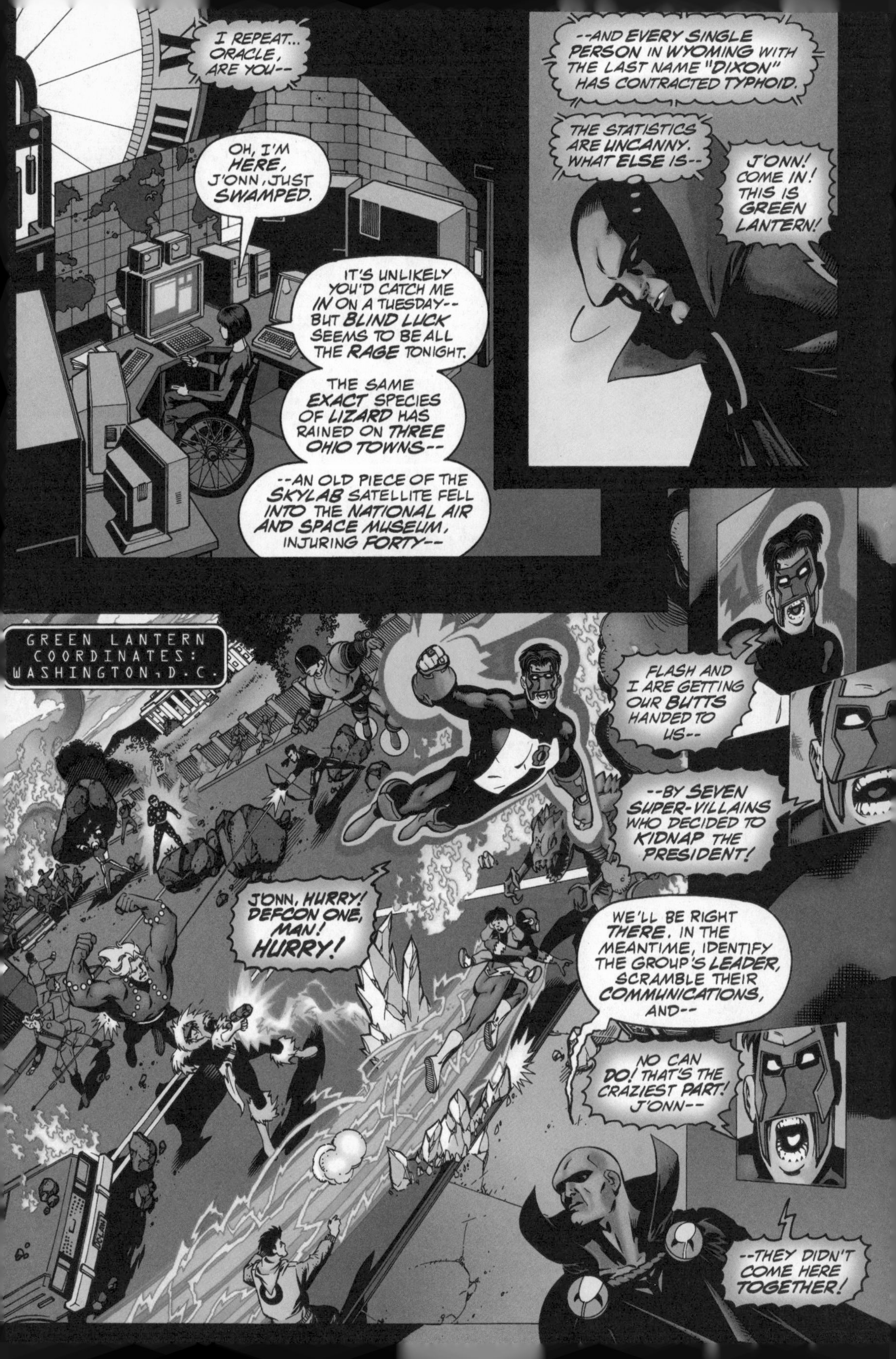
I REPEAT... ORACLE, ARE YOU--
OH, I'M HERE, J'ONN, JUST SWAMPED.
IT'S UNLIKELY YOU'D CATCH ME IN ON A TUESDAY-- BUT BLIND LUCK SEEMS TO BE ALL THE RAGE TONIGHT.
THE SAME EXACT SPECIES OF LIZARD HAS RAINED ON THREE OHIO TOWNS--
--AN OLD PIECE OF THE SKYLAB SATELLITE FELL INTO THE NATIONAL AIR AND SPACE MUSEUM, INJURING FORTY--
--AND EVERY SINGLE PERSON IN WYOMING WITH THE LAST NAME "DIXON" HAS CONTRACTED TYPHOID.
THE STATISTICS ARE UNCANNY. WHAT ELSE IS--
J'ONN! COME IN! THIS IS GREEN LANTERN!
GREEN LANTERN COORDINATES: WASHINGTON, D.C.
FLASH AND I ARE GETTING OUR BUTTS HANDED TO US--
--BY SEVEN SUPER-VILLAINS WHO DECIDED TO KIDNAP THE PRESIDENT!
J'ONN, HURRY! DEFCON ONE, MAN! HURRY!
WE'LL BE RIGHT THERE. IN THE MEANTIME, IDENTIFY THE GROUP'S LEADER, SCRAMBLE THEIR COMMUNICATIONS, AND--
NO CAN DO! THAT'S THE CRAZIEST PART! J'ONN--
--THEY DIDN'T COME HERE TOGETHER!

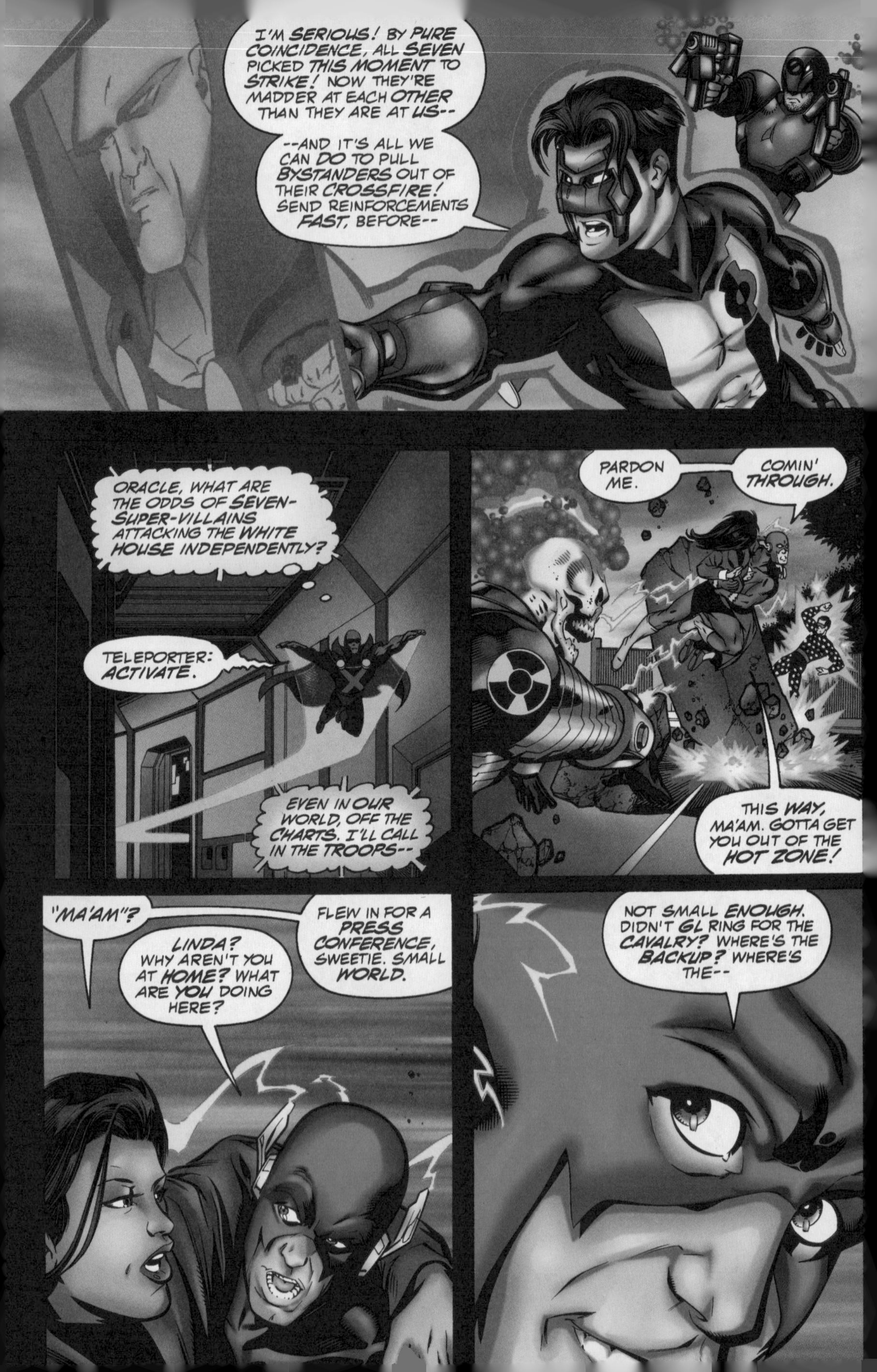
I'M SERIOUS! BY PURE COINCIDENCE, ALL SEVEN PICKED THIS MOMENT TO STRIKE! NOW THEY'RE MADDER AT EACH OTHER THAN THEY ARE AT US--
--AND IT'S ALL WE CAN DO TO PULL BYSTANDERS OUT OF THEIR CROSSFIRE! SEND REINFORCEMENTS FAST, BEFORE--
ORACLE, WHAT ARE THE ODDS OF SEVEN-SUPER-VILLAINS ATTACKING THE WHITE HOUSE INDEPENDENTLY?
TELEPORTER: ACTIVATE.
EVEN IN OUR WORLD, OFF THE CHARTS. I'LL CALL IN THE TROOPS--
PARDON ME.
COMIN' THROUGH.
THIS WAY, MA'AM. GOTTA GET YOU OUT OF THE HOT ZONE!
"MA'AM"?
LINDA? WHY AREN'T YOU AT HOME? WHAT ARE YOU DOING HERE?
FLEW IN FOR A PRESS CONFERENCE, SWEETIE. SMALL WORLD.
NOT SMALL ENOUGH. DIDN'T GL RING FOR THE CAVALRY? WHERE'S THE BACKUP? WHERE'S THE--

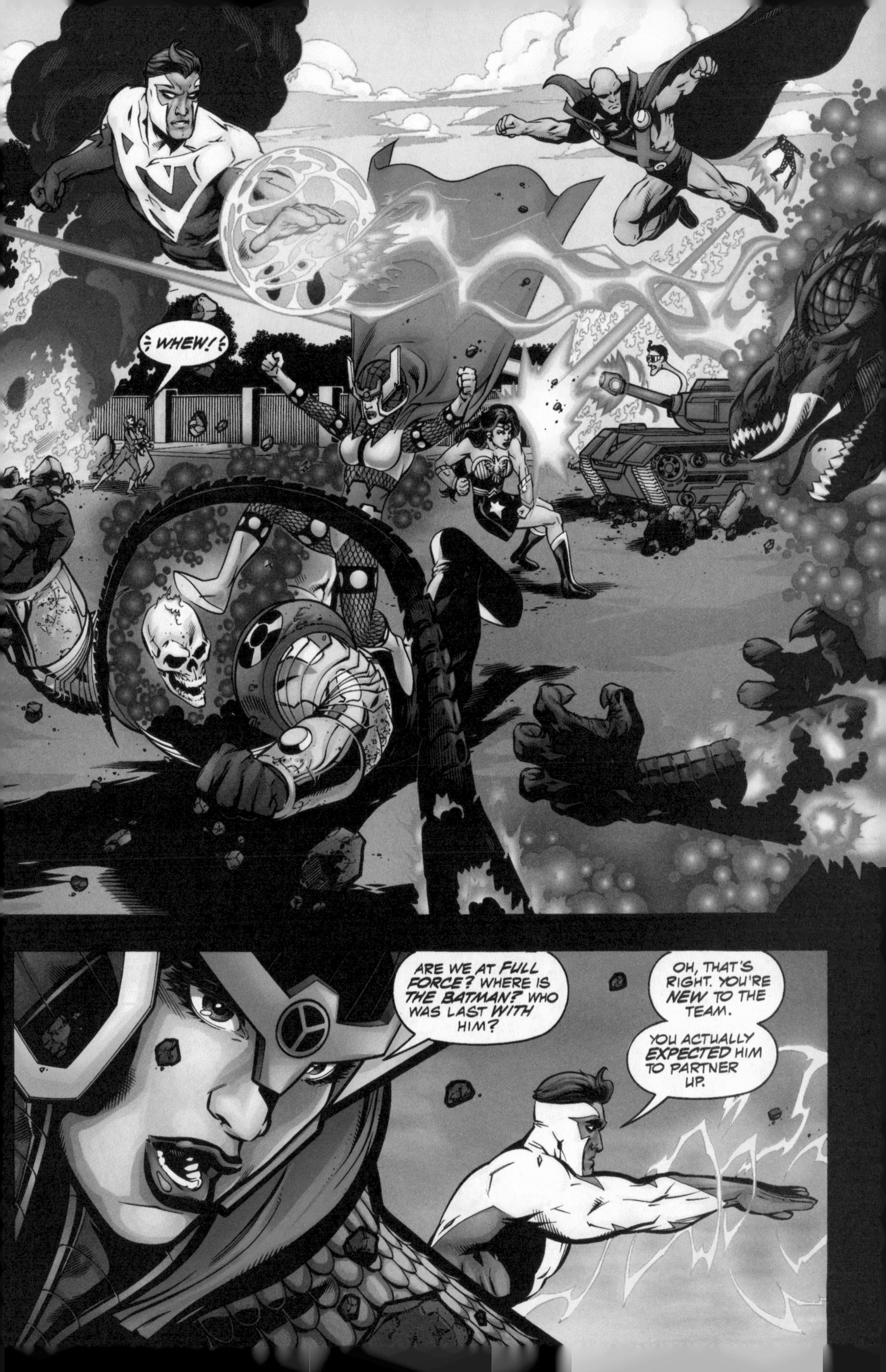
WHEW!
ARE WE AT FULL FORCE? WHERE IS THE BATMAN? WHO WAS LAST WITH HIM?
OH, THAT'S RIGHT. YOU'RE NEW TO THE TEAM.
YOU ACTUALLY EXPECTED HIM TO PARTNER UP.

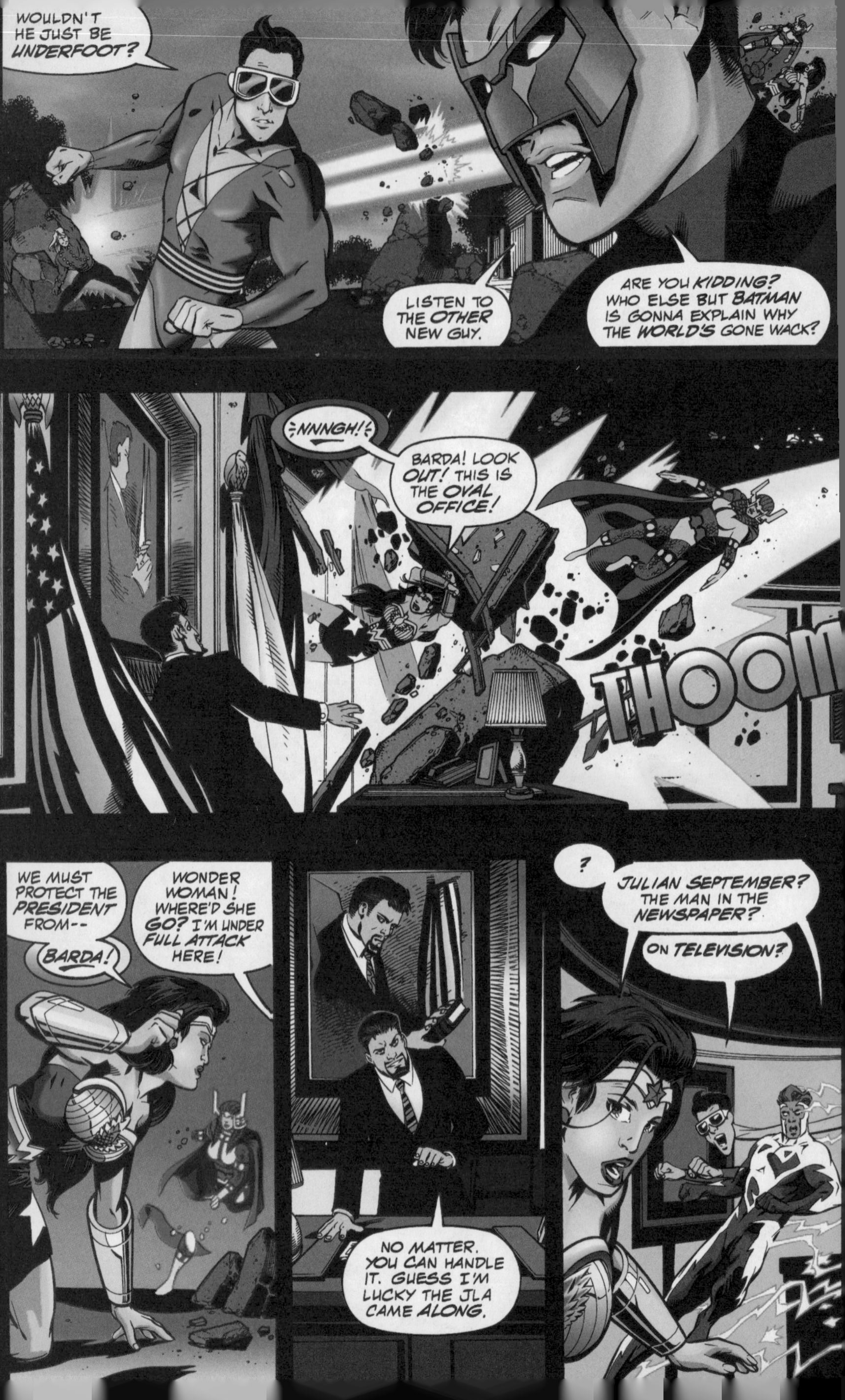
WOULDN'T HE JUST BE UNDERFOOT?
LISTEN TO THE OTHER NEW GUY.
ARE YOU KIDDING? WHO ELSE BUT BATMAN IS GONNA EXPLAIN WHY THE WORLD'S GONE WACK?
NNNGH!
BARDA! LOOK OUT! THIS IS THE OVAL OFFICE!
THOOM
WE MUST PROTECT THE PRESIDENT FROM--
BARDA!
WONDER WOMAN! WHERE'D SHE GO? I'M UNDER FULL ATTACK HERE!
NO MATTER. YOU CAN HANDLE IT. GUESS I'M LUCKY THE JLA CAME ALONG.
?
JULIAN SEPTEMBER? THE MAN IN THE NEWSPAPER?
ON TELEVISION?

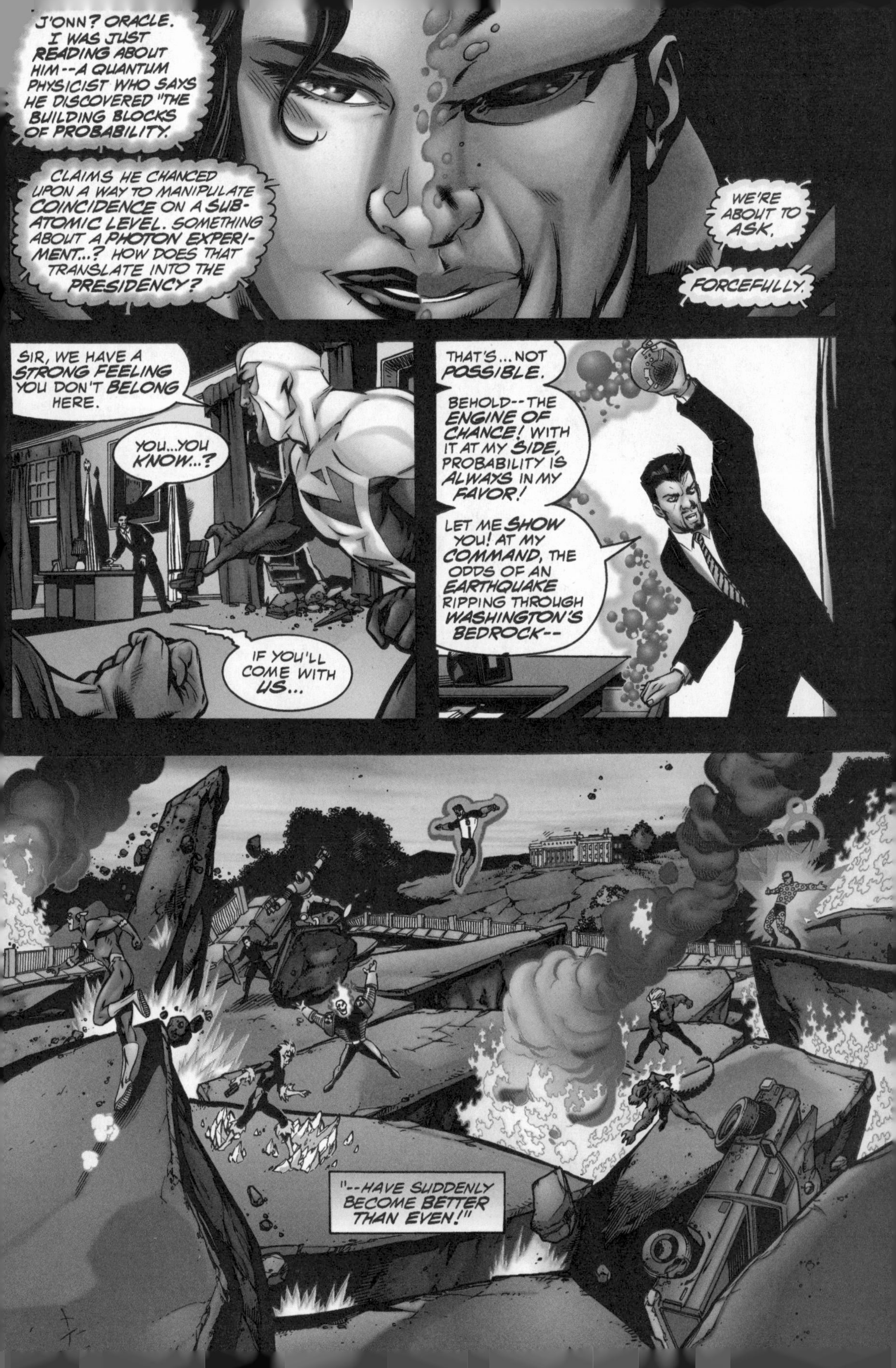
J'ONN? ORACLE. I WAS JUST READING ABOUT HIM--A QUANTUM PHYSICIST WHO SAYS HE DISCOVERED "THE BUILDING BLOCKS OF PROBABILITY.
CLAIMS HE CHANCED UPON A WAY TO MANIPULATE COINCIDENCE ON A SUB-ATOMIC LEVEL. SOMETHING ABOUT A PHOTON EXPERIMENT...? HOW DOES THAT TRANSLATE INTO THE PRESIDENCY?
WE'RE ABOUT TO ASK.
FORCEFULLY.
SIR, WE HAVE A STRONG FEELING YOU DON'T BELONG HERE.
YOU...YOU KNOW...?
IF YOU'LL COME WITH US...
THAT'S...NOT POSSIBLE.
BEHOLD--THE ENGINE OF CHANCE! WITH IT AT MY SIDE, PROBABILITY IS ALWAYS IN MY FAVOR!
LET ME SHOW YOU! AT MY COMMAND, THE ODDS OF AN EARTHQUAKE RIPPING THROUGH WASHINGTON'S BEDROCK--
"--HAVE SUDDENLY BECOME BETTER THAN EVEN!"

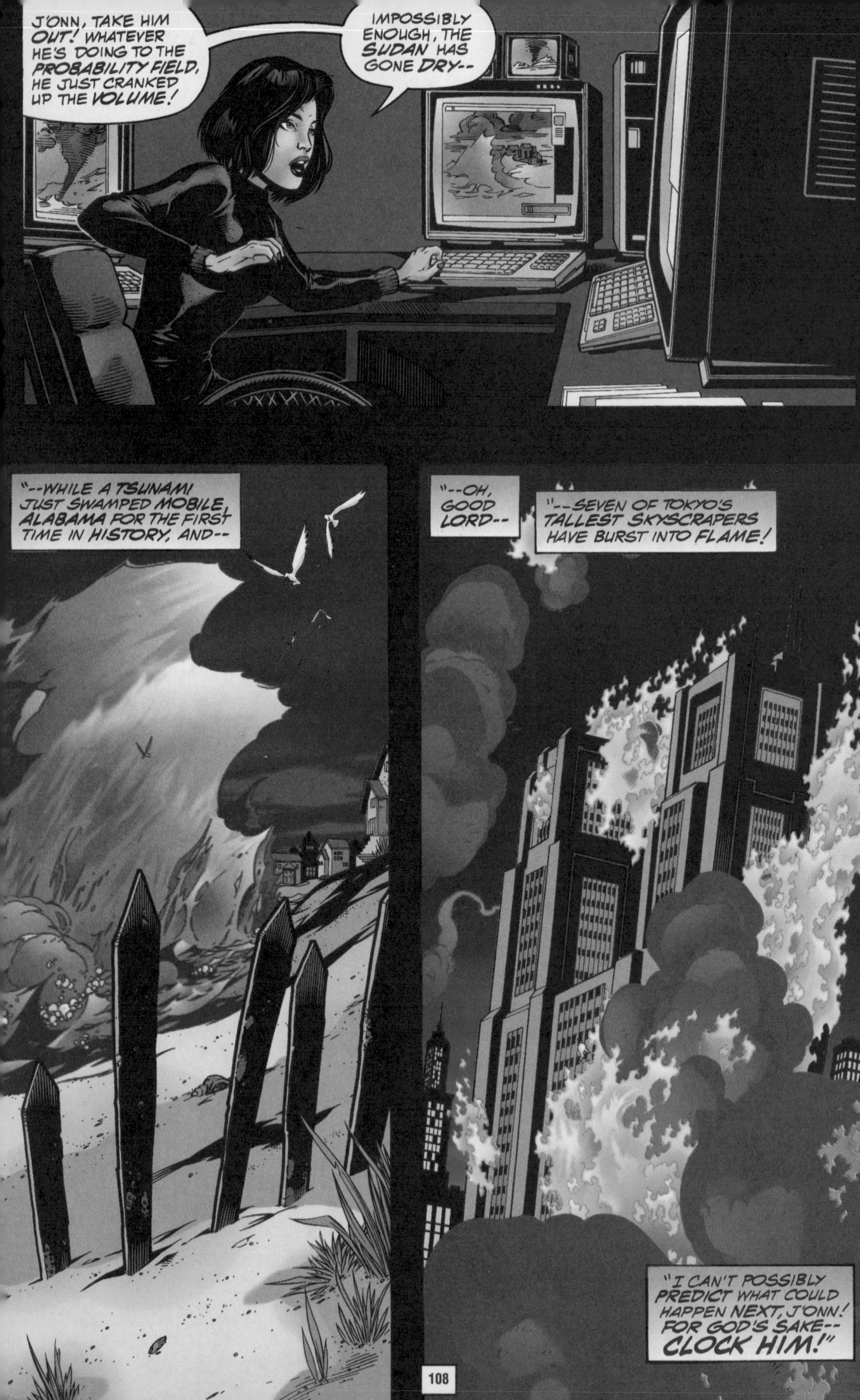
J'ONN, TAKE HIM OUT! WHATEVER HE'S DOING TO THE PROBABILITY FIELD, HE JUST CRANKED UP THE VOLUME!
IMPOSSIBLY ENOUGH, THE SUDAN HAS GONE DRY--
"--WHILE A TSUNAMI JUST SWAMPED MOBILE, ALABAMA FOR THE FIRST TIME IN HISTORY, AND--
"--OH, GOOD LORD--
"--SEVEN OF TOKYO'S TALLEST SKYSCRAPERS HAVE BURST INTO FLAME!
"I CAN'T POSSIBLY PREDICT WHAT COULD HAPPEN NEXT, J'ONN! FOR GOD'S SAKE-- CLOCK HIM!"

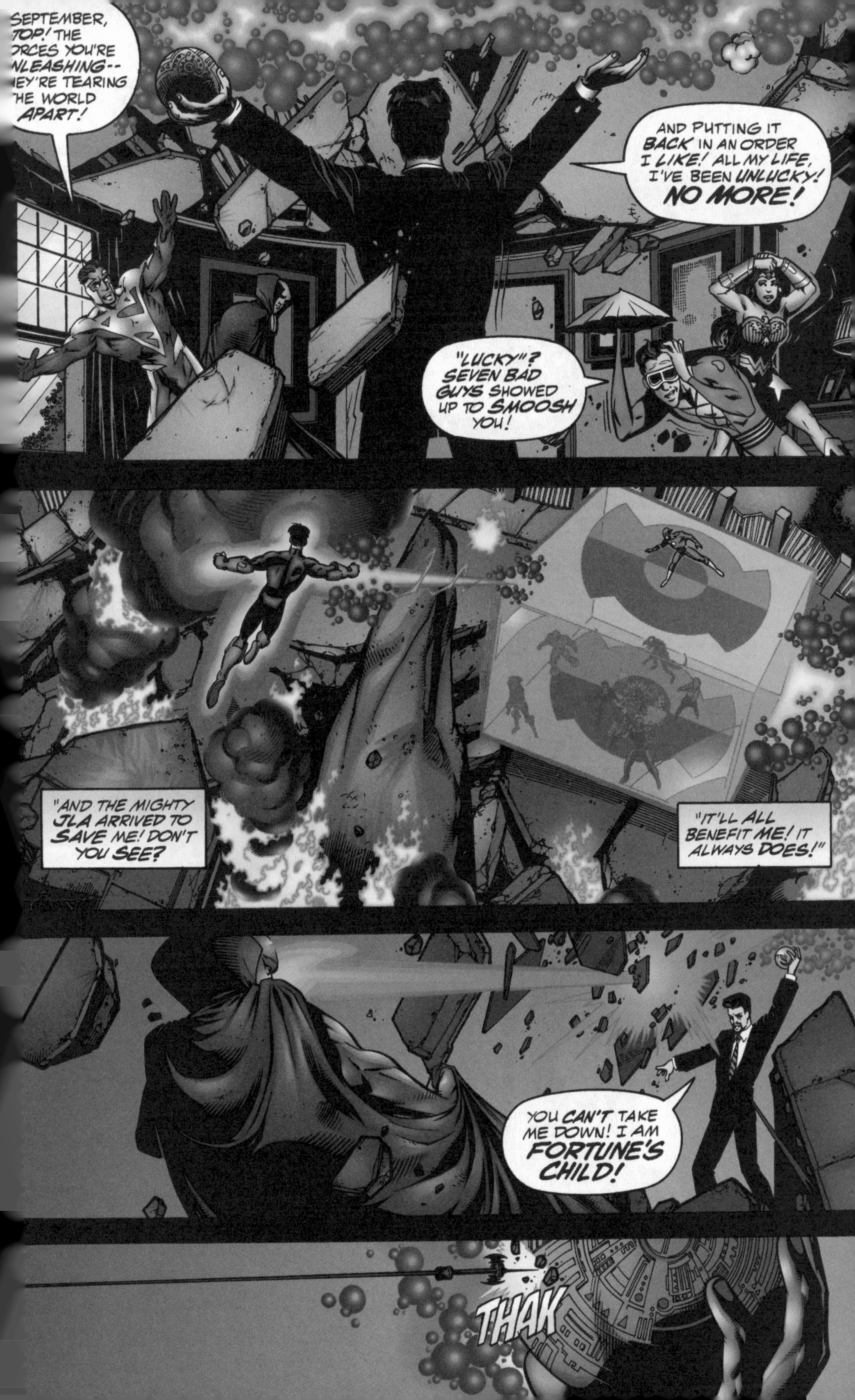
SEPTEMBER, STOP! THE FORCES YOU'RE UNLEASHING-- THEY'RE TEARING THE WORLD APART!
AND PUTTING IT BACK IN AN ORDER I LIKE! ALL MY LIFE, I'VE BEEN UNLUCKY! NO MORE!
"LUCKY"? SEVEN BAD GUYS SHOWED UP TO SMOOSH YOU!
"AND THE MIGHTY JLA ARRIVED TO SAVE ME! DON'T YOU SEE?
"IT'LL ALL BENEFIT ME! IT ALWAYS DOES!"
YOU CAN'T TAKE ME DOWN! I AM FORTUNE'S CHILD!
THAK

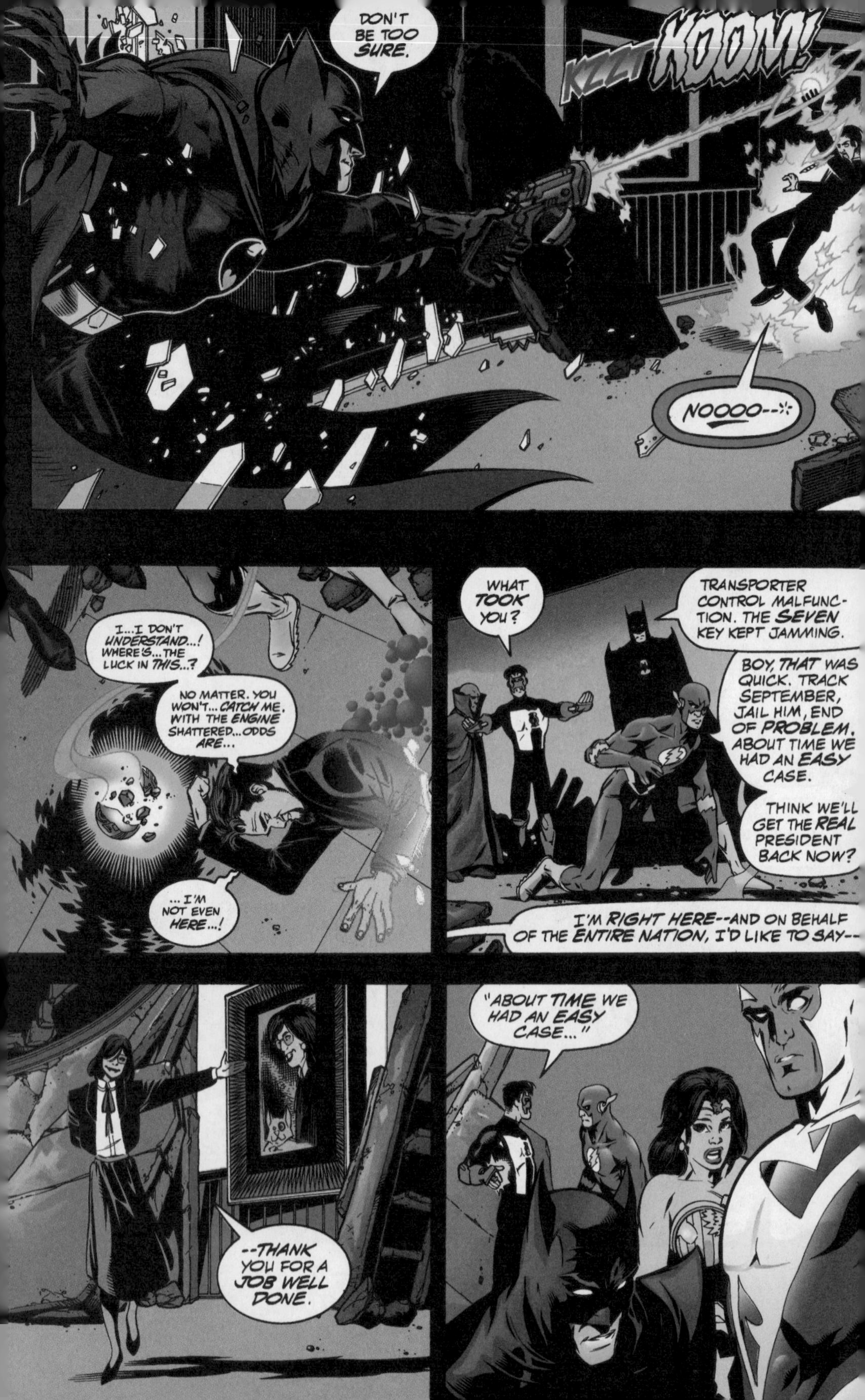
DON'T BE TOO SURE.
KZZZT KOOM!
NOOOO--
I...I DON'T UNDERSTAND...! WHERE'S...THE LUCK IN THIS...?
NO MATTER. YOU WON'T...CATCH ME. WITH THE ENGINE SHATTERED...ODDS ARE...
... I'M NOT EVEN HERE...!
WHAT TOOK YOU?
TRANSPORTER CONTROL MALFUNCTION. THE SEVEN KEY KEPT JAMMING.
BOY, THAT WAS QUICK. TRACK SEPTEMBER, JAIL HIM, END OF PROBLEM. ABOUT TIME WE HAD AN EASY CASE.
THINK WE'LL GET THE REAL PRESIDENT BACK NOW?
I'M RIGHT HERE--AND ON BEHALF OF THE ENTIRE NATION, I'D LIKE TO SAY--
--THANK YOU FOR A JOB WELL DONE.
"ABOUT TIME WE HAD AN EASY CASE..."

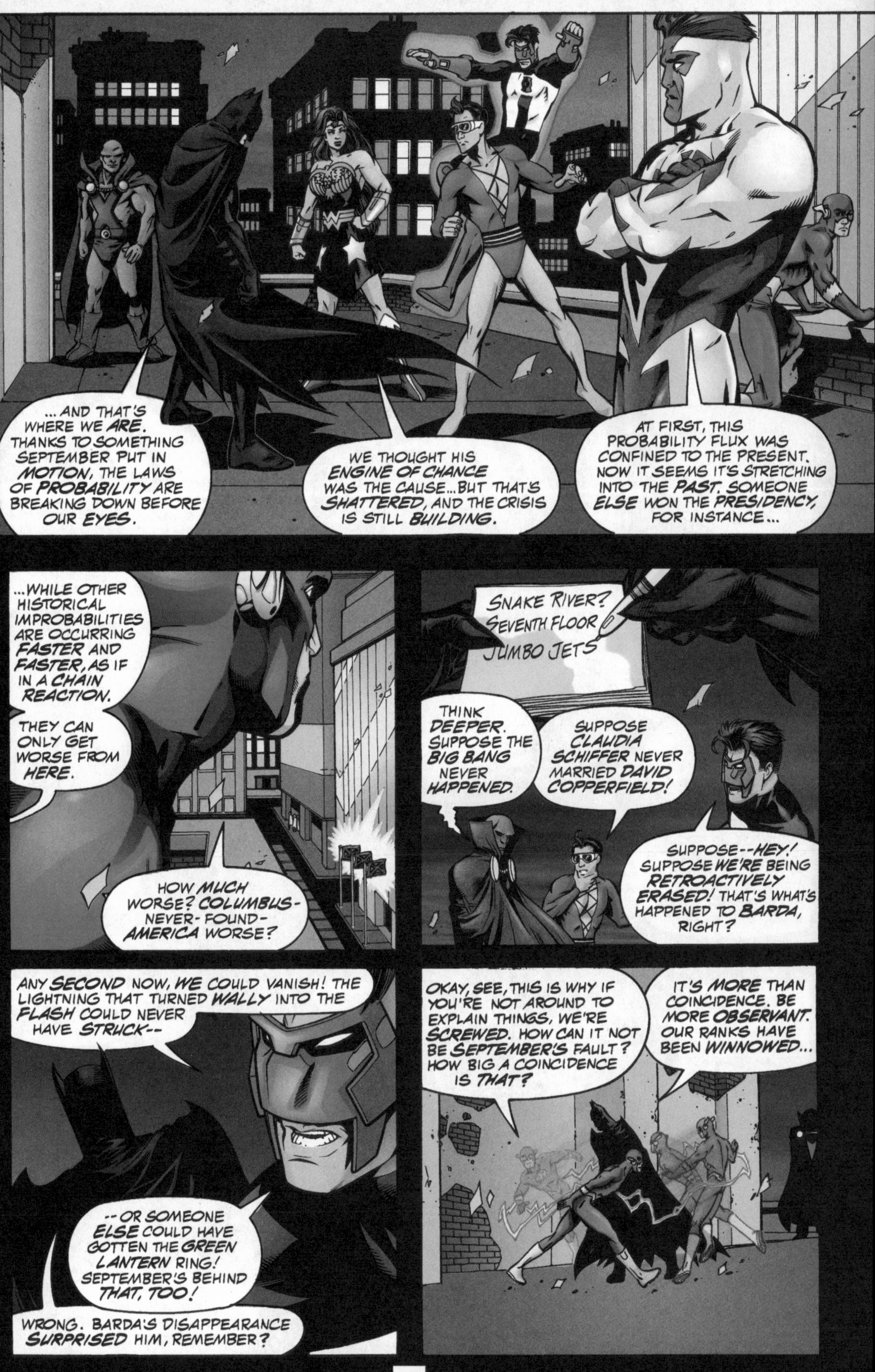

...AND THAT'S WHERE WE ARE. THANKS TO SOMETHING SEPTEMBER PUT IN MOTION, THE LAWS OF PROBABILITY ARE BREAKING DOWN BEFORE OUR EYES.
WE THOUGHT HIS ENGINE OF CHANCE WAS THE CAUSE...BUT THAT'S SHATTERED, AND THE CRISIS IS STILL BUILDING.
AT FIRST, THIS PROBABILITY FLUX WAS CONFINED TO THE PRESENT. NOW IT SEEMS IT'S STRETCHING INTO THE PAST. SOMEONE ELSE WON THE PRESIDENCY, FOR INSTANCE...
...WHILE OTHER HISTORICAL IMPROBABILITIES ARE OCCURRING FASTER AND FASTER, AS IF IN A CHAIN REACTION.
THEY CAN ONLY GET WORSE FROM HERE.
HOW MUCH WORSE? COLUMBUS-NEVER-FOUND-AMERICA WORSE?
SNAKE RIVER? SEVENTH FLOOR JUMBO JETS
THINK DEEPER. SUPPOSE THE BIG BANG NEVER HAPPENED.
SUPPOSE CLAUDIA SCHIFFER NEVER MARRIED DAVID COPPERFIELD!
SUPPOSE--HEY! SUPPOSE WE'RE BEING RETROACTIVELY ERASED! THAT'S WHAT'S HAPPENED TO BARDA, RIGHT?
ANY SECOND NOW, WE COULD VANISH! THE LIGHTNING THAT TURNED WALLY INTO THE FLASH COULD NEVER HAVE STRUCK--
--OR SOMEONE ELSE COULD HAVE GOTTEN THE GREEN LANTERN RING! SEPTEMBER'S BEHIND THAT, TOO!
WRONG. BARDA'S DISAPPEARANCE SURPRISED HIM, REMEMBER?
OKAY, SEE, THIS IS WHY IF YOU'RE NOT AROUND TO EXPLAIN THINGS, WE'RE SCREWED. HOW CAN IT NOT BE SEPTEMBER'S FAULT? HOW BIG A COINCIDENCE IS THAT?
IT'S MORE THAN COINCIDENCE. BE MORE OBSERVANT. OUR RANKS HAVE BEEN WINNOWED...

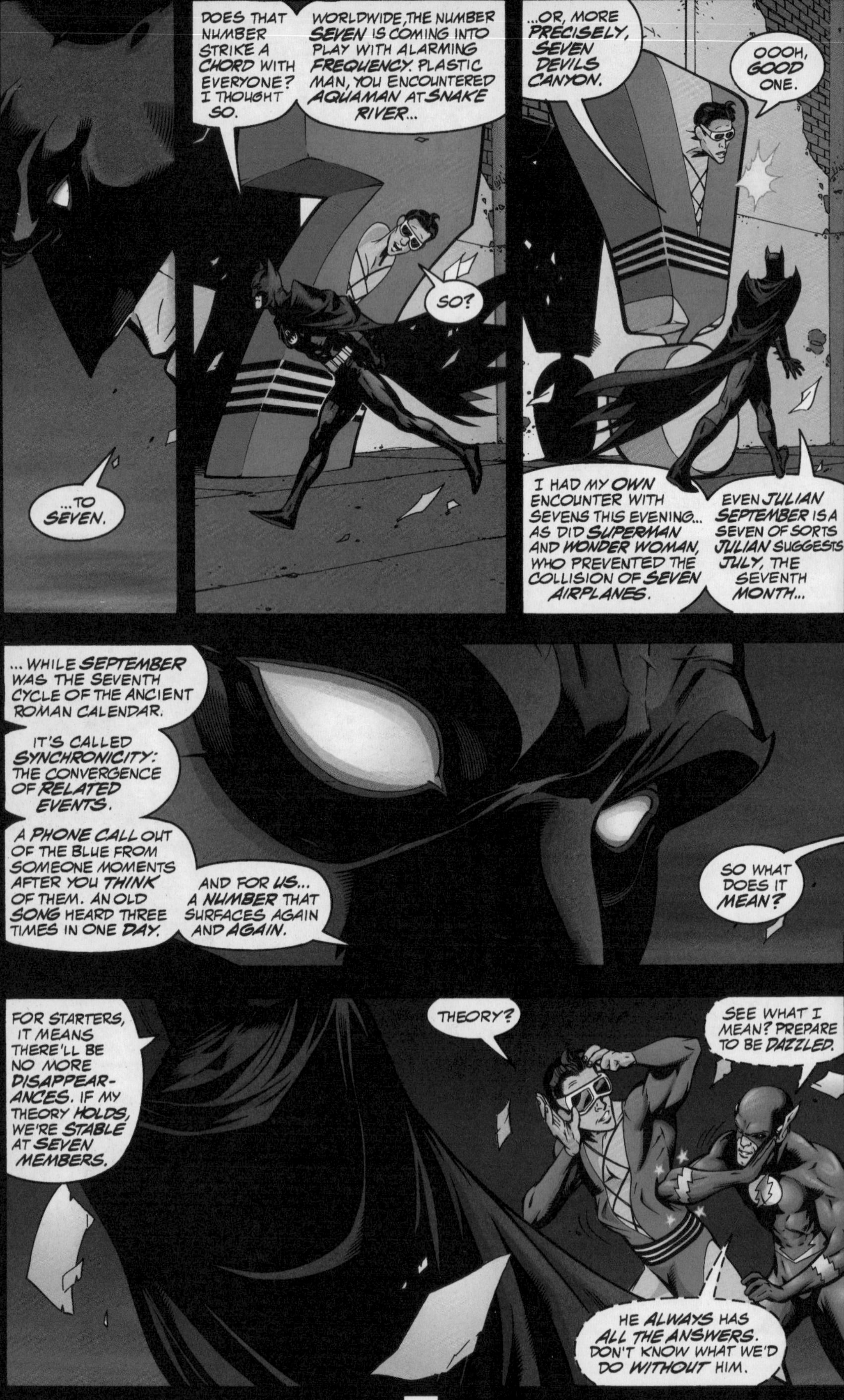

...TO SEVEN.
DOES THAT NUMBER STRIKE A CHORD WITH EVERYONE? I THOUGHT SO.
WORLDWIDE, THE NUMBER SEVEN IS COMING INTO PLAY WITH ALARMING FREQUENCY. PLASTIC MAN, YOU ENCOUNTERED AQUAMAN AT SNAKE RIVER...
SO?
...OR, MORE PRECISELY, SEVEN DEVILS CANYON.
OOOH, GOOD ONE.
I HAD MY OWN ENCOUNTER WITH SEVENS THIS EVENING... AS DID SUPERMAN AND WONDER WOMAN, WHO PREVENTED THE COLLISION OF SEVEN AIRPLANES.
EVEN JULIAN SEPTEMBER IS A SEVEN OF SORTS. JULIAN SUGGESTS JULY, THE SEVENTH MONTH...
...WHILE SEPTEMBER WAS THE SEVENTH CYCLE OF THE ANCIENT ROMAN CALENDAR.
IT'S CALLED SYNCHRONICITY: THE CONVERGENCE OF RELATED EVENTS.
A PHONE CALL OUT OF THE BLUE FROM SOMEONE MOMENTS AFTER YOU THINK OF THEM. AN OLD SONG HEARD THREE TIMES IN ONE DAY.
AND FOR US... A NUMBER THAT SURFACES AGAIN AND AGAIN.
SO WHAT DOES IT MEAN?
FOR STARTERS, IT MEANS THERE'LL BE NO MORE DISAPPEAR-ANCES. IF MY THEORY HOLDS, WE'RE STABLE AT SEVEN MEMBERS.
THEORY?
SEE WHAT I MEAN? PREPARE TO BE DAZZLED.
HE ALWAYS HAS ALL THE ANSWERS. DON'T KNOW WHAT WE'D DO WITHOUT HIM.

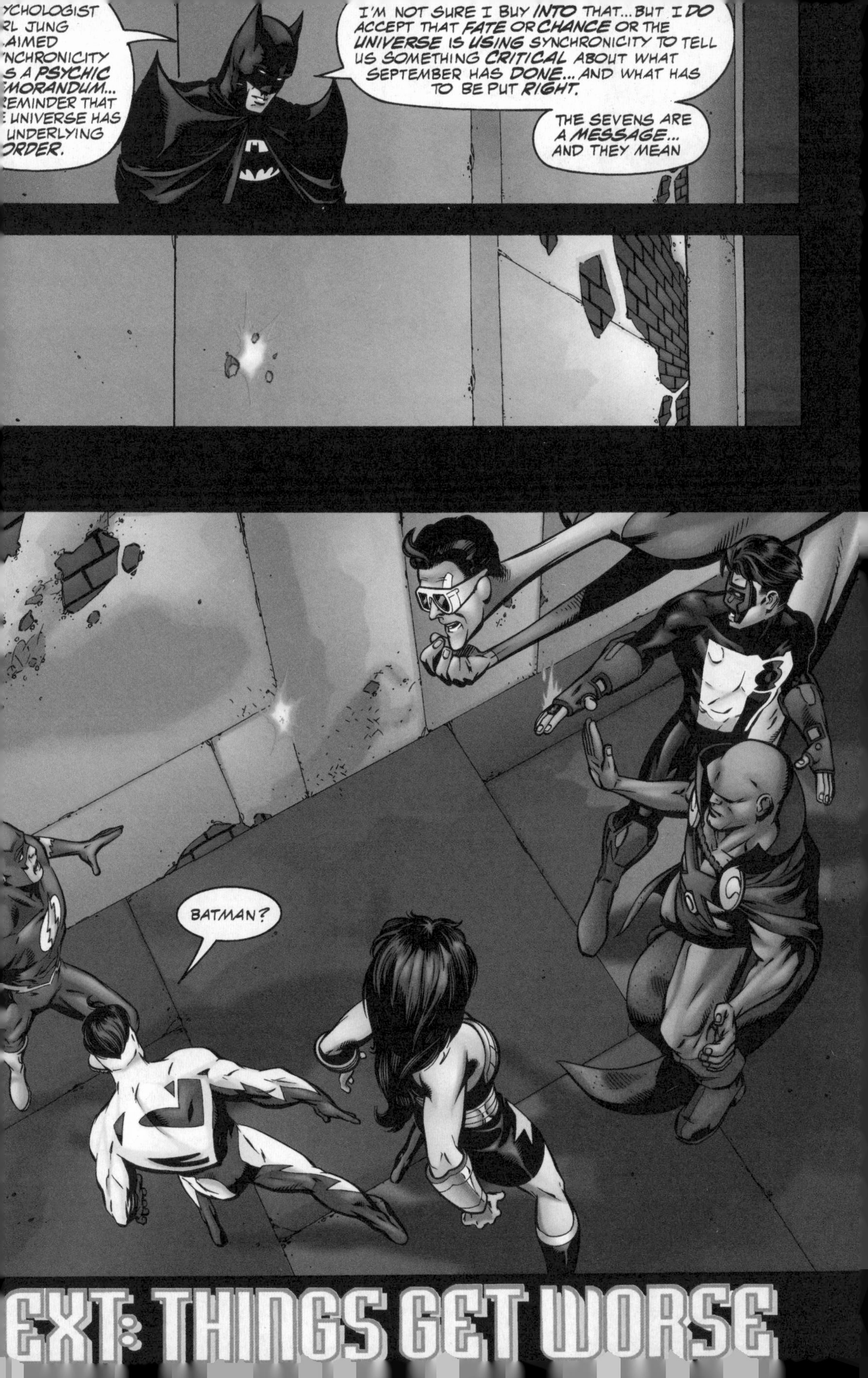
YCHOLOGIST
RL JUNG
AIMED
YNCHRONICITY
S A PSYCHIC
MORANDUM...
REMINDER THAT
E UNIVERSE HAS
UNDERLYING
ORDER.
I'M NOT SURE I BUY INTO THAT... BUT I DO ACCEPT THAT FATE OR CHANCE OR THE UNIVERSE IS USING SYNCHRONICITY TO TELL US SOMETHING CRITICAL ABOUT WHAT SEPTEMBER HAS DONE... AND WHAT HAS TO BE PUT RIGHT.
THE SEVENS ARE A MESSAGE... AND THEY MEAN
BATMAN?
EXT: THINGS GET WORSE

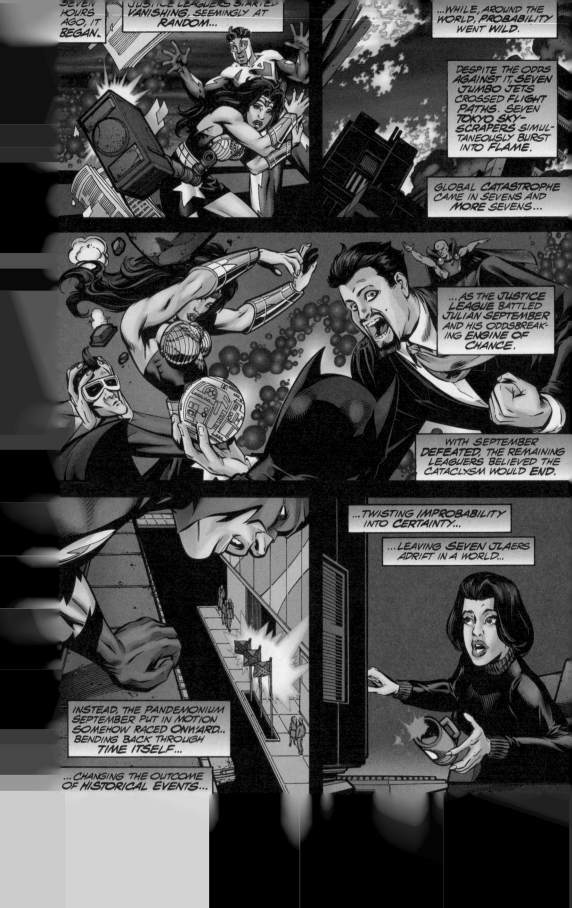

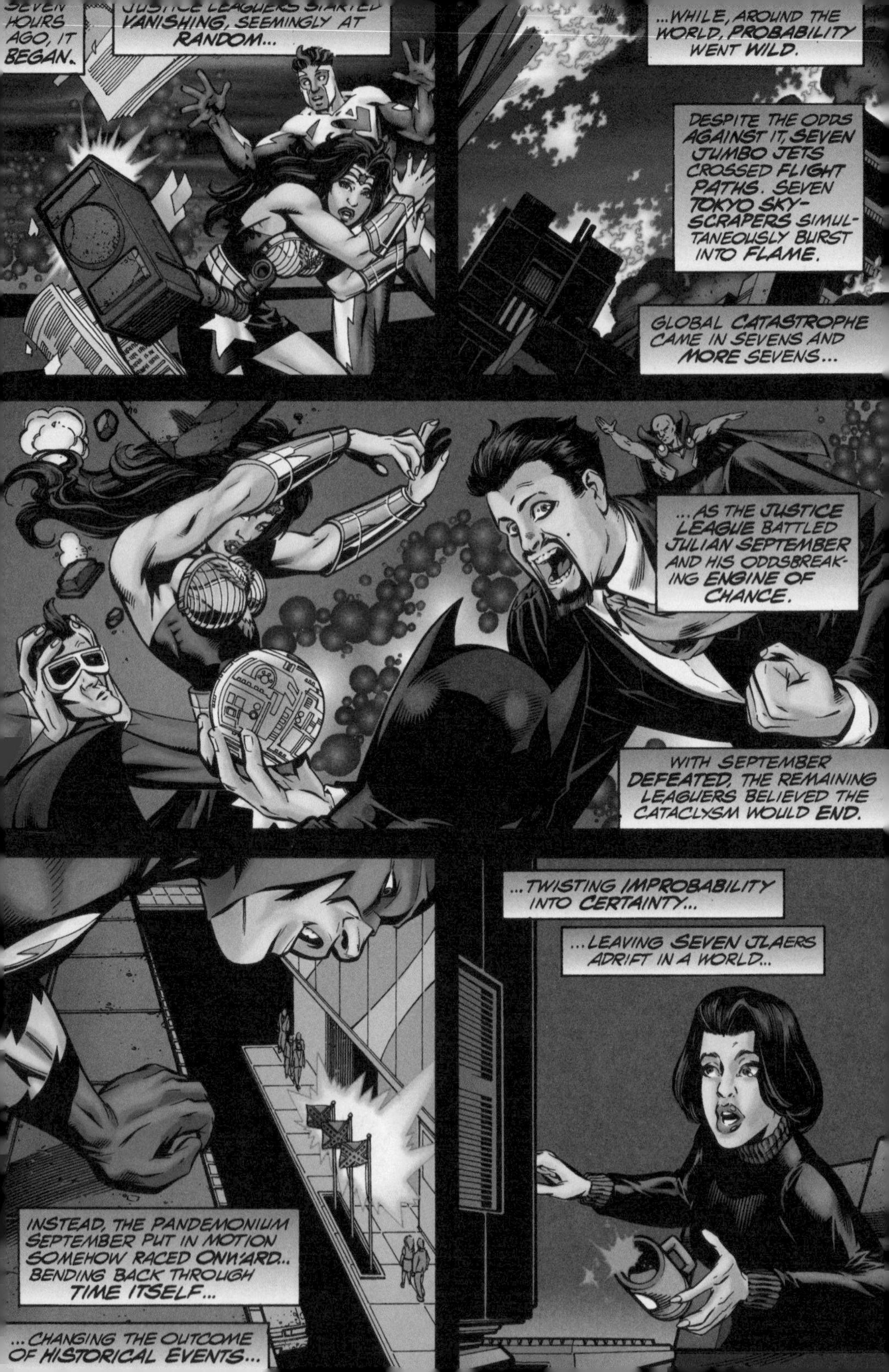
SEVEN HOURS AGO, IT BEGAN.
JUSTICE LEAGUERS STARTED VANISHING, SEEMINGLY AT RANDOM...
...WHILE, AROUND THE WORLD, PROBABILITY WENT WILD.
DESPITE THE ODDS AGAINST IT, SEVEN JUMBO JETS CROSSED FLIGHT PATHS. SEVEN TOKYO SKY-SCRAPERS SIMUL-TANEOUSLY BURST INTO FLAME.
GLOBAL CATASTROPHE CAME IN SEVENS AND MORE SEVENS...
...AS THE JUSTICE LEAGUE BATTLED JULIAN SEPTEMBER AND HIS ODDSBREAK-ING ENGINE OF CHANCE.
WITH SEPTEMBER DEFEATED, THE REMAINING LEAGUERS BELIEVED THE CATACLYSM WOULD END.
INSTEAD, THE PANDEMONIUM SEPTEMBER PUT IN MOTION SOMEHOW RACED ONWARD.. BENDING BACK THROUGH TIME ITSELF...
...CHANGING THE OUTCOME OF HISTORICAL EVENTS...
...TWISTING IMPROBABILITY INTO CERTAINTY...
...LEAVING SEVEN JLAERS ADRIFT IN A WORLD...

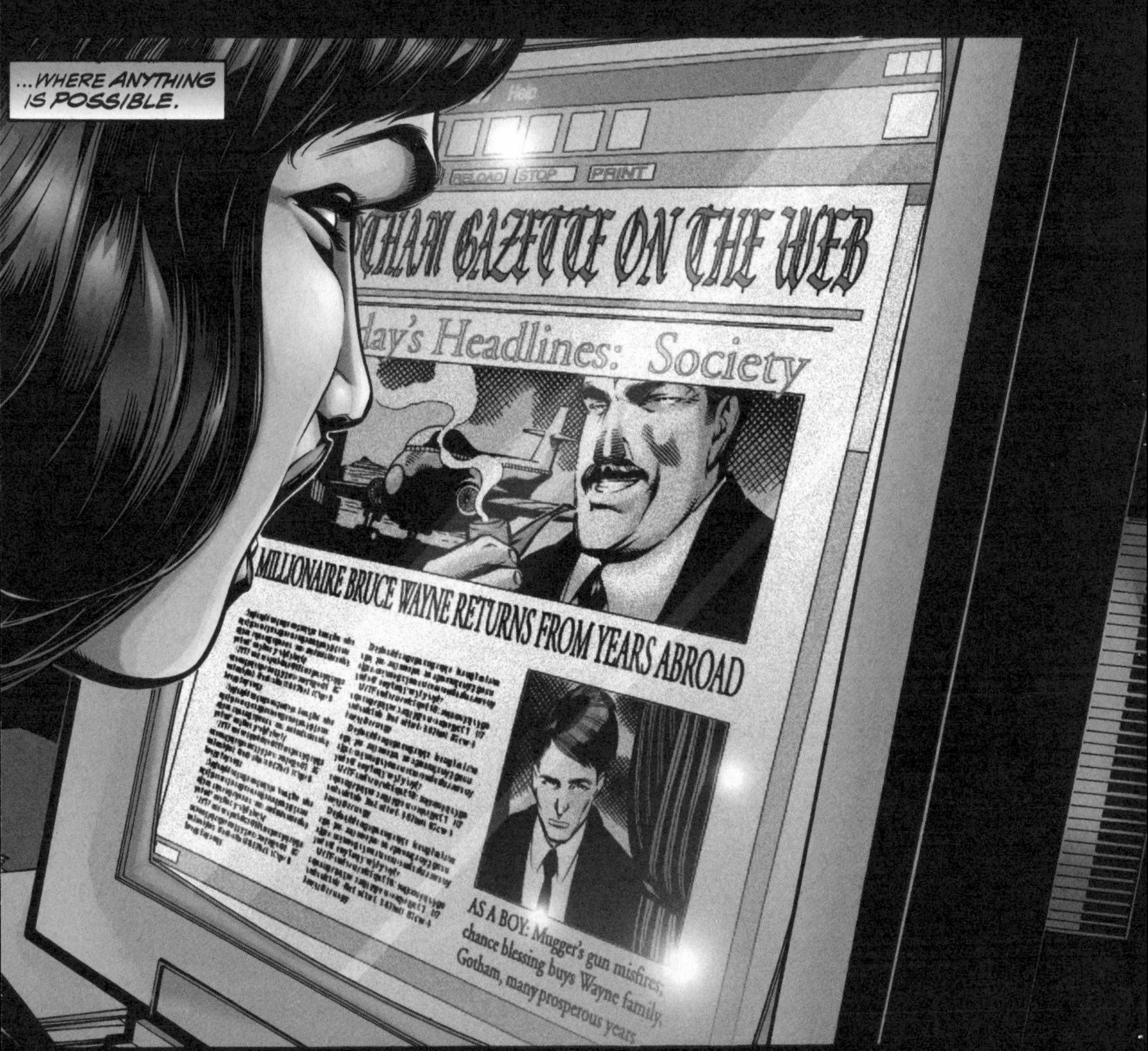
...WHERE ANYTHING IS POSSIBLE.
Help
RELOAD STOP PRINT
THAM GAZETTE ON THE WEB
day's Headlines: Society
MILLIONAIRE BRUCE WAYNE RETURNS FROM YEARS ABROAD
AS A BOY: Mugger's gun misfires; chance blessing buys Wayne family, Gotham, many prosperous years

SEVEN SOLDIERS OF PROBABILITY

MARK WAID-guest writer
HOWARD PORTER-penciller
JOHN DELL & WALDEN WONG-inkers
KEN LOPEZ-letterer
PAT GARRAHY-colorist
HEROIC AGE-separations
L.A. WILLIAMS-ass't editor
DAN RASPLER-editor

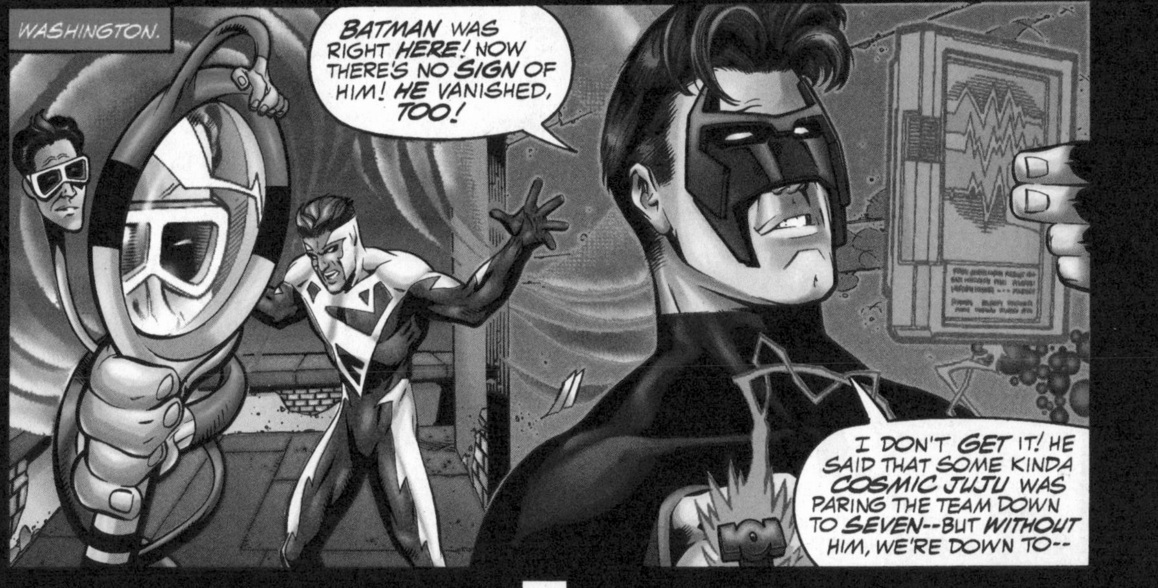
WASHINGTON.
BATMAN WAS RIGHT HERE! NOW THERE'S NO SIGN OF HIM! HE VANISHED, TOO!
I DON'T GET IT! HE SAID THAT SOME KINDA COSMIC JUJU WAS PARING THE TEAM DOWN TO SEVEN--BUT WITHOUT HIM, WE'RE DOWN TO--

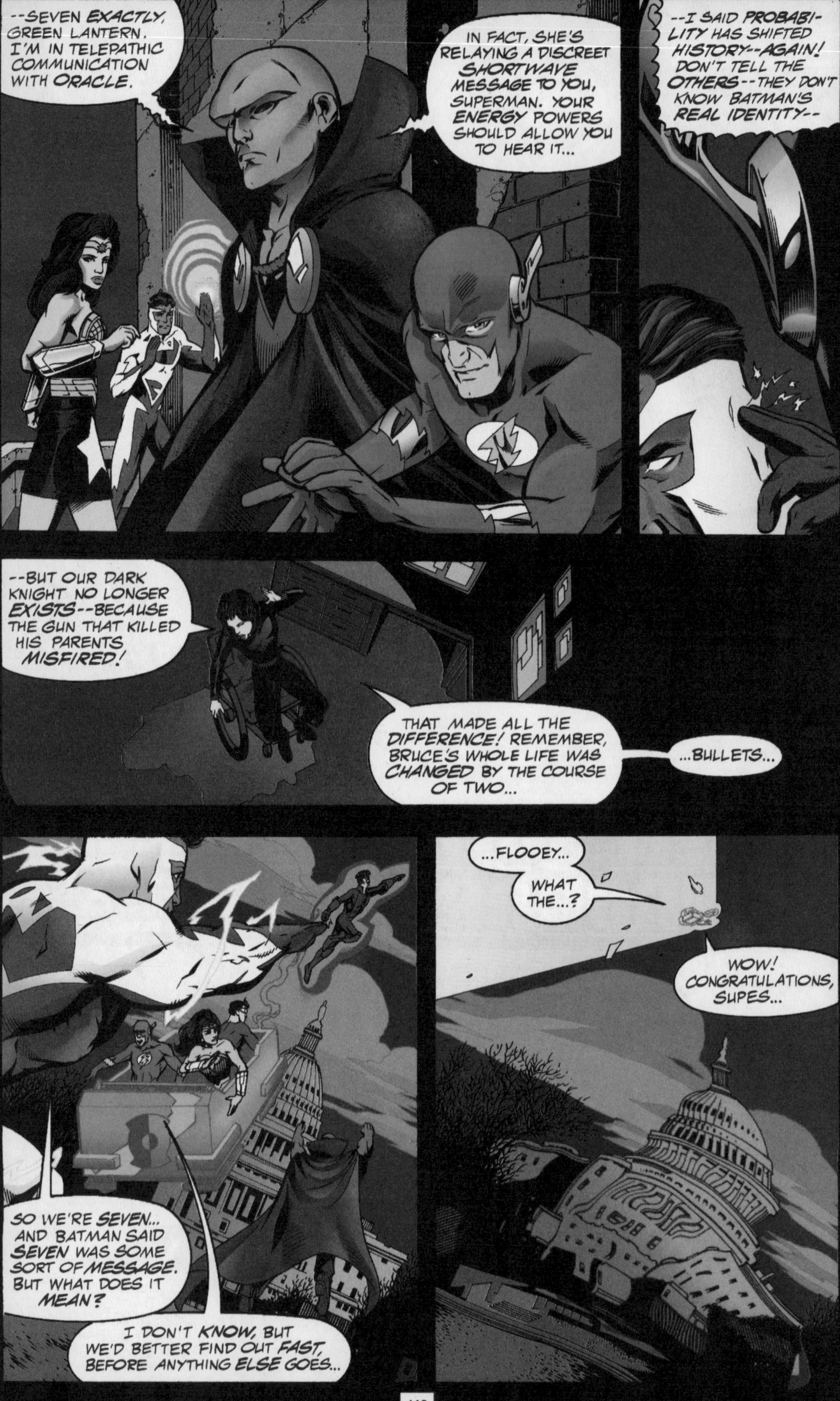
--SEVEN EXACTLY, GREEN LANTERN. I'M IN TELEPATHIC COMMUNICATION WITH ORACLE.
IN FACT, SHE'S RELAYING A DISCREET SHORTWAVE MESSAGE TO YOU, SUPERMAN. YOUR ENERGY POWERS SHOULD ALLOW YOU TO HEAR IT...
--I SAID PROBABILITY HAS SHIFTED HISTORY--AGAIN! DON'T TELL THE OTHERS--THEY DON'T KNOW BATMAN'S REAL IDENTITY--
--BUT OUR DARK KNIGHT NO LONGER EXISTS--BECAUSE THE GUN THAT KILLED HIS PARENTS MISFIRED!
THAT MADE ALL THE DIFFERENCE! REMEMBER, BRUCE'S WHOLE LIFE WAS CHANGED BY THE COURSE OF TWO...
...BULLETS...
SO WE'RE SEVEN... AND BATMAN SAID SEVEN WAS SOME SORT OF MESSAGE. BUT WHAT DOES IT MEAN?
I DON'T KNOW, BUT WE'D BETTER FIND OUT FAST, BEFORE ANYTHING ELSE GOES...
...FLOOEY...
WHAT THE...?
WOW! CONGRATULATIONS, SUPES...

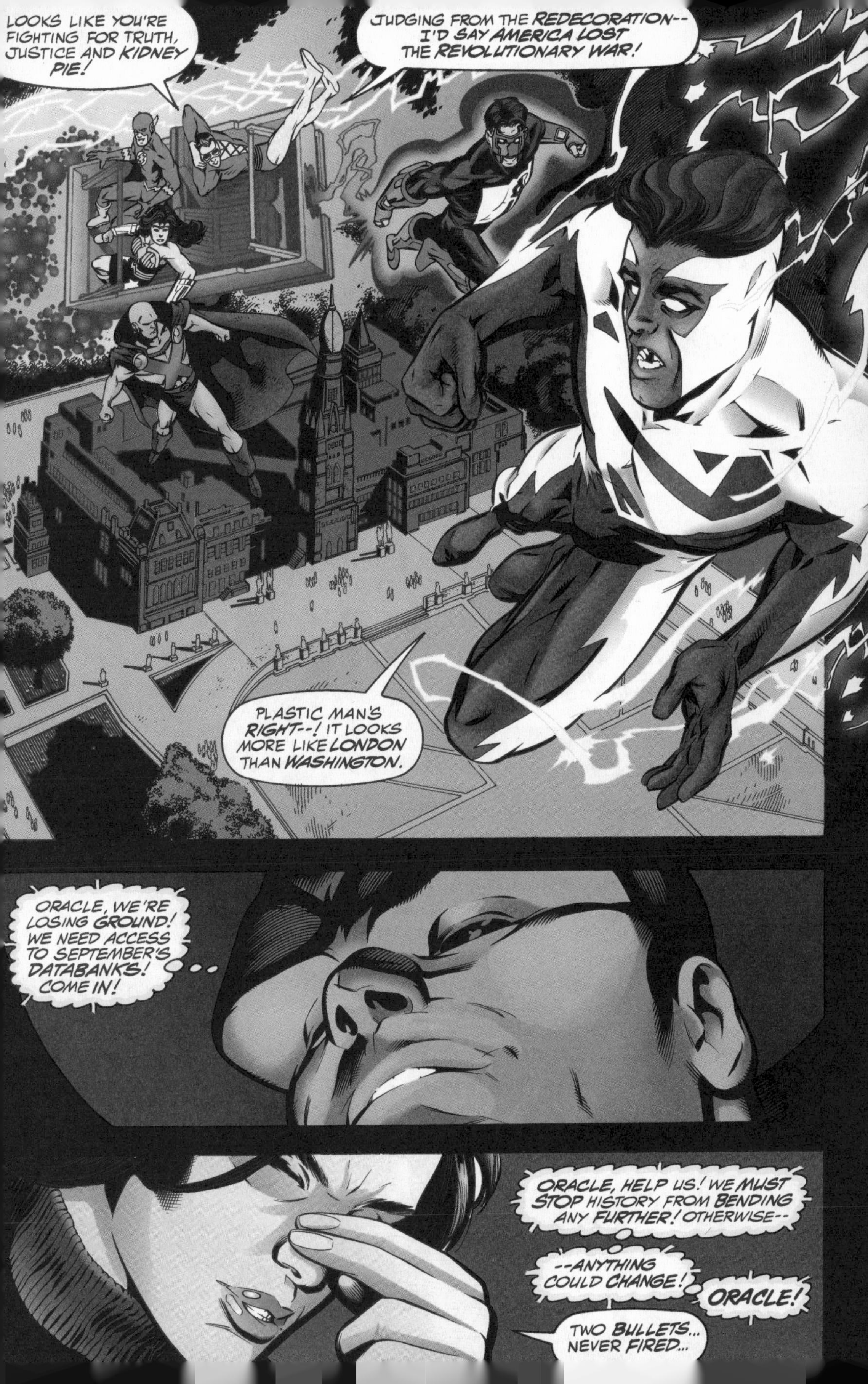
LOOKS LIKE YOU'RE FIGHTING FOR TRUTH, JUSTICE AND KIDNEY PIE!
JUDGING FROM THE REDECORATION-- I'D SAY AMERICA LOST THE REVOLUTIONARY WAR!
PLASTIC MAN'S RIGHT--! IT LOOKS MORE LIKE LONDON THAN WASHINGTON.
ORACLE, WE'RE LOSING GROUND! WE NEED ACCESS TO SEPTEMBER'S DATABANKS! COME IN!
ORACLE, HELP US! WE MUST STOP HISTORY FROM BENDING ANY FURTHER! OTHERWISE--
--ANYTHING COULD CHANGE!
ORACLE!
TWO BULLETS... NEVER FIRED...

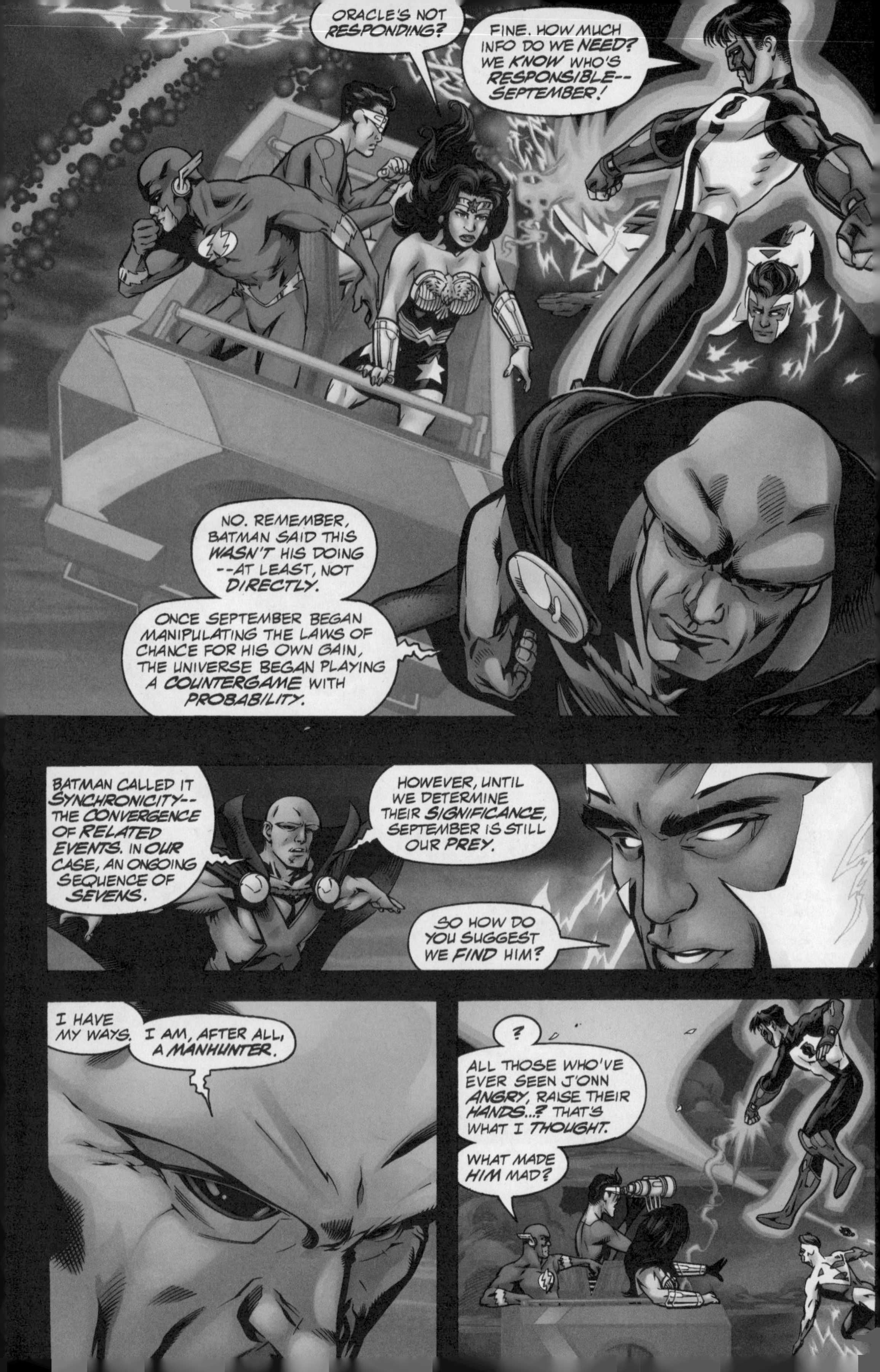

ORACLE'S NOT RESPONDING?
FINE. HOW MUCH INFO DO WE NEED? WE KNOW WHO'S RESPONSIBLE-- SEPTEMBER!
NO. REMEMBER, BATMAN SAID THIS WASN'T HIS DOING --AT LEAST, NOT DIRECTLY.
ONCE SEPTEMBER BEGAN MANIPULATING THE LAWS OF CHANCE FOR HIS OWN GAIN, THE UNIVERSE BEGAN PLAYING A COUNTERGAME WITH PROBABILITY.
BATMAN CALLED IT SYNCHRONICITY-- THE CONVERGENCE OF RELATED EVENTS. IN OUR CASE, AN ONGOING SEQUENCE OF SEVENS.
HOWEVER, UNTIL WE DETERMINE THEIR SIGNIFICANCE, SEPTEMBER IS STILL OUR PREY.
SO HOW DO YOU SUGGEST WE FIND HIM?
I HAVE MY WAYS.
I AM, AFTER ALL, A MANHUNTER.
?
ALL THOSE WHO'VE EVER SEEN J'ONN ANGRY, RAISE THEIR HANDS...? THAT'S WHAT I THOUGHT.
WHAT MADE HIM MAD?

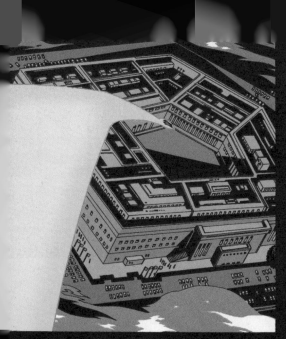

FILE
ROOM
Security
Clearance
A-1
ONLY

September, Julian
Security Clearance
Required

BLOODY COMPUTING MACHINES ARE *DOWN* AGAIN. WE'LL HAVE TO GO TO *PAPER*--

HELLO? WHO'S *THERE*? THIS IS A RESTRICTED AREA!

AS WELL IT *SHOULD* BE.

YOUR *MAJESTY*--?

GIVE ME EVERYTHING WE *HAVE* ON THIS MAN AND HIS LIKELY *WHEREABOUTS*-- IMMEDIATELY.

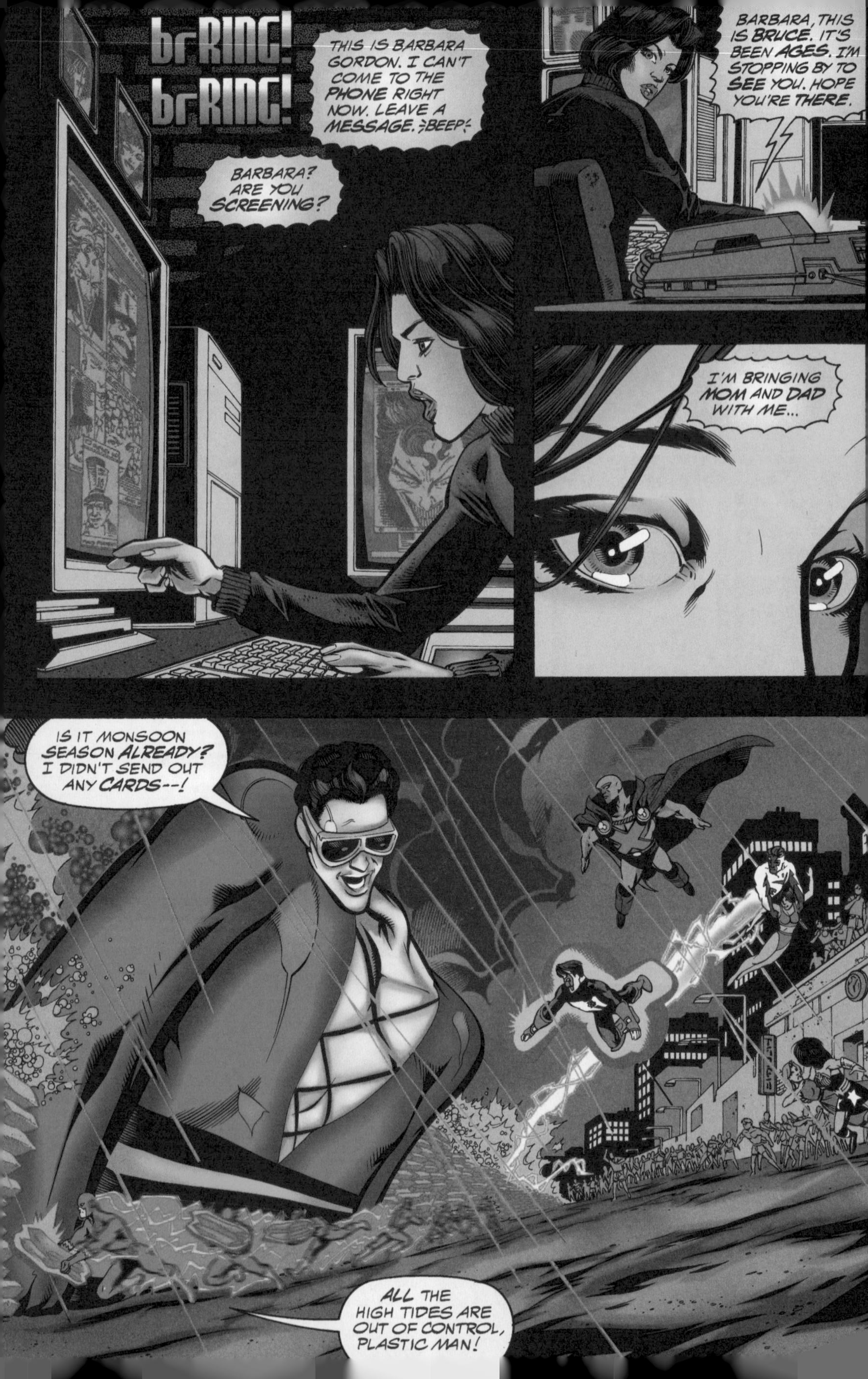
brRING! brRING!
THIS IS BARBARA GORDON. I CAN'T COME TO THE PHONE RIGHT NOW. LEAVE A MESSAGE. BEEP
BARBARA? ARE YOU SCREENING?
BARBARA, THIS IS BRUCE. IT'S BEEN AGES. I'M STOPPING BY TO SEE YOU. HOPE YOU'RE THERE.
I'M BRINGING MOM AND DAD WITH ME...
IS IT MONSOON SEASON ALREADY? I DIDN'T SEND OUT ANY CARDS--!
ALL THE HIGH TIDES ARE OUT OF CONTROL, PLASTIC MAN!

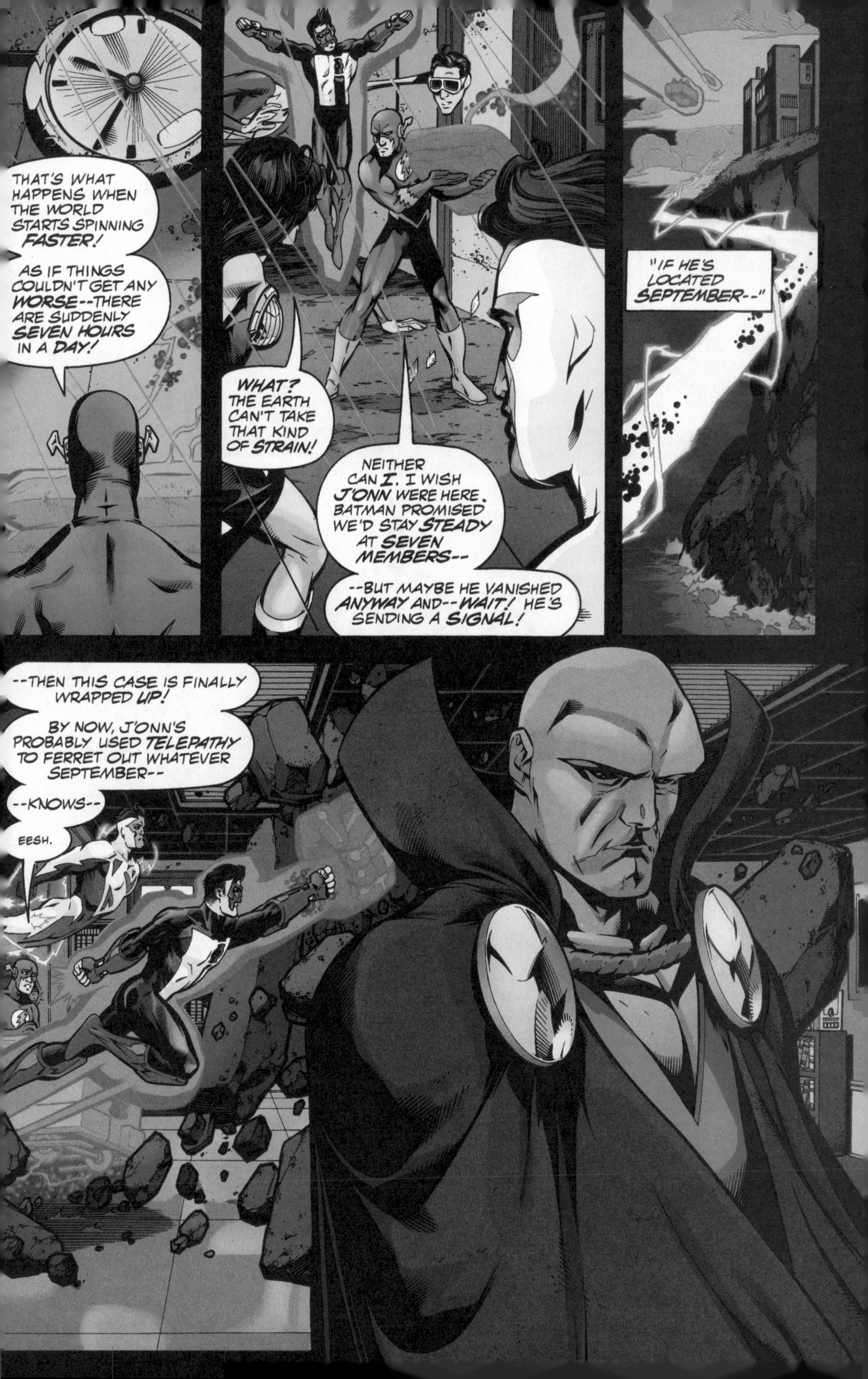
THAT'S WHAT HAPPENS WHEN THE WORLD STARTS SPINNING FASTER!
AS IF THINGS COULDN'T GET ANY WORSE--THERE ARE SUDDENLY SEVEN HOURS IN A DAY!
WHAT? THE EARTH CAN'T TAKE THAT KIND OF STRAIN!
NEITHER CAN I. I WISH J'ONN WERE HERE. BATMAN PROMISED WE'D STAY STEADY AT SEVEN MEMBERS--
--BUT MAYBE HE VANISHED ANYWAY AND--WAIT! HE'S SENDING A SIGNAL!
"IF HE'S LOCATED SEPTEMBER--"
--THEN THIS CASE IS FINALLY WRAPPED UP!
BY NOW, J'ONN'S PROBABLY USED TELEPATHY TO FERRET OUT WHATEVER SEPTEMBER--
--KNOWS--
EESH.

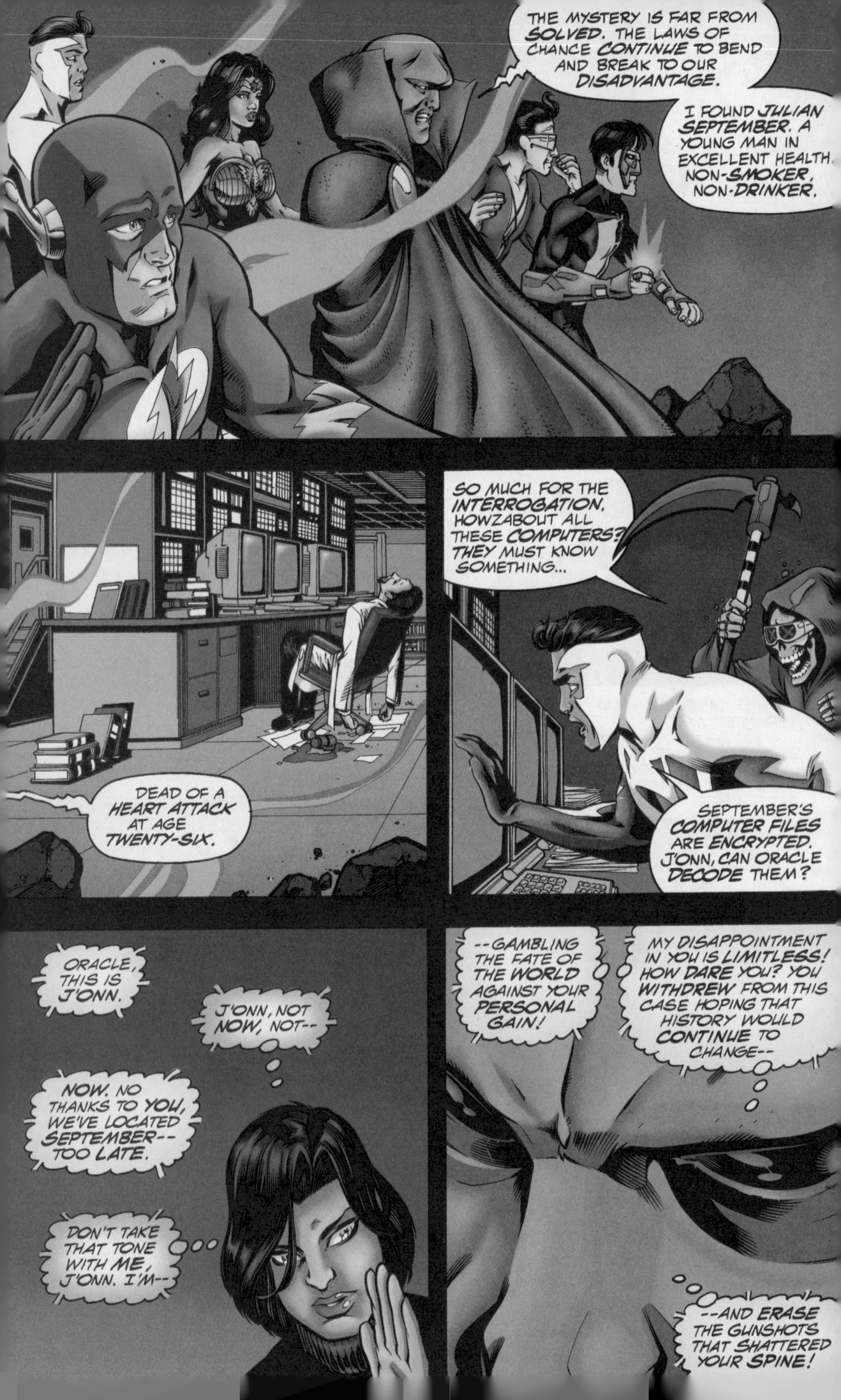
THE MYSTERY IS FAR FROM SOLVED. THE LAWS OF CHANCE CONTINUE TO BEND AND BREAK TO OUR DISADVANTAGE.
I FOUND JULIAN SEPTEMBER. A YOUNG MAN IN EXCELLENT HEALTH. NON-SMOKER. NON-DRINKER.
DEAD OF A HEART ATTACK AT AGE TWENTY-SIX.
SO MUCH FOR THE INTERROGATION. HOWZABOUT ALL THESE COMPUTERS? THEY MUST KNOW SOMETHING...
SEPTEMBER'S COMPUTER FILES ARE ENCRYPTED. J'ONN, CAN ORACLE DECODE THEM?
ORACLE, THIS IS J'ONN.
J'ONN, NOT NOW, NOT--
NOW. NO THANKS TO YOU, WE'VE LOCATED SEPTEMBER-- TOO LATE.
DON'T TAKE THAT TONE WITH ME, J'ONN. I'M--
MY DISAPPOINTMENT IN YOU IS LIMITLESS! HOW DARE YOU? YOU WITHDREW FROM THIS CASE HOPING THAT HISTORY WOULD CONTINUE TO CHANGE--
--GAMBLING THE FATE OF THE WORLD AGAINST YOUR PERSONAL GAIN!
--AND ERASE THE GUNSHOTS THAT SHATTERED YOUR SPINE!

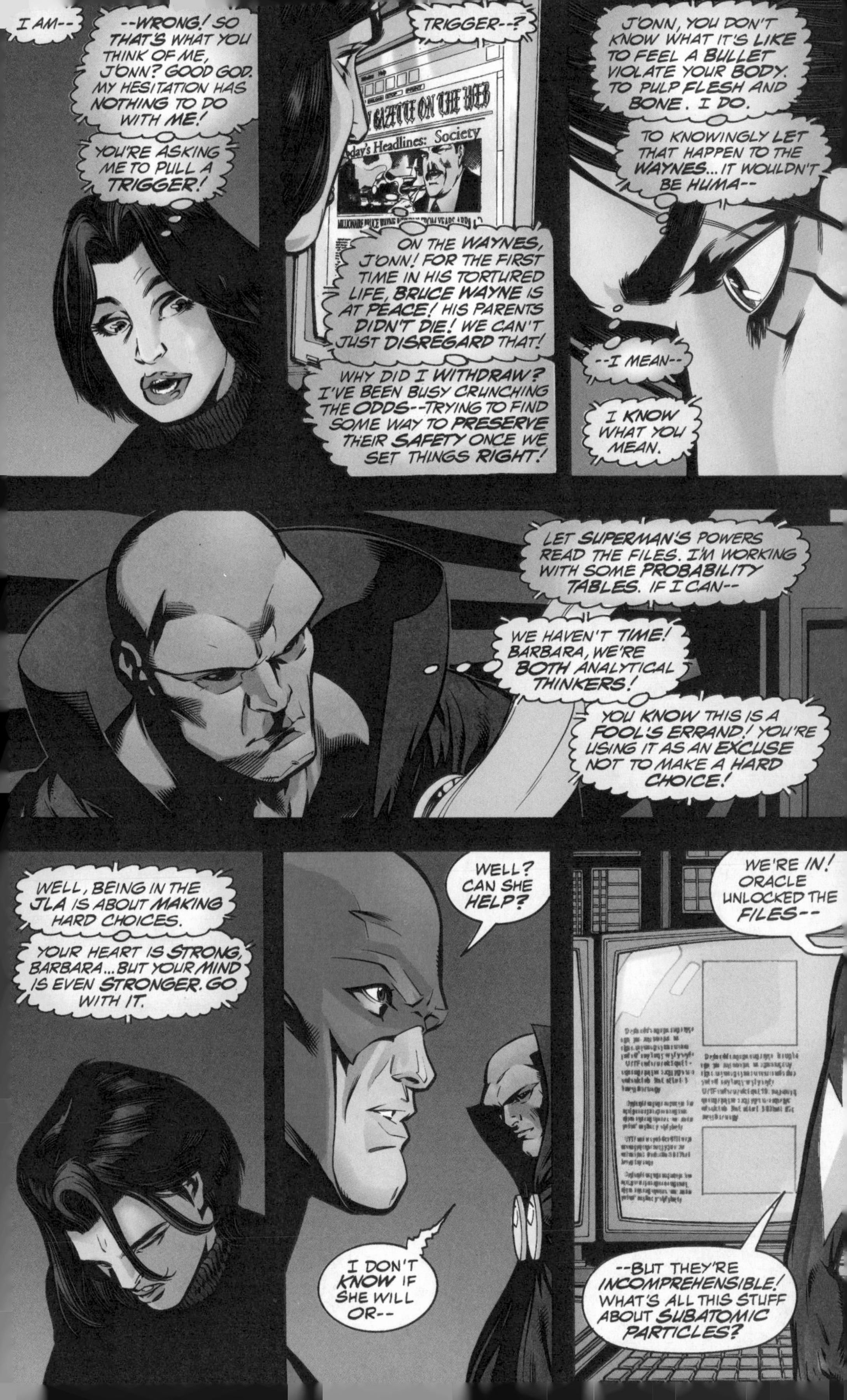
I AM--
--WRONG! SO THAT'S WHAT YOU THINK OF ME, J'ONN? GOOD GOD. MY HESITATION HAS NOTHING TO DO WITH ME!
YOU'RE ASKING ME TO PULL A TRIGGER!
TRIGGER--?
GAZETTE ON THE WEB
day's Headlines: Society
ON THE WAYNES, J'ONN! FOR THE FIRST TIME IN HIS TORTURED LIFE, BRUCE WAYNE IS AT PEACE! HIS PARENTS DIDN'T DIE! WE CAN'T JUST DISREGARD THAT!
WHY DID I WITHDRAW? I'VE BEEN BUSY CRUNCHING THE ODDS--TRYING TO FIND SOME WAY TO PRESERVE THEIR SAFETY ONCE WE SET THINGS RIGHT!
J'ONN, YOU DON'T KNOW WHAT IT'S LIKE TO FEEL A BULLET VIOLATE YOUR BODY. TO PULP FLESH AND BONE. I DO.
TO KNOWINGLY LET THAT HAPPEN TO THE WAYNES... IT WOULDN'T BE HUMA--
--I MEAN--
I KNOW WHAT YOU MEAN.
LET SUPERMAN'S POWERS READ THE FILES. I'M WORKING WITH SOME PROBABILITY TABLES. IF I CAN--
WE HAVEN'T TIME! BARBARA, WE'RE BOTH ANALYTICAL THINKERS!
YOU KNOW THIS IS A FOOL'S ERRAND! YOU'RE USING IT AS AN EXCUSE NOT TO MAKE A HARD CHOICE!
WELL, BEING IN THE JLA IS ABOUT MAKING HARD CHOICES.
YOUR HEART IS STRONG, BARBARA... BUT YOUR MIND IS EVEN STRONGER. GO WITH IT.
WELL? CAN SHE HELP?
I DON'T KNOW IF SHE WILL OR--
WE'RE IN! ORACLE UNLOCKED THE FILES--
--BUT THEY'RE INCOMPREHENSIBLE! WHAT'S ALL THIS STUFF ABOUT SUBATOMIC PARTICLES?

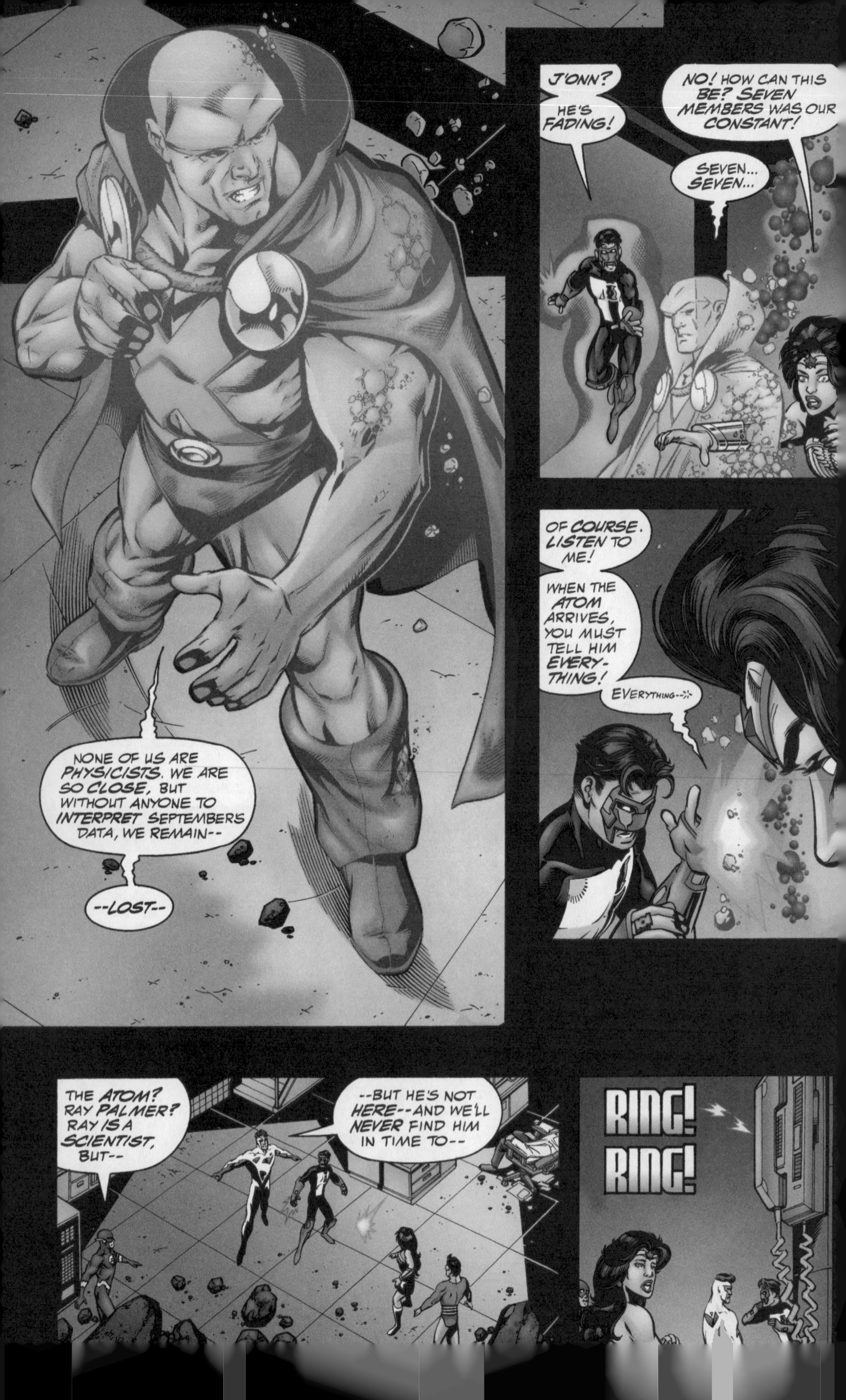
NONE OF US ARE PHYSICISTS. WE ARE SO CLOSE, BUT WITHOUT ANYONE TO INTERPRET SEPTEMBER'S DATA, WE REMAIN--
--LOST--
J'ONN?
HE'S FADING!
NO! HOW CAN THIS BE? SEVEN MEMBERS WAS OUR CONSTANT!
SEVEN... SEVEN...
OF COURSE. LISTEN TO ME!
WHEN THE ATOM ARRIVES, YOU MUST TELL HIM EVERYTHING!
EVERYTHING--
THE ATOM? RAY PALMER? RAY IS A SCIENTIST, BUT--
--BUT HE'S NOT HERE--AND WE'LL NEVER FIND HIM IN TIME TO--
RING! RING!

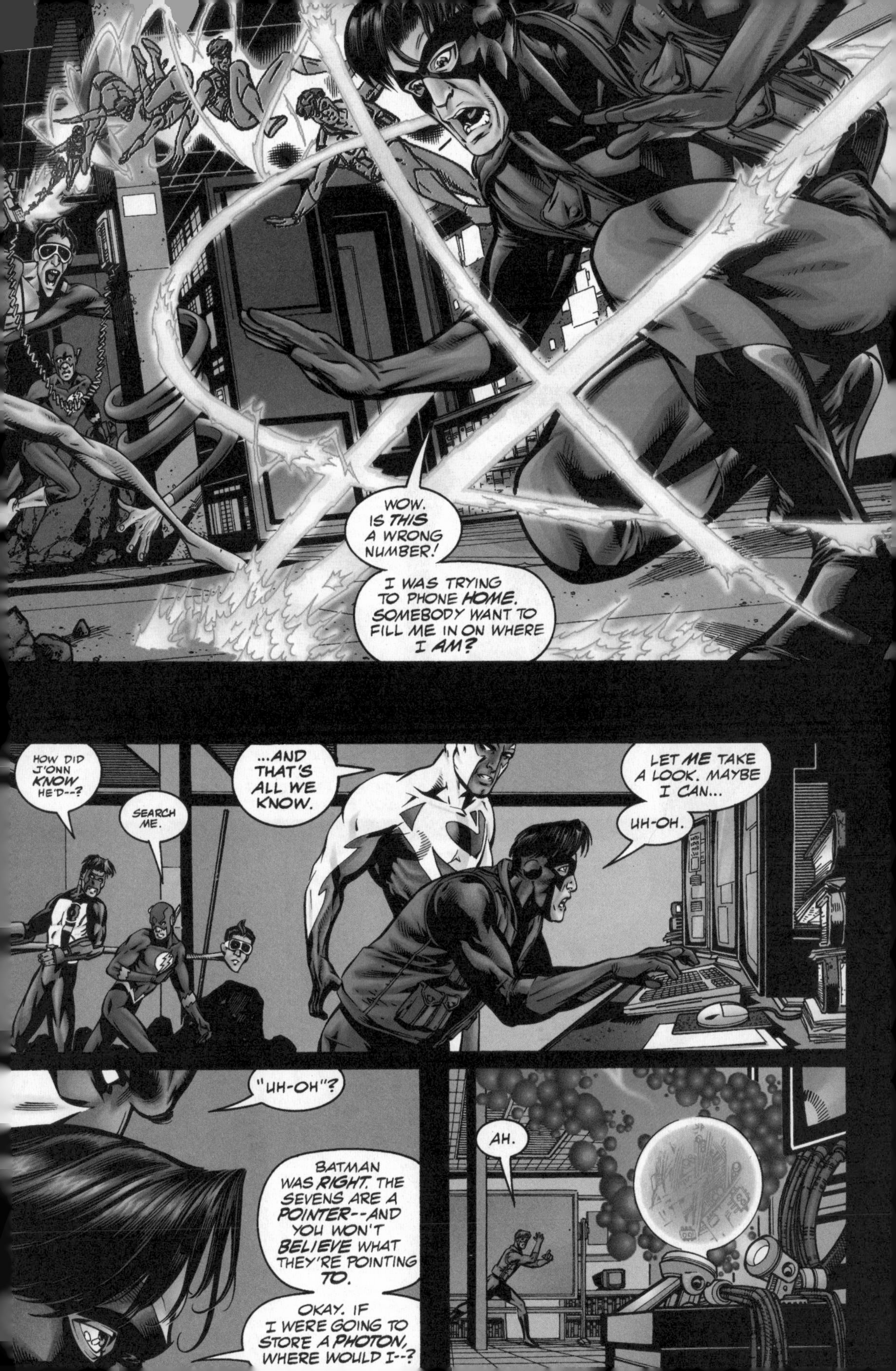

WOW. IS THIS A WRONG NUMBER!
I WAS TRYING TO PHONE HOME. SOMEBODY WANT TO FILL ME IN ON WHERE I AM?
HOW DID J'ONN KNOW HE'D--?
SEARCH ME.
...AND THAT'S ALL WE KNOW.
LET ME TAKE A LOOK. MAYBE I CAN...
UH-OH.
"UH-OH"?
AH.
BATMAN WAS RIGHT. THE SEVENS ARE A POINTER--AND YOU WON'T BELIEVE WHAT THEY'RE POINTING TO.
OKAY. IF I WERE GOING TO STORE A PHOTON, WHERE WOULD I--?

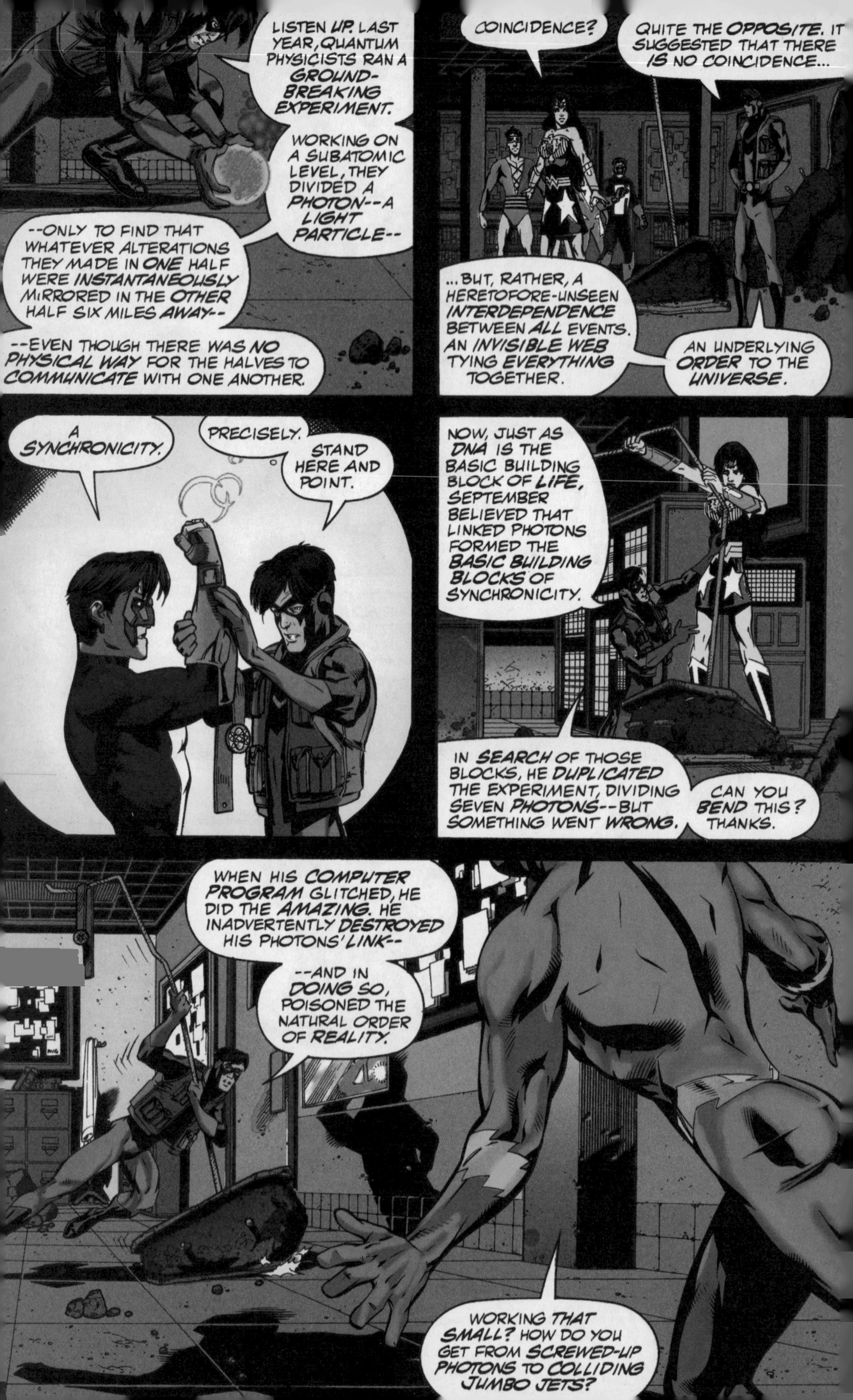
LISTEN UP. LAST YEAR, QUANTUM PHYSICISTS RAN A GROUND-BREAKING EXPERIMENT.
WORKING ON A SUBATOMIC LEVEL, THEY DIVIDED A PHOTON--A LIGHT PARTICLE--
--ONLY TO FIND THAT WHATEVER ALTERATIONS THEY MADE IN ONE HALF WERE INSTANTANEOUSLY MIRRORED IN THE OTHER HALF SIX MILES AWAY--
--EVEN THOUGH THERE WAS NO PHYSICAL WAY FOR THE HALVES TO COMMUNICATE WITH ONE ANOTHER.
COINCIDENCE?
QUITE THE OPPOSITE. IT SUGGESTED THAT THERE IS NO COINCIDENCE...
...BUT, RATHER, A HERETOFORE-UNSEEN INTERDEPENDENCE BETWEEN ALL EVENTS. AN INVISIBLE WEB TYING EVERYTHING TOGETHER.
AN UNDERLYING ORDER TO THE UNIVERSE.
A SYNCHRONICITY.
PRECISELY.
STAND HERE AND POINT.
NOW, JUST AS DNA IS THE BASIC BUILDING BLOCK OF LIFE, SEPTEMBER BELIEVED THAT LINKED PHOTONS FORMED THE BASIC BUILDING BLOCKS OF SYNCHRONICITY.
IN SEARCH OF THOSE BLOCKS, HE DUPLICATED THE EXPERIMENT, DIVIDING SEVEN PHOTONS--BUT SOMETHING WENT WRONG.
CAN YOU BEND THIS? THANKS.
WHEN HIS COMPUTER PROGRAM GLITCHED, HE DID THE AMAZING. HE INADVERTENTLY DESTROYED HIS PHOTONS' LINK--
--AND IN DOING SO, POISONED THE NATURAL ORDER OF REALITY.
WORKING THAT SMALL? HOW DO YOU GET FROM SCREWED-UP PHOTONS TO COLLIDING JUMBO JETS?

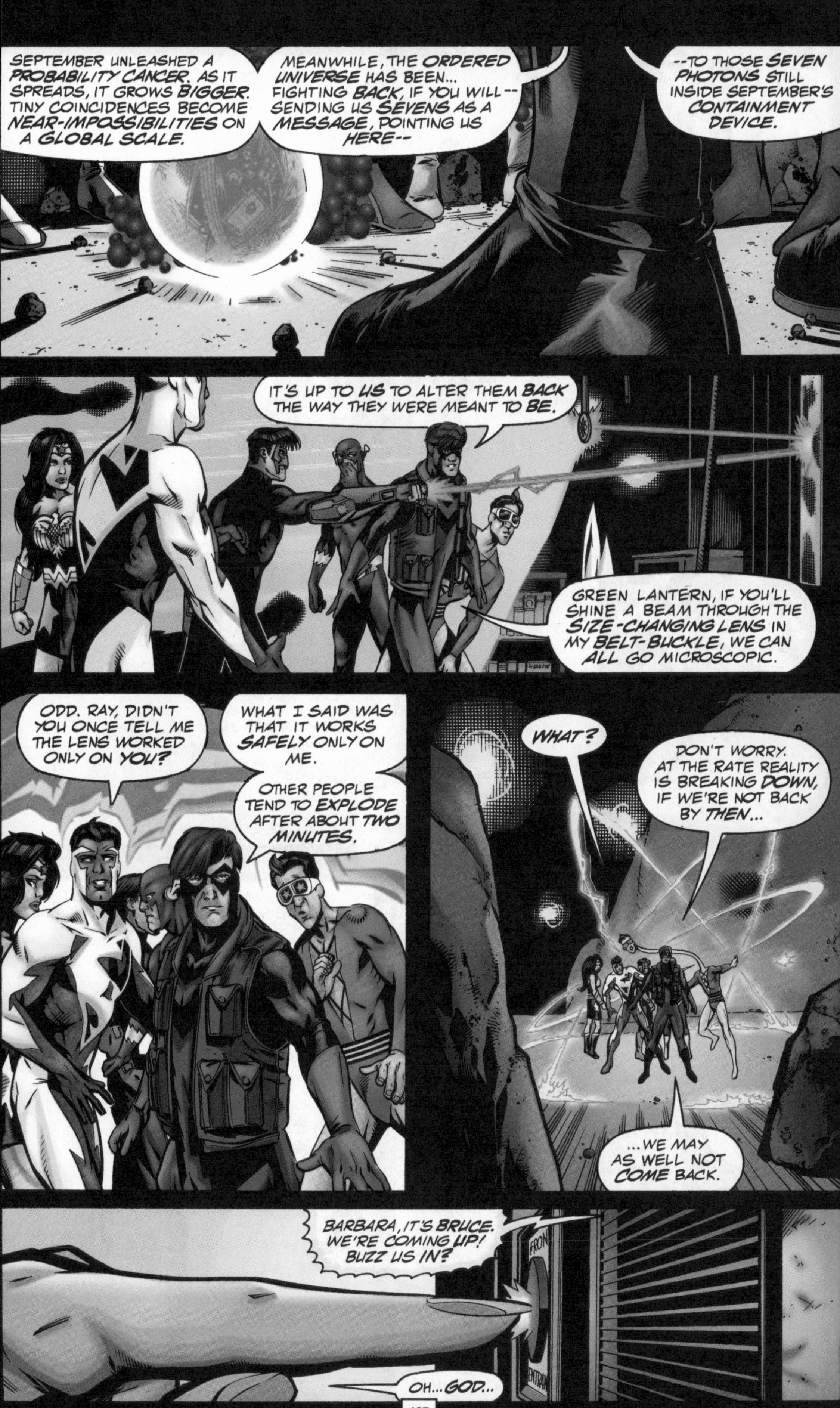
SEPTEMBER UNLEASHED A PROBABILITY CANCER. AS IT SPREADS, IT GROWS BIGGER. TINY COINCIDENCES BECOME NEAR-IMPOSSIBILITIES ON A GLOBAL SCALE.
MEANWHILE, THE ORDERED UNIVERSE HAS BEEN... FIGHTING BACK, IF YOU WILL-- SENDING US SEVENS AS A MESSAGE, POINTING US HERE--
--TO THOSE SEVEN PHOTONS STILL INSIDE SEPTEMBER'S CONTAINMENT DEVICE.
IT'S UP TO US TO ALTER THEM BACK THE WAY THEY WERE MEANT TO BE.
GREEN LANTERN, IF YOU'LL SHINE A BEAM THROUGH THE SIZE-CHANGING LENS IN MY BELT-BUCKLE, WE CAN ALL GO MICROSCOPIC.
ODD. RAY, DIDN'T YOU ONCE TELL ME THE LENS WORKED ONLY ON YOU?
WHAT I SAID WAS THAT IT WORKS SAFELY ONLY ON ME.
OTHER PEOPLE TEND TO EXPLODE AFTER ABOUT TWO MINUTES.
WHAT?
DON'T WORRY. AT THE RATE REALITY IS BREAKING DOWN, IF WE'RE NOT BACK BY THEN...
...WE MAY AS WELL NOT COME BACK.
BARBARA, IT'S BRUCE. WE'RE COMING UP! BUZZ US IN?
OH...GOD...

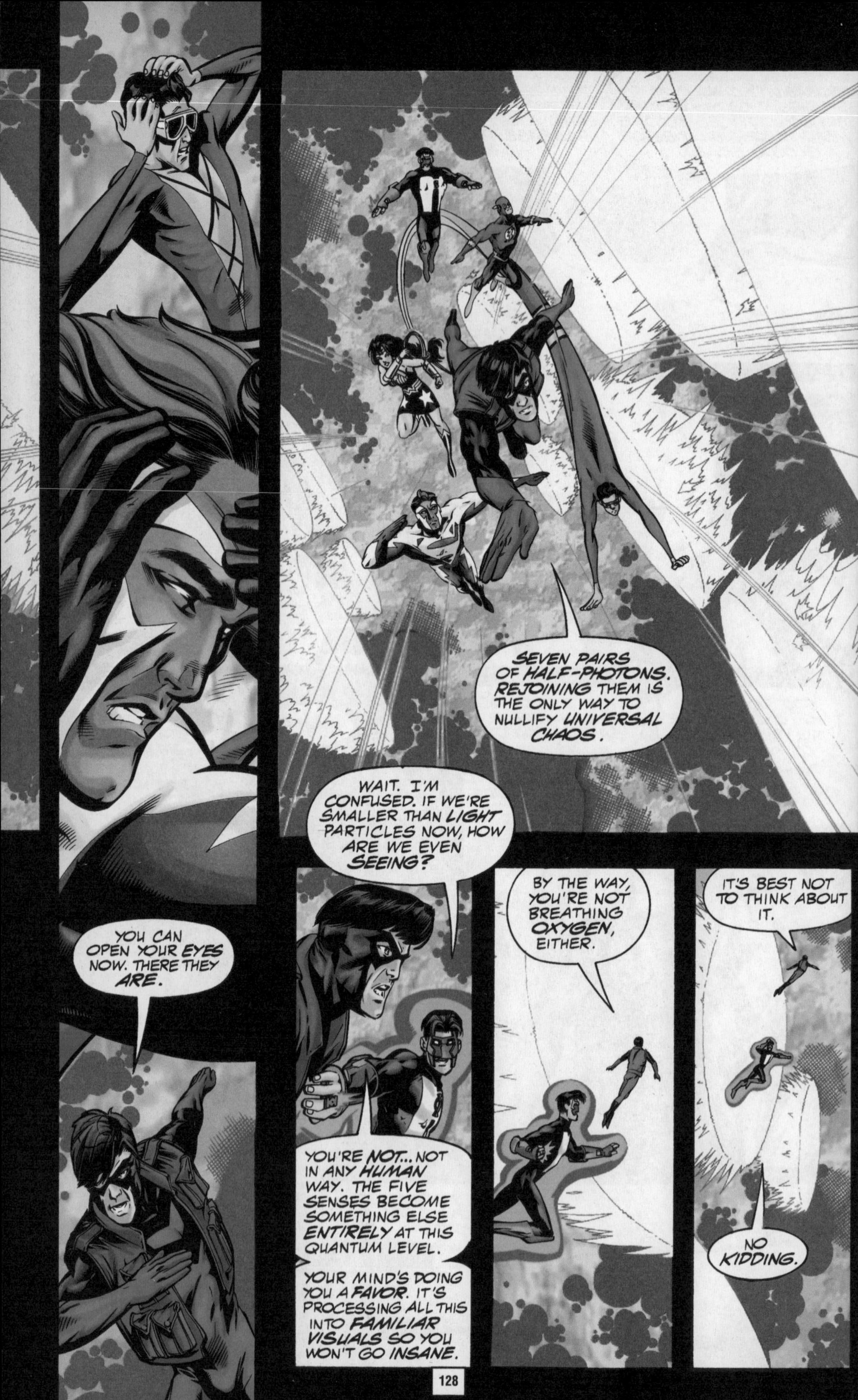

SEVEN PAIRS OF HALF-PHOTONS. REJOINING THEM IS THE ONLY WAY TO NULLIFY UNIVERSAL CHAOS.
YOU CAN OPEN YOUR EYES NOW. THERE THEY ARE.
WAIT. I'M CONFUSED. IF WE'RE SMALLER THAN LIGHT PARTICLES NOW, HOW ARE WE EVEN SEEING?
YOU'RE NOT... NOT IN ANY HUMAN WAY. THE FIVE SENSES BECOME SOMETHING ELSE ENTIRELY AT THIS QUANTUM LEVEL.
YOUR MIND'S DOING YOU A FAVOR. IT'S PROCESSING ALL THIS INTO FAMILIAR VISUALS SO YOU WON'T GO INSANE.
BY THE WAY, YOU'RE NOT BREATHING OXYGEN, EITHER.
IT'S BEST NOT TO THINK ABOUT IT.
NO KIDDING.

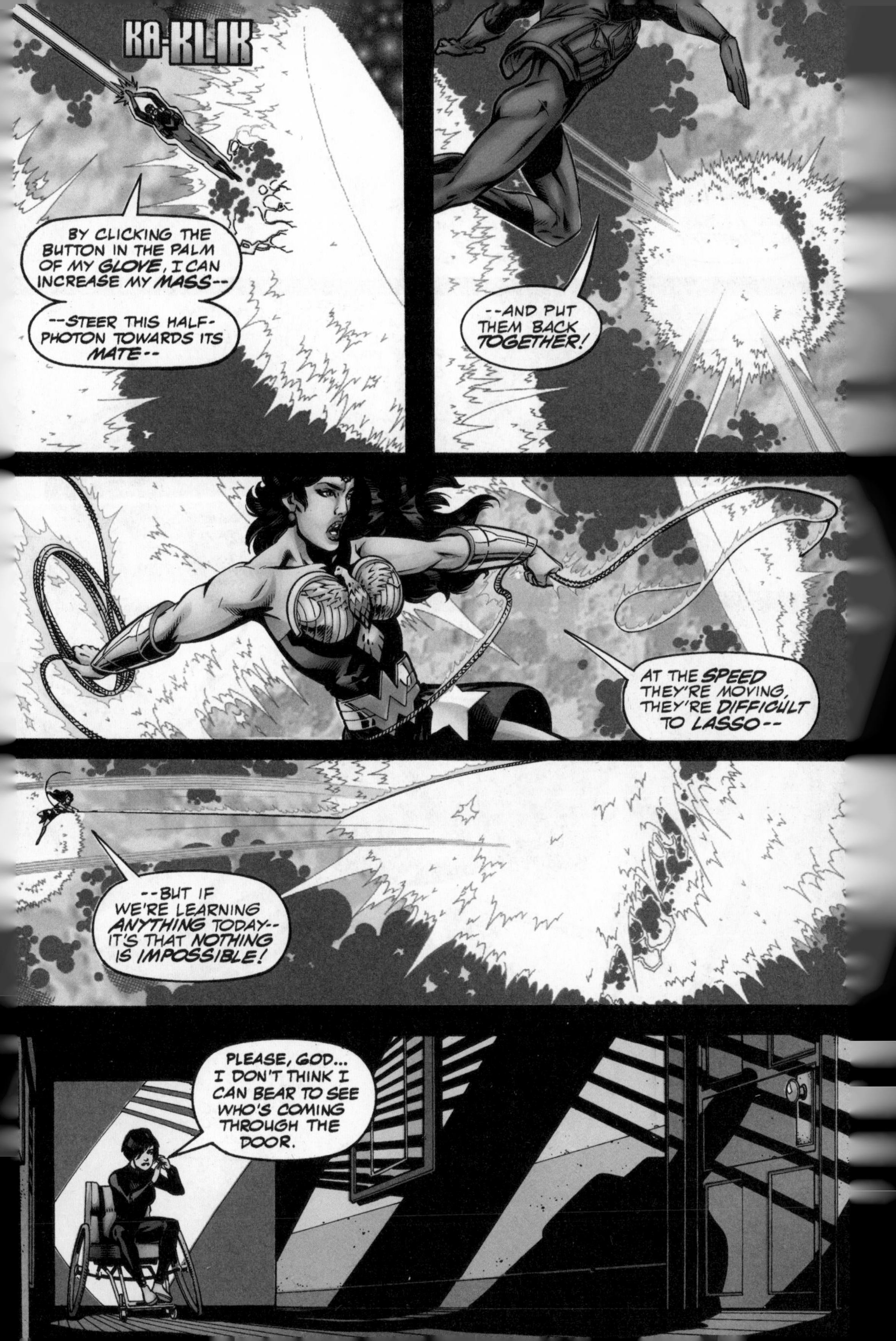
KA-KLIK
BY CLICKING THE BUTTON IN THE PALM OF MY GLOVE, I CAN INCREASE MY MASS--
--STEER THIS HALF-PHOTON TOWARDS ITS MATE--
--AND PUT THEM BACK TOGETHER!
AT THE SPEED THEY'RE MOVING, THEY'RE DIFFICULT TO LASSO--
--BUT IF WE'RE LEARNING ANYTHING TODAY--IT'S THAT NOTHING IS IMPOSSIBLE!
PLEASE, GOD... I DON'T THINK I CAN BEAR TO SEE WHO'S COMING THROUGH THE DOOR.

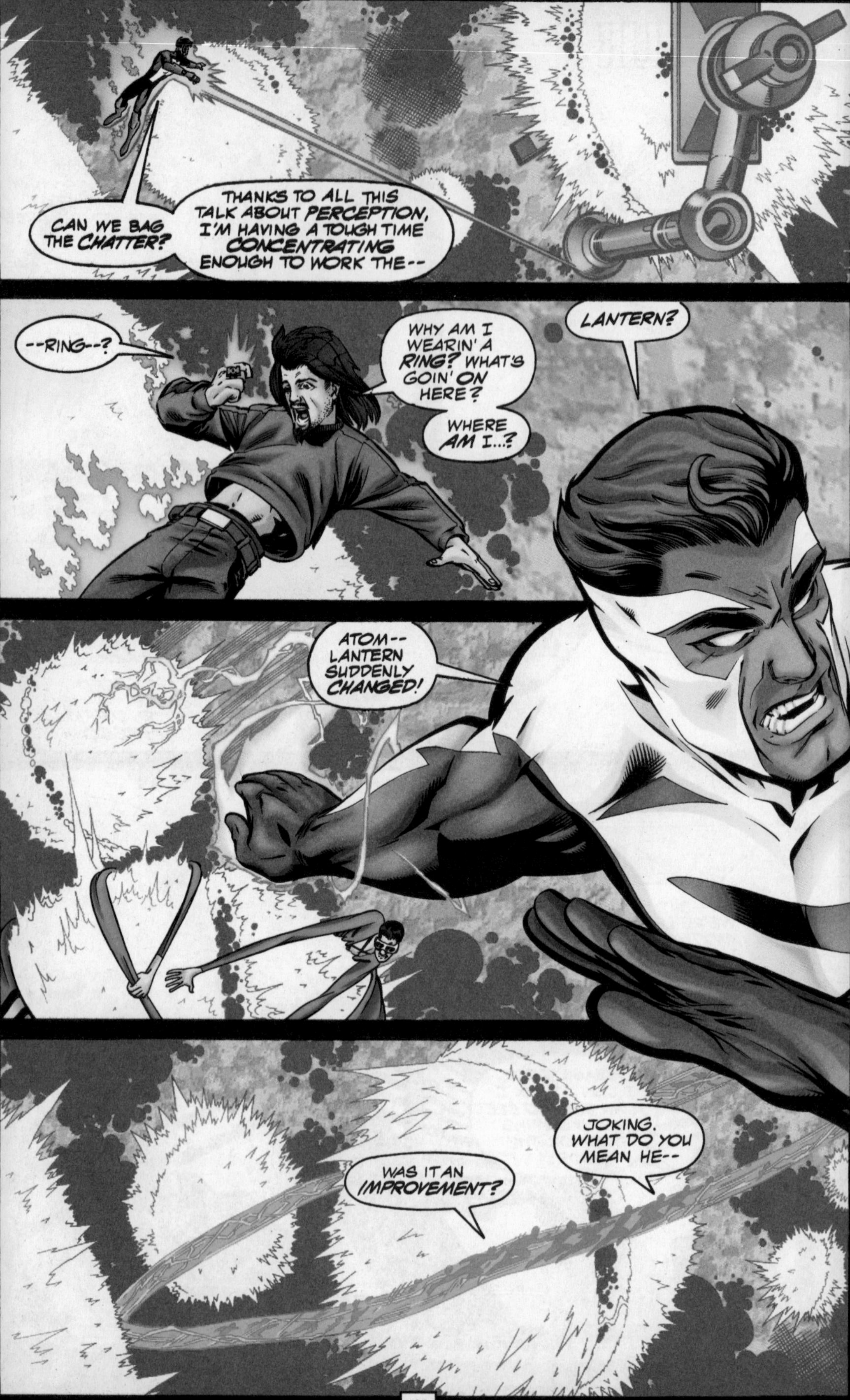
CAN WE BAG THE CHATTER?
THANKS TO ALL THIS TALK ABOUT PERCEPTION, I'M HAVING A TOUGH TIME CONCENTRATING ENOUGH TO WORK THE--
--RING--?
WHY AM I WEARIN' A RING? WHAT'S GOIN' ON HERE?
WHERE AM I...?
LANTERN?
ATOM-- LANTERN SUDDENLY CHANGED!
WAS IT AN IMPROVEMENT?
JOKING. WHAT DO YOU MEAN HE--

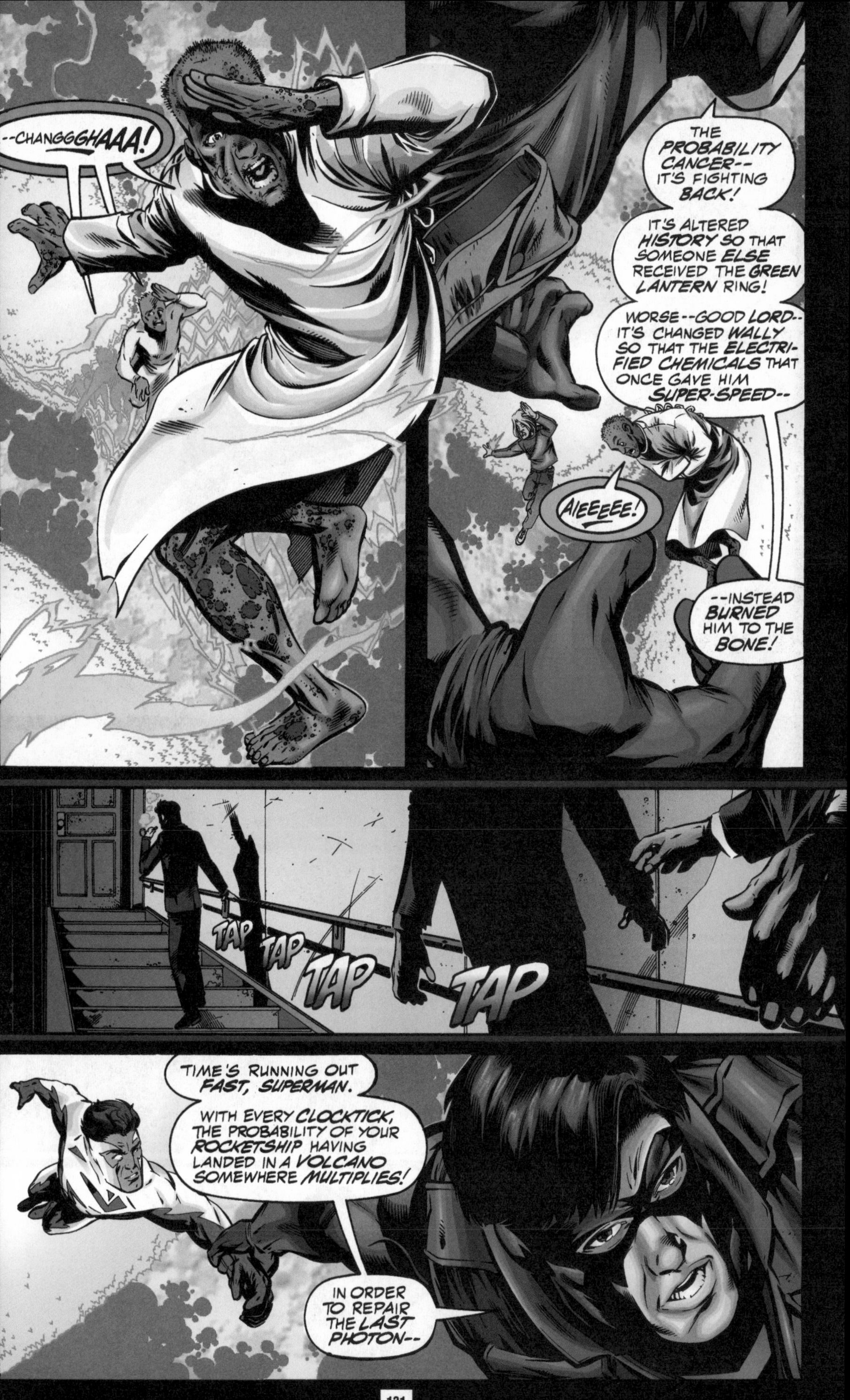
--CHANGGGHAAA!
THE PROBABILITY CANCER-- IT'S FIGHTING BACK!
IT'S ALTERED HISTORY SO THAT SOMEONE ELSE RECEIVED THE GREEN LANTERN RING!
WORSE--GOOD LORD-- IT'S CHANGED WALLY SO THAT THE ELECTRIFIED CHEMICALS THAT ONCE GAVE HIM SUPER-SPEED--
AIEEEEE!
--INSTEAD BURNED HIM TO THE BONE!
TAP
TAP
TAP
TAP
TIME'S RUNNING OUT FAST, SUPERMAN.
WITH EVERY CLOCKTICK, THE PROBABILITY OF YOUR ROCKETSHIP HAVING LANDED IN A VOLCANO SOMEWHERE MULTIPLIES!
IN ORDER TO REPAIR THE LAST PHOTON--

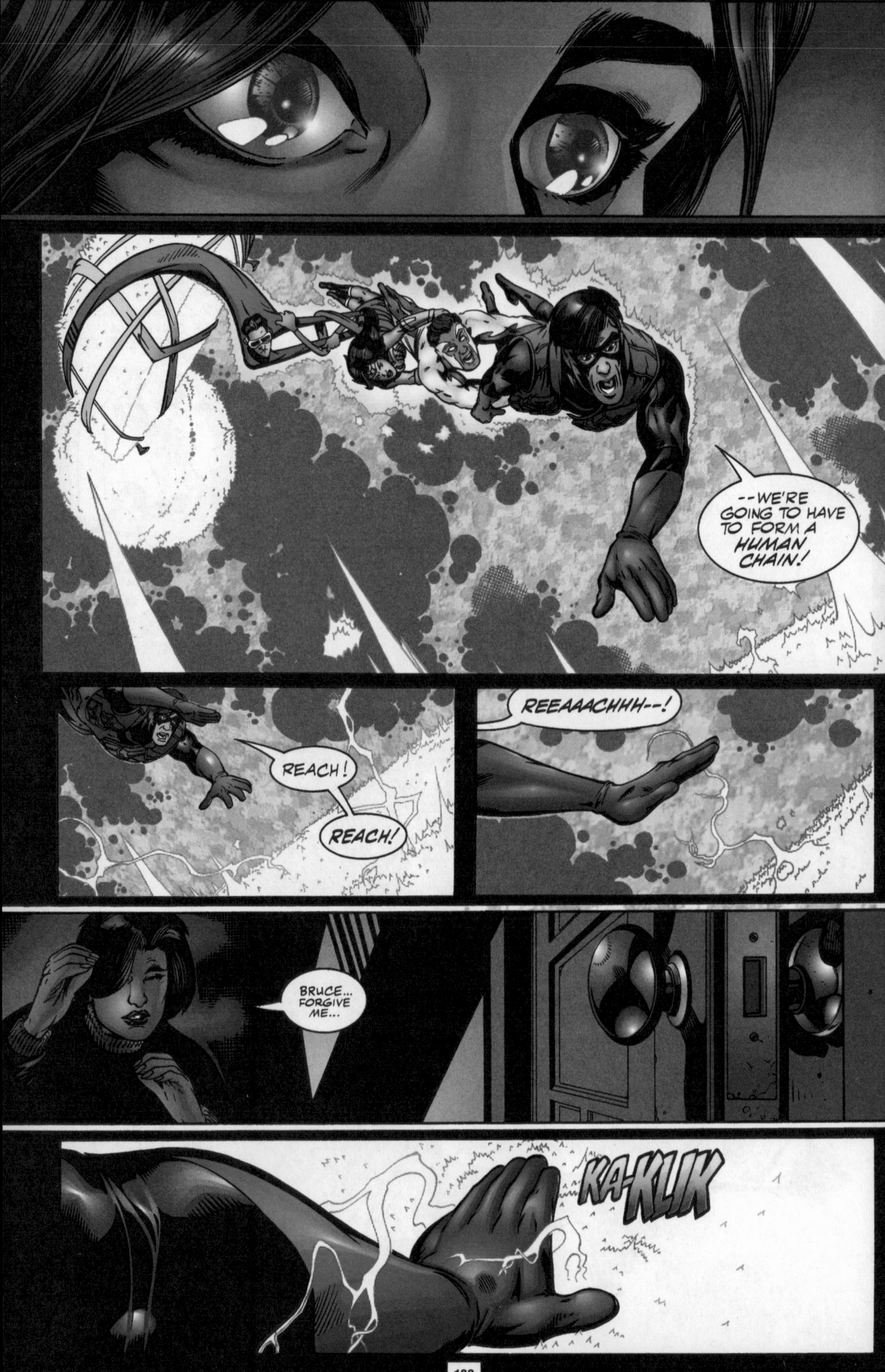
--WE'RE GOING TO HAVE TO FORM A HUMAN CHAIN!
REACH!
REACH!
REEAAACHHH--!
BRUCE... FORGIVE ME...
KA-KLIK

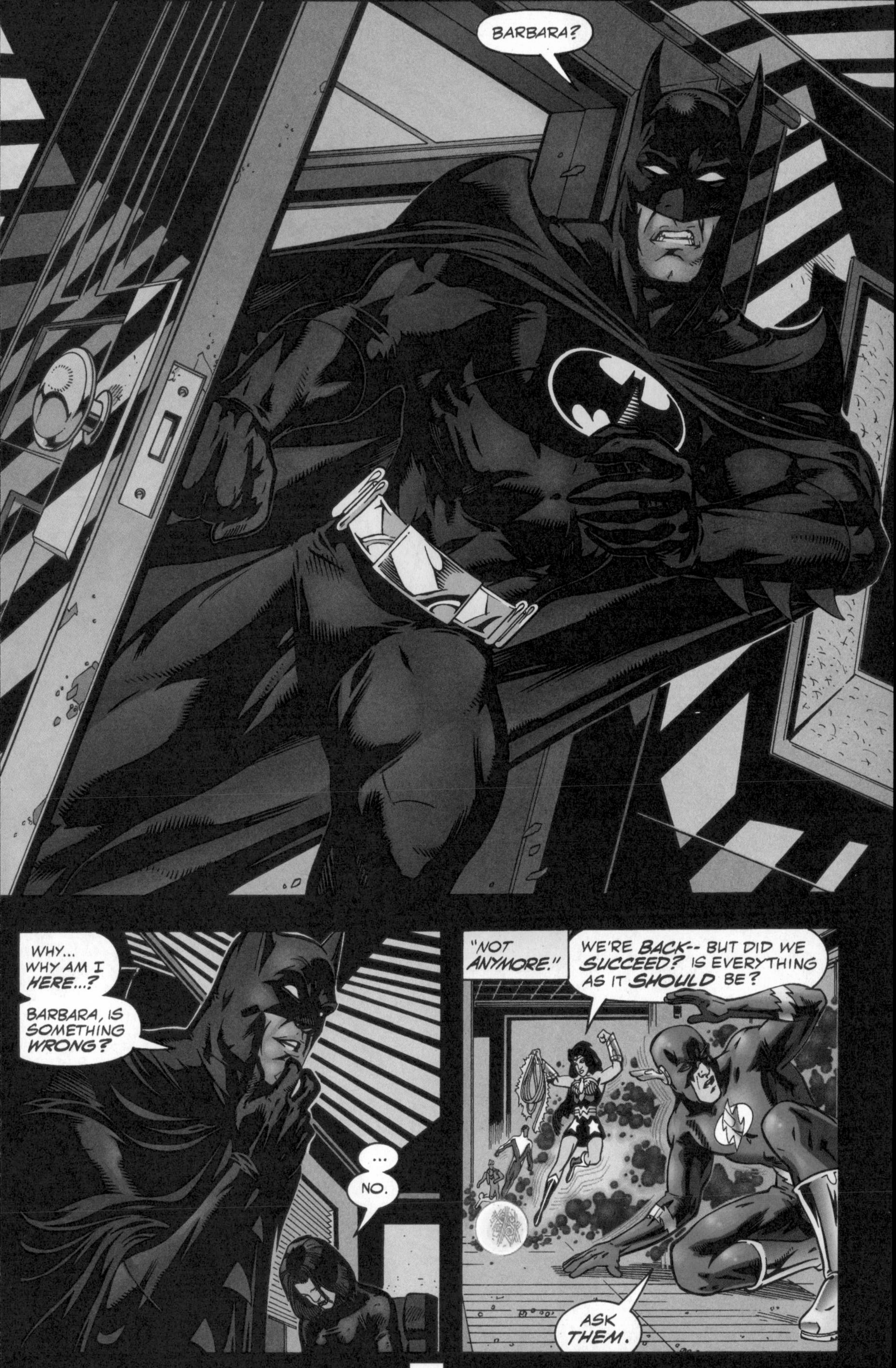
BARBARA?
WHY... WHY AM I HERE...?
BARBARA, IS SOMETHING WRONG?
...
NO.
"NOT ANYMORE."
WE'RE BACK-- BUT DID WE SUCCEED? IS EVERYTHING AS IT SHOULD BE?
ASK THEM.

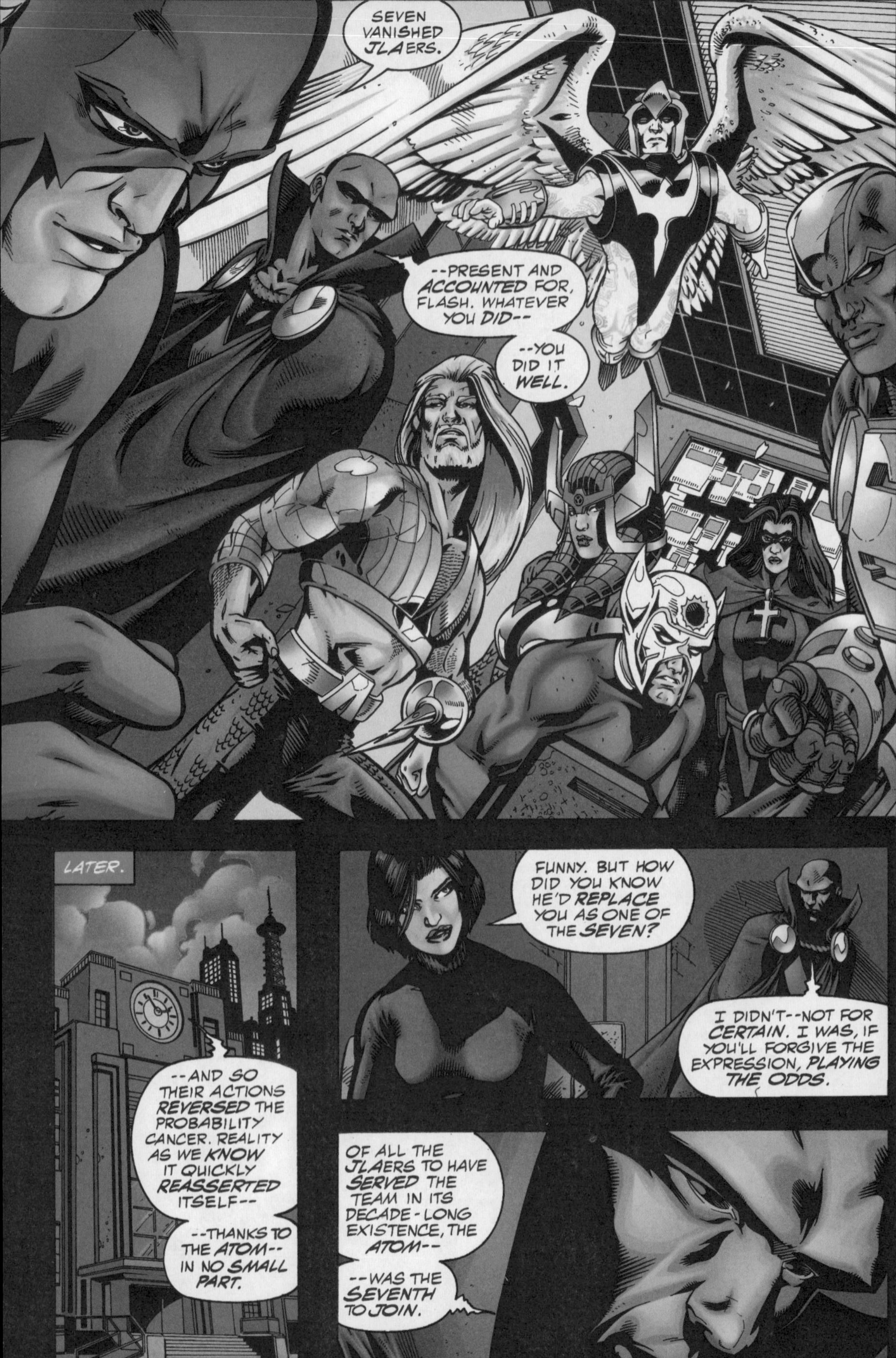
SEVEN VANISHED JLAERS.
--PRESENT AND ACCOUNTED FOR, FLASH. WHATEVER YOU DID--
--YOU DID IT WELL.
LATER.
--AND SO THEIR ACTIONS REVERSED THE PROBABILITY CANCER. REALITY AS WE KNOW IT QUICKLY REASSERTED ITSELF--
--THANKS TO THE ATOM--IN NO SMALL PART.
FUNNY. BUT HOW DID YOU KNOW HE'D REPLACE YOU AS ONE OF THE SEVEN?
I DIDN'T--NOT FOR CERTAIN. I WAS, IF YOU'LL FORGIVE THE EXPRESSION, PLAYING THE ODDS.
OF ALL THE JLAERS TO HAVE SERVED THE TEAM IN ITS DECADE-LONG EXISTENCE, THE ATOM--
--WAS THE SEVENTH TO JOIN.

I APOLOGIZE FOR MISJUDG-ING YOUR MOTIVES, BARBARA. CLEARLY, WE DO NOT GIVE YOU ENOUGH CONSIDERATION.

THE LEAGUE IS CAPABLE OF BUILDING A WATCHTOWER ON THE MOON, SURELY WE COULD ENGINEER A PROSTHESIS FOR YOUR LEGS...

THANK YOU, BUT NO. I HAVE LITTLE INTEREST IN BEING HALF-ROBOT.

YOU DO MISS YOUR MOBILITY...?

MORE THAN WORDS CAN EXPRESS. AND I DREAM OF THE MEDICAL BREAK-THROUGHS THAT MIGHT SOMEDAY RESTORE IT.

BUT IN THE MEANTIME, I'VE WORKED HARD TO TREAT WHAT HAPPENED TO ME AS AN OPPOR-TUNITY, NOT A HANDICAP.

I CONCENTRATE ON THE GOOD I CAN DO NOW THAT I'VE BEEN FORCED TO EXERCISE MY MIND.

DESPITE HIS EVIL, J'ONN, SEPTEMBER HAD THE RIGHT NOTION.

"SOMETIMES OUR ONLY COMFORT COMES FROM BELIEVING THAT THERE IS NO CHANCE.

"THAT WHATEVER HAPPENS IN THIS WORLD...

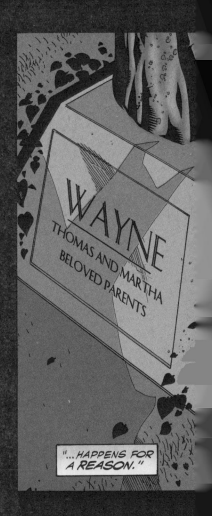

WAYNE
THOMAS AND MARTHA
BELOVED PARENTS

"...HAPPENS FOR A REASON."

THE END

MYSTERY IN SPACE

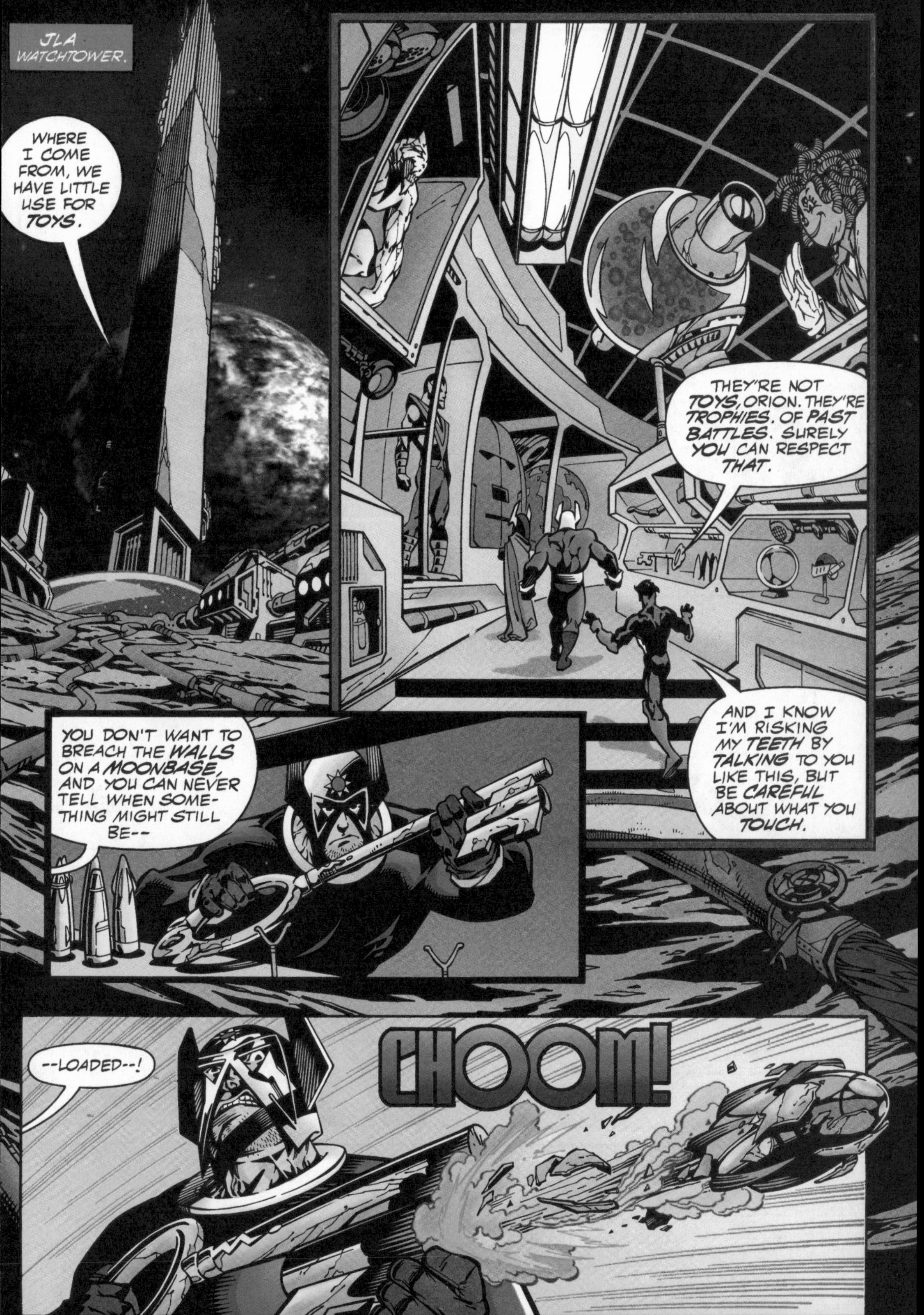
JLA WATCHTOWER.
WHERE I COME FROM, WE HAVE LITTLE USE FOR TOYS.
THEY'RE NOT TOYS, ORION. THEY'RE TROPHIES. OF PAST BATTLES. SURELY YOU CAN RESPECT THAT.
AND I KNOW I'M RISKING MY TEETH BY TALKING TO YOU LIKE THIS, BUT BE CAREFUL ABOUT WHAT YOU TOUCH.
YOU DON'T WANT TO BREACH THE WALLS ON A MOONBASE, AND YOU CAN NEVER TELL WHEN SOME-THING MIGHT STILL BE--
--LOADED--!
CHOOM!

WHAT THE--?
OH, IT'S YOU!
PLEASE... BE MY GUEST!

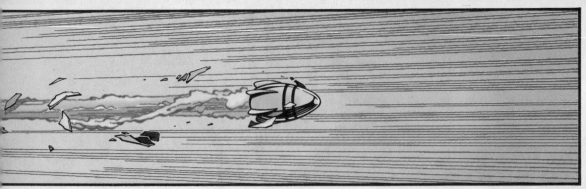

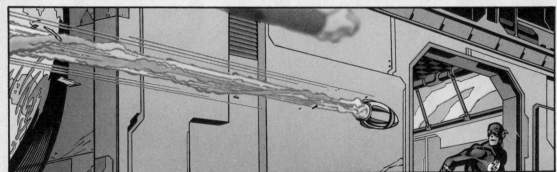

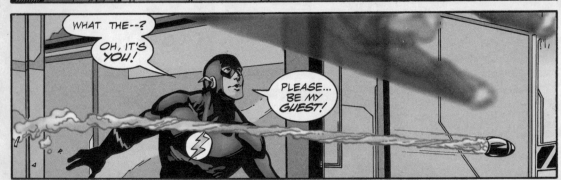

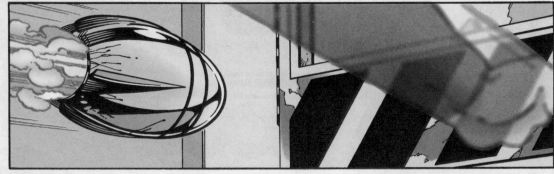

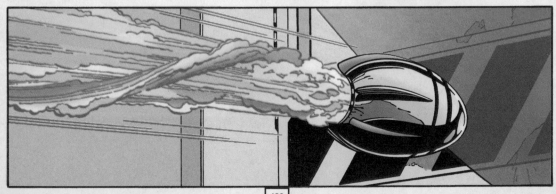

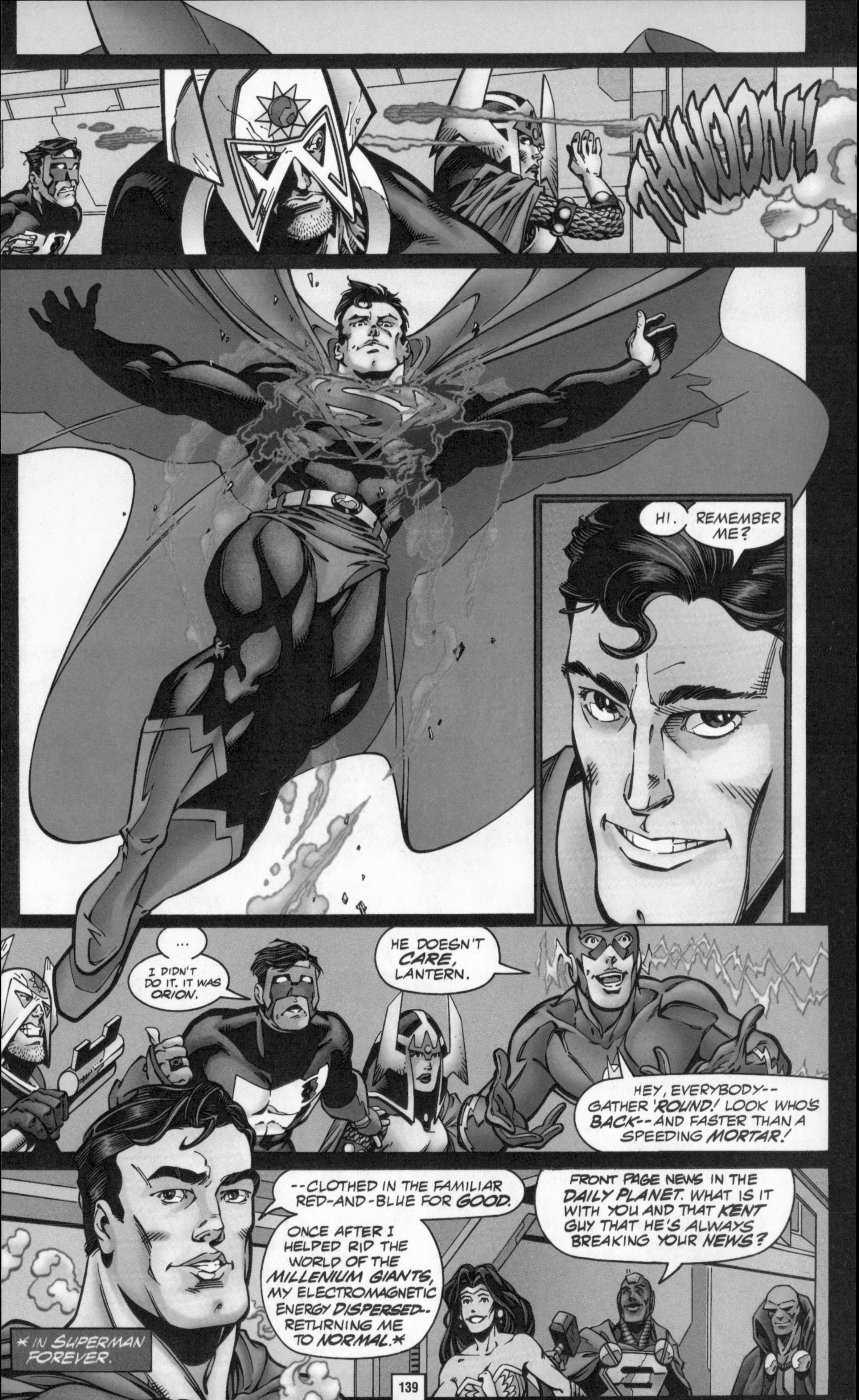
WHOOM!
HI. REMEMBER ME?
...
I DIDN'T DO IT. IT WAS ORION.
HE DOESN'T CARE, LANTERN.
HEY, EVERYBODY-- GATHER 'ROUND! LOOK WHO'S BACK--AND FASTER THAN A SPEEDING MORTAR!
--CLOTHED IN THE FAMILIAR RED-AND-BLUE FOR GOOD.
ONCE AFTER I HELPED RID THE WORLD OF THE MILLENIUM GIANTS, MY ELECTROMAGNETIC ENERGY DISPERSED-- RETURNING ME TO NORMAL.*
FRONT PAGE NEWS IN THE DAILY PLANET. WHAT IS IT WITH YOU AND THAT KENT GUY THAT HE'S ALWAYS BREAKING YOUR NEWS?
* IN SUPERMAN FOREVER.

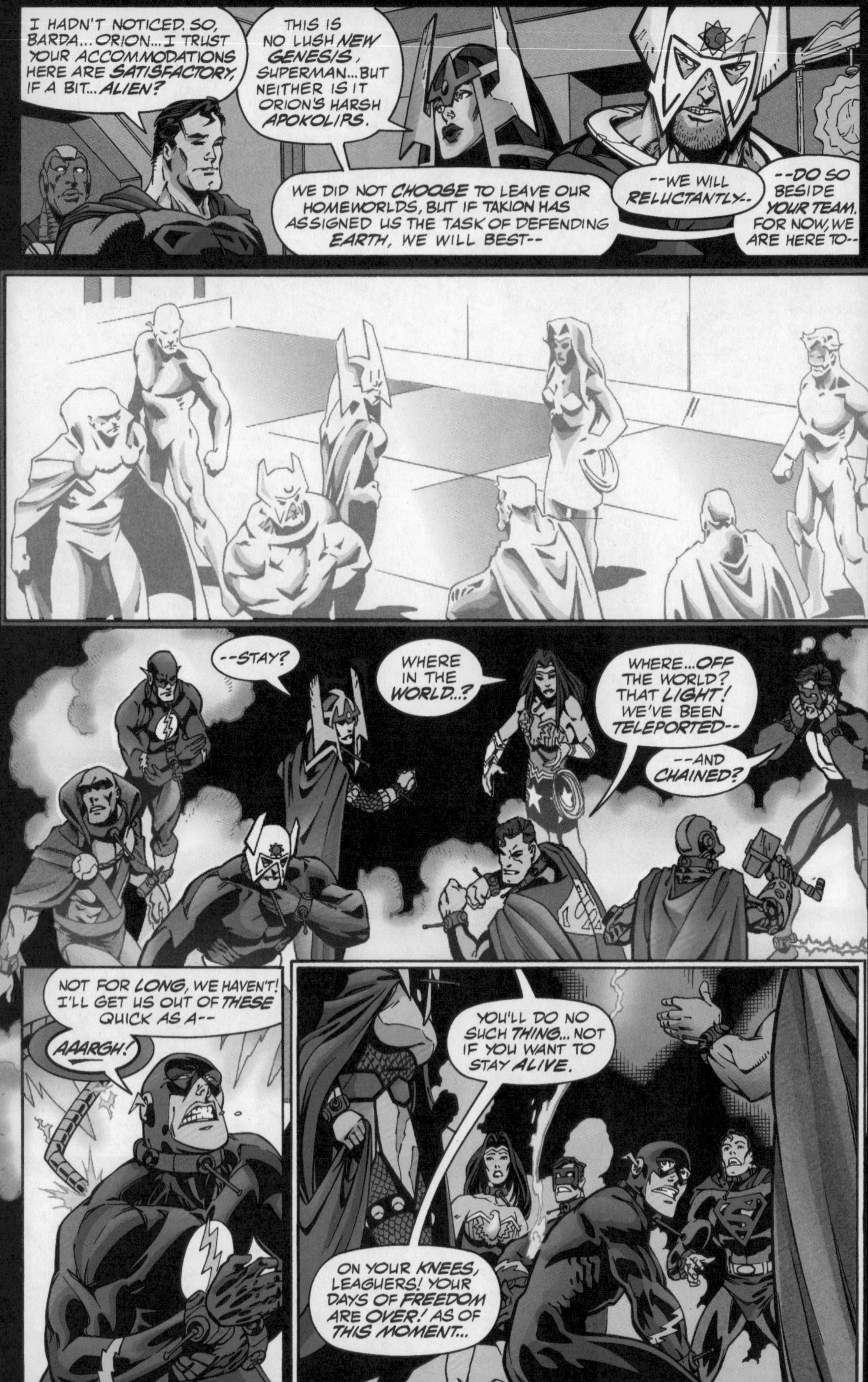

I HADN'T NOTICED. SO, BARDA... ORION... I TRUST YOUR ACCOMMODATIONS HERE ARE SATISFACTORY, IF A BIT... ALIEN?
THIS IS NO LUSH NEW GENESIS, SUPERMAN... BUT NEITHER IS IT ORION'S HARSH APOKOLIPS.
WE DID NOT CHOOSE TO LEAVE OUR HOMEWORLDS, BUT IF TAKION HAS ASSIGNED US THE TASK OF DEFENDING EARTH, WE WILL BEST--
--WE WILL RELUCTANTLY--
--DO SO BESIDE YOUR TEAM. FOR NOW, WE ARE HERE TO--
--STAY?
WHERE IN THE WORLD..?
WHERE... OFF THE WORLD? THAT LIGHT! WE'VE BEEN TELEPORTED--
--AND CHAINED?
NOT FOR LONG, WE HAVEN'T! I'LL GET US OUT OF THESE QUICK AS A--
AAARGH!
YOU'LL DO NO SUCH THING... NOT IF YOU WANT TO STAY ALIVE.
ON YOUR KNEES, LEAGUERS! YOUR DAYS OF FREEDOM ARE OVER! AS OF THIS MOMENT...

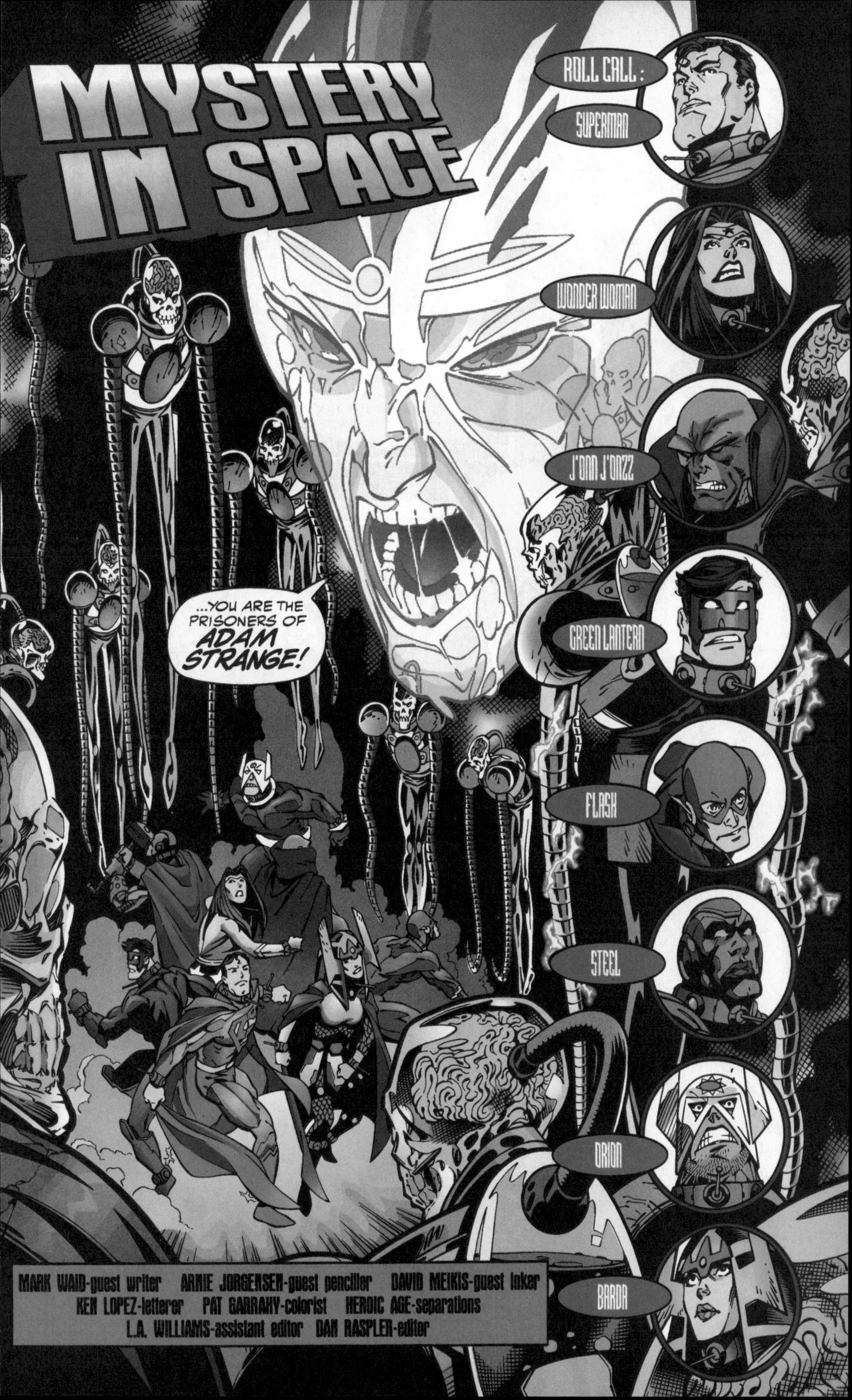
MYSTERY IN SPACE
ROLL CALL:
SUPERMAN
WONDER WOMAN
J'ONN J'ONZZ
GREEN LANTERN
FLASH
STEEL
ORION
BARDA
...YOU ARE THE PRISONERS OF ADAM STRANGE!
MARK WAID-guest writer ARNIE JORGENSEN-guest penciller DAVID MEIKIS-guest inker
KEN LOPEZ-letterer PAT GARRAHY-colorist HEROIC AGE-separations
L.A. WILLIAMS-assistant editor DAN RASPLER-editor

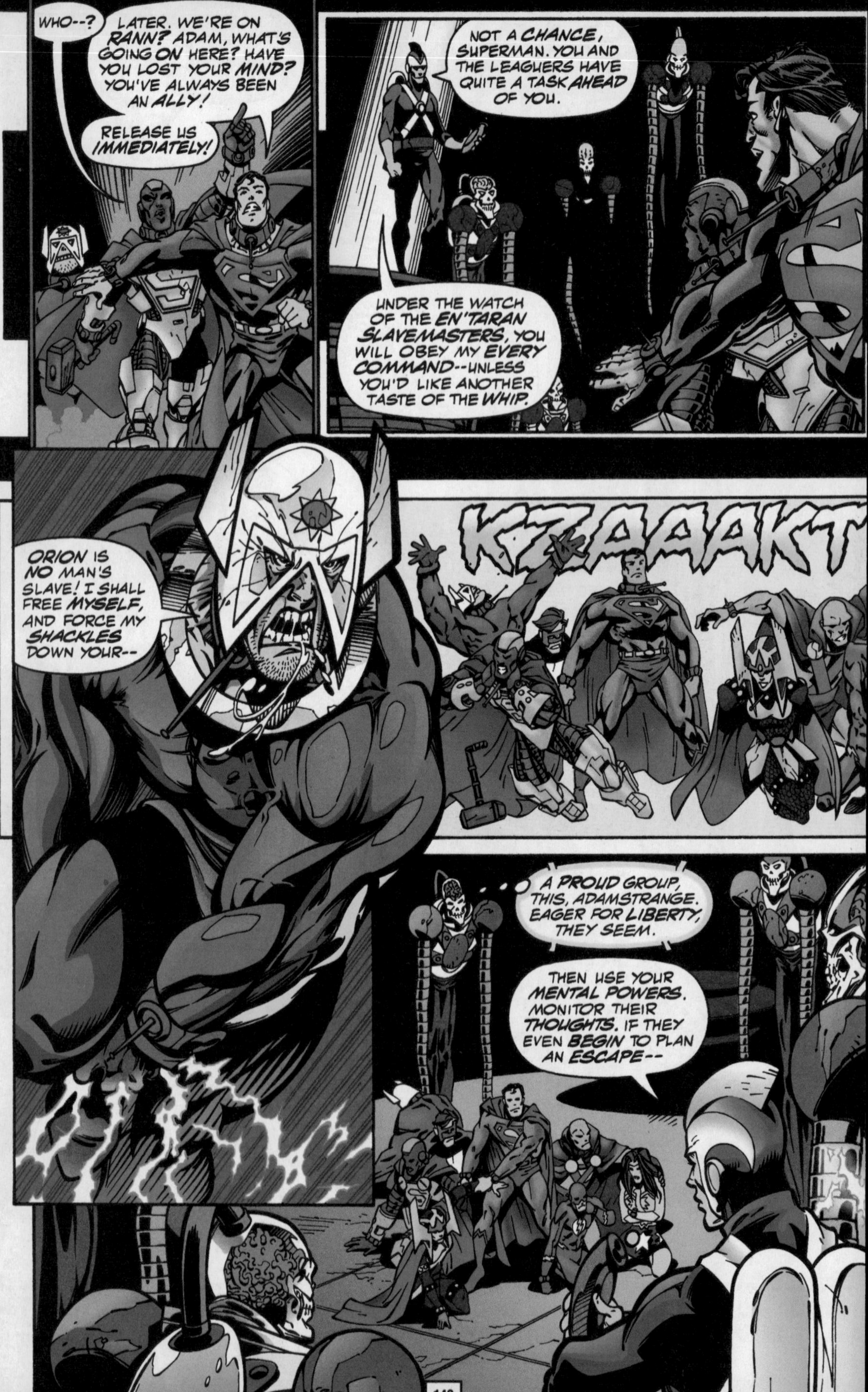
WHO--?
LATER. WE'RE ON RANN? ADAM, WHAT'S GOING ON HERE? HAVE YOU LOST YOUR MIND? YOU'VE ALWAYS BEEN AN ALLY!
RELEASE US IMMEDIATELY!
NOT A CHANCE, SUPERMAN. YOU AND THE LEAGUERS HAVE QUITE A TASK AHEAD OF YOU.
UNDER THE WATCH OF THE EN'TARAN SLAVEMASTERS, YOU WILL OBEY MY EVERY COMMAND--UNLESS YOU'D LIKE ANOTHER TASTE OF THE WHIP.
ORION IS NO MAN'S SLAVE! I SHALL FREE MYSELF, AND FORCE MY SHACKLES DOWN YOUR--
KZAAAKT
A PROUD GROUP, THIS, ADAMSTRANGE. EAGER FOR LIBERTY, THEY SEEM.
THEN USE YOUR MENTAL POWERS. MONITOR THEIR THOUGHTS. IF THEY EVEN BEGIN TO PLAN AN ESCAPE--

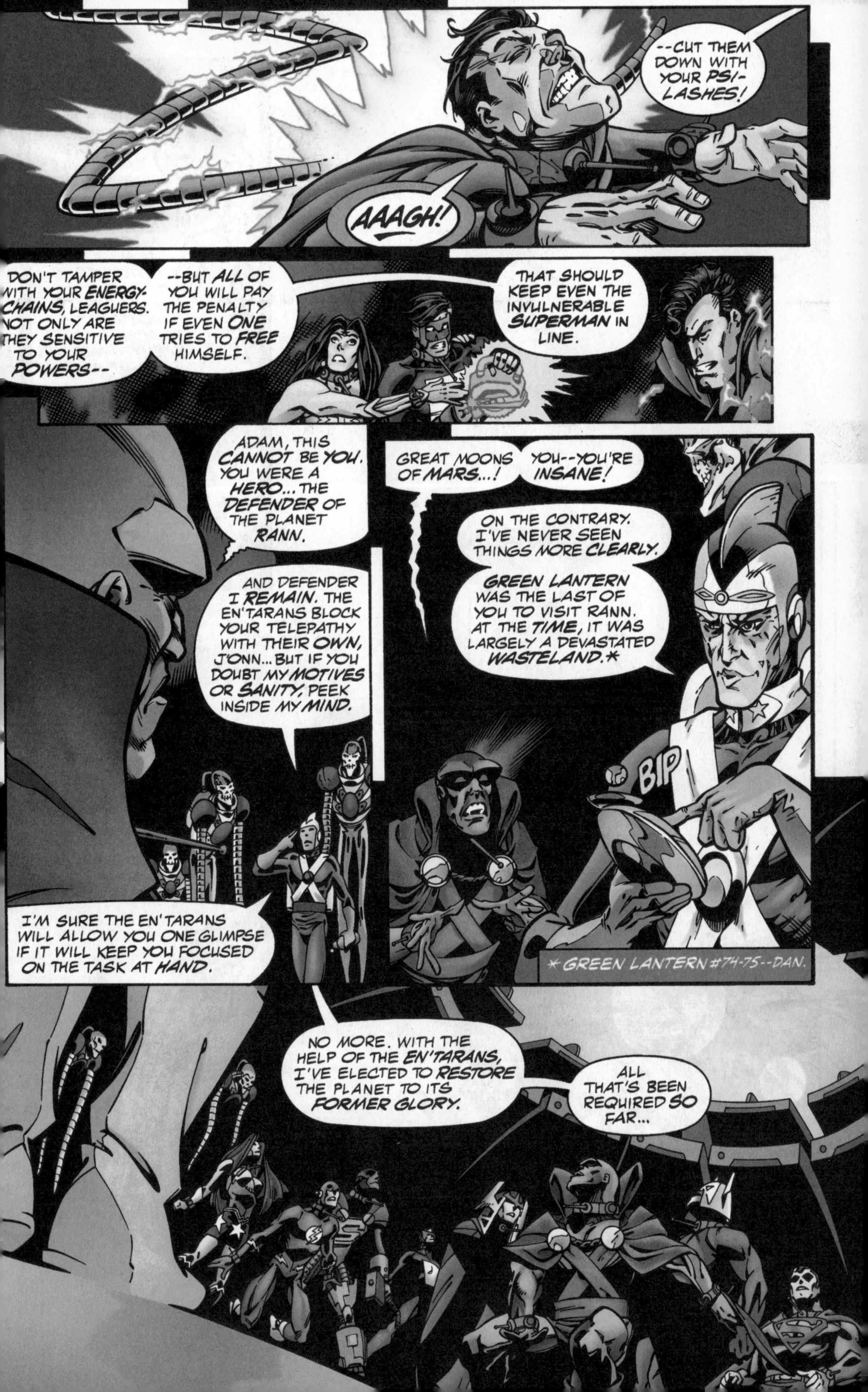
--CUT THEM DOWN WITH YOUR PSI-LASHES!
AAAGH!
DON'T TAMPER WITH YOUR ENERGY-CHAINS, LEAGUERS. NOT ONLY ARE THEY SENSITIVE TO YOUR POWERS--
--BUT ALL OF YOU WILL PAY THE PENALTY IF EVEN ONE TRIES TO FREE HIMSELF.
THAT SHOULD KEEP EVEN THE INVULNERABLE SUPERMAN IN LINE.
ADAM, THIS CANNOT BE YOU. YOU WERE A HERO... THE DEFENDER OF THE PLANET RANN.
AND DEFENDER I REMAIN. THE EN'TARANS BLOCK YOUR TELEPATHY WITH THEIR OWN, J'ONN... BUT IF YOU DOUBT MY MOTIVES OR SANITY, PEEK INSIDE MY MIND.
I'M SURE THE EN'TARANS WILL ALLOW YOU ONE GLIMPSE IF IT WILL KEEP YOU FOCUSED ON THE TASK AT HAND.
GREAT MOONS OF MARS...!
YOU--YOU'RE INSANE!
ON THE CONTRARY. I'VE NEVER SEEN THINGS MORE CLEARLY.
GREEN LANTERN WAS THE LAST OF YOU TO VISIT RANN. AT THE TIME, IT WAS LARGELY A DEVASTATED WASTELAND.*
BIP
* GREEN LANTERN #74-75--DAN.
NO MORE. WITH THE HELP OF THE EN'TARANS, I'VE ELECTED TO RESTORE THE PLANET TO ITS FORMER GLORY.
ALL THAT'S BEEN REQUIRED SO FAR...

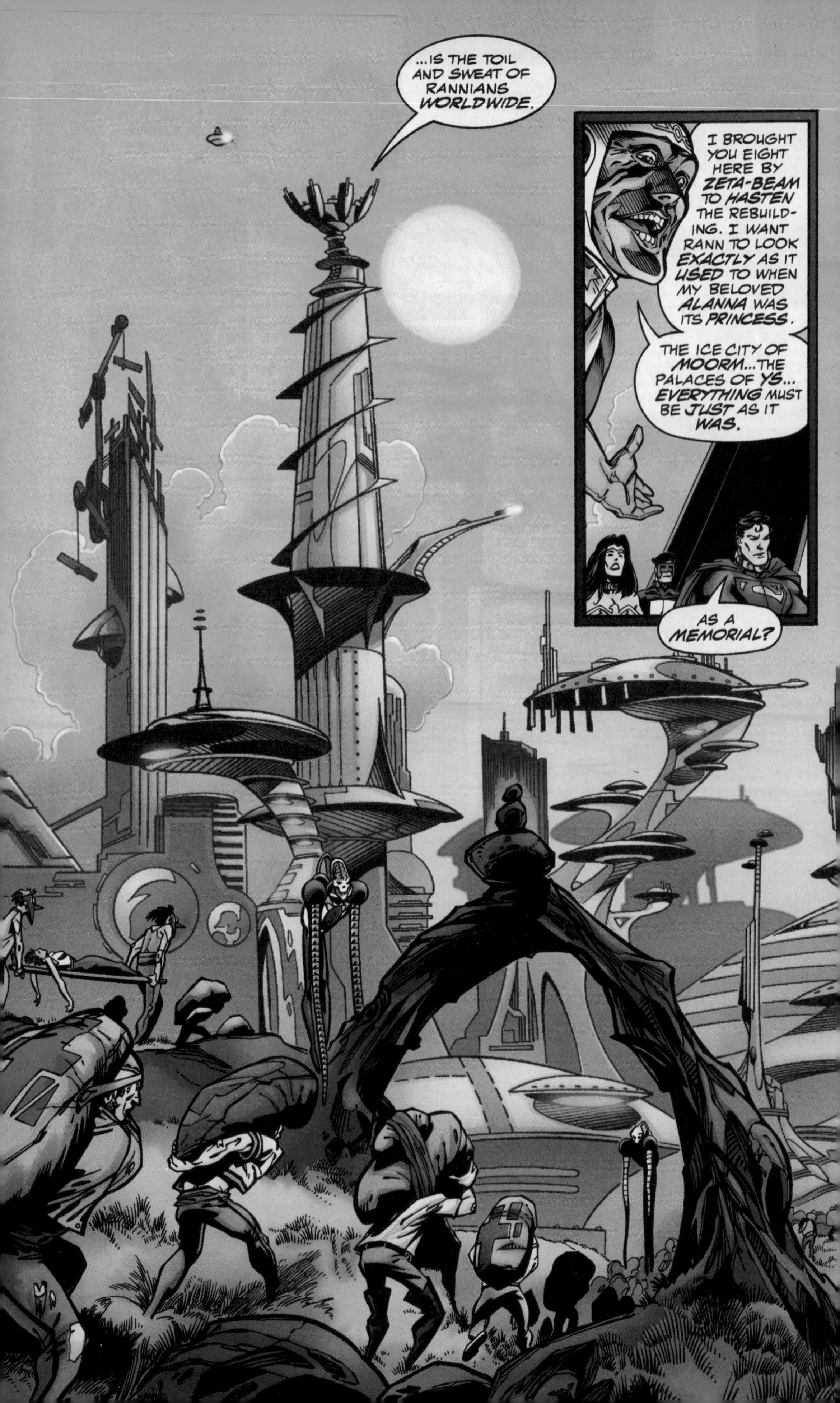
...IS THE TOIL AND SWEAT OF RANNIANS WORLDWIDE.
I BROUGHT YOU EIGHT HERE BY ZETA-BEAM TO HASTEN THE REBUILDING. I WANT RANN TO LOOK EXACTLY AS IT USED TO WHEN MY BELOVED ALANNA WAS ITS PRINCESS.
THE ICE CITY OF MOORM...THE PALACES OF YS... EVERYTHING MUST BE JUST AS IT WAS.
AS A MEMORIAL?

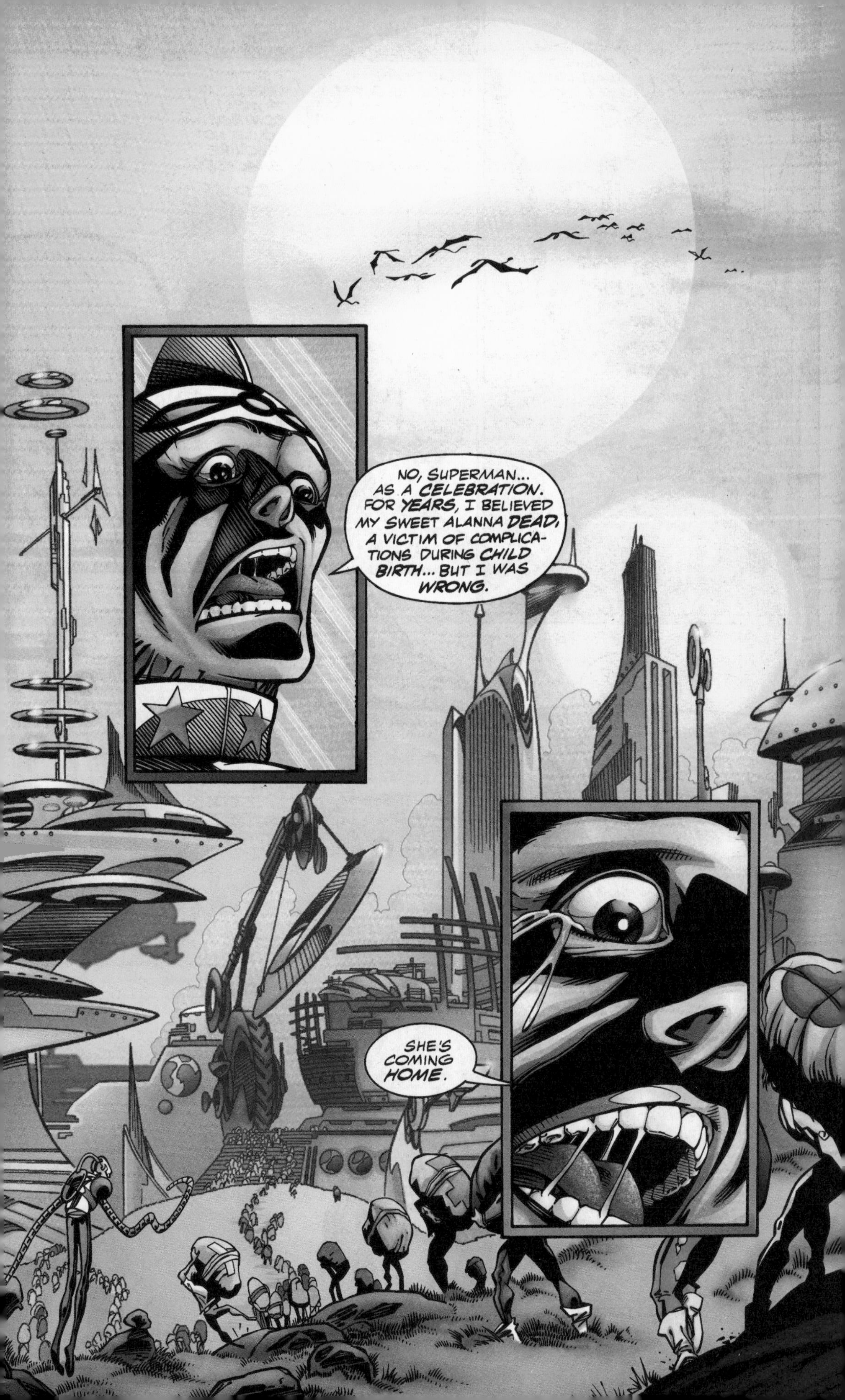
NO, SUPERMAN... AS A CELEBRATION. FOR YEARS, I BELIEVED MY SWEET ALANNA DEAD, A VICTIM OF COMPLICATIONS DURING CHILD BIRTH... BUT I WAS WRONG.
SHE'S COMING HOME.

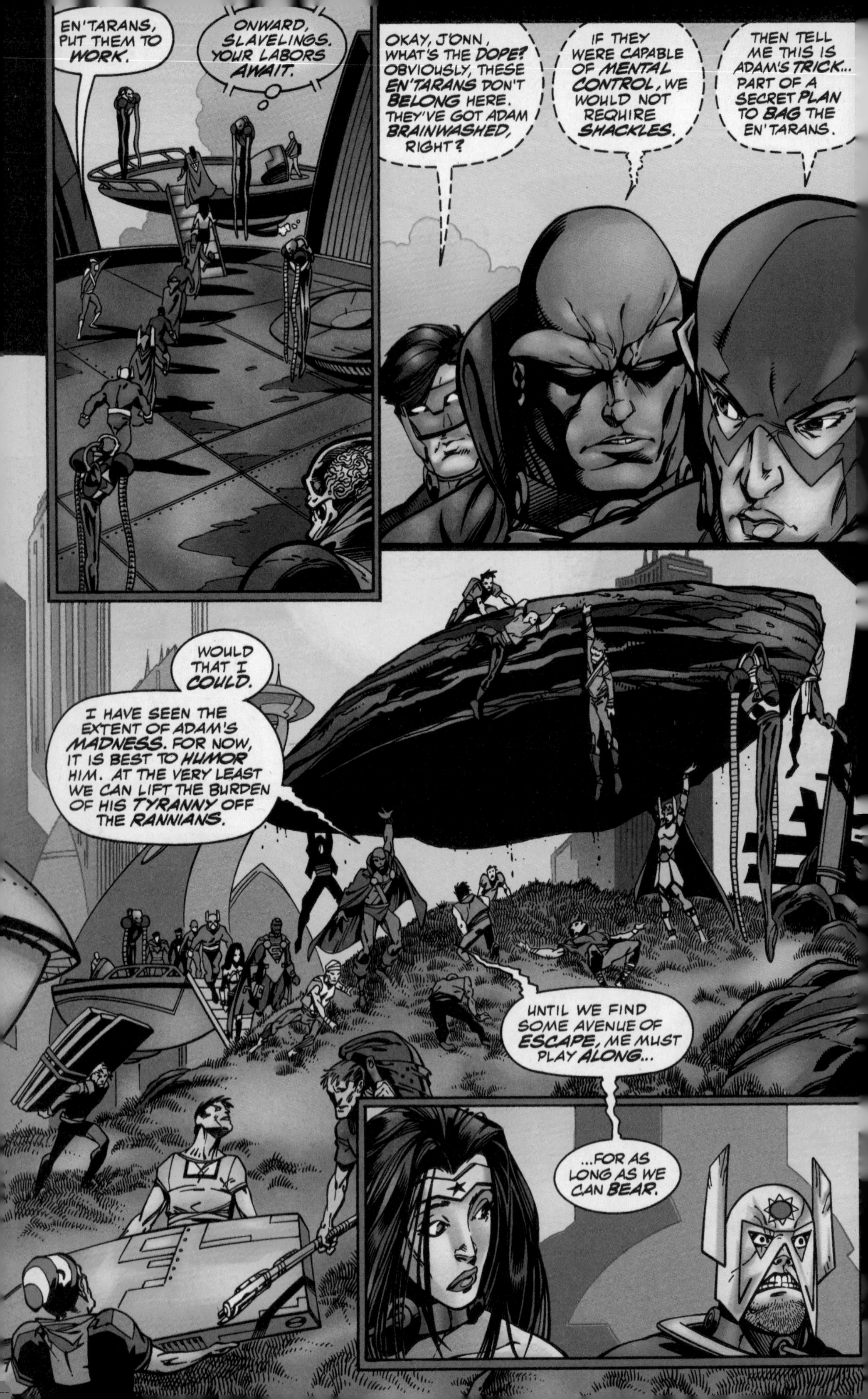
EN'TARANS, PUT THEM TO WORK.
ONWARD, SLAVELINGS. YOUR LABORS AWAIT.
OKAY, J'ONN, WHAT'S THE DOPE? OBVIOUSLY, THESE EN'TARANS DON'T BELONG HERE. THEY'VE GOT ADAM BRAINWASHED, RIGHT?
IF THEY WERE CAPABLE OF MENTAL CONTROL, WE WOULD NOT REQUIRE SHACKLES.
THEN TELL ME THIS IS ADAM'S TRICK... PART OF A SECRET PLAN TO BAG THE EN'TARANS.
WOULD THAT I COULD.
I HAVE SEEN THE EXTENT OF ADAM'S MADNESS. FOR NOW, IT IS BEST TO HUMOR HIM. AT THE VERY LEAST WE CAN LIFT THE BURDEN OF HIS TYRANNY OFF THE RANNIANS.
UNTIL WE FIND SOME AVENUE OF ESCAPE, ME MUST PLAY ALONG...
...FOR AS LONG AS WE CAN BEAR.

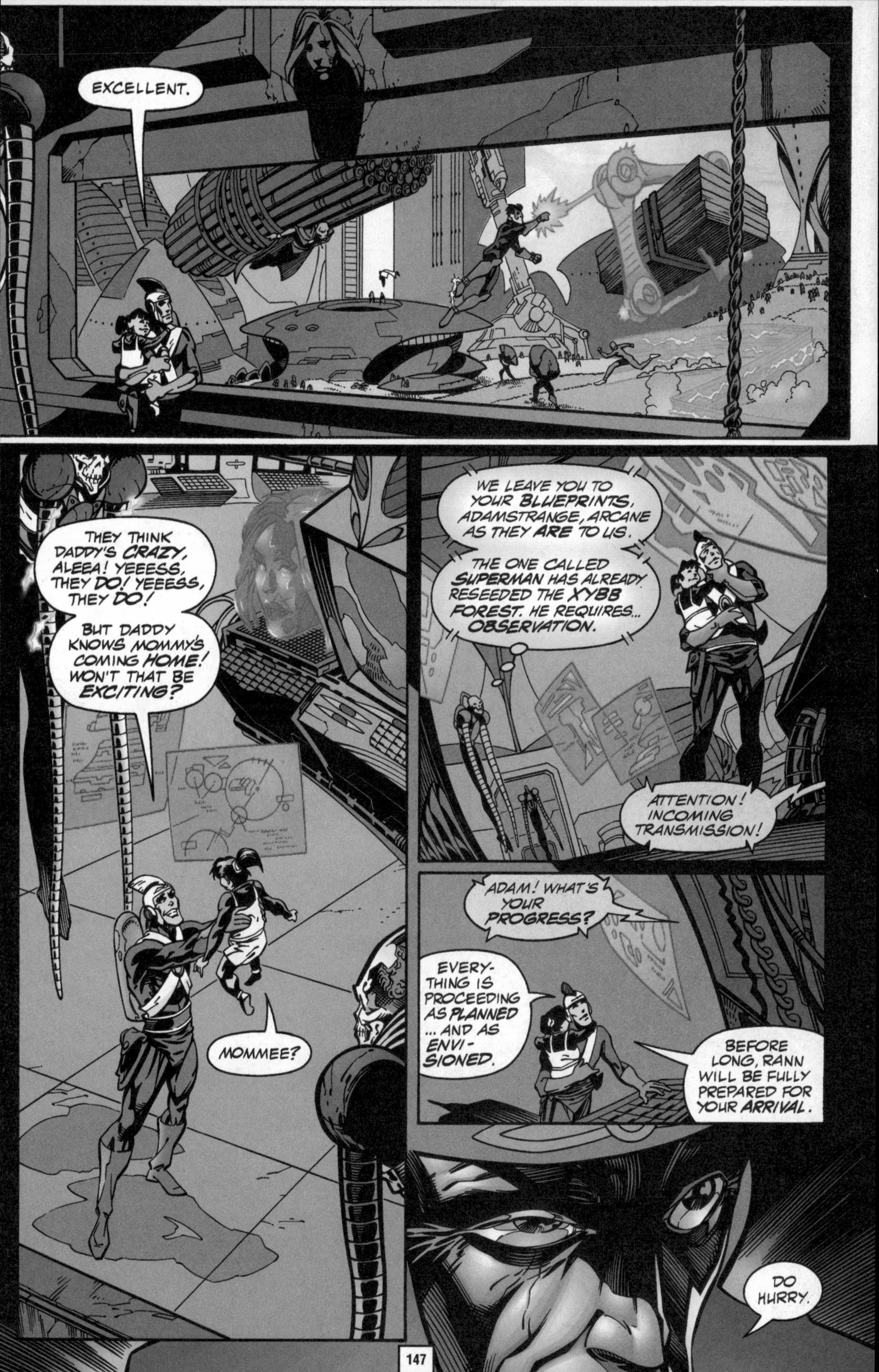

EXCELLENT.
THEY THINK DADDY'S CRAZY, ALEEA! YEEESS, THEY DO! YEEESS, THEY DO!
BUT DADDY KNOWS MOMMY'S COMING HOME! WON'T THAT BE EXCITING?
MOMMEE?
WE LEAVE YOU TO YOUR BLUEPRINTS, ADAMSTRANGE, ARCANE AS THEY ARE TO US.
THE ONE CALLED SUPERMAN HAS ALREADY RESEEDED THE XYBB FOREST. HE REQUIRES... OBSERVATION.
ATTENTION! INCOMING TRANSMISSION!
ADAM! WHAT'S YOUR PROGRESS?
EVERY-THING IS PROCEEDING AS PLANNED ... AND AS ENVI-SIONED.
BEFORE LONG, RANN WILL BE FULLY PREPARED FOR YOUR ARRIVAL.
DO HURRY.

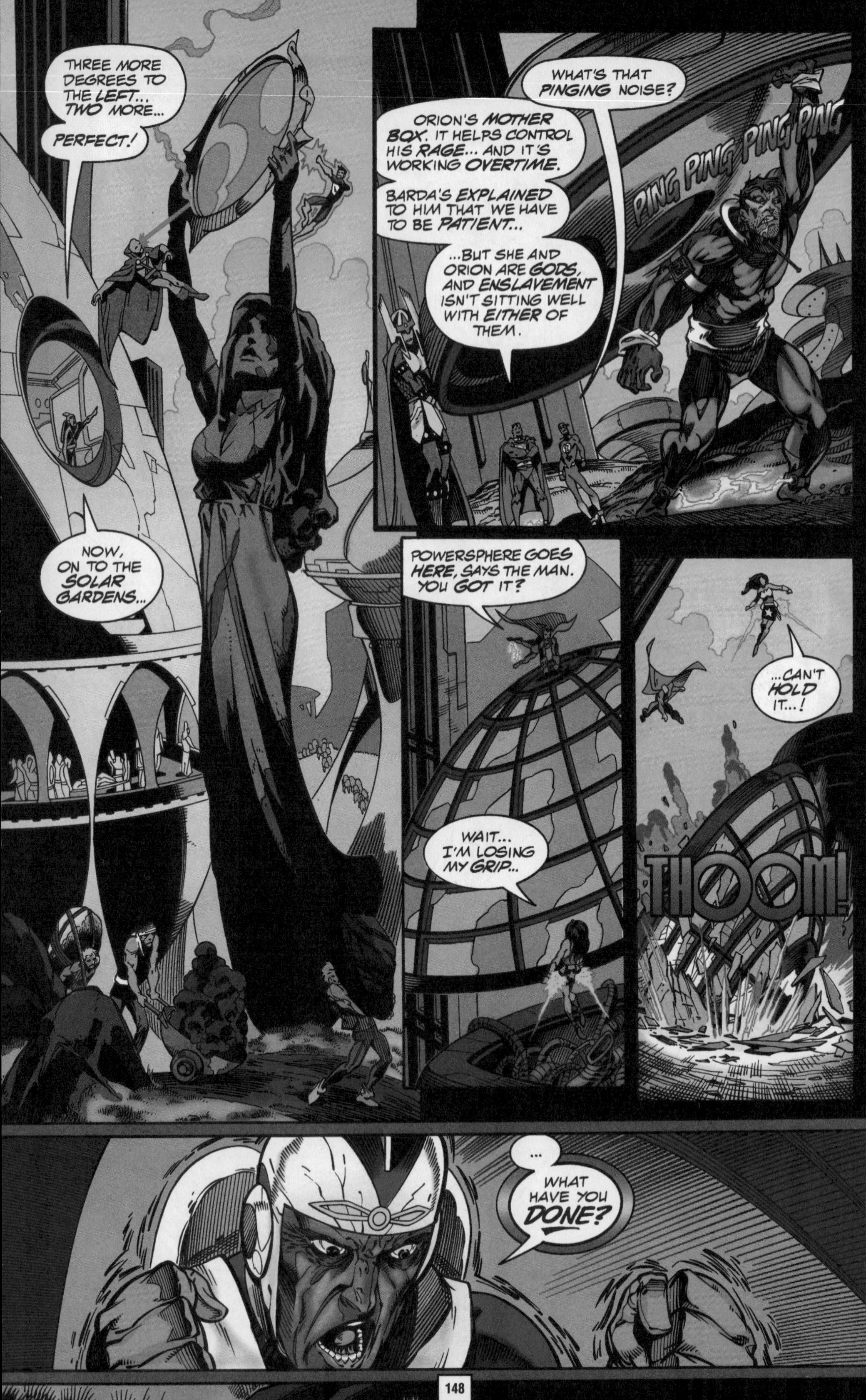
THREE MORE DEGREES TO THE LEFT... TWO MORE...
PERFECT!
NOW, ON TO THE SOLAR GARDENS...
WHAT'S THAT PINGING NOISE?
ORION'S MOTHER BOX. IT HELPS CONTROL HIS RAGE... AND IT'S WORKING OVERTIME.
BARDA'S EXPLAINED TO HIM THAT WE HAVE TO BE PATIENT...
...BUT SHE AND ORION ARE GODS, AND ENSLAVEMENT ISN'T SITTING WELL WITH EITHER OF THEM.
PING PING PING PING PING
POWERSPHERE GOES HERE, SAYS THE MAN. YOU GOT IT?
WAIT... I'M LOSING MY GRIP...
...CAN'T HOLD IT...!
THOOM!
... WHAT HAVE YOU DONE?

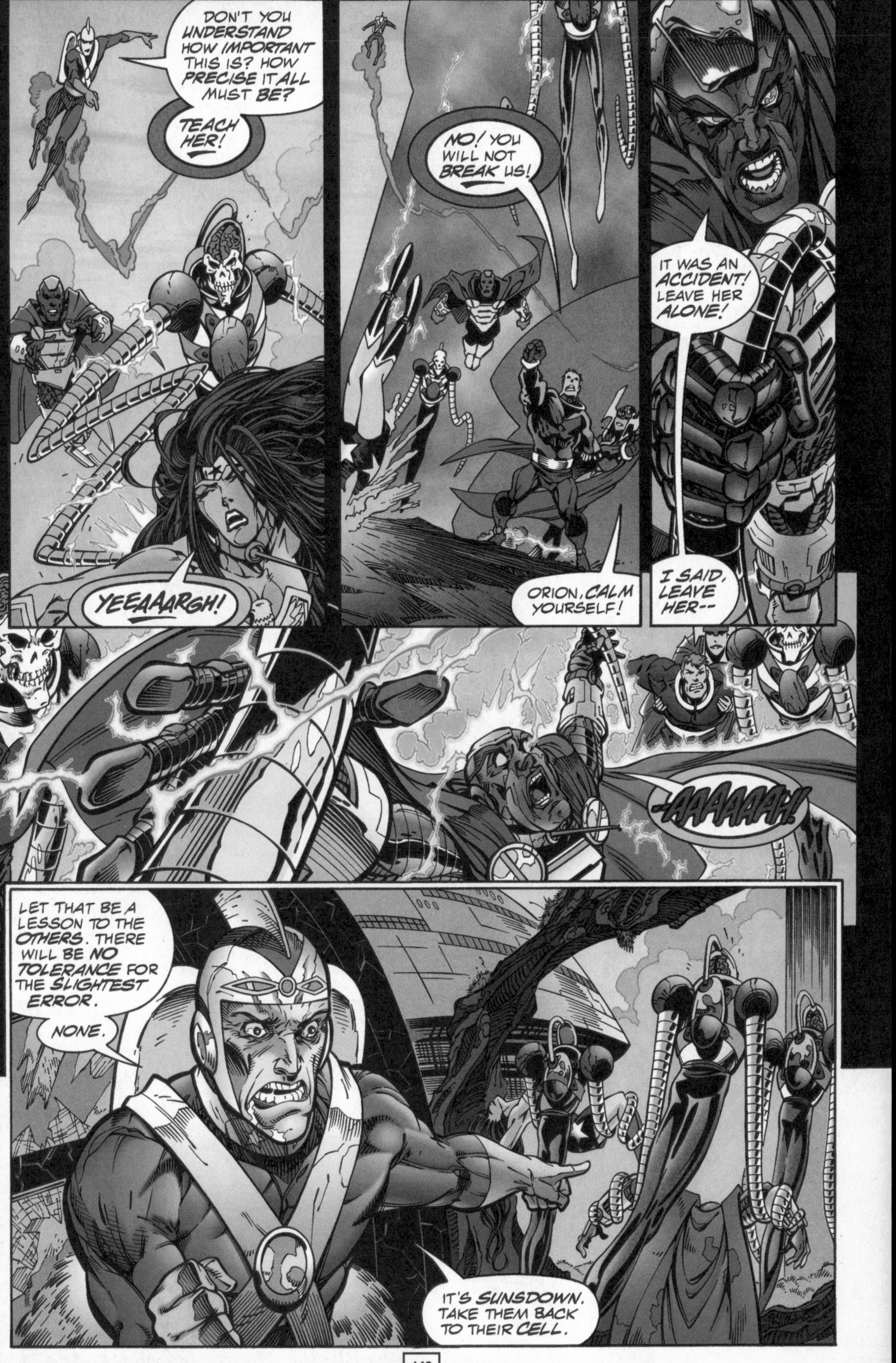
DON'T YOU UNDERSTAND HOW IMPORTANT THIS IS? HOW PRECISE IT ALL MUST BE?
TEACH HER!
YEEAAARGH!
NO! YOU WILL NOT BREAK US!
ORION, CALM YOURSELF!
IT WAS AN ACCIDENT! LEAVE HER ALONE!
I SAID, LEAVE HER--
-AAAAAAH!
LET THAT BE A LESSON TO THE OTHERS. THERE WILL BE NO TOLERANCE FOR THE SLIGHTEST ERROR.
NONE.
IT'S SUNSDOWN. TAKE THEM BACK TO THEIR CELL.

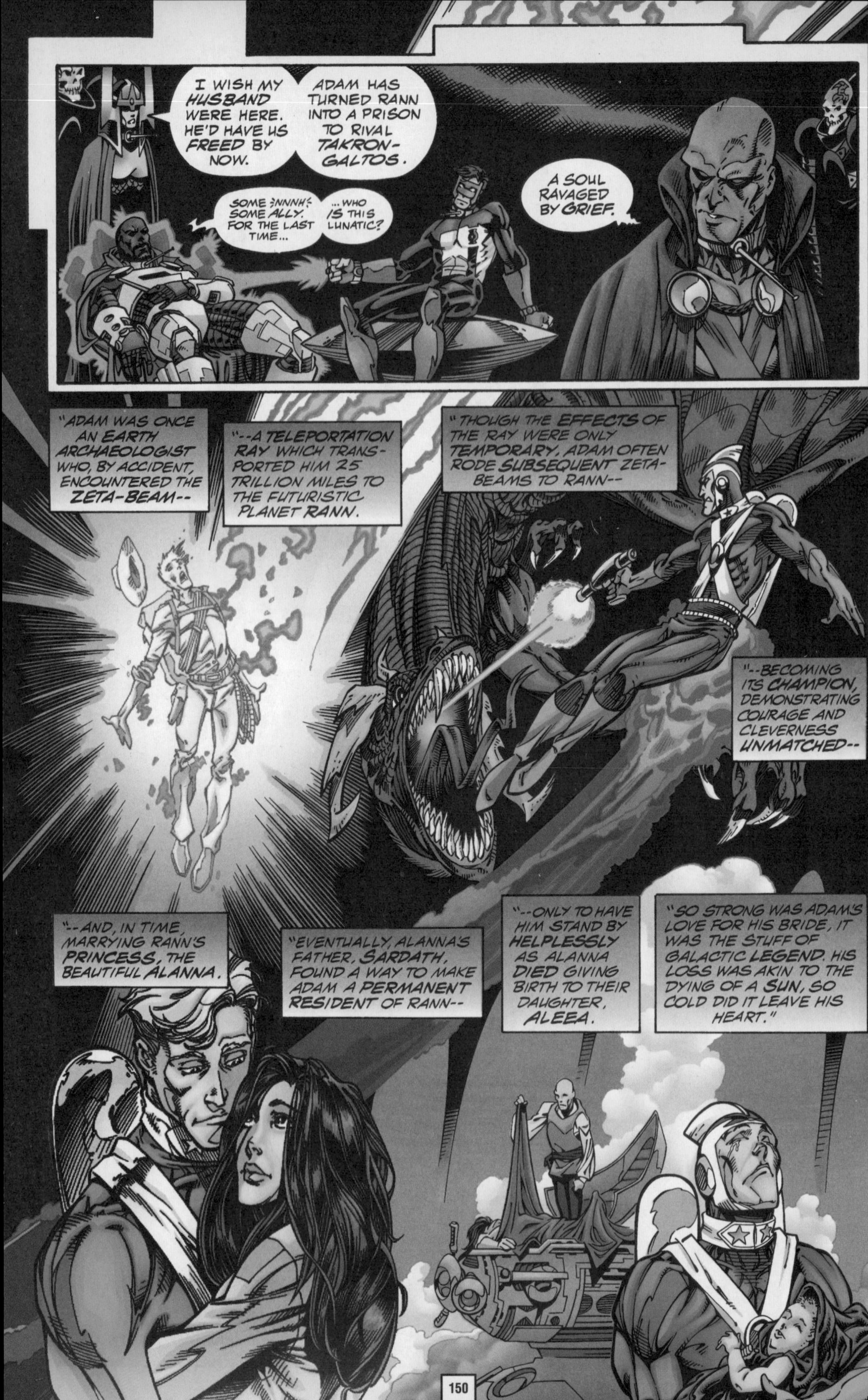
I WISH MY HUSBAND WERE HERE. HE'D HAVE US FREED BY NOW.
ADAM HAS TURNED RANN INTO A PRISON TO RIVAL TAKRON-GALTOS.
SOME ≷NNNH≶ SOME ALLY. FOR THE LAST TIME...
...WHO IS THIS LUNATIC?
A SOUL RAVAGED BY GRIEF.
"ADAM WAS ONCE AN EARTH ARCHAEOLOGIST WHO, BY ACCIDENT, ENCOUNTERED THE ZETA-BEAM--
"--A TELEPORTATION RAY WHICH TRANS-PORTED HIM 25 TRILLION MILES TO THE FUTURISTIC PLANET RANN.
"THOUGH THE EFFECTS OF THE RAY WERE ONLY TEMPORARY, ADAM OFTEN RODE SUBSEQUENT ZETA-BEAMS TO RANN--
"--BECOMING ITS CHAMPION, DEMONSTRATING COURAGE AND CLEVERNESS UNMATCHED--
"--AND, IN TIME, MARRYING RANN'S PRINCESS, THE BEAUTIFUL ALANNA.
"EVENTUALLY, ALANNA'S FATHER, SARDATH, FOUND A WAY TO MAKE ADAM A PERMANENT RESIDENT OF RANN--
"--ONLY TO HAVE HIM STAND BY HELPLESSLY AS ALANNA DIED GIVING BIRTH TO THEIR DAUGHTER, ALEEA.
"SO STRONG WAS ADAM'S LOVE FOR HIS BRIDE, IT WAS THE STUFF OF GALACTIC LEGEND. HIS LOSS WAS AKIN TO THE DYING OF A SUN, SO COLD DID IT LEAVE HIS HEART."

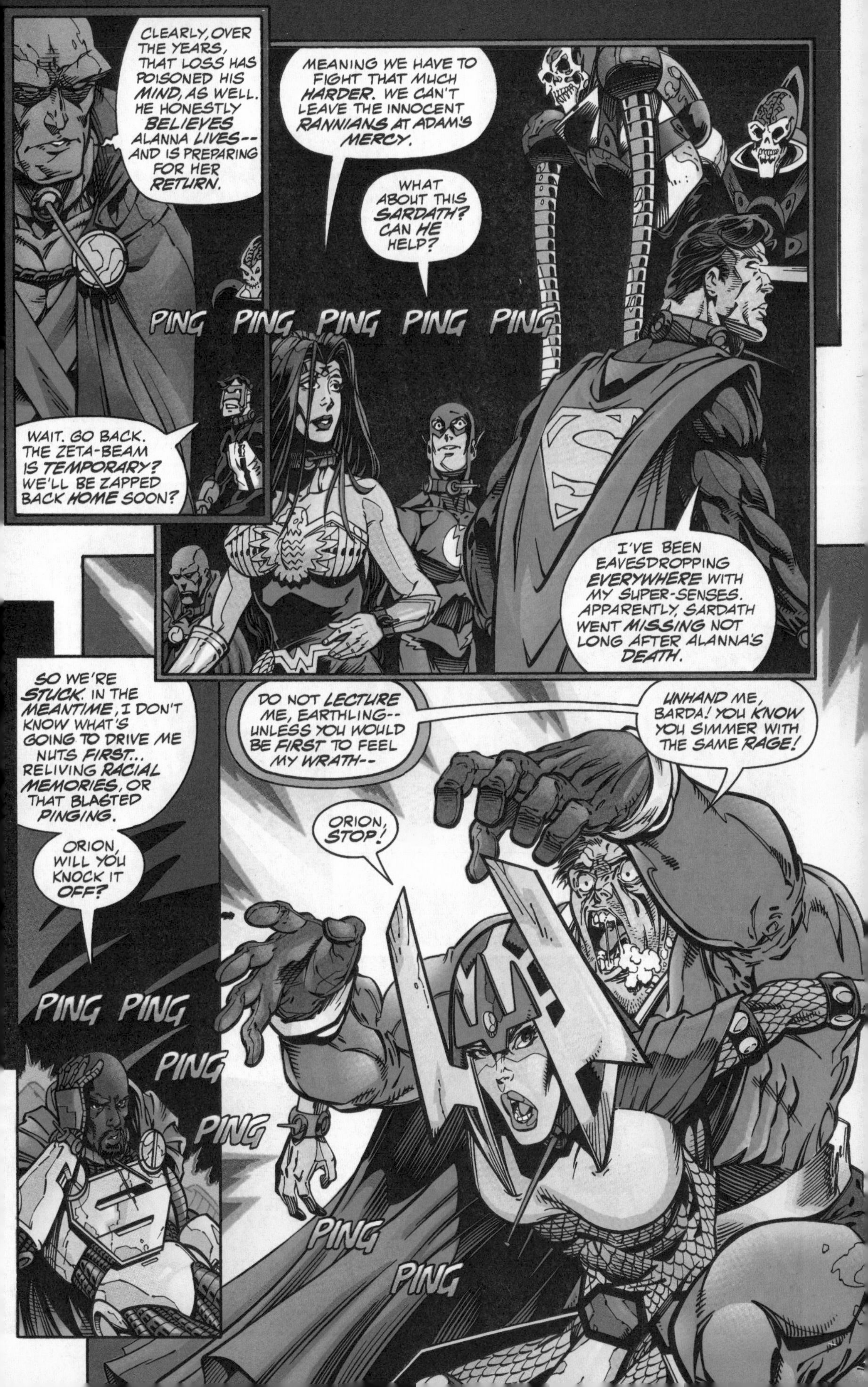
CLEARLY, OVER THE YEARS, THAT LOSS HAS POISONED HIS MIND, AS WELL. HE HONESTLY BELIEVES ALANNA LIVES-- AND IS PREPARING FOR HER RETURN.
MEANING WE HAVE TO FIGHT THAT MUCH HARDER. WE CAN'T LEAVE THE INNOCENT RANNIANS AT ADAM'S MERCY.
WHAT ABOUT THIS SARDATH? CAN HE HELP?
PING PING PING PING PING
WAIT. GO BACK. THE ZETA-BEAM IS TEMPORARY? WE'LL BE ZAPPED BACK HOME SOON?
I'VE BEEN EAVESDROPPING EVERYWHERE WITH MY SUPER-SENSES. APPARENTLY, SARDATH WENT MISSING NOT LONG AFTER ALANNA'S DEATH.
SO WE'RE STUCK. IN THE MEANTIME, I DON'T KNOW WHAT'S GOING TO DRIVE ME NUTS FIRST... RELIVING RACIAL MEMORIES, OR THAT BLASTED PINGING.
ORION, WILL YOU KNOCK IT OFF?
DO NOT LECTURE ME, EARTHLING-- UNLESS YOU WOULD BE FIRST TO FEEL MY WRATH--
UNHAND ME, BARDA! YOU KNOW YOU SIMMER WITH THE SAME RAGE!
ORION, STOP!
PING PING
PING
PING
PING
PING

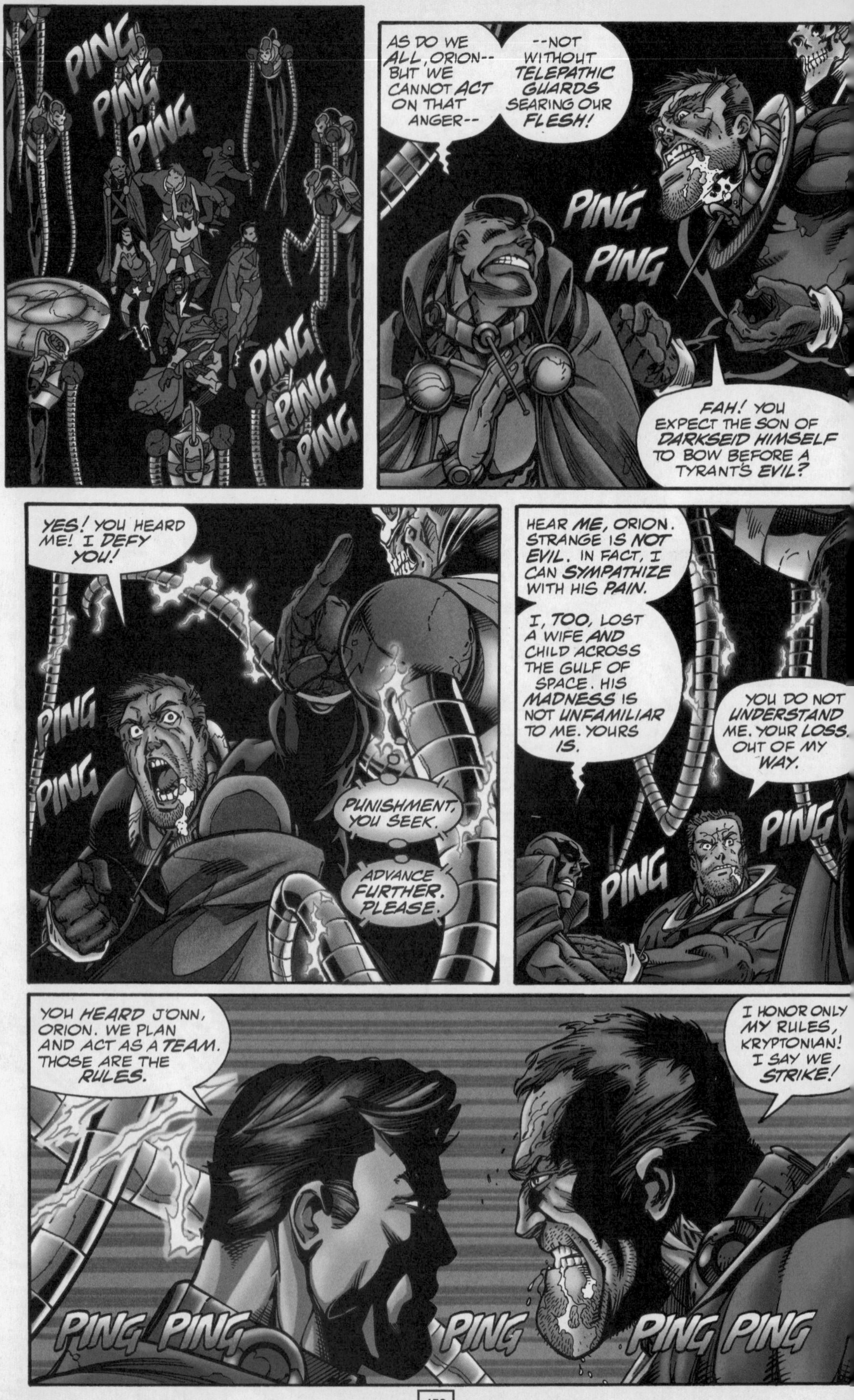
PING
PING
PING
PING
PING
PING
AS DO WE ALL, ORION-- BUT WE CANNOT ACT ON THAT ANGER--
--NOT WITHOUT TELEPATHIC GUARDS SEARING OUR FLESH!
PING
PING
FAH! YOU EXPECT THE SON OF DARKSEID HIMSELF TO BOW BEFORE A TYRANT'S EVIL?
YES! YOU HEARD ME! I DEFY YOU!
PING
PING
PUNISHMENT, YOU SEEK.
ADVANCE FURTHER. PLEASE.
HEAR ME, ORION. STRANGE IS NOT EVIL. IN FACT, I CAN SYMPATHIZE WITH HIS PAIN.
I, TOO, LOST A WIFE AND CHILD ACROSS THE GULF OF SPACE. HIS MADNESS IS NOT UNFAMILIAR TO ME. YOURS IS.
YOU DO NOT UNDERSTAND ME. YOUR LOSS. OUT OF MY WAY.
PING
PING
YOU HEARD J'ONN, ORION. WE PLAN AND ACT AS A TEAM. THOSE ARE THE RULES.
I HONOR ONLY MY RULES, KRYPTONIAN! I SAY WE STRIKE!
PING PING
PING
PING PING

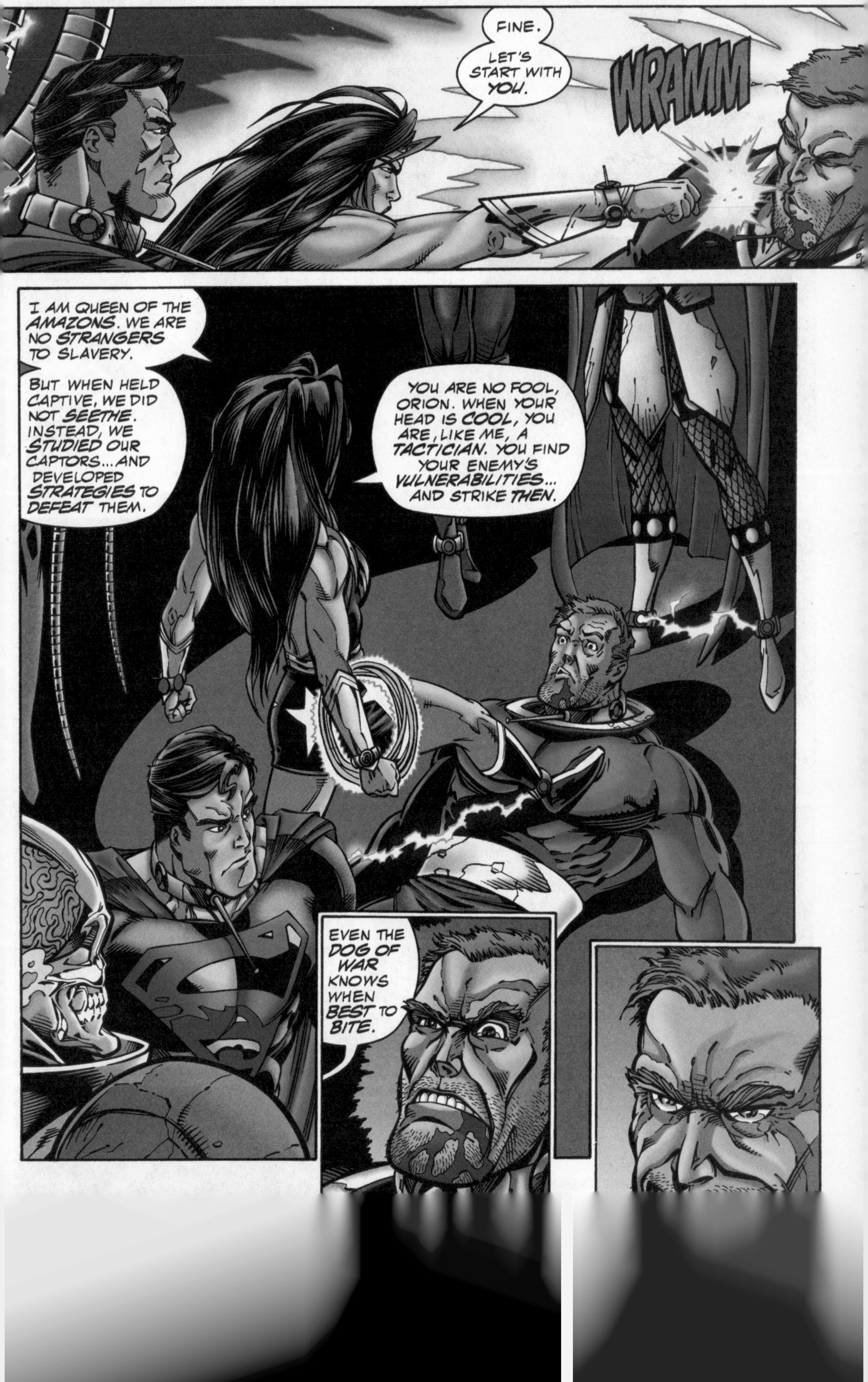
FINE.
LET'S START WITH YOU.
WRAMM
I AM QUEEN OF THE AMAZONS. WE ARE NO STRANGERS TO SLAVERY.
BUT WHEN HELD CAPTIVE, WE DID NOT SEETHE. INSTEAD, WE STUDIED OUR CAPTORS... AND DEVELOPED STRATEGIES TO DEFEAT THEM.
YOU ARE NO FOOL, ORION. WHEN YOUR HEAD IS COOL, YOU ARE, LIKE ME, A TACTICIAN. YOU FIND YOUR ENEMY'S VULNERABILITIES... AND STRIKE THEN.
EVEN THE DOG OF WAR KNOWS WHEN BEST TO BITE.

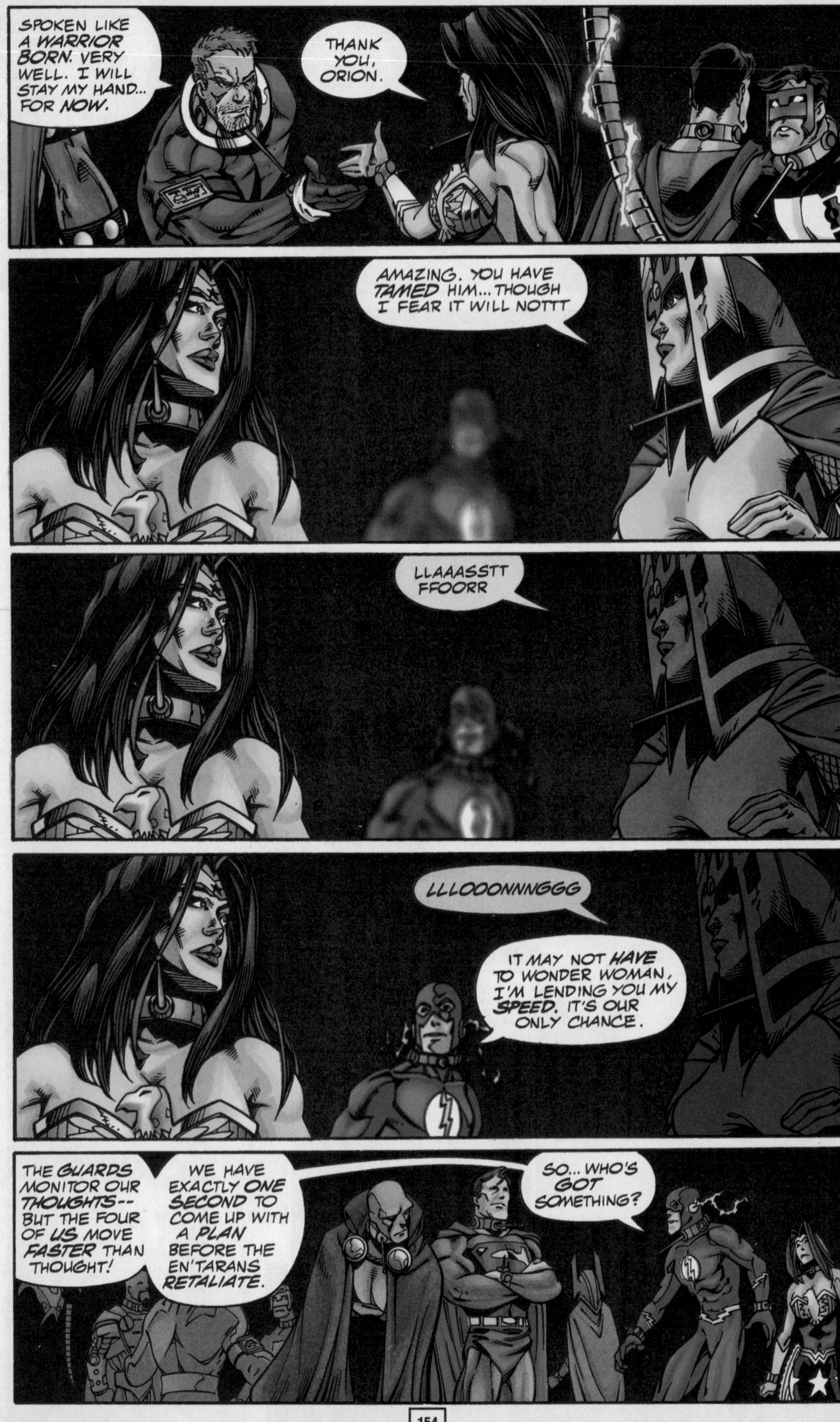
SPOKEN LIKE A WARRIOR BORN. VERY WELL. I WILL STAY MY HAND... FOR NOW.
THANK YOU, ORION.
AMAZING. YOU HAVE TAMED HIM... THOUGH I FEAR IT WILL NOTTT
LLAAASSTT FFOORR
LLLOOONNNGGG
IT MAY NOT HAVE TO WONDER WOMAN, I'M LENDING YOU MY SPEED. IT'S OUR ONLY CHANCE.
THE GUARDS MONITOR OUR THOUGHTS-- BUT THE FOUR OF US MOVE FASTER THAN THOUGHT!
WE HAVE EXACTLY ONE SECOND TO COME UP WITH A PLAN BEFORE THE EN'TARANS RETALIATE.
SO... WHO'S GOT SOMETHING?

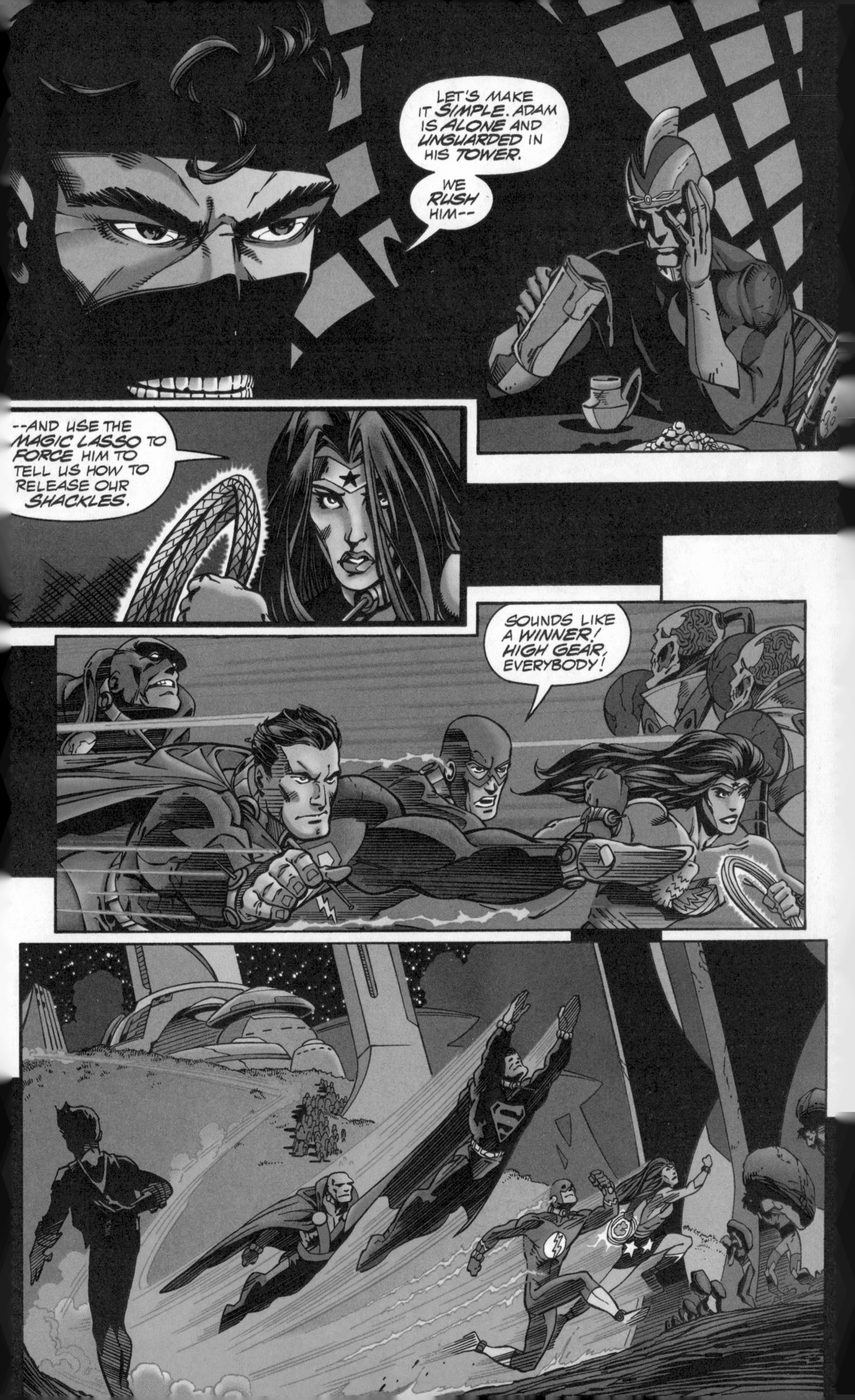
LET'S MAKE IT SIMPLE. ADAM IS ALONE AND UNGUARDED IN HIS TOWER.
WE RUSH HIM--
--AND USE THE MAGIC LASSO TO FORCE HIM TO TELL US HOW TO RELEASE OUR SHACKLES.
SOUNDS LIKE A WINNER! HIGH GEAR, EVERYBODY!

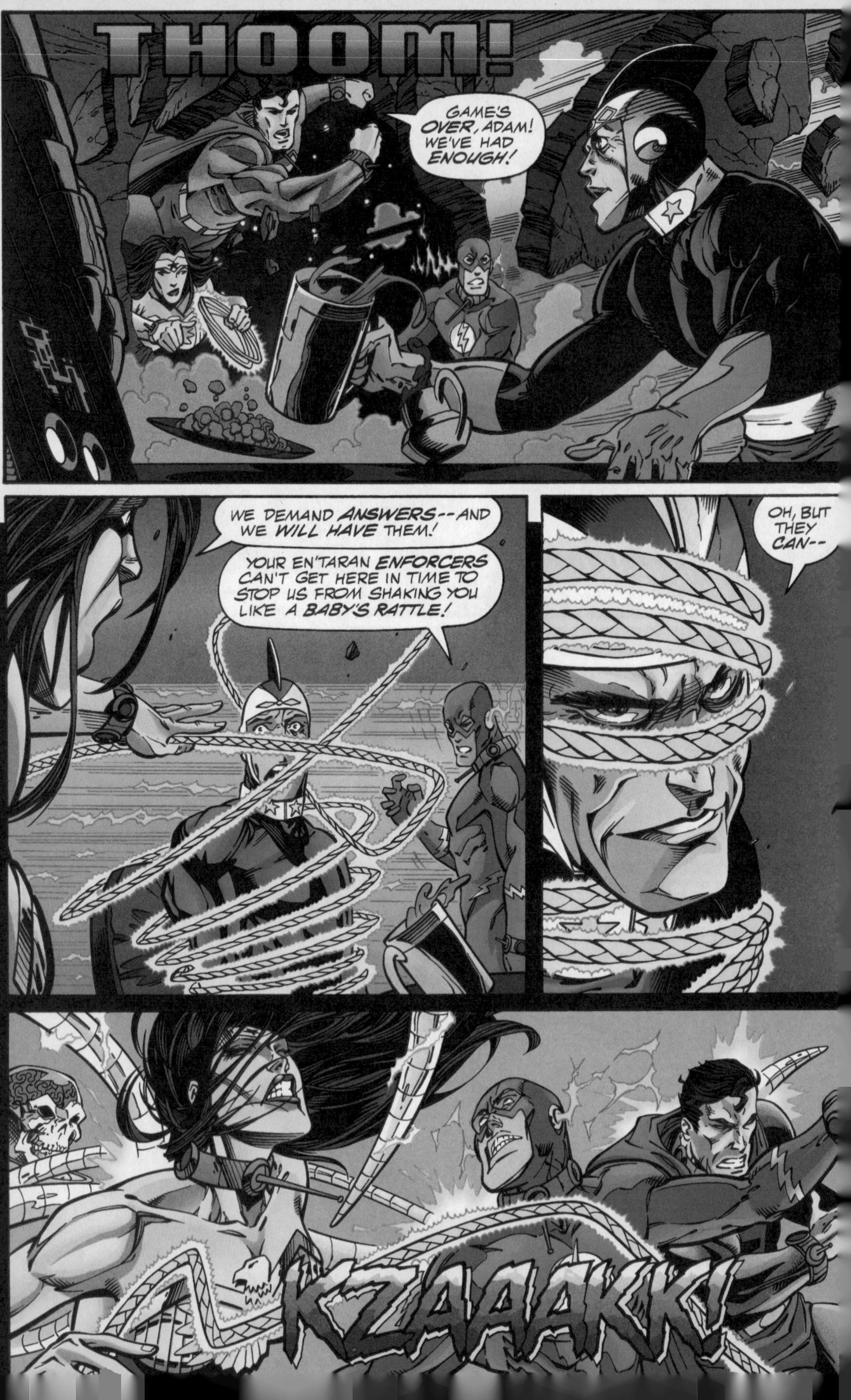
THOOM!
GAME'S OVER, ADAM! WE'VE HAD ENOUGH!
WE DEMAND ANSWERS--AND WE WILL HAVE THEM!
YOUR EN'TARAN ENFORCERS CAN'T GET HERE IN TIME TO STOP US FROM SHAKING YOU LIKE A BABY'S RATTLE!
OH, BUT THEY CAN--
KZAAAKK!

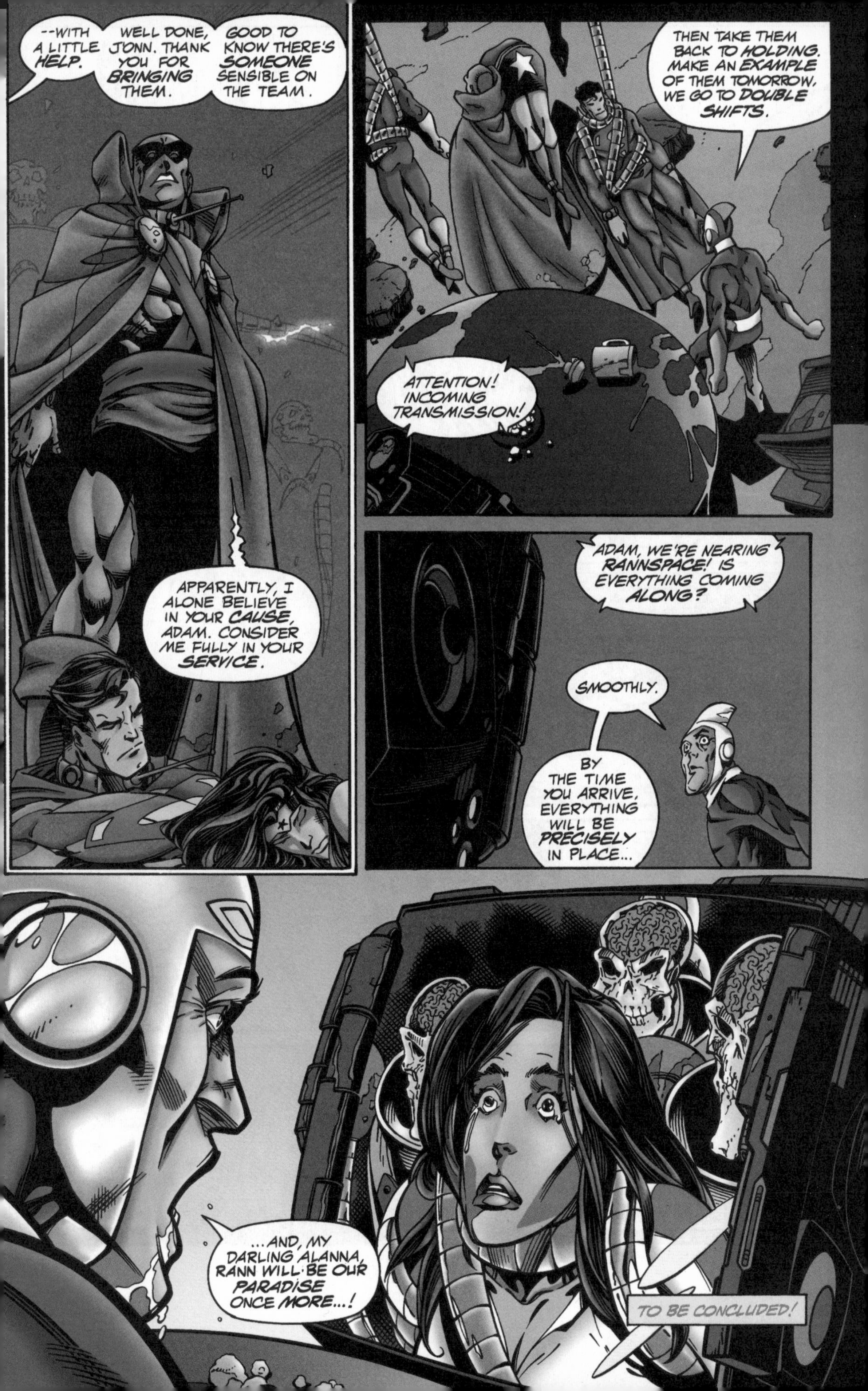
--WITH A LITTLE HELP.
WELL DONE, J'ONN. THANK YOU FOR BRINGING THEM.
GOOD TO KNOW THERE'S SOMEONE SENSIBLE ON THE TEAM.
APPARENTLY, I ALONE BELIEVE IN YOUR CAUSE, ADAM. CONSIDER ME FULLY IN YOUR SERVICE.
THEN TAKE THEM BACK TO HOLDING. MAKE AN EXAMPLE OF THEM TOMORROW, WE GO TO DOUBLE SHIFTS.
ATTENTION! INCOMING TRANSMISSION!
ADAM, WE'RE NEARING RANNSPACE! IS EVERYTHING COMING ALONG?
SMOOTHLY.
BY THE TIME YOU ARRIVE, EVERYTHING WILL BE PRECISELY IN PLACE...
...AND, MY DARLING ALANNA, RANN WILL BE OUR PARADISE ONCE MORE...!
TO BE CONCLUDED!

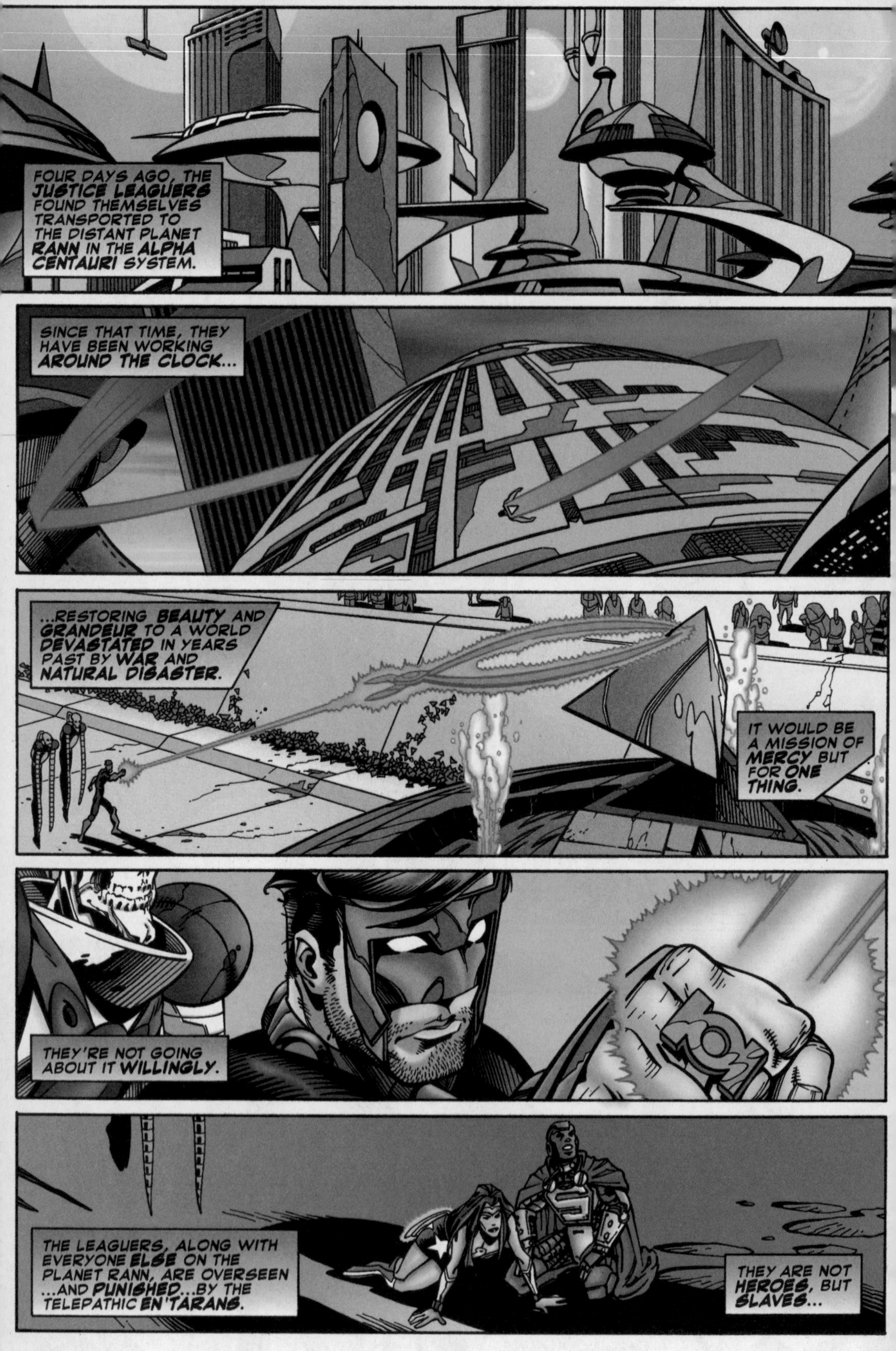
FOUR DAYS AGO, THE JUSTICE LEAGUERS FOUND THEMSELVES TRANSPORTED TO THE DISTANT PLANET RANN IN THE ALPHA CENTAURI SYSTEM.
SINCE THAT TIME, THEY HAVE BEEN WORKING AROUND THE CLOCK...
...RESTORING BEAUTY AND GRANDEUR TO A WORLD DEVASTATED IN YEARS PAST BY WAR AND NATURAL DISASTER.
IT WOULD BE A MISSION OF MERCY BUT FOR ONE THING.
THEY'RE NOT GOING ABOUT IT WILLINGLY.
THE LEAGUERS, ALONG WITH EVERYONE ELSE ON THE PLANET RANN, ARE OVERSEEN ...AND PUNISHED...BY THE TELEPATHIC EN'TARANS.
THEY ARE NOT HEROES, BUT SLAVES...

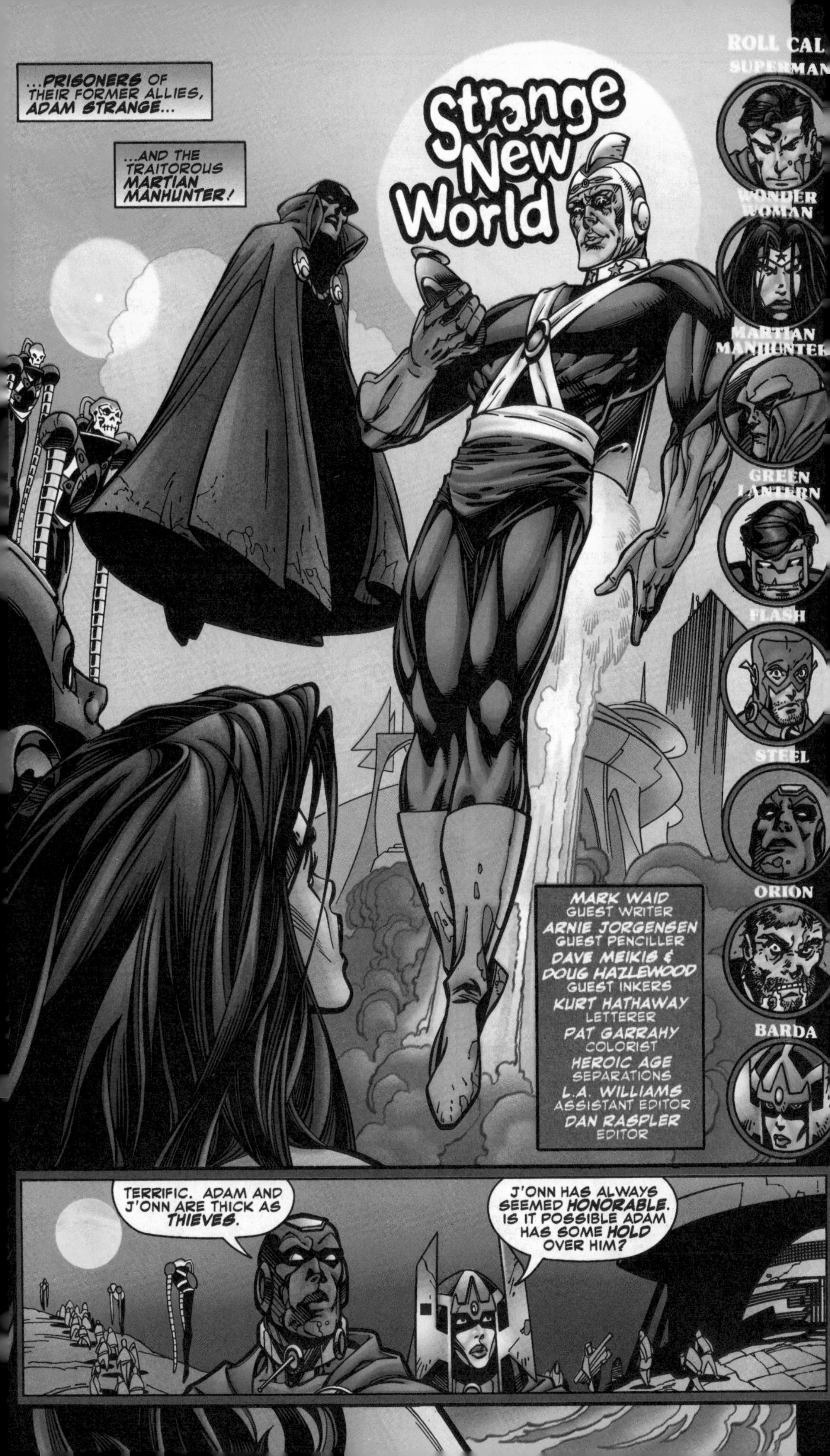
...PRISONERS OF THEIR FORMER ALLIES, ADAM STRANGE...
...AND THE TRAITOROUS MARTIAN MANHUNTER!
Strange New World
ROLL CAL
SUPERMAN
WONDER WOMAN
MARTIAN MANHUNTER
GREEN LANTERN
FLASH
STEEL
ORION
BARDA
MARK WAID GUEST WRITER
ARNIE JORGENSEN GUEST PENCILLER
DAVE MEIKIS & DOUG HAZLEWOOD GUEST INKERS
KURT HATHAWAY LETTERER
PAT GARRAHY COLORIST
HEROIC AGE SEPARATIONS
L.A. WILLIAMS ASSISTANT EDITOR
DAN RASPLER EDITOR
TERRIFIC. ADAM AND J'ONN ARE THICK AS THIEVES.
J'ONN HAS ALWAYS SEEMED HONORABLE. IS IT POSSIBLE ADAM HAS SOME HOLD OVER HIM?

THEY HAVE SOME WEIRD *BOND.* SOMETHING ABOUT BOTH OF THEM HAVING LOST THEIR *FAMILIES.* GIVEN THE *CIRCUM-STANCES,* MY COMPASSION'S A LITTLE *SHALLOW.*

PLUS, *ADAM'S* GONE *CRAZY.* HE THINKS HIS WIFE'S COMING BACK FROM THE DEAD. ISN'T THAT WHY HE'S GOT US *WORKING* THIS HARD?

TO *REBUILD* RANN--*EXACTLY*--FOR *HER?* GOD, GET ME *OUT* OF HERE...!

PING PING PIN

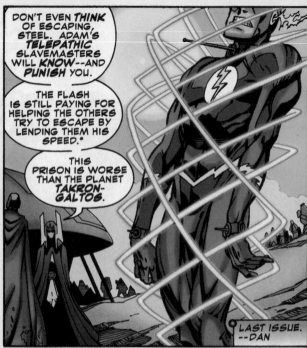

DON'T EVEN *THINK* OF ESCAPING, STEEL. ADAM'S *TELEPATHIC* SLAVEMASTERS WILL *KNOW*--AND *PUNISH* YOU.

THE FLASH IS STILL PAYING FOR HELPING THE OTHERS TRY TO ESCAPE BY LENDING THEM HIS SPEED.*

THIS PRISON IS WORSE THAN THE PLANET *TAKRON-GALTOS.*

*LAST ISSUE. --DAN

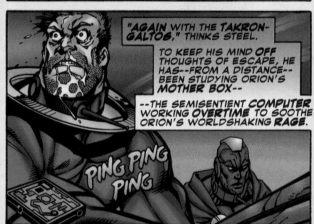

"AGAIN WITH THE TAKRON-GALTOS," THINKS STEEL.

TO KEEP HIS MIND *OFF* THOUGHTS OF ESCAPE, HE HAS--FROM A DISTANCE--BEEN STUDYING ORION'S *MOTHER BOX*--

--THE SEMISENTIENT *COMPUTER* WORKING *OVERTIME* TO SOOTHE ORION'S WORLDSHAKING *RAGE.*

PING PING PING

SO ADEPT AT ANALYZING TECHNOLOGY IS STEEL THAT HE'S GROWN TO IMAGINE A *KINSHIP* WITH THE MOTHER BOX--

--A VAGUE *UNDER-STANDING* OF HOW IT *REGULATES* ORION'S *MOODS*--HOW IT--

PING PING PING PING

--*MANIPULATES*--

--*HIS*--

--*MIND*--

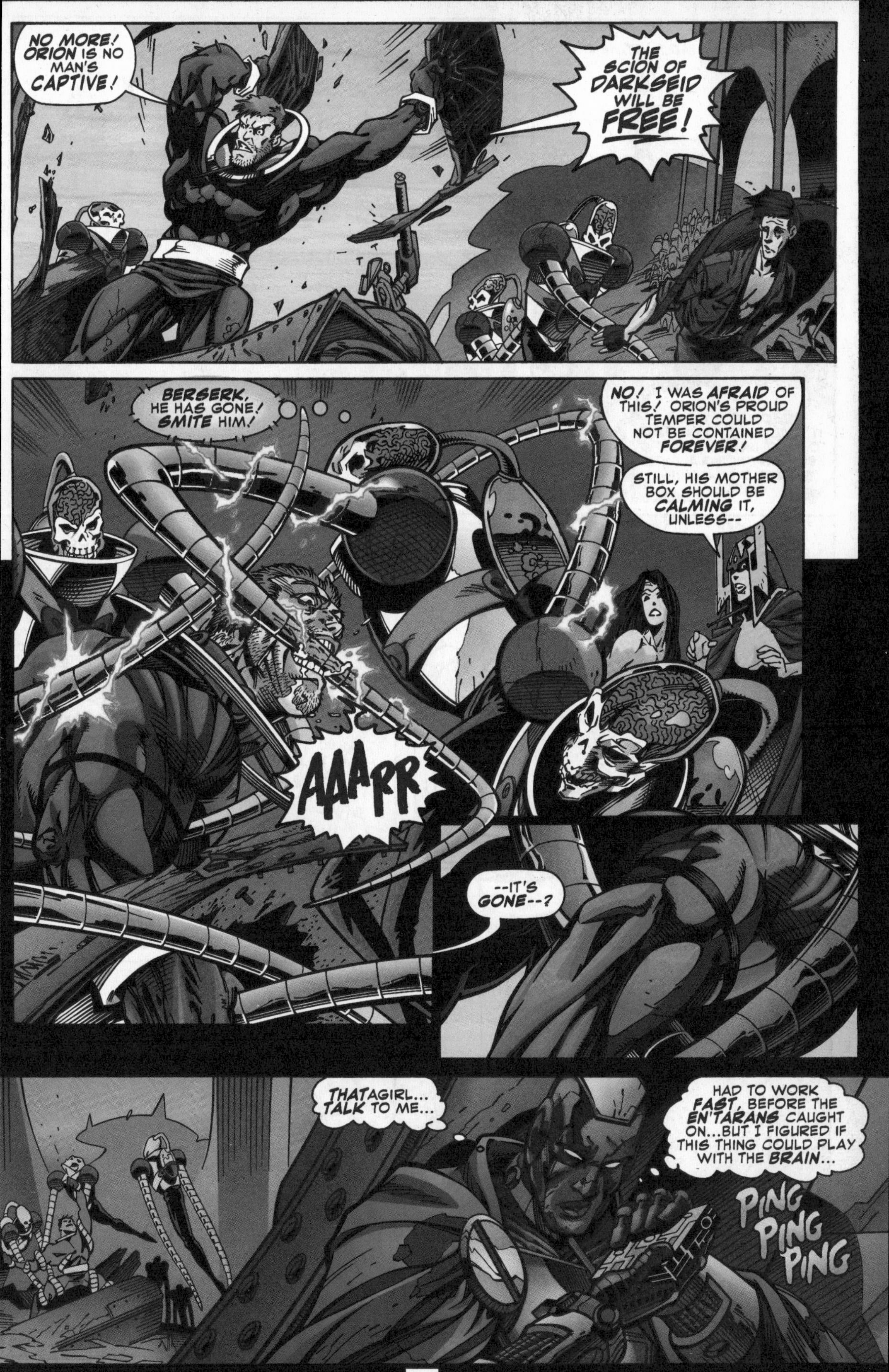
NO MORE! ORION IS NO MAN'S CAPTIVE!
THE SCION OF DARKSEID WILL BE FREE!
BERSERK, HE HAS GONE! SMITE HIM!
NO! I WAS AFRAID OF THIS! ORION'S PROUD TEMPER COULD NOT BE CONTAINED FOREVER!
STILL, HIS MOTHER BOX SHOULD BE CALMING IT, UNLESS--
AAARR
--IT'S GONE--?
THATAGIRL... TALK TO ME...
HAD TO WORK FAST, BEFORE THE EN'TARANS CAUGHT ON...BUT I FIGURED IF THIS THING COULD PLAY WITH THE BRAIN...
PING PING PING

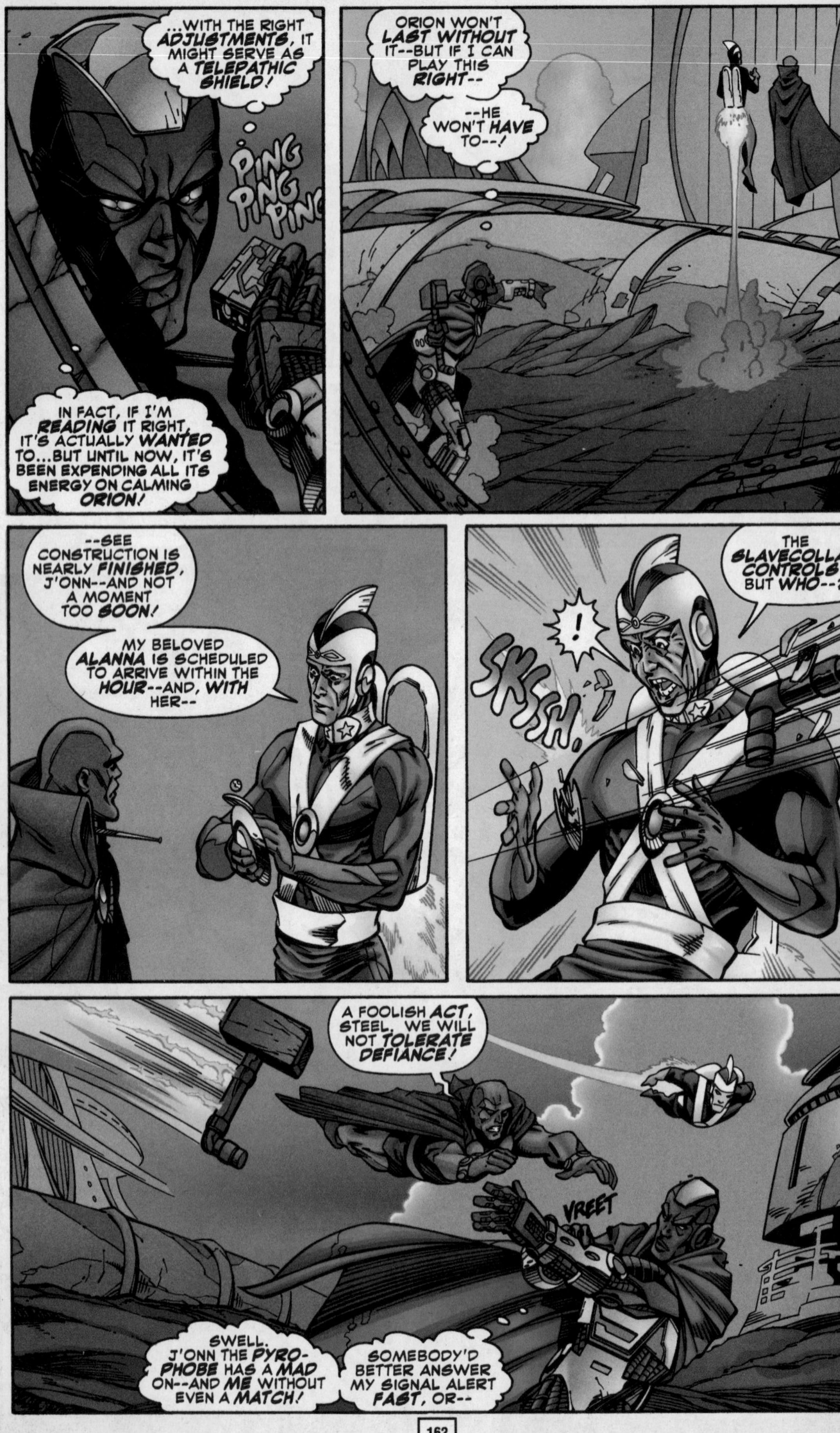
...WITH THE RIGHT ADJUSTMENTS, IT MIGHT SERVE AS A TELEPATHIC SHIELD!
PING PING PING
IN FACT, IF I'M READING IT RIGHT, IT'S ACTUALLY WANTED TO...BUT UNTIL NOW, IT'S BEEN EXPENDING ALL ITS ENERGY ON CALMING ORION!
ORION WON'T LAST WITHOUT IT--BUT IF I CAN PLAY THIS RIGHT--
--HE WON'T HAVE TO--!
--SEE CONSTRUCTION IS NEARLY FINISHED, J'ONN--AND NOT A MOMENT TOO SOON!
MY BELOVED ALANNA IS SCHEDULED TO ARRIVE WITHIN THE HOUR--AND, WITH HER--
!
SKSH.
THE SLAVECOLLAR CONTROLS! BUT WHO--?
A FOOLISH ACT, STEEL. WE WILL NOT TOLERATE DEFIANCE!
VREET
SWELL. J'ONN THE PYRO-PHOBE HAS A MAD ON--AND ME WITHOUT EVEN A MATCH!
SOMEBODY'D BETTER ANSWER MY SIGNAL ALERT FAST, OR--

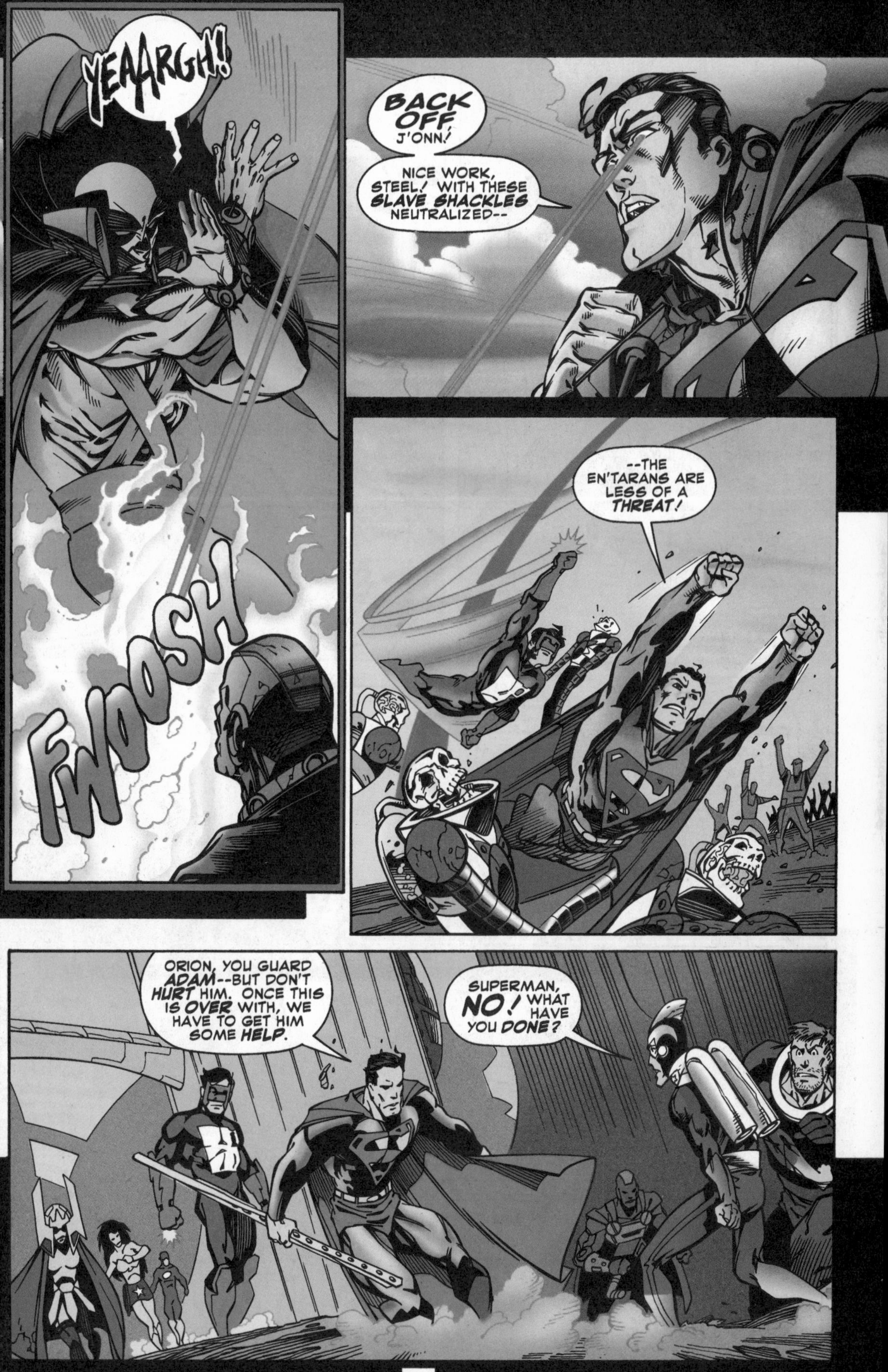
YEAARGH!
BACK OFF, J'ONN!
NICE WORK, STEEL! WITH THESE SLAVE SHACKLES NEUTRALIZED--
FWOOSH
--THE EN'TARANS ARE LESS OF A THREAT!
ORION, YOU GUARD ADAM--BUT DON'T HURT HIM. ONCE THIS IS OVER WITH, WE HAVE TO GET HIM SOME HELP.
SUPERMAN, NO! WHAT HAVE YOU DONE?

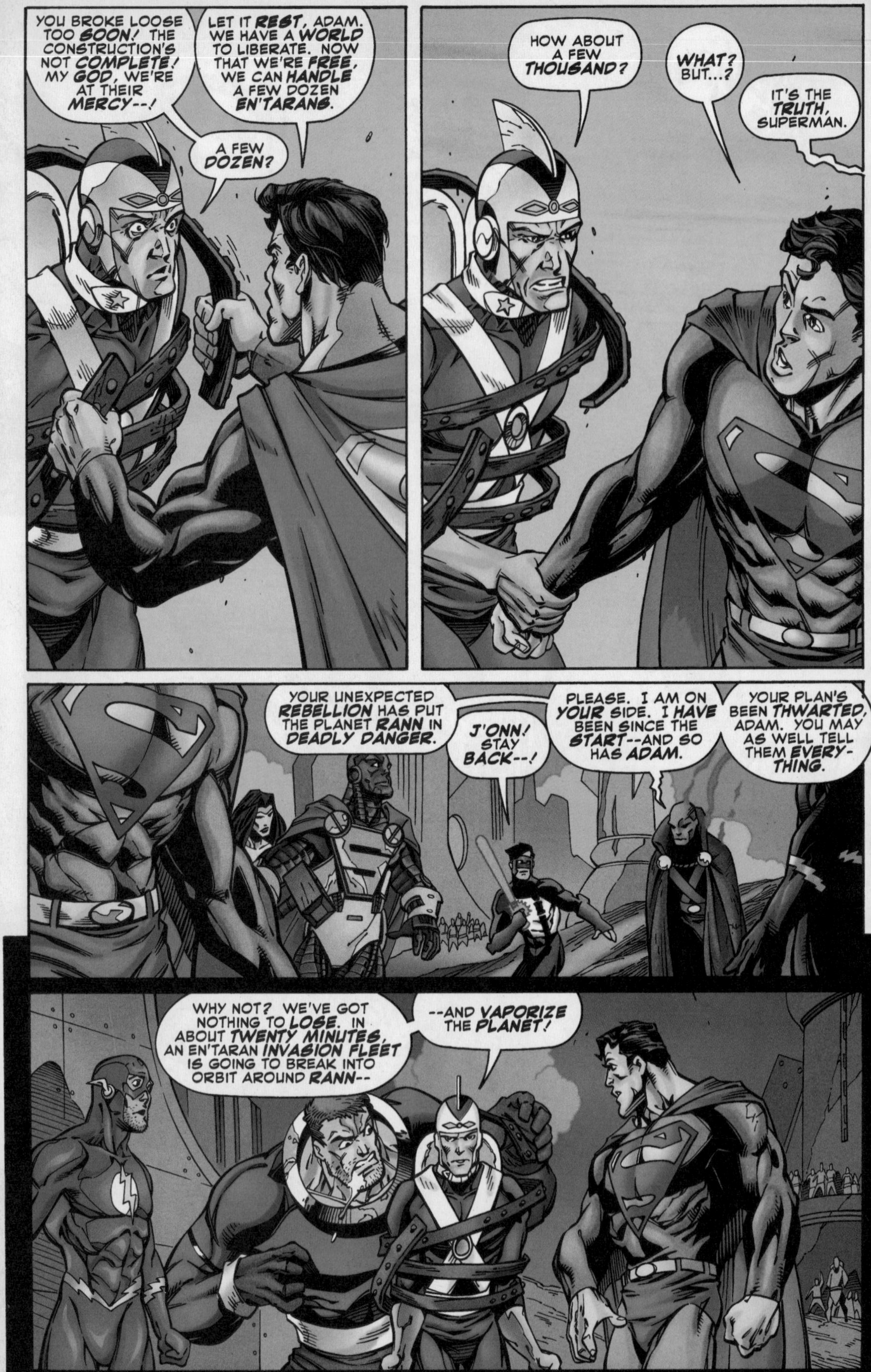
YOU BROKE LOOSE TOO SOON! THE CONSTRUCTION'S NOT COMPLETE! MY GOD, WE'RE AT THEIR MERCY--!
LET IT REST, ADAM. WE HAVE A WORLD TO LIBERATE. NOW THAT WE'RE FREE, WE CAN HANDLE A FEW DOZEN EN'TARANS.
A FEW DOZEN?
HOW ABOUT A FEW THOUSAND?
WHAT? BUT...?
IT'S THE TRUTH, SUPERMAN.
YOUR UNEXPECTED REBELLION HAS PUT THE PLANET RANN IN DEADLY DANGER.
J'ONN! STAY BACK--!
PLEASE. I AM ON YOUR SIDE. I HAVE BEEN SINCE THE START--AND SO HAS ADAM.
YOUR PLAN'S BEEN THWARTED, ADAM. YOU MAY AS WELL TELL THEM EVERYTHING.
WHY NOT? WE'VE GOT NOTHING TO LOSE. IN ABOUT TWENTY MINUTES, AN EN'TARAN INVASION FLEET IS GOING TO BREAK INTO ORBIT AROUND RANN--
--AND VAPORIZE THE PLANET!

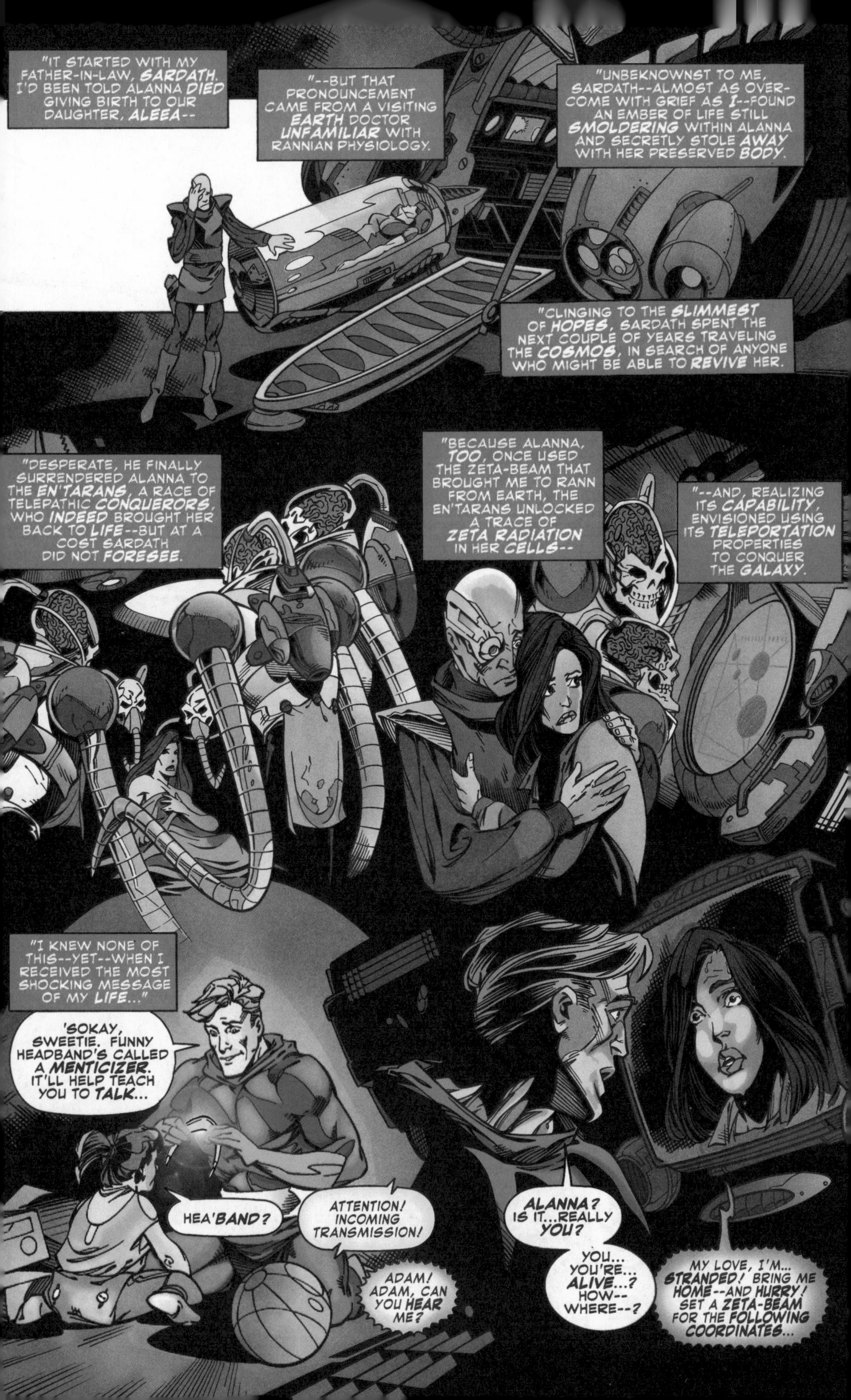
"IT STARTED WITH MY FATHER-IN-LAW, SARDATH. I'D BEEN TOLD ALANNA DIED GIVING BIRTH TO OUR DAUGHTER, ALEEA--
"--BUT THAT PRONOUNCEMENT CAME FROM A VISITING EARTH DOCTOR UNFAMILIAR WITH RANNIAN PHYSIOLOGY.
"UNBEKNOWNST TO ME, SARDATH--ALMOST AS OVERCOME WITH GRIEF AS I--FOUND AN EMBER OF LIFE STILL SMOLDERING WITHIN ALANNA AND SECRETLY STOLE AWAY WITH HER PRESERVED BODY.
"CLINGING TO THE SLIMMEST OF HOPES, SARDATH SPENT THE NEXT COUPLE OF YEARS TRAVELING THE COSMOS, IN SEARCH OF ANYONE WHO MIGHT BE ABLE TO REVIVE HER.
"DESPERATE, HE FINALLY SURRENDERED ALANNA TO THE EN'TARANS, A RACE OF TELEPATHIC CONQUERORS, WHO INDEED BROUGHT HER BACK TO LIFE--BUT AT A COST SARDATH DID NOT FORESEE.
"BECAUSE ALANNA, TOO, ONCE USED THE ZETA-BEAM THAT BROUGHT ME TO RANN FROM EARTH, THE EN'TARANS UNLOCKED A TRACE OF ZETA RADIATION IN HER CELLS--
"--AND, REALIZING ITS CAPABILITY, ENVISIONED USING ITS TELEPORTATION PROPERTIES TO CONQUER THE GALAXY.
"I KNEW NONE OF THIS--YET--WHEN I RECEIVED THE MOST SHOCKING MESSAGE OF MY LIFE..."
'SOKAY, SWEETIE. FUNNY HEADBAND'S CALLED A MENTICIZER. IT'LL HELP TEACH YOU TO TALK...
HEA'BAND?
ATTENTION! INCOMING TRANSMISSION!
ADAM! ADAM, CAN YOU HEAR ME?
ALANNA? IS IT...REALLY YOU?
YOU... YOU'RE... ALIVE...? HOW-- WHERE--?
MY LOVE, I'M... STRANDED! BRING ME HOME--AND HURRY! SET A ZETA-BEAM FOR THE FOLLOWING COORDINATES...

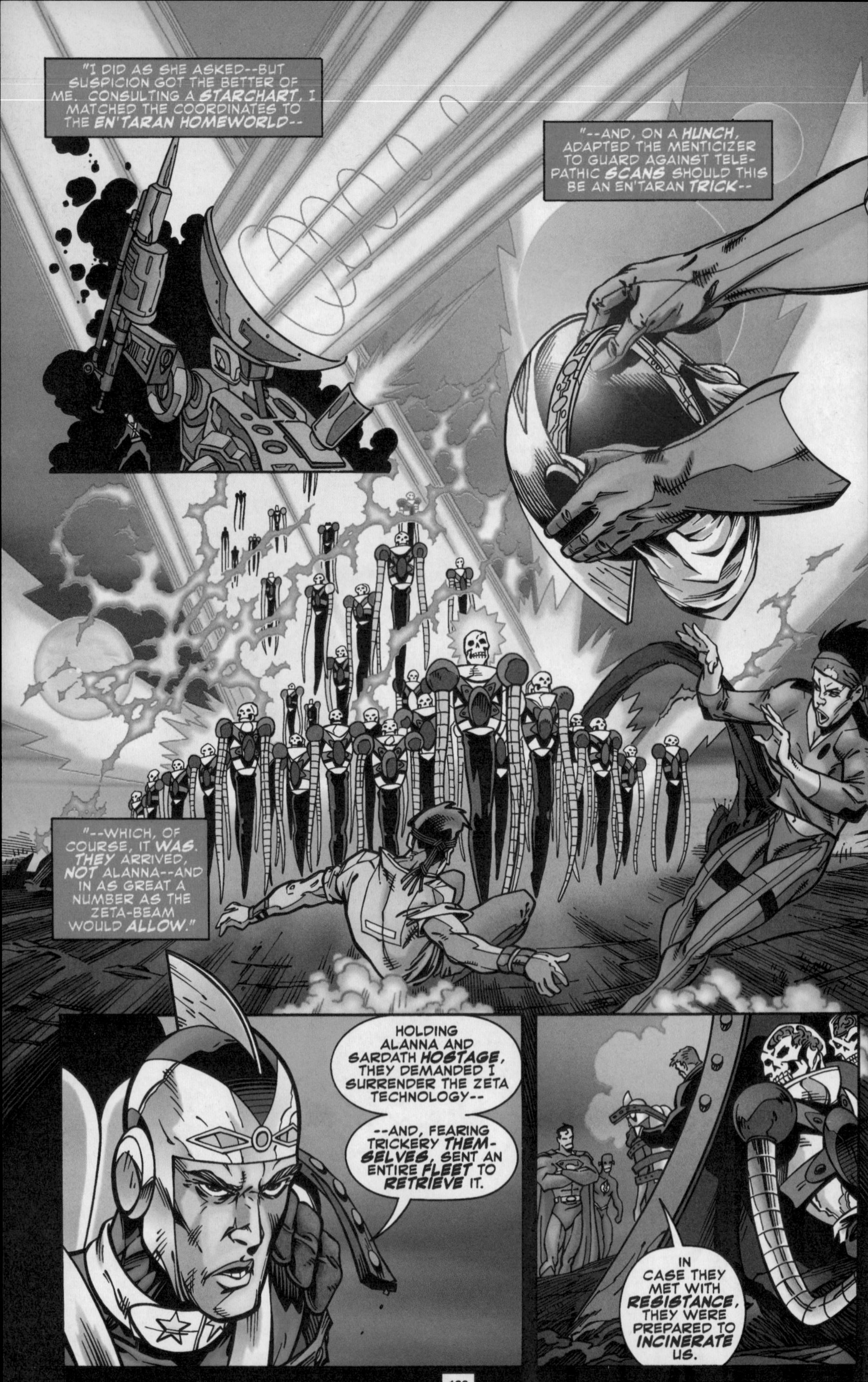
"I DID AS SHE ASKED--BUT SUSPICION GOT THE BETTER OF ME. CONSULTING A STARCHART, I MATCHED THE COORDINATES TO THE EN'TARAN HOMEWORLD--
"--AND, ON A HUNCH, ADAPTED THE MENTICIZER TO GUARD AGAINST TELEPATHIC SCANS SHOULD THIS BE AN EN'TARAN TRICK--
"--WHICH, OF COURSE, IT WAS. THEY ARRIVED, NOT ALANNA--AND IN AS GREAT A NUMBER AS THE ZETA-BEAM WOULD ALLOW."
HOLDING ALANNA AND SARDATH HOSTAGE, THEY DEMANDED I SURRENDER THE ZETA TECHNOLOGY--
--AND, FEARING TRICKERY THEMSELVES, SENT AN ENTIRE FLEET TO RETRIEVE IT.
IN CASE THEY MET WITH RESISTANCE, THEY WERE PREPARED TO INCINERATE US.

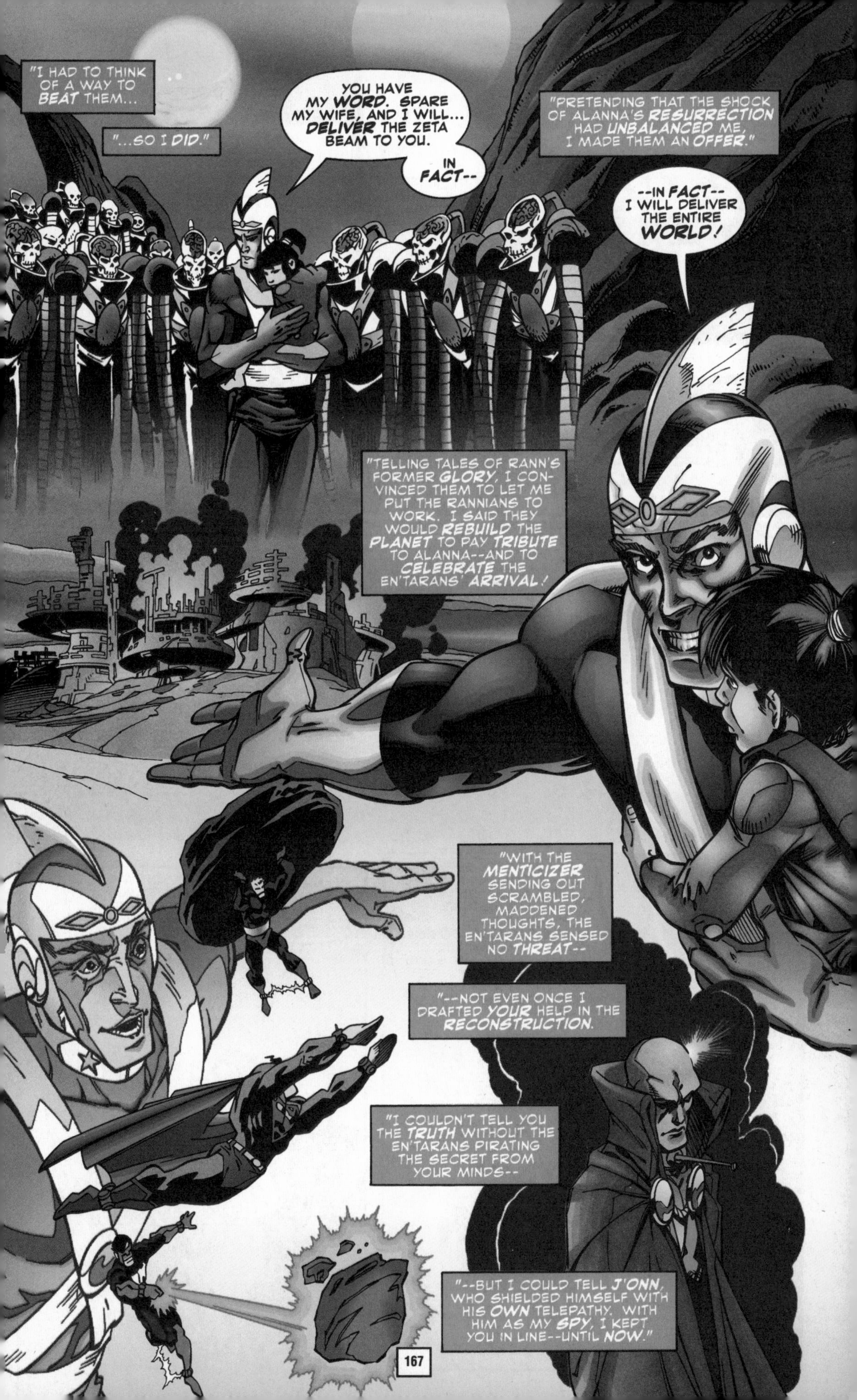
"I HAD TO THINK OF A WAY TO BEAT THEM...
"...SO I DID."
YOU HAVE MY WORD. SPARE MY WIFE, AND I WILL... DELIVER THE ZETA BEAM TO YOU.
IN FACT--
"PRETENDING THAT THE SHOCK OF ALANNA'S RESURRECTION HAD UNBALANCED ME, I MADE THEM AN OFFER."
--IN FACT-- I WILL DELIVER THE ENTIRE WORLD!
"TELLING TALES OF RANN'S FORMER GLORY, I CONVINCED THEM TO LET ME PUT THE RANNIANS TO WORK. I SAID THEY WOULD REBUILD THE PLANET TO PAY TRIBUTE TO ALANNA--AND TO CELEBRATE THE EN'TARANS' ARRIVAL!
"WITH THE MENTICIZER SENDING OUT SCRAMBLED, MADDENED THOUGHTS, THE EN'TARANS SENSED NO THREAT--
"--NOT EVEN ONCE I DRAFTED YOUR HELP IN THE RECONSTRUCTION.
"I COULDN'T TELL YOU THE TRUTH WITHOUT THE EN'TARANS PIRATING THE SECRET FROM YOUR MINDS--
"--BUT I COULD TELL J'ONN, WHO SHIELDED HIMSELF WITH HIS OWN TELEPATHY. WITH HIM AS MY SPY, I KEPT YOU IN LINE--UNTIL NOW."

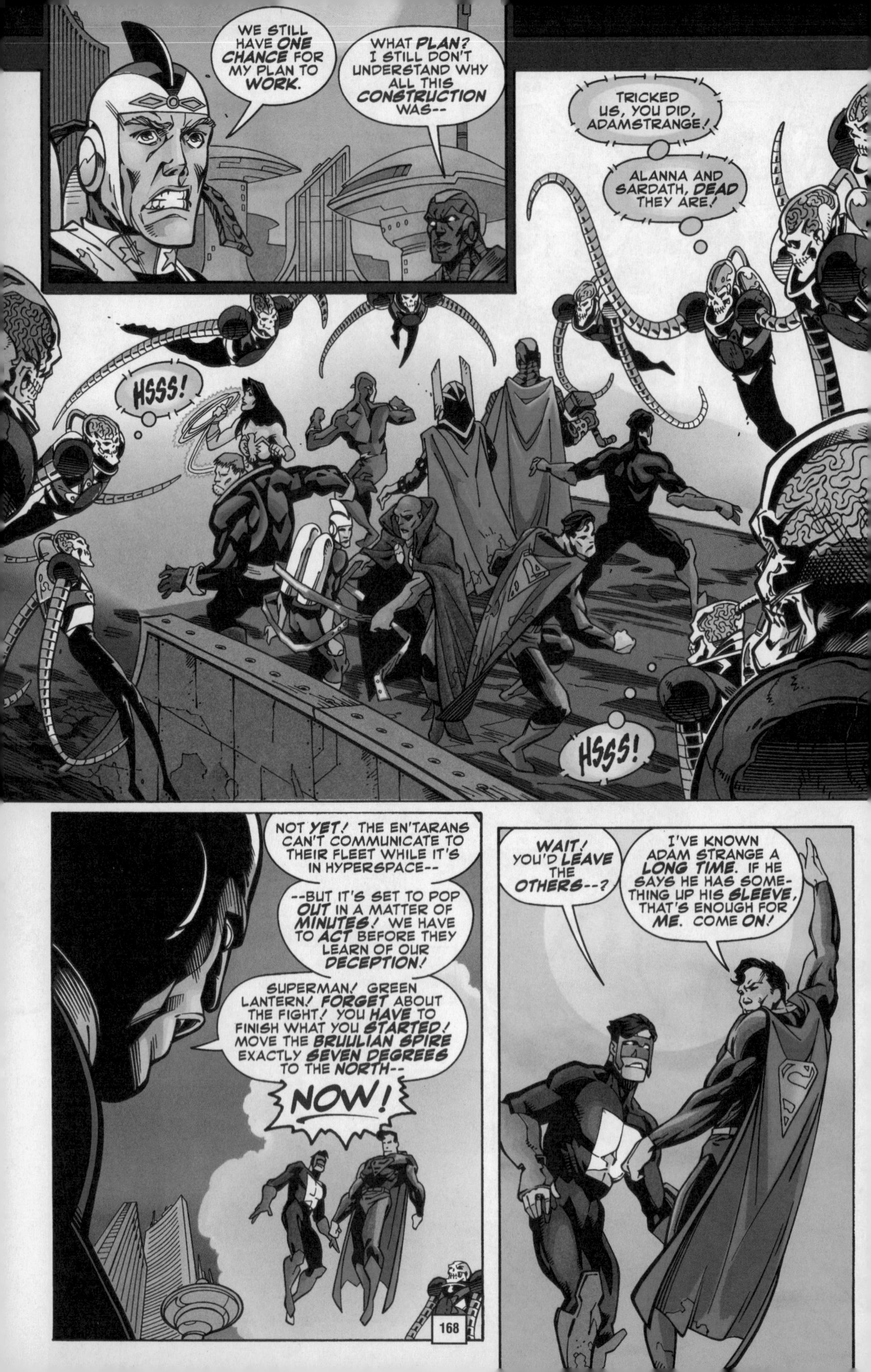
WE STILL HAVE ONE CHANCE FOR MY PLAN TO WORK.
WHAT PLAN? I STILL DON'T UNDERSTAND WHY ALL THIS CONSTRUCTION WAS--
TRICKED US, YOU DID, ADAMSTRANGE!
ALANNA AND SARDATH, DEAD THEY ARE!
HSSS!
HSSS!
NOT YET! THE EN'TARANS CAN'T COMMUNICATE TO THEIR FLEET WHILE IT'S IN HYPERSPACE--
--BUT IT'S SET TO POP OUT IN A MATTER OF MINUTES! WE HAVE TO ACT BEFORE THEY LEARN OF OUR DECEPTION!
SUPERMAN! GREEN LANTERN! FORGET ABOUT THE FIGHT! YOU HAVE TO FINISH WHAT YOU STARTED! MOVE THE BRUULIAN SPIRE EXACTLY SEVEN DEGREES TO THE NORTH--
NOW!
WAIT! YOU'D LEAVE THE OTHERS--?
I'VE KNOWN ADAM STRANGE A LONG TIME. IF HE SAYS HE HAS SOMETHING UP HIS SLEEVE, THAT'S ENOUGH FOR ME. COME ON!

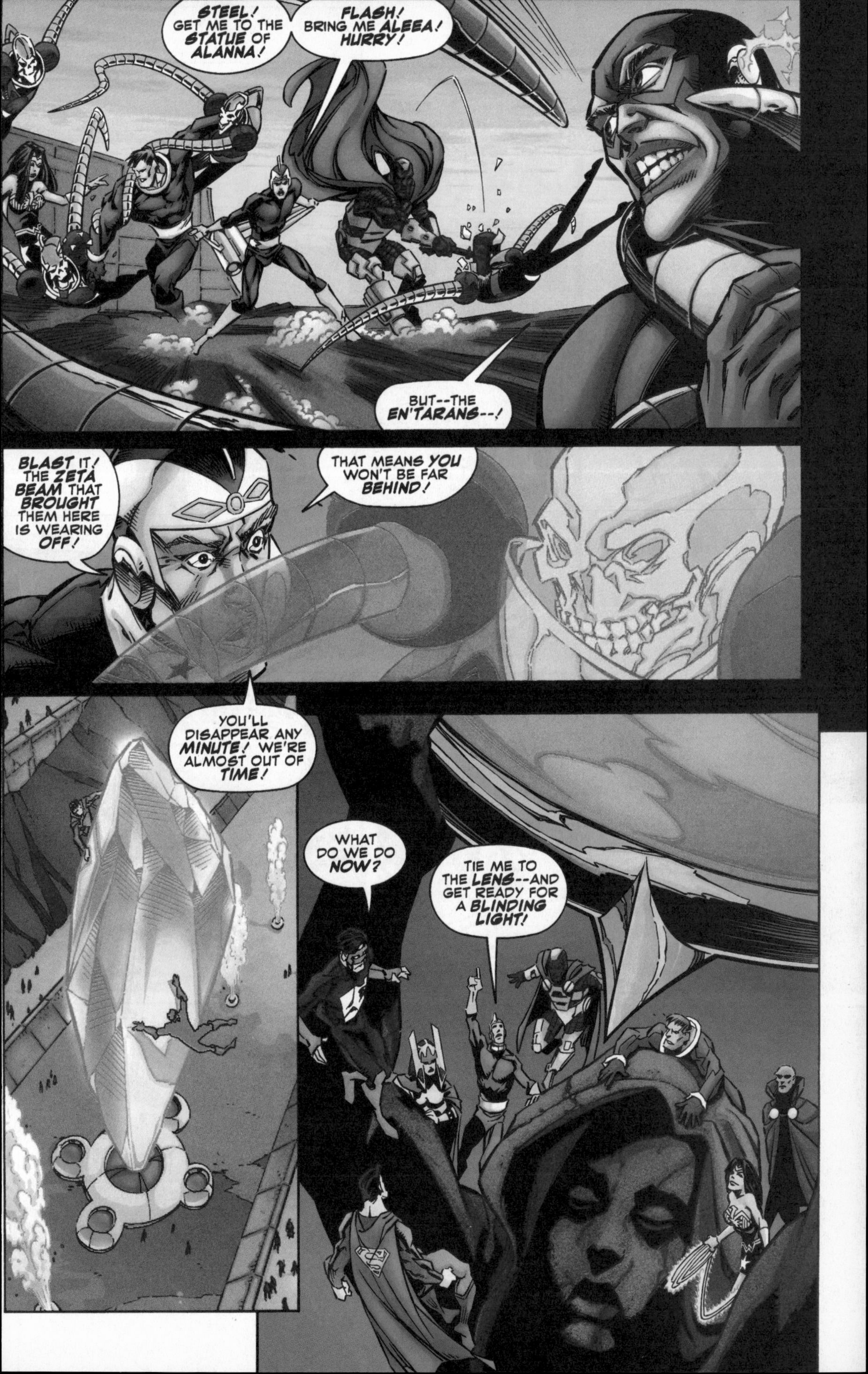
STEEL! GET ME TO THE STATUE OF ALANNA!
FLASH! BRING ME ALEEA! HURRY!
BUT--THE EN'TARANS--!
BLAST IT! THE ZETA BEAM THAT BROUGHT THEM HERE IS WEARING OFF!
THAT MEANS YOU WON'T BE FAR BEHIND!
YOU'LL DISAPPEAR ANY MINUTE! WE'RE ALMOST OUT OF TIME!
WHAT DO WE DO NOW?
TIE ME TO THE LENS--AND GET READY FOR A BLINDING LIGHT!

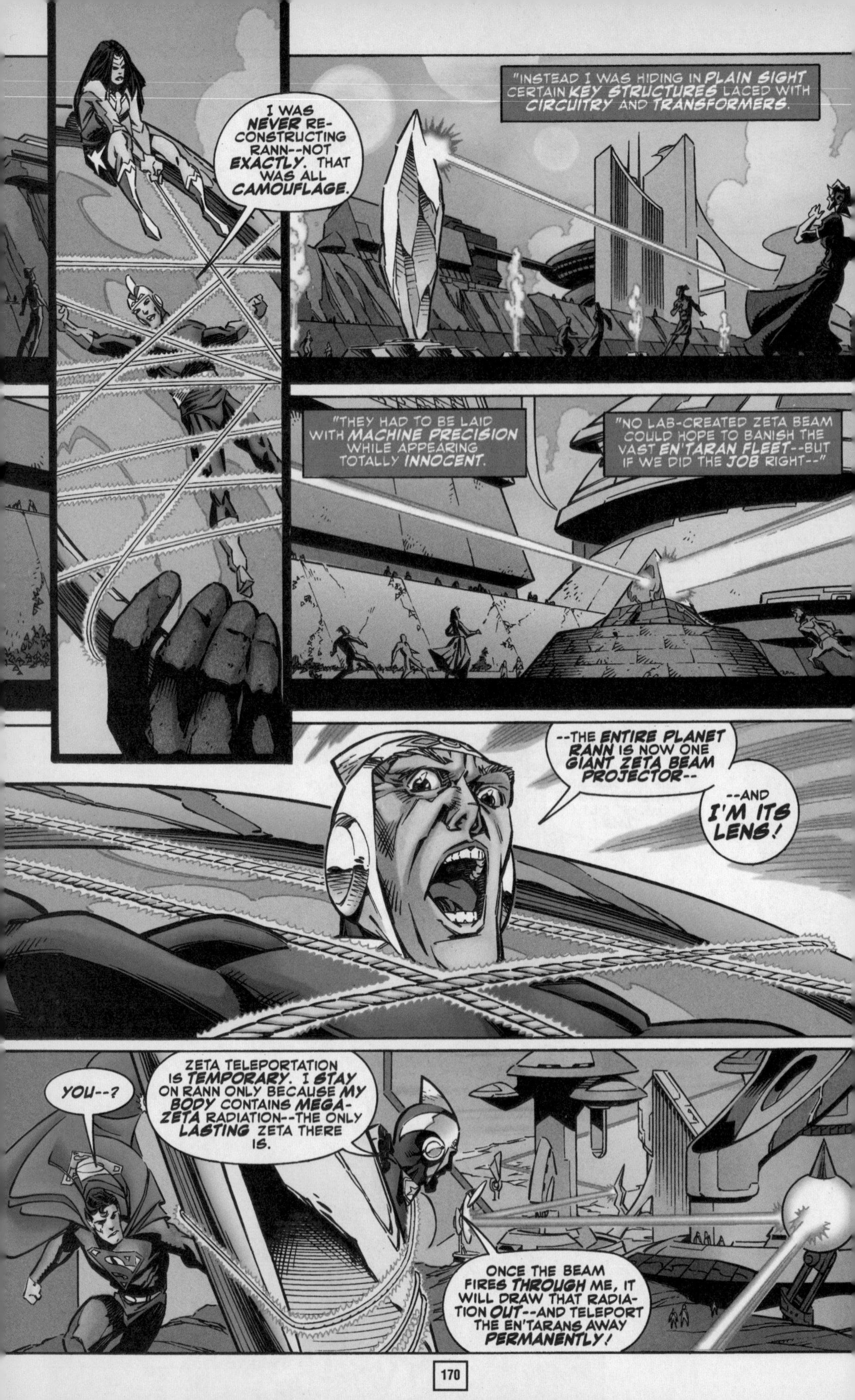
I WAS NEVER RE-CONSTRUCTING RANN--NOT EXACTLY. THAT WAS ALL CAMOUFLAGE.
"INSTEAD I WAS HIDING IN PLAIN SIGHT. CERTAIN KEY STRUCTURES LACED WITH CIRCUITRY AND TRANSFORMERS.
"THEY HAD TO BE LAID WITH MACHINE PRECISION WHILE APPEARING TOTALLY INNOCENT.
"NO LAB-CREATED ZETA BEAM COULD HOPE TO BANISH THE VAST EN'TARAN FLEET--BUT IF WE DID THE JOB RIGHT--"
--THE ENTIRE PLANET RANN IS NOW ONE GIANT ZETA BEAM PROJECTOR--
--AND I'M ITS LENS!
YOU--?
ZETA TELEPORTATION IS TEMPORARY. I STAY ON RANN ONLY BECAUSE MY BODY CONTAINS MEGA-ZETA RADIATION--THE ONLY LASTING ZETA THERE IS.
ONCE THE BEAM FIRES THROUGH ME, IT WILL DRAW THAT RADIATION OUT--AND TELEPORT THE EN'TARANS AWAY PERMANENTLY!

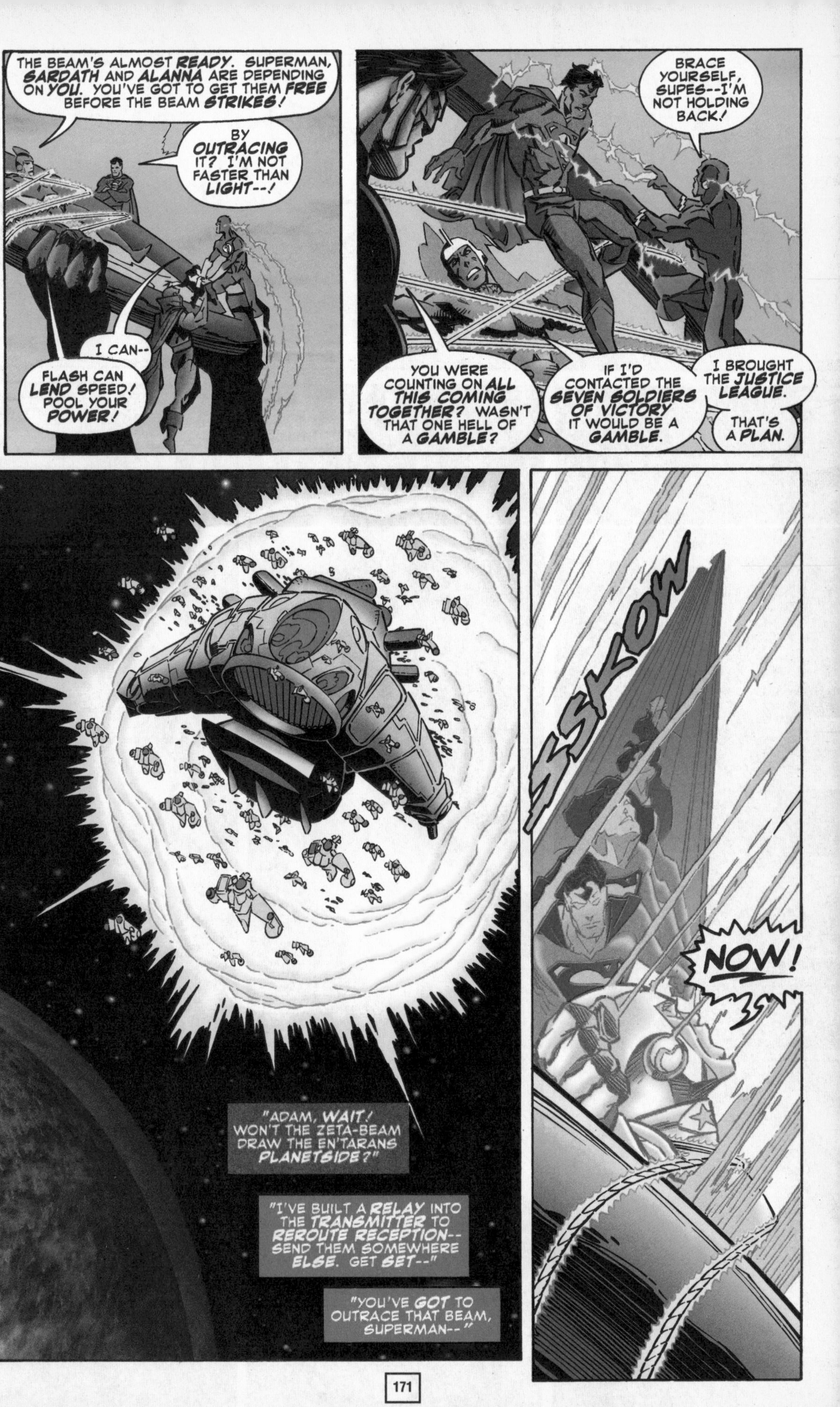
THE BEAM'S ALMOST READY. SUPERMAN, SARDATH AND ALANNA ARE DEPENDING ON YOU. YOU'VE GOT TO GET THEM FREE BEFORE THE BEAM STRIKES!
BY OUTRACING IT? I'M NOT FASTER THAN LIGHT--!
I CAN--
FLASH CAN LEND SPEED! POOL YOUR POWER!
BRACE YOURSELF, SUPES--I'M NOT HOLDING BACK!
YOU WERE COUNTING ON ALL THIS COMING TOGETHER? WASN'T THAT ONE HELL OF A GAMBLE?
IF I'D CONTACTED THE SEVEN SOLDIERS OF VICTORY IT WOULD BE A GAMBLE.
I BROUGHT THE JUSTICE LEAGUE.
THAT'S A PLAN.
"ADAM, WAIT! WON'T THE ZETA-BEAM DRAW THE EN'TARANS PLANETSIDE?"
"I'VE BUILT A RELAY INTO THE TRANSMITTER TO REROUTE RECEPTION--SEND THEM SOMEWHERE ELSE. GET SET--"
"YOU'VE GOT TO OUTRACE THAT BEAM, SUPERMAN--"
SSKOW
NOW!

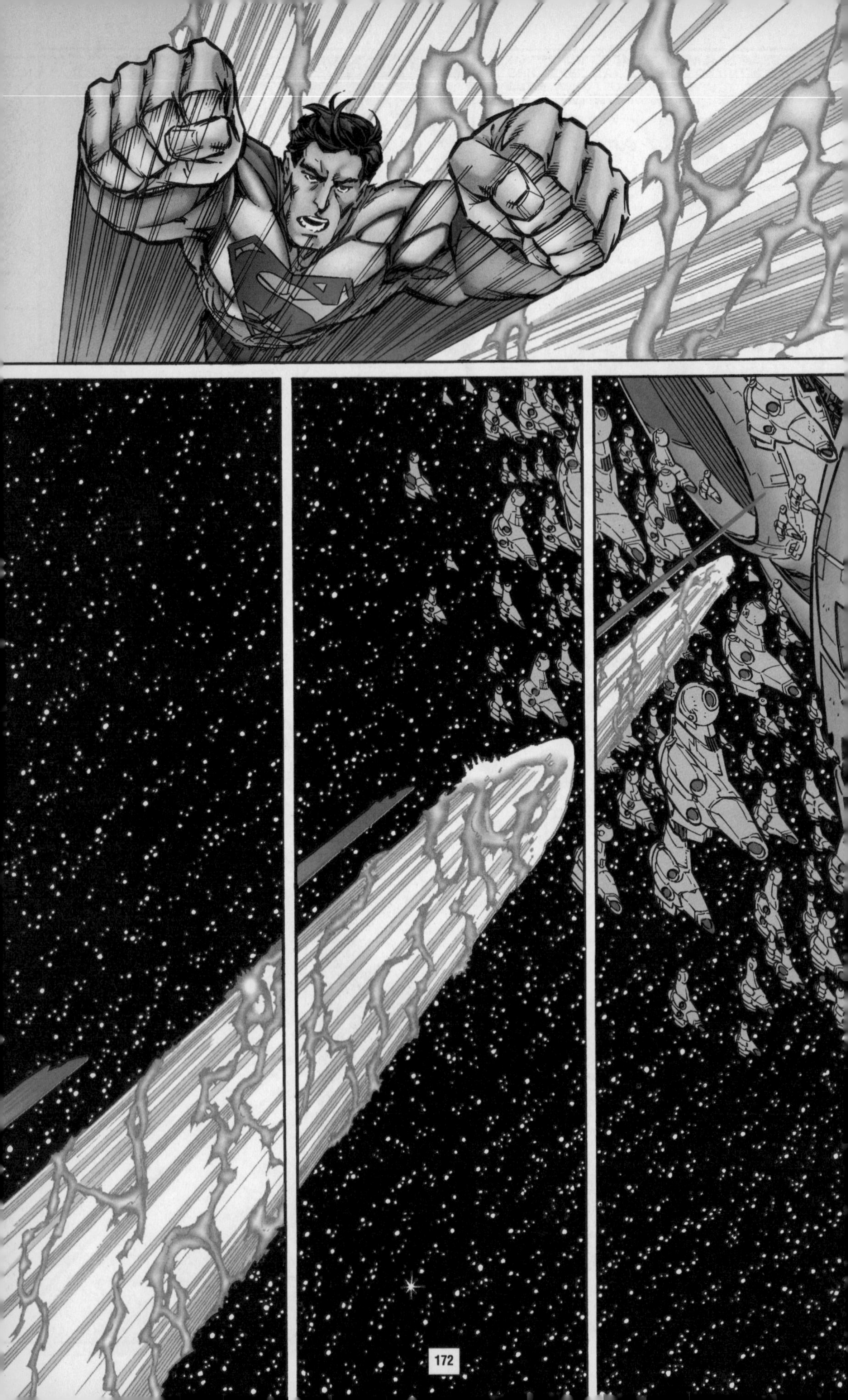

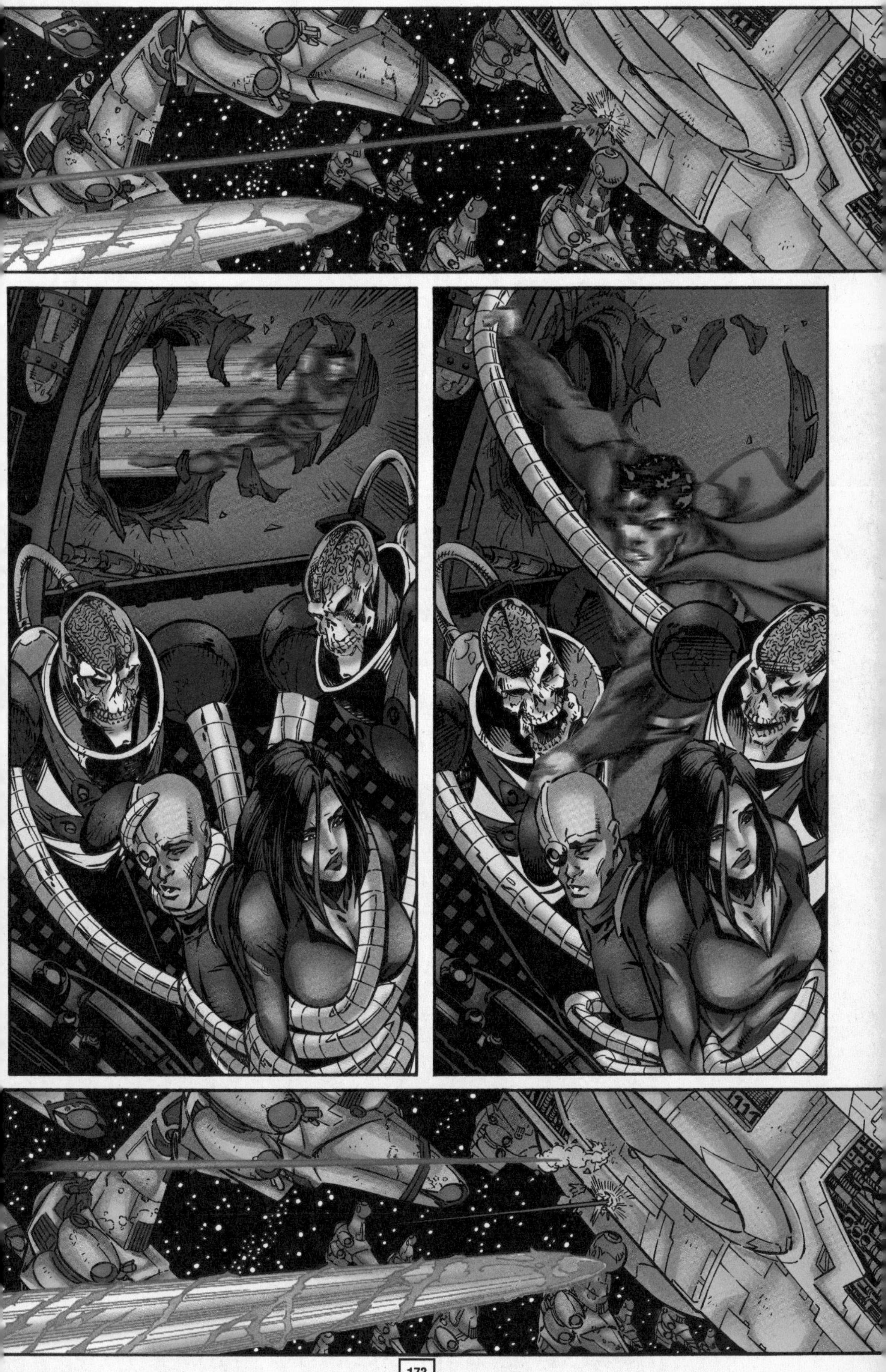

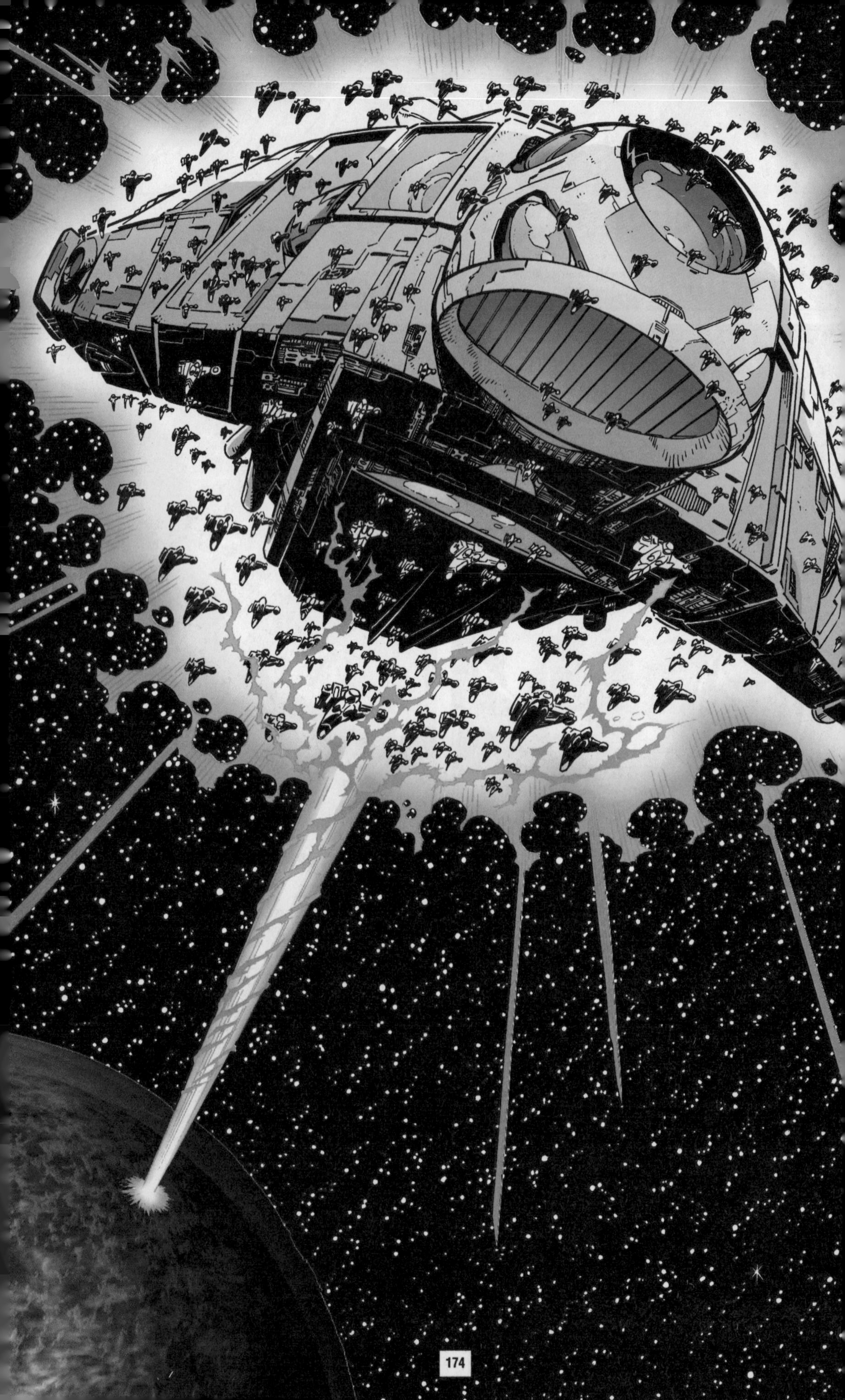

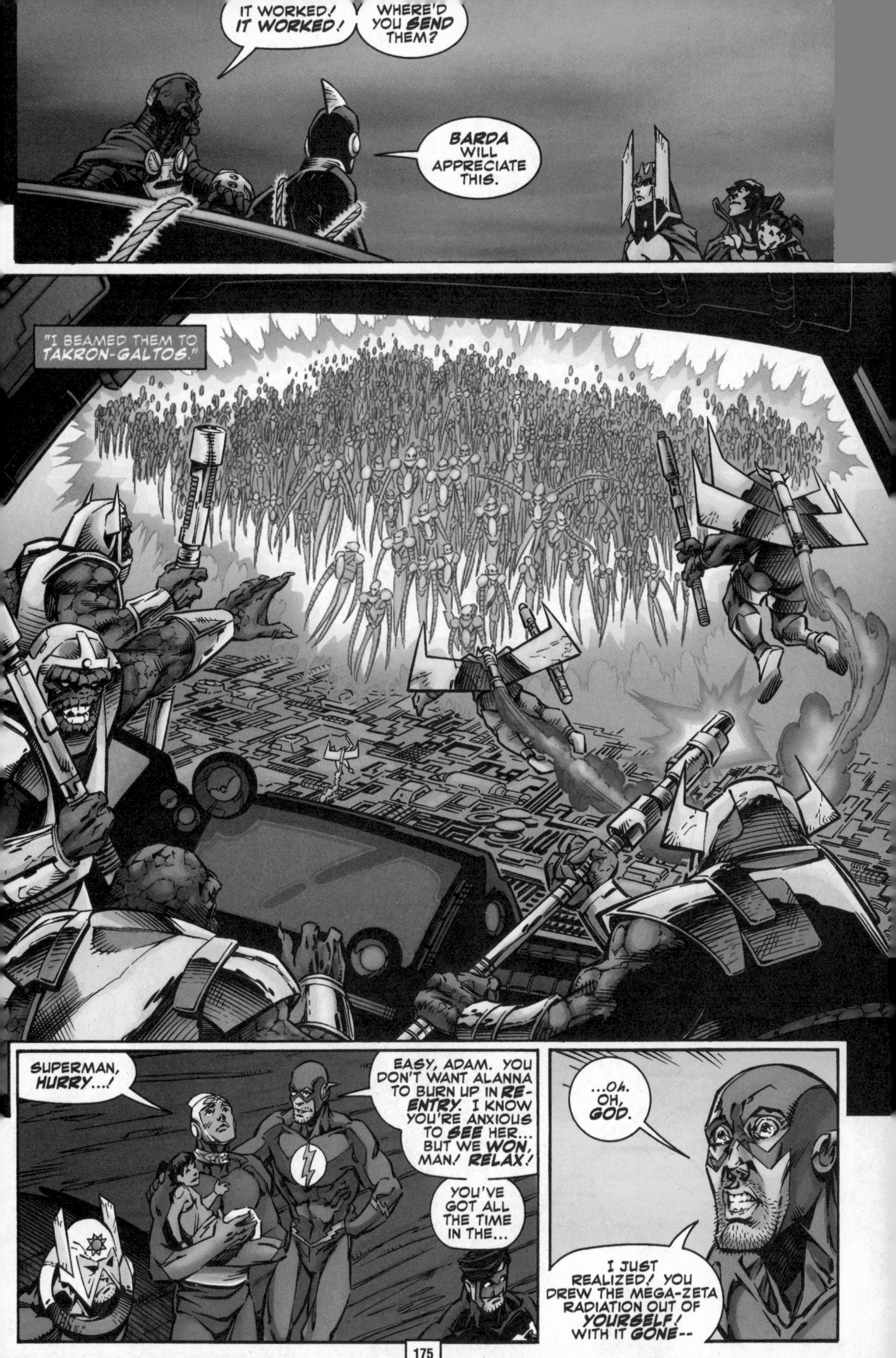
IT WORKED! IT WORKED!
WHERE'D YOU SEND THEM?
BARDA WILL APPRECIATE THIS.
"I BEAMED THEM TO TAKRON-GALTOS."
SUPERMAN, HURRY...!
EASY, ADAM. YOU DON'T WANT ALANNA TO BURN UP IN RE-ENTRY. I KNOW YOU'RE ANXIOUS TO SEE HER... BUT WE WON, MAN! RELAX!
YOU'VE GOT ALL THE TIME IN THE...
...Oh. OH, GOD.
I JUST REALIZED! YOU DREW THE MEGA-ZETA RADIATION OUT OF YOURSELF! WITH IT GONE--

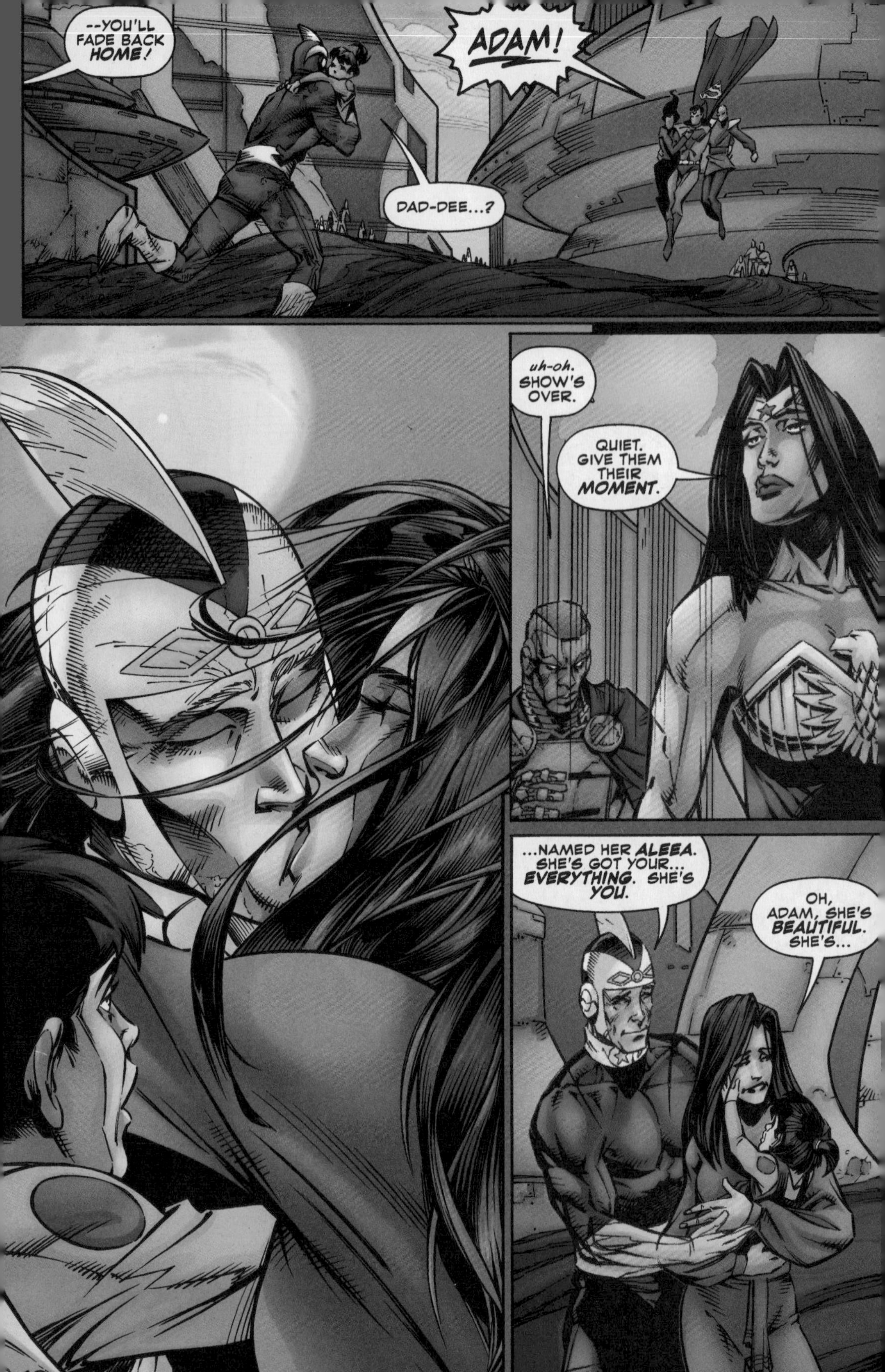
--YOU'LL FADE BACK HOME!
ADAM!
DAD-DEE...?
uh-oh. SHOW'S OVER.
QUIET. GIVE THEM THEIR MOMENT.
...NAMED HER ALEEA. SHE'S GOT YOUR... EVERYTHING. SHE'S YOU.
OH, ADAM, SHE'S BEAUTIFUL. SHE'S...
19

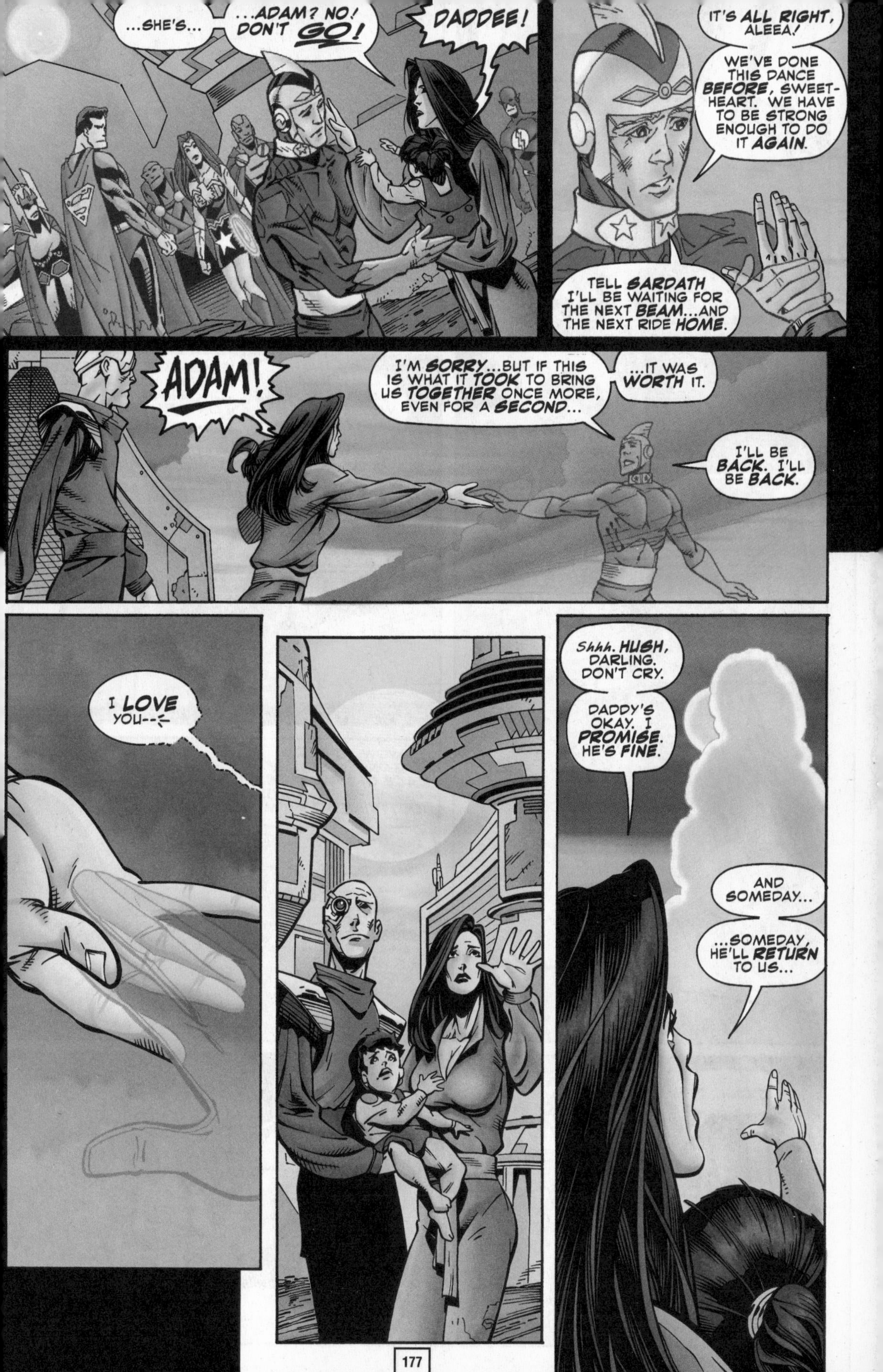
...SHE'S...
...ADAM? NO! DON'T GO!
DADDEE!
IT'S ALL RIGHT, ALEEA!
WE'VE DONE THIS DANCE BEFORE, SWEET-HEART. WE HAVE TO BE STRONG ENOUGH TO DO IT AGAIN.
TELL SARDATH I'LL BE WAITING FOR THE NEXT BEAM...AND THE NEXT RIDE HOME.
ADAM!
I'M SORRY...BUT IF THIS IS WHAT IT TOOK TO BRING US TOGETHER ONCE MORE, EVEN FOR A SECOND...
...IT WAS WORTH IT.
I'LL BE BACK. I'LL BE BACK.
I LOVE YOU--
Shhh. HUSH, DARLING. DON'T CRY.
DADDY'S OKAY. I PROMISE. HE'S FINE.
AND SOMEDAY...
...SOMEDAY, HE'LL RETURN TO US...

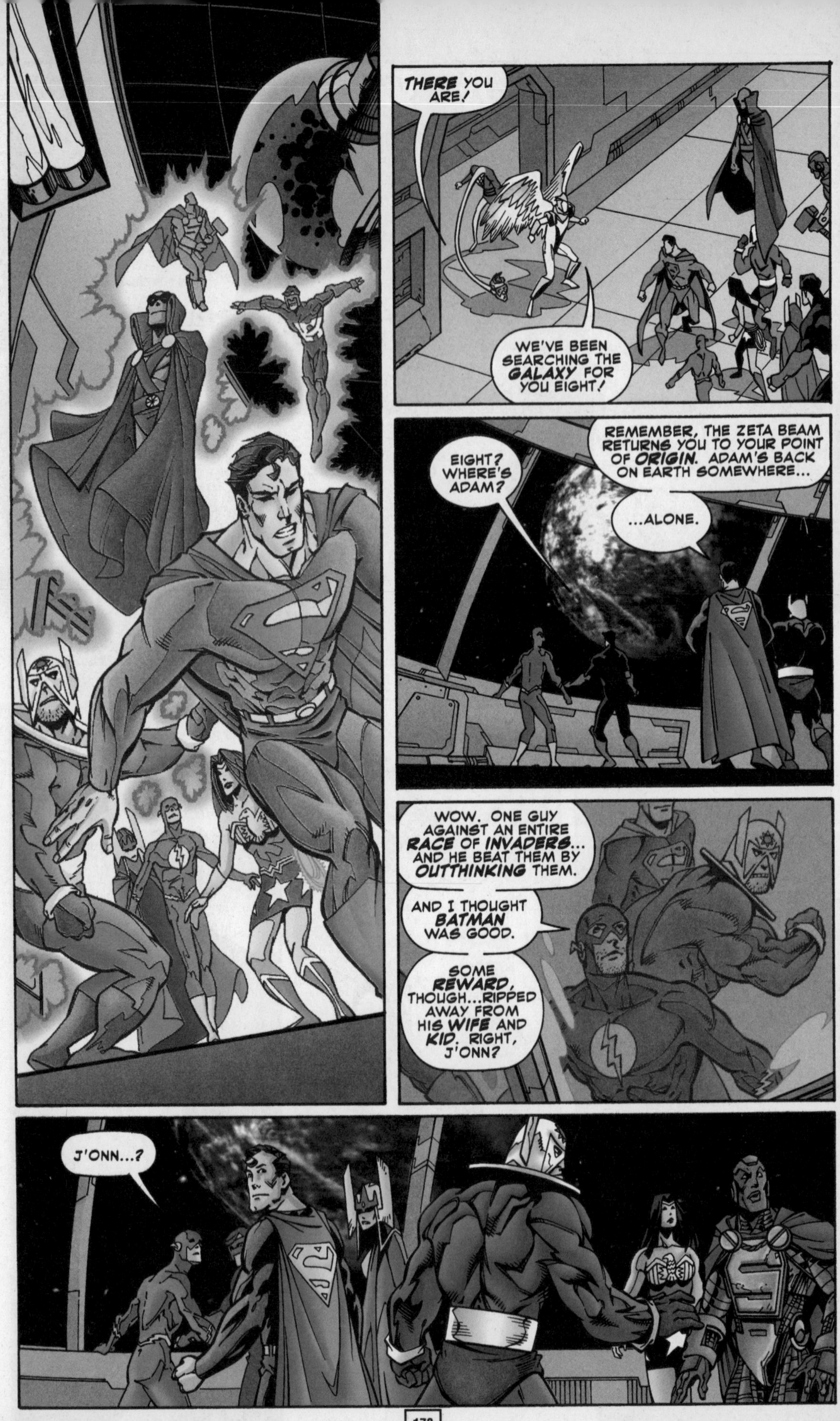

THERE YOU ARE!
WE'VE BEEN SEARCHING THE GALAXY FOR YOU EIGHT!
EIGHT? WHERE'S ADAM?
REMEMBER, THE ZETA BEAM RETURNS YOU TO YOUR POINT OF ORIGIN. ADAM'S BACK ON EARTH SOMEWHERE...
...ALONE.
WOW. ONE GUY AGAINST AN ENTIRE RACE OF INVADERS... AND HE BEAT THEM BY OUTTHINKING THEM.
AND I THOUGHT BATMAN WAS GOOD.
SOME REWARD, THOUGH...RIPPED AWAY FROM HIS WIFE AND KID. RIGHT, J'ONN?
J'ONN...?

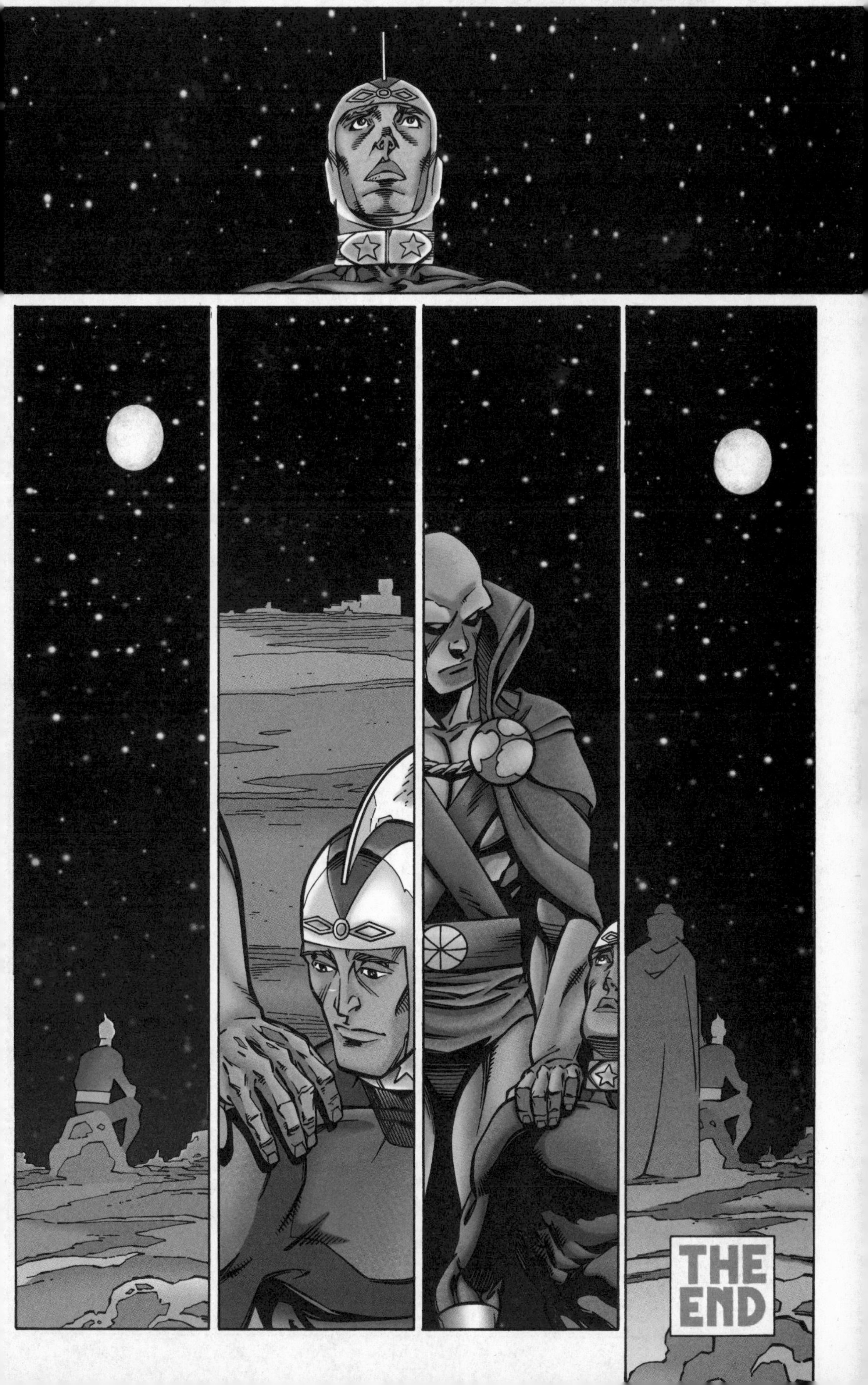
THE END

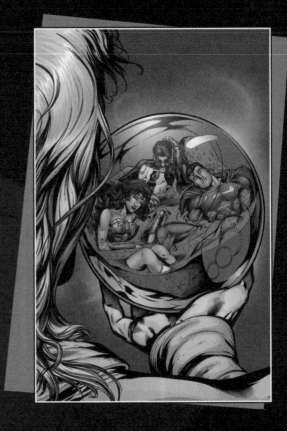

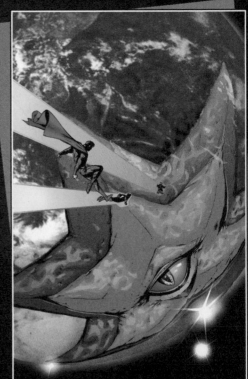

RETURN OF THE
CONQUEROR

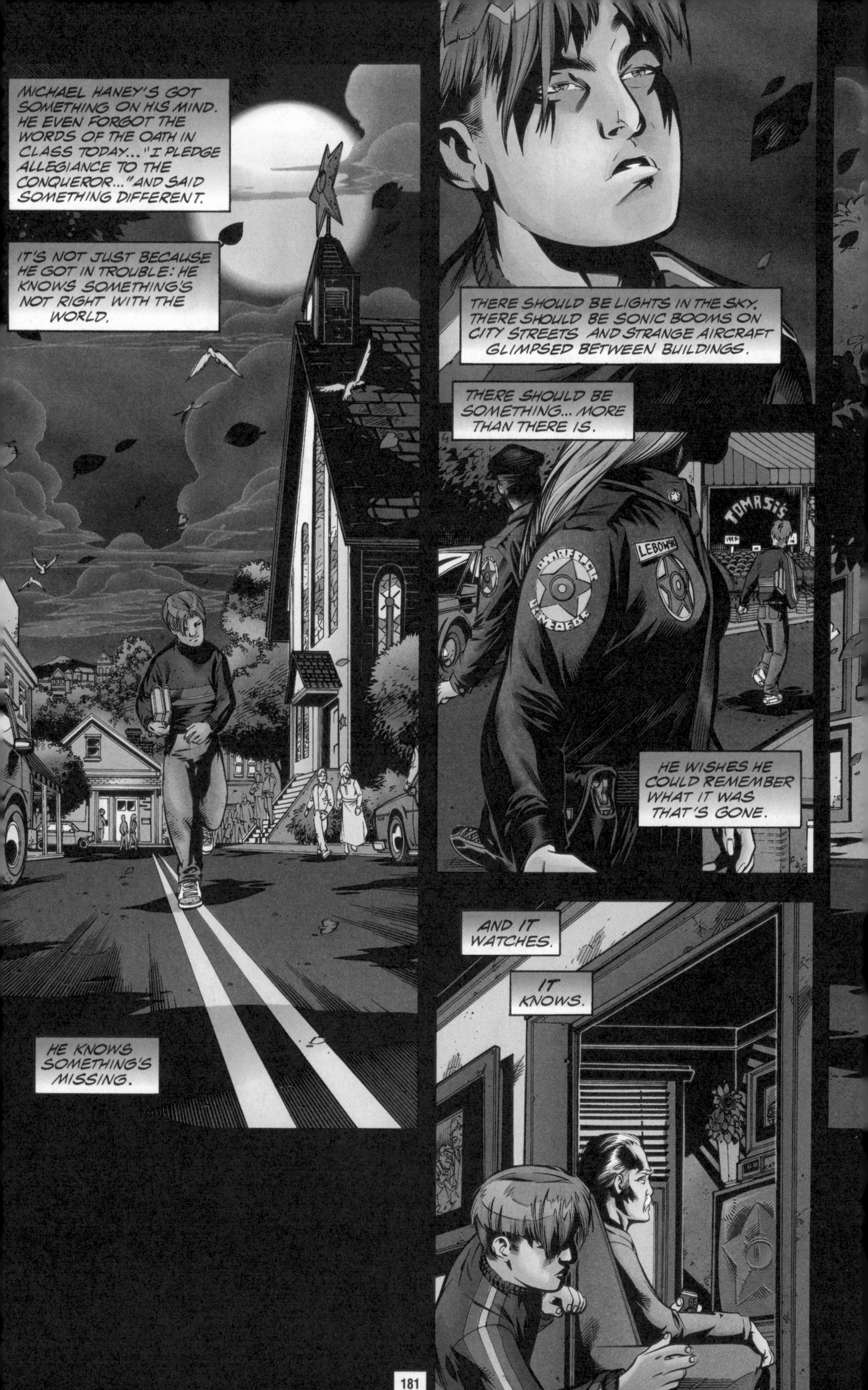
MICHAEL HANEY'S GOT SOMETHING ON HIS MIND. HE EVEN FORGOT THE WORDS OF THE OATH IN CLASS TODAY... "I PLEDGE ALLEGIANCE TO THE CONQUEROR..." AND SAID SOMETHING DIFFERENT.
IT'S NOT JUST BECAUSE HE GOT IN TROUBLE: HE KNOWS SOMETHING'S NOT RIGHT WITH THE WORLD.
HE KNOWS SOMETHING'S MISSING.
THERE SHOULD BE LIGHTS IN THE SKY. THERE SHOULD BE SONIC BOOMS ON CITY STREETS AND STRANGE AIRCRAFT GLIMPSED BETWEEN BUILDINGS.
THERE SHOULD BE SOMETHING... MORE THAN THERE IS.
LEBOWSKI
TOMASI'S
HE WISHES HE COULD REMEMBER WHAT IT WAS THAT'S GONE.
AND IT WATCHES.
IT KNOWS.

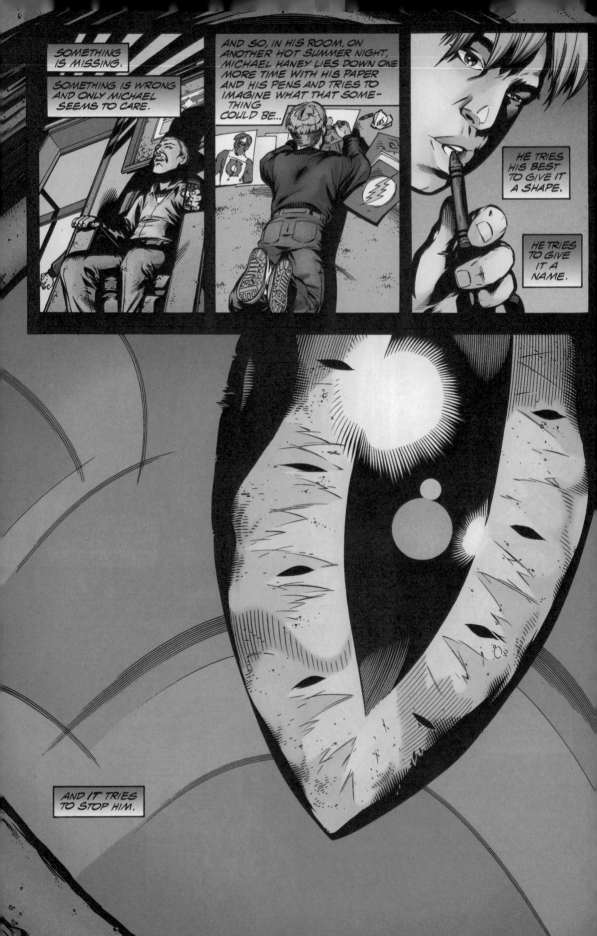

SOMETHING IS MISSING.

SOMETHING IS WRONG AND ONLY MICHAEL SEEMS TO CARE.

AND SO, IN HIS ROOM, ON ANOTHER HOT SUMMER NIGHT, MICHAEL HANEY LIES DOWN ONE MORE TIME WITH HIS PAPER AND HIS PENS AND TRIES TO IMAGINE WHAT THAT SOMETHING COULD BE...

HE TRIES HIS BEST TO GIVE IT A SHAPE.

HE TRIES TO GIVE IT A NAME.

AND IT TRIES TO STOP HIM.

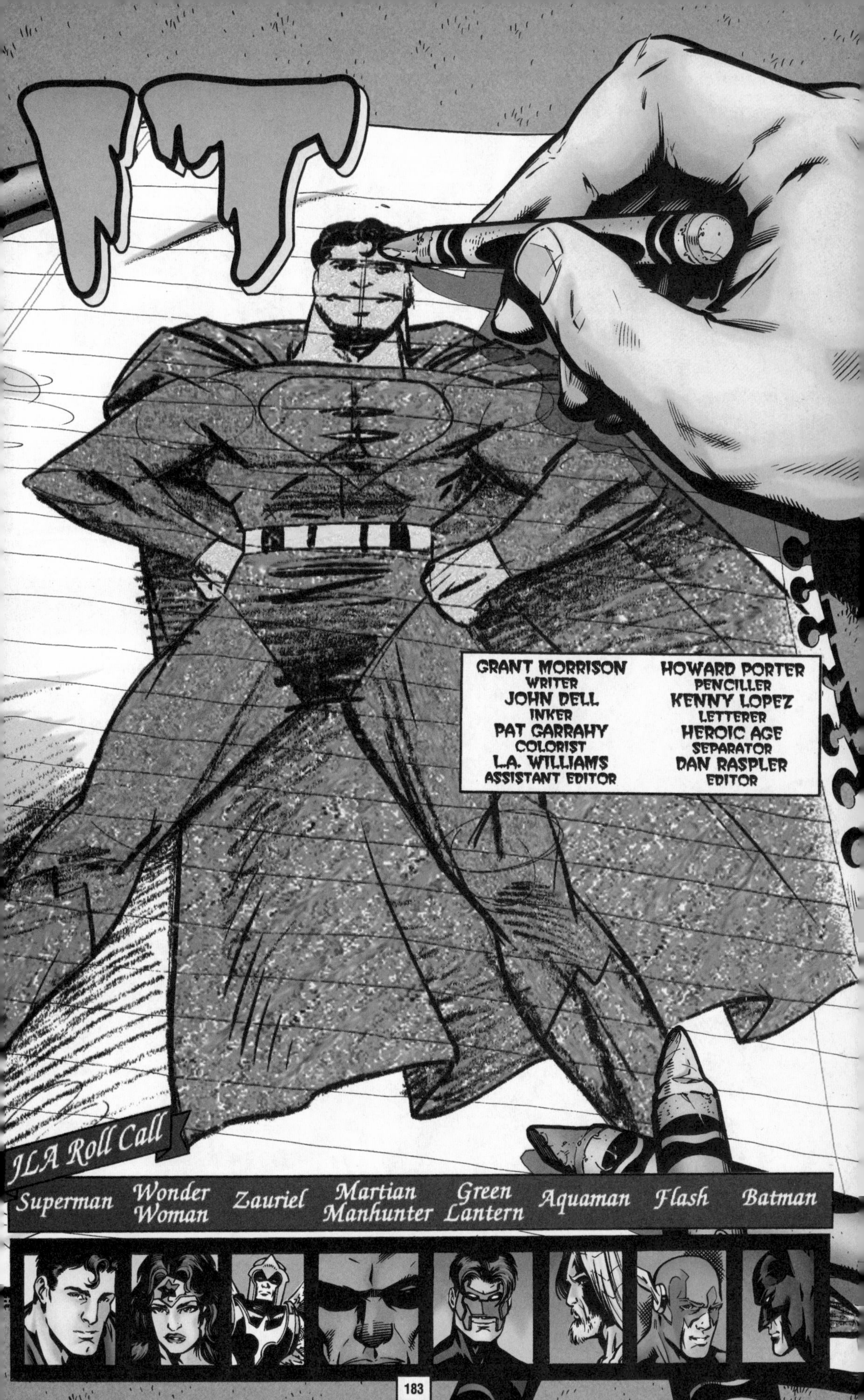

GRANT MORRISON
WRITER
HOWARD PORTER
PENCILLER
JOHN DELL
INKER
KENNY LOPEZ
LETTERER
PAT GARRAHY
COLORIST
HEROIC AGE
SEPARATOR
L.A. WILLIAMS
ASSISTANT EDITOR
DAN RASPLER
EDITOR
JLA Roll Call
Superman
Wonder Woman
Zauriel
Martian Manhunter
Green Lantern
Aquaman
Flash
Batman

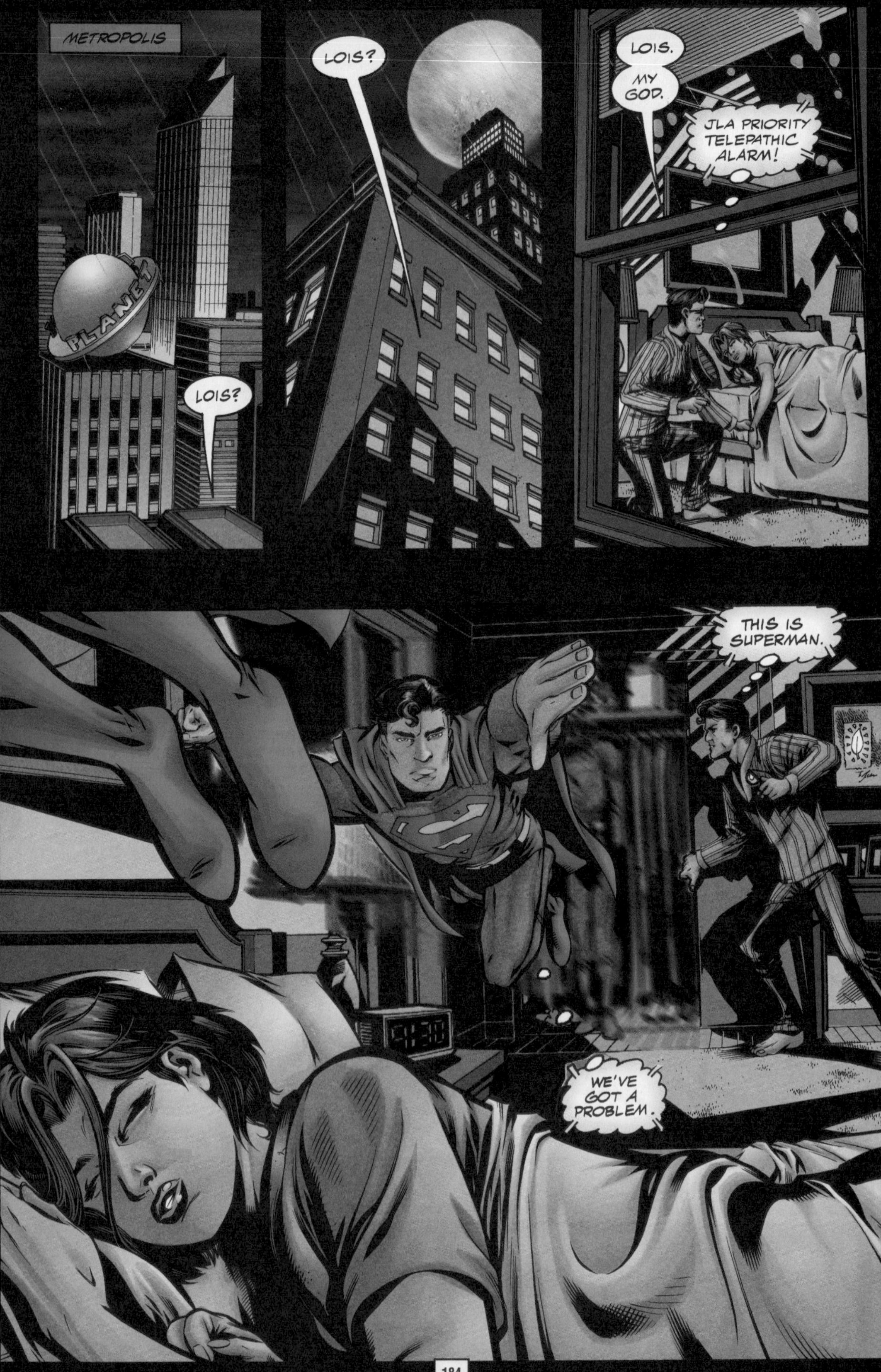
METROPOLIS
LOIS?
LOIS?
LOIS.
MY GOD.
JLA PRIORITY TELEPATHIC ALARM!
THIS IS SUPERMAN.
WE'VE GOT A PROBLEM.

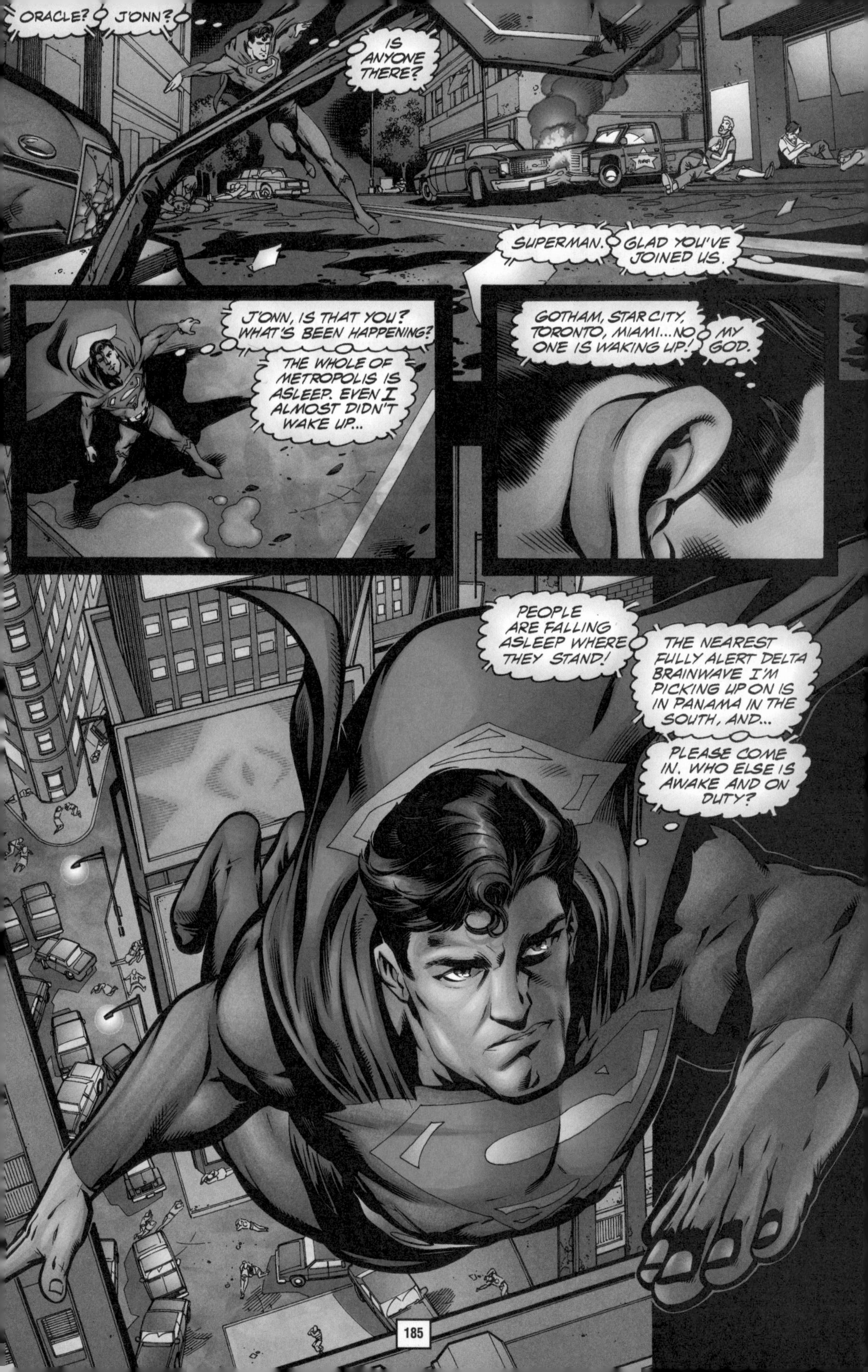
ORACLE?
J'ONN?
IS ANYONE THERE?
SUPERMAN.
GLAD YOU'VE JOINED US.
J'ONN, IS THAT YOU? WHAT'S BEEN HAPPENING?
THE WHOLE OF METROPOLIS IS ASLEEP. EVEN I ALMOST DIDN'T WAKE UP...
GOTHAM, STAR CITY, TORONTO, MIAMI...NO ONE IS WAKING UP!
MY GOD.
PEOPLE ARE FALLING ASLEEP WHERE THEY STAND!
THE NEAREST FULLY ALERT DELTA BRAINWAVE I'M PICKING UP ON IS IN PANAMA IN THE SOUTH, AND...
PLEASE COME IN. WHO ELSE IS AWAKE AND ON DUTY?

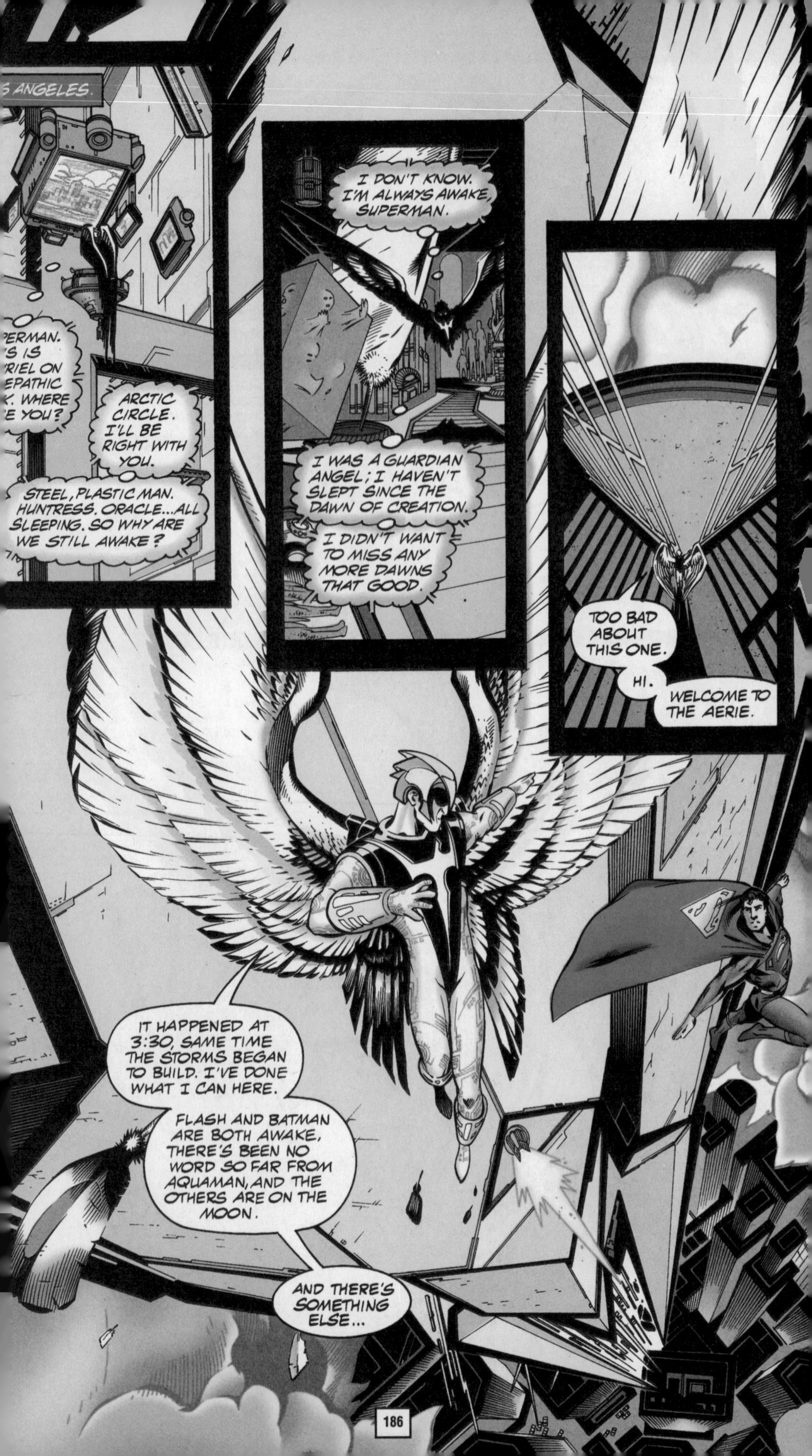
S ANGELES.
PERMAN.
'S IS
RIEL ON
EPATHIC
K. WHERE
E YOU?
ARCTIC CIRCLE. I'LL BE RIGHT WITH YOU.
STEEL, PLASTIC MAN. HUNTRESS. ORACLE...ALL SLEEPING. SO WHY ARE WE STILL AWAKE?
I DON'T KNOW. I'M ALWAYS AWAKE, SUPERMAN.
I WAS A GUARDIAN ANGEL; I HAVEN'T SLEPT SINCE THE DAWN OF CREATION.
I DIDN'T WANT TO MISS ANY MORE DAWNS THAT GOOD.
TOO BAD ABOUT THIS ONE.
HI.
WELCOME TO THE AERIE.
IT HAPPENED AT 3:30, SAME TIME THE STORMS BEGAN TO BUILD. I'VE DONE WHAT I CAN HERE.
FLASH AND BATMAN ARE BOTH AWAKE, THERE'S BEEN NO WORD SO FAR FROM AQUAMAN, AND THE OTHERS ARE ON THE MOON.
AND THERE'S SOMETHING ELSE...

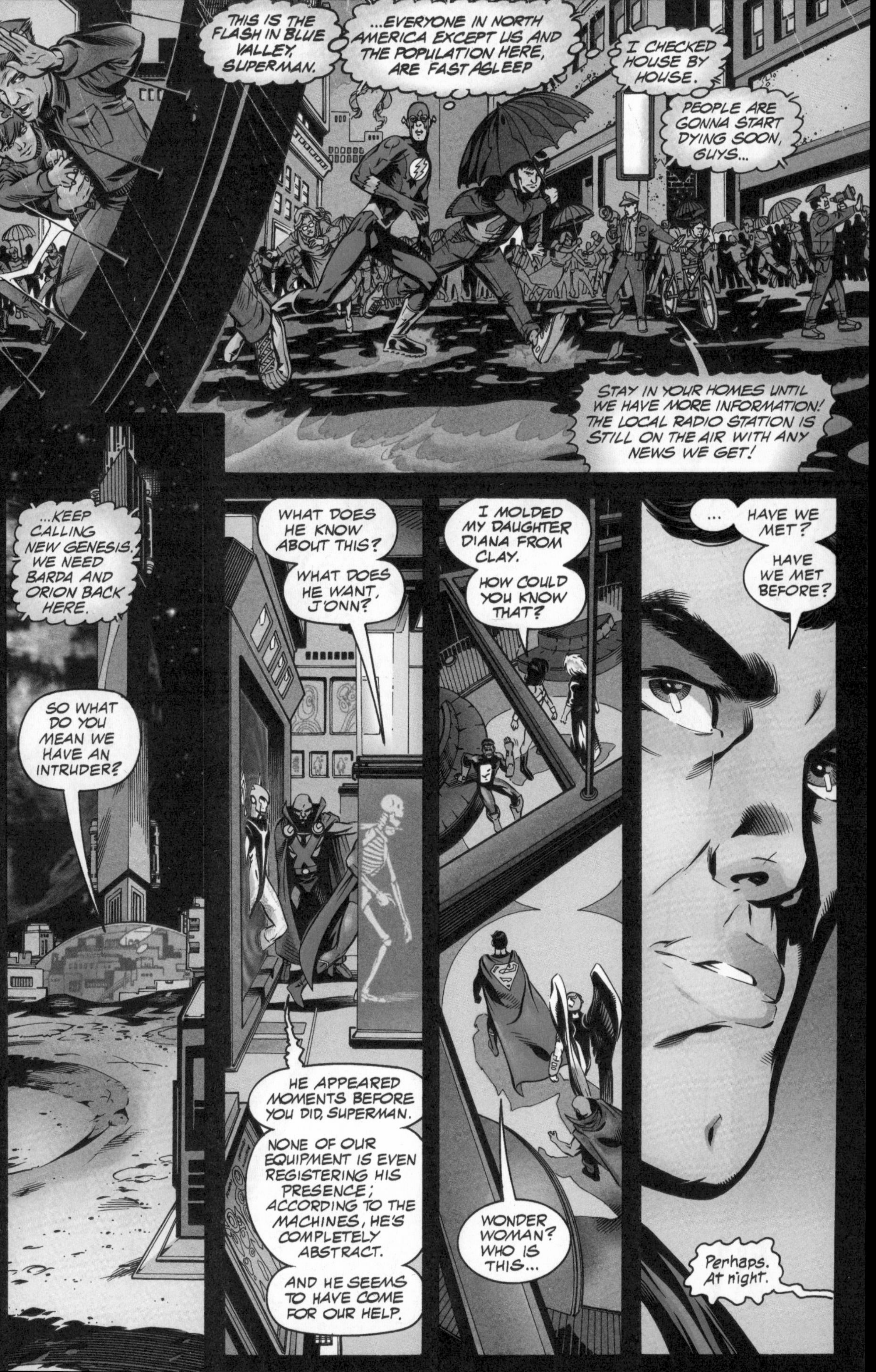
THIS IS THE FLASH IN BLUE VALLEY, SUPERMAN.
...EVERYONE IN NORTH AMERICA EXCEPT US AND THE POPULATION HERE, ARE FAST ASLEEP
I CHECKED HOUSE BY HOUSE.
PEOPLE ARE GONNA START DYING SOON, GUYS...
STAY IN YOUR HOMES UNTIL WE HAVE MORE INFORMATION! THE LOCAL RADIO STATION IS STILL ON THE AIR WITH ANY NEWS WE GET!
...KEEP CALLING NEW GENESIS. WE NEED BARDA AND ORION BACK HERE.
SO WHAT DO YOU MEAN WE HAVE AN INTRUDER?
WHAT DOES HE KNOW ABOUT THIS?
WHAT DOES HE WANT, J'ONN?
HE APPEARED MOMENTS BEFORE YOU DID, SUPERMAN.
NONE OF OUR EQUIPMENT IS EVEN REGISTERING HIS PRESENCE; ACCORDING TO THE MACHINES, HE'S COMPLETELY ABSTRACT.
AND HE SEEMS TO HAVE COME FOR OUR HELP.
I MOLDED MY DAUGHTER DIANA FROM CLAY.
HOW COULD YOU KNOW THAT?
WONDER WOMAN? WHO IS THIS...
...
HAVE WE MET?
HAVE WE MET BEFORE?
Perhaps. At night.

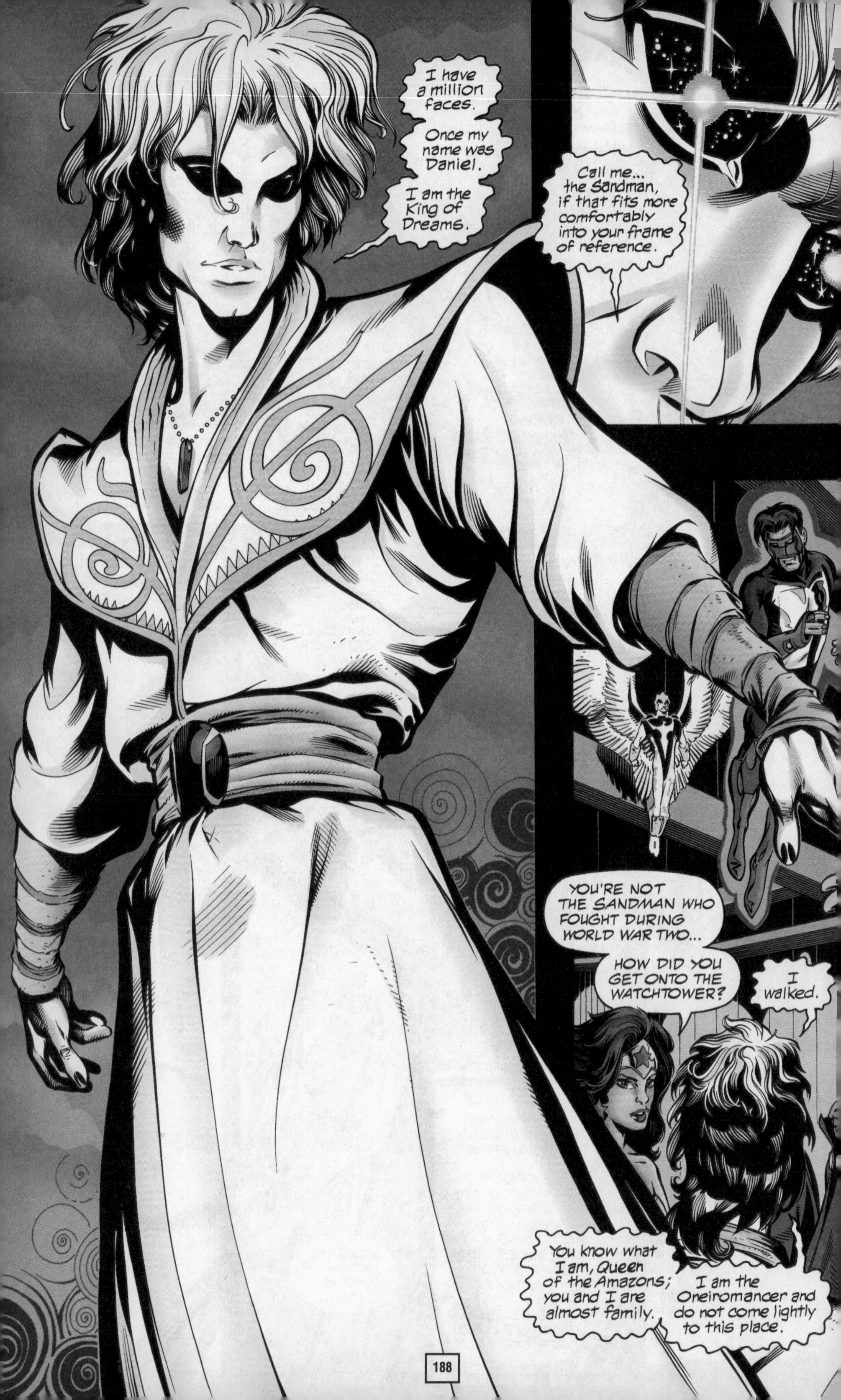

I have a million faces.
Once my name was Daniel.
I am the King of Dreams.
Call me... the Sandman, if that fits more comfortably into your frame of reference.
YOU'RE NOT THE SANDMAN WHO FOUGHT DURING WORLD WAR TWO...
HOW DID YOU GET ONTO THE WATCHTOWER?
I walked.
You know what I am, Queen of the Amazons; you and I are almost family.
I am the Oneiromancer and do not come lightly to this place.

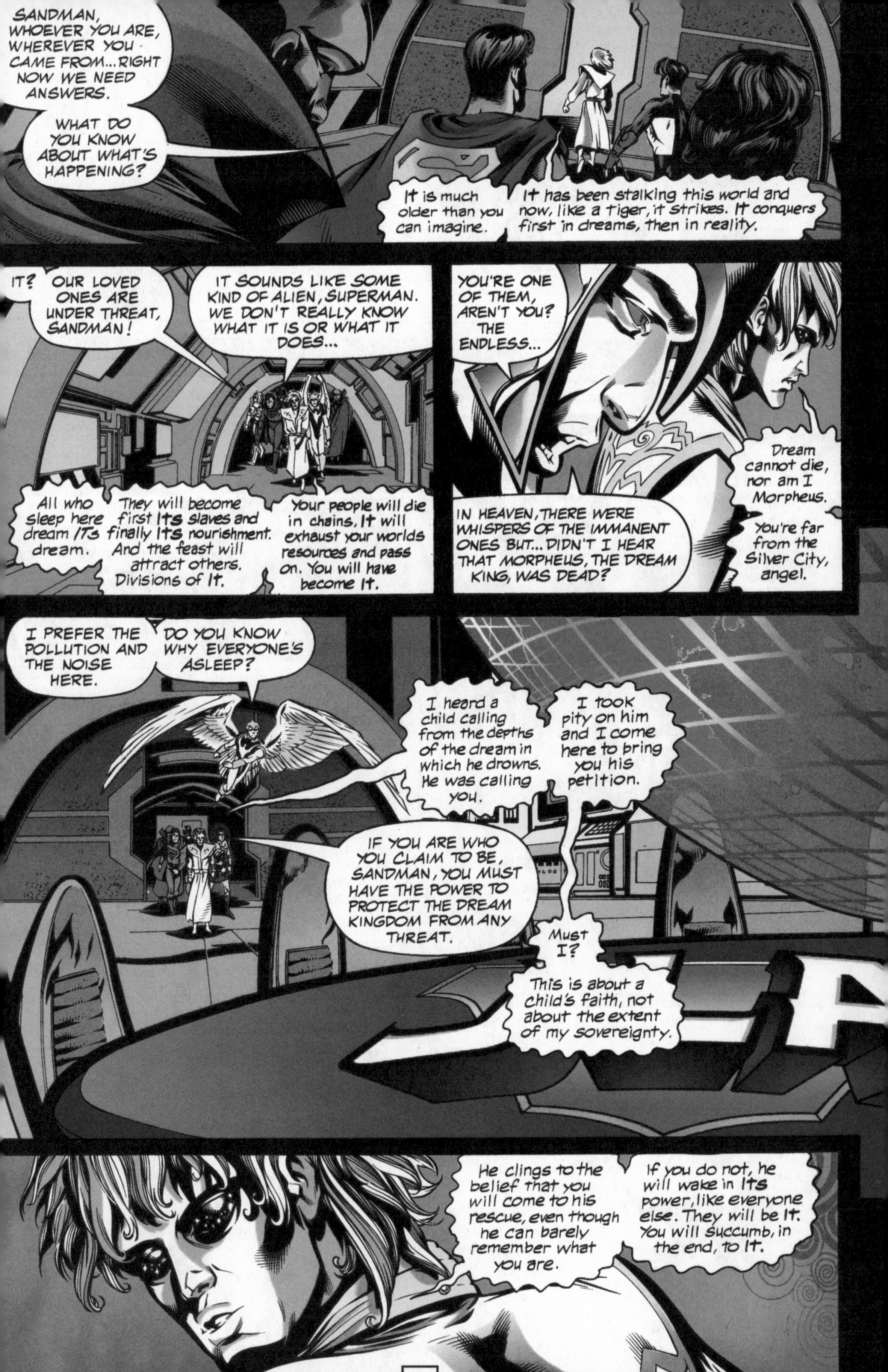

SANDMAN, WHOEVER YOU ARE, WHEREVER YOU CAME FROM... RIGHT NOW WE NEED ANSWERS.
WHAT DO YOU KNOW ABOUT WHAT'S HAPPENING?
It is much older than you can imagine.
It has been stalking this world and now, like a tiger, it strikes. It conquers first in dreams, then in reality.
IT?
OUR LOVED ONES ARE UNDER THREAT, SANDMAN!
IT SOUNDS LIKE SOME KIND OF ALIEN, SUPERMAN. WE DON'T REALLY KNOW WHAT IT IS OR WHAT IT DOES...
All who sleep here dream ITS dream.
They will become first ITS slaves and finally ITS nourishment. And the feast will attract others. Divisions of IT.
Your people will die in chains. IT will exhaust your worlds resources and pass on. You will have become IT.
YOU'RE ONE OF THEM, AREN'T YOU? THE ENDLESS...
IN HEAVEN, THERE WERE WHISPERS OF THE IMMANENT ONES BUT... DIDN'T I HEAR THAT MORPHEUS, THE DREAM KING, WAS DEAD?
Dream cannot die, nor am I Morpheus.
You're far from the Silver City, angel.
I PREFER THE POLLUTION AND THE NOISE HERE.
DO YOU KNOW WHY EVERYONE'S ASLEEP?
I heard a child calling from the depths of the dream in which he drowns. He was calling you.
I took pity on him and I come here to bring you his petition.
IF YOU ARE WHO YOU CLAIM TO BE, SANDMAN, YOU MUST HAVE THE POWER TO PROTECT THE DREAM KINGDOM FROM ANY THREAT.
Must I?
This is about a child's faith, not about the extent of my sovereignty.
He clings to the belief that you will come to his rescue, even though he can barely remember what you are.
If you do not, he will wake in ITS power, like everyone else. They will be IT. You will succumb, in the end, to IT.

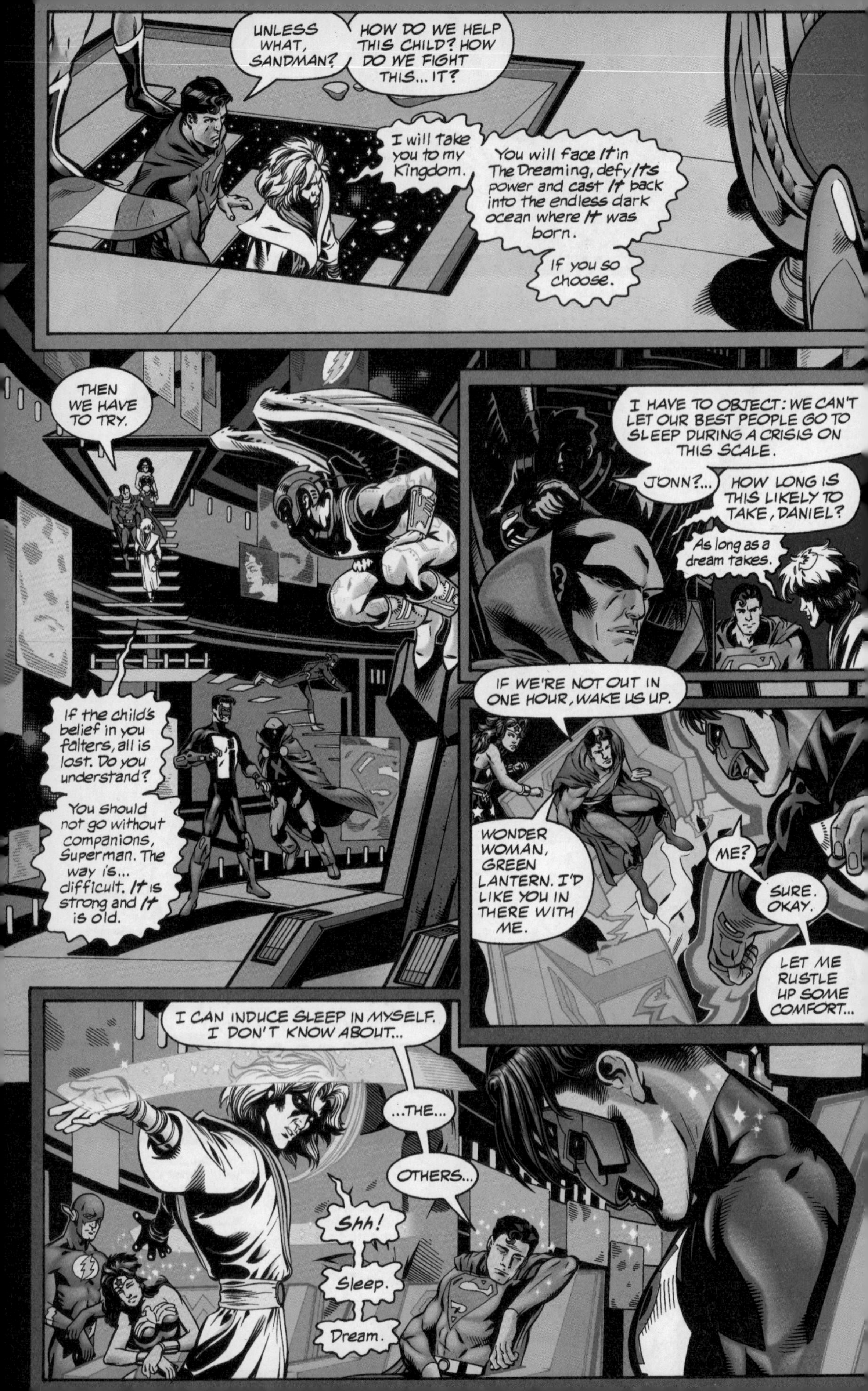
UNLESS WHAT, SANDMAN?
HOW DO WE HELP THIS CHILD? HOW DO WE FIGHT THIS... IT?
I will take you to my Kingdom.
You will face It in The Dreaming, defy Its power and cast It back into the endless dark ocean where It was born.
If you so choose.
THEN WE HAVE TO TRY.
If the child's belief in you falters, all is lost. Do you understand?
You should not go without companions, Superman. The way is... difficult. It is strong and It is old.
I HAVE TO OBJECT: WE CAN'T LET OUR BEST PEOPLE GO TO SLEEP DURING A CRISIS ON THIS SCALE.
J'ONN?...
HOW LONG IS THIS LIKELY TO TAKE, DANIEL?
As long as a dream takes.
IF WE'RE NOT OUT IN ONE HOUR, WAKE US UP.
WONDER WOMAN, GREEN LANTERN. I'D LIKE YOU IN THERE WITH ME.
ME?
SURE. OKAY.
LET ME RUSTLE UP SOME COMFORT...
I CAN INDUCE SLEEP IN MYSELF. I DON'T KNOW ABOUT...
...THE...
OTHERS...
Shh!
Sleep.
Dream.

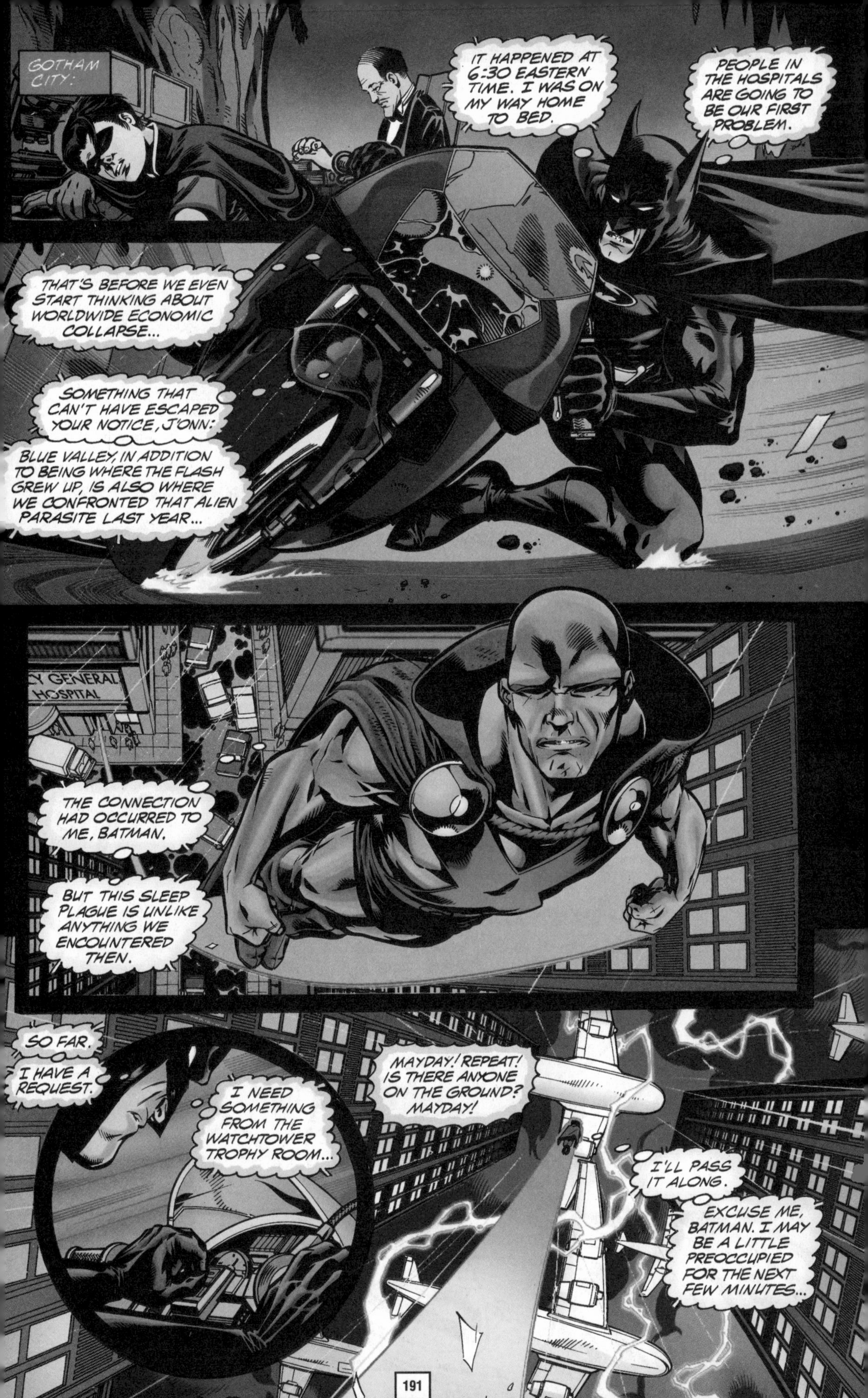
GOTHAM CITY:
IT HAPPENED AT 6:30 EASTERN TIME. I WAS ON MY WAY HOME TO BED.
PEOPLE IN THE HOSPITALS ARE GOING TO BE OUR FIRST PROBLEM.
THAT'S BEFORE WE EVEN START THINKING ABOUT WORLDWIDE ECONOMIC COLLAPSE...
SOMETHING THAT CAN'T HAVE ESCAPED YOUR NOTICE, J'ONN:
BLUE VALLEY, IN ADDITION TO BEING WHERE THE FLASH GREW UP, IS ALSO WHERE WE CONFRONTED THAT ALIEN PARASITE LAST YEAR...
CY GENERAL HOSPITAL
THE CONNECTION HAD OCCURRED TO ME, BATMAN.
BUT THIS SLEEP PLAGUE IS UNLIKE ANYTHING WE ENCOUNTERED THEN.
SO FAR.
I HAVE A REQUEST.
I NEED SOMETHING FROM THE WATCHTOWER TROPHY ROOM...
MAYDAY! REPEAT! IS THERE ANYONE ON THE GROUND? MAYDAY!
I'LL PASS IT ALONG.
EXCUSE ME, BATMAN. I MAY BE A LITTLE PREOCCUPIED FOR THE NEXT FEW MINUTES...

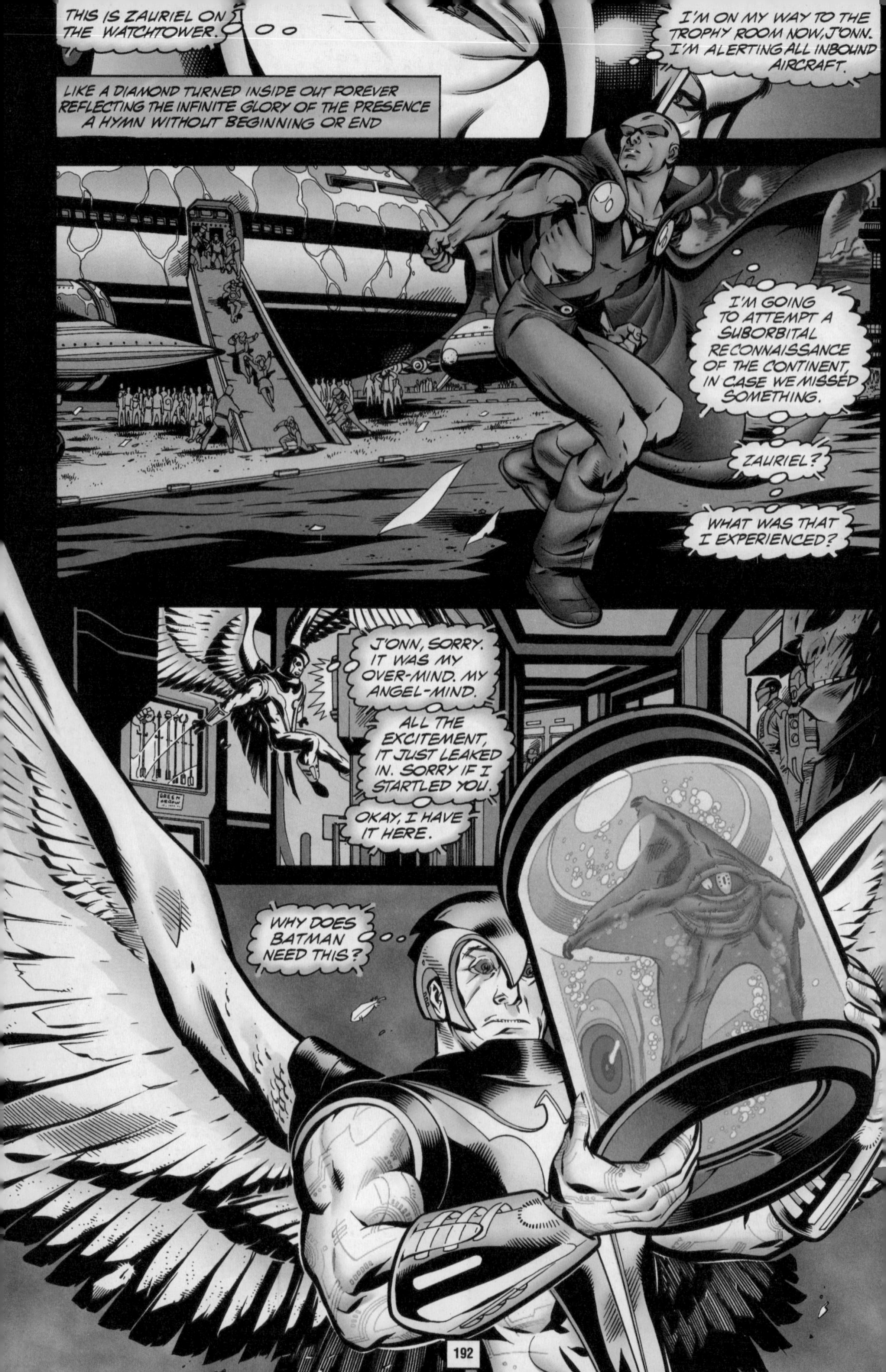
THIS IS ZAURIEL ON THE WATCHTOWER.
I'M ON MY WAY TO THE TROPHY ROOM NOW, J'ONN. I'M ALERTING ALL INBOUND AIRCRAFT.
LIKE A DIAMOND TURNED INSIDE OUT FOREVER REFLECTING THE INFINITE GLORY OF THE PRESENCE A HYMN WITHOUT BEGINNING OR END
I'M GOING TO ATTEMPT A SUBORBITAL RECONNAISSANCE OF THE CONTINENT, IN CASE WE MISSED SOMETHING.
ZAURIEL?
WHAT WAS THAT I EXPERIENCED?
J'ONN, SORRY. IT WAS MY OVER-MIND. MY ANGEL-MIND.
ALL THE EXCITEMENT, IT JUST LEAKED IN. SORRY IF I STARTLED YOU.
OKAY, I HAVE IT HERE.
WHY DOES BATMAN NEED THIS?

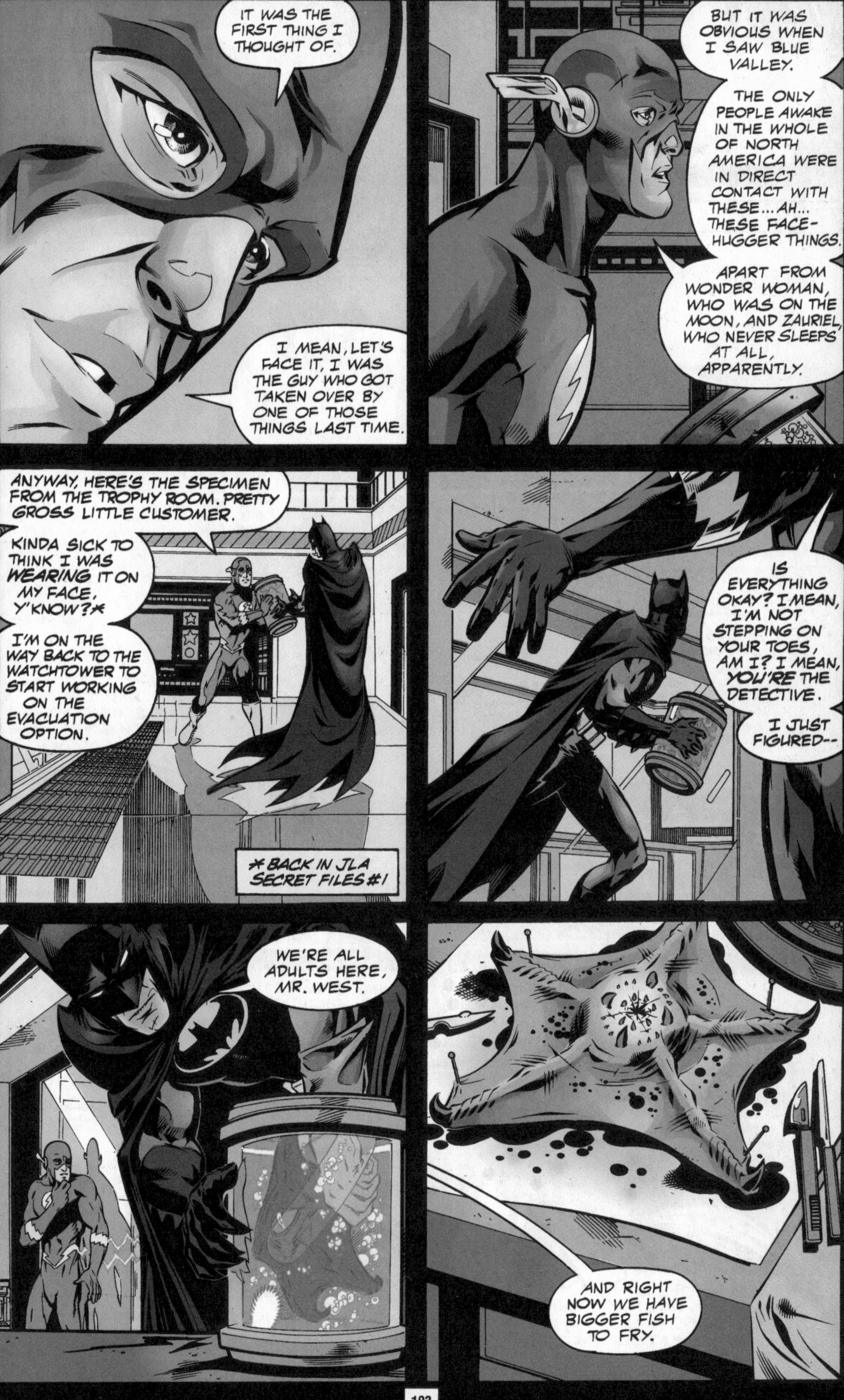
IT WAS THE FIRST THING I THOUGHT OF.
I MEAN, LET'S FACE IT, I WAS THE GUY WHO GOT TAKEN OVER BY ONE OF THOSE THINGS LAST TIME.
BUT IT WAS OBVIOUS WHEN I SAW BLUE VALLEY.
THE ONLY PEOPLE AWAKE IN THE WHOLE OF NORTH AMERICA WERE IN DIRECT CONTACT WITH THESE... AH... THESE FACE-HUGGER THINGS.
APART FROM WONDER WOMAN, WHO WAS ON THE MOON, AND ZAURIEL, WHO NEVER SLEEPS AT ALL, APPARENTLY.
ANYWAY, HERE'S THE SPECIMEN FROM THE TROPHY ROOM. PRETTY GROSS LITTLE CUSTOMER.
KINDA SICK TO THINK I WAS WEARING IT ON MY FACE, Y'KNOW?*
I'M ON THE WAY BACK TO THE WATCHTOWER TO START WORKING ON THE EVACUATION OPTION.
*BACK IN JLA SECRET FILES #1
IS EVERYTHING OKAY? I MEAN, I'M NOT STEPPING ON YOUR TOES, AM I? I MEAN, YOU'RE THE DETECTIVE.
I JUST FIGURED--
WE'RE ALL ADULTS HERE, MR. WEST.
AND RIGHT NOW WE HAVE BIGGER FISH TO FRY.

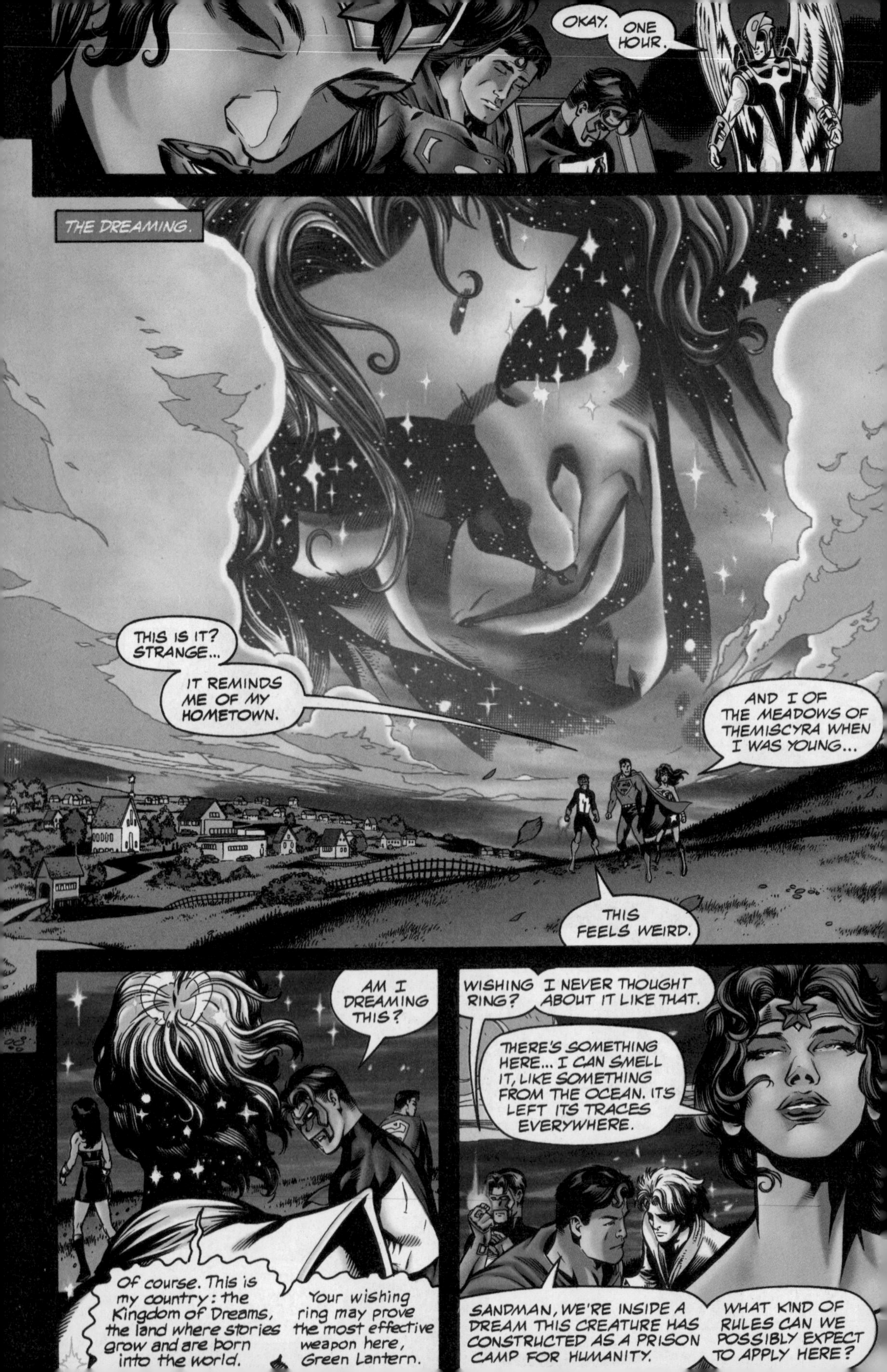
OKAY. ONE HOUR.
THE DREAMING.
THIS IS IT? STRANGE...
IT REMINDS ME OF MY HOMETOWN.
AND I OF THE MEADOWS OF THEMISCYRA WHEN I WAS YOUNG...
THIS FEELS WEIRD.
AM I DREAMING THIS?
Of course. This is my country: the Kingdom of Dreams, the land where stories grow and are born into the world.
Your wishing ring may prove the most effective weapon here, Green Lantern.
WISHING RING?
I NEVER THOUGHT ABOUT IT LIKE THAT.
THERE'S SOMETHING HERE... I CAN SMELL IT, LIKE SOMETHING FROM THE OCEAN. IT'S LEFT ITS TRACES EVERYWHERE.
SANDMAN, WE'RE INSIDE A DREAM THIS CREATURE HAS CONSTRUCTED AS A PRISON CAMP FOR HUMANITY.
WHAT KIND OF RULES CAN WE POSSIBLY EXPECT TO APPLY HERE?

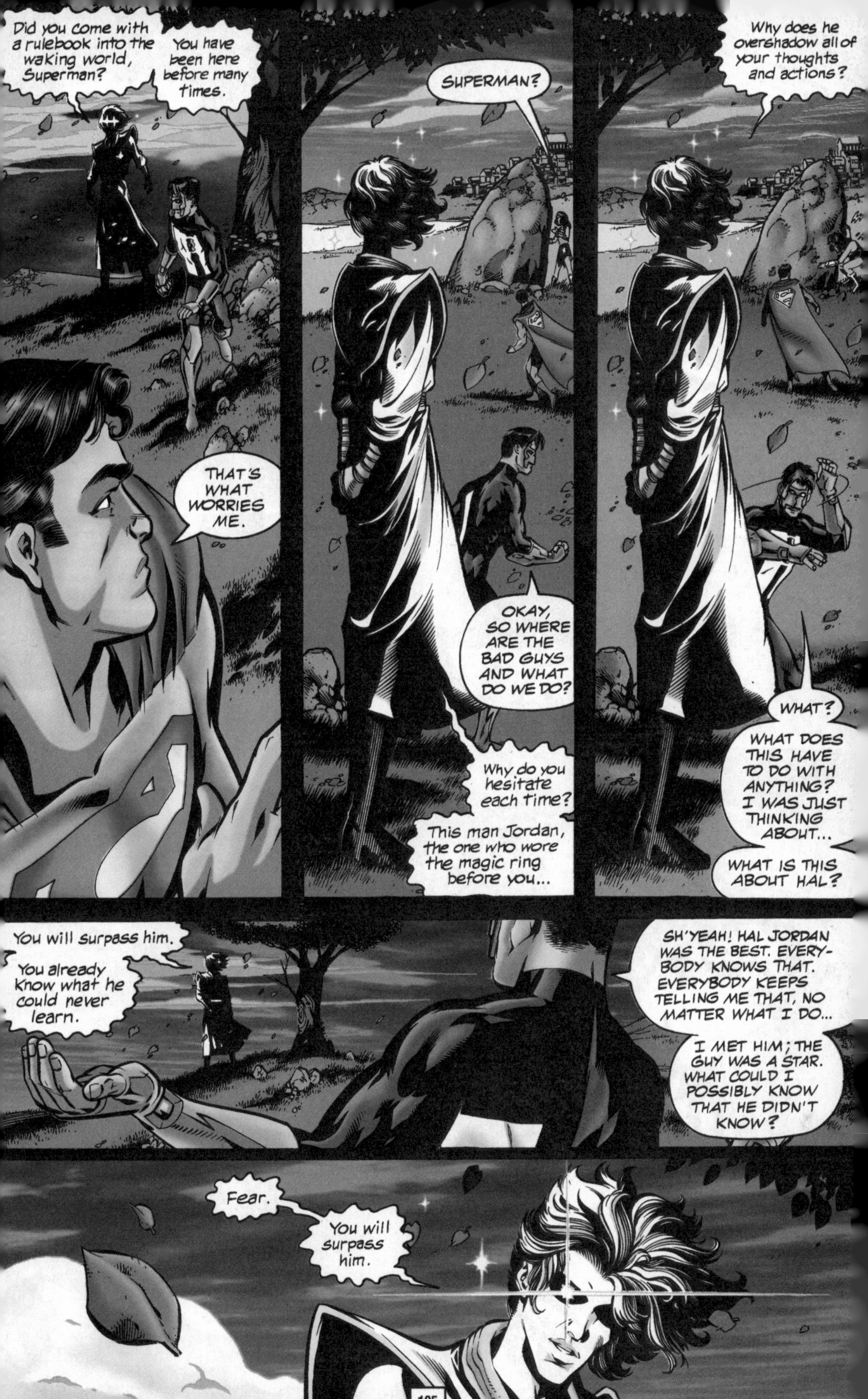

Did you come with a rulebook into the waking world, Superman?
You have been here before many times.
THAT'S WHAT WORRIES ME.
SUPERMAN?
OKAY, SO WHERE ARE THE BAD GUYS AND WHAT DO WE DO?
Why do you hesitate each time?
This man Jordan, the one who wore the magic ring before you...
Why does he overshadow all of your thoughts and actions?
WHAT?
WHAT DOES THIS HAVE TO DO WITH ANYTHING? I WAS JUST THINKING ABOUT...
WHAT IS THIS ABOUT HAL?
You will surpass him.
You already know what he could never learn.
SH'YEAH! HAL JORDAN WAS THE BEST. EVERYBODY KNOWS THAT. EVERYBODY KEEPS TELLING ME THAT, NO MATTER WHAT I DO...
I MET HIM; THE GUY WAS A STAR. WHAT COULD I POSSIBLY KNOW THAT HE DIDN'T KNOW?
Fear.
You will surpass him.

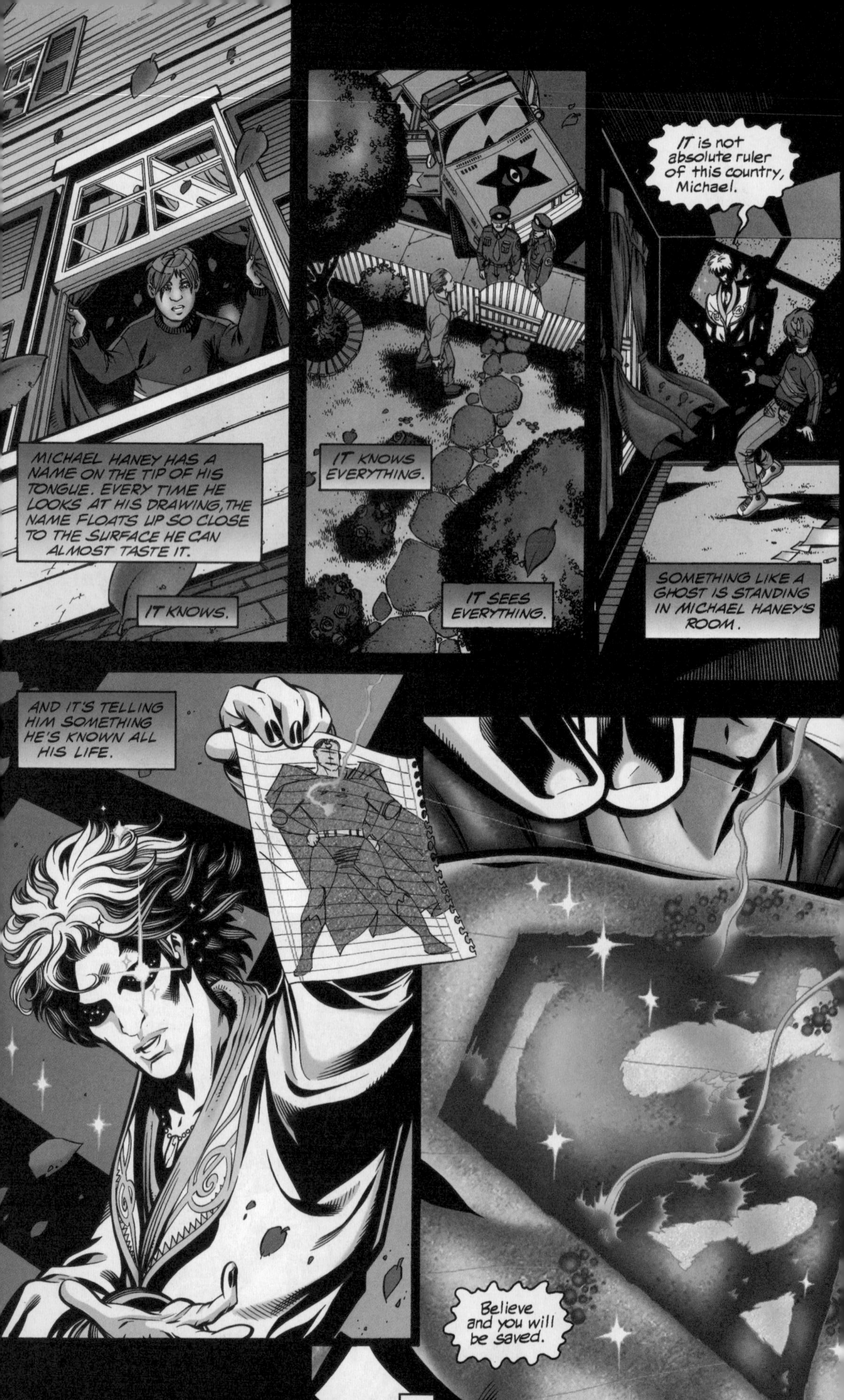

MICHAEL HANEY HAS A NAME ON THE TIP OF HIS TONGUE. EVERY TIME HE LOOKS AT HIS DRAWING, THE NAME FLOATS UP SO CLOSE TO THE SURFACE HE CAN ALMOST TASTE IT.
IT KNOWS.
IT KNOWS EVERYTHING.
IT SEES EVERYTHING.
IT is not absolute ruler of this country, Michael.
SOMETHING LIKE A GHOST IS STANDING IN MICHAEL HANEY'S ROOM.
AND IT'S TELLING HIM SOMETHING HE'S KNOWN ALL HIS LIFE.
Believe and you will be saved.

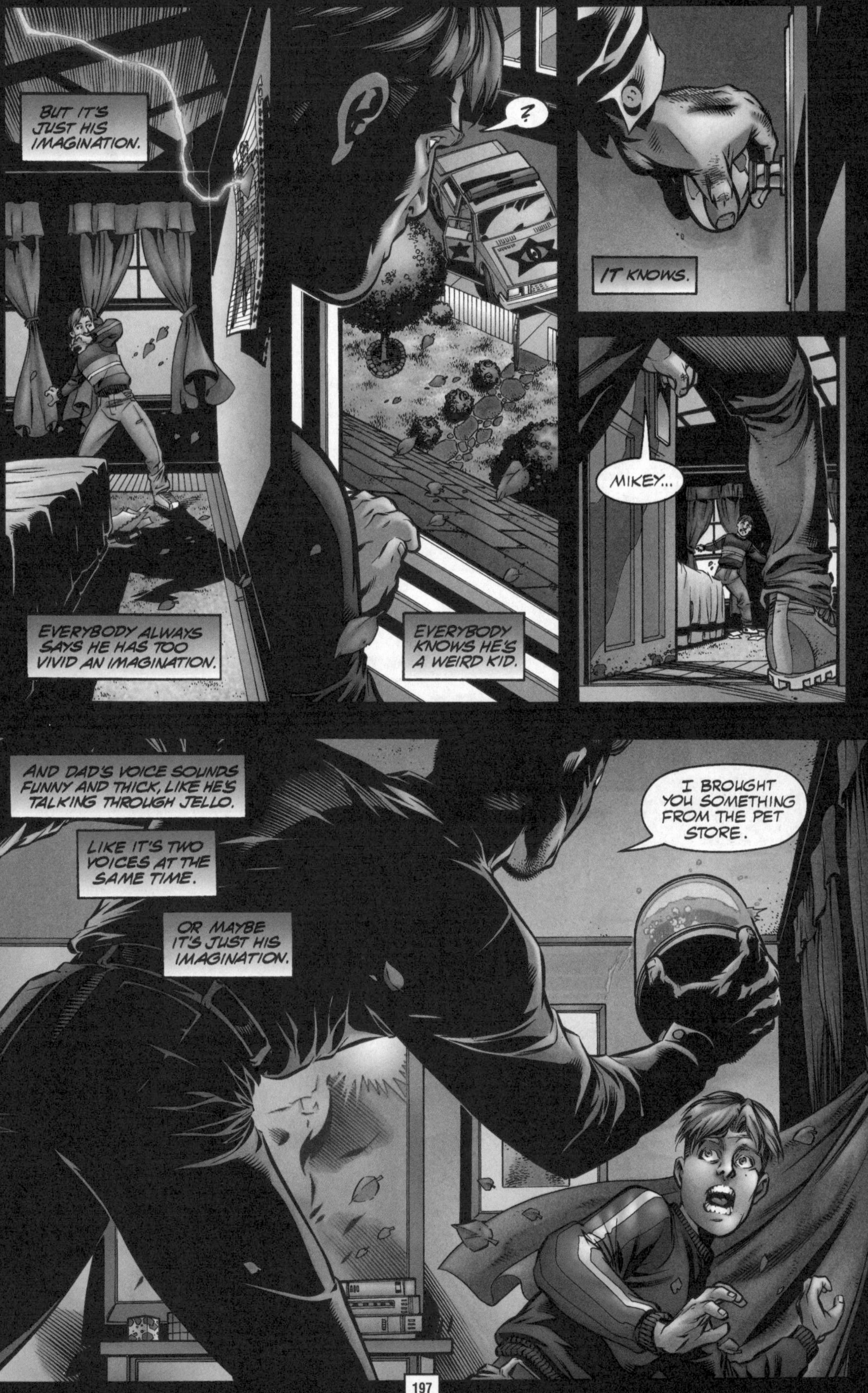

BUT IT'S JUST HIS IMAGINATION.
EVERYBODY ALWAYS SAYS HE HAS TOO VIVID AN IMAGINATION.
?
EVERYBODY KNOWS HE'S A WEIRD KID.
IT KNOWS.
MIKEY...
AND DAD'S VOICE SOUNDS FUNNY AND THICK, LIKE HE'S TALKING THROUGH JELLO.
LIKE IT'S TWO VOICES AT THE SAME TIME.
OR MAYBE IT'S JUST HIS IMAGINATION.
I BROUGHT YOU SOMETHING FROM THE PET STORE.

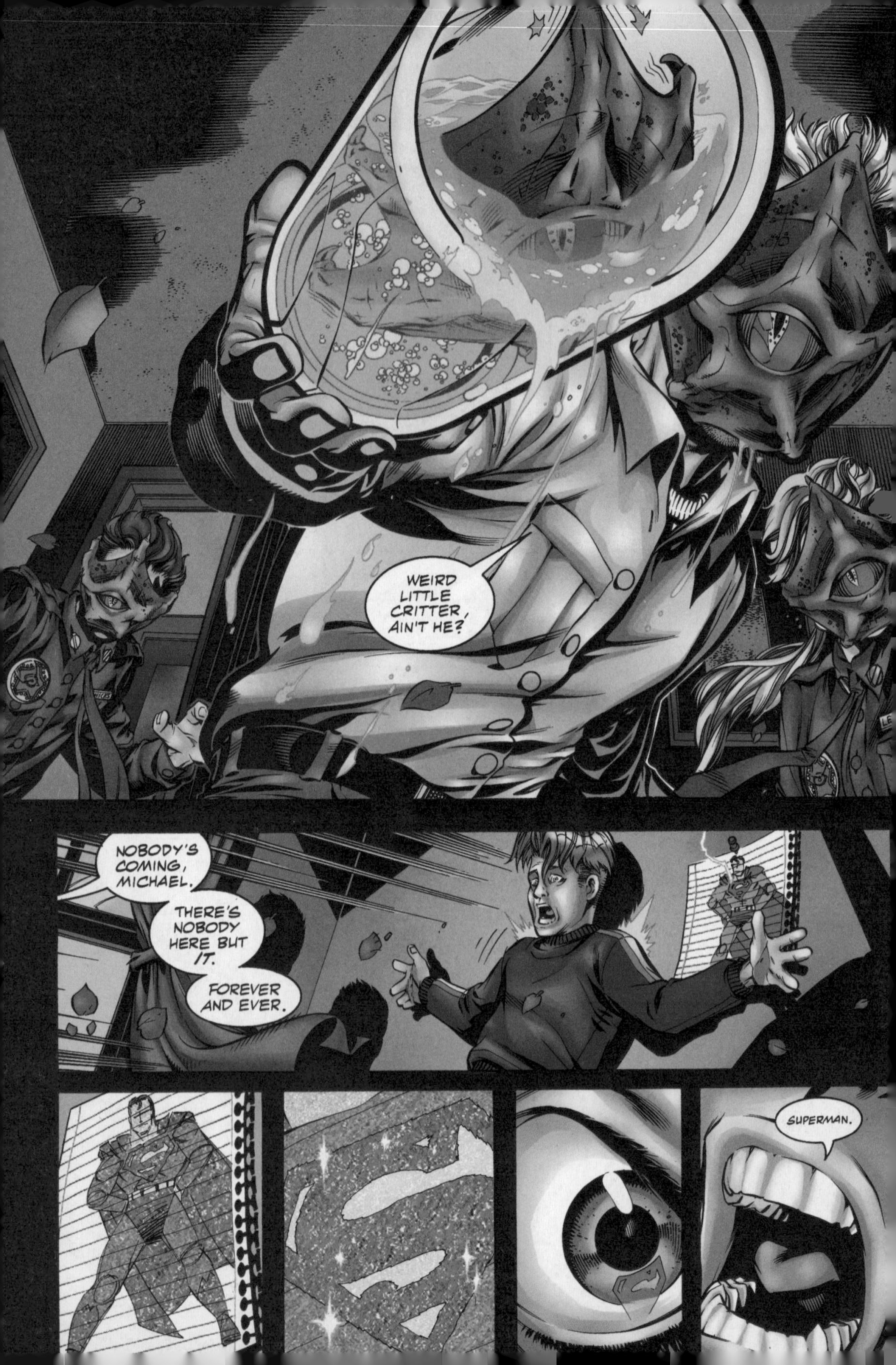
WEIRD LITTLE CRITTER, AIN'T HE?
NOBODY'S COMING, MICHAEL.
THERE'S NOBODY HERE BUT IT.
FOREVER AND EVER.
SUPERMAN.

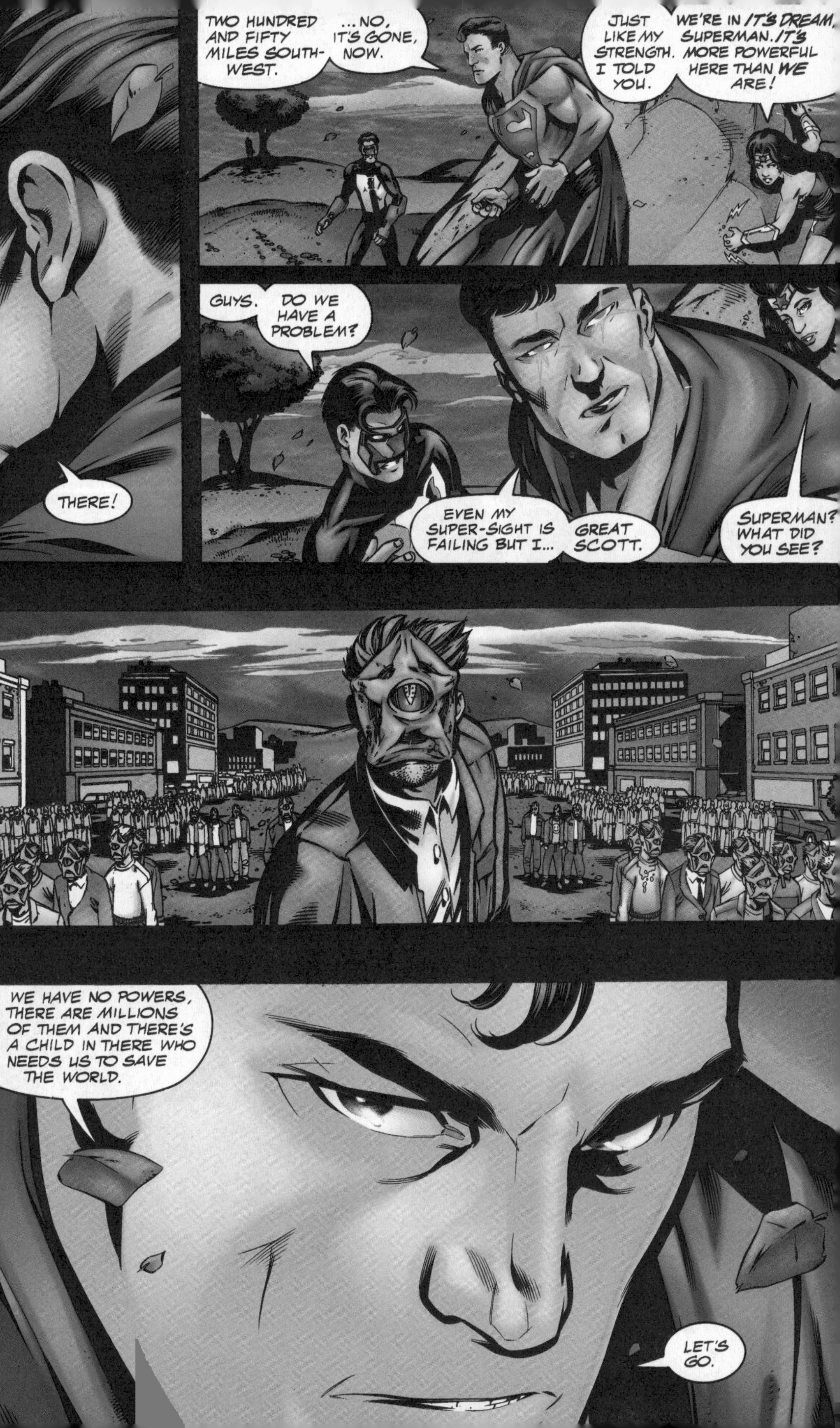
TWO HUNDRED AND FIFTY MILES SOUTH-WEST.
...NO, IT'S GONE, NOW.
JUST LIKE MY STRENGTH. I TOLD YOU.
WE'RE IN IT'S DREAM, SUPERMAN. IT'S MORE POWERFUL HERE THAN WE ARE!
THERE!
GUYS.
DO WE HAVE A PROBLEM?
EVEN MY SUPER-SIGHT IS FAILING BUT I...
GREAT SCOTT.
SUPERMAN? WHAT DID YOU SEE?
WE HAVE NO POWERS, THERE ARE MILLIONS OF THEM AND THERE'S A CHILD IN THERE WHO NEEDS US TO SAVE THE WORLD.
LET'S GO.

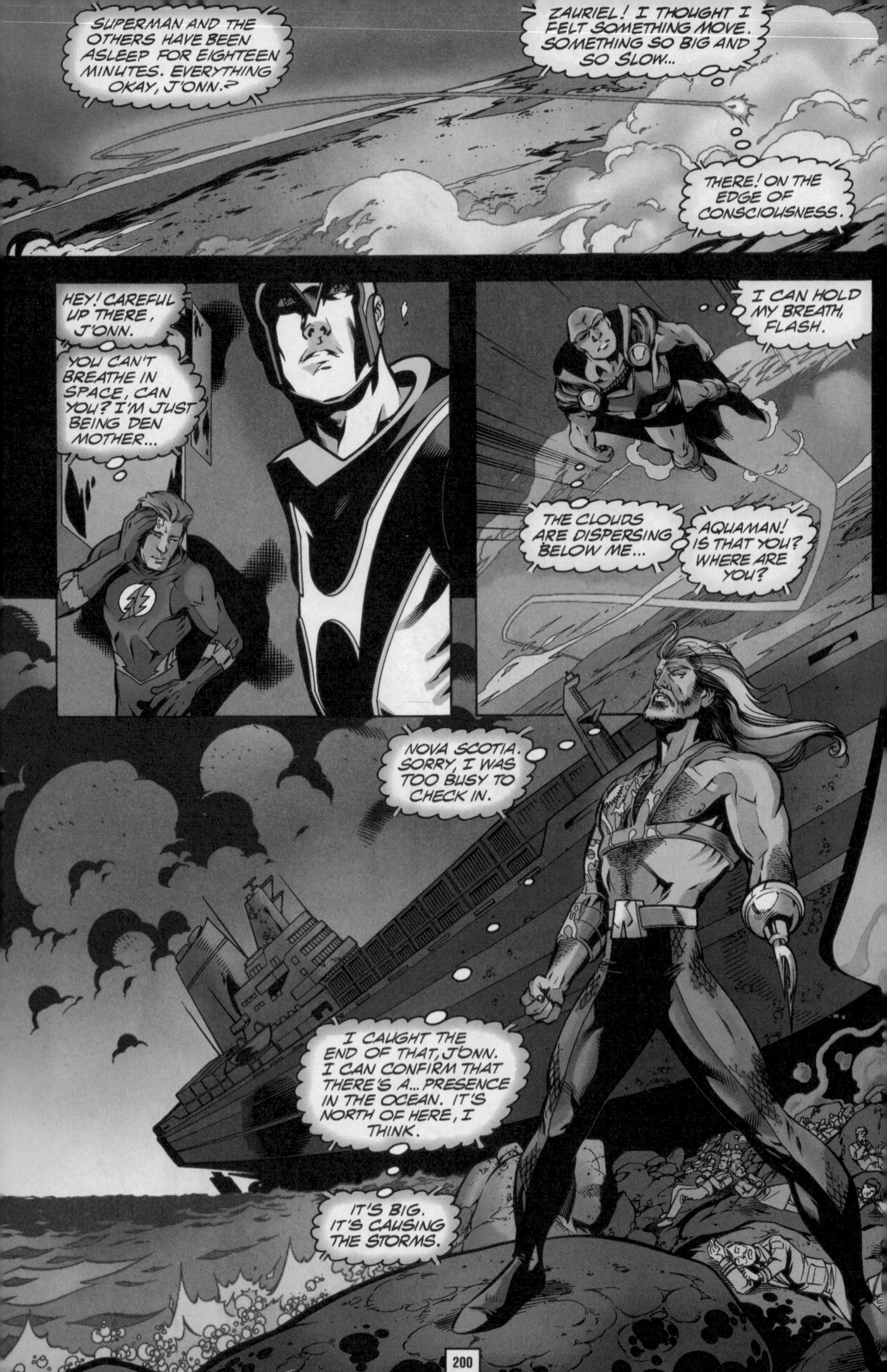
SUPERMAN AND THE OTHERS HAVE BEEN ASLEEP FOR EIGHTEEN MINUTES. EVERYTHING OKAY, J'ONN.?
ZAURIEL! I THOUGHT I FELT SOMETHING MOVE. SOMETHING SO BIG AND SO SLOW...
THERE! ON THE EDGE OF CONSCIOUSNESS.
HEY! CAREFUL UP THERE, J'ONN.
YOU CAN'T BREATHE IN SPACE, CAN YOU? I'M JUST BEING DEN MOTHER...
I CAN HOLD MY BREATH, FLASH.
THE CLOUDS ARE DISPERSING BELOW ME...
AQUAMAN! IS THAT YOU? WHERE ARE YOU?
NOVA SCOTIA. SORRY, I WAS TOO BUSY TO CHECK IN.
I CAUGHT THE END OF THAT, J'ONN. I CAN CONFIRM THAT THERE'S A... PRESENCE IN THE OCEAN. IT'S NORTH OF HERE, I THINK.
IT'S BIG. IT'S CAUSING THE STORMS.

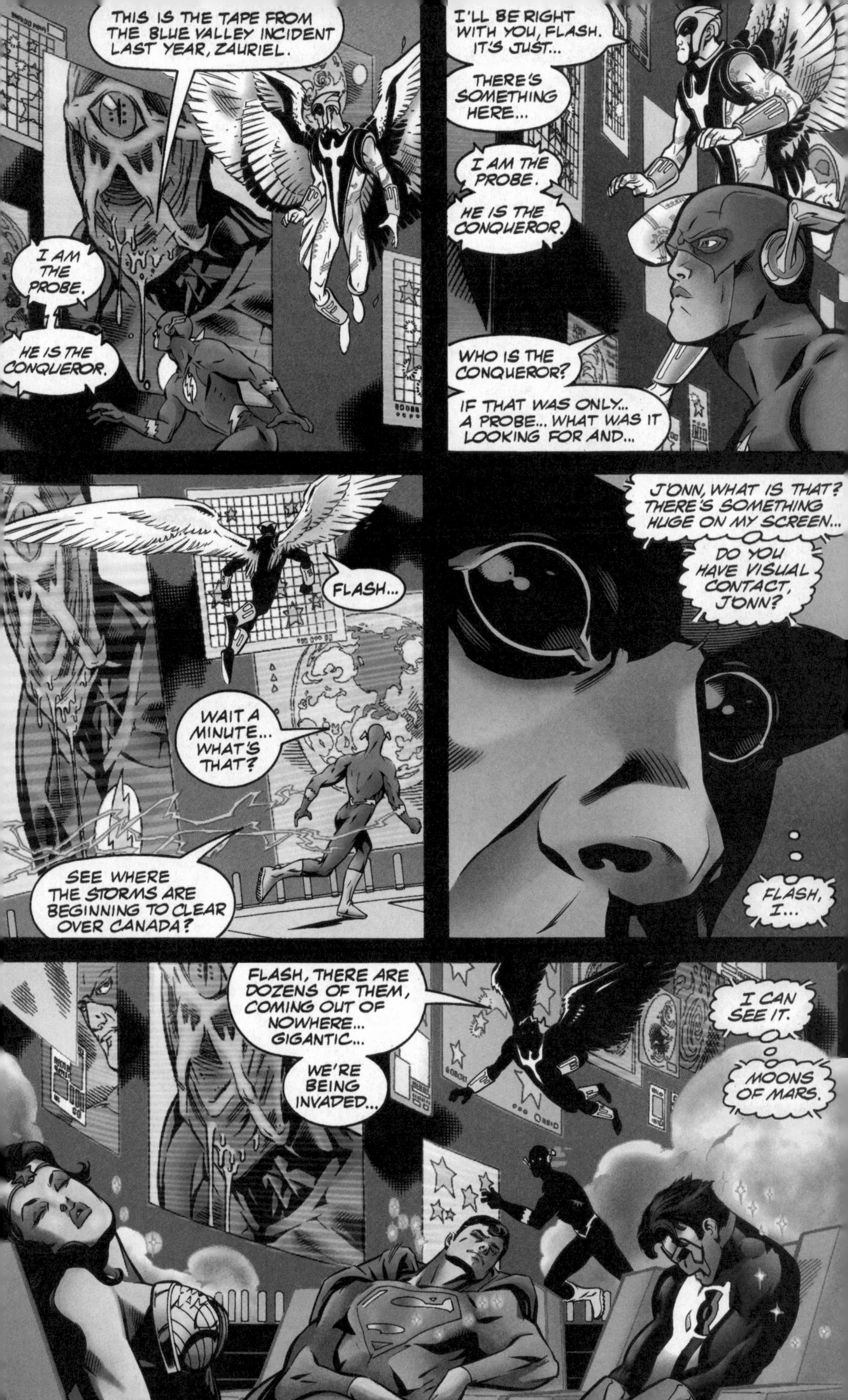
THIS IS THE TAPE FROM THE BLUE VALLEY INCIDENT LAST YEAR, ZAURIEL.
I AM THE PROBE.
HE IS THE CONQUEROR.
I'LL BE RIGHT WITH YOU, FLASH. IT'S JUST...
THERE'S SOMETHING HERE...
I AM THE PROBE.
HE IS THE CONQUEROR.
WHO IS THE CONQUEROR?
IF THAT WAS ONLY... A PROBE... WHAT WAS IT LOOKING FOR AND...
FLASH...
WAIT A MINUTE... WHAT'S THAT?
SEE WHERE THE STORMS ARE BEGINNING TO CLEAR OVER CANADA?
J'ONN, WHAT IS THAT? THERE'S SOMETHING HUGE ON MY SCREEN...
DO YOU HAVE VISUAL CONTACT, J'ONN?
FLASH, I...
FLASH, THERE ARE DOZENS OF THEM, COMING OUT OF NOWHERE... GIGANTIC...
WE'RE BEING INVADED...
I CAN SEE IT.
MOONS OF MARS.

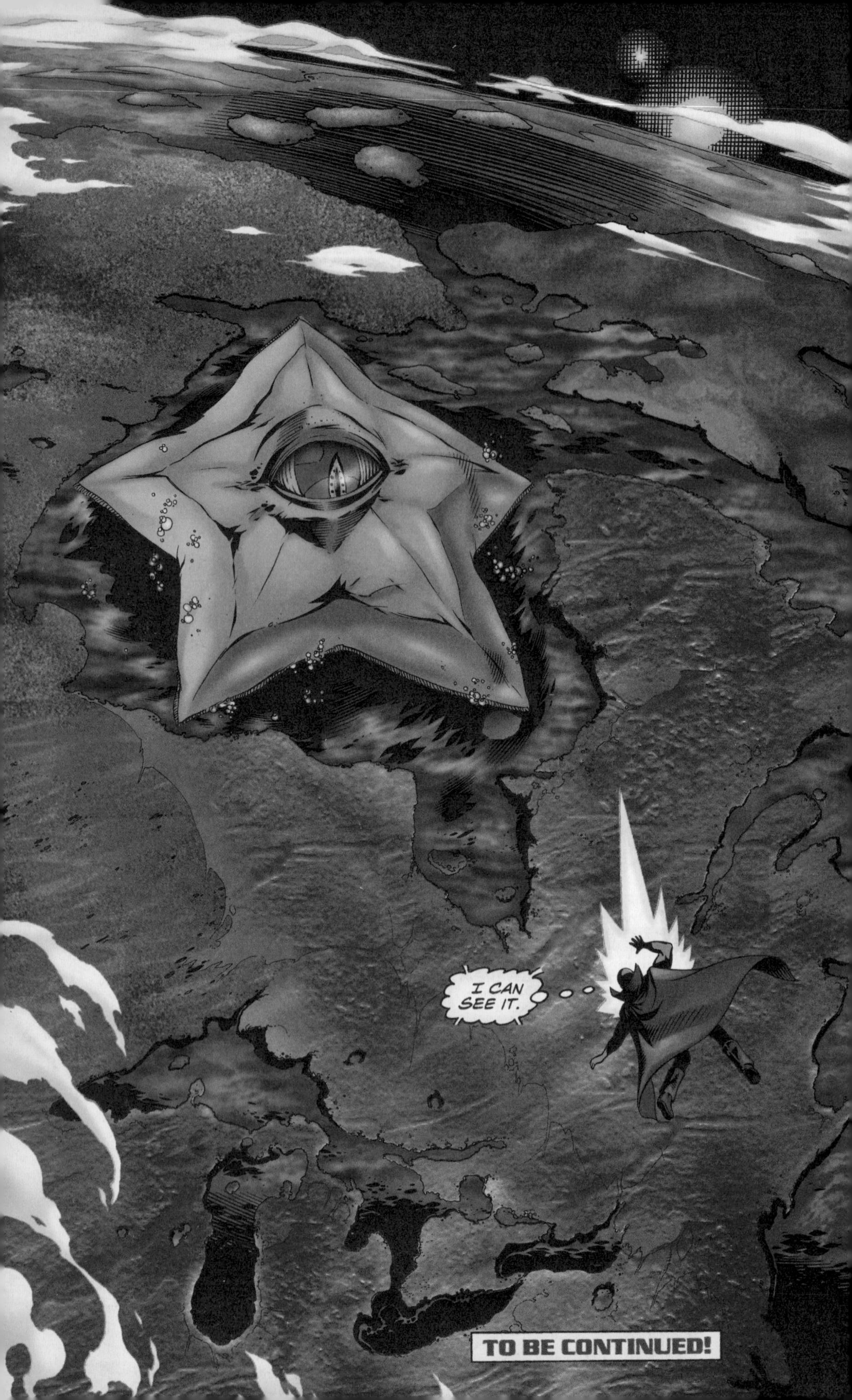
I CAN SEE IT.
TO BE CONTINUED!

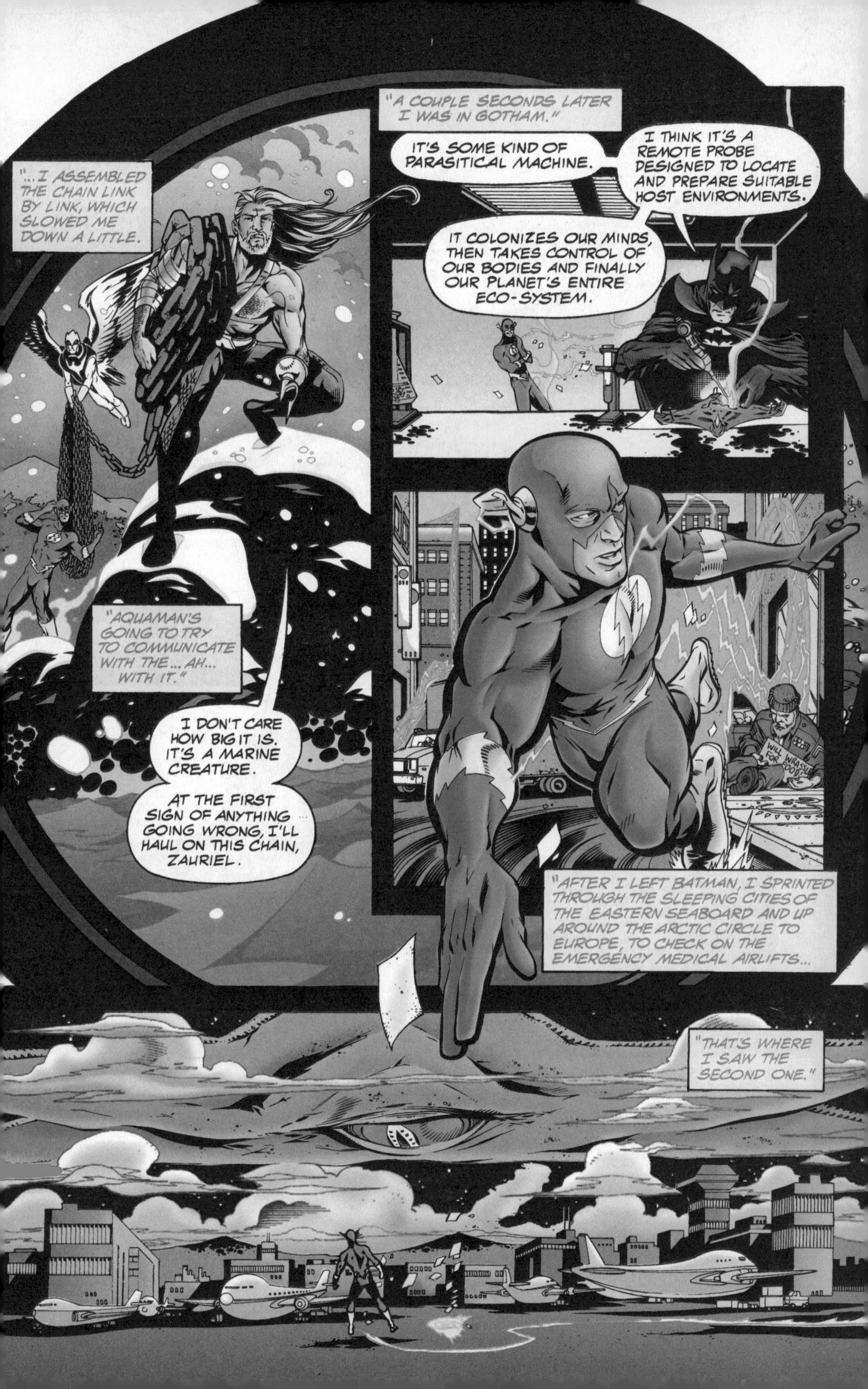

"...I ASSEMBLED THE CHAIN LINK BY LINK, WHICH SLOWED ME DOWN A LITTLE.
"AQUAMAN'S GOING TO TRY TO COMMUNICATE WITH THE... AH... WITH IT."
I DON'T CARE HOW BIG IT IS. IT'S A MARINE CREATURE.
AT THE FIRST SIGN OF ANYTHING GOING WRONG, I'LL HAUL ON THIS CHAIN, ZAURIEL.
"A COUPLE SECONDS LATER I WAS IN GOTHAM."
IT'S SOME KIND OF PARASITICAL MACHINE.
I THINK IT'S A REMOTE PROBE DESIGNED TO LOCATE AND PREPARE SUITABLE HOST ENVIRONMENTS.
IT COLONIZES OUR MINDS, THEN TAKES CONTROL OF OUR BODIES AND FINALLY OUR PLANET'S ENTIRE ECO-SYSTEM.
"AFTER I LEFT BATMAN, I SPRINTED THROUGH THE SLEEPING CITIES OF THE EASTERN SEABOARD AND UP AROUND THE ARCTIC CIRCLE TO EUROPE, TO CHECK ON THE EMERGENCY MEDICAL AIRLIFTS...
"THAT'S WHERE I SAW THE SECOND ONE."

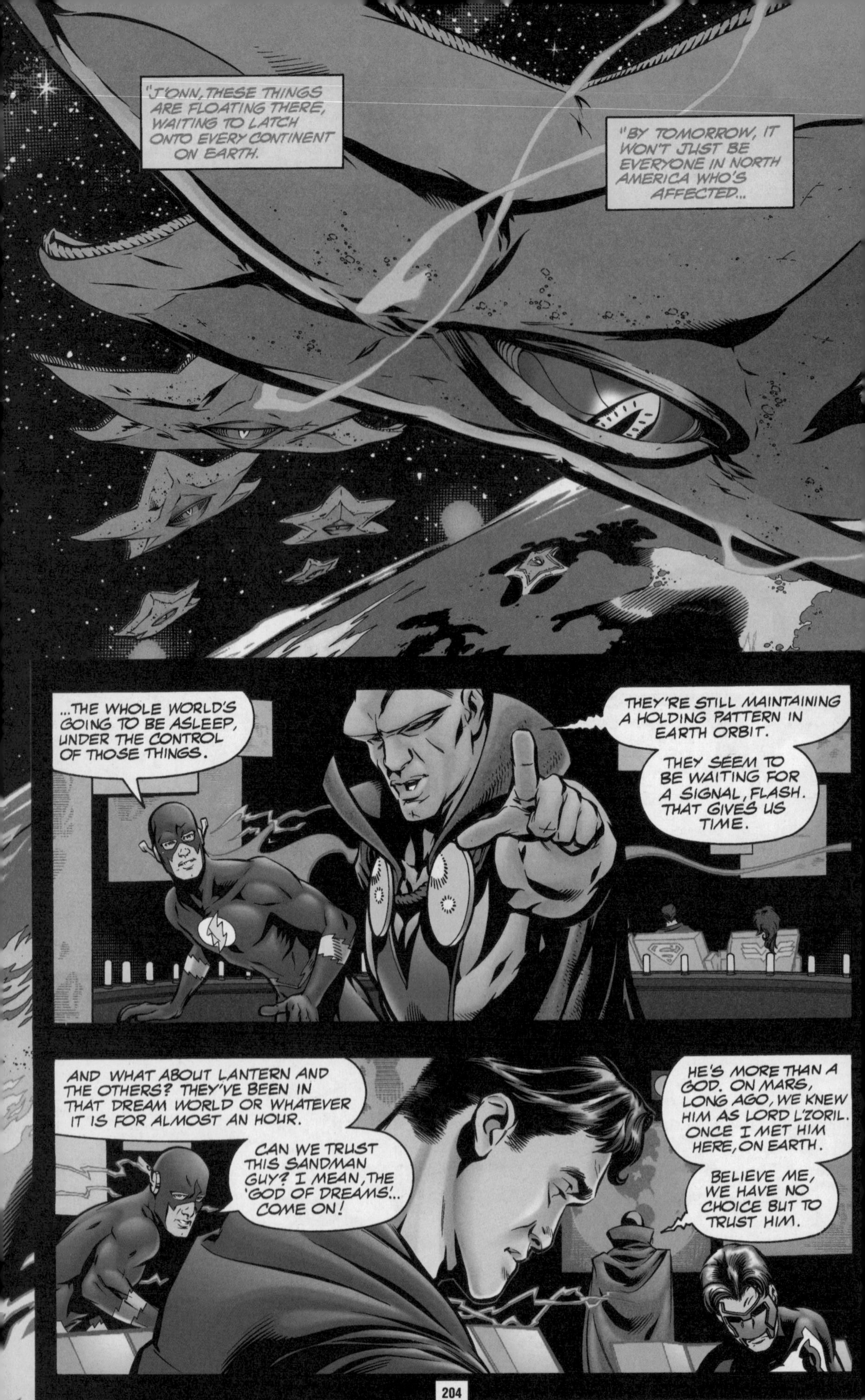
"J'ONN, THESE THINGS ARE FLOATING THERE, WAITING TO LATCH ONTO EVERY CONTINENT ON EARTH.
"BY TOMORROW, IT WON'T JUST BE EVERYONE IN NORTH AMERICA WHO'S AFFECTED...
...THE WHOLE WORLD'S GOING TO BE ASLEEP, UNDER THE CONTROL OF THOSE THINGS.
THEY'RE STILL MAINTAINING A HOLDING PATTERN IN EARTH ORBIT.
THEY SEEM TO BE WAITING FOR A SIGNAL, FLASH. THAT GIVES US TIME.
AND WHAT ABOUT LANTERN AND THE OTHERS? THEY'VE BEEN IN THAT DREAM WORLD OR WHATEVER IT IS FOR ALMOST AN HOUR.
CAN WE TRUST THIS SANDMAN GUY? I MEAN, THE 'GOD OF DREAMS'... COME ON!
HE'S MORE THAN A GOD. ON MARS, LONG AGO, WE KNEW HIM AS LORD L'ZORIL. ONCE I MET HIM HERE, ON EARTH.
BELIEVE ME, WE HAVE NO CHOICE BUT TO TRUST HIM.

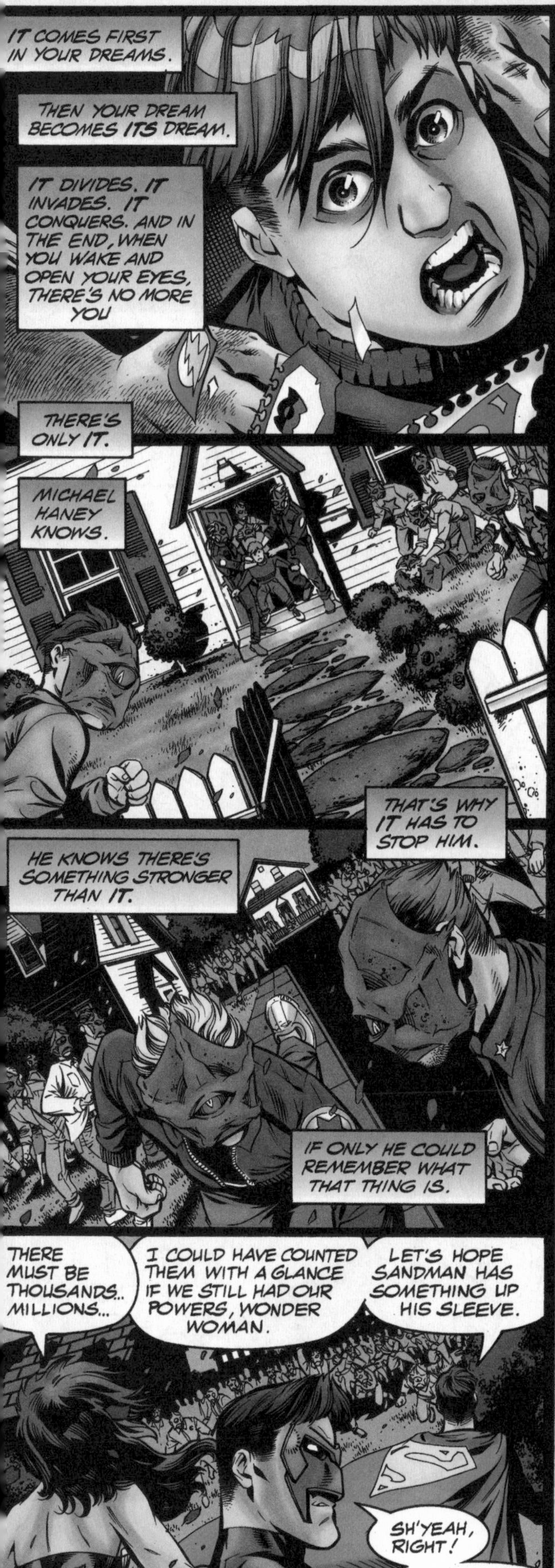
IT COMES FIRST IN YOUR DREAMS.
THEN YOUR DREAM BECOMES ITS DREAM.
IT DIVIDES. IT INVADES. IT CONQUERS. AND IN THE END, WHEN YOU WAKE AND OPEN YOUR EYES, THERE'S NO MORE YOU
THERE'S ONLY IT.
MICHAEL HANEY KNOWS.
HE KNOWS THERE'S SOMETHING STRONGER THAN IT.
THAT'S WHY IT HAS TO STOP HIM.
IF ONLY HE COULD REMEMBER WHAT THAT THING IS.
THERE MUST BE THOUSANDS.. MILLIONS...
I COULD HAVE COUNTED THEM WITH A GLANCE IF WE STILL HAD OUR POWERS, WONDER WOMAN.
LET'S HOPE SANDMAN HAS SOMETHING UP HIS SLEEVE.
SH'YEAH, RIGHT!
WHERE'D HE DISAPPEAR TO?
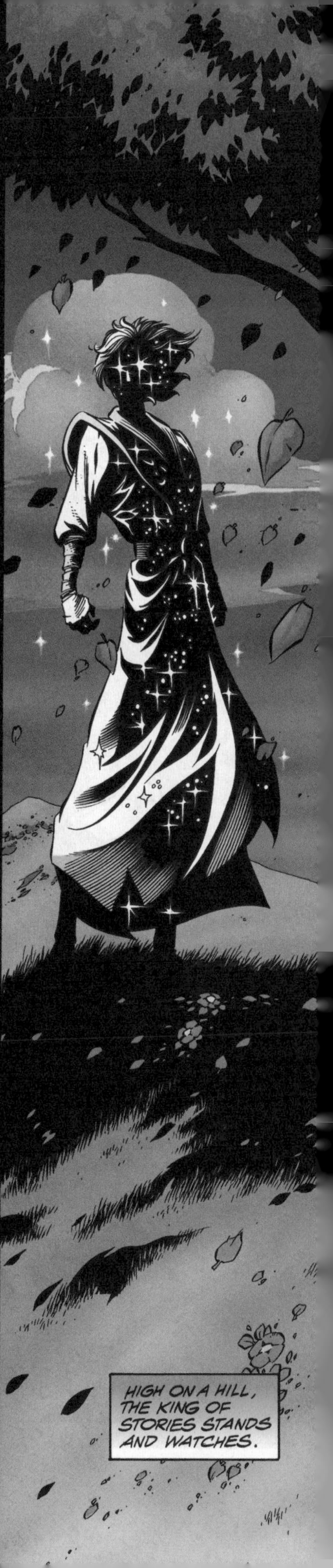
HIGH ON A HILL, THE KING OF STORIES STANDS AND WATCHES.

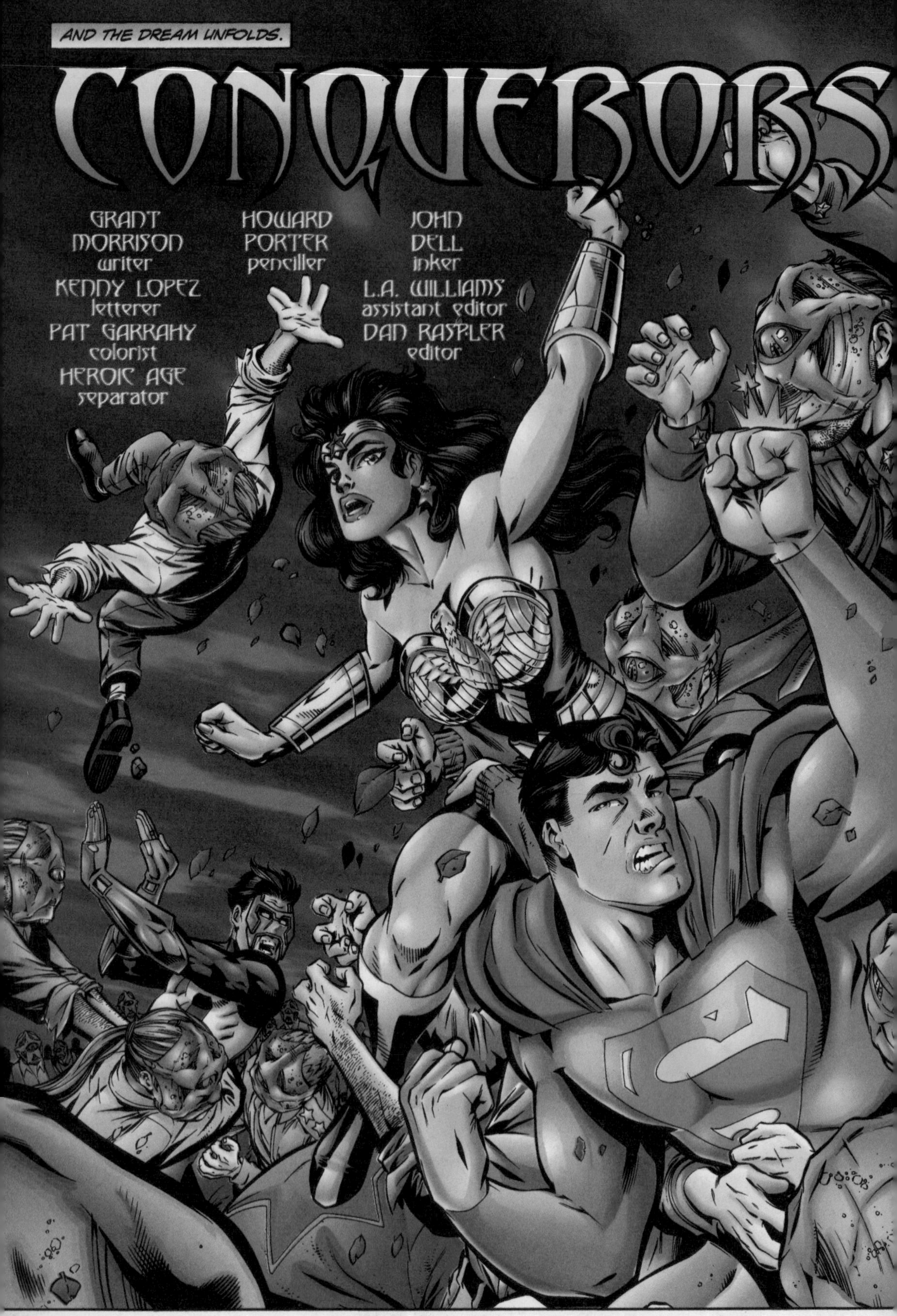
AND THE DREAM UNFOLDS.
CONQUERORS
GRANT MORRISON writer
HOWARD PORTER penciller
JOHN DELL inker
KENNY LOPEZ letterer
L.A. WILLIAMS assistant editor
PAT GARRAHY colorist
DAN RASPLER editor
HEROIC AGE separator

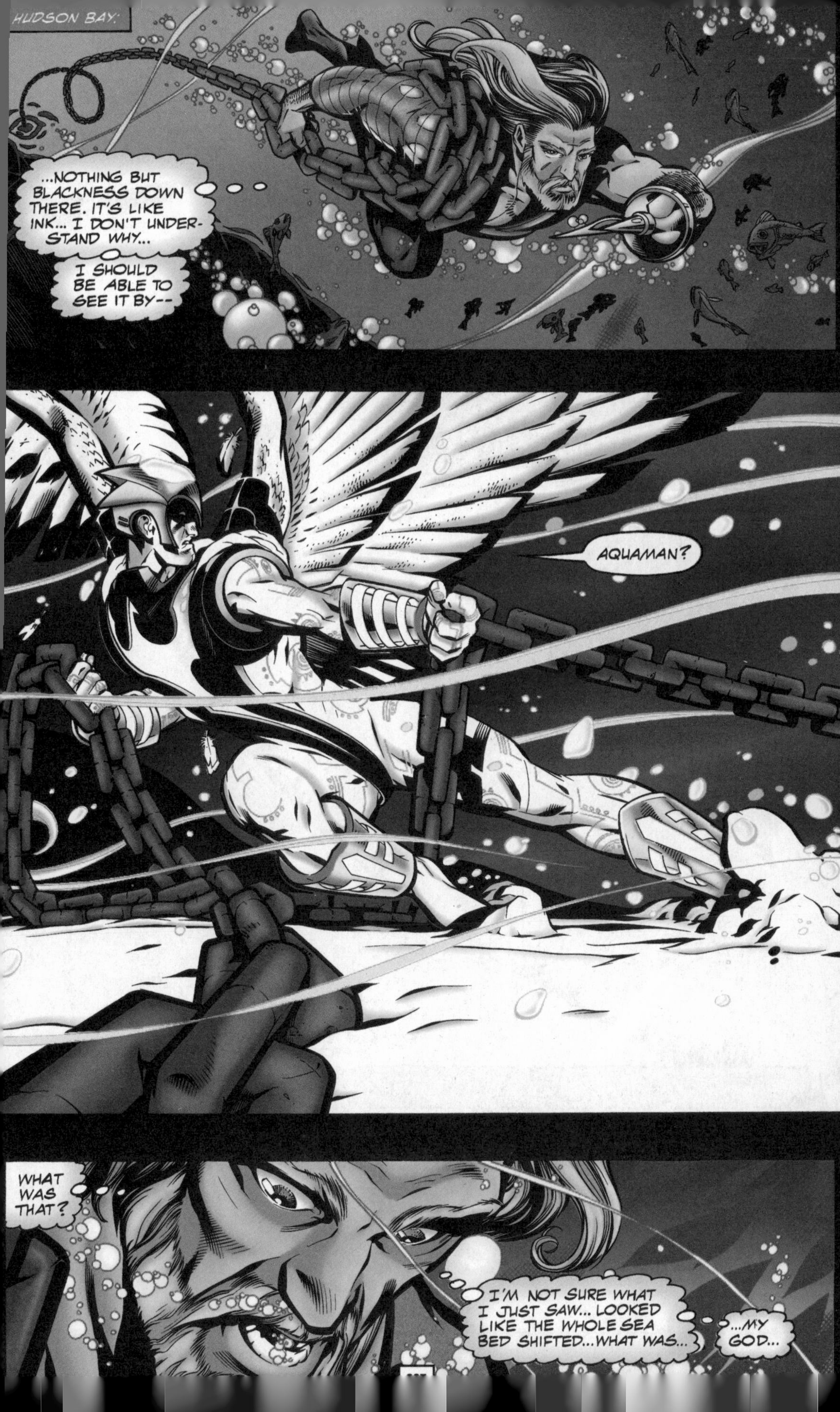

HUDSON BAY:
...NOTHING BUT BLACKNESS DOWN THERE. IT'S LIKE INK... I DON'T UNDER-STAND WHY...
I SHOULD BE ABLE TO SEE IT BY--
AQUAMAN?
WHAT WAS THAT?
I'M NOT SURE WHAT I JUST SAW... LOOKED LIKE THE WHOLE SEA BED SHIFTED...WHAT WAS...
...MY GOD...

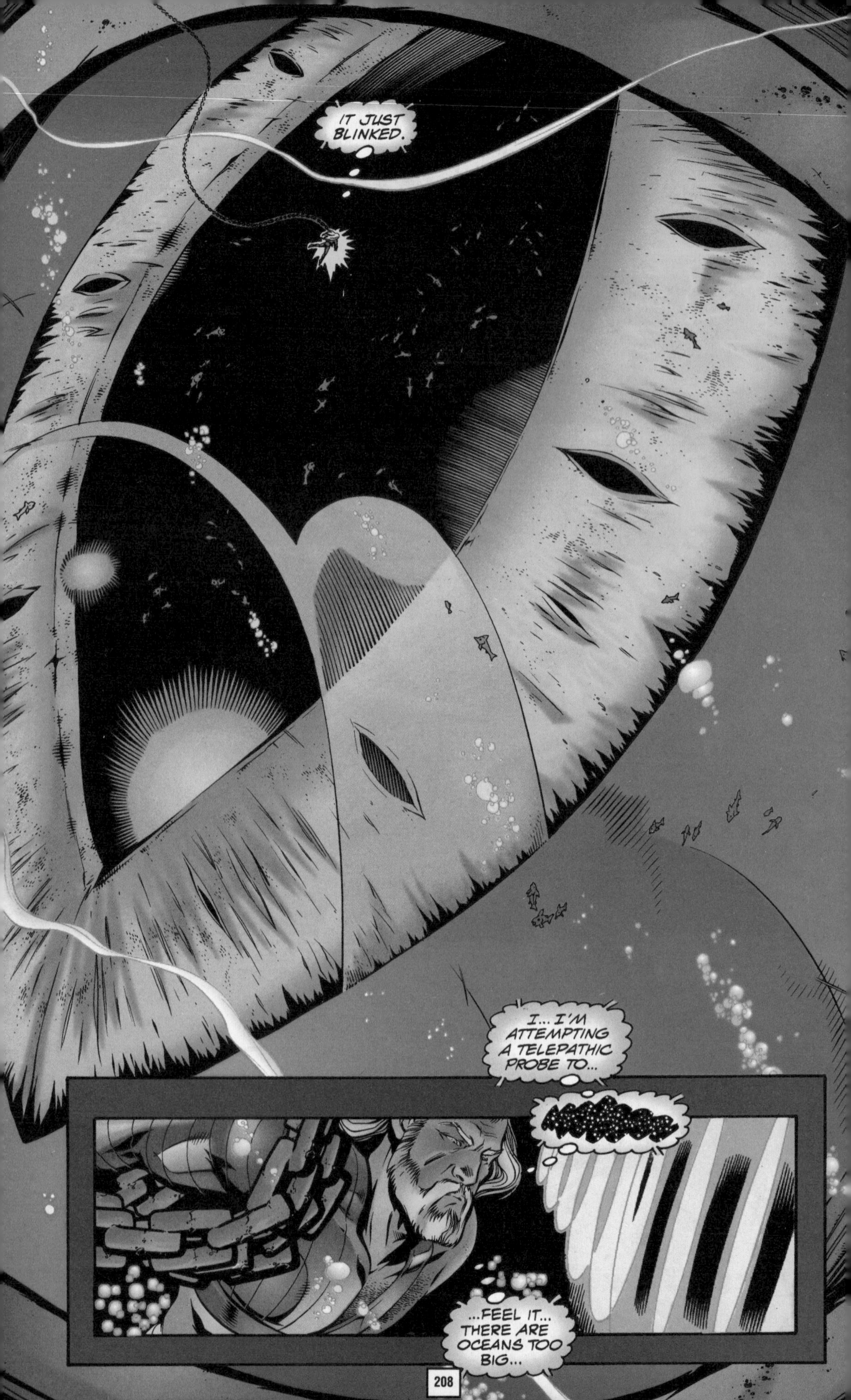
IT JUST BLINKED.
I... I'M ATTEMPTING A TELEPATHIC PROBE TO...
...FEEL IT... THERE ARE OCEANS TOO BIG...

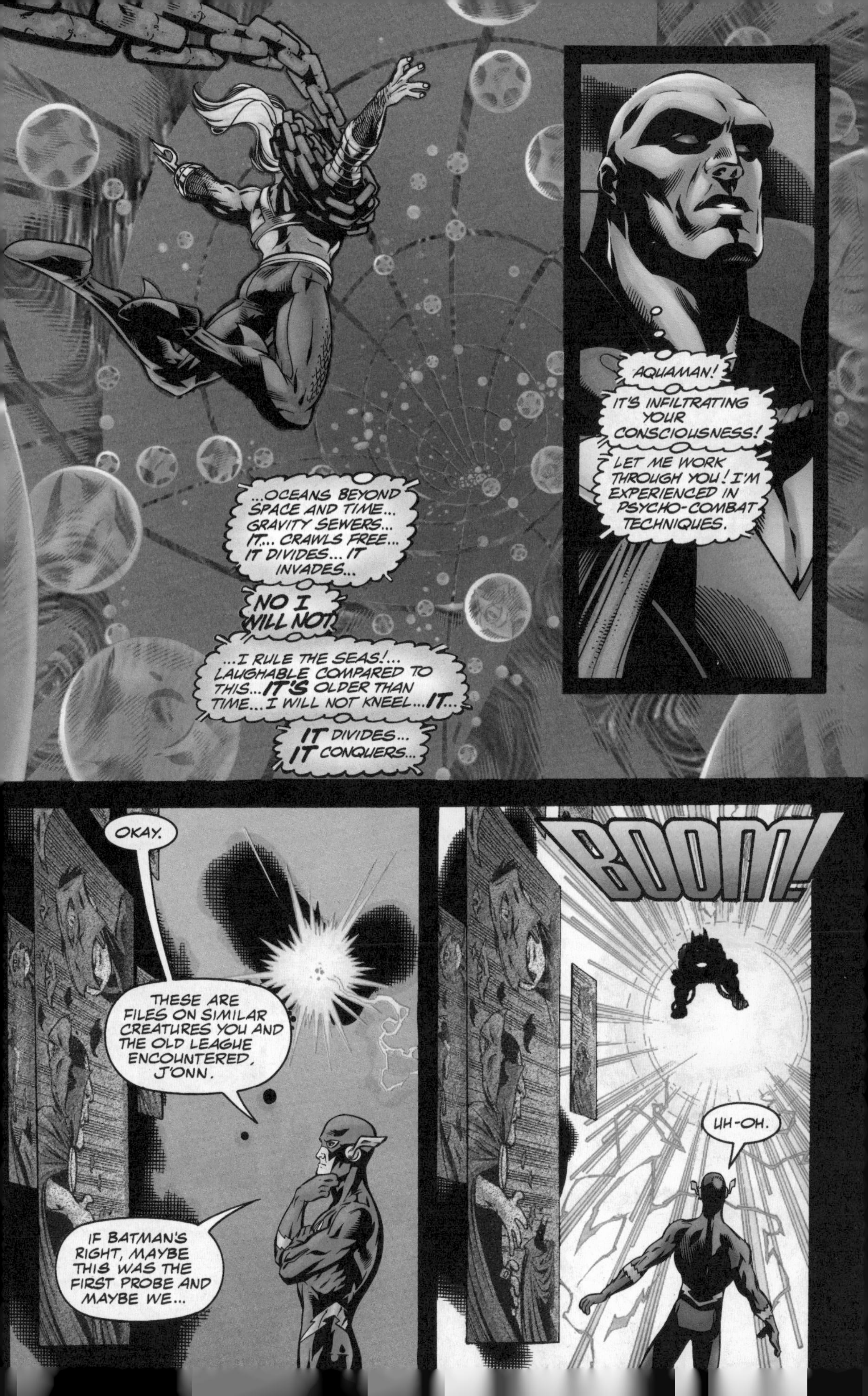
...OCEANS BEYOND SPACE AND TIME... GRAVITY SEWERS... IT... CRAWLS FREE... IT DIVIDES... IT INVADES...
NO I WILL NOT
...I RULE THE SEAS!... LAUGHABLE COMPARED TO THIS...IT'S OLDER THAN TIME...I WILL NOT KNEEL...IT...
IT DIVIDES... IT CONQUERS...
AQUAMAN!
IT'S INFILTRATING YOUR CONSCIOUSNESS!
LET ME WORK THROUGH YOU! I'M EXPERIENCED IN PSYCHO-COMBAT TECHNIQUES.
OKAY.
THESE ARE FILES ON SIMILAR CREATURES YOU AND THE OLD LEAGUE ENCOUNTERED, J'ONN.
IF BATMAN'S RIGHT, MAYBE THIS WAS THE FIRST PROBE AND MAYBE WE...
BOOM!
UH-OH.

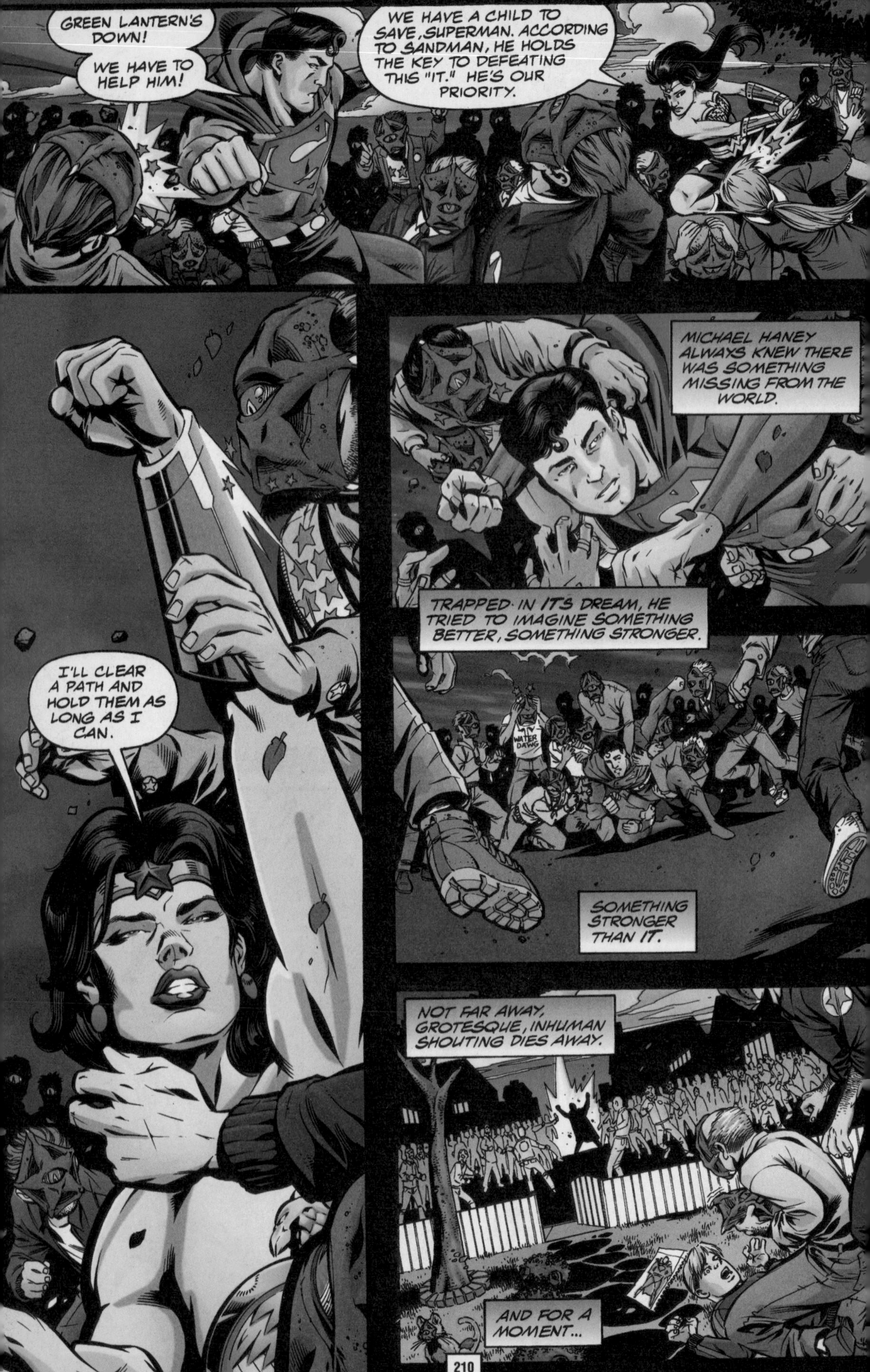
GREEN LANTERN'S DOWN!
WE HAVE TO HELP HIM!
WE HAVE A CHILD TO SAVE, SUPERMAN. ACCORDING TO SANDMAN, HE HOLDS THE KEY TO DEFEATING THIS "IT." HE'S OUR PRIORITY.
I'LL CLEAR A PATH AND HOLD THEM AS LONG AS I CAN.
MICHAEL HANEY ALWAYS KNEW THERE WAS SOMETHING MISSING FROM THE WORLD.
TRAPPED IN ITS DREAM, HE TRIED TO IMAGINE SOMETHING BETTER, SOMETHING STRONGER.
WATER DAWG
SOMETHING STRONGER THAN IT.
NOT FAR AWAY, GROTESQUE, INHUMAN SHOUTING DIES AWAY.
AND FOR A MOMENT...

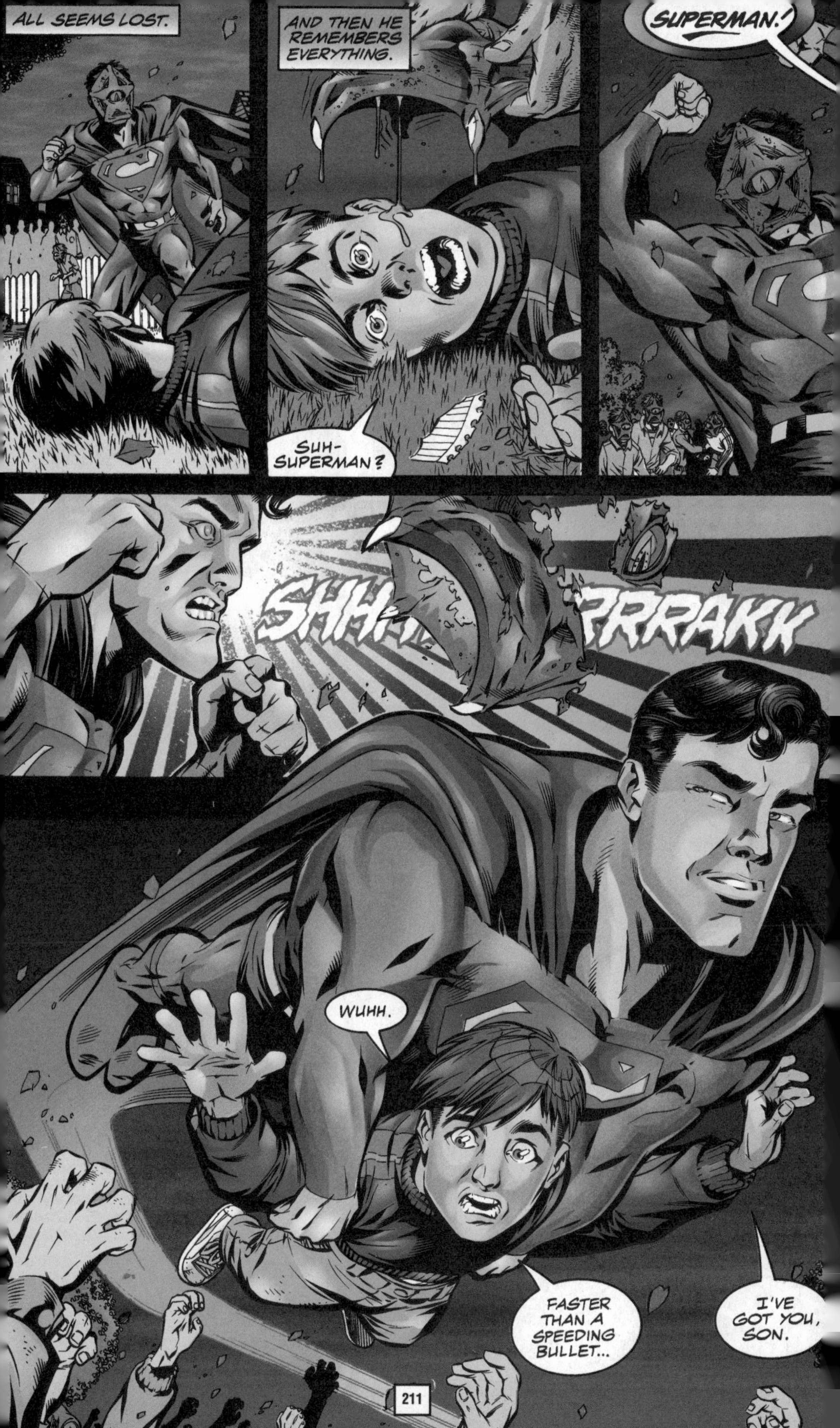
ALL SEEMS LOST.
AND THEN HE REMEMBERS EVERYTHING.
SUH-SUPERMAN?
SUPERMAN!
WUHH.
FASTER THAN A SPEEDING BULLET...
I'VE GOT YOU, SON.

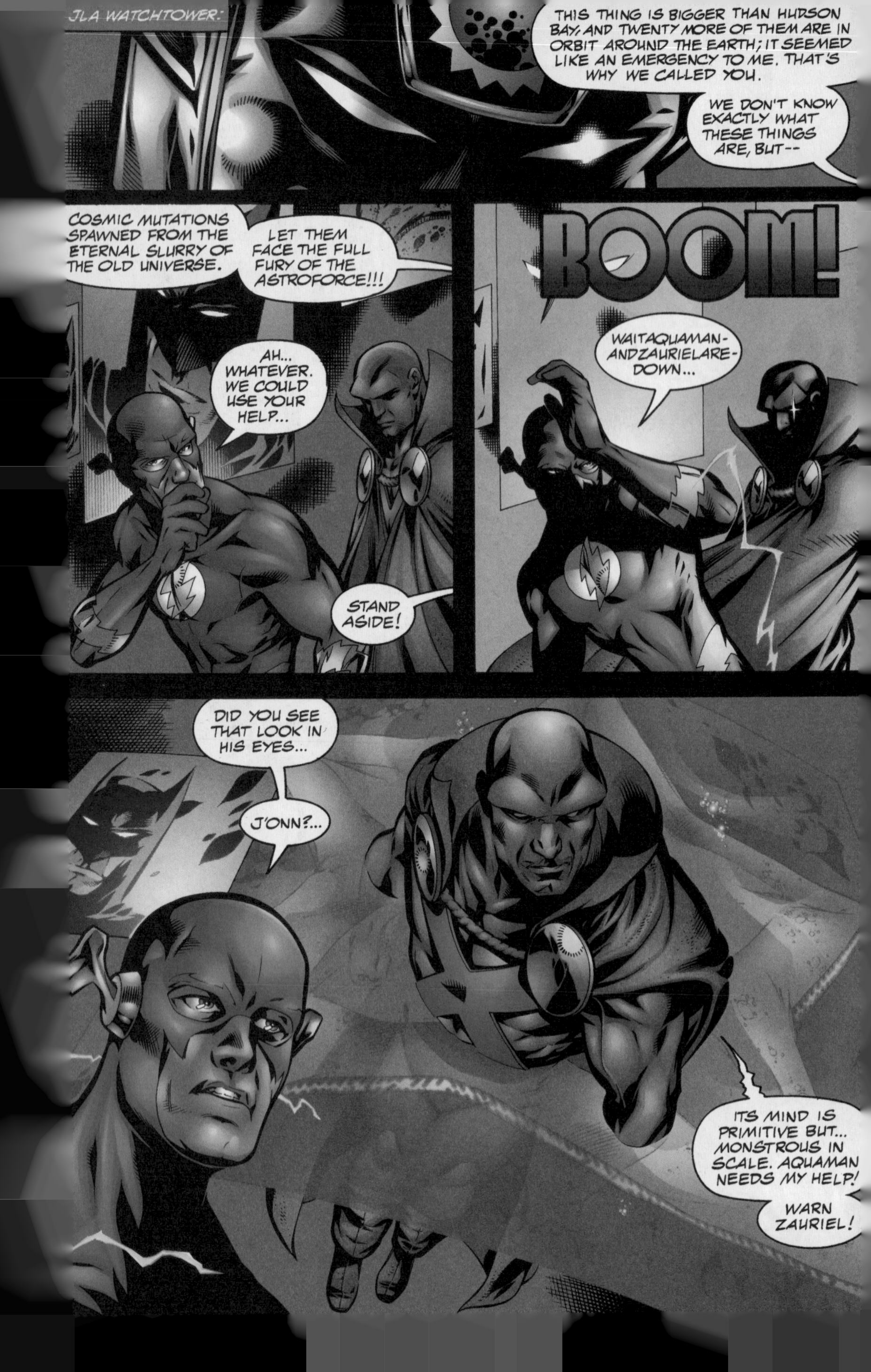
JLA WATCHTOWER:
THIS THING IS BIGGER THAN HUDSON BAY, AND TWENTY MORE OF THEM ARE IN ORBIT AROUND THE EARTH; IT SEEMED LIKE AN EMERGENCY TO ME. THAT'S WHY WE CALLED YOU.
WE DON'T KNOW EXACTLY WHAT THESE THINGS ARE, BUT--
COSMIC MUTATIONS SPAWNED FROM THE ETERNAL SLURRY OF THE OLD UNIVERSE.
LET THEM FACE THE FULL FURY OF THE ASTROFORCE!!!
AH... WHATEVER. WE COULD USE YOUR HELP...
STAND ASIDE!
BOOM!
WAITAQUAMAN-ANDZAURIELARE-DOWN...
DID YOU SEE THAT LOOK IN HIS EYES...
J'ONN?...
ITS MIND IS PRIMITIVE BUT... MONSTROUS IN SCALE. AQUAMAN NEEDS MY HELP!
WARN ZAURIEL!

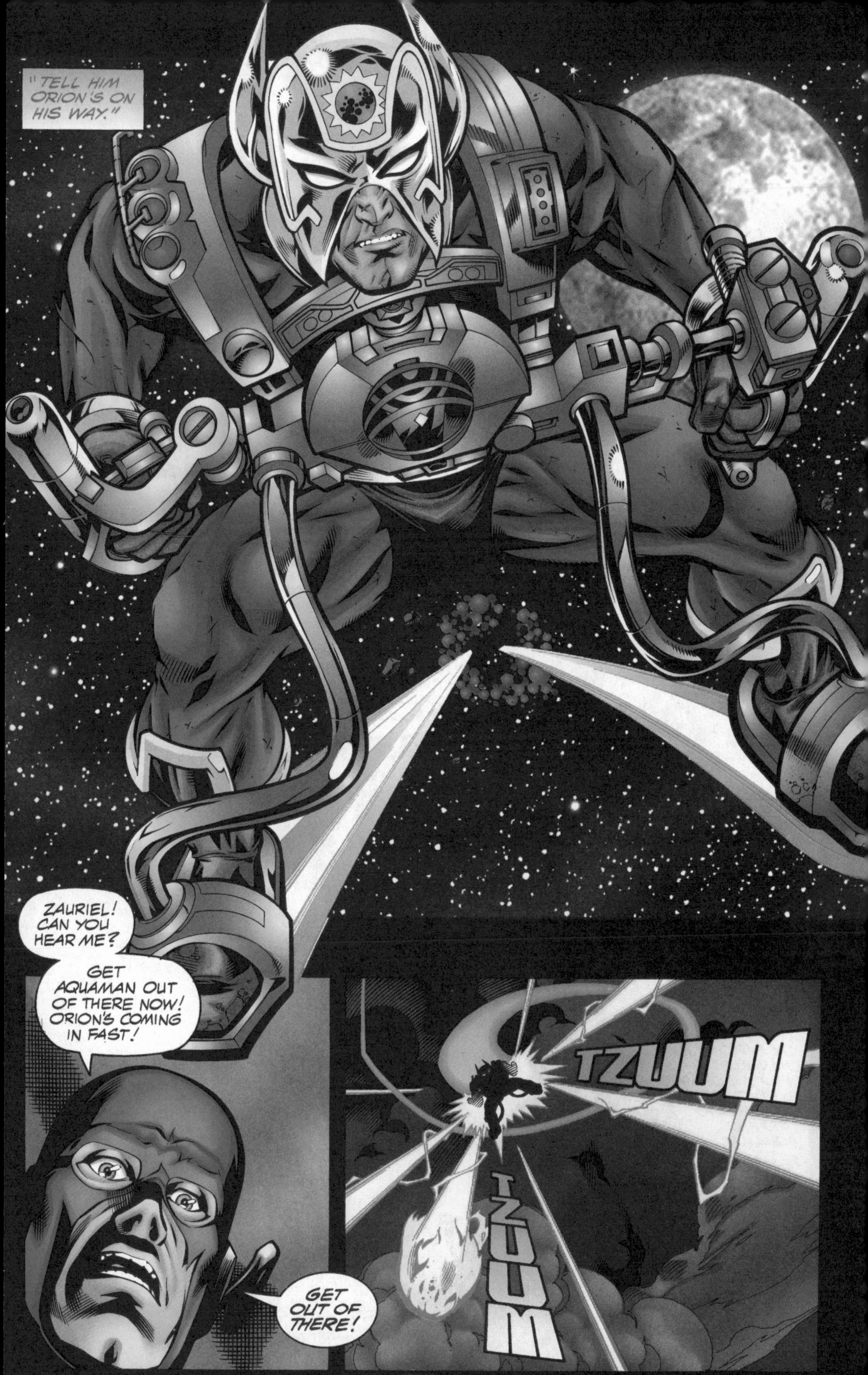
"TELL HIM ORION'S ON HIS WAY."
ZAURIEL! CAN YOU HEAR ME?
GET AQUAMAN OUT OF THERE NOW! ORION'S COMING IN FAST!
GET OUT OF THERE!
TZUUM
TZUUM

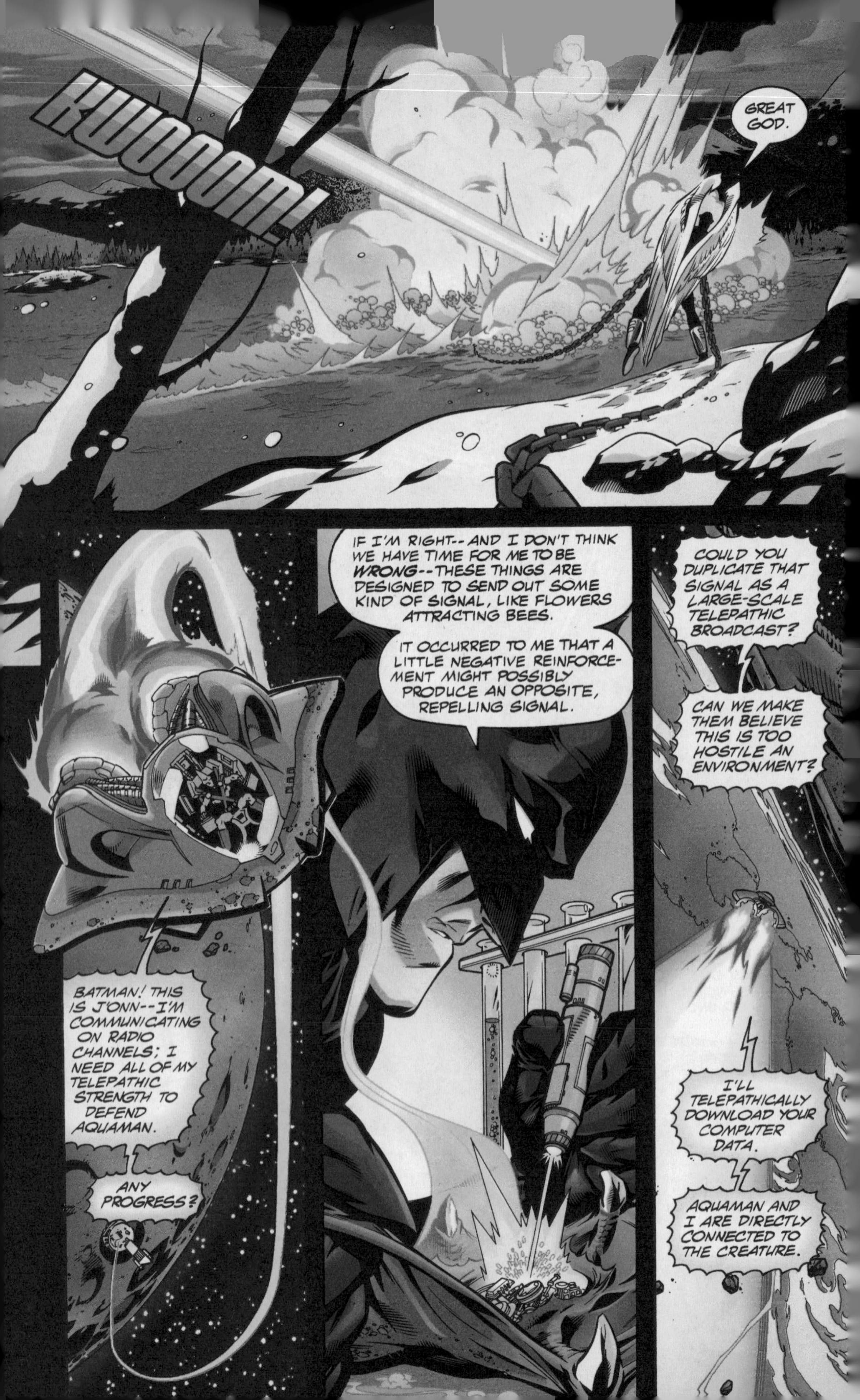

KWOOOOM!
GREAT GOD.
BATMAN! THIS IS J'ONN--I'M COMMUNICATING ON RADIO CHANNELS; I NEED ALL OF MY TELEPATHIC STRENGTH TO DEFEND AQUAMAN.
ANY PROGRESS?
IF I'M RIGHT-- AND I DON'T THINK WE HAVE TIME FOR ME TO BE WRONG--THESE THINGS ARE DESIGNED TO SEND OUT SOME KIND OF SIGNAL, LIKE FLOWERS ATTRACTING BEES.
IT OCCURRED TO ME THAT A LITTLE NEGATIVE REINFORCEMENT MIGHT POSSIBLY PRODUCE AN OPPOSITE, REPELLING SIGNAL.
COULD YOU DUPLICATE THAT SIGNAL AS A LARGE-SCALE TELEPATHIC BROADCAST?
CAN WE MAKE THEM BELIEVE THIS IS TOO HOSTILE AN ENVIRONMENT?
I'LL TELEPATHICALLY DOWNLOAD YOUR COMPUTER DATA.
AQUAMAN AND I ARE DIRECTLY CONNECTED TO THE CREATURE.

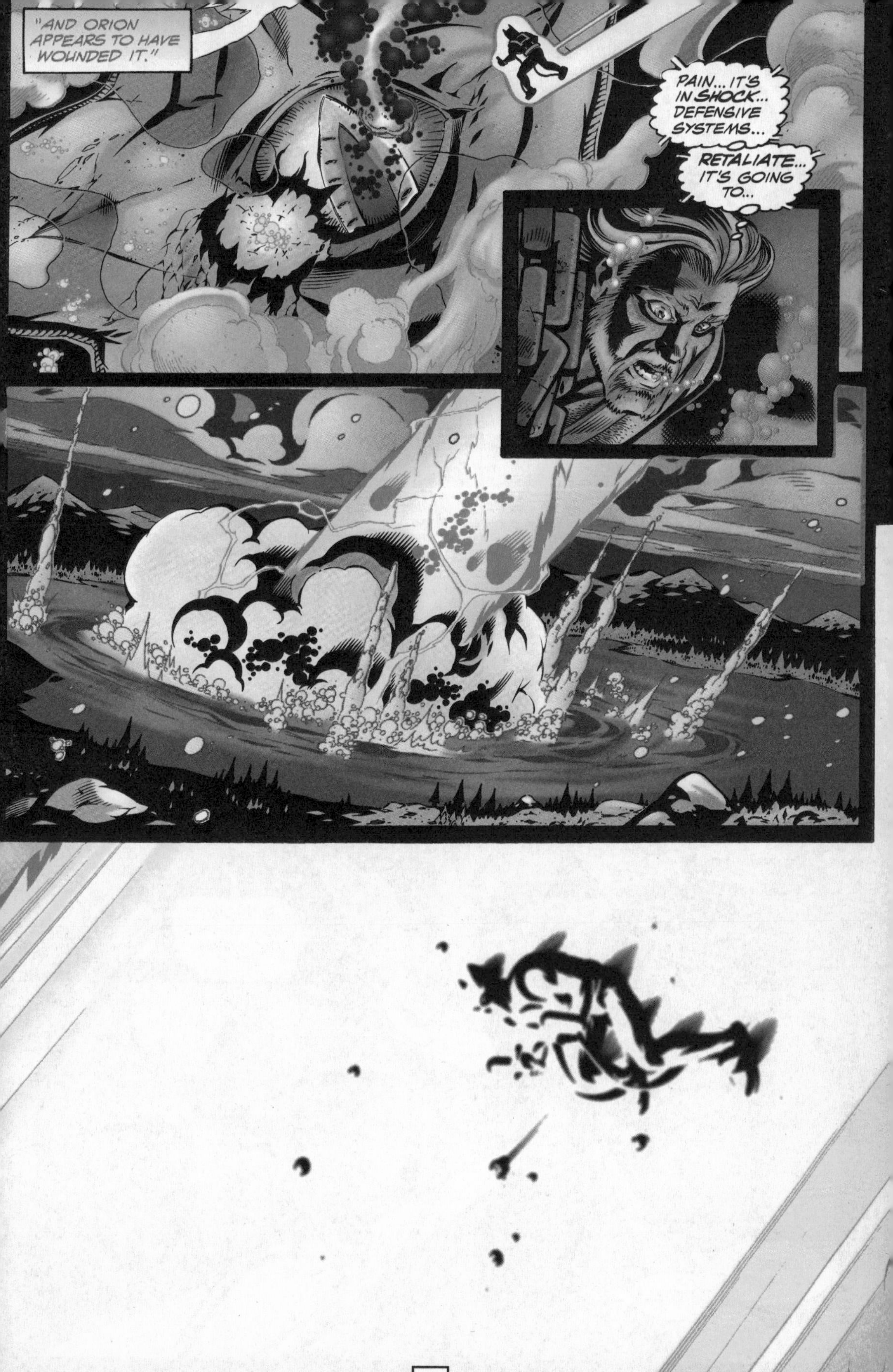
"AND ORION APPEARS TO HAVE WOUNDED IT."
PAIN... IT'S IN SHOCK... DEFENSIVE SYSTEMS...
RETALIATE... IT'S GOING TO...

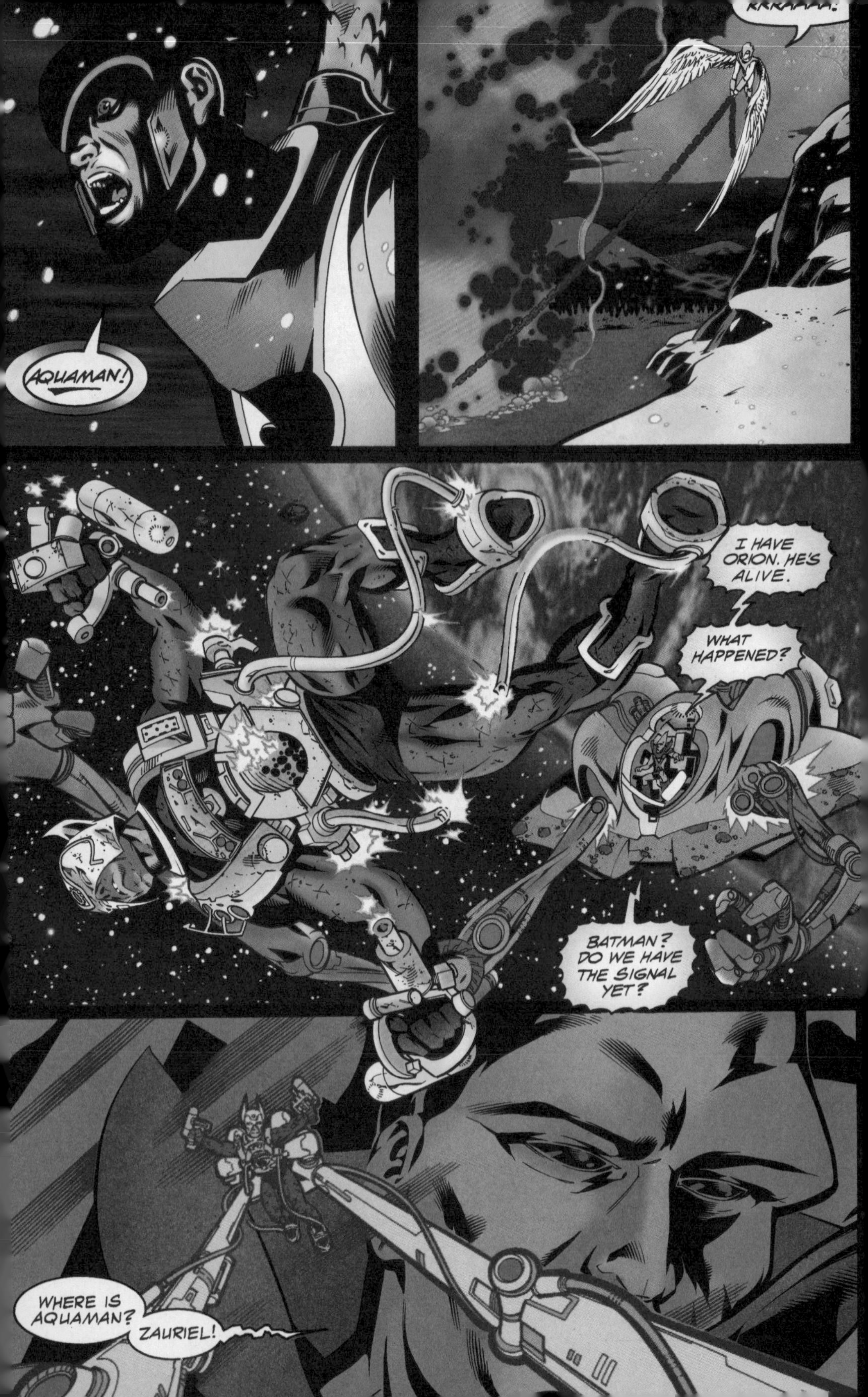
AQUAMAN!
KRRAAAA!
I HAVE ORION. HE'S ALIVE.
WHAT HAPPENED?
BATMAN? DO WE HAVE THE SIGNAL YET?
WHERE IS AQUAMAN?
ZAURIEL!

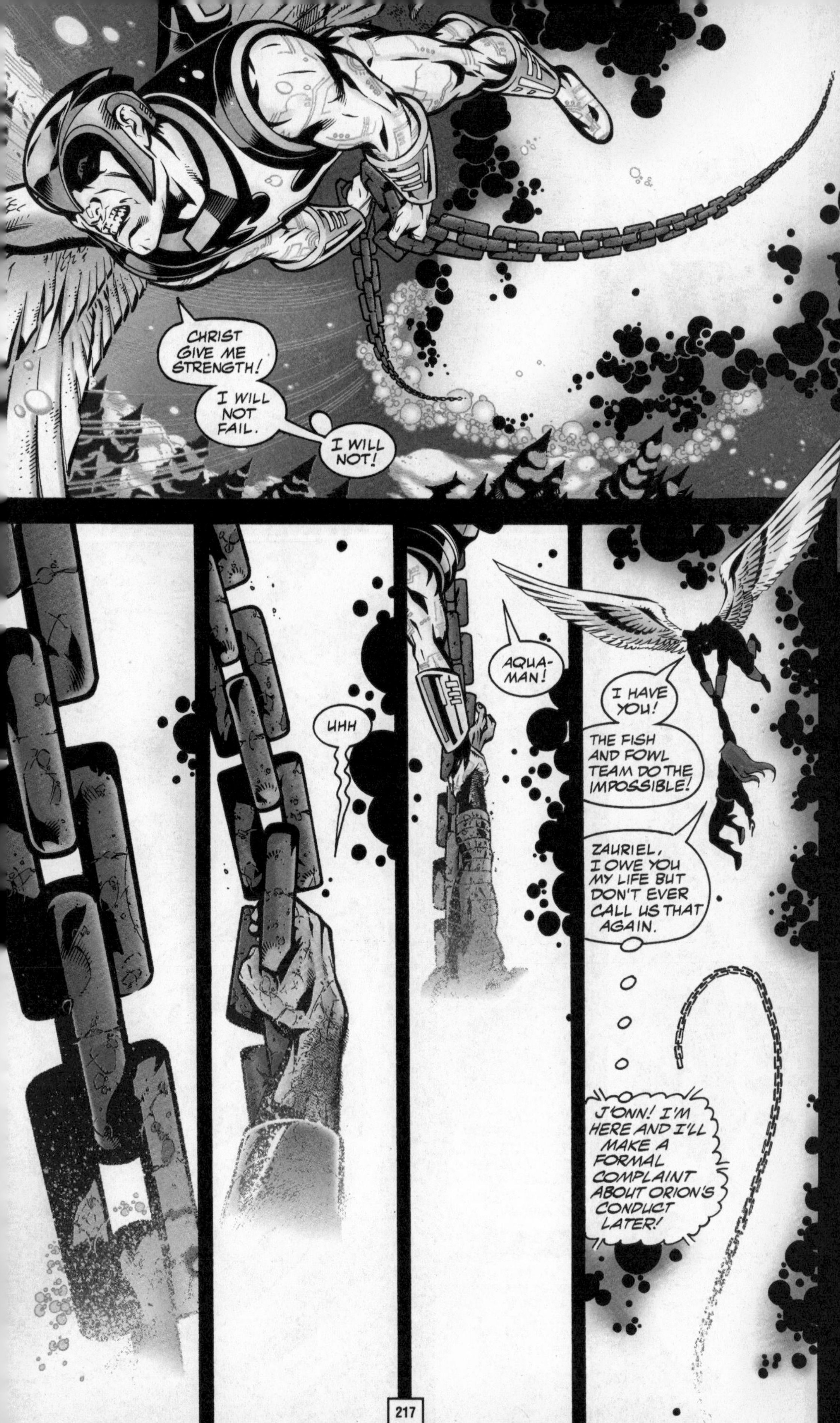
CHRIST GIVE ME STRENGTH!
I WILL NOT FAIL.
I WILL NOT!
UHH
AQUA-MAN!
I HAVE YOU!
THE FISH AND FOWL TEAM DO THE IMPOSSIBLE!
ZAURIEL, I OWE YOU MY LIFE BUT DON'T EVER CALL US THAT AGAIN.
J'ONN! I'M HERE AND I'LL MAKE A FORMAL COMPLAINT ABOUT ORION'S CONDUCT LATER!

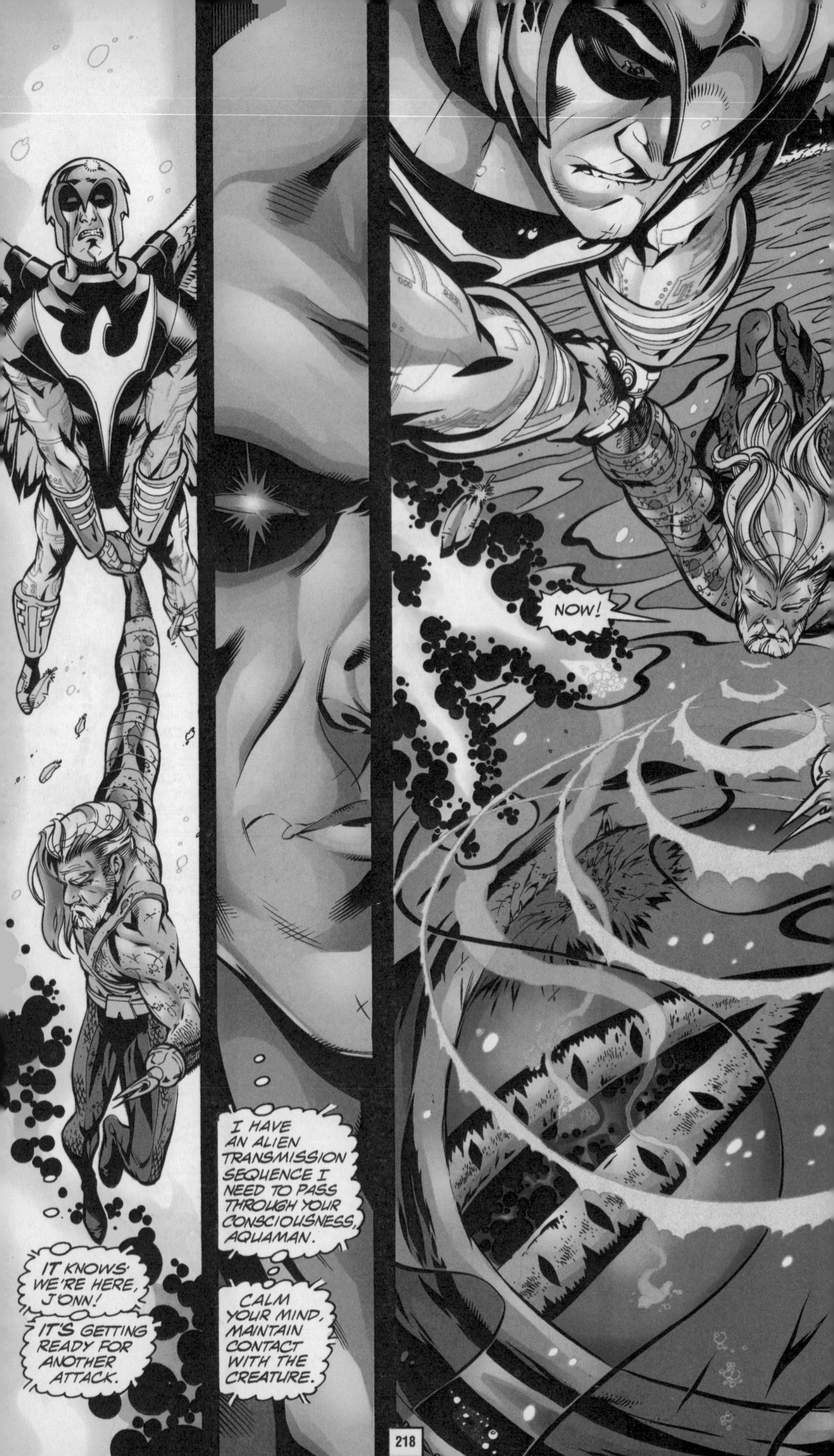
IT KNOWS WE'RE HERE, J'ONN!
IT'S GETTING READY FOR ANOTHER ATTACK.
I HAVE AN ALIEN TRANSMISSION SEQUENCE I NEED TO PASS THROUGH YOUR CONSCIOUSNESS, AQUAMAN.
CALM YOUR MIND, MAINTAIN CONTACT WITH THE CREATURE.
NOW!

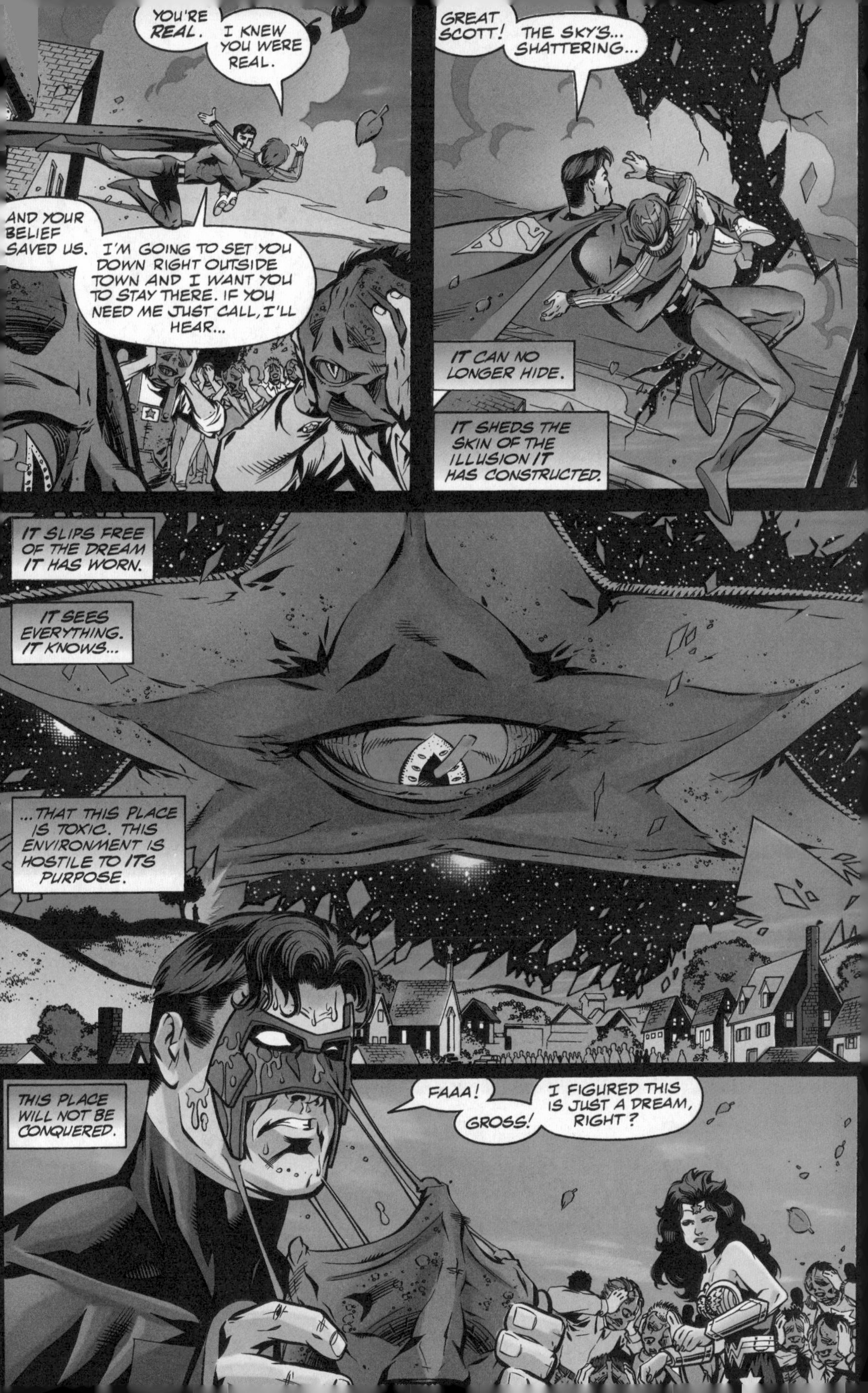
YOU'RE REAL.
I KNEW YOU WERE REAL.
AND YOUR BELIEF SAVED US.
I'M GOING TO SET YOU DOWN RIGHT OUTSIDE TOWN AND I WANT YOU TO STAY THERE. IF YOU NEED ME JUST CALL, I'LL HEAR...
GREAT SCOTT!
THE SKY'S... SHATTERING...
IT CAN NO LONGER HIDE.
IT SHEDS THE SKIN OF THE ILLUSION IT HAS CONSTRUCTED.
IT SLIPS FREE OF THE DREAM IT HAS WORN.
IT SEES EVERYTHING. IT KNOWS...
...THAT THIS PLACE IS TOXIC. THIS ENVIRONMENT IS HOSTILE TO ITS PURPOSE.
THIS PLACE WILL NOT BE CONQUERED.
FAAA!
GROSS!
I FIGURED THIS IS JUST A DREAM, RIGHT?

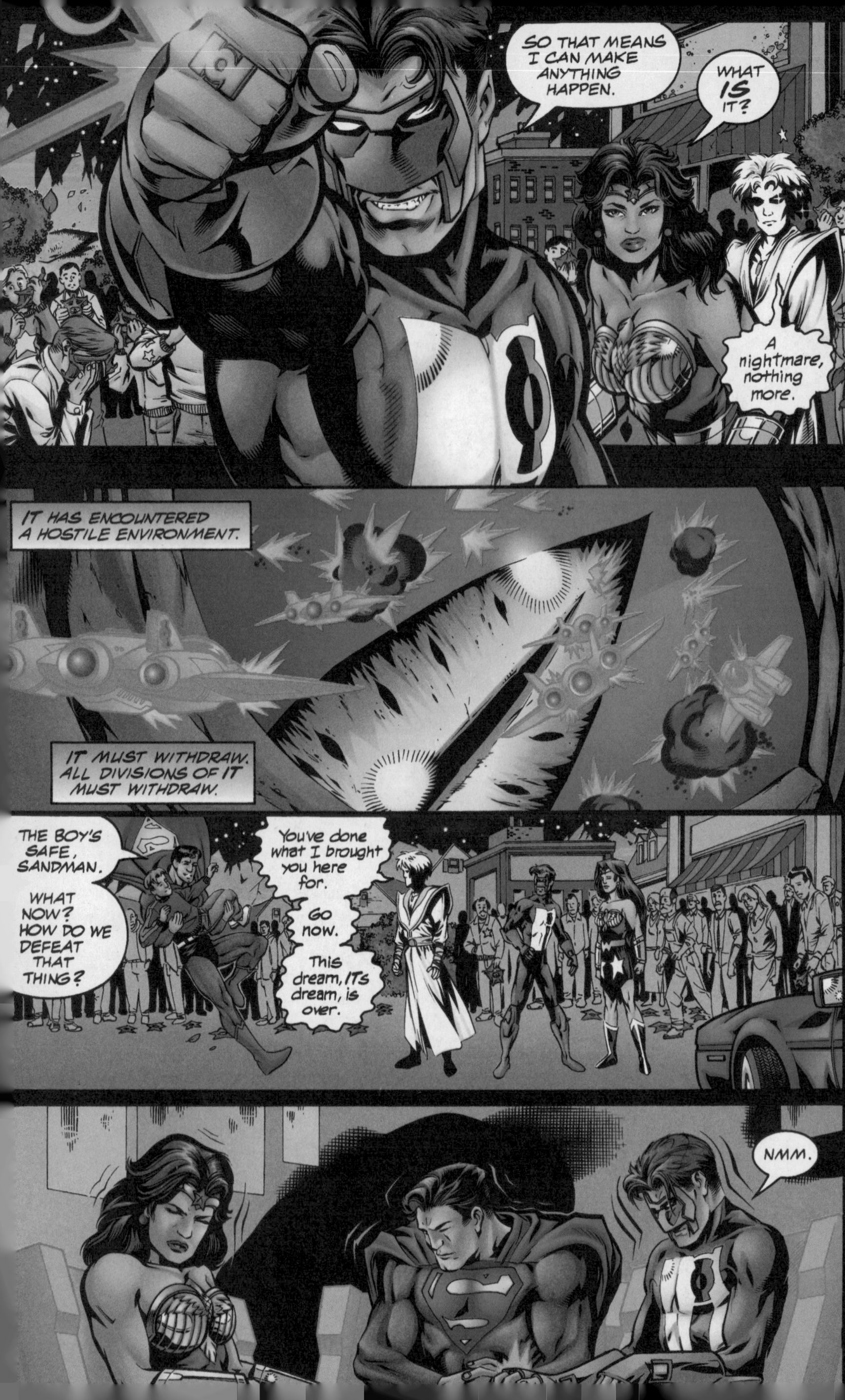
SO THAT MEANS I CAN MAKE ANYTHING HAPPEN.
WHAT IS IT?
A nightmare, nothing more.
IT HAS ENCOUNTERED A HOSTILE ENVIRONMENT.
IT MUST WITHDRAW. ALL DIVISIONS OF IT MUST WITHDRAW.
THE BOY'S SAFE, SANDMAN.
WHAT NOW? HOW DO WE DEFEAT THAT THING?
You've done what I brought you here for.
Go now.
This dream, ITs dream, is over.
NMM.

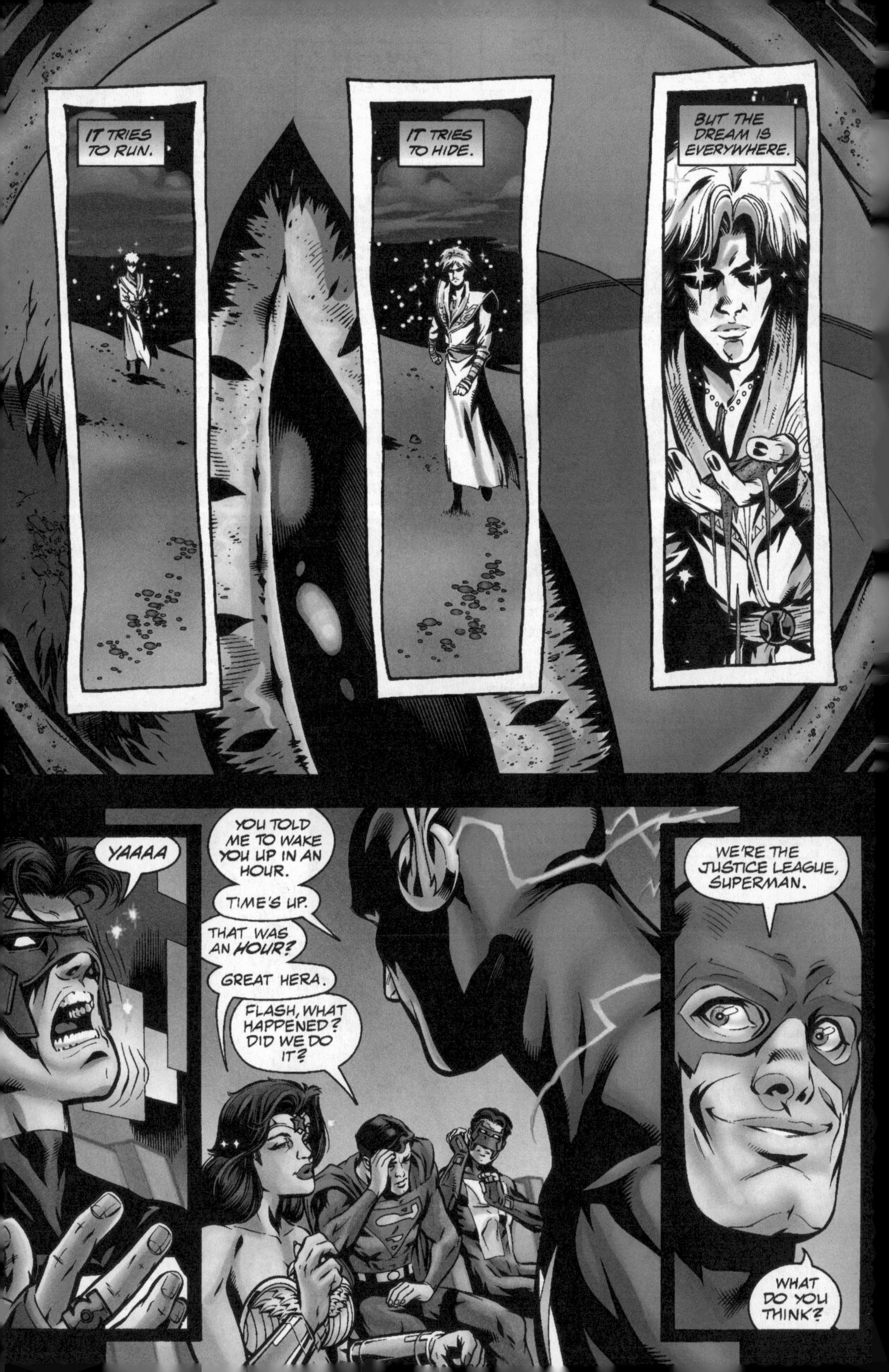
IT TRIES TO RUN.
IT TRIES TO HIDE.
BUT THE DREAM IS EVERYWHERE.
YAAAA
YOU TOLD ME TO WAKE YOU UP IN AN HOUR.
TIME'S UP.
THAT WAS AN HOUR?
GREAT HERA.
FLASH, WHAT HAPPENED? DID WE DO IT?
WE'RE THE JUSTICE LEAGUE, SUPERMAN.
WHAT DO YOU THINK?

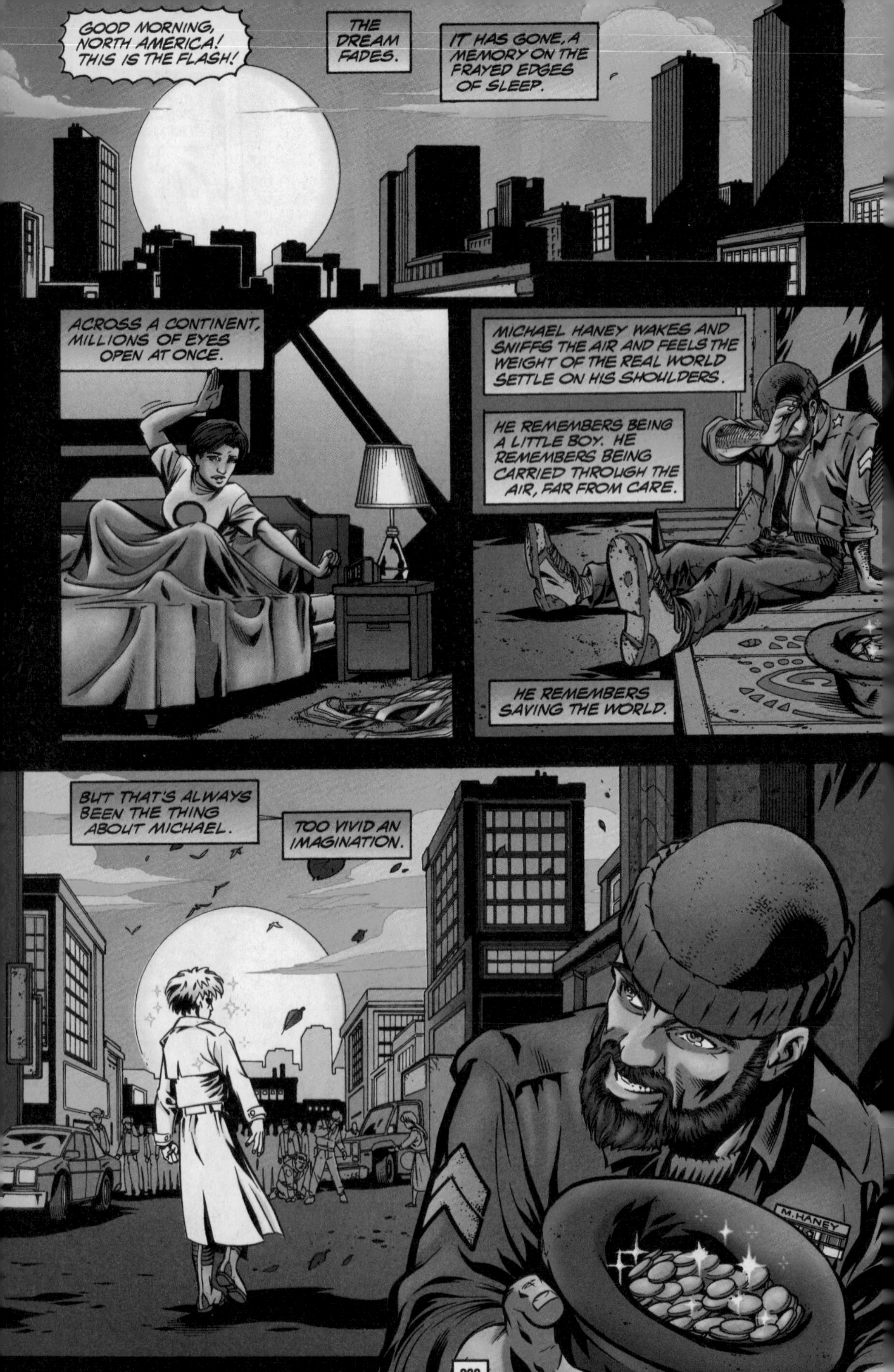
GOOD MORNING, NORTH AMERICA! THIS IS THE FLASH!
THE DREAM FADES.
IT HAS GONE, A MEMORY ON THE FRAYED EDGES OF SLEEP.
ACROSS A CONTINENT, MILLIONS OF EYES OPEN AT ONCE.
MICHAEL HANEY WAKES AND SNIFFS THE AIR AND FEELS THE WEIGHT OF THE REAL WORLD SETTLE ON HIS SHOULDERS.
HE REMEMBERS BEING A LITTLE BOY. HE REMEMBERS BEING CARRIED THROUGH THE AIR, FAR FROM CARE.
HE REMEMBERS SAVING THE WORLD.
BUT THAT'S ALWAYS BEEN THE THING ABOUT MICHAEL.
TOO VIVID AN IMAGINATION.
M. HANEY

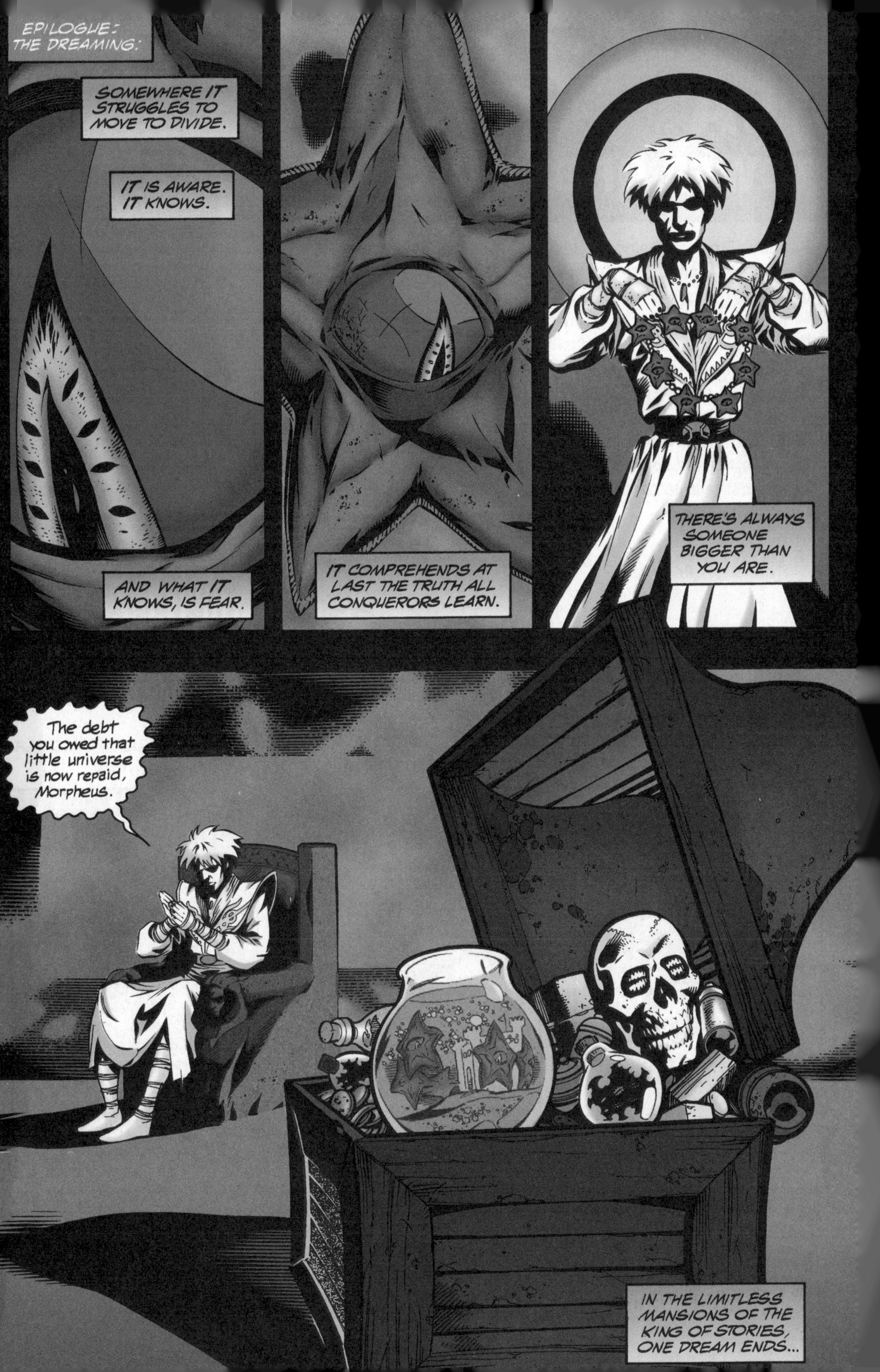
EPILOGUE: THE DREAMING:
SOMEWHERE IT STRUGGLES TO MOVE TO DIVIDE.
IT IS AWARE. IT KNOWS.
AND WHAT IT KNOWS, IS FEAR.
IT COMPREHENDS AT LAST THE TRUTH ALL CONQUERORS LEARN.
THERE'S ALWAYS SOMEONE BIGGER THAN YOU ARE.
The debt you owed that little universe is now repaid, Morpheus.
IN THE LIMITLESS MANSIONS OF THE KING OF STORIES, ONE DREAM ENDS...

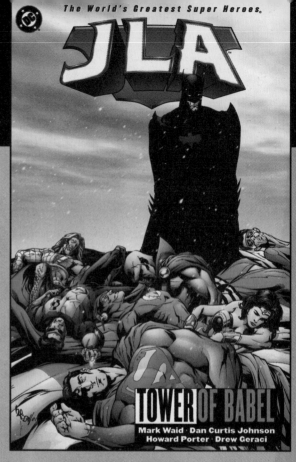

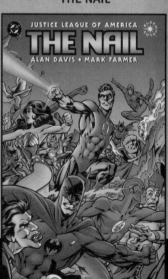

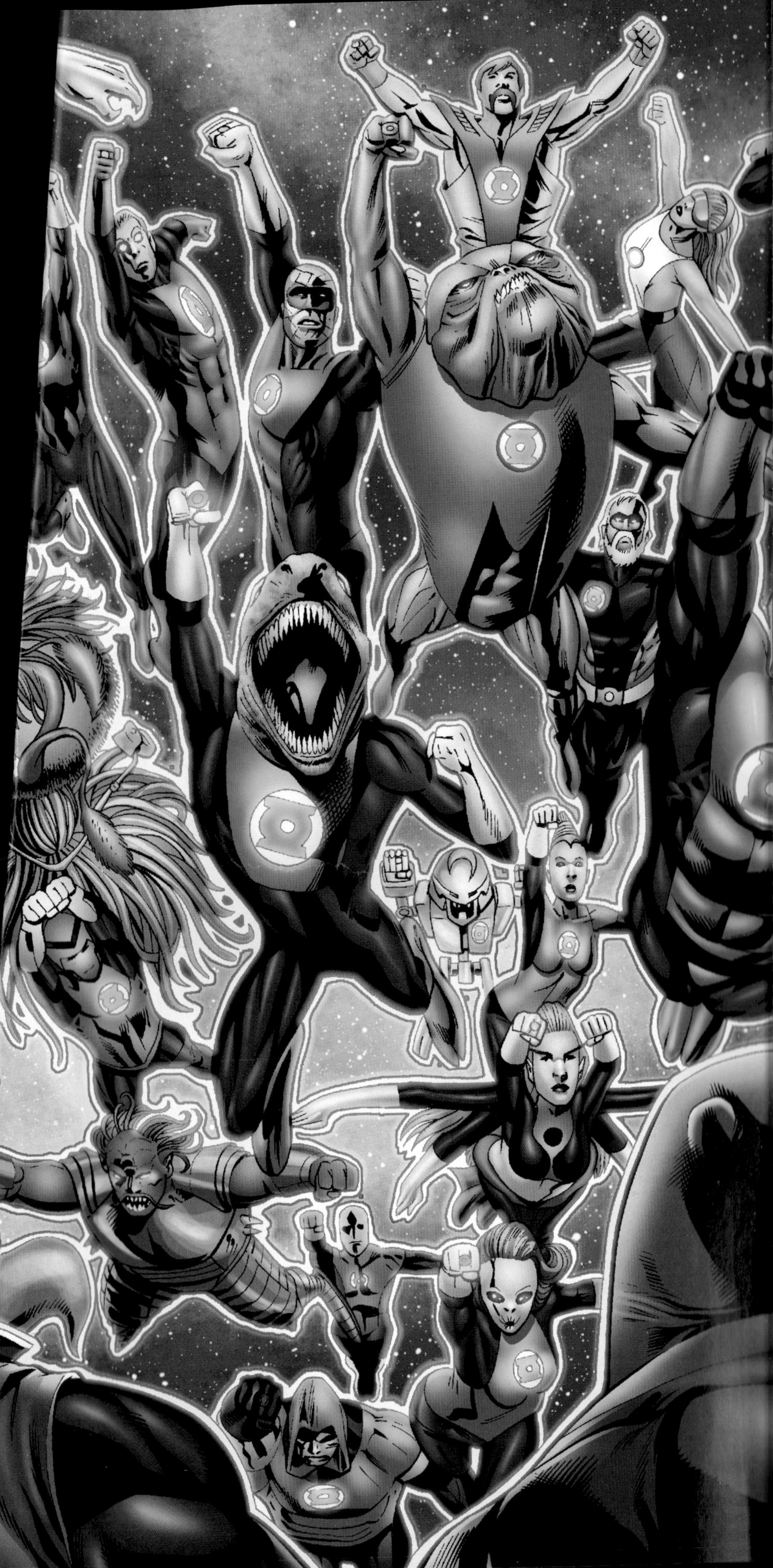

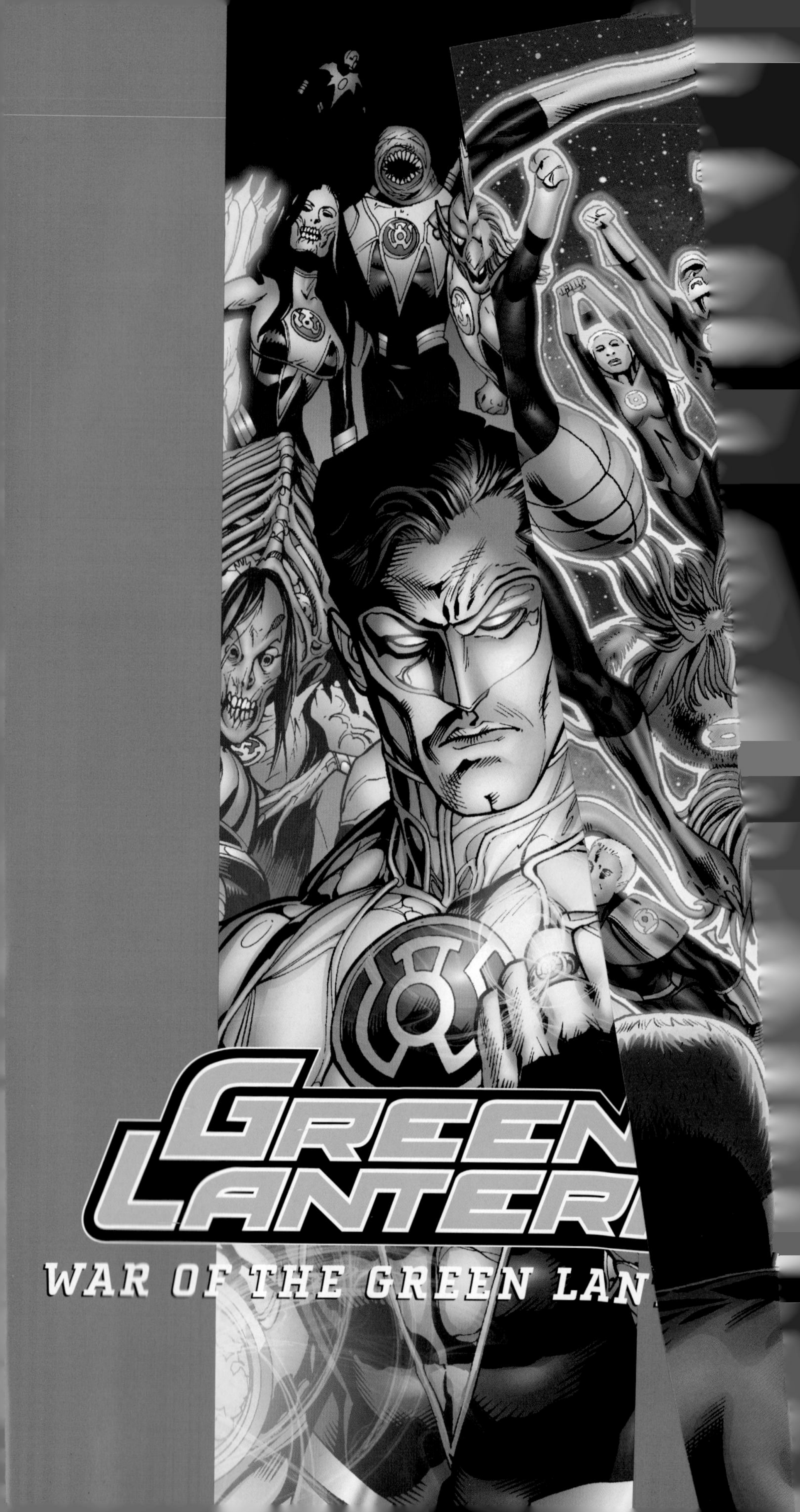
GREEN
LANTER
WAR OF THE GREEN LAN